SOCIAL JUSTICE FOR CHILDREN AND YOUNG PEOPLE

According to the Convention on the Rights of the Child, the goal of a social justice approach for children is to ensure that children "are better served and protected by justice systems, including the security and social welfare sectors." Despite this worthy goal, the United Nations documents how children are rarely viewed as stakeholders in justice rules of law. Child justice issues are often dealt with as separate from larger justice and security issues, and when justice issues for children are addressed, it is often through a siloed rather than a comprehensive approach. This volume actively challenges the current youth social justice paradigm through terminology and new approaches that place children and young people front and center in the social justice conversation. Through international consideration, children and young people worldwide are incorporated into the social justice conversation.

Caroline S. Clauss-Ehlers is an associate professor and the program/clinical coordinator for the Programs in School Counseling and Counseling Psychology in the Department of Educational Psychology at Rutgers, the State University of New Jersey. Her research and writing focuses on cultural resilience, trauma, bilingualism, and work with children and their families within diverse community contexts. She has edited/coedited/authored four books and numerous articles in this area. Dr. Clauss-Ehlers served as the chair of the American Psychological Association Task Force on Re-envisioning the Multicultural Guidelines for the 21st Century, a group that wrote the *Multicultural Guidelines: An Ecological Approach to Context, Identity, and Intersectionality* (2017).

Dr. Aradhana Bela Sood is a senior professor of child mental health policy at Virginia Commonwealth University. She has spent thirty years providing tertiary care to children with serious emotional disturbance and in the past decade shifted her focus to prevention efforts particularly in under-resourced populations. Recognized for her contributions to public mental health work by state and national organizations, Dr. Sood has spread her prevention efforts across infancy, childhood, and transition-age youth. She has edited two books on mental health policy and prevention in children's mental health.

Mark D. Weist is a professor in clinical-community and school psychology in the Department of Psychology at the University of South Carolina. In his prior position at the University of Maryland, he founded the Center for School Mental Health, providing leadership in the advancement of school mental health (SMH) policies and programs. He has edited or developed twelve books and has published and presented widely on diverse topics in SMH. He is currently coleading a regional conference and leading two randomized controlled trials focused on improving the effectiveness and impact of SMH.

Social Justice for Children and Young People

INTERNATIONAL PERSPECTIVES

Edited by

CAROLINE S. CLAUSS-EHLERS

Rutgers, The State University of New Jersey

ARADHANA BELA SOOD

Virginia Commonwealth University

MARK D. WEIST

University of South Carolina

CAMBRIDGE
UNIVERSITY PRESS

University Printing House, Cambridge CB2 8BS, United Kingdom

One Liberty Plaza, 20th Floor, New York, NY 10006, USA

477 Williamstown Road, Port Melbourne, VIC 3207, Australia

314-321, 3rd Floor, Plot 3, Splendor Forum, Jasola District Centre, New Delhi - 110025, India

103 Penang Road, #05-06/07, Visioncrest Commercial, Singapore 238467

Cambridge University Press is part of the University of Cambridge.

It furthers the University's mission by disseminating knowledge in the pursuit of education, learning and research at the highest international levels of excellence.

www.cambridge.org
Information on this title: www.cambridge.org/9781108447034
DOI: 10.1017/9781108551830

© Caroline S. Clauss-Ehlers, Aradhana Bela Sood and Mark D. Weist 2020

This publication is in copyright. Subject to statutory exception and to the provisions of relevant collective licensing agreements, no reproduction of any part may take place without the written permission of Cambridge University Press.

First published 2020
First paperback edition 2022

A catalogue record for this publication is available from the British Library

Library of Congress Cataloging in Publication data
NAMES: Clauss-Ehlers, Caroline S., editor. | Sood, Aradhana Bela, editor. | Weist, Mark D., editor.
TITLE: Social justice for children and young people : international perspectives / edited by Caroline S. Clauss-Ehlers, Rutgers University, New Jersey, Aradhana Bela Sood, Virginia Commonwealth University, Mark D. Weist, University of South Carolina.
DESCRIPTION: Cambridge, United Kingdom ; New York, NY : Cambridge University Press, 2020.
IDENTIFIERS: LCCN 2019059931 (print) | LCCN 2019059932 (ebook) | ISBN 9781108427685 (hardback) | ISBN 9781108551830 (ebook)
SUBJECTS: LCSH: Children's rights. | Children – Legal status, laws, etc.. | Social justice.
CLASSIFICATION: LCC HQ789 .S59 2020 (print) | LCC HQ789 (ebook) | DDC 323.3/52–dc23
LC record available at https://lccn.loc.gov/2019059931
LC ebook record available at https://lccn.loc.gov/2019059932

ISBN 978-1-108-42768-5 Hardback
ISBN 978-1-108-44703-4 Paperback

Cambridge University Press has no responsibility for the persistence or accuracy of URLs for external or third-party internet websites referred to in this publication, and does not guarantee that any content on such websites is, or will remain, accurate or appropriate.

CSCE – To Olliver, Sabrina, and Isabel in support of a just world for children everywhere

ABS – To my mother, Sushila, a just soul. To the children of the Bon Air Juvenile Justice System and the East End of Richmond, VA: your stories keep me humble and inspire me to speak for justice

MDW – To the memory of Stan, my second father, with much gratitude and love

Contents

List of Contributors		page xi
Foreword by Terrence J. Roberts		xxvii

PART I SOCIAL JUSTICE AND HUMAN RIGHTS FOR CHILDREN AND YOUNG PEOPLE 1

1 Introduction: An Urgent Call to Understand the Status of Children and Young People within a Social Justice Paradigm 3
  Caroline S. Clauss-Ehlers, Aradhana Bela Sood, Cara Lomaro, and Mark D. Weist

2 The Language of Social Justice for Children and Young People: Key Terms and Guiding Principles 20
  Becca McBride

3 Social Determinants of Health: Children and the Consequences of Socially Unjust Policies 35
  Aradhana Bela Sood, Danny T. K. Avula, and Tara Warman Wiley

4 Health and Mental Health Disparities: Application of the Health Capability Paradigm for Children and Young People 52
  Scott J. Hunter and Khalid I. Afzal

PART II INTERNATIONAL SOCIAL JUSTICE ISSUES THAT HAVE AN IMPACT ON CHILDREN AND YOUNG PEOPLE 69

5 Children and Poverty: A Global Approach 71
  Nathalie O. Iotti and Tomas Jungert

6	Educational Access for Women and Girls As a Social Justice Issue: Ghana As a Case Study Lynn Pasquerella and Dawn Michele Whitehead	91
7	The Youngest Victims: Children and Young People Affected by War James Garbarino, Amy E. Governale, and Danielle Nesi	106
8	Lesbian, Gay, Bisexual, Transgender, and Queer Youth and Social Justice Susan W. Jones, Aradhana Bela Sood, Nancy Bearss, and Caroline S. Clauss-Ehlers	123
9	Social Justice for Child Immigrants Shawn S. Sidhu and Balkozar S. Adam	138
10	Social Justice for Children and Young People with Disabilities Elizabeth H. Jensen and Judith R. Harrison	153
11	Critical School Mental Health Praxis (CrSMHP): A Framework for Change Jennifer Ulie-Wells, Katherine Richardson Bruna, and Carrie Romo	175
12	Family-School Partnerships within Tiered Systems of Support to Increase Access, Improve Equity, and Promote Positive Outcomes for All Children and Families S. Andrew Garbacz, Christopher H. Vatland, Laura Kern, Nathaniel P. von der Embse, Tanya Novotnak, Devon R. Minch, and Mark D. Weist	194
13	Social Justice and School Discipline: Schoolwide Positive Behavioral Interventions and Supports (SWPBIS) Jessica Swain-Bradway, Satish Moorthy, and Milaney Leverson	211
14	Understanding Body Respect As a Social Justice Issue for Young People Sigrún Daníelsdóttir	228

PART III REGIONAL AND COUNTRY CASE STUDIES ON SOCIAL JUSTICE FOR YOUTH   245

| 15 | The Need for Bridging the Gap between the Academy and Public Services in Brazil: Two Case Reports
Cristina de Andrade Varanda, Fernanda Dreux Miranda Fernandes, and Cibelle Albuquerque de la Higuera Amato | 247 |

16	The Education of Migrant Children in China's Cities Donghui Zhang and Tanja Sargent	260
17	Inequalities in Healthcare for Children and Adolescents in Colombia Erwin H. Hernandez-Rincon and Yahira Rossini Guzmán-Sabogal	273
18	Learning for Psychology via the Cuban Program of Care for People Affected by the Chernobyl Accident: 1990–2011 Alexis Lorenzo Ruiz	285
19	Learning from the Perspectives of At-Risk Resilient Ethiopian Students: How School-Based Resilience Arises from Connectedness, Competence, and Contribution Maura Mulloy	302
20	Social Justice for Children and Young People: A Qualitative Case Study of India Rajeev Seth, Riti Chandrashekhar, Shubhangi Kansal, and Vijayluxmi Bose	316
21	Israel: Features of Injustice in the Context of Educational Opportunities Audrey Addi-Raccah and Moshe Israelashvili	331
22	Social Justice for Children and Young People in Mexico María Elena Figueroa-Díaz and Liliana López Levi	347
23	Social Justice for Children and Young People in Norway Torill Larsen, Ingrid Holsen, and Helga Bjørnøy Urke	361
24	Social Justice and Children in Pakistan Sana Younus, Aisha Sanober Chachar, and Ayesha Irshad Mian	374
25	The Impact of Decades of Political Violence on Palestinian Children in the Gaza Strip and the West Bank Abdel Aziz Mousa Thabet	388
26	Social Justice Issues for Children and Young People in Peru and Other Latin American Countries Renato D. Alarcón	402
27	Social Justice and Adolescent Health: A Case Study of Rwanda Agnes Binagwaho, Kirstin Scott, and Kateri Donahoe	419

28 Ending Mental Health Stigma and Discrimination: Young People Creating a Fairer Scotland 437
Amy Quinn, Ellie Moyes, Oliver McLuckie, Kirsten Roberts, and Doriana DeGradi, Supported by Laura Sharpe, Calum Irving, Wendy Halliday, and Clare McArthur

29 Violence Exposure among Children and Young People: A South African Case Study 450
Theophilus Lazarus, Gershom Lazarus, Eugene Emory, Katelyn Reardon, and Eva Kuzyk

30 Youth Participatory Action Research in Urban Public Education: Underrepresented Youth Addressing Social Justice in the United States 460
Jack Baker, Paul Flaspohler, Katelyn Wargel, and Tammy Schwartz

PART IV CONCLUSION 477

31 Conclusion: Being a Change Agent for Social Justice for Children and Youth 479
Caroline S. Clauss-Ehlers, Mark D. Weist, Aradhana Bela Sood, and Cara Lomaro

Contributors

Dr. Balkozar S. Adam is a child and adolescent psychiatrist with decades of experience working with children and their families. She is board certified in psychiatry and child and adolescent psychiatry. She is a distinguished fellow of both the APA and the AACAP. She is a member of the American College of Psychiatrists. Dr. Adam works closely with diverse populations, focusing on providing culturally sensitive care to patients. She is currently working at the University of Missouri–Columbia as a child and adolescent psychiatrist and clinical professor of psychiatry.

Audrey Addi-Raccah, PhD, is an associate professor at the School of Education at Tel-Aviv University. She is the head of the unit of sociology of education and community. Her research is concerned with sociology of education and educational management with a focus on educational inequality, school effects, teachers' and school principals' work, and parental involvement in education. She is currently examining the social position and influence of parent leadership in a school founded by the Israel Science Foundation and is engaged in a large-scale research project on school improvement.

Khalid I. Afzal, MD, is a board-certified adult, and child and adolescent psychiatrist, and an associate professor of psychiatry and behavioral neuroscience in the University of Chicago Pritzker School of Medicine and Biological Sciences. He is the director of the Pediatric Consultation–Liaison Service in UChicago Medicine and Comer Children's Hospital. He trained at Texas Tech University Health Sciences Center for his adult psychiatry residency, and at the University of Chicago for his child fellowship. He is interested in global mental health, the psychosomatic manifestations of illness, cultural aspects of psychiatric presentations, and creative family interventions for depression, anxiety, attention-deficit hyperactivity disorder (ADHD), and disruptive behavior disorders. His research includes pediatric mental health awareness in minority populations in the United States and in low- and middle-income countries. His research team has published the first-ever suicide screening pathway for pediatric hospitals, and he has presented both nationally and internationally on his research and clinical practice.

Dr. Renato D. Alarcón is a professor emeritus and consultant in the Department of Psychiatry and Psychology at Mayo Clinic College of Medicine, Rochester, Minnesota. He also holds the Honorio Delgado Chair at the Universidad Peruana Cayetano Heredia (UPCH) School of Medicine, in Lima, Peru. He completed his psychiatric residency and fellowships in psychosomatic medicine and clinical psychopharmacology at Johns Hopkins Hospital and earned his MPH at the Hopkins School of Public Health. After eight years of academic work at his alma mater in Lima, he returned to the United States and occupied leadership positions in the Departments of Psychiatry at the University of Alabama in Birmingham and Emory University School of Medicine before joining the Mayo Clinic. The author or coauthor of more than 250 articles, and the author or editor of nineteen books and eighty-two book chapters, Dr. Alarcón is the senior editor of *Psiquiatría (Psychiatry)*, the most widely used psychiatric textbook in Latin America, and a board member of several publications in the continent. He has received, among other distinctions, the American Psychiatric Association's (APA) Simon Bolivar (1999) and George Tarjan (2011) Awards, and the World Association of Cultural Psychiatry's Jean Garrabé (2016) Award. He is also an APA Distinguished Life Fellow and a Psychiatric Association of Latin America (APAL) Master of Latin American Psychiatry. The National Institute of Mental Health in Peru made him the first recipient of the Honorio Delgado Gold Medal in 2016, and the National Academy of Medicine in Peru incorporated him as a full member in 2017. He was a member of the APA's DSM-5 Task Force (1999–2013), and he currently belongs to the APA's DSM Steering Committee. His fields of academic and clinical interest include mood and personality disorders, psychiatric diagnosis, global mental health, and cultural psychiatry.

Cristina de Andrade Varanda is a psychologist, postdoctorate, and PhD in rehabilitation science from the School of Medicine of the University of São Paulo, with a master's degree in experimental psychology from the Institute of Psychology of the University of São Paulo. She is a full professor of psychology at Paulista University in Brazil, and a research leader of the Group of Studies and Research in Psychology and Cognition (GEPESPSI) at Paulista University. Dr. Andrade Varanda has published articles on autism, psycholinguistics, and children's language and behavior.

Danny T. K. Avula, MD, MPH, is the public health director for the City of Richmond and Henrico County. He is board certified in pediatrics and preventive medicine, and practices clinically as a pediatric hospitalist. In 2013, Dr. Avula was appointed to Virginia's State Board of Social Services, where he served as chairman from 2018 to 2019. He has devoted much of his personal life to learning how to be a good neighbor in a racially and socioeconomically diverse neighborhood experiencing the challenges of gentrification and displacement of long-term residents. His work has been featured nationally by the Centers for Disease Control (CDC), MSNBC, and on the Technology, Entertainment and Design (TED) circuit with his TEDx talk entitled "Dependence Isn't a Dirty Word."

Jack Baker is a graduate student in clinical psychology at Miami University, with interests in school-based mental health and interpersonal violence prevention. He graduated from the University of Virginia in 2016 with a degree in youth and social innovation. His experiences in youth participatory action research have fostered an interest in merging the fields of social justice and clinical psychology to provide more space for the voices of all youth to be heard.

Nancy Bearss began practice as a physician's assistant (PA) in 1981 with a focus on prevention and adolescent medicine after receiving her undergraduate degree at Bucknell University, her PA certification at Essex Community College in Baltimore, and her MPH at Johns Hopkins University School of Public Health. Her primary work has been in school-based health centers in Maryland and Delaware. In 2004, Ms. Bearss left clinical medicine to teach at the PA program at Towson University, and in 2009, she returned to primary care and school-based health. In 2019, Ms. Bearss retired from clinical medicine. She continues to lecture at Towson University for the Allied Health Program.

Professor Agnes Binagwaho, MD, M(Ped), PHD, is the vice chancellor of the University of Global Health Equity (UGHE). She has held high-level government positions, serving as the executive secretary of Rwanda's National AIDS Control Commission, the permanent secretary of the Ministry of Health, and for five years as the minister of health. She is a senior advisor to the director general of the World Health Organization. She is a professor of pediatrics at UGHE, a senior lecturer at Harvard Medical School, and an adjunct clinical professor of pediatrics at the School of Medicine at Dartmouth. Since 2016, she has been a member of the American National Academy of Medicine, and since 2017, she has been a fellow of the African Academy of Sciences.

Ms. Vijayluxmi Bose has an MS in communication studies from Emerson College in Boston. She is a former faculty member at the AJK Mass Communication Research Centre, Jamia Millia Islamia, the Public Health Foundation of India, and Delhi University. She drafted the "Regional Communication Strategy for Birth Defects Prevention" of the World Health Organization and has facilitated the Indian Child Protection Medical Professionals Network. She is the coauthor of a publication in the *Oschner Journal* titled "Social Determinants of Child Marriage in Rural India," and she provides technical support to the Bal Umang Drishya Sanstha nongovernmental organization.

Katherine Richardson Bruna is an associate professor in the School of Education at Iowa State University (ISU). She is the founding director and professor-in-charge of the ISU 4 U Promise, a university-school-community "promise program" partnership that, since 2012, has served two high-needs elementary schools in urban Des Moines neighborhoods that are experiencing rapid ethnic diversification. At ISU, she teaches courses on multicultural and bilingual education and on interpretive inquiry methods.

Dr. Aisha Sanober Chachar completed her MBBS at Isra University, Pakistan. She completed her adult psychiatry residency at Aga Khan University in 2015, and worked in a faculty position at the Department of Psychiatry, Aga Khan University for two years. She is currently a child and adolescent psychiatry postgraduate trainee at Aga Khan University.

Ms. Riti Chandrashekhar utilizes her background in applied psychology as a research associate at Bal Umang Drishya Sanstha (BUDS).

Caroline S. Clauss-Ehlers is an associate professor and the program/clinical coordinator for the programs in school counseling and counseling psychology in the Department of Educational Psychology at Rutgers, The State University of New Jersey. Her research and writing focuses on cultural resilience, trauma, bilingualism, and work with children and their families within diverse community contexts. She has edited, coedited, co-authored, and authored books and numerous articles in this area. She has served as the chair of the American Psychological Association's Task Force on Re-envisioning the Multicultural Guidelines for the 21st Century, a group who wrote *Multicultural Guidelines: An Ecological Approach to Context, Identity, and Intersectionality* (2017) (see www.apa.org/about/policy/multicultural-guidelines).

Sigrún Daníelsdóttir, M.Sc, Cand. Psych, is a child and adolescent psychologist and project manager for mental health promotion at the Directorate of Health in Iceland. Her work centers largely on mental health promotion in schools and local communities, and she has headed several policy development efforts in areas such as school mental health promotion and suicide prevention. She is also a body image researcher, writer, and activist, and collaborates nationally and internationally on initiatives to advance body respect and equality.

Kateri Donahoe, MPH, is a research associate in the office of the vice chancellor at the University of Global Health Equity (UGHE) in Rwanda. She earned an MPH in global health and a BA in international relations, both from Boston University. She has previously worked and conducted research on maternal and reproductive healthcare, gender-based violence, and human rights issues. Since joining UGHE in 2017, Ms. Donahoe has supported research efforts in the areas of universal access to healthcare, implementation science, and equitable healthcare delivery.

Dr. Eugene Emory is a professor of psychology, psychiatry, and behavioral sciences and the director of the Center for Prenatal Assessment and Human Development at Emory University. His research in developmental neuroscience focuses on prenatal cognition and brain imaging. His previous work includes studies of fetal and infant neurobehavioral development and reproductive stress. His professional areas of expertise include developmental and clinical neuropsychology.

Fernanda Dreux Miranda Fernandes, PhD, is a speech-language pathologist (SLP) and audiologist, and an associate professor in the communication sciences and disorders program at the School of Medicine of the University of São Paulo. She has a doctorate in linguistics and semiotics and has published more than 120 papers. Dr. Fernandes is also a former president of the Brazilian SLP Association, a member of the board of the International Association of Logopedics and Phoniatrics, and an American Speech-Language-Hearing Association (ASHA) fellow.

Dr. María Elena Figueroa-Díaz is an associate professor at the National Autonomous University of Mexico and the Metropolitan Autonomous University. She has a PhD in sociology from the National Autonomous University of Mexico. Previously, she studied philosophy and human development. Her work focuses on cultural policies, gender, social inequalities and life projects, representations of the future, and the relationship between culture and territory.

Paul Flaspohler is an associate professor of clinical psychology at Miami University (of Ohio) and the director of research and evaluation for the Center for School-Based Mental Health Programs. Dr. Flaspohler received his PhD in clinical-community psychology from the University of South Carolina and completed his internship at the Consultation Center at the Yale School of Medicine. In addition to applied research in community development and program evaluation, Dr. Flaspohler assists community organizations and schools with identifying needs and developing solutions for community problems.

S. Andrew Garbacz is an assistant professor in the school psychology program in the Department of Educational Psychology at the University of Wisconsin–Madison. His work focuses on enhancing and integrating family-school-community collaboration within school and community systems. He coleads the Family-School-Community Alliance dedicated to advancing family-school-community collaboration in multitiered systems of support. He has received the Lightner Witmer Award from Division 16 of the American Psychological Association and a family-school partnership award from the National Association of School Psychologists.

James Garbarino, PhD, holds the Maude C. Clarke Chair in Humanistic Psychology and was founding director of the Center for the Human Rights of Children at Loyola University Chicago. Among the books he has authored are: *Listening to Killers: Lessons Learned from My 20 Years As a Psychological Expert*

Witness in Murder Cases (2015), *Miller's Children: Why Giving Teenage Killers a Second Chance Matters for All of Us* (2018), and *Lost Boys: Why Our Sons Turn Violent and How We Can Save Them* (1999). In 1989, he received the American Psychological Association's Award for Distinguished Professional Contributions to Public Service.

Amy E. Governale, PhD, is a visiting assistant professor of psychology at North Park University. Her research uses an ecological systems framework to explore contexts that promote well-being among under-serviced youth. This includes examining after-school program participation among low-income, ethnically diverse adolescents in the United States, and the impacts of trauma and political violence exposure on child development in global settings.

Yahira Rossini Guzmán-Sabogal, MD, PhD, is a medical specialist in psychiatry from the National University of Colombia, and a specialist in bioethics at the University of La Sabana in Colombia. Dr. Guzmán-Sabogal earned a PhD in applied medical research from the University of Navarra in Spain, and is currently the director of the psychiatry and mental health research group at the University of La Sabana. Dr. Guzmán-Sabogal has served as the administrator for The Carter Center Scholarship for Journalists in Mental Health in Colombia. Currently, Dr. Guzmán-Sabogal is the director of professors and the Research Faculty of Medicine at the University of La Sabana. Dr. Guzmán-Sabogal is a member of the Scientific Committee of the Colombian Psychiatric Association.

Judith R. Harrison, PhD, is an assistant professor in the Department of Educational Psychology, Special Education at Rutgers University in New Brunswick, New Jersey. Dr. Harrison was a special education teacher and counselor for more than twenty years in public schools. Her research interests include the effectiveness, acceptability, and feasibility of classroom-based strategies for youth with emotional and behavioral disorders and attention-deficit hyperactivity disorder.

Erwin H. Hernandez-Rincon, MD, MSc, PhD, is a physician with master's degrees in government and health management and primary care research, and a PhD in clinical research. He is an associate professor at the Center for Studies in Community Health, School of Medicine, Universidad de La Sabana (Colombia). Dr. Hernandez-Rincon has experience in public health, community health, and primary care in vulnerable populations.

Cibelle Albuquerque de la Higuera Amato is a speech-language pathologist with a master's degree in experimental physiopathology from the School of Medicine of the University of São Paulo and a PhD in general linguistics from the School of Philosophy, Letters and Human Sciences of the University of São Paulo. Dr. Higuera Amato is a professor in the postgraduate program in developmental disorders at Mackenzie Presbyterian University, and a professor in the Program of

Improvement in Speech and Hearing Therapy in Child Psychiatry, Hospital das Clínicas, School of Medicine, University of São Paulo. Dr. Higuera Amato is a member of the Brazilian Society of Speech-Language Pathologists.

Ingrid Holsen, PhD, is currently a professor at the Department for Health Promotion and Development at the University of Bergen. Professor Holsen's primary research interests are youth participatory action research, mental health and positive youth development, and implementation and evaluation of health promotion efforts in schools.

Scott J. Hunter, PhD, is a professor of psychiatry and behavioral neuroscience, and pediatrics in the University of Chicago Pritzker School of Medicine and Biological Sciences Division, and the director of neuropsychology for UChicago Medicine and Comer Children's Hospital. He obtained his PhD in clinical and developmental psychology from the University of Illinois at Chicago, an internship at Northwestern University Medical School, and postdoctoral fellowships in pediatric neuropsychology and neurodevelopmental disorders at the University of Rochester School of Medicine and Dentistry. His research focuses on trajectories of attention and executive functioning in individuals with neurodevelopmental and medical conditions, with an emphasis on the impact of socioeconomic factors, including homelessness and healthcare disparities, on neurocognitive and behavioral development. A former chair of the American Psychological Association's (APA) Committee on Professional Practice and Standards, Dr. Hunter is coauthor of the 2017 update of the APA Multicultural Guidelines for the practice of professional psychology.

Nathalie O. Iotti is a research assistant in the Department of Psychology at the University of Turin, Italy. Nathalie is a licensed psychologist who works with children and adolescents. Currently, she is studying to become a psychotherapist. Her research interests lie in the area of psychology, ranging from bullying to clinical psychology and child abuse and neglect. She is presently conducting research examining bystander roles of adolescents witnessing school bullying. Outside of professional interests, she reads, hikes, plays the guitar, and enjoys traveling widely with her family.

Moshe Israelashvili is a professor in the school counseling program at the School of Education, Tel Aviv University, Israel. His PhD thesis (social psychology) was on "the emergence of feelings of injustice." His current studies focus on times of transition, in pursuit of preventing maladjustment (e.g., school maladjustment). Recently, he edited (with Professor John L. Romano, the University of Minnesota) *The Cambridge Handbook of International Prevention Science* (2017, Cambridge University Press), and (with Professor Fadia Nasser Abo-Alhija, Tel Aviv University) *Education in the Arab Society of Israel* (in press, Mofet Publishing House).

Elizabeth H. Jensen has been working in the mental health field in an array of facilities ranging from inpatient, outpatient, residential treatment, the Department of Corrections, and the Department of Justice, and with students from grades 7 to 12. Her educational background in individual counseling modalities, substance abuse, and marriage, family, and couples counseling has provided her a platform from which to approach the many issues that arise in the mental health field.

Dr. Susan W. Jones received a doctor of medicine degree from the Virginia Commonwealth University School of Medicine, a psychiatry residency at the University of Alabama Hospitals, and a fellowship in child and adolescent psychiatry from Virginia Commonwealth University (VCU) at the Virginia Treatment Center for Children. She practiced as a community child psychiatrist for twenty-three years and is an assistant professor at VCU. Her expertise is in eating disorders, children with trauma histories, and working with gender-expansive children and educating the next generation of providers. She provides embedded child psychiatry services to a multidisciplinary clinic for gender-expansive children at VCU.

Tomas Jungert, PhD, is an associate professor in the Department of Psychology at Lund University, Sweden. Tomas completed his PhD at Linköping University, Sweden, and did his postdoc at McGill University, Canada. His research interests lie in the area of psychology, ranging from motivation and need satisfaction in different contexts to bullying and educational psychology. He is currently conducting research examining bystander roles of adolescents witnessing school bullying. Outside of professional interests, he reads, writes, plays tennis, and enjoys traveling widely with his family.

Shubhangi Kansal has worked as a research associate at Bal Umang Drishya Sanstha (BUDS), and has a background in applied psychology. She is currently a master's student at Leipzig University.

Laura Kern is a postdoctoral scholar at the University of South Florida. She practiced law for more than ten years, receiving her JD from Quinnipiac University. After her son was diagnosed with autism, she received a master of arts in special education and doctorate in educational psychology with a focus on special education at the University of Connecticut's Neag School of Education as well as certificates in evaluation and positive behavior intervention and support. Her research interests include the intersection of policy with educational practice, the reduction of aggressive behaviors in schools, and the implementation of multitiered systems of support.

Eva Kuzyk is an undergraduate student earning her BS in neuroscience and behavioral biology at Emory University. She is an intern at the Center for Prenatal Assessment and Human Development at Emory University and the Grady Trauma Project. Her academic interests lie in the area of trauma and mental health development in young people.

List of Contributors xix

Torill Larsen, PhD, is currently a professor at the Department for Health Promotion and Development at the University of Bergen and the vice dean for research at Western Norway University of Applied Science. Professor Larsen's primary research interests are children and adolescents' health, positive youth development, implementation of health promotion efforts in schools, teacher training, and school leadership.

Gershom Lazarus is originally from South Africa and is currently pursuing a PhD in clinical psychology at Emory University with a focus in neuropsychology. His research interests include the link between maternal stress and fetal developmental outcomes and the use of an intervention targeting maternal physiological functioning to improve fetal neurodevelopment. He has also been interested in cross-cultural mental healthcare.

Dr. Theophilus Lazarus completed a postdoctoral fellowship in clinical and forensic neuropsychology at the University of North Carolina Wilmington under the direction of Dr. Antonio E. Puente, a former president of the American Psychological Association (APA) and the National Academy of Neuropsychology. Dr. Lazarus teaches, conducts research, and practices as a forensic and clinical neuropsychologist and has assessed more than 5,000 cases of infant and childhood traumatic brain injury. His special interest is researching the mental health and legal protection needs of infant and childhood survivors of traumatic brain injury.

Milaney Leverson is a licensed school psychologist with eight years of school practice experience, and has worked for the past seven years as a regional technical assistance coordinator supporting and training schools in positive behavioral interventions and supports (PBIS) and culturally responsive practices in the state of Wisconsin. Milaney has collaborated with other state PBIS teams to embed culturally responsive practices in their PBIS trainings and supports and has presented at state, national, and international conferences on the topic of creating culturally responsive PBIS systems. Milaney is a founding member of the Equity Work Group with the National PBIS Center.

Cara Lomaro is an undergraduate student at Rutgers University, studying psychology and women and gender studies. She is in her third year as a research assistant with Dr. Caroline S. Clauss-Ehlers and has assisted with the revised American Psychological Association's Multicultural Guidelines, among other projects. Most recently, Cara has worked on two chapters for *The Cambridge Handbook of Community Psychology: Interdisciplinary and Contextual Perspectives* (to be published by Cambridge University Press, anticipated publication date in 2020) that examine mental health and social media, and the impact of climate change on communities, respectively.

Dr. Liliana López Levi is a full-time professor at the Department of Politics and Culture at the Metropolitan Autonomous University, Xochimilco campus, in

Mexico City, where she is the head of the state management and political systems research area, as well as the head of the society and territory specialization belonging to the social science PhD program. Dr. López Levi received her bachelor's degree, master's degree, and PhD in geography from the National Autonomous University of Mexico. Her research and writing focus on the relationship between imaginaries and territory, political culture, and cultural spaces.

Alexis Lorenzo Ruiz, Lic. Psychology, Rostov-on-Don University, Russia (1988), Master's degree in health psychology, Medical University of Havana (1996). Full-time professor at the University of Havana, Cuba. Doctor in psychological sciences, National University Interior Ministry, Kharkov Ukraine (2000). Chief discipline clinical and health psychology. Psychology faculty at the University of Havana. National research project coordinator Psychological well-being and health. President of the Cuban Society of Psychology. Founding member Latin American Network Psychology Emergencies and Disasters. Short-Term Scholar University of Connecticut (UCONN) PostDoc Institute for Collaboration on Health, Intervention and Policy (InCHIP) to conduct research in the field of psychology (August 2017–January 2018).

Becca McBride is a specialist on the intersection between learning, government policy, and human rights. Her book *The Globalization of Adoption: Individuals, States, and Agencies across Borders* explores how governments learn about solutions to child welfare challenges from non-state actors. She holds a PhD in international relations and political theory from Vanderbilt University, and an MA in Eurasian, Russian, and East European studies from Georgetown University. She has held diverse professional positions, including assistant professor of political science at Calvin College, Russian political and leadership analyst at the Central Intelligence Agency, and her current role as learning and development manager at Deloitte.

Ayesha Irshad Mian is an internationally renowned child and adolescent psychiatrist. Dr. Mian is an MBBS graduate from Aga Khan University (AKU). Currently, she shares a joint appointment as the chair of the Department of Psychiatry and the dean of students at AKU. Dr. Mian cochairs the International Relations Committee of the American Academy of Child and Adolescent Psychiatry (AACAP), serves on the Executive Council of the International Association for Child and Adolescent Psychiatry and Allied Professions (IACAPAP) as a codirector of the Donald J. Cohen Fellowship Program, and has been awarded the prestigious Distinguished Fellowship by the AACAP. She has recently been recognized with a lifetime achievement award from the University of Missouri–Columbia's International Center for Psychosocial Trauma and the University's Child and Adolescent Psychiatry Alumni Association.

Devon R. Minch is a technical assistance specialist for the Florida Positive Behavioral Interventions & Support (FLPBIS) Project. Dr. Minch provides training and technical assistance to Florida school districts to implement positive behavior interventions and supports (PBIS) within K–12 public schools in the state. Devon coleads the Family-School-Community Alliance, a partner organization to the National PBIS Technical Assistance Center, focused on supporting and expanding research and practice on family engagement within tiered systems of supports.

Satish Moorthy has worked for more than sixteen years in the educational, social service, and mental health fields serving children and youth with special needs. He has supported positive behavioral interventions and supports (PBIS) in New York City school districts since 2009. Mr. Moorthy has worked in the field of human rights as a policy advocate, mental health practitioner, and teacher for immigrant and refugee children and youth in Chicago, IL. He holds a dual master's degree in public policy and clinical social work from the University of Chicago, and a bachelor's degree in English literature from the University of California, Berkeley. Mr. Moorthy is an elected board member of the international Association for Positive Behavior Support (APBS).

Maura Mulloy, PhD, is a licensed psychologist, mindfulness teacher, and researcher, and the author of *Resilience-Building Schools for At-Risk Youth: Developing the Social, Emotional and Motivational Foundations of Academic Success* (Civic Research Institute). After living and working for seven years in Ethiopia and Haiti, she has returned home to the United States with her husband and three young daughters. She is the director of research and development at the Thrive Center for Emerging Adults in Columbia, MD, where she works clinically with young adults, teaches mindfulness, and co-runs a parent support group. Dr. Mulloy received her BA from Yale University, her PhD from The Catholic University of America, and her postdoctoral training from University of Maryland at Baltimore's Center for School Mental Health.

Danielle Nesi, MA, is a doctoral student in the developmental psychology program at Loyola University Chicago. Her general research interests include forensic developmental psychology and issues related to juvenile justice. Danielle's most current work investigates risk and resiliency in adolescents and emerging adults, and interventions to promote positive outcomes for justice-involved individuals.

Tanya Novotnak is a doctoral student in the school psychology program at the University of Wisconsin–Madison. She holds BAs in psychology and French from Knox College in Galesburg, Illinois, and an MS in educational psychology from the University of Wisconsin–Madison. Before studying school psychology, Tanya worked as an educator in community programs and schools in the United States and Benin, West Africa. Tanya studies family-school and community-school partnerships that promote positive environments for adolescent development and learning.

Lynn Pasquerella, president of the Association of American Colleges and Universities, has served as the eighteenth president of Mount Holyoke College, the provost at the University of Hartford, and the vice provost for academic affairs and dean of the graduate school at the University of Rhode Island, where she began her career as a professor. A philosopher whose work has combined teaching and scholarship with local and global engagement, Pasquerella is the host of Northeast Public Radio's *The Academic Minute,* a member of the advisory board of the Newman's Own Foundation, and president of the Phi Beta Kappa Society.

Katelyn Reardon graduated from Emory University in May 2019 and plans to pursue a master's degree in the future. She currently assists with research in the Emory University Department of Neuropsychology. Her research interests include effects of trauma on neurodevelopment and behavior, predictors of childhood externalizing problems in high-risk populations, maladaptive behaviors and adjustment, and therapeutic interventions targeting child and adult psychopathology.

Terrence J. Roberts, PhD, is one of the "Little Rock Nine" who desegregated Central High School in Little Rock, Arkansas, in 1957. As a fifteen-year-old eleventh grader, he joined eight other students and became one of the first nine Black students to go to a formerly segregated public high school in Little Rock. Dr. Roberts is CEO of Terrence Roberts Consulting, a management consultant firm devoted to fair and equitable practices in business and industry. Additionally, he is coprincipal of Roberts & Roberts, LLC, a consulting firm offering assistance to groups who wish to engage in substantive conversations about race and the issues related to race in America. A graduate of California State University, Los Angeles (BA) and the University of California, Los Angeles (UCLA) (MSW), Dr. Roberts obtained his PhD in psychology from Southern Illinois University in Carbondale, Illinois. *Lessons from Little Rock,* a memoir by Dr. Roberts, was published on October 1, 2009. In this book, Dr. Roberts describes his experience at Central High School and talks about the salient lessons of that episode. On February 1, 2010, his second book, *Simple, Not Easy: Reflections on Community, Social Responsibility, and Tolerance,* was published. The essays in this volume seek to guide the reader toward more socially responsible positions in life.

Carrie Romo, MS. Ed., is an educator and activist from Kansas City, Kansas. She attended Central College in Pella, Iowa, where she quickly found her calling toward social justice and equity. As a freshman, she got involved with the White Privilege Conference, which she credits with helping her channel her confusion and anger into education and action. She currently serves as a planning member for the nonprofit organization The Privilege Institute.

Tanja Sargent received her PhD in education and sociology from the University of Pennsylvania. She is now an associate professor in the Department of Educational Theory, Policy and Administration at the Rutgers Graduate School of Education in

New Jersey, where she teaches courses in comparative education and society and education in contemporary China. Her research focuses on issues of educational reform in contemporary China, including the role of professional teachers' learning communities in the implementation of curricular and pedagogical reforms.

Dr. Tammy Schwartz is the director of the Urban Cohort and a faculty member in the College of Education, Health and Society at Miami University. Her deepest interests include the educational experiences of children who are marginalized for any reason and the preparation of resilient and community-minded teachers who are equipped to ensure their success. Her passion for this work is rooted in her history as an urban child living with poverty and as an urban public school teacher. She holds great hope for the future of public education.

Kirstin Woody Scott, MPhil, PhD, is a student at Harvard Medical School. She graduated from the University of California, Davis with degrees in neurobiology and classics. She earned a master of public health degree from the University of Cambridge, and then worked in healthcare politics before becoming a Rotary Ambassadorial Scholar in Nicaragua. Prior to beginning medical school, she completed her PhD in health policy at Harvard, concentrating on political analysis and global health quality. Since 2013, she has supported a variety of health policy research initiatives in Rwanda.

Dr. Rajeev Seth is a US-trained, American board-certified senior consultant pediatrician, with a special interest in realizing child rights and protection for all children. Dr. Seth leads Bal Umang Drishya Sanstha (BUDS) (www.buds.in), a registered nonprofit organization formed with the objective of advancing the well-being, education, health, and welfare of underprivileged children in several urban slums and rural poor marginalized communities in India. Dr. Seth has been elected president of the International Society for Prevention of Child Abuse and Neglect (ISPCAN). He works hard to develop partnerships and expand the reach of its network with other regional, national, and international organizations interested in protecting the rights of children. Dr. Seth is a former chair of the Indian Child Abuse Neglect and Child Labour (ICANCL) Group. Dr. Seth has several academic publications, awards, and grants to his credit.

Shawn S. Sidhu is an assistant professor of psychiatry at the University of New Mexico (UNM), and he currently serves as training director for the UNM Child and Adolescent Psychiatry Fellowship Program. Dr. Sidhu has been both providing mental health evaluations for asylum-seeking immigrants, and training individuals along the border in how to provide such evaluations. His work along the border also involves building capacity at the border, and liaising with academic departments, immigration attorneys, community nonprofit organizations, and local chapters of the National Alliance on Mental Illness. He hopes to one day build a Southwestern Network for Survivors of Torture.

Dr. Aradhana Bela Sood is a senior professor of child mental health policy at Virginia Commonwealth University (VCU). She has spent thirty years providing tertiary care to children with serious emotional disturbance and in the past decade shifted her focus to prevention efforts, particularly in under-resourced populations. Recognized for her contributions to public mental health work by state and national organizations, Dr. Sood has engaged in prevention efforts that span infancy, childhood, and transition-age youth. She has edited two books on mental health policy and prevention in children's mental health.

Dr. Jessica Swain-Bradway is the executive director for Northwest PBIS Network. Her regional and national research and implementation of schoolwide positive behavioral interventions and supports (SWPBIS) focus on the expansion of "traditional" PBIS to include comprehensive supports in response to the stressors and demands students, teachers, families, and communities face. Jessica has expertise in aligning restorative practices, mental health practices, including trauma-informed care, and academic Response to Intervention (RtI) into the SWPBIS framework.

Professor Abdel Aziz Mousa Thabet is a Palestinian child and adolescent psychiatrist who was educated in Palestine, Austria, and the United Kingdom in child psychiatry. He is a professor emeritus at Al Quds University, and he is now affiliated with the Center for Refugee Studies at York University. He is running a clinical setting in Gaza City seeing adult and child victims of trauma and political violence. Over the past three decades, Professor Thabet has conducted research on the prevalence of mental health problems and the evaluation of intervention methods in dealing with children in Gaza and the West Bank.

Jennifer Ulie-Wells is the founder and executive director of the Please Pass the Love Youth Mental Health Initiative, which provides systemic training and support for thousands of educators, schools, and districts across Iowa, and she is an adjunct at Drake University. In 2018, she launched an online school mental health literacy program in collaboration with Drake and the Iowa State Education Association (ISEA). She works in a variety of local and national school mental health capacities. As an educator activist, her research interests reside in the intersectionality of school mental health, specifically racial/cultural trauma.

Helga Bjørnøy Urke has a PhD in health promotion from the University of Bergen, Norway. Her main area of research is related to social aspects of child and adolescent health and well-being. She is currently an associate professor at the Department of Health Promotion and Development at the University of Bergen.

Christopher H. Vatland is a research assistant professor at the University of South Florida. In his capacity there, Dr. Vatland coordinates community support activities for the Florida Center for Inclusive Communities, which is a University Center for Excellence in Developmental Disabilities (UCEDD). He also manages and collaborates on a range of research, technical assistance, and development projects related to school-based and family-based supports as well as family-school engagement.

Nathaniel P. von der Embse is an assistant professor of school psychology at the University of South Florida. Dr. von der Embse serves as an associate editor for the *Journal of School Psychology*, and his research interests include universal screening for behavioral and mental health, teacher stress and student test anxiety, and training educators in population-based mental health services. He has received the Lightner Witmer Award for early career scholarship from Division 16 of the American Psychological Association.

Katelyn Wargel is a clinical psychology doctoral student and graduate assistant at Miami University (of Ohio). Katelyn has received a bachelor of science degree in management and a bachelor of arts degree in communication from Purdue University, and a master of public administration degree from Indiana University–Purdue University Indianapolis. In her training at Miami University, Katelyn conducts applied research in community settings with the goal of empowering stakeholders to continually evaluate and improve upon effective mental health initiatives in schools and communities.

Mark D. Weist is a professor in clinical-community and school psychology in the Department of Psychology at the University of South Carolina. In his prior position at the University of Maryland, he founded the Center for School Mental Health, providing leadership in the advancement of school mental health (SMH) policies and programs. He has edited or developed twelve books and has published and presented widely on diverse topics in SMH. He is currently coleading a regional conference (see www.schoolbehavioralhealth.org), and leading two randomized controlled trials focused on improving the effectiveness and impact of SMH.

Dawn Michele Whitehead is the vice president of the Office of Global Citizenship for Campus, Community and Careers at the Association of American Colleges and Universities (AAC&U) in Washington, DC. In her work with AAC&U, she collaborates with colleges and universities to advance practices, strategies, and innovative projects for integrative global learning across the undergraduate curriculum. She also works with institutions to make clear curricular connections among courses in general education and the majors to provide students with quality liberal education experiences. She has published work on global learning, global service learning, curricular reform, and education in Ghana. Prior to joining AAC&U, Whitehead served as the director of curriculum internationalization at Indiana University–Purdue University Indianapolis, where she also served as faculty director for global service learning programs in Costa Rica, Ghana, and Kenya and taught in the International Studies Department. She earned her PhD at Indiana University

Bloomington in education policy studies with a doctoral minor in international and comparative education and a concentration in African studies.

Tara Warman Wiley is a public health communications specialist with Richmond City Health District. She is the coordinator for Culture of Health Richmond, a health equity data-sharing and storytelling project that celebrates bold ideas and voices to improve racial and social justice and health outcomes in Greater Richmond. Tara is a former assistant professor of research writing at Virginia Commonwealth University. She holds an MFA in creative writing from Syracuse University.

Dr. Sana Younus graduated as the first fellow from the pioneering child and adolescent psychiatry fellowship program at Aga Khan University, Pakistan, in 2018. She completed her MBBS at Dow Medical College, followed by post-graduation studies in adult psychiatry at Aga Khan University. She was a recipient of the Donald J. Cohen Fellowship at the International Association of Child and Adolescent Psychiatry and Allied Professions in 2018. She was also awarded the Paramjit Joshi International Scholar's Award by the American Academy of Child and Adolescent Psychiatry the same year.

Donghui Zhang received her PhD from the Graduate School of Education, the University of Pennsylvania, and is now working as an associate professor in the School of Education, Renmin University of China. Her research interests include educational policy, education, culture and society, and comparative education. For the past ten years, she has been involved in research projects on the education of rural migrant children and ethnic minority children in Chinese cities.

Foreword

Years ago, during my first semester in college, I chanced upon a work by Lisa Richette entitled *The Throwaway Children*. It was difficult reading for me; the idea that children would be so misused and abused, even by those who were assigned to care for them, was way outside my comfort zone. I could find no rationale for such a reality. Later, I read Ernest Becker's *The Birth and Death of Meaning*, in which he writes: "It is the task of culture to provide for each and every single individual the firm conviction that he or she is an object of primary value in a world of meaningful action." Obviously our society has failed to meet that standard, especially when it is applied to children.

The authors of this text have set out to rectify this heinous situation. By presenting evidence that helps readers develop a critical awareness of the plight of children around the globe and offering a plethora of reform measures, they seek to enlist the time and talent of all who wish to see meaningful change. Unless and until we choose to include children and young people in our fight for social justice, we run the risk of disabling the very ones to whom we are to pass the batons we received from those who lived before us.

Unfortunately the "us-them" and "we-they" dichotomies we embrace as a natural part of our life has done more damage than we realize. When these egregious fictive beliefs are imposed upon children and young people, we miss opportunities to transfer whatever useful information we have to the generations who follow. This work will educate, inspire, and hopefully transform readers who will opt to sign up as warriors dedicated to saving the lives and souls of the many children we continue to "throw away"!

–Terrence J. Roberts, PhD

PART I

Social Justice and Human Rights for Children and Young People

1

Introduction

An Urgent Call to Understand the Status of Children and Young People within a Social Justice Paradigm

Caroline S. Clauss-Ehlers, Aradhana Bela Sood, Cara Lomaro, and Mark D. Weist

INTRODUCTION

The goal of a social justice approach for children is "to ensure that children, defined by the Convention on the Rights of the Child as all persons under the age of eighteen, are better served and protected by justice systems, including the security and social welfare sectors" (United Nations Secretary General [UNSG], 2008, p.1). Despite this worthy goal, the United Nations (UN) documents how children are rarely viewed as stakeholders in rules of law. Child justice issues are often dealt with as separate from larger justice and security issues, and when justice issues for children are addressed, it is often through a siloed, rather than a comprehensive, approach. The UN concludes: "Access to justice, though increasingly recognized as an important strategy for protecting the rights of vulnerable groups, and thus for fighting poverty, rarely takes children into account" (United Nations Secretary General [UNSG], 2008, p.2).

The Convention on the Rights of the Child (CRC) (UN General Assembly, 1989) was adopted in 1989 and provides provisions for child justice and human rights specifically for people younger than eighteen years of age. The CRC has been ratified by every member country of the United Nations with the exception of the United States. It states: "Recalling that, in the Universal Declaration of Human Rights, the United Nations has proclaimed that childhood is entitled to special care and assistance" (UN General Assembly, 1989, p.1).

The CRC document consists of a preamble and fifty-four articles focused on the rights of the child. For example, Article 2.1 says: "States Parties shall respect and ensure the rights set forth in the present Convention to each child within their jurisdiction without discrimination of any kind, irrespective of the child's or his or her parent's or legal guardian's race, colour, sex, language, religion, political or other opinion, national, ethnic or social origin, property, disability, birth or other status" (CRC, 1989, 1990, p. 2). The CRC offers broad support for families whose role it is to protect and raise their children. For example, Article 5 says: "States Parties shall respect the responsibilities, rights and duties of parents or, where applicable, the members of the extended family or community as provided for by local custom, legal guardians or other persons legally responsible for the child, to provide, in a manner consistent with the evolving capacities of the child, appropriate direction and guidance in the exercise by the child of the rights recognized in the present Convention" (CRC, 1989, 1990, p. 2). It also encourages governmental justice sectors and welfare entities to implement programs that support children and families, thus promoting their human rights. For example, Article 4 says: "States Parties shall undertake all appropriate legislative, administrative, and other measures for the implementation of the rights recognized in the present Convention. With regard to economic, social and cultural rights, States Parties shall undertake such measures to the maximum extent of their available resources and, where needed, within the framework of international co-operation" (CRC, 1989, 1990, p. 2). Also notable about the CRC is that it underscores children's right to have a say in issues related to social justice. That is, Article 12.1 says: "States Parties shall assure to the child who is capable of forming his or her own views the right to express those views freely in all matters affecting the child, the views of the child being given due weight in accordance with the age and maturity of the child." The CRC outlines how children's human rights are on par with those of adults (CRC, 1989, 1990, p. 4).

Rationale

As preliminary discussions emerged about the possibility of writing this book, it was striking for the coeditors to acknowledge that no volume with a similar focus existed on the market. A review of current publications indicated no comprehensive book specifically focused on promoting social justice for children and young people from an international perspective, in contrast to a number of contributions focused on adults. One book focused on children was identified, but an international perspective was not taken and only the experience of early childhood was considered (as opposed to addressing adolescence as well).

We took this gap in the literature to be indicative of the UN contention that "children are yet to be viewed as key stakeholders in rule of law initiatives" (UNSG, 2008, p. 1). This volume, the first of its kind, seeks to address this gap by presenting an overall international framework to understand the guiding social justice principles for children and young people. This volume also seeks to present a working understanding of how these principles are operationalized (or not operationalized) globally through the inclusion of country case studies.

Country case studies reflect the experiences of low- and lower-middle-income economies as well as upper-middle- and high-income economies based on current World Bank country classifications (World Bank, n.d.). Understanding the country experience is important given societal trends toward globalization. The coeditors also thought it was important to consider the ways in which countries might partner and support one another around social justice issues that have an impact on children and young people. By documenting and understanding how nations seek to support their children, it is hoped that countries can share models and resources across boundaries and borders.

The rationale for a comprehensive volume that actively incorporates children and young people as critical social justice stakeholders is presented in the context of these serious limitations. This volume actively challenges the current social justice paradigm with new approaches that place children and young people front and center in the social justice conversation. Advancing approaches to improve social justice for children and young people around the world are presented, with the UN guiding principles for justice for children as an underlying framework (UN, 2008).

Hence, UN guiding principles for justice for children are "based on international legal norms and standards" and underscore the approach taken in this book (UNSG, 2008, p. 2). The UN asserts that the guiding principles encompass international rule of law standards toward all justice efforts concerning children (UN, 2008). The rationale for a common approach is to help the UN "leverage support through partners working on broader agendas around rule of law, including governance, security, social welfare and justice sector reform in which justice for children can easily be integrated" (p. 2). The guiding principles for a UN approach to justice for children are:

1. Ensuring that the best interests of the child is given primary consideration
2. Guaranteeing fair and equal treatment of every child, free from all kinds of discrimination
3. Advancing the right of the child to express his or her views freely and to be heard
4. Protecting every child from abuse, exploitation and violence
5. Treating every child with dignity and compassion
6. Respecting legal guarantees and safeguards in all processes
7. Preventing conflict with the law as a crucial element of any juvenile justice policy
8. Using deprivation of liberty of children only as a measure of last resort and for the shortest appropriate period of time
9. Mainstreaming children's issues in all rule of law efforts. (UN, 2008, p. 1)

With these guiding principles in mind, the purpose of this volume is to respond to gaps in practice and the literature via contributing chapters that reflect critical trends in social justice for children and young people from an international perspective. Chapters represent four areas that construct this book's framework: (1) social justice and human rights for children and young people; (2) international social justice issues for children and young people; (3) region and country case studies on social justice for children and young people; and (4) a platform for recommendations and reform. Tables and/or figures in each chapter are numbered with the chapter number followed by their chronological presentation (e.g., the first table in Chapter 5 is labeled Table 5.1). The first section, on social justice and human rights, introduces the reader to key concepts and terminology in the social justice literature. A review of the status of research and limitations is also provided.

While themes reflected throughout the nine guiding principles connect with each chapter, specific guiding principles are relevant for each section. Part I, "Social Justice and Human Rights for Children and Young People," provides an overview and reviews key concepts and terminology relevant to social justice and human rights for children and young people. The UN approach toward justice for children and related rule of law principles and frameworks are also discussed. Guiding principles 6, 7, and 9, which deal with rules of law as they concern justice for children, are key guidelines reflected in Part I. For instance, Chapter 2, "The Language of Social Justice for Children and Young People," provides a foundation to understand political processes and structures that either advocate for children or promote vulnerabilities. This foundational chapter helps the reader understand how children and young people are "embedded" in state and international procedures and policies. Chapter 3, "Social Determinants of Health," examines how health outcomes can be linked to socially determined variables such as housing, transportation, educational access, and nutrition. The chapter discusses how these factors are influenced by political structures that in turn influence policy outcomes, including those that have an impact on children and young people. Chapter 4, "Health and Mental Health Disparities," incorporates Ruger's health capability paradigm that views healthcare as a basic human right that, as applied to children, justifies equity in healthcare among society's youngest members.

Part II, "International Social Justice Issues That Have an Impact on Children and Young People," focuses on ten specific international social justice issues that have an impact on children and young people. While procedures of law are reflected throughout these chapters, thus incorporating UN guiding principles 6, 7, and 9, the specific issues and their impact on children's agency, quality of life, and life outcomes reflect guiding principles 1, 2, 3, 4, 5, and 8 – each of which considers the best interests, human rights, and dignity of children. In addition, chapters discuss each challenge to child and youth social justice from an international framework given the interconnectedness of nations and an increasing shift toward globalization via advances in transportation and technology. The ten topics presented in Part II include children and poverty (Chapter 5); educational access for women and girls (Chapter 6); children and young people affected by war (Chapter 7); the rights of lesbian, gay, bisexual, transgender, and queer youth (LGBTQ) (Chapter 8); social justice for children and adolescents who are immigrants (Chapter 9); social justice for children and young people with disabilities (Chapter 10); school mental health as a social justice framework for young people (Chapter 11); the role of family-school partnerships in promoting positive academic, social, and behavioral outcomes (Chapter 12); school-wide positive behavioral interventions and support (SWPBIS) (Chapter 13); and the impact of weight stigma on children's lives (Chapter 14).

Part III, "Regional and Country Case Studies on Social Justice for Youth," incorporates discussion about the ways in which the nine guiding principles may or may not be reflected in national policies and infrastructures. Given that social justice parameters tend to focus on the experience of adults, these national and international conversations about social justice efforts for children, as reflected in this book's country case studies, are important. Regional and country case studies present region/country parameters, barriers to social justice for young people, considerations related to rebuilding capacity, and programmatic examples.

It is also important to note some of the critical limitations in incorporating country case studies. More than once, for instance, the coeditors invited international colleagues to write a case study about their nation and were informed by invitees that they were not able to write such a chapter. These colleagues feared national retribution or personal consequences if they published something that brought attention to the injustices their countries were engaging in toward children. Such concerns about sharing the truth of children's national experiences speak to the importance of advocacy, appropriate political infrastructures designed to support child justice, and the need for free speech and open communication to promote reform.

While the coeditors were not able to include the voices of these countries in this volume, a hope is that the themes presented across chapters can inform and advocate for these country experiences in some meaningful way. Regional/country case studies that are included in this volume capture the experiences of Brazil, China, Colombia, Cuba, Ethiopia, India, Israel, Mexico, Norway, Pakistan, Palestine, Peru and Latin America, Rwanda, Scotland, South Africa, and the United States. Country case studies provide an opportunity to explore how nations implement social justice frameworks focused on youth. Such exploration includes what countries can learn from one another as they seek to close gaps in addressing youth social justice issues in addition to barriers related to developing social justice frameworks for children.

Part IV is the volume's conclusion. This chapter presents lessons learned and from them derives action-oriented strategies to promote social justice for children and young people. The chapter discusses how such efforts encompass two themes: (1) those related to engagement in social justice for children and young people, and (2) themes that focus on supporting a global infrastructure that promotes social justice for children and young people.

Social Justice Frameworks

The UN guiding principles are accompanied by a framework with "two tracks" that focus on aspects of child justice efforts. The first track concerns aspects of the framework that "ensure greater attention to children in rule of law initiatives" (UNSG, 2008, p. 1). The second track focuses on "additional interventions necessary to strengthen rule of law efforts in terms of justice for children specially and to guarantee full respect for child rights" (UNSG, 2008, p. 1). Both aspects of the framework seek to strengthen rules of law that address child justice issues. Four overall aspects of the UN framework promote social justice for children. They are as follows:

1. A constitution or its equivalent, and a legal framework and the implementation thereof (i.e., considering issues related to social justice for children when laws and policies are implemented at national and international levels);
2. Institutions of justice, governance, security, and human rights (i.e., rules of law regarding human rights, justice institutions, security, and governance must incorporate children's justice issues);
3. Transitional justice processes and mechanisms (i.e., children's issues need to be integrated into transitional processes and mechanisms); and
4. A public and civil society that contributes to strengthening the rule of law and that holds public officials and institutions accountable (i.e., children need to be included in these efforts through initiatives and processes such as child rights education, legal awareness, including children in identifying legal issues they care about, providing legal services for children, promoting children's access to justice systems not run by the state, offering programs for children in crisis situations, and raising awareness of children's rights when they experience justice systems as victims).

Country case studies provide international examples that consider the extent to which these frameworks are incorporated in national social justice infrastructures for children and young people.

Current Social Justice Models for Children and Young People: Opportunities and Barriers

While the coeditors took a global approach to exploring current social justice models in the literature, a search of journal articles focused on social justice for children and young people over the past ten years revealed that most articles were based in the United States, with the exception of journal articles from Canada (McLaughlin, Gray, & Wilson, 2015; Schmidt, 2014) and Israel (Lavie-Ajayi & Krumer-Nevo, 2013). Many of the articles were case studies or analyses (Schmidt, 2014). The lack of international models of social justice for children that specifies regional needs is viewed as a significant gap in the literature. The coeditors encouraged the exploration and dissemination of research on social justice models for children that reflect approaches outside of North America.

Of the social justice models that do exist, several are currently sought out for teaching and promoting social justice for youth. One such framework is the social justice youth development model (SJYD). As Ginwright and Cammarota (2002) explain, two components that make up SJYD are self-awareness and critical consciousness. According to the model, self-awareness works by strengthening youths' knowledge of their own identity whereas critical consciousness teaches them to critique the world and institutions around them (Pryor & Outley, 2014). Ginwright and Cammarota (2002) contend that "critical consciousness and social action provide young people with tools to understand and change the underlying causes of social and historical processes that perpetuate the problems they face daily" (p. 88). Through this model, youth consider themselves, their communities, and their world in order to identify issues and to make possible changes a reality (Cammarota, 2011).

Positive Youth Development (PYD) is another program of social justice for children and young people that focuses on expanding young people's skill sets, values, attitudes, and competency as they grow into adults (Eccles & Gootman, 2002; Lerner, Taylor, & von Eye, 2002). Positive Youth Development stresses dual participation from youth and adults in a collaborative effort to improve decision-making skills (Eccles & Gootman, 2002). While young people engage in programs outside of school, they are able to form bonds with adults that help them transition into a more secure and safe adulthood (Gambone et al., 2006; Holden et al., 2004).

Both models focus on empowering youth so they believe they can create positive change around them. While PYD works to develop young people's skills and put them to use in social action projects, SJYD is more applicable to larger-scale projects and longer political campaigns (Ross, 2011). Another way young people engage in social justice efforts is through their school curricula and programs. Similar to the concept of critical thinking central to SJYD, rethinking or critiquing what is learned in school equips youth with the information they need to participate in the "real world." This can be achieved by focusing on identities of historical figures who combated oppression, incorporating issues within one's own community, or incorporating a curriculum where cultural and linguistic aspects of youths' identities are represented. By focusing on oppressed groups throughout the study of history and not just during civil rights units, students grow more aware of and informed about the way their society came to be (Clauss-Ehlers et al., 2019; Schmidt, 2014).

Learning about their personal communities provides youth with an understanding of their surroundings so as to further identify issues and advocate for positive change (Cammarota, 2011). Molding curricula to reflect young people's culture and language has the potential to strengthen their sense of self and identity. Social studies curricula in particular can provide a basis of knowledge for youth advocacy (Schmidt, 2014; Shirley, 2017).

Social justice youth programming has been implemented in communities in a variety of ways. One way has been to incorporate social justice education into school curricula. While this is an easily accessible option for youth, it is not always available, and many times it has to be congruent with an already existing curriculum (Cammarota, 2011). Institutionally, social justice can also be promoted through work with youth in professional settings such as social work. Professionals who work with youth have a critical role in developing youth consciousness and awareness. These models are often influenced by social, political, and economic climates and take into consideration the biopsychosocial aspects of the environment (Clauss-Ehlers et al., 2019; McLaughlin et al., 2015). Another option involves independent organizations that offer programs such as after school extracurricular activities. Recreational spaces often provide youth with a productive environment for the development of the self-awareness and critical consciousness that are central to the SJYD framework (Pryor & Outley, 2014).

Program Examples

The Healthy Options for Prevention and Education (HOPE) Coalition, based in Worcester, Massachusetts, is a "youth-adult partnership" with a mission to "reduce youth violence and substance use and promote adolescent mental health and youth voice in the City of Worcester" (see www.hopecoalitionwoo.org/). The HOPE Coalition has a mental health model that "integrates mental health counselors into youth organizations to address stigma, transportation and other access barriers" (see www.hopecoalitionwoo.org/hope-mental-health). It also has a peer leader campaign where peer leaders are actively engaged in their communities.

In one initiative, youth conducting research about their community developed a plan of action to combat smoking. Many of the youth had personal experiences with tobacco-related deaths or illnesses in their families. They found disproportionate numbers of advertisements for tobacco products as well as access to them in and around their town (Roberge, 2015). Youth began to confront this issue by compiling their research into a PowerPoint presentation delivered to the community. Their efforts garnered support from the adults and officials in attendance, including city council members, health committee members, and a state senator.

In partnership with these officials, youth were able to inspire and promote the Act to Control Youth Access to Tobacco and even presented at the bill's hearing. At the end of the three-year project, the youth reported feeling a sense of accomplishment in raising awareness and developing relationships with the adults with whom they worked. Overall, they felt empowered by learning communication skills, tobacco facts, and how to work in groups (Ross, 2011).

In Tucson, Arizona, the Social Justice Education Project is a student-run research project implemented in three high schools. Similar to a community-based participatory research (CBPR) approach, the Social Justice Education Project requires youth to develop critical consciousness through engagement in a participatory action research (PAR) project. The goal of the program is to foster educational engagement among Latinx youth by "[teaching] students research skills and allow[ing] them to use their research to address inequities that students of color experience in public schools" (as cited in http://democraticeducation.org/index.php/library/resource/social_justice_education_project/). Critical consciousness was developed through involvement in PAR research. The research prompted students to be more aware of their communities as well as have a stronger understanding of global issues. These types of programs increase academic achievement as well as community involvement (Cammarota, 2011).

A program centered in Israel called Berosh Acher (In a Different Mind-Set) involves partnerships with government institutions and nongovernmental organizations (NGOs) to promote youth development (Lavie-Ajayi & Krumer-Nevo, 2013). The Berosh Acher approach centers on forming relationships with underrepresented youth through the intervention of street youth workers. Street youth workers spend most of their time working and residing in the same community, which is thought to build community relationships. Through these relationships, street youth workers encourage youth to make less-risky choices and connect them to social and educational services. In the Berosh Acher model, street youth workers promote social capital among the youth, providing resources and connections through which to navigate social structures and institutions (Lavie-Ajayi & Krumer-Nevo, 2013). This model also seeks to foster transformation and understanding through the development of counter narratives among youth. This involves youth placing their identities and behaviors in the context of their experiences.

Despite such promising programs, institutional barriers have inhibited social justice education. Education policies that serve to regulate testing, curricula, and accountability disproportionately affect urban communities of color, and are among some of the largest factors of educational attrition (Ingersoll, Merrill, & Stuckey, 2014; Dover, Henning, & Agarwal-Rangnath, 2016). Common core state standards that focus on standardized tests and curricula can limit teachers' ability to tailor their lessons to what they want to teach. While some teachers can incorporate their own social justice lessons into a set curriculum, this understandably requires more effort. Teacher performance assessments can also contribute to undermining educators' authority as well, encouraging them to work toward an external objective rather than their own personal teaching goals (Dover et al., 2016).

For professional youth workers, their personal social justice focus can be at odds with that of their institution. Establishments may not be designed for social justice purposes and view youth work as the need to control, monitor, and restrain problematic behavior (Lavie-Ajayi & Krumer-Nevo, 2013). This approach is counter to popular frameworks focused on empowering youth, particularly those with limited social capital. Due to this lack of connection, youth workers may have to work against current establishments to provide equal opportunities for young people (Lavie-Ajayi & Krumer-Nevo, 2013).

International Structural Challenges to Meet the Needs of Children

The previous section speaks to the resilience of youth and the modeling of a futuristic and positive orientation about life despite the odds they face. Yet, across nations, children are for the most part dependent on parents and caregivers for the negotiation of predictable and expected struggles of life. Parent mental health and decision-making capacity are intricately linked to child well-being. Although it is challenging to extrapolate the prevalence of adverse childhood events (ACEs) (Felitti & Anda, 2010) worldwide, Cohen et al. (2006) studied the neurocognitive functioning of 1,659 otherwise healthy adults (no current or prior diagnosis of major depression, anxiety, substance abuse, or neurological brain disorder) from the United States, Australia, England, and the Netherlands and found how ubiquitous childhood stress was across countries. The occurrence and age of onset of nineteen ACEs were assessed by the self-administered Early Life Stress Questionnaire (ELSQ, Sanders & Becker-Lausen, 1995), and current symptoms of stress, depression, and anxiety by the Depression Anxiety Stress Scale (DASS, Lovibond & Lovibond, 1995).

The relationship of specific ACEs to DASS symptoms was examined. Participants reported relatively high prevalence of ACEs. Only 27.6 percent of the sample reported no ACEs, while 39.5 percent reported one or two significant experiences and 32.9 percent reported more than two ACEs. Rates of most ACEs were quite similar across the three continents. Various ACEs were significantly associated with current DASS severity, particularly ACEs involving emotional abuse, neglect, family conflict, violence, and breakup. This finding that nearly one-third of the sample reported three or more ACEs as children suggests a high prevalence of early life stress in otherwise healthy "normal" adults around the world. Prior to the age of eighteen, a significant percentage of children worldwide live with an adult who has experienced domestic violence in the past year, an adult who is dependent on alcohol or drugs, or a parent who has severe mental health problems (Cleaver, Unell, & Aldgate, 2011). These ACEs cause them to have poor physical and mental health in adulthood.

Although prevention of ACEs is the best strategy to improve the quality of a child's life, in practical terms, it is often only when problems escalate to a crisis point for children is their plight recognized and addressed formally. By the time youth are in crisis, their suffering (e.g., employment, psychological and physical health) is at a moderate or severe level of distress and intervention is more costly (Franey, Geffner, & Flaconer, 2001). Thus, the opportunity to act preemptively or preventively to support a child's development is lost. The international case studies and chapters in this volume that discuss abuse, child marriage, child labor, regional wars, and social determinants of health underscore how ACEs have an impact on children, youth, and families in their life course.

In addition to physical and mental health vulnerabilities that children and youth face because of their dependence on adults with whom they live, other structural international causes of children being vulnerable to socially unjust outcomes stem from the interlinked global economy that has evolved in the past century (Pollack, 2004). Globalization has contributed to the exploitation of children and youth based on where they live. The unintended and, in some circumstances, intended consequences of the globalization of the world economy have created nations of haves and have nots with a disproportionate negative effect on the children and youth of those countries where there are few to advocate for their rights.

In the postcolonial era, the world has been broadly demarcated economically into the northern global economy (Eurocentric: e.g., England, Netherlands, Portugal, Spain) and the southern global economy (e.g., Central America, South Asia, the Caribbean, Africa) (Goldsmith, 1996). As countries from the northern hemisphere were forced to or decided to leave the countries in the southern hemisphere that they had colonized for their indigenous resources, they left in place infrastructures of poor governance and exploitation of the local populations by lending them money for projects with low potential to add value to the local economy. The increasingly high levels of national debt in these countries eat into social projects directed at children's health or education (Roodman, 2001). Dismantling of trade barriers and inadequate labor laws have led to exploitation of children and women in sweatshops in order to manufacture low-cost products at a fraction of the wages that a worker in the northern/western hemisphere would command (Varley, 1998). Work conditions for the children include long hours of work without breaks, inadequate food, and very poor pay, which are common practices in countries that operate under the Free Trade Zone agreements, where humane labor practices are sacrificed to attract investment (Goldsmith, 1996; Varley, 1998).

The dividends of these projects rarely make it to the children and create increasing debt burden to entities such as the International Monetary Fund and the World Bank (Bello, 2000). The inability to return the debt or even the high interest on the debt forces these countries to face austerity measures, which translates into giving up resources for children in the form of adequate food, housing, and social programs (Bello, 2000; Northcott, 1999). It has been reported that if the debt burden was forgiven for just African countries, 7 million children would be saved from starvation (United Nations Development Programme, 1997). In other words, the inequities in available economic resources lead to a crippling cycle of exploitation of indigenous resources by powerful countries, borrowing capital at high interest in order to sustain failing structures, and excessive debt leading to austerity measures, which directly has an impact on the most voiceless and vulnerable in any nation – the children.

Children facing starvation are as vulnerable psychologically as those who are perpetual witnesses to wars. Yet corporations in the northern global economy continue to support trade policies that worsen this problem of debt and encourage the exploitation of children in labor markets, patterns that implicitly sanction starvation (Bello, 2000). In relationship to war, generations of children in some countries are chronically exposed to wars over which there is no control. In summary, worldwide policies create structural paradigms supporting exploitation of children. International case studies comparing low-income economies and high-income economies illustrate how issues that have an impact on social justice for children and young people present both differing and shared experiences across countries. It is also encouraging to note that some low-income economies like that of Rwanda are beginning to focus more purposefully on social justice issues for children and youth.

An awareness of what is morally just and what should be the basic rights of children as delineated in the guiding principles of the UN charter on the rights of children can help governments start examining their policies and how they directly or indirectly affect children and youth. The section in this book that presents case studies from around the world demonstrates the variability in the manner in which government policies have an impact on the treatment of children: this can be both positive and negative; this section examines how children's developmental needs to live in safe and nurturing environments are sometimes sacrificed in regional wars and how cultural norms that do not value or elevate children's rights/needs play into unjust treatment of youth sometimes deliberately (e.g., using children for manual labor) and at other times inadvertently and as an unintended consequence of a political decision (Cohen et al., 2006).

Failing to help children has social, educational, and economic costs. The majority of mental health issues that affect adults have their onset before the age of twenty-five (Kessler et al., 2005). High rates of infant mortality, child abuse, and illnesses like HIV/AIDS transmitted through infected parents; substance-exposed infants and the downstream effects of toxic stress on dysregulated children and youth; child marriages; adolescent pregnancies; inadequate safety nets in the form of poor-quality foster care – all create social harm to children and, by extension, to society. The rationale for publishing this volume is to highlight the specific injustice to a segment of society who do not have a voice in the broad social and political landscape of the world, yet they are the foundation of global society as they age into adulthood. Our current children and youth are the ones who will eventually craft policies and guidelines for a more just, stable, and equitable world.

International Strategies to Expand and Promote Social Justice for Children and Youth

The Community of Practice (COP) strategy (see Wenger, McDermott, & Snyder, 2002) offers much promise to deepen collaboration focused on improving social justice for children and youth. Communities of Practice focus on relationship building and convening people to share ideas and solutions, to provide mutual support, and to progress from discussion to dialogue to collaboration to policy and practice change. These COPs deepen the work and promote quality and sustainability of change efforts through strengthened and expanded relationships and more effective ideas and solutions to challenges, as the collective intellect is smarter (Cashman et al., 2014). They also emphasize a *shared agenda*, with families/youth, schools, mental healthcare systems, and other youth-serving systems (e.g., child welfare, juvenile justice, primary care) sharing responsibility, working together, and providing mutual support in the advancement of initiatives and programs that help children and youth (Andis et al., 2002). Two COPs focused on mental health in schools (a major emphasis for each of the three editors) and making a difference for social justice and children and youth are reviewed in the following section.

School Mental Health International Leadership Exchange (SMHILE). Recognizing the rapid emergence of more comprehensive mental healthcare services in schools (see Weist, 1997), the International Alliance for Child and Adolescent Mental Health in Schools (INTERCAMHS) (see www.intercamhs.org) emerged in the early 2000s to provide a forum for global dialogue on the advancement of school mental health (SMH). From its beginnings, the SMH field has had a social justice emphasis, addressing the inequity of poor access to and poor quality of services for children and youth receiving care from more traditional mental health settings (Hoover-Stephan et al., 2007). Through the COP strategy, INTERCAMHS created a forum for leaders and stakeholders from around the world to discuss and collaborate on advancing SMH, with a view toward building global capacity for the field of school mental health while improving the quality of schools and reducing inequities in care (Rowling & Weist, 2004). It also promoted collaboration between governmental and nongovernmental organizations (Vince-Whitman et al., 2007), facilitated research-stakeholder collaboration toward more genuinely conducted and impactful research (Short, Weist, Manion, & Evans, 2012), and promoted systematic partnerships between nations, such as the Canada-US School Mental Health Alliance (Wells et al., 2011).

However, as a global COP, INTERCAMHS began losing momentum in the early 2010s. This was related to some challenges in leadership and a pattern of decreasing dialogue and meetings over time. Recognizing this developing gap, the School Mental Health International Leadership Exchange (SMHILE) (see www.smhile.com) was developed in 2013 to reenergize a COP focused on building global capacity for SMH; SMHILE assisted in the development of world conferences on mental health promotion and SMH in London in 2014 and South Carolina in the United States in 2015, and more recently hosted a conference on mental health promotion within the education system in Sweden in 2018, connecting to the work of the International Initiative for Mental Health Leadership (see www.imhl.org).

Notably, SMHILE focuses on five themes: (1) cross-sector collaboration in building systems of care, (2) meaningful youth and family engagement, (3) workforce development and mental health literacy, (4) implementation of evidence-based practices, and (5) ongoing monitoring and quality assurance. In addition to promoting social justice for children in the world in relation to increased likelihood of receiving needed mental healthcare services (Weist et al., 1999), the second theme area for SMHILE focuses on meaningful youth and family engagement as a critical social justice issue. That is, school mental health programming for children and youth is generally not informed or led by youth and families (Weist, Garbacz, Lane, & Kincaid, 2017). To address this significant concern, SMHILE-led training events have focused on this second theme, and one of the members of its Core Leadership Team (CLT) is a youth leader. In addition, a number of CLT members have children struggling with emotional/behavioral challenges, and members will incorporate an understanding of these experiences while planning strategies to strengthen family and youth leadership in guiding SMH.

Family-School-Community Alliance (FSCA). Following the development of an e-book on family engagement and leadership (Weist et al., 2017) sponsored by the US National Center for Positive Behavioral Interventions and Supports (see www.pbis.org), the Family-School-Community Alliance (FSCA) emerged in 2017. The FSCA is led by faculty from the University of Wisconsin–Madison (UWM) and the University of South Florida (USF). Members include researchers, policy leaders, teachers, clinicians, family advocates, and youth and family leaders. Annual meetings have been held at UWM in 2017 and 2018 and at USF in 2019. The mission of the FSCA is to *promote family, youth, and community engaged partnerships in research, practice, and policy to improve prevention and intervention in the systems and practices of positive behavioral interventions and supports and related multi-tiered systems of support (MTSS) toward improvement in valued outcomes* (www.fscalliance.org).

According to the FSCA website (www.fscalliance.org), four core values undergird the work of this COP: (1) Schools, facilities, and programs proactively reach out to families to establish family-school partnerships. (2) Schools, facilities, and programs empower families to reach out to professionals in order to engage with them in partnership. (3) Families, youth, community members, educators, and related personnel engage together within the MTSS to co-identify priorities, co-create plans, carry out shared plans, and share in decision-making and evaluation of programs. (4) Interactions between families, youth, community members, educators, and related personnel are multidirectional; as interactions evolve, partners are responsive to changes and adapt accordingly.

Importantly, both SMHILE and FSCA are also purposefully addressing the social justice issue of students needing and/or receiving mental healthcare services with negative labels that end up stigmatizing and harming them. For example, use of terms like "psychopathology" and "emotional disturbance," and diagnostic labels such as "borderline personality disorder," "bipolar disorder," and "conduct disorder" often negatively affects the way professionals (e.g., teachers, counselors) treat students. Use of these labels should be avoided, along with taking other steps to assure that children and youth presenting mental health challenges are treated no differently than children and youth not presenting with these problems (see Weist, Mellin, Garbacz, & Anderson-Butcher, 2019).

CONCLUSION

Social Justice for Children and Young People: International Perspectives provides a comprehensive, international approach to social justice for children and young people that is not currently identified in the literature. This text presents a theoretical base that defines key concepts and international social justice models. This volume includes a section on regional and country experiences that highlight how key concepts and theories are implemented across the globe. Given significant gaps in the literature, coupled with the reality that children are often overlooked in justice efforts, this book provides a much-needed resource for educators, policy makers, elected officials, healthcare and mental healthcare professionals, educators, advocates, medical professionals, and those concerned with rules of law. This book has an underlying advocacy theme. It is hoped that this volume will inspire readers to engage in social justice efforts for children and young people in their respective regions/countries.

REFERENCES

Andis, P., Cashman, J., Praschil, R., et al. (2002). A strategic and shared agenda to advance mental health in schools through family and system partnerships. *International Journal of Mental Health Promotion*, 4, 28–35.

Bello, W. (2000). Building an iron cage. The Bretton Woods institutions, the WTO, and the south. In S. Anderson (ed.), *Views from the south: The effects of globalization and WTO on third world countries* (pp. 59–90). Chicago: Food First Books and International Forum on Globalization.

Cammarota, J. (2011). From hopelessness to hope: Social justice pedagogy in urban education and youth development. *Urban Education*, 46(4), 828–844.

Cashman, J., Linehan, P., Purcell, L., et al. (2014). *Leading by convening: A blueprint for authentic engagement*. Alexandria, VA: National Association of State Directors of Special Education.

Clauss-Ehlers, C. S., Chiriboga, D., Hunter, S. J., Roysircar, G., & Tummala-Narra, P. (2019). APA Multicultural Guidelines executive summary: Ecological approach to context, identity, and intersectionality. *American Psychologist*, 74(2), 232–244.

Cleaver, H., Unell, I., & Aldgate, J. (2011). *Children's needs – Parenting capacity. Child abuse: Parental mental illness, learning disability, substance misuse and domestic violence* (2nd ed.). London: Stationary Office.

Cohen, R. A., Hitsman, B. L., Paul, R. H., et al. (2006). Early life stress and adult emotional experience: An international perspective. *International Journal of Psychiatry in Medicine*, 36(1), 35–52. Retrieved from https://doi.org/10.2190/5R62-9PQY-0NEL-TLPA.

Dover, A. G., Henning, N., & Agarwal-Rangnath, R. (2016). Reclaiming agency: Justice-oriented social studies teachers respond to changing curricular standards. *Teaching and Teacher Education*, 59, 457–467.

Eccles, J., & Gootman, J. (eds.). (2002). *Community programs to promote youth development*. Washington, DC: National Academy Press.

Felitti, V. J., & Anda, R. F. (2010). The relationship of adverse childhood experiences to adult health, well-being, social function, and healthcare. In R. Lanius, E. Vermetten, & C. Pain (eds.), *The impact of early life trauma on health and disease: The hidden epidemic* (pp. 77–87). New York: Cambridge University Press.

Franey, K., Geffner, R., & Flaconer, R. (2001). *The cost of child maltreatment: Who pays? We all do*. San Diego, CA: Family Violence & Sexual Assault Institute, 1–243.

Gambone, M., Yu, H., Lewis-Charp, H., Sipe, C., & Lacoe, J. (2006). Outcomes of youth organizing and other approaches. *Journal of Community Practice, 14*, 235–253.

Ginwright, S., & Cammarota, J. (2002). New terrain in youth development: The promise of a social justice approach. *Social Justice, 29*(4), 82–95.

Goldsmith, E. (1996). Development as colonialism. In J. Mander & E. Goldsmith (eds.), *The case against the global economy* (pp. 253–266). San Francisco, CA: Sierra Club Books.

Holden, D., Messeri, P., Evans, W., Crankshaw, E., & Ben-Davies, M. (2004). Conceptualizing youth empowerment within tobacco control. *Health Education & Behavior, 31*, 548–563.

Hoover-Stephan, S., Weist, M. D., Kataoka, S., Adelsheim, S., & Mills, C. (2007). Transformation of children's mental health services: The role of school mental health. *Psychiatric Services, 58*, 1330–1338.

Ingersoll, R., Merrill, L., & Stuckey, D. (2014). Seven trends: The transformation of the teaching force. Consortium for Policy Research in Education (CPRE), University of Pennsylvania.

Kessler, R. C., et al. (2005). Prevalence, severity, and comorbidity of 12-month DSM-IV disorders in the National Comorbidity Survey Replication. *Archives of General Psychiatry, 62*(6), 593–602.

Lavie-Ajayi, M., & Krumer-Nevo, M. (2013). In a different mindset: Critical youth work with marginalized youth. *Children and Youth Services Review, 35*, 1698–1704.

Lerner, R., Taylor, C., & von Eye, A. (2002). Positive youth development: Thriving as a basis of personhood and civil society. *New Directions for Youth Development: Theory, Practice, Research, 95*, 11–33.

Loes, C., Pascarella, E., & Umbach, P. (2012). Effects of diversity experiences on critical thinking skills: Who benefits? *Journal of Higher Education, 83*(1), 1–25.

Lovibond, S.H., & Lovibond, P.F. (1995). *Manual for the Depression Anxiety Stress Scales* (2nd Ed.). Sydney: Psychology Foundation.

McLaughlin, A. M., Gray, E., & Wilson, M. (2015). Child welfare workers and social justice: Mending the disconnect. *Children and Youth Services Review, 59*, 177–183.

Northcott, M. (1999). *Life after debt: Christianity and global justice*. London: Society for Promoting Christian Knowledge.

Pollack, R. J. (2004). Social justice and the global economy: New challenges for social work in the 21st century. *Social Work, 49*(2), 281–290.

Pryor, B. N. K., & Outley, C. W. (2014). Just spaces: Urban recreation centers as sites for social justice youth development. *Journal of Leisure Research, 46*(3), 272–290.

Roberge, A. (2015, February 20). HOPE Coalition helps Worcester youth weed out tobacco. *Telegram.com*, Worcester, MA.

Roodman, D. M. (2001). *Still waiting for the jubilee: Pragmatic solutions for the Third World debt crisis*. Washington, DC: Worldwatch Institute.

Ross, L. (2011). Sustaining youth participation in a long-term tobacco control initiative: Consideration of a social justice perspective. *Youth & Society, 43*(2), 681–704.

Rowling, L., & Weist, M. D. (2004). Promoting the growth, improvement and sustainability of school mental health programs worldwide. *International Journal of Mental Health Promotion, 6*(2), 3–11.

Ruger, J. P. (2016). The health capability paradigm and the right to health care in the United States. *Theoretical Medicine and Bioethics, 37*, 275–292.

Sanders, B., & Becker-Lausen, E. (1995). The measurement of psychological maltreatment: Early data on the child abuse and trauma scale. *Child Abuse & Neglect* 19, 315–323.

Schmidt, S. J. (2014). Civil rights continued: How history positions young people to contemplate sexuality (in)justice. *Equity & Excellence in Education*, 47(3), 353–369.

Shirley, V. J. (2017). Indigenous social justice pedagogy: Teaching into the risks and cultivating the heart. *Critical Questions in Education*, 8(2), 163–177.

Short, K., Weist, M. D., Manion, I., & Evans, S. W. (2012). Tying together research and practice: Using ROPE for successful partnerships in school mental health. *Administration and Policy in Mental Health and Mental Health Services Research*, 39, 238–247.

World Bank (n.d.). World Bank country and lending groups. Retrieved from https://datahelpdesk.worldbank.org/knowledgebase/articles/906519-world-bank-country-and-lending-groups.

UN General Assembly, Convention on the Rights of the Child, 20 November 1989, United Nations, Treaty Series, vol. 1577, p. 3, available at: www.refworld.org/docid/3ae6b38fo.html

United Nations Development Programme (1997). Human Development Report, Geneva.

United Nations Secretary General (UNSG) (2008). *Guidance note of the secretary-general: UN approach to justice for children*. Retrieved from www.unicef.org/protection/RoL_Guidance_Note_UN_Approach_Justice_for_Children_FINAL.pdf.

Varley, P. (ed.) (1998). *The sweatshop quandary: Corporate responsibility on the global frontier*. Washington, DC: Investor Responsibility Center.

Vince-Whitman, C., Belfer, M., Oommen, M., et al. (2007). The role of international organizations to promote school-based mental health. In S. Evans, M. D. Weist, & Z. Serpell (eds.), *Advances in school-based mental health interventions* (pp. 22:1–22:14). New York: Civic Research Institute.

Weist, M. D. (1997). Expanded school mental health services: A national movement in progress. In T. H. Ollendick & R. J. Prinz (eds.), *Advances in clinical child psychology, Volume 19* (pp. 319–352). New York: Plenum Press.

Weist, M. D., Garbacz, A., Lane, K., & Kincaid, D. (2017). Enhancing progress for meaningful family engagement in all aspects of positive behavioral interventions and supports and multi-tiered systems of support. In M. D. Weist, A. Garbacz, K. Lane, & D. Kincaid (eds.), *Aligning and integrating family engagement in positive behavioral interventions and supports (PBIS): Concepts and strategies for families and schools in key contexts* (pp. 1–8). Center for Positive Behavioral Interventions and Supports. Eugene: University of Oregon Press.

Weist, M. D., Kutcher, S., & Wei, Y. (2015). The global advancement of school mental health for adolescents. In S. Kutcher, Y. Wei, & M. D. Weist (eds.), *School mental health: Global challenges and opportunities* (pp. 1–5). Cambridge, UK: Cambridge University Press.

Weist, M. D., Mellin, E., Garbacz, S. A., & Anderson-Butcher, D. (2019). Reducing the use of language that stigmatizes students. National Association of School Psychologists. *Communique*, 47(8), 1, 22–23.

Weist, M. D., Myers, C. P., Hastings, E., Ghuman, H., & Han, Y. (1999). Psychosocial functioning of youth receiving mental health services in the schools vs. community mental health centers. *Community Mental Health Journal*, 35, 69–81.

Weist, M. D., Short, K., McDaniel, H., & Bode, A. (2016). The School Mental Health International Leadership Exchange (SMHILE): Working to advance the field through opportunities for global networking. *International Journal of Mental Health Promotion*, 18(1), 1–7.

Wells, G., Biewener, M., Vince-Whitman, C., et al. (2011). The formation of the Canada-United States School Mental Health Alliance. *Advances in School Mental Health Promotion*, 4(3), 42–54.

Wenger, E., McDermott, R., & Snyder, W. M. (2002). *Cultivating communities of practice: A guide to managing knowledge*. Boston, MA: Harvard Business School.

2

The Language of Social Justice for Children and Young People

Key Terms and Guiding Principles

Becca McBride

The author recalls discussing female genital mutilation (FGM) in her human rights class. She explained to her students how many girls who live through war are separated from their parents and left to be cared for by other family members, adults, or institutions. After such separations, some relatives may flee the country with their family members' daughters in order to escape the practice of FGM, thus becoming refugees. These situations represent intense child vulnerability. War and violence disrupt children's family lives, and legal status as a dependent can shift from parents to relatives or from parents to institutional care.

Many girls (and the relatives seeking to protect them) become refugees so as to avoid having their personal security and health undermined through FGM. According to the United Nations International Children's Emergency Fund (UNICEF), for instance, more than 80 percent of girls older than fifteen years old in seven African countries, including Egypt, Sudan, Sierra Leone, Mali, and Guinea, have undergone FGM (UNICEF, 2013). These statistics demonstrate the state- and international-level structures in which vulnerability among girls is situated. Understanding such childhood vulnerability requires recognizing the political structures that both cause vulnerability and offer a range of solutions.

This chapter seeks to provide a foundational grasp of the political structures in which social justice advocacy for children is positioned. This is an important basis for a book on social justice for children for three reasons. First, if we do not understand the political structures that can be the root causes of vulnerability, we cannot accurately assess how to correct them for society as a whole or for individual children. Second, political structures provide the common language around which the international community understands child vulnerability. Third, effective advocates can activate these structures as tools to remedy child vulnerability in many cases.

To orient the reader to the structures and procedures in which children are embedded at the state and international levels, this chapter proceeds in three main sections. The first section explains the international human rights regime surrounding social justice advocacy, and clarifies the key concepts that emerge out of the associated legal and institutional frameworks. The second section spells out how state- and international-level institutions and treaties articulate child rights, and identifies potential areas for tension between those articulated rights. The third and final section provides an overview of the multiple levels of actors who collaborate to pursue social justice advocacy for children.

THE INTERNATIONAL HUMAN RIGHTS REGIME AND CHILD ADVOCACY

All children have a legal identity as part of a family (a child) and as part of a country (a citizen). Yet they are a unique type of citizen in any country, because they interact with the government through advocates, whether that is parents or other advocates (e.g., a legal guardian). Social justice advocacy for children can occur either within a national political system or across international borders. The international child rights regime arose out of recognition that national governments are often the cause of child vulnerability, and children lack many of the typical tools for holding governments accountable (Simmons, 2009; see pp. 307–312). In this reality, most often the solution to child vulnerability comes from outside actors.

The governments most influential in developing the human rights regime were the governments we typically consider to be highly protective of vulnerable children. They are the governments that have well-developed social welfare systems, smaller populations of children in institutional care, and norms and legal frameworks that provide for child rights; the language surrounding social justice for children reflects the norms in these countries and mirrors their institutions (Simmons, 2009; see pp. 312–317). This section unpacks the political and normative foundation of the human rights regime by first exploring the complex interaction between state governments and the international system around human rights, second identifying the key documents of the international human rights regime that were designed to protect children, and third examining the key concepts that emerge out of these documents.

The Interaction between Domestic and International Regimes

What is the international human rights regime, and why is it such an important foundation for understanding international advocacy for children? "Regime" refers to the overlapping sets of norms, laws, and institutions around a certain issue area. Before we can outline how children are protected in the international human rights regime, it's important to understand the complex interaction between domestic and international regimes. More specifically, it's crucial to understand how domestic regimes *differ* from international regimes, and how domestic regimes *influence* whether states commit to and comply with international regimes.

Regimes can be either domestic or international. For example, at the domestic level, we often talk about regimes in terms of "democratic regime" or "authoritarian regime." Let's look at democratic regimes as an example. Democracies have certain norms about how citizens should be protected that characterize their governments (Simmons, 2009; see pp. 24–25). Democratic legislatures design laws to reinforce those norms and to articulate how they should be respected. For instance, the norm of parental responsibility for children, which is common in democratic states, is often encoded into laws that protect parental rights. Courts and child welfare institutions then implement and negotiate these laws. When we say a state has a "democratic regime," we are referring to the norms, laws, and institutional arrangements that are typical to democracies. Although democracies can differ in terms of the specifics of their laws or institutions (parliament vs. presidency, for example), in general they share similar norms, they encode these norms into laws, and they have institutions that ensure those laws are applied consistently.

Authoritarian regimes, on the other hand, often have fewer laws protecting individuals, and these laws are often not consistently applied to all citizens. This difference is most evident for issues like FGM, because democracies are more likely to have norms and laws protecting children from cultural practices that threaten their physical well-being, while autocracies are less likely to have laws protecting children in the same way, or to consistently apply them where they do exist. Even though transitioning democracies, like Gambia, for example, still have patterns of individuals practicing FGM, the democratic government seeks to implement and to consistently apply the laws to protect young girls (Peyton & Jahateh, 2018).

The term "regime" can also describe *international* political arrangements around certain issue areas. For example, when we talk about the "international child rights regime," we are referring to overlapping norms, treaties, and institutions around protecting children and ensuring they have what they need to thrive, regardless of their political, social, or geographic situation. This child rights regime articulates how children should be protected (norms), lays out how governments should do it (treaties), and seeks to hold governments accountable to those standards (institutions).

In domestic regimes, members (citizens) are (tacitly) committed to the laws of their government by virtue of being citizens, and governments maintain compliance to laws through a combination of hard-power mechanisms, like the threat of prison, and soft-power mechanisms, like cultural influences. International regimes, like the child rights regime, operate in an environment with no centralized authority that ensures governments actually follow through on what they promise to do. The practical implication is that governments decide which international laws they will commit to following, and they decide when they will actually follow those international laws or break them (Simmons, 2009; see p. 4). We see examples all the time of governments disregarding their treaty commitments when the short-term gains outweigh the perceived long-term costs of noncompliance.

To make the picture even more complex, scholars have identified that a state's domestic regime (i.e., Are they a democracy or not?) has an impact on how they commit to and comply with international law in somewhat counterintuitive ways (Hafner-Burton & Tsutsui, 2005). Scholars have noticed that while established democracies are more likely to respect and protect human rights than authoritarian governments, they are also *less likely* to commit to human rights treaties than authoritarian governments with worse human rights records (Hathaway, 2007; Moravcsik, 2000). Why might this be the case?

Democracies are accountable internally to their citizens and externally to other states in the international system. Therefore, their human rights records, and their ability to comply with treaty obligations, have an impact on internal election prospects and external relationships with other democracies. Additionally, democracies have stronger rule-of-law constraints (like checks and balances between branches of government) that make signing, ratifying, and implementing treaties much more procedurally complicated and time-consuming (Hathaway, 2007; Simmons, 2009). Because of these constraints, democracies are more likely to consider their ability to comply with treaties before they commit to them, and the length of time to fully implement treaties is much longer (Fearon, 1998; Von Stein, 2005). The stronger this domestic and international accountability and the more complicated the procedural constraints, the more likely democracies like the United States will appear to be "false negatives" in treaty commitments (Simmons, 2009; see pp. 17–19). They will appear to devalue a treaty because of lack of commitment, when really the barrier to commitment is connected with institutional constraints, not normative values (Hathaway, 2007; Moravcsik, 2000).

Authoritarian systems, on the other hand, have lower levels of accountability both to their citizens and to external state and non-state actors. The lack of transparent elections prevents internal accountability. Single-party and military authoritarian systems are especially less likely to invest in building a reputation that facilitates cooperation with other states (Mattes & Rodriguez, 2014). While transitioning systems defy this trend (Moravcsik, 2000) (e.g., when new democracies transition out of authoritarianism), consolidated authoritarian systems appear less concerned with internal or external perceptions of their human rights records. Moreover, authoritarian systems often lack the rule-of-law constraints that lengthen the process of treaty commitment for consolidated democracies. In fact, for stronger authoritarian systems that lack checks and balances between branches of government, the process of signing, ratifying, and implementing a treaty merely requires the approval of the leader. Therefore, it costs less for authoritarian governments to commit to treaties because noncompliance with treaty commitments is much less risky for authoritarian governments than it is for democracies (Simmons, 2010).

These complex dynamics result in the paradox of treaty commitment and compliance. Authoritarian governments are *more* likely to commit to international treaties on a variety of topics, but they are *less* likely to comply with those commitments. Democracies, on the other hand, take longer to commit and often never reach the point at which they do commit to treaties. They are more likely to comply with treaties once they do commit, however, and in many cases, they comply even if they haven't committed to the treaty (Simmons, 2009; see pp. 17–19). For child advocacy, this trend is especially prevalent, because children are a group that is even less capable of holding their governments accountable. Thus, we often see countries committing quickly and easily to treaties designed to protect children, but compliance with these treaties is problematic.

Protecting Children through the International Human Rights Regime

How do these unique challenges of the international system, especially the self-selecting nature of international treaties, influence how children are protected in the international human rights regime? Western nations dominated the formation of the human rights regime (Simmons, 2009; see pp. 24–40), and Western understandings of childhood dominate the child welfare narrative (Simmons, 2009; see pp. 312–319). This is a particular challenge for child protection because there is broader diversity in cultural understandings of the role of the child in society and in the family than there is for other areas of human rights. For example, in Western nations, the age of responsibility is typically sixteen or older and legally tends to be eighteen. This influences the age at which children are expected to contribute financially to the family, are permitted to marry, and are recruited into the military. In many developing countries, children are expected to work much younger, are allowed to marry much younger, and are even recruited into the military much younger (Barone, 2015). Norms around child rights are perhaps some of the most contested norms in the international system, which makes it a particularly hard domain in which to shape governments' behavior and to hold them accountable for protecting the children under their care.

The key human rights document pertaining to children is the Convention on the Rights of the Child (CRC), which entered into force in 1990. The CRC is an umbrella convention that accomplishes two main goals. First, the treaty articulates the rights that children have to participate in decisions that have an impact on them; receive protection from discrimination, neglect, or exploitation and other types of harm; and receive provision of their basic needs so they can thrive. Second, the treaty identifies which parties are responsible for protecting children and providing for their needs.

Under the umbrella of the CRC are several optional protocols and specialized documents that explain how these responsible parties should implement and protect the rights reserved for children in unique situations. For example, the Hague Convention on the Protection of Children and Co-operation in Intercountry Adoption, which entered into force in 1993, serves as a coordination mechanism for states processing adoptions across borders and monitors state behavior in order to ensure child protection in that situation of enhanced child vulnerability. The Optional Protocol on the Sale of Children, Child Prostitution, and Child Pornography, which entered into force in 2000, clarifies children's enhanced vulnerability to exploitation through forced movement across borders. This includes sex and labor trafficking, organ trafficking, and underage marriage. Similarly, the Optional Protocol on the Involvement of Children in Armed Conflict, which also entered into force in 2000, clarifies children's enhanced vulnerability in armed conflicts that use children as soldiers. All these treaties, along with other regional and specialized treaties, build on the rights and responsibilities the CRC articulates, and provide states with guidance on how to best protect children in conditions of enhanced vulnerability.

Just as is true for other treaties in the human rights regime, states self-select into commitment to the CRC and other child rights treaties, and their implementation looks different depending on the system, the type of government, and the quality of institutions within each state. However, a web of international institutions assists with implementation, especially for states that lack institutional quality, and monitors states' compliance with treaty obligations. The United Nations Committee on the Rights of the Child is the key institution monitoring and reporting on state compliance, while UNICEF works with national governments to implement the provisions of the treaties. Additionally, the Hague Conference on Private International Law provides guidance on implementation and monitoring for the treaty upon intercountry adoption.

Commitment to the CRC is almost universal, with only the United States not having fully ratified the treaty. Aspects of the treaty remain controversial in the United States, and the same institutional constraints mentioned earlier in this chapter have prevented full US commitment, despite the strong role the United States played in drafting key components of the treaty (Smolin, 2006).[1] But despite the near universal commitment to the CRC, compliance with the treaty has remained a challenge. Many of the states whose behavior advocates would hope to most influence to protect children within their borders have failed to follow through on their treaty commitments in this area. The next section explores some of these key areas of tension in child protection and advocacy.

Key Concepts in Social Justice Advocacy for Children

The first important concept is who qualifies as a child. All the key documents on child rights define children as any human under the age of eighteen (CRC, Article 1). Reflecting the 1959 Declaration of the Rights of the Child, the CRC reminds that children are physically and mentally immature and need an enhanced level of care, safeguards, and legal protection (CRC, Preamble). This definition is an excellent example of how political processes have influenced the language and practices surrounding social justice for children. It is a distinctly Western notion that childhood lasts until age eighteen (Barone, 2015). The fact that Western countries were more influential in the process of articulating child rights means that human rights documents leave little room for non-Western understandings of childhood (Cohen, 1998). The lack of diverse cultural perspectives on children, both in the formation of the child rights regime, and in the language used to describe children, shapes the ongoing potential for dialogue between powerful Western nations and developing countries around child welfare.

A second key concept relates to understanding what is meant by child vulnerability, and distinguishing that from orphan status. Because children always need an advocate to achieve agency in political systems, we understandably perceive orphanhood as the pinnacle of vulnerability for children. Therefore, it is common to hear people use the word "orphan" to describe vulnerable children. In reality, a child under eighteen is only an orphan when both parents have died or terminated their parental rights. In many countries, those conditions render the child available for domestic or international adoption by a nonrelative. But child vulnerability, as discussed throughout this volume, comes in many forms that may or may not be related to a child's parental status. Thus, the term "vulnerable child" refers to a wide spectrum of conditions that have an impact on a child's ability to thrive, while the term "orphan" only applies to the child's parental status.

A third key concept is "children's rights." All humans have their rights articulated within the Universal Declaration of Human Rights, including humans under the age of eighteen. But because children lack physical and emotional maturity, they need enhanced care and protection. Thus, the CRC articulates rights that are specific to children in this condition of diminished maturity. Some of those rights are redundant with universal human rights, but are reiterated in order to remind that they are particularly difficult to protect for children. Others are unique to children, and require unique frameworks for their provision. For example, the right to a national identity is a universal human right that is particularly difficult to protect for children because they lack the ability to secure and protect that identity without parental advocacy. The right to an education, however, is specific to children and adolescents who are still in an early developmental stage in life and need education in order to secure opportunities later in life. The term "children's rights" is the recognition that basic human rights, as well as rights specific to humans in the developmental stages of childhood and adolescence, are particularly difficult to secure without some type of parental or adult advocacy.

ARTICULATED CHILD RIGHTS AND TENSIONS BETWEEN RIGHTS

The global human rights regime addresses each of the key issues explored in this volume, both in the CRC and in its optional protocols and specialized documents; this section examines them in light of the focus and organization of this volume. In general, we can group the themes presented in this volume into three main corresponding categories: (1) quality-of-life concerns around issues like poverty alleviation, health improvement, and educational provisions; (2) the protection of basic rights in conditions of enhanced vulnerability like civil war, extreme violence, and trafficking; and (3) identity rights that are especially difficult for children to safeguard like cultural rights, national identity rights, and family rights. Violation of each of these categories of rights renders individual children more physically, emotionally, and socially vulnerable, which is the primary focus of this book. This section first identifies how these rights are articulated in the CRC, and then highlights potential areas of tension between articulated rights.

All rights in the CRC are situated within the need for a child's "full and harmonious development of his or her personality" (CRC, Preamble, p. 1). States are charged with both protecting and enabling children's right to thrive in all the categories previously mentioned. For example, states have the responsibility to promote children's general quality of life by providing the things they need to thrive, including acceptable standards of childcare (CRC, Article 3); the highest standards of health care (CRC, Article 24); a standard of living adequate for their physical, mental, spiritual, moral, and social development (CRC, Article 27); access to adequate education (CRC, Articles 28 and 29); and access to rest and leisure (CRC, Article 31). Moreover, the CRC identifies several conditions of enhanced vulnerability that require special provisions like abuse and neglect (CRC, Article 19); economic exploitation (CRC, Article 32); drug abuse (CRC, Article 33); sexual exploitation (CRC, Article 34); abduction or trafficking (CRC, Article 35); and torture, inhumane punishment, or unlawful detention (CRC, Article 36). The document also charges governments with enabling children's physical, emotional, and psychological recovery if they have suffered these conditions of enhanced vulnerability (CRC, Article 39).

Finally, the CRC identifies several identity rights that are essential for a child to thrive and especially difficult to secure for children in general and for vulnerable children in particular. For example, the preamble affirms that traditions and cultural values are important for the "protection and harmonious development of the child" (CRC, Preamble, p. 2). The CRC also affirms that children have the right to acquire a national identity from birth (CRC, Article 7, section 1; UN General Assembly, 1990), and that states should respect the right of a child to preserve his or her national identity (CRC, Article 8, section 1). The document also articulates that children should not be separated from their parents against their parents' will (CRC, Article 9); separated from one or more parents across state borders (CRC, Article 10); or suffer unlawful interference with their privacy, family, home, or correspondence (CRC, Article 16). While these identity and cultural rights were previously articulated for all humans, the CRC is distinctive in its identification of the unique difficulties associated with securing these rights for children.

In addition to these articulated rights, the CRC contains recurring language that does not articulate rights but nonetheless repeatedly highlights priorities in the protection of children. First, the CRC continually claims that in every decision, the primary consideration should be the "best interests of the child" (CRC, Articles 3, 9, 18, 20, 21, 37, 40). Although this language is frequently used, the CRC includes little guidance on exactly what is in the best interest of the child, or how that is to be determined, and by whom (Wallace, 2003). The only consensus concerning the best interest of the child is that the child's family is an important unit within which the best interest of the child is to be determined, unless that family is unable or unwilling to properly care for the child. For instance, the CRC affirms that the family is the primary unit for the growth and well-being of children, and that children should grow up in a family environment in order to ensure their "full and harmonious development" (CRC, Preamble, p. 1). Thus, when children are permanently or temporarily deprived of their family environments, they fall under the protection of the state as an advocate to replace the family (CRC, Article 20).

This overarching language in the document, combined with the focus in the preamble on the full and harmonious development of the child, represents the first space for a conflict concerning the rights of vulnerable children. The language presents no articulated right to a *family*, but rather the recognition that a family is an important context for child development and flourishing. So despite many articulated rights related to a child's family of birth, if the child has been separated from that family, he or she does not have an articulated right to be placed in a different family. Many groups that advocate for international adoption appeal to a child's "right to a family," but this right is not directly enumerated in the primary document articulating child rights. This is an important (yet subtle) distinction, because many advocacy groups undermine their advocacy by using this language that appeals to an unarticulated right. A more effective approach would be to stress that when a child's birth family is determined to be unavailable or detrimental for a child's flourishing, other solutions can supplement that care so as to reduce vulnerability.

Beyond this conflict between the themes of the document and the lack of an articulated right to a family, there is also potential for conflict over the rights that are directly articulated. For example, children have a right to be protected from discrimination, abuse, and exploitation. But they also have a right to be protected from separation from their birth parents against their parents' will, and from unlawful interference with their privacy, family, and home. Sometimes these two sets of rights can directly conflict each other, especially when it is the parents perpetuating the abuse or exploitation. For example, differences in belief on appropriate means of discipline or education can lead to interference in the child's family. Going back to the statistics presented at the beginning of this chapter, the example presented demonstrates how relatives may support FGM as a cultural practice while girls and other family members might disagree with the relatives who support it and seek protection from the practice. These cases are incredibly difficult to mediate both legally and socially.

One of the most clearly recognized areas for tension in the articulated rights is the conflict between the right to an education and the right to a cultural identity. In Article 29, children are given the right to an education with five qualities. First, the education must be focused on developing the child's personality, talents, and mental and physical abilities to their fullest potential. Second, the education must be focused on developing the child's respect for human rights and fundamental freedoms, and for the principles enshrined in the Charter of the United Nations. Third, the education must be focused on developing respect for the child's parents; for his or her own cultural identity, language, and values; for the national values of the country in which the child is living; for the country from which he or she may originate; and for civilizations different from his or her own. Fourth, the education must be focused on preparing the child for "responsible life in a free society, in the spirit of understanding, peace, tolerance, equality of sexes, and friendship among all peoples, ethnic, national and religious groups and persons of indigenous origin" (CRC, Article 29, p. 9). Fifth, the education must be focused on developing "respect for the natural environment" (CRC, Article 29, p. 9). In Article 30, each child is given the right to "enjoy his or her own culture, to profess and practice his or her own religion, or to use his or her own language (p. 9)."

The tensions in these two back-to-back articles are quite profound, rendering them highly aspirational but difficult to achieve in reality. In fact, these two articles are at the heart of opposition to the CRC in the United States (Smolin, 2006). Some sections of Article 29 aspire to a highly tolerant education that instills in children respect for diversity of all types. Other sections focus on the particularity of cultural and religious beliefs and practices, leaving some flexibility for children to be educated in those traditions. But what about cases where particular religious or cultural traditions are intolerant of other religious or cultural traditions? Is educating a child to believe that one religious perspective is true, for example, tantamount to teaching them to be intolerant of other religious traditions? This key tension has caused opposition to the treaty in the United States amongst advocates for religious education, who fear that ratification of the treaty would endanger religious education within the United States (Smolin, 2006).

The challenge then becomes how to navigate these tensions, especially for advocates seeking social justice for vulnerable children. It is not feasible to create a guide to each conflict in rights. However, we can still rely upon guiding criteria that can help us more effectively mediate between conflicting rights. These guiding criteria help in multiple ways: (1) they provide a method of carefully thinking through decisions (on the individual level) and policy (at the state level); (2) they provide common language we can use to justify decisions; and (3) they provide a means of assessing decisions after they have been made and implemented.

One such guiding criterion is to identify whose *rights are being protected* in the decision to privilege one right (or set of rights) over another. Often the rights of children, vulnerable children in particular, get intertwined with the rights of others involved with the children. For example, when considering vulnerable children who are available for adoption, we are also confronted with the rights of birth parents, adoptive parents, caretakers investing in the children, and even the children's siblings. Because children often the most vulnerable of all parties involved, their rights are the most likely to be violated. Advocates can help courts navigate tensions between rights by continually placing the rights of children in the center of the discussion.

A second guiding criterion is to identify whose *interests are being served* in the decision to privilege one right (or set of rights) over another. Often, multiple groups' interests are served by the decision to privilege one set of rights over another. Taking the same example, does the decision to privilege one right over another establish long-term practices that serve the interests of adoption agencies or other advocating groups more than the children who need to be protected? Or, perhaps, are the interests of institutions like orphanages also being served? If there is little difference in the protection of children between the two choices, it is important to ensure that special interest groups aren't benefiting from the current situation in a way that could jeopardize child protection in later situations. For example, the decision to open an adoption relationship between two countries has the potential to protect vulnerable children. But it also has the potential to enhance child vulnerability if either country lacks the institutional strength to monitor the relationship adequately. Identifying other benefiting groups *beyond* vulnerable children in a decision can expose ulterior motives that might influence the calculation of which rights to privilege in each decision.

THE OVERLAPPING NETWORK OF CHILD ADVOCATES

This final section discusses the overlapping responsibilities of the state, the community, and the individual in advocating for vulnerable children. Before discussing each of these actors in turn, it is first important to think about how the characteristics of vulnerable children have important implications for their protection. Two important dimensions must be considered when thinking about vulnerable children: their location and the circumstances that render them vulnerable. First, vulnerable children have a political and an immediate location, and both are important to keep in mind when considering responsibility for their care. On one hand, the political location signals the long-term potential of providing for the care and legal protection of children who lack parental advocacy. On the other hand, vulnerable children's immediate location has important implications for whether their immediate needs are being met, as well as the availability of long-term solutions.

For political location, some vulnerable children are located within countries that have a social welfare system designed to care for them, while others are located within countries that may lack the capacity to care for or protect children. In fact, these systems tend to have more vulnerable children because the conditions that undermine effective social welfare provision are typically the same conditions that render children vulnerable. For example, extremely poor countries may have disproportionately more families without the resources to care for children; this same lack of resources also makes it difficult to build institutions at the state level that can care for vulnerable children.

Vulnerable children also have an immediate location. In the worst cases, vulnerable children lack not only parental advocacy; they may also lack food and shelter and basic life provisions. In other cases, vulnerable children have lost parental advocacy, but they are provided for through some type of kin care, or care from others in their community. For instance, vulnerable children can be housed in orphanages, group foster care homes, or families in their community. In other cases, vulnerable children are still located with their families, but those families lack the resources and/or capacity to provide for their care. These children not only lack basic provisions, but they are also at risk of losing their parental advocacy due to extenuating circumstances like extreme poverty or natural disasters.

The second dimension that is vital to consider is the circumstances that render children vulnerable. Children who are vulnerable because one or both parents have died, or because their parents have terminated their legal rights, have certain long-term solutions available to them that other children with ambiguous legal situations lack. Moreover, because many countries do not consider parenting to be a role that can be legally assigned or terminated, it can be difficult to identify children's legal status regarding their parents. This problem is magnified in countries with overwhelming numbers of vulnerable children, because the system can lack the capacity to track and document the status of all vulnerable children.

Yet other causes render children vulnerable without making them eligible for long-term solutions. For example, think back to the chaos following the 2010 earthquake in Haiti. Many children were separated from their families because of the earthquake, and several adoption agencies started processing adoptions to the United States in the aftermath. The difficulty with this situation was that many of the children still had living parents who very much wanted to be reunited with their children (Thompson, 2010). The US and Haitian governments had to step in quickly in order to prevent children from being removed from Haiti, even in the difficult post-earthquake situation that significantly reduced these children's immediate standard of living.

Another situation of child vulnerability that does not render children eligible for long-term solutions is when children are vulnerable *within* their family unit, or temporarily separated from their parents, for example in situations of abuse. In these cases, a different set of solutions is appropriate within the children's birth country, such as temporary and longer-term foster care. It is only when children have never known their parents, or when they have been separated from their parents permanently, that a combination of domestic and international solutions can be more helpful.

The three main sets of actors advocating for vulnerable children have distinct yet overlapping responsibilities to that end. The first level of actors, the state, is responsible for providing and enforcing a framework that protects the rights of vulnerable children within that state. Vulnerable children have lost their parental advocacy, and the primary responsibility for their care rests in the hands of the state. In the best of circumstances, the state has a child welfare system in place so as to provide for vulnerable children. But we know that even the most developed countries, with the most advanced institutional capacity, still have deficits in their child welfare systems. Additionally, often the conditions that render children vulnerable are the same conditions that undermine the state's ability to provide for vulnerable children. For example, if extreme poverty within a state renders many children vulnerable, those same conditions of poverty make it less likely that the state has resources to care for them. To effectively care for vulnerable children, two other sets of actors must step in when the state fails.

The second level of actors, the organizational level, can take several different forms. For example, nongovernmental organizations (NGOs) focused on caring for vulnerable children operate both within state borders and across national borders. These organizations range from subject matter experts on particular aspects of child vulnerability (e.g., health issues) to faith-based organizations advocating for particular approaches to child vulnerability in general (Keck & Sikkink, 1998; Simmons, 2009). On the other hand, intergovernmental organizations (IGOs) like the United Nations, the Hague Conference on Private International Law, and many other regional organizations, work collaboratively with governments in order to articulate rights and responsibilities, influence governments to commit to pursuing those responsibilities, and monitor state behavior as they seek to enforce treaties. In this way, intergovernmental and nongovernmental organizations collaborate across borders and partner so as to globally advocate for and care for vulnerable children.

The third level of actors, the individual, represents professionals from a variety of disciplines that implement best practices across political, cultural, and social contexts, identify and report violations of those standards, and enable healing in children who have experienced enhanced vulnerability. For example, legal professionals advocate for the legal protection of children in conditions of enhanced vulnerability, stepping into the role that parents typically perform. Psychologists promote healing in children who have suffered systematic and episodic abuse at the hands of their political system and violent actors. Development professionals work with governments to build the institutional support needed to correct systematic abuse and vulnerability. The state, organizational, and individual levels of actors all work collaboratively, within the larger political structures that shape and constrain their potential for influence.

CONCLUSION

This volume addresses a critical gap in the literature around children in the international system by identifying the ways in which children are relevant stakeholders in international social justice issues. Because children need advocates to have access to their governments and international bodies, they are already operating from a position of vulnerability. But as the introductory issue of FGM demonstrated, children are also more likely to be victims of situations that increase their vulnerability, which can separate them from the parental advocacy they need to thrive and fully develop.

One of the key goals of this volume is to present a social justice framework that successfully incorporates children and young people as stakeholders in the process, and to demonstrate how such an expanded framework can better advocate for children in a variety of issue areas. To support that overall goal, this chapter has provided a foundation for understanding the political structures, dynamics, and language in which advocacy for vulnerable children is situated, especially as it crosses international borders. First, it has presented the overlapping norms, treaties, and institutions of the international human rights regime, and demonstrated how those apply specifically to children. Second, it has clarified some of the key concepts emerging out of those documents and institutions and shown how they are used to discuss vulnerable children. Third, it has identified the rights articulated in the treaties that provide for children's human rights, and illuminated potential areas of conflict between the articulated rights. Finally, it has mapped out the levels of actors responsible for social justice advocacy for children, and revealed how their roles and responsibilities overlap.

Note

1. For a full discussion of the controversial aspects of the treaty within the United States, see Smolin (2006).

REFERENCES

Barone, F. (2015). A cross-cultural perspective on childhood. *Human relations area files: Cultural information for education and research.* New Haven, CT: Yale University. hraf.yale.edu/a-cross-cultural-perspective-on-childhood/

Cohen, C. P. (1998). Role of the United States in drafting the Convention on the Rights of the Child: Creating a new world for children. *Loyola Poverty Law Journal, 4,* 9ff.

Fearon, J. D. (1998). Bargaining, enforcement, and international cooperation. *International Organization,* 52(2), 269–305.

Hafner-Burton, E. M., & Tsutsui, K. (2005). Human rights in a globalizing world: The paradox of empty promises. *American Journal of Sociology,* 110(5), 1373–1411.

Hague Conference for Private International Law (1993). *Hague Convention on Protection of Children and Co-operation in Respect to Intercountry Adoption.*

Hathaway, O. A. (2007). Why do countries commit to human rights treaties? *Journal of Conflict Resolution,* 51(4), 588–621.

Keck, M., & Sikkink, K. (1998). *Activists beyond borders: Transnational activist networks in international politics.* Ithaca, NY: Cornell University Press.

Mattes, M., & Rodriguez, M. (2014). Autocracies and international cooperation. *International Studies Quarterly,* 58(3), 527–538.

McBride, B. (2016). *The globalization of adoption: Individuals, states, and agencies across borders.* New York: Cambridge University Press.

Moravcsik, A. (2000). The origins of human rights regimes: Democratic delegation in postwar Europe. *International Organization*, 54(2), 217–252.
Peyton, N., & Jahateh, L. (2018, January 23). With newfound democracy, Gambia faces resurgence in FGM and child marriage. Reuters, Thomson Reuters Foundation. www.reuters.com/article/us-gambia-women-fgm/with-newfound-democracy-gambia-faces-resurgence-in-fgm-and-child-marriage-idUSKBN1FC0XA
Powell, E. J., & Staton, J. K. (2009). Domestic judicial institutions and human rights treaty violation. *International Studies Quarterly*, 53(1), 149–174.
Simmons, B. (2009). *Mobilizing for human rights: International law in domestic politics.* New York: Cambridge University Press.
Simmons, B. (2010). Treaty compliance and violation. *Annual Review of Political Science*, 13, 273–296.
Smolin, D. M. (2006). Overcoming religious objections to the Convention on the Rights of the Child. *Emory International Law Review*, 20, 81–110.
Thompson, G. (2010). After Haiti quake, the chaos of U.S. adoptions. *New York Times*, August 3, 2010. www.nytimes.com/2010/08/04/world/americas/04adoption.html?pagewanted=all&_r=0
UN General Assembly. (1990). *Convention on the Rights of the Child.*
UN General Assembly. (2001). *Optional Protocol to the Convention on the Rights of the Child on the Sale of Children, Child Prostitution and Child Pornography.*
UN General Assembly. (2001). *Optional Protocol to the Convention on the Rights of the Child on the Use of Children in Armed Conflict.*
United Nations International Children's Emergency Fund (UNICEF). (2013). *Female genital mutilation/cutting: A statistical overview and exploration of the dynamics of change.* New York: United Nations International Children's Emergency Fund.
Von Stein, J. (2005). Do treaties constrain or screen? Selection bias and treaty compliance. *American Political Science Review*, 99(4), 611–622.
Vreeland, J. R. (2008). Political institutions and human rights: Why dictatorships enter into the United Nations Convention against Torture. *International Organization*, 62(1), 65–101.
Wallace, S. R. (2003). International adoption: The most logical solution to the disparity between the numbers of orphaned and abandoned children in some countries and families and individuals wishing to adopt in others. *Arizona Journal of International and Comparative Law*, 20, 689–724.

3

Social Determinants of Health

Children and the Consequences of Socially Unjust Policies

Aradhana Bela Sood, Danny T. K. Avula, and Tara Warman Wiley

Janae is a smart and capable twenty-one-year-old Black woman who has lived in the same low-income urban neighborhood all her life.[1] She graduated from the local public high school and received grants to take a few community college classes, but after dealing with the frustrations of unreliable transportation to campus and trying to manage many more urgent priorities, she decided to put classes on hold and focus on making money. She shares an apartment with her mother, who suffers from lupus and is on long-term disability, and her younger brother and sister, and works as a part-time cashier at a discount store down the street from their apartment. Janae sometimes dates men from the neighborhood, but is cautious about letting anyone in. Her father has been gone since she was a small child, and her mother has had a number of boyfriends, a few who were violent with her, one who was violent with Janae and her siblings, and one who touched Janae inappropriately. Most of the time, Janae feels responsible for taking care of her mother, brother, and sister – she uses her mother's Supplemental Nutrition Assistance Plan (SNAP) card to buy groceries at the discount store where she works or at the corner grocery, and she makes sure there is always food at home. She promises her family that she will always be there when they need her, but she dreams of going back to school and having new experiences and a career that makes her feel proud. Janae worries a lot about what she's missing, and the worrying sometimes makes her tired and depressed, and at other times it makes her want to go out and party and forget about all her responsibilities.

Caitlin is an intelligent twenty-one-year-old White woman who is a college junior at a large state university 100 miles from her hometown.[2] She grew up living with her mother, father, and younger brother in a green, spacious upper-middle-class suburb and attended some of the best public schools in the state. Her parents were very health-focused: they enrolled her in sports at an early age and made sure she ate healthy meals. Caitlin's mother was treated for depression throughout Caitlin's childhood and was at times unavailable emotionally, which led Caitlin to rely on academics and athletics for praise and self-worth. Because she devoted herself to swimming for years, Caitlin was offered a scholarship to join the women's swim team at the university she now attends. In her sophomore year, she was sexually assaulted at a fraternity party but was supported by her parents in seeking action against the perpetrator and receives ongoing counseling in order to help her to navigate her feelings. Whenever school or life overwhelms her, she gets in the car her parents bought her and drives home for the weekend, where her father cooks her favorite foods and she has space to relax and reconnect with childhood friends, though sometimes she heads back to school early if her mother's depression is making her uncomfortable. Caitlin is a biology major but hasn't decided yet what she will do for a career – she is thinking of being a physical therapist, but she knows she has time to decide and that her parents will help when it's time to pursue graduate school.

No life experience determines a person's future absolutely, but the systems of support and opportunity we experience from the moment we are conceived and throughout our lives have a powerful effect on our ability to enjoy good health and personal fulfillment. Looking at these two case studies, it is possible that Janae will accomplish her goals of attending school and pursuing a meaningful career while still supporting her family, but her lack of personal support, financial resources, and transportation, along with a history of untreated trauma and no role models for how to build a different future, make it much harder for her to realize her dream. Caitlin, on the other hand, has had all of the economic and environmental advantages a person needs to enjoy good health: quality schools, a green suburban neighborhood, consistent access to resources, and emotional and clinical support for overcoming barriers to thriving. Caitlin's life has not been free of challenges, but the factors that determine her ability to thrive – the social determinants of health – are consistently in her favor when compared with Janae's experience.

In this chapter, we examine the nature of social determinants of health – how they shape all aspects of our lives and either enhance or limit our ability to enjoy health and opportunity. In addition, we study the structural roots of these social determinants – the systemic values and prejudices that result in policies and investments that promote health for some communities and limit it for others over the course of generations. Finally, we explore the protective factors that can be built to disrupt negative social determinants of health – equity-driven improvements to policies, programs, and investments – and explore ways the City of Richmond, Virginia, is working collectively to build these protective factors in its most vulnerable communities today.

Note that the case studies presented at the start of this chapter were selected because of the differences between them – Black/White, urban/suburban, low-income/higher-income, single-parent/two-parent household – represent common and stark disparities that affect health and opportunity for many Americans. They are not intended as a comprehensive account of all social determinants: for example, native language and citizenship status (Walker, Strom Williams, & Egede, 2016) are both powerful determinants of health and opportunity, and gender identity and religious affiliation are strong predictors of whether a person will experience prejudice and a resulting lack of access to opportunities and supports. The case studies are a framework for understanding the nature of social determinants of health and how we can begin to build a more equitable future for every person. We hope this chapter will serve as a launching point for readers to consider the role they can play personally and professionally in disrupting the challenges others experience because of their socioeconomic circumstances.

DEFINING SOCIAL DETERMINANTS OF HEALTH

The social environment a child is born into is not a variable he or she can control: the race, age, education level, physical and emotional health, and neighborhood of residence of a child's parents heavily determine access to support and opportunity at every phase of life. Essentially, social determinants of health (SDOH) are supports that act as shock absorbers against lifelong stress or – if protective factors are lacking – contribute to stress and limitations that negatively affect health and well-being. According to the WHO Commission (Solar, 2010), SDOH fall broadly into two categories: structural determinants that refer to (a) a society's prevailing socioeconomic and political structures that influence public policy and determine social welfare, housing quality, public safety, environmental quality, and employment and educational opportunity; and (b) an individual's place within that society related to race, ethnicity, gender, and class; and intermediary determinants including living and working conditions, personal behavior, biology, and other circumstantial factors that affect individuals living with a community strengthened or weakened by the structural factors listed earlier (WHO Commission on Social Determinants of Health, 2005).

The structural and intermediary determinants listed previously in this chapter are evident in Janae and Caitlin's stories: Janae grew up in a low-income urban community where the public schools are likely of a lower quality than the suburban schools Caitlin attended. Black children are also likely to be graded more harshly, referred to special education, and punished more frequently and severely in school and more likely to drop out than their White peers regardless of intellectual ability (Office of Minority Health, Office of the Director, CDC, 2005). Black students in majority-Black schools in low-income neighborhoods are also less likely to have access to college and career counseling and formal supports for transitioning to postsecondary education, limiting their long-term potential for making economic gains.

With limited transportation access and an abundance of convenience and corner stores in her neighborhood, Janae most likely consumed prepackaged foods regularly, and experienced lower-quality nutrition throughout her life. Lack of access to healthy foods can contribute to poorer health outcomes over the life course as well as form habits and preferences for less healthy foods even if the ability to access or afford quality food improves. Growing up in an affordable apartment in a densely populated urban neighborhood most likely also exposed Janae to poorer air quality and mold, dust, or other allergens, possibly increasing the amount of time she was ill and absent from school in childhood. Black children, especially those living in densely populated urban areas and/or low-income housing, are disproportionately affected by uncontrolled pediatric asthma (Williams, Sternthal, & Wright, 2009), which is exacerbated by environmental triggers and an ability to access regular medical care or to afford costly inhalers. Uncontrolled asthma in childhood (Krieger & Higgins, 2002) can ultimately result in lower academic achievement and poorer social outcomes given limited capacity for physical activity, lifelong financial stability, and reduced life expectancy. Poor neighborhood conditions generally characterized by vacant and blighted properties, lack of green space, low access to resources and transportation, and lack of general community safety are also strongly correlated to increased risk of hypertension, HIV/AIDS, obesity, and respiratory illness as well as increased risk of untreated mental health challenges (Link & Phelan, 1995).

A less tangible but perhaps more powerful social determinant is Janae's race. Regardless of whether she and Caitlin have the same intellectual capacity, assuming they both live in the United States today, systemic racial prejudice persists and greatly determines health and opportunity. Janae is less likely to be given educational and employment opportunities (Scott & Wilson, 2011) or to receive equal pay, equal consideration and attention by medical care providers, and equal treatment by law enforcement based on her race alone (US Bureau of Justice Statistics, 2018). Even adjusting for educational and economic status, racism is linked to poorer postnatal health outcomes in babies born to Black mothers (Alhusen, Bower, Epstein, & Sharps, 2016). Black adults also experience higher rates of cardiovascular disease (CDC, n.d.a).

In addition, Janae's traumatic experiences of her father's absence and physical and sexual violence in childhood have a dramatic impact on her ability to thrive. Adverse childhood experiences (ACEs) are childhood events that significantly impact brain development and behavioral patterns, and include exposure to emotional abuse, physical abuse, sexual abuse, emotional or physical neglect, exposure to parental substance abuse, parental separation or divorce, domestic violence, parental mental illness (including suicide/attempt), or parental incarceration (Felitti & Anda, 2010). The number of ACEs sustained in childhood is strongly correlated with poor physical and mental health outcomes in adulthood, even after accounting for high educational achievement and improved economic status (Felitti & Anda, 2010). Without interventions to help develop coping skills and resilience, these events during childhood continue to affect adult decision-making around healthcare, exercise, relationships, and sense of self-worth even if a person is not consciously thinking about them. While Caitlin too experienced trauma in the form of her mother's depression and a sexual assault, she received treatment that is more likely to build her capacity for resilience, or the ability to overcome adversity and pursue a healthy and fulfilling life. Ongoing stressors in Janae's life, such as realistic fears about her mother's relationships and poor health, further impede her resilience as her emotional energy is diverted from meeting her own needs.

In understanding social determinants of health, it is equally important to understand not only *what* they are but *why* they are (Priest et al., 2013). Social determinants are a result of being born in a certain place and situation, but the systemic factors that influence health and opportunity – housing (US Department of Health and Human Services, 2009), school quality, neighborhood safety, employment opportunity, access to resources and transportation – are the result of *choices* made by political and private sector leaders over the course of generations that prioritized investment in some communities and deprioritized others (Pollack, Egerter, Sadegh-Nobari, Dekker, & Braverman, 2008). For example, in Richmond in the mid-twentieth century, government leaders chose to build Interstate 95 directly *through* the thriving Black neighborhood of Jackson Ward, tearing down many structures in the neighborhood, reducing home and business values, and negatively impacting air quality and community safety. They further chose to cluster four public housing communities in Richmond's majority-black East End and later built an adult detention center within walking distance of those public housing communities. These decisions, followed by decades of disinvestment in public schools, parks, and roads in the East End, have branded the community as undesirable to generations of future residential and commercial investors.

Black children born in the East End of Richmond are more likely to experience lifelong challenges as a result of their social determinants of health, but these social determinants are not permanent and inevitable: they are *conditional* and dependent entirely upon our collective willingness to see them persist. In order to disrupt the limiting factors of health and opportunity experienced by so many people in low-income communities and communities of color, we need to be bold in highlighting the *policies, programs, investments*, and *assumptions* that drive health inequalities (Ku, 2003). How can we build upon the strengths of communities and provide families with the resources they need to help their children succeed academically, socially, and economically and live long and healthy lives (RAND Corporation, 2005)? How must our values and priorities shift? How might life look different for both Janae and Caitlin if we dedicate ourselves personally and professionally to disrupting the root causes of inequity whenever possible?

UNDERSTANDING PROTECTIVE FACTORS

Stakeholders in local government, healthcare systems, schools, foundations, and community organizations who seek to improve outcomes for children and families whose social determinants of health limit their ability to thrive must build programs and pursue policy changes that address the *risk factors* of poor health and personal stability. While it may take generations to address larger systemic challenges such as racial prejudice, underfunded schools, and limited employment opportunities and transportation access for residents of low-income communities, positive change and potential for thriving can be developed for families and communities when risk factors are addressed in four key areas:

- Family – Youth are at increased risk for negative outcomes when they live in families with high levels of conflict or violence, when parents lack knowledge or willingness to engage around setting boundaries or modeling healthy behaviors, when parents are absent from the household, or when they struggle with alcohol, drug abuse, or mental illness (Tsey, Whiteside, Deemal, & Gibson, 2003).
- Community – Youth are at increased risk for negative outcomes when they live in unsafe neighborhoods with limited access to healthy recreation and social engagement, when they perceive their neighborhood as a place where drugs or guns are easily available, when they change residences frequently in childhood and have a limited sense of belonging to their home or neighborhood, or when they feel discriminated against by the behavior of others or by the condition of their neighborhood in general (Wickrama, Merten, & Wickrama, 2012).
- School – Youth who struggle academically for reasons such as unidentified learning disabilities, repeating at least one grade, experiencing bullying with no adult intervention, or feeling that they do not belong in their school environment are less likely to experience physical, mental, and social well-being or financial self-sufficiency in adulthood (Huang, Cheng, & Theise, 2013).
- Peer-Individual – Youth who exhibit rebellious or violent behaviors or who experiment with drugs at an early age, who associate with peers who use drugs or are involved in gangs, who experience repeated bullying or dating violence, or who work more than twenty hours per week during the school year are at increased risk for physical, mental, social, and economic challenges throughout their lifetime (Settipani et al., 2018).

Addressing these risk factors involves creating programs and resources to help youth and families develop social and emotional skills and personal habits to improve their short- and long-term outcomes, but it also means *building relationships and trust* in communities that have historically experienced disinvestment and prejudice and that therefore may be less inclined to trust outside providers and organizations. Understanding the power of *protective factors* to improve health outcomes is essential to building not only programs and access that enhance them but also trust and understanding that can drastically improve outcomes for individual youth and families and, over time, for entire communities who engage with these supports. According to the Child Welfare Information Gateway (2014):

Protective factors are conditions or attributes in individuals, families, communities, or the larger society that, when present, mitigate or eliminate risk in families and communities [and] increase the health and well-being of children and families. Protective factors help parents to find resources, supports, or coping strategies that allow them to parent effectively, even under stress (p. 1).

The Center for the Study of Social Policy (CSSP) developed a protective factors framework that is currently in use by providers in more than thirty states (Child Welfare Information Gateway, 2014). The CSSP divides protective factors into five strengths-building categories:

- Parental Resilience – The ability of parents to navigate and rebound from stress and seek help when necessary and to build healthy relationships with others, including their own children, and to model healthy lifestyle choices and social behaviors at home and in the community;
- Social Connections – Building and sustaining positive relationships with friends, family, neighbors, and other community members, and a belief that members of the community are invested in each other's lives and have the capacity to work together to affect change in their shared circumstances;
- Concrete Supports in Times of Need – Families have access to support services to meet basic needs such as food, housing, clothing, healthcare, and transportation, and support for navigating critical issues such as substance abuse, mental health challenges, or domestic violence;
- Knowledge of Parenting and Child Development – Parents use positive discipline strategies, are actively involved in their children's lives at home and at school, and promote positive development by making healthy lifestyle choices at home such as a nutritious diet, exercise, positive social engagement, and reliable routines;
- Social and Emotional Competence of Children – A child's ability to interact positively with others at home and school, to regulate his or her emotions and communicate feelings, and to engage to the best of his or her ability academically and socially at school. A child's social and emotional competence depends not only on how he or she engages with others at home, at school, and in the community but also on an inherent sense of belonging, self-worth, and positive potential.

In communities with high rates of poverty, family instability, and chronic disinvestment in schools, housing, and community resources, these protective factors are often difficult for families to establish and maintain. Many families are too overwhelmed by daily stressors to advocate for themselves or to educate themselves about resources for their children even when these are available. Access to quality education is considered essential not only to attainment of success in life but also to social cohesion and economic stability (Gradstein & Justman, 2002). However, many barriers stand in the way of families effectively advocating for their children. For example, a request for a child study team evaluation in an under-resourced school district may be met with refusal despite state and federal laws that support the concept. This is partially because individual schools and community centers in neighborhoods that face multiple social inequities often lack the financial resources to fund programming to help families and youth build these protective factors. Broader partnerships with local government, foundations, healthcare systems, and other stakeholders are typically necessary before structures can be put into place to enhance these protective factors in a community. Many of these efforts are often funded with grants, and the life of these grants is frequently short-lived. In a conversation with community leaders and families in the East End of Richmond, parents describe schools that are frigid in the winter and sweltering in the summer as there is no local funding to support heating and air conditioning (Village Conversation, 2018). This lies in contrast to well-furnished and environmentally comfortable schools within a twenty-minute drive to suburban Richmond.

Finally, programs designed to enhance protective factors are most effective when they are both evidence-based and designed in partnership with community members in order to ensure that they are culturally and linguistically appropriate and appealing to the community. Developing programs in partnership with the community also improves the credibility of the program, as community members who are engaged in program development and implementation can act as ambassadors for the program and build relationships more easily with program participants who share their background and experiences. A public health approach that uses a primary, secondary, and tertiary prevention and intervention framework (Gordon, 1983) and incorporates a wraparound system of care (Winters & Metz, 2009) is one key way to start addressing health disparities and inequities (Pauly, Macdonald, Hancock, Martin, & Perkin, 2013). The following case studies provide examples of initiatives in Richmond, Virginia.

CASE STUDIES: FAMILY STABILITY, COMMUNITY CARE, AND YOUTH DEVELOPMENT IN RICHMOND, VIRGINIA

In Richmond, stakeholders across sectors have been collaborating extensively to develop programs and resources in order to boost protective factors and promote resilience in our most vulnerable communities. Richmond is a dynamic city in the midst of an economic and cultural transformation. An influx of diverse new businesses, revitalization of historic neighborhoods, a growing population of educated young professionals, burgeoning arts and culinary scenes, and the explosive growth of Virginia Commonwealth University (VCU) in the city center have energized Richmond's landscape over the past decade. These positive changes, however, stand in stark contrast to the concentrated intergenerational poverty and systemic marginalization that persist disproportionately among the city's African American residents. Decades of racially motivated housing practices and planning decisions have created entrenched education, health, and housing inequities and a steep disparity in quality of life from neighborhood to neighborhood. The current citywide poverty rate is 25.5 percent with a child poverty rate of 39.5 percent, including eighteen clustered census tracts where child poverty exceeds 80 percent (US Census, n.d.). Concentrated poverty, especially in East End neighborhoods surrounding six major public housing communities, has resulted in a physical landscape characterized by deterioration, substandard housing, and abandoned industrial and commercial sites. Each census tract that contains a public housing community in Richmond is a designated Health Profession Shortage Area, and 48 percent of Richmond qualifies as a food desert. Given this lack of access to healthy food and fitness opportunities, 36.7 percent of African American residents are obese citywide compared to 23.6 percent of white residents, and African American and Latino low-income residents experience disproportionate rates of heart disease, cancer, and diabetes (US Census, n.d.). However, income is an even greater predictor of obesity, with a rate of 39.8 percent among those who make less than $35,000/year and 19 percent for those with incomes above $75,000 (US Census, n.d.). Opportunities to pursue preventive self-care or to navigate pathways out of poverty are further limited among many low-income families given that 35 percent of all adults have not earned a high school diploma and 58 percent of households with children are led by single parents (US Census, n.d.). As a result, an alarming number of residents experience poor health outcomes, fractured family structures, personal and community trauma, and a general lack of hope and power. A 2015 analysis by the Equal Opportunity Project at Harvard found Richmond to be among the worst 2 percent of all county units in the United States – the forty-eighth worst out of 2,478 – in fostering upward mobility (Chetty, Friedman, Hendren, Jones, & Porter, 2018). In addition, a study by the VCU Center for Society and Health shows that residents of public housing complexes in Richmond have a life expectancy of up to twenty years less than residents of more affluent neighborhoods (Virginia Commonwealth University Center on Society and Health, 2015).

Now, partners in public health, local government, education, philanthropy, and the nonprofit, faith-based, and community sectors are coming together to build protective factors that support youth and families in all stages of life and all areas of risk. Successful local efforts include growing free, high-quality after school programs that engage both youth and parents; clinical support for parents and children who have experienced trauma; expanded services to reduce opioid overdose rates and provide access to affordable substance abuse treatment; case management to help families transitioning out of public housing find affordable, high-quality alternatives in the private market; and initiatives to engage youth and families in preventing community violence and improving community safety.

The following are three in-depth examples of local initiatives that enhance protective factors, each of which was developed and is operated in partnership with the community in order to maximize relevance and impact.

Cultivating Agency and Access through Public Housing Resource Centers

Through on-site clinical care, health and life skills education, and individualized navigation support, resource centers are helping residents to practice preventive self-care and embark on pathways to self-sufficiency while reshaping the culture of healthcare utilization in low-income communities. The Richmond City Health Department (RCHD) currently operates eight resource centers, six of which are located in public housing, one of which is located at Broad Rock Elementary School within a low-income community, and one of which is located in the Southwood apartment community where primarily Hispanic/Latino/Latinx residents live. Resource centers are staffed by nurses and nurse practitioners who provide clinical services based on a financial eligibility sliding scale, including screening and treatment for sexually transmitted infections, family planning, cancer prevention, and chronic disease prevention. In addition, resource centers train and employ community healthcare workers (CHWs), all of whom are current or recent residents of the communities they serve. The CHWs provide navigation support for primary care, healthcare coverage, social services, and support groups, as well as community outreach and education, and help clients to pursue self-sufficiency by providing navigation support for housing options, education and social supports, and the Center for Workforce Innovation. The RCHD resource centers serve more than 1,600 unduplicated patients per year and conduct more than 2,200 patient visits. In addition, CHWs lead or facilitate more than 400 classes and 450 outreach events that connect public housing residents to education, physical fitness, nutrition education, and parenting resources, demonstrating both the strong service capacity of CHWs and an interest in improved health and/or expanded health knowledge among residents (Richmond City Health District, 2018).

In addition to the services they provide, the CHWs themselves are a powerful example of positive change in Richmond's most vulnerable communities. When the program began, CHWs worked part-time without benefits, but their impact on health outcomes and relationship building in their communities was clear, and all CHWs employed by the RCHD are now full-time, salaried employees. The CHWs also advocated to the Commonwealth of Virginia to create a statewide certification process for CHWs to maintain a standard of care and improve employability, and founded the Virginia Community Health Worker Association, which has more than 200 members statewide and provides a platform for professional development, advocacy, and mutual support among CHWs across urban and rural localities (Virginia Community Health Worker Association, 2019). The CHWs have advocated to Richmond City Council, presented at national conferences, and worked alongside residents of the communities they serve to promote policy changes with the local housing authority. Their success is a clear demonstration of what can happen when local leaders choose to invest in change from within a community and build upon the strengths of community members, creating not only better access to healthcare and case management for the community as a whole but also opportunities for meaningful employment at a living wage for the CHWs themselves.

By locating programs and services in public housing communities and ensuring that residents play a role in informing and facilitating programming, resource centers cultivate change from within and help residents to see clinical care, wellness education, recreation, and access to local produce as features of their community rather than external interventions. In addition, working with trained peers builds trust among residents and models healthy community engagement and lifestyle choices. As public housing communities are redeveloped nationwide, Richmond's resource centers demonstrate the broad impact of empowering public housing residents to help one another navigate personal health, nutrition, fitness, and self-sufficiency.

Improving Child Health through Parental Resilience and Cooperation through the Virginia Family and Fatherhood Initiative

Operated through the RCHD in partnership with faith-based, nonprofit, and community partners across the state, the Virginia Family and Fatherhood Initiative (VFFI) is committed to strengthening fathers' and mothers' ability to co-parent and reduce their own barriers to thriving in order to improve family life and long-term outcomes for their children. Using a socio-ecological model (CDC, n.d.b) to create change at interpersonal, institutional, community, and public policy levels, the VFFI helps parents build knowledge, self-sufficiency, and accountability while also creating partnerships and shared responsibility for family stabilization. The VFFI offers comprehensive parenting support through a twenty-one-hour fatherhood development program and a fifteen-hour motherhood development program designed by the National Partnership for Community Leadership (NPCL). These curricula help both parents improve parenting and co-parenting skills, build resilience when faced with personal and family trauma, and aid in the navigation of education, employment, and housing opportunities. Trained peer educators facilitate the programs and are able to build rapport and trust with the mothers and fathers who participate based on their common lived experiences and cultural backgrounds. In addition to sessions at faith-based and community centers, the VFFI operates the motherhood and fatherhood development programs inside jails and substance abuse treatment centers, providing parents who are separated from their children a powerful opportunity to reflect on their choices, and to build skills and confidence that have the power to transform their family relationships and restore a sense of purpose as parents upon release. In 2015 and 2016, 490 fathers, including those who are incarcerated or residents of a substance abuse treatment center, completed the fatherhood development program, and 102 mothers completed the motherhood development program. Among program graduates, 75 percent of fathers reported increased knowledge of and an improved attitude toward responsible parenting, and 78 percent of mothers reported improved knowledge and attitudes. To date, thirty-seven community members, many of whom reside in low-income communities, have been trained to offer these curricula to their peers (Virginia Family and Fatherhood Initiative, 2015).

By brokering resources between partners and leveraging relationships of trust with a unifying commitment to parents and children, the VFFI offers a new way of thinking about child health equity and reducing poverty and social disparities to support whole family thriving.

After School Care Centers As an Entry Point for a Public Health Approach to Reduce Social Inequities in Care

A recent study of the East End of Richmond (Virginia Commonwealth University Center on Society and Health, 2015) reported that residents have a life expectancy of sixty-seven years. This is the second lowest in the city and sixteen years lower than areas of Richmond with the highest life expectancy that are located just five to ten miles away. Parental health and its impact on child well-being are inextricably linked. For example, untreated parental depression and anxiety can lead to significant morbidity in children (Herba, Glover, Ramchandani, & Rondon, 2016). The Peter Paul Development Center (PPDC) is an after school program that serves children and families in the East End of Richmond. The Richmond Promise Neighborhoods (RPN) Community Action Network is an initiative housed within the PPDC that works to reduce the burden of social determinants of health on well-being. The RPN is a grassroots collaborative of neighbors and service providers (nonprofits, schools, healthcare providers, etc.) who meet regularly to reduce service siloes, share information, and support the well-being of families throughout the East End. Some activities under the RPN include:

1) Goal-Directed Families, a long-term, voluntary parent group ($N \sim 40$) that works with family support staff and a mental healthcare provider and other peers to improve well-being through setting and achieving concrete family goals. Within this subset of families, self-report data using the Child Behavior Checklist (CBCL, Achenbach & Rescorla, 2001) provides information about how parents perceives their families' functioning. These data are used to develop an individualized approach to mobilize resources that reduce risk factors, enhance and support protective factors, and facilitate engagement with care providers and social supports that are otherwise routinely available to populations not at risk for health and social inequity. The RPN plans to expand this public health approach to 100 percent of families served by the organization while gathering data regarding outcomes.

2) The RPN Community Action Network Partner Survey (CPS), a self-report data collection tool, has been implemented so as to collect data on each organizational partner (N = 55) who is a member of the RPN regarding services it provides and the perceived impact of the community action network on the organization.
3) The Shared Family Survey (SFS) is a self-report data collection tool that collects family- and neighborhood-level information on participants in the Goal-Directed Families program in order to support the work of family-support staff. The CPS and SFS were developed in consultation with an academic research partner so as to balance service needs and research rigor. The group also plans to expand data collection using the SFS to other partners in the RPN who service clients so that it can improve data-driven strategies related to wellness throughout the East End. The data collected will be used to further refine plans to coordinate community healthcare needs proximal to where residents live and fast tracking of clinical mental healthcare services, and the ongoing use of data-driven strategic planning with the goal of reducing the severity of factors related to social determinants of health in clients supported by the SFS/Goal-Directed Families program over time. This process will encourage conversations around large-scale data collection, sharing, and dissemination among Community Action Network (CAN) partners and participants in the Goal-Directed Families program. It is hoped that the types of decision makers who might use the results of the proposed research to advance a culture of health would be local lawmakers, hospital systems, and insurance companies, clinician advocacy groups, and resident/patient advocacy groups. These groups are typically interested in engaging with communities in order to improve coordinated access and continued engagement with support services.

One example of the effectiveness of this approach was the case of a single mother who was connected to care through feedback she received on the CBCL she had filled out for her children.[3] The woman was given a safe space to address the depression and anxiety that had been preventing her from leaving her home except to pick up her children. She was also able to talk with a qualified staff member from the RPN about her loss of employment, the stress about one of her children's underperformance in school, and morbid obesity in another child. She also was frightened about deaths related to guns on her block. The RPN worked to create a plan for her that included rapid connection to a mental healthcare provider (fast tracking and adequate treatment), applying for and being hired by an employer after the resolution of her depression, one child being referred to an obesity clinic with guided education regarding healthy nutrition and exercise, and education regarding advocacy to the school guidance counselor for an individualized education plan (IEP). As far as change in housing to a safer area, conversations with the housing authority were not successful, but regardless of this lingering issue, life for the family as a whole gradually began to move in a positive direction. More importantly, the mother's confidence in advocating for and accessing resources has improved significantly. She is now using her own experience to provide peer support to other families.

JANAE AND CAITLIN IN AN EQUITABLE FUTURE

We began this discussion of social determinants with two capable, promising young women who have faced significant challenges throughout their lives, but only one of them had the resources and personal support that are typically necessary to overcome those challenges and live fully to her potential. Over the course of her life, Janae's capacity to thrive has been limited not by her talents or her dreams but by the lack of resources available to her and her family. How different might Janae's life be if her mother had been able to connect with a CHW at a resource center and discuss options for affordable care for her medical condition, alternative housing, and any other supports she needed? How might Janae's mother's choices as a parent have changed if she had participated in a program like the VFFI and been given a safe space to reflect on how the partners she chose were affecting her family? How much more prepared for college and navigating the pressures of adult life might Janae be if she had engaged in a community of support and empowerment like the Peter Paul Development Center over the course of her childhood?

It is important to note that none of the supports described in the case studies above can erase the deeper systemic challenges Janae faces. She is still more likely to attend an underfunded and underperforming school, to experience prejudice because of her skin color or socioeconomic background, and to experience stress or physical illness based on community violence, air quality, housing quality, and limited access to healthy food and recreation in her community. At the same time that Richmond is building programmatic supports for families, we are working to change policies and investments to ensure equitable access to high-quality public education and affordable housing, green space, and transportation. Programs like the VFFI and the PPDC help community members to thrive despite the circumstances they face in their homes and communities, but true health equity means strengthening the fabric of those communities through long-term reinvestment in infrastructure and opportunity so that future generations have fewer obstacles to overcome from the start. Building toward health equity also means partnering with residents so they are agents of change in their own lives and communities rather than recipients of better outside support. Only by disrupting the root causes of health disparities and social injustice and establishing protective factors that promote safety and health and create pathways to opportunity for every resident can we hope to see lasting change for Janae and so many others like her who deserve every opportunity to thrive.

Notes

1. Case studies have been de-identified to protect confidentiality.
2. Case studies have been de-identified to protect confidentiality.
3. Case studies have been de-identified to protect confidentiality.

REFERENCES

Achenbach, T. M., & Rescorla, L. A. (2001). *Manual for the ASEBA School-Age Forms & Profiles*. Burlington: University of Vermont, Research Center for Children, Youth, & Families.

Alhusen, J. L., Bower, K. M., Epstein, E., & Sharps, P. (2016). Racial discrimination and adverse birth outcomes: An integrative review. *Journal of Midwifery & Women's Health*, 61(6), 707–720. doi:10.1111/jmwh.12490

Centers for Disease Control and Prevention (CDC) (n.d.a). Age-specific excess deaths associated with stroke among racial/ethnic minority populations – United States, 1997. *Morbidity and Mortality Weekly Report 2000*, 49(5), 94–97.

Centers for Disease Control and Prevention (CDC) (n.d.b). The social ecological model: A framework for prevention. Retrieved from www.cdc.gov/violenceprevention/overview/social-ecologicalmodel.html.

Chetty, R., Friedman, J., Hendren, N., Jones, M., & Porter, S. (2018). The Opportunity Atlas: Mapping the childhood roots of social mobility. Opportunity Insights. Harvard University. Retrieved from https://opportunityinsights.org/wp-content/uploads/2018/10/atlas_paper.pdf.

Child Welfare Information Gateway (2014). *Protective Factors Approaches in Child Welfare*. Washington, DC: US Department of Health and Human Services.

Commission on Social Determinants of Health (2008). Closing the gap in a generation: Health equity through action on the social determinants of health. In *Final Report of the Commission on Social Determinants of Health* (pp. 1–256). Geneva: World Health Organization.

Felitti, V. J., & Anda, R. F. (2010). The relationship of adverse childhood experiences to adult health, well-being, social function, and healthcare. In R. Lanius, E. Vermetten, & C. Pain (eds.), *The Impact of Early Life Trauma on Health and Disease: The Hidden Epidemic* (pp. 77–87). New York: Cambridge University Press.

Gordon, R. S., Jr. (1983). An operational classification of disease prevention. *Public Health Reports*, 98(2), 107–109.

Gradstein, M., & Justman, M. (2002). Education, social cohesion, and economic growth. *American Economic Review*, 92(4), 1192–1204. Retrieved from http://proxy.library.vcu.edu/login?url=https://search.proquest.com/docview/233034055?accountid=14780.

Herba, C. M., Glover, V., Ramchandani, P. G., & Rondon, M. B. (2016, October 3). Maternal depression and mental health in early childhood: An examination of underlying mechanisms in low-income and middle-income countries. *Lancet Psychiatry*, (10), 983–992. doi:10.1016/S2215-0366(16)30148-1. Epub 2016 Sep 17.

Huang, K., Cheng, S., & Theise, R. (2013). School contexts as social determinants of child health: Current practices and implications for future public health practice. *Public Health Reports*, 128(6_suppl3), 21–28. doi:10.1177/00333549131286s304.

Krieger, J., & Higgins, D. L. (2002). Housing and health: Time again for public health action. *American Journal of Public Health*, 92(5), 758–768.

Ku, L. (2003, May 7). Charging the poor more for health care: Cost-sharing in Medicaid. Center on Budget and Policy Priorities. Retrieved from www.cbpp.org/archiveSite/5-7-03health.pdf.

Link, B., & Phelan, J. (1995). Social conditions as fundamental causes of disease. *Journal of Health and Social Behavior*, 80–94. Retrieved from www.jstor.org/stable/2626958.

Office of Minority Health, Office of the Director, CDC (2005). Health disparities experienced by black or African Americans – United States. *Morbidity and Mortality Weekly Report*, 54(1), 1–3. Retrieved from www.cdc.gov/mmwr/preview/mmwrhtml/mm5401a1.htm.

Pauly, B., Macdonald, M., Hancock, T., Martin, W., & Perkin, K. (2013). Reducing health inequities: The contribution of core public health services in BC. *BMC Public Health*, 13(1). doi:10.1186/1471-2458-13-550

Pollack, C., Egerter, S., Sadegh-Nobari, T., Dekker, M., & Braverman, P. (2008). Where we live matters for our health: The links between housing and health. Issue Brief #2. Princeton, NJ: Robert Wood Johnson Foundation, Commission to Build a Healthier America.

Potterf, J. E., & Pohl, J. R. (2018). A black teen, a white cop, and a city in turmoil: Analyzing newspaper reports on Ferguson, Missouri and the death of Michael Brown. *Journal of Contemporary Criminal Justice*, 34(4), 421–441. doi:10.1177/1043986218787732

Priest, N., Paradies, Y., Trenerry, B., et al. (2013). A systematic review of studies examining the relationship between reported racism and health and wellbeing for children and young people. *Social Science & Medicine*, 95, 115–127. Retrieved from www.sciencedirect.com/science/article/pii/S0277953612007927.

RAND Corporation (2005). Does neighborhood deterioration lead to poor health? Santa Monica, CA: RAND Corporation.

Richmond City Health District (2019). Retrieved from www.institutephi.org/our-work-in-action/community-health-worker-initiatives/richmond-city-health-district-community-advocates/.

Scott, A. J., & Wilson, R. F. (2011). Social determinants of health among African Americans in a rural community in the Deep South: An ecological exploration. *Rural and Remote Health*, 11, 1634. (Online), 2011. Retrieved from www.ncbi.nlm.nih.gov/pubmed/21299335.

Settipani, C. A., Hawke, L. D., Virdo, G., et al. (2018). Social determinants of health among youth seeking substance use and mental health treatment. *Journal of the Canadian Academy of Child and Adolescent Psychiatry*, 27(4), 213–221.

Solar, Irwin A. (2010). A conceptual framework for action on the social determinants of health. Social Determinants of Health Discussion Paper 2 (Policy and Practice). WHO Library Cataloguing-in-Publication Data A conceptual framework for action on the social determinants of health. Pp 27–30.

Strengthening Families and the Protective Factors Framework (2019). Center for the Study of Social Policy. Retrieved from https://cssp.org/resource/about-strengthening-families-and-the-protective-factors-framework/.

Tsey, K., Whiteside, M., Deemal, A., & Gibson, T. (2003). Social determinants of health, the "control factor" and the family wellbeing empowerment program. *Australasian Psychiatry*, 11(1_suppl), 34–39. doi:10.1046/j.1038-5282.2003.02017.x

US Bureau of Justice Statistics (2018, January). Prisoners in 2016, 8, table 6, pp. 1–2.

US Census (n.d.). American Fact Finder: 2013–2017 American Community Survey 5-Year Estimates. Retrieved from https://factfinder.census.gov/faces/nav/jsf/pages/community_facts.xhtml?src=bkmk.

US Department of Health and Human Services (2009). *Surgeon General's Call to Action to Promote Healthy Homes*. Washington, DC: US Department of Health and Human Services, Office of the Surgeon General.

Village Conversation (2018, October). Richmond City Health District, Inspire Work Group on Youth Violence Prevention. Unpublished communication.

Virginia Commonwealth University Center on Society and Health (2015). Mapping life expectancy: 20 years in Richmond, VA. Retrieved from https://societyhealth.vcu.edu/work/the-projects/mapsrichmond.html.

Virginia Community Health Worker Association (2019, May). Certification and training overview. Retrieved from www.chwva.org/certification-training.

Virginia Family and Fatherhood Initiative (2015). Child wellbeing and family fragmentation: Solutions for healthy families. Retrieved from https://virginiafamilies.org/scholars-corner/A-Public-Health-Report–Child-Wellbeing-and-Family-Fragmentation-Solutions-for-Healthy-Families(Final-12–4-15).pdf.

Walker, R. J., Strom Williams, J., & Egede, L. E. (2016). Influence of race, ethnicity and social determinants of health on diabetes outcomes. *American Journal of the Medical Sciences*, 351(4), 366–373. doi:10.1016/j.amjms.2016.01.008

Wickrama, T., Merten, M. J., Wickrama, K. A. S. (2012, March). Early community influence on young adult physical health: Race/ethnicity and gender differences. *Advances in Life Course Research*, 17(1), 25–33. Retrieved from https://doi.org/10.1016/j.alcr.2012.01.001.

Williams, D. R., Sternthal, M., & Wright, R. J. (2009). Social determinants: Taking the social context of asthma seriously. *Pediatrics*, 123(Suppl. 3), S174–S184. doi:10.1542/peds.2008-2233H.

Winters, N. C., & Metz, W. P. (2009). The wraparound approach in systems of care. *Psychiatric Clinics of North America*, 32(1), 135–151. doi:10.1016/j.psc.2008.11.007.

4

Health and Mental Health Disparities

Application of the Health Capability Paradigm for Children and Young People

Scott J. Hunter and Khalid I. Afzal

INTRODUCTION

In 2011, shortly after his election as the mayor of Chicago, Illinois, Rahm Emanuel presented his first budget, for the third largest city in the United States, to the city council and the general public. At a time of continued uncertainty about the city's finances, one of the mayor's initial responses to addressing the significant budgetary concerns for the city was to propose the closure of one-half of the city's community mental healthcare clinics (Joravsky, 2013). This was in addition to proposing the closure of fifty-four elementary schools, as well as several high schools, serving nearly 12,000 youths across the city (Gordon et al., 2018; Joravsky, 2013; Strauss, 2018). This action was proposed as a potential means of saving the city "an estimated $2.2 million with the closings" (Joravsky, 2013). Notably, almost every one of the community mental healthcare programs being proposed for closure was situated in the south and west sides of the city, areas highly segregated and predominantly populated by African American, Latino, and other non-White communities. The one north side area included, Rogers Park, is also well known as a home for a substantially diverse population, including citizens from around the world, many of whom have recently immigrated to the United States. Without surprise, the mayor's proposal was met with howls of anger and frustration from the communities affected by the closures (Strauss, 2018). In addition, the mental healthcare services community in the city equally cried foul, aware that negative effects would certainly be experienced given the demands for care that were already not being well met. Immediately, community activists and residents from these areas, many individuals who were utilizing the services of these programs, identified how the closures would impact their daily lives. They shared their stories about their need for available in-community mental healthcare to the broader public, through interviews and protests, and in hearings before the city council. Yet, as was expected and as reflected in ongoing reporting about the move to close the centers, the die was cast. Joravsky (2013) reiterated, in his review of the experience, what is well known in Chicago – that "the odds were against them [i.e., the clients of the community mental healthcare programs and the community activists]. The harsh fact remains that the clinics serve a particularly vulnerable constituency that doesn't typically have access to the mayor: poor people with mental health issues."

By 2012, all of the proposed clinics were closed, or "consolidated" as the mayor attempted to suggest (Byrne, 2018), and the communities were deprived immediately of required resources for mental healthcare (Quinn, 2018). This included not only the provision of psychological therapies but also direct access to medications clients were utilizing in order to address their psychiatric illnesses, and ongoing case management services. And despite the mayor's suggestions that resources were available to these individuals across sites still open in the city, the majority of clients from the closed mental healthcare programs were unable to successfully transfer their care (Quinn, 2018; Strauss, 2018). While the city offered allocations of a minimal amount of money (e.g., $500,000; see Joravsky, 2013) so as to cover care with already unavailable private mental healthcare providers (who typically only accepted individuals with private insurance or who could pay out of pocket for their care), most individuals were forced to attempt to obtain care either from the remaining overburdened community mental healthcare programs located outside of their communities, or to forego treatment until symptoms were no longer manageable and they required emergency care (Quinn, 2018). Additionally, with the closing of the centers, 125 medical employees of the city, the majority persons of color who regularly served some of the poorest and most vulnerable members of Chicago's populace, were fired by the mayor and the Chicago City Council (Joravsky, 2013). As a result of the closings, numerous citizens requiring support for post-traumatic stress disorder, anxiety disorders, depressive disorders, psychotic spectrum disorders, and substance abuse disorders were left with very limited assistance or care available to them in or near their community of residence.

Accompanying this trauma was a companion move by the mayor and his appointed team at the Chicago Public Schools to close a significant number of neighborhood-based public elementary schools; in 2013, this was complete, with a total of forty-nine elementary schools and one high school closed (Gordon et al., 2018; Strauss, 2018). The combined effect of these two actions led to severe challenges for families with complicated needs, living in areas of the city with limited resources. As a result, a crisis of significant concern emerged in these communities in Chicago, regarding available assistance and support for mental healthcare needs. This crisis is in fact one that sadly remains to this date incompletely addressed, with compounding unmet challenges, including overcrowded classroom conditions, subpar special education supports, schools with no available social workers or counselors, and a lack of resources or services to address multigenerational trauma (Gordon et al., 2018) and the impact of community violence (Quinn, 2018). Altogether, this is a crisis fueled by continued substantial limitations on mental healthcare and minimal available resources, specifically in areas requiring these services most desperately (Quinn, 2018).

Further impacting this issue has been a growing difficulty, across both city and state, with funding and paying for the even more limited resources available for health and mental healthcare in Illinois. This challenge rose in response to a multiyear budget impasse that unfolded following the subsequent election of Bruce Rauner as the governor of Illinois, an impasse that served to defund numerous additional community-based health and mental healthcare programs, further increasing the absence of ongoing primary medical care on top of already minimized access to mental healthcare (Mendoza, 2018).

As Chicago and Illinois have struggled over the past eight years to attempt to turn this situation around, a situation of diminished opportunity for support for communities struggling with poverty and low resources, a prominent question has been just who has the right to care, both for medical and mental health needs. How can that be determined in an equitable way, given an awareness of costs and unequal distribution of options for care (Jost & Pollack, 2018)? Unsurprisingly, Chicago is not alone in attempting to address this question; it is indeed a question being asked across the United States, one of the richest countries in the world (Cheng, Emmanuel, Levy, & Jenkins, 2015; Flores, 2010). Multiple studies have revealed that the model being utilized for supporting access to care in the United States is one that, even following the initiation of the Patient Protection and Affordable Care Act (PPACA or ACA; 42 USC 18001, 2010), remains inadequate and unjust in its provisions for supporting public healthcare needs, despite seeing some change in disparities in healthcare access since ACA implementation (Griffin et al., 2017; Jost & Pollack, 2018; Oberlander, 2016). Limitations in access to care are readily found in a majority of settings across the country (Gaffney & McCormick, 2017; Jost & Pollack, 2018; Maruthappu, Ologunde, & Gunarajasingam, 2013; Oberlander, 2016). The impact of these limitations is often experienced by those who most directly require integrated health and mental healthcare services: persons residing in low-resourced communities, who are often segregated in these communities with regard to accessible transportation, available local care providers, and adequate support services to assist with obtaining care. These failures in ensuring that resources are available further aggravate and extend the challenges under-resourced communities experience, given the combined stresses of financial insecurity, inadequate housing, poor educational opportunity, and increased risk for community violence and trauma (Jost & Pollack, 2018; Quinn, 2018). Additionally, communities with low resources are often reliant on their local hospital emergency rooms for both medical and psychiatric care, centers often lacking in resources for providing just that needed level of care (Quinn, 2018). As one egregious example in Chicago (and actually across the state of Illinois itself) has shown, only one hospital is now available, with very limited beds, for individuals presenting with co-occurring mental and physical health conditions. Instead, the majority of these individuals are treated in a haphazard manner, through limited mental health consultation resources while housed on a medical unit where training to address the impact of co-occurring challenges is often limited among the medical team (T. Koogler, 2019, personal communication). The question that continuously gets posed, across communities and within the harsh political climate that currently defines the United States, is how this is in fact ethical, as an example of just and beneficent care (Pollack, 2019). To the providers in the trenches, attempting to assist these affected community members, the answer is a resounding no.

This chapter is premised on the belief that ethical medical and mental healthcare require a social justice framework, one that takes as its principle stance that healthcare is a human right. Utilizing Ruger's (2010, 2016) health capability paradigm, a philosophical model developed from the Aristotelian theory of good, where "human flourishing is the end of all political activity" (Ruger, 2010, p. 45), we consider how, both within the United States itself and globally, the engagement of a perspective of positive rights regarding health and healthcare is required when approaching how to best address social disparities and access to medical and mental health treatment. We first consider the health capability paradigm and how it conceptually frames, within a social justice perspective, the right to health and the provision of healthcare for children and youth. We next explore how this model can be considered more directly within a discussion of how dual medical and mental healthcare is currently practiced in our program at the University of Chicago Medicine, a tertiary-care hospital system located on the south side of Chicago, in the Hyde Park neighborhood, and in Harvey, Illinois, a south suburb – areas where a majority of patients referred and treated are from lower- to lower-middle-class socioeconomic communities, and who utilize Medicaid as their primary source of insurance for healthcare. We focus specifically on the provision of forms of medical and mental healthcare that are often the least considered and subsequently unreimbursed by Medicaid: neuropsychological assessment and consultation/liaison for mental health needs in patients with medical conditions, which are among the most requested ancillary services for youth when ensuring more effective outcomes for their health needs. We next present a case that addresses the application of the health capability paradigm within a child and adolescent psychiatric care setting, with a goal of addressing how policies within the United States regarding negative rights have amplified the disparities in care that are both available and can be maintained. We end with a discussion of how communities, locally within the United States, but also perhaps globally, can better engage this model as a means for justifying more equitable and conscientious care for their residents.

THE HEALTH CAPABILITY PARADIGM AND HEALTHCARE DISPARITIES FOR YOUTH

Ruger, in her seminal text *Health and Social Justice*, presents a cogent philosophical model of health as a right and a mechanism for individual and social agency. As a theory situated in "a particular view of the good life: human flourishing, which values health intrinsically and more highly than non-intrinsic or solely instrumental social goods, such as income" (2010, p. 3), Ruger's model of health capability, "a person's ability to be healthy" (p. 3), is comprised of both a right to a functional health status and a recognition of the agency individuals hold in determining how to best achieve that status. Necessary to this model is the idea that health is foundational as a value and a social priority; it is a prerequisite for an individual's having sufficient capacity to care for and adapt to the demands that life imposes. As the model has developed in its continued iterations (cf. Ruger, 2016), it has identified as key society's requirement for recognizing health as a right, arguing that without health, there is no clear path to individual effectiveness or autonomy, let alone full participation in society itself.

Underlying the health capability model is the argument that, as contemporary philosophers and sociopolitical theorists Martha Nussbaum (2003) and Amartya Sen (1992) have discussed, society's obligation to maintain and improve health capabilities in people is founded in a commitment to their flourishing. Ruger has suggested that a key contribution to health management and scientific investigations regarding aspects of health should be an emphasis on how to best foster and support access to care and intervention as means for ensuring that individuals can develop, grow, and engage in opportunities that will promote successful educational and economic outcomes. Ruger recognizes nonetheless how this emphasis may vary with regard to cultural and vocational opportunities a particular society may have available. Yet this primary emphasis on health is first and foremost a right required for individuals to flourish within society. This can allow for the articulation of choices among the best options possible so as to achieve this goal.

Central to the health capability paradigm is the recognition that a right to health also stands concurrent with a right to equal access to care that ensures the obtainment of health. Additionally, a moral responsibility exists to provide all citizens within a society with access to the same range of care, care that is not minimal or just adequate, or, as has become the norm with the ACA, tiered, but instead care that is optimal for all. Quality of care determines how well health is achieved and maintained; as such, all individuals hold the right to a quality of care that is necessary and sufficient for ensuring that they are healthy. As Ruger has stated, "high-quality care is morally necessary because it will help people function best, given their circumstances" (2016, p. 283). Notably as well, "equal access does not mean equal outcomes, however. Equal health outcomes are impossible to achieve, given human diversity" (p. 283). This is a recognition, within the model, that ethical responsibilities are held by individuals, as well as providers and institutions that seek to support health. All are engaged in a process where information, guidance, and direct care are made available in order to enhance the advocacy and agency of the community toward achieving the goal of common health.

Political challenges abound when considering how to best organize and then implement approaches to ensuring health as a form of justice. Multiple efforts have been proposed across the world, with select countries (e.g., Cuba, the Scandinavian countries, and Canada) placing greater emphasis on positive rights that include equal access to healthcare and its requirements given available resources (Ruger, 2010), versus others, such as the United States, where determinations have been made supporting individual autonomy within a marketplace system, and decisions have focused on negative rights (i.e., "'negative' rights, unlike 'positive' rights, do not impose an obligation on others to provide you with something" [Bradley, 2010, p. 838]), where health is not viewed as a requirement for all (Christopher & Caruso, 2015; Ruger, 2016). Through the articulation of the health capability paradigm, Ruger (2010, 2016) has proposed a shared health governance model, whereby all institutions collaborate with the public toward the development of health agency (i.e., the capacity individuals hold to determine their own choices and how to achieve them, with specific regard toward the maintenance and promotion of health) and an overarching set of environmental policies and conditions that support and maintain health. It allows for choice; individuals make determinations based on need, not solely on access. Particularly, "this approach fosters consensus on distributive principles and procedures; provides incompletely theorized agreements as a method for achieving that consensus; emphasizes costs and effectiveness for assessing health policies and laws; and encourages collaborative problem-solving ... central to justice" (Ruger, 2016, p. 283).

UNDERSTANDING HEALTHCARE DISPARITIES IN MENTAL HEALTH

Chicago is not alone as a city within the United States where differences abound in the availability of adequate and sufficient healthcare. Daily, articles are published in newspapers and presented on news programs about the challenges for a substantial set of families when seeking access to healthcare for their children. Similarly, we read frequently about the profound discrepancies that exist worldwide in regard to available resources for healthcare, let alone nutrition and housing, that contribute to holding a semblance of health itself. Numbers are staggering in terms of the morbidity and mortality of poverty (Fritzell, Kangas, Hertzmann, Blomgren, & Hiilamo, 2013; Khullar & Chokshi, 2018); to have such limited resources available serves as a profound injustice, limiting chances for a full life, as well as for taking advantage of educational and vocational opportunities across time. Without adequate health, or the means to support it, youth are left with limitations as opposed to capacities.

Efforts have been at play within the United States to mitigate the losses of opportunity that have existed for the majority of the country's history, specifically for those who have reduced resources typically available to them (Ortega, Rodriguez, & Bustamante, 2015; Silvers, 2013). The establishment of Social Security and Medicare as means toward securing greater independence with aging helped set in motion a move toward a more liberal process regarding health, yet no constitutional protection for health exists in the United States, neither is there a guaranteed right to healthcare to support that goal, save for prisoners (cf. *Estelle v. Gamble*, US Supreme Court, 1976; Ruger, 2010), who do receive a semblance of healthcare as a guaranteed right. What has been established, principally at the federal level, is a statutory right to healthcare. Through interpretation of the Constitution (Article I, Section 8), Congress is identified as holding the power to "regulate interstate commerce and to tax and spend for the general welfare" (Ruger, 2016, p. 277). To date, Congress has established Medicare, Medicaid, the State Children's Health Insurance Program (SCHIP), and the ACA as means by which healthcare is made available ostensibly to all, albeit at a restricted and highly varied level depending on state interpretations and actions, save for Medicare, which remains federally funded and dictated (Moseley, 2008; Ruger, 2010). The most pertinent statutory provisions for children and youth are Medicaid, SCHIP, and the ACA. Each is, however, represented quite unevenly; while the mandate for these programs is federal, the funding is highly variable, and with differences in how services are made available and provided for by the states themselves (Moseley, 2008). Individuals who do not qualify for these programs fall readily through the cracks in terms of available services (Moseley, 2008; Ruger, 2010).

In Illinois, a state once considered a model for its investment in and allocations of mental healthcare (Visotsky, 2005), many years of decisions by politicians across the spectrum have affected both how well services are funded and how provision of services is determined (Quinn, 2018). As an example, Illinois now ranks eighteenth for mental and behavioral care access for children and youth (Huen-Johnson, Menchine, Goldman, & Seabury, 2018; Mental Health America, 2018). This has contributed to difficulties in obtainment of healthcare and mental healthcare for typically functioning and impacted children and youth, as well as those with underlying neurodevelopmental conditions and physical disabilities (Quinn, 2018). Over time, resources have tightened in regard to access to specific forms of care; with reductions in funding, agencies and medical centers that have traditionally been the main sites for providing appropriate healthcare services have been reduced in regard to key staffing positions, as well as have closed settings where care was available (Quinn, 2018). Consolidations in multiple areas across the state have created shortages in available care; this has hampered efforts to promote health from infancy through emerging adulthood. Schools throughout the state have seen an increase in the need to support health issues with their students, as well as nursing care, pediatrics consultations, school psychologists and social workers, and allied health therapists all laid off and programs downsized (Gordon et al., 2018). Families, particularly those with more limited socioeconomic means but also those situated within the middle class, with private insurance coverage, have all found access to needed care quite limited and difficult to obtain (Huen-Johnson et al., 2018).

In Chicago, adding the closures of local community mental healthcare facilities to the already challenging mix of restricted healthcare options for residents of the south side has led to a significant demand for emergent services, particularly for children and youth (Quinn, 2018). One of the most pernicious situations for many families is the intersection of health and mental health needs. Challenges with available resources for maintaining health, including adequate housing, a violence-free environment in which to live, appropriate and consistent supports within the school setting to help manage learning needs, and access to a range of nutritional options for food, have all aggregated to create a much higher risk for medical needs. Health that allows the pursuit of educational and leisure goals is significantly hampered in these settings. And without readily accessible healthcare, difficulties increase and compound for many residents in these deprived environments. Most often, this leaves the best option the emergency department of the nearest hospital (Huen-Johnson et al., 2018; Quinn, 2018). But this option is fraught with difficulty in both immediately addressing the health needs of the individuals seeking care, and in being able to assist these individuals in obtaining the necessary aftercare resources they require so as to improve their health status and combat their vulnerabilities across time.

This is the daily challenge that occurs within our Department of Psychiatry and Behavioral Neuroscience and its Section of Child and Adolescent Psychiatry. Consultation regarding stabilization and management of the psychosocial and behavioral needs of children and youth experiencing medical illness is provided through triage and management services, directed by one of us (KIA). Determining the interaction between physical and mental health, with a full recognition of the environmental and economic demands on patients and their families, becomes a key element of provision of care. Deciding what is the best approach is not always just; best practices, supported by empirical studies regarding mood and behavioral conditions and their management, are generally the goal, but they are not always easily supported, either by the institution or by its reliance on a system that is unreliable in its determinations regarding care access and length. Challenges include insurance restrictions, lack of availability of medications on a pharmacy panel, and unavailability of beds at hospitals within reasonable distance for the family.

Of note, with our program at The University of Chicago Medicine and Comer Children's Hospital, only a small group of faculty providers is available at any given time for providing consultation/liaison for children and their needs. Follow-up care, specifically for the intersection of health and mental health concerns, that can also address the wider systems of care needs that exist for many of the youth seen, is limited. For example, while medication management may be possible, given its limitations on time allocation and the ability to go for longer periods of time once mood or behavioral needs are stable, ongoing therapeutic interventions, such as psychotherapy or consultation, are more difficult to start, let alone provide with consistency. Referrals into the community cannot readily be engaged; this is particularly the case for families on Medicaid, where few providers are available and care periods are often quite limited (Quinn, 2018).

The provision of broader auxiliary care, often required for differential diagnosis and guidance regarding how to understand the impact of disease, its treatment, and its course on cognitive and behavioral development, such as referral for neuropsychological assessment, is even more restricted, both by the state's Medicaid mandates for care coverage (e.g., Medicaid in Illinois does not pay for psychological or neuropsychological assessment; Illinois Department of Healthcare and Family Services, 2016) and limitations on access by private insurers to manage care. This leaves many children, particularly those experiencing difficulties with learning due to attentional, executive functioning, and memory challenges that may be secondary to their medical condition, without needed treatment with required pharmacological agents. Additionally, the family is unable to obtain a clear understanding of what supports are required to allow them to return to school and home. To amplify this point, as demonstrated repeatedly across multiple studies (Kim et al., 2013; Middlebrooks & Audage, 2008; Suglia, Duarte, Sandel, & Wright, 2010), increased stress from emotional, behavioral, and environmental insults (e.g., lack of educational supports, inaccessibility of treatment resources, returning to an unsafe home environment) contributes to slower recovery following medical intervention, and increases risk for complications and poorer outcomes.

These issues underlie the need to refocus our questions regarding how to best obtain a socially just healthcare environment, and to aim for equity in resource allocation, as well as options for choice at earlier periods in time. As the health capability paradigm guides us, our efforts must be redirected toward promoting health as a right and a means for greater choice in personal decision-making regarding health. As discussed earlier, given the demands placed on tertiary care settings and their resources, emergency care may be a sole means for obtaining intervention for some communities. Once a child requires a broader set of resources to meet health needs, limitations are frequently confronted and as a result, de facto rationing of care can occur (Moseley, 2008; Ruger, 2010). Yet providers can intervene in ways in order to prevent potential injustice at the individual level. More specifically, the choices and decisions clinicians make about available care options, within a framework of even limited opportunities for care, may serve to enhance health agency for their patients and clients. This may then provide a wider impact on the community, by ensuring that an equal set of potential supports and interventions is available, regardless of the ability to pay.

A CASE OF DUAL HEALTHCARE AND MENTAL HEALTHCARE DISPARITIES

To support a more efficacious approach to managing and supporting childhood health, based on the health capability paradigm and its goals for fostering just care and equitable support, we present the following case as an example. This case is a composite based on multiple youths seen by our program; the identifiers are not specific to any one child who has been treated.

Andy S. is an eight-year-old Latino male with a history of tuberous sclerosis and intractable epilepsy.[1] He resides on the far south side of Chicago with his biological parents, one of whom (his mother) was born in the United States, and one of whom (his father) immigrated to the United States from Mexico when he was a young child. Andy has two siblings, a five-year-old sister and a twenty-month-old brother. Both parents speak Spanish within the home and the children are being raised bilingually. Andy's father is an HVAC technician and his mother primarily stays at home taking care of the children, although she does work part time for a local market when she can. Neither parent is consistently insured, due to seasonal changes in Andy's father's employment. As part of SCHIP, the children have Medicaid coverage as their health insurance, and primary care is provided through a local healthcare center run by a community-based nonprofit.

Andy's diagnosis of tuberous sclerosis is believed to be due to a likely spontaneous genetic mutation, as no other family members are known to have the disorder. Andy was born full term with no reported complications during the pregnancy, delivery, or immediate perinatal period. Andy experienced his first seizure when he was four months old; this was a generalized seizure, but without status. He was taken to the local hospital, where he experienced several more seizures, and was stabilized and then transferred for further assessment and care at The University of Chicago Medicine's Comer Children's Hospital. While Andy was undergoing evaluation, further seizure activity was observed, and following a twenty-four-hour EEG and imaging, he was diagnosed with tuberous sclerosis. Efforts to treat his seizures were complicated by poor response to the initial antiseizure medications utilized; he required polypharmacological approaches to manage his intractable epilepsy, which are known to have an accumulated negative effect on cognitive development (Felix & Hunter, 2010). At age three, Andy underwent neurosurgery involving a right frontal resection, in an effort to control his epilepsy. He was seizure-free for nine months following surgery, but then started having episodes of head dropping, staring, and lip twitching. These seizures lasted between ten and twenty seconds, and included episodes of staring and face twitching on occasion. Medications were reintroduced, with continued need for polypharmacological management to date.

Developmental milestones were all met slowly and early intervention services were provided through the public school system starting at age two. Over the course of the initial two years following neurosurgery, Andy showed increased challenge with language development, and behavioral regulation difficulties emerged, including hyperactivity and aggression. Feeding, bowel and bladder control issues and difficulties with sleep regulation were all present as well. Andy was followed by his Comer Children's team across multiple specialties, including pediatric neurology, developmental and behavioral pediatrics, and child and adolescent psychiatry. To date, he remains on multiple antiseizure medications, as well as additional medications for behavioral management and sleep regulation. He has been intermittently hospitalized for monitoring of his seizure activity, but no further surgery has been considered.

Accompanying his neurosurgical intervention plan, Andy has completed several neuropsychological evaluations in order to assess his cognitive functioning, both pre- and postsurgical. Andy holds a primary diagnosis of mild neurocognitive disorder due to another medical condition, secondary to his tuberous sclerosis and epilepsy, and the side effects of his seizure medications; this diagnosis is reflective of the broad-based impact his medical conditions have on his cognitive functioning, particularly his language, attention, memory, and executive functioning development. He also shows difficulties consistent with diagnosis of an autism spectrum disorder (ASD), including his echolalia, lack of social reciprocity, poor eye contact, stereotyped behaviors (e.g., rocking and occasional hand flapping), and rigid/inflexible behavior. His ASD diagnosis was initially made with his second neuropsychological evaluation, and further corroborated with a repeat neuropsychological evaluation four years later, as part of ongoing medical and educational planning.

Management of Andy's psychiatric needs has progressed, in response to continued adherence to routines that can often lead to anger outbursts. Andy additionally engages in self-injurious behaviors, like head banging, scratching, hitting, and biting, that can complicate parenting and provision of special education services. He has shown disruptive outbursts and aggressive behaviors toward family members, teachers, and medical staff. Hunger and fatigue have been identified as triggers for aggression and episodes of self-injurious behavior. Andy's behaviors have made it very hard for his family to leave the house with him, and his parents and teachers are afraid that his head banging may increase his vulnerability to seizures. Care is complicated and challenging for the family; Andy's siblings cannot consistently receive the range of attention and care they require, due to Andy's significant symptom presentation and needs.

Andy is essentially nonverbal, with an inconsistent use of words. The family has used a picture exchange communication system (PECS) around the house so as to support communication. He received developmental and speech therapy through early intervention programming through age three, and occupational therapy (OT), speech therapy, and physical therapy (PT) through a local Easter Seals program. Andy remains in diapers, cannot dress himself without assistance, and requires help in feeding. He is enrolled in a public school near the family's home, with an individualized education plan (IEP) in place under a classification of "Other Health Impairment" to address his medical conditions and an accompanying classification of ASD. Challenges in consistency with his programming, both in the school setting and with Easter Seals, have been experienced, due to difficulties in staffing (i.e., his school has been unable to hire an appropriate aide and he has gone through repeat changes in therapists due to funding variabilities with Easter Seals). The psychiatry team (i.e., the psychiatrist and neuropsychologist) have recommended applied behavioral analysis (ABA) therapy as a medical necessity for Andy, to address the severely limiting perseverating symptoms, the associated distress to Andy and his family, and the ongoing lack of progress with the therapies and interventions he has been receiving at school. However, Andy's Medicaid provider has denied coverage for ABA therapy, stating that his presentation "does not meet medical necessity" because it is not perceived as "severe enough" to warrant this level of intervention. Legal assistance has been required from a local pro bono program that works with families being treated by the medical center in order to appeal this Medicaid decision. It took two appeals before a state-level review approved ABA therapy. Yet, despite coverage for ABA services after this review, Andy's parents have been consistently unable to find local providers willing to accept Andy's Medicaid insurance. Additionally, the school district has indicated that it does not currently have an available ABA resource for Andy within the classroom setting. As a result, his progress at school and at home, given his significant comorbid psychiatric and medical needs, continues to suffer.

A REFRAMING USING THE HEALTH CAPABILITY PARADIGM AS A MODEL OF JUSTICE

Andy's case is a useful one for considering how we struggle regularly to effectively frame health as a human right, and must work aggressively on a daily basis to make available the resources required to support ongoing development and progress toward a best possible outcome for children and youth experiencing medical and mental health needs. Across multiple levels of service provision, failures are often confronted, even under the best of circumstances. This sadly can reflect a system that has come to prioritize limited options for care for a limited number of people, and within a hierarchy of access as a result of the ability to pay. Despite a system being developed and implemented that is ideally supposed to help meet the needs for health maintenance, Illinois Medicaid, underlying access to care can at times be hampered by confusing-seeming and arbitrary-feeling bureaucratic determinations. When examined more closely, decisions for care are challenged both by financial limitations at the state level (Quinn, 2018), and by failures to understand and implement appropriate standards of care supported by research that are strongly recommended even federally (e.g., empirical guidelines for the implementation of ABA and other supported therapies in ASD; Volkmar et al., 2014). Notably, Illinois is one of forty-eight states in the United States that have laws requiring insurance coverage of ASD treatment services. Although Medicaid did not cover some of the services provided to Andy, including the neuropsychological evaluations conducted for Andy in concert with his epilepsy surgery, and the follow-up assessment four years later, decision-making on the part of the medical team and agreements by the hospital administration allowed for the assurance of appropriate diagnostic and management services for Andy's medical needs. Collaboration with legal resources further assisted the family in ensuring that appropriate medical interventions were ultimately approved. Nonetheless, difficulties in obtaining access to necessary care remained present. Specifically, the ABA therapies recommended for Andy are not readily available to many patients requiring such services across the state (Olsen, 2017), particularly when federal or state monies are required to cover these services (e.g., Medicaid or Medicare), and are often only available for those who either can pay out of pocket or who have private insurance that covers the service. With regard to Andy and his family, further legal support remains required so as to attempt to arrange for appropriate therapies within the school setting at a minimum.

This highlights the absence of justice when considering the right to healthcare for children and youth and reinforces the need for a commitment to identifying and acknowledging that health is a right for all individuals within the United States and across the world, as reflected in the many chapters of this book. As Ruger (2010, 2016) has discussed, to provide for health within a framework of human rights, decisions regarding access and availability to care are required. It is not a *Cadillac level of care* necessarily that is required, but it is also not the case that we as a society should be allowing for insufficient and under-supported care either. Ruger (2010, 2016) has outlined a positive path, one ethically and morally situated, that recognizes health as a right, one absolutely required for children and youth to prosper and survive. With that right comes the societal responsibility of ensuring an equal and equitable path for healthcare, in regard to both physical and mental health needs. To attain the capacity to flourish, we must recommit ourselves to ensure there is a right to a just opportunity; health is a means for ensuring this occurs.

Efforts at achieving such a path are not unknown globally. As discussed earlier, multiple countries across the world have identified a process for determining both what is a minimum consistent level of access to care appropriate to ensuring uniform health for communities, and for identifying a means of allocating resources, both financially and in regard to personnel responsible for providing care, in order to ensure that care is available. What Ruger (2010) has provided is an outline for decision-making; what is most required is a citizenry committed to ensuring that these decisions are effectively made. Using Andy as an example, several particular steps become evident for ensuring a maximal consideration of shared access and available health opportunity. We see first and foremost that a political commitment to developmental success is required; in the United States, strides are being made toward states implementing uniform goals of early childhood education. Similarly, early health screenings and monitoring within the context of such programs can serve to foster greater engagement in health for enrolled children and their parents. The University of Chicago Medicine has partnered with the public schools in areas of greater economic need to provide in-school clinics, where yearly screenings and emergent healthcare can be accessed for all attendees through mobile pediatric units. This approach is not unique to either our medical center or to Chicago itself; Illinois's Department of Public Health and the Department of Healthcare and Family Services collaborate with multiple medical centers across the state to provide access to mobile health units within communities of reduced resources. The challenge is that this is tied directly to legislative decisions regarding financial allocations, and decisions can at times be capricious. Where change is most required, and where a commitment is needed regarding seeing health as a human right, is in terms of how the public views access. Sadly, differing economic models within political structures serve to influence this decision. Ruger reminds us that the decision required to counteract this influence is one that is communitarian and equitable. Social justice requires a commitment to others over just ourselves and our personal options (Ruger, 2016).

Note

1. Case studies have been de-identified to protect confidentiality.

REFERENCES

Bradley, A. (2010). Positive rights, negative rights, and health care. *Journal of Medical Ethics*, 36, 838–841.

Byrne, J. (2018, October 24). Mayor Rahm Emanuel's public health chief defends mental health clinic closures, but critic says patients were missed. *Chicago Tribune*. Retrieved from www.chicagotribune.com/news/local/politics/ct-met-rahm-emanuel-mental-health-services-20181024-story.html.

Cheng, T. L., Emmanuel, M. A., Levy, D. J., & Jenkins, R. R. (2015). Child health disparities: What can a clinician do? *Pediatrics*, 136, 961–968.

Christopher, A. S., & Caruso, D. (2015). Promoting health as a human right in the post-ACA United States. *American Medical Association Journal of Ethics*, 17, 958–965.

Felix, L., & Hunter, S. J. (2010). Pediatric aspects of epilepsy. In J. Donders & S. J. Hunter (eds.), *Principles and practice of lifespan developmental neuropsychology* (pp. 359–369). Cambridge, UK: Cambridge University Press.

Flores, G. (2010). Technical report: Racial and ethnic disparities in the health and health care of children. *Pediatrics*, 125, e979–e1020. doi:10.1542/peds.2010-0188

Fritzell, J., Kangas, O., Hertzmann, J. B., Blomgren, J., & Hiilamo, H. (2013). Cross-temporal and cross-national poverty and mortality rates among developed countries. *Journal of Environmental and Public Health*, 915490. doi:10.1155/2013/915490

Gaffney, A., & McCormick, D. (2017). The Affordable Care Act: Implications for health-care equity. *Lancet*, 389, 1442–1452. doi:10.1016/S0140-6736(17)30786-9

Gordon, M. F., de la Torre, M., Cowhy, J. R., et al. (2018). *School closings in Chicago: Staff and student experiences and academic outcomes*. Chicago, IL: University of Chicago Consortium on School Research.

Griffin, K., Evans, L., & Bor, J. (2017). The Affordable Care Act reduced socioeconomic disparities in health care access. *Health Affairs*, 36. doi:10.1377/hltaff.2017.0083

Huen-Johnson, H., Menchine, M., Goldman, D., & Seabury, J. (2018, May). *The cost of mental illness: Illinois facts and figures*. Los Angeles: University of Southern California Leonard D. Schaeffer Center for Health Policy and Economics.

Illinois Department of Healthcare and Family Services (2016, January). *Managed care manual for Medicaid providers*. Springfield: Illinois Department of Healthcare and Family Services.

Jost, T., & Pollack, H. A. (2016). Making health care truly affordable after health reform. *Journal of Law, Medicine, and Ethics*, 44, 546–554.

Joravsky, B. (2013, March 26). Before the schools, Mayor Emanuel closed the clinics. *Chicago Reader*. Retrieved from www.chicagoreader.com/chicago/mayor-emanuel-closes-city-mental-health-clinics/Content?oid=9145051.

Khullar, D., & Chokshi, D. A. (2018). Health, income, and poverty: Where we are and what could help. *Health Affairs Health Policy Brief*. doi:10.137/hbp20180817.901.935

Kim, P., Evans, G. W., Angstradt, M., et al. (2013). Effects of childhood poverty and chronic stress on emotion regulatory brain function in adulthood. *Proceedings of the National Academy of Sciences*, 110, 18442–18447.

Maruthappu, M., Ologunde, R., & Gunarajasingam, A. (2013). Is health care a right? Health reforms in the USA and their impact upon the concept of care. *Annals of Medicine and Surgery*, 2, 15–17.

Mendoza, S. (2018, September 18). *Consequences of Illinois' 2015–2017 budget impasse and fiscal outlook*. Springfield: Office of the Illinois Comptroller. Retrieved from https://illinoiscomptroller.gov/financial-data/find-a-report/special-fiscal/consequences-of-illinois-2015-2017-budget-impasse-and-fiscal-outlook/.

Mental Health America (2018). Access to care: State rankings. Retrieved from www.mentalhealthamerica.net/issues/ranking-states.

Middlebrooks, J. S., & Audage, N. C. (2008). *The effects of childhood stress on health across the lifespan*. Atlanta, GA: Centers for Disease Control and Prevention, National Center for Injury Prevention and Control.

Moseley, G. B. (2008). The U.S. health care non-system, 1908–2008. *American Medical Association Journal of Ethics*, 10, 324–331.

Nussbaum, M. C. (2003). Capabilities as fundamental entitlements: Sen and social justice. *Feminist Economics*, 9, 33–59.

Oberlander, J. (2016). Implementing the Affordable Care Act: The promise and limits of health care reform. *Journal of Health Politics, Policy, and Law*, 41, 803–826. doi:10.1215/03616878-3620953

Olsen, D. (2017, January 2). Autism program clients face more cutbacks connected with state funding. *State-Journal Register*. Retrieved from www.sj-r.com/news/20170102/autism-program-clients-face-more-cutbacks-connected-with-state-funding.

Ortega, A. N., Rodriguez, H. P., & Bustamante, A. V. (2015). Policy dilemmas in Latino health care and implementation of the Affordable Care Act. *Annual Review of Public Health*, 36, 525–544.

Patient Protection and Affordable Care Act. 42 USC 18001 2010.

Pollack, H. A. (2019, February 13). *Medicaid policies to serve severely disadvantaged populations*. Lecture to the MacLean Center for Clinical Medical Ethics 37th Annual Lecture Series: Improving value to the US healthcare System. Chicago, IL: University of Chicago Pritzker School of Medicine.

Quinn, M. (2018, October). *Mental breakdown*. Governing: The states and localities. Governing. Retrieved from www.governing.com/topics/health-human-services/gov-chicago-mental-health.html.

Ruger, J. P. (2010). *Health and social justice*. Oxford, UK: Oxford University Press.

Ruger, J. P. (2016). The health capability paradigm and the right to health care in the United States. *Theoretical Medicine and Bioethics*, 37, 275–292. doi:10.1007/s11017-016-9371-y.

Sen, A. (1992). *Inequality reexamined*. Cambridge, MA: Harvard University Press.

Silvers, J. B. (2013). The Affordable Care Act: Objectives and likely results in an imperfect world. *Annals of Family Medicine*, 11, 402–405. doi:10.1370/afm.1567.

Strauss, V. (2018, May 24). Chicago promised that closing nearly 50 schools would help kids in 2013. A new report says it didn't. *Washington Post*. Retrieved from www.washingtonpost.com

/news/answer-sheet/wp/2018/05/24/chicago-promised-that-closing-nearly-50-schools-would-help-kids-in-2013-a-new-report-says-it-didnt/?utm_term=.b11a3e9d6f66.

Suglia, S. F., Duarte, C. S., Sandel, M. T., & Wright, R. J. (2010). Social and environmental stressors in the home and childhood asthma. *Journal of Epidemiology and Community Health*, 64, 636–642. doi:10.1136/jech.2008.082942.

Visotsky, H. M. (2005). Mental health. In *The electronic encyclopedia of Chicago*. Chicago: Chicago Historical Society. Retrieved from www.encyclopedia.chicagohistory.org/pages/811.html.

Volkmar, F., Siegel, M., Woodbury-Smith, M., et al. (2014). Practice parameter for the assessment and treatment of children and adolescents with autism spectrum disorder. *Journal of the American Academy of Child and Adolescent Psychiatry*, 53, 237–257.

PART II

International Social Justice Issues That Have an Impact on Children and Young People

5

Children and Poverty

A Global Approach

Nathalie O. Iotti and Tomas Jungert

CHILDREN AND POVERTY: A GLOBAL APPROACH

In this chapter we define poverty and its effects on child development, provide statistics on poverty for industrialized and developing countries, discuss the experience of children living in poverty worldwide, and suggest rules of law to address poverty among young people and children.

DEFINING POVERTY

According to *Merriam-Webster's Online Dictionary* (n.d.), *poverty* is "the state of one who lacks a usual or socially acceptable amount of money or material possessions" (no page number). As demonstrated, this definition is formulated mostly in economic terms, as that is the idea of poverty most people have. The definition is not wrong, but it is very limited, and the reasons why are described in the following paragraphs. First, poverty is defined in current terms; second, criticisms that surround the definition of poverty are discussed; and, finally, a number of poverty measures that are both fair and accurate are mentioned.

Absolute poverty. *Absolute poverty* is calculated as the food expenditure necessary to meet dietary recommendations, supplemented by a small allowance for nonfood goods. It is measured with respect to families and not to individuals and adjusted for number of family members (United Nations Educational, Scientific and Cultural Organization [UNESCO], 2017). According to this definition, *income poverty* is when a family fails to meet a certain state-established threshold that differs across countries. This definition is not concerned with broader quality-of-life issues or with the level of inequality in society (Engle & Black, 2008). The measure that is most commonly used to calculate income is the International Poverty Line, developed by the World Bank and set at US $1.90 per person per day since October 2015 (United Nations International Children's Emergency Fund [UNICEF], 2016). The problem with using a linear measure is that small increases in a person's income cannot be appreciated or contribute to a significant change to that person's quality of life. Furthermore, the line does not measure important aspects, such as access to clean water or medical services and education, and, therefore, it does not provide a clear picture of a person's actual resources and their impact on quality of life and opportunities.

Relative poverty. *Relative poverty*, instead, defines poverty in relation to the economic status of other members of society – that is, it considers people poor if they fall below the prevailing standards of living in a given societal context (UNESCO, 2017). Relative poverty usually occurs when households receive 50 percent less income than average median outcomes. The basic needs perspective goes beyond the definition of income poverty and adds the need for provision by a community of the basic social services necessary to prevent individuals from falling into poverty in the first place. In other words, it recognizes a series of social services, such as education, access to medical care, etc., that cater to basic human needs. If these are lacking, the individual can be considered poor.

Finally, the empowerment (or capability) perspective implies that poverty translates into a lack of some basic capability to function, or agency (UNESCO, 2017). *Agency* is the ability to undertake purposeful actions; it includes individual factors, such as education and self-confidence, and collective and family factors, such as cultural organization, identity, and having a voice (Engle & Black, 2008). Poverty stifles agency because it limits the individual's range of choices and the feeling of having an effect on one's environment. Poverty limits where and if one studies, what kind of, if any, medical services are available, what type of jobs one has, and access to healthy food choices. In other words, poverty limits personal freedom and, consequently, agency.

Criticisms. Several criticisms surround these definitions of poverty (see Table 5.1). First of all, note that both of the definitions of poverty provided are largely concerned with income and consumption and less with individual well-being. This is not wrong per se, but can be very limited (UNESCO, 2017). Second, relying on household-level measures might mask the fact that people within the household, especially children, have inadequate resources allocated to them and might be deprived in other dimensions (UNICEF, 2016). Third, poverty and poverty escape are seen by some researchers and policy makers as individual conditions or as conditions that are linked to social exclusion factors that prevent categories of people, or groups, from escaping poverty (Engle & Black, 2008). By *poverty escape* we mean the transition from a state of want or lack of services and necessities to a state where access to said services and necessities is permitted. This distinction is relevant because the former does not take into account societal factors, while the latter does.

Finally, poverty is a dynamic process and can be intermittent, with families cycling in and out of poverty over short periods of time, a figure that does not appear when measuring absolute poverty. The current authors of this chapter agree with all criticisms cited, and believe that better measures and definitions of poverty should be provided, measures that are both fair and accurate. *Fair* refers to measures that

TABLE 5.1 *Definitions and critiques of the term* poverty

Poverty	Definition	Criticism
Poverty	State of one who lacks a usual or socially acceptable amount of money or material possessions	Formulated mostly in economic terms. Very limited
Absolute poverty	Food expenditure necessary to meet dietary recommendations, supplemented by a small allowance for nonfood goods	Not sufficiently concerned with individual well-being. Does not consider gaps between the current level of poverty and the historical standard
Relative poverty	Poverty in relation to the economic status of other members of society. People are poor if they fall below the prevailing standards of living in a given societal context.	Not sufficiently concerned with individual well-being. Does not help determine whether incomes have increased over time

take into account societal- and country-level factors, as well as children's needs, and *accurate* refers to recording the actual extent of the phenomenon.

Multidimensional Poverty Index and other measures. One measure that the authors of this chapter believe is fair and accurate is the Multidimensional Poverty Index (MPI), a tool designed to enhance poverty data. The index covers three dimensions of disadvantage: health, education, and material deprivation, that are measured by ten weighted indicators. The indicators are: nutrition, child mortality, years of schooling, school attendance, type of cooking fuel, sanitation, safe drinking water, electricity, flooring, and asset ownership. The MPI data reports can be disaggregated – that is, separated into their component parts – for children, and count individuals as poor when they are disadvantaged in relation to at least one-third of the indicators. Its most recent findings indicate that 1.6 billion people lived in multidimensional poverty in 2015 (UNICEF, 2016). This means that 1.6 billion people were deprived with regard to their health, education, or living standards during the year 2015. This figure will rise by 2030 if no precautions are taken, both because of population growth and because a higher proportion of children will be poor due to climate change, wars, and shifting political power balances (UNICEF, 2016).

Another measure is the Multiple Overlapping Deprivation Analysis (MODA), developed by UNICEF. This measure was designed to make analyses of child poverty and deprivation worldwide more equitable. Children, rather than the household, are the unit of analysis since children experience poverty differently than do adults (UNICEF, 2016). This differential experience is because, for children, deprivation can have severe outcomes on their development, as explained in the following paragraphs.

EFFECTS OF POVERTY ON CHILD DEVELOPMENT

Child development is the ordered emergence of the interdependent skills of sensorimotor, cognitive-language, and socioemotional functioning that depend upon children's physical well-being, their families, and their larger social network. In all countries, poverty is a chronic stress for children and their families that can interfere with successful adjustment to developmental tasks, including school achievement (Engle & Black, 2008). As Engle and Black report: "Children raised in low-income families are at risk for academic and social problems as well as poor health and well-being, which can in turn undermine educational achievement" (2008, p. 244). This means that poverty is a serious threat to normative child development.

Developmental systems theory (DST) is useful in explaining the multiple mechanisms linking poverty with child education and development. Developmental systems theory is based on ecological theory (Bronfenbrenner, 1979) and conceptualizes interactions across multiple levels, extending from basic biological processes to interactions at the individual, family, school, community, and cultural levels. Interactions are bidirectional, which means that changes in one aspect of the system may affect relations and processes throughout the system (Engle & Black, 2008).

Furthermore, families act as the primary socializing agents for their children. In addition to providing basic necessities, such as food, shelter, and clothing, families help transmit cultural and educational values, thus allowing children to adapt to societal demands and opportunities. Early child–parent interactions help children learn regulatory processes and socialize them into their culture (Engle & Black, 2008).

Direct effects. Poverty can influence child development and education by increasing risk factors, limiting protective factors, and stifling opportunities for stimulation and enrichment. One example of this is the fact that children from families facing poverty are at risk for both undernutrition and overweight, conditions that are both associated with food insecurity (Engle & Black, 2008). Food insecurity is the state of being unable to consistently access or afford adequate, nutritious food. The literature suggests that many of the effects of poverty on children are influenced by a lack of household resources (e.g., Coleman, 1990; Cook et al., 2006). For instance, children growing up in poverty experience risks in their homes and communities, such as illnesses, family stress, and crowding (Engle & Black, 2008; Parker, Greer, & Zuckerman, 1988).

Moderated effects. The effects of poverty vary across the characteristics of families and children. For example, families whose parents have low educational attainment and poor decision-making skills may have more difficulty protecting their children from the effects of poverty than families with more education and better decision-making skills (Engle & Black, 2008). This shows how education plays an important role in individual development and how it can aid people in escaping poverty.

Moderated effects can also be protective, such as when families invest in materials and activities that are educational and enriching for their children, protecting them effectively from the effects of poverty. This is called the family investment model, whereby parental occupation, education, and family education play a role in the investments that families make in their children, which in turn has an effect on their development and well-being (Conger & Donnellan, 2007). Family characteristics may also influence child development through a process known as social selection, where individual differences in parental traits may lead to differences in family income and, in turn, have an impact on child development (Conger & Donnellan, 2007). For example, parents who have prosocial attributes may transmit these values to their children, protecting them from the negative effects of poverty.

Mediated effects. In the mediated effects model, the effects of poverty lead to disruptions in family functioning, which in turn have negative repercussions on child development (Engle & Black, 2008). This is also known as the family stress model (Conger & Conger, 2002), whereby negative economic pressure is put on the family and combined with the parents' emotional and behavioral problems. This leads to interparental conflict and low warmth-support, which in turn leads to less nurturing and involved parenting, therefore having a negative influence on child development and well-being (Conger & Conger, 2002).

Transactional effects. In the transactional effects model, the effects of poverty reverberate through the relations between families and children, incorporating both moderated and mediated effects (Engle & Black, 2008). For example, the caregivers of temperamentally difficult children may be less likely to exhibit responsive and nurturing caregiving and may be more likely to report depressive symptoms than the caregivers of temperamentally easy children (Engle & Black, 2008). The negative symptoms of maternal depression on children's development can be exacerbated by a child's difficult temperament, and a similar relationship might exist in times of poverty. In a similar manner, the aforementioned family investment model predicts that parents are more likely to invest in educational resources, even in times of poverty, when they perceive their children as bright or academically gifted (Conger & Donnellan, 2007).

Community effects. Developmental systems theory also highlights the role of poverty in influencing neighborhood, community, and cultural patterns (Engle & Black, 2008). Families with few resources tend to live in low-income neighborhoods, which often are characterized by high density, crime, and fewer opportunities for socialization (Black & Krishnakumar, 1998). Furthermore, the schools in these neighborhoods tend to have a higher ratio of students per teacher and to be underfunded, beset by disciplinary problems, staffed by overwhelmed teachers, and confronted with difficulties meeting their educational mandates (Engle & Black, 2008; Murnane, 2007). Actually, it is important to note that community-level variables account less for children's academic performance than family-level variables (Leventhal & Brooks-Gunn, 2000). This is in line with the family stress model that suggests the effects of community-level poverty may be mediated by family patterns and behaviors (Conger & Conger, 2002). Furthermore, moving out of low-income neighborhoods does not necessarily result in the disappearance of the negative effects of persistent poverty (Ackerman, Brown, & Izard, 2004; Ackerman, Izard, Kobak, Brown, & Smith, 2007). The impact of intermittent poverty on child outcomes is similar to that of persistent poverty. A possible interpretation for this lack of difference can be found in the early effects model, which suggests poor behavioral and academic patterns established in preschool persist, even if environmental conditions improve (Entwisle, Alexander, & Olson, 2005).

STATISTICS

Low- and middle-income countries. In 2012, the number of people living in extreme poverty worldwide was nearly half of what it had been at the end of the 1990s. The decline in poverty has since continued throughout the world, and today 11 percent of the world's population lives in extreme poverty, which likely is the lowest rate in millennia. However, some important differences emerge in this development when comparing regions. For example, the pace of progress in the Middle East and North Africa has been quite slow after years of progress. The rates of monetary poverty seem stagnant in parts of these regions, and are even on the rise by some estimates (UNICEF, 2016).

Data using broader poverty lines give a sense of the global and universal nature of poverty (see Table 5.2). In 2012, more than 2 billion people in low- and middle-income countries lived on less than US $3.10 per day and were considered as living under "moderate" poverty. Of these people, nearly 900 million lived in South Asia, some 500 million lived in East Asia and the Pacific, and about 72 million lived in Latin America and the Caribbean. About 50 million people in the Middle East and North Africa lived on less than $3.10 per day in 2008, which is the latest year for which reliable surveys are available. Worldwide, more than 3 billion people remained vulnerable to poverty in 2012 as they lived on less than $5.00 per day (UNICEF, 2016).

The experience of Latin America highlights the need to look beyond poverty thresholds. From the mid-1990s to 2011, extreme poverty fell by half in that region, thanks to rising incomes, which were a consequence of global trade, the market economy (Hart, 2007), and pensions and other social transfers. Despite this remarkably positive development, a study in 2008–2009 found that 81 million children and adolescents in Latin America and the Caribbean were affected by at least one

TABLE 5.2 *Percentage of population living below various international poverty lines, by World Bank Region, 2012*

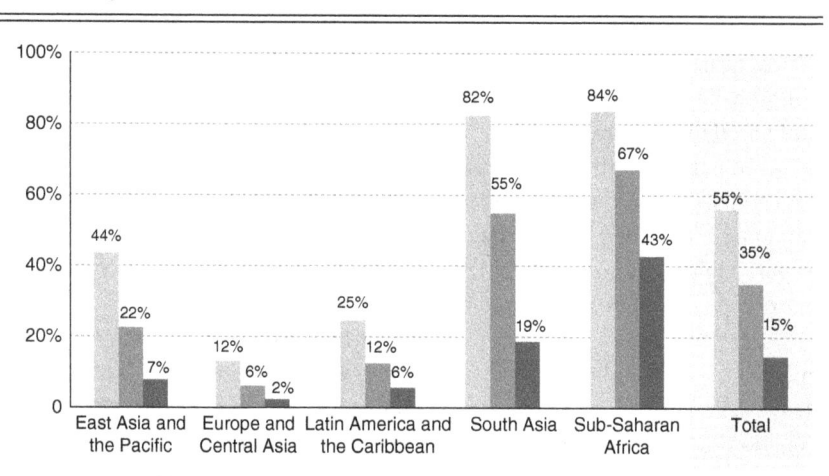

Region	People vulnerable to poverty (less than $5.00 a day)	People living in moderate poverty (less than $3.10 a day)	People living in extreme poverty (less than $1.90 a day)
East Asia and the Pacific	44%	22%	7%
Europe and Central Asia	12%	6%	2%
Latin America and the Caribbean	25%	12%	6%
South Asia	82%	55%	19%
Sub-Saharan Africa	84%	67%	43%
Total	55%	35%	15%

Note: Total refers to low- and middle-income countries available in PovcalNet. Data were not available for the Middle East and North Africa at the time of calculation. All estimates are based on purchasing power parity figures (current international $) extrapolated from the 2011 International Comparison Program (ICP) benchmark estimates. The figure of US $5.00/day is not an official international poverty line used by the World Bank.
Source: World Bank (2016).

moderate or severe deprivation of their rights to education, nutrition, housing, sanitation, drinking water, or access to information. However, by 2012, there were more people in Latin America's middle class than in the ranks of the extreme poor. Yet 38 percent of the population lived on a daily income of between $4.00 and $10.00 per day in 2013, indicating there is a risk that people in Latin America might slip back into extreme poverty (UNICEF, 2016).

Another study of multidimensional poverty that focused on children in sub-Saharan Africa presented disturbing results. In the thirty countries for which comparable data were available, 247 million out of the 368 million children under age eighteen experienced two to five deprivations that threatened their survival and development. Examples of such deprivation ranged from physical and sexual abuse to insecure and dangerous housing conditions and institutional rearing. As an example, a child born in Sierra Leone today is about thirty times more likely to die before age five than a child born in the United Kingdom. Women in sub-Saharan Africa face a 1-in-36 lifetime risk of maternal mortality, and in Chad, the country with the most alarming situation, women face a 1-in-18 risk (UNICEF, 2016). These risks should be compared to risk of 1 in 3,300 in high-income countries.

Noticeable regional variations appear in the broad neonatal trend. In sub-Saharan Africa, nearly one in ten babies die before their first birthday and about one-third of children die before they reach age five. Overall, the geographical distribution of global child mortality is changing. Worldwide, child deaths are highly concentrated. In 2015, about 80 percent of these deaths occurred in South Asia and sub-Saharan Africa, and almost half occurred in just five countries: the Democratic Republic of the Congo, Ethiopia, India, Nigeria, and Pakistan. According to the 2011 World Development Report, children from these five countries are more than twice as likely to be undernourished as children in low- and middle-income countries, and twice as likely to die before age five. Among the twenty countries with the highest child mortality rates, ten fall into the World Bank's list of fragile contexts (UNICEF, 2016). The World Bank defines a fragile context to be within a country that (a) is entitled to assistance (i.e., a donation) from the International Development Association (IDA); (b) has had a UN peacekeeping mission in the prior three years; and (c) has received a "governance" score of less than 3.2 (as per the Country Performance and Institutional Assessment [CPIA] index of the World Bank). However, the base on which a "fragile" country is distinguished from a "non-fragile" country remains far from precise and has been debated (see, e.g., Woolcock, 2014).

On the positive side, the proportion of poverty has never been as low as it is today. For example, the mortality rate of children before age five was 41 in 1,000 in 2016, which is likely the lowest in millennia. It is probable that education and democratization can improve this development even further. If all mothers achieved secondary education, 1.5 million fewer annual deaths would occur of children under age five in sub-Saharan Africa and 1.3 million fewer in South Asia (UNICEF, 2016). This decrease in annual deaths of children could be achieved as many risks could be avoided. A few examples are the reduction of the risk of death by drowning due to increased supervision, risk and water safety education, and safe rescue skills, as well as the reduction of the risk of potential deadly effects of toxic chemicals, through hazard labeling of products in their daily life, and due to increased knowledge about such dangers, which helps mothers avert poisoning and accidents. Other examples of how increased maternal education may reduce deaths are that children would be protected from environmental threats and suspected exposure to environmental stressors as education may help mothers identify hazards in household situations, make correct diagnoses, manage, and treat their children with illnesses derived from environmental stressors.

Furthermore, infant mortality has declined since the introduction of multiparty elections in sub-Saharan African countries when they resulted in the installation of a new chief executive. Democratization may result in declined infant mortality in many ways. For example, Kudamatsu (2012) shows that among the key mechanisms in which democratization helps reduce child mortality is improvements in maternal healthcare provision, increased probability that a mother breastfeeds her child, and increased household access to toilets. Decreases in child mortality did not happen when dictators stayed in power by winning multiparty elections or when a new chief executive took office undemocratically (Kudamatsu, 2012). Thus, democratization may be an important way of promoting development in the poorest countries, because an elected government will promote more practices, make maternal healthcare more accessible, and invest in the provision of better sanitation facilities, all of which is beneficial for the survival of children (Kudamatsu, 2012). Table 5.2 presents the percentage of the population living below various international poverty lines as per the World Bank Region, 2012.

High-income countries. Relative poverty, which is of particular significance in richer countries, can also affect the lives of children. Relative poverty means poverty in relation to the economic status of other members of society – that is, it considers people poor if they fall below the prevailing standards of living in a given societal context (UNESCO, 2017). Fewer opportunities to be educated, healthy, and nourished puts children at a disadvantage and limits their life chances compared to peers.

For example, eight years after the onset of the 2008 financial crisis, the slowness of economic recovery, high levels of unemployment, financial pressure, and rising inequality threatened the hopes of a generation of children in high-income countries. Meanwhile, children and poor families continued to feel the effects of deficit reduction programs that governments initiated in response to the crisis.

In 2014, in forty-one of the most affluent countries, nearly 77 million children lived in monetary poverty. Taking precrisis levels as an anchor point, child poverty rates increased in twenty-three high-income countries after 2008 (UNICEF, 2016). In five countries, child poverty rates increased by more than 50 percent. In most European Union countries, the proportion of children in poverty is higher than that of adults (see Figure 5.1). This is a worrying datum because it means that child poverty might be underrepresented by official surveys if we take into account the usual definitions of poverty. These data show that much work remains to be done even in high-income countries in terms of policy making and application. For example, as shown in Figure 5.1, about 40 percent of children in Romania and about every third child in Bulgaria and Spain are living below the poverty threshold (60 percent of median equalized income after social transfers), while only about 20 percent of the adults in these countries are living below the poverty threshold.

EXPERIENCES OF POVERTY

Throughout this chapter, the authors have reported that children and young people raised in poverty are at enlarged risk for a host of negative outcomes.

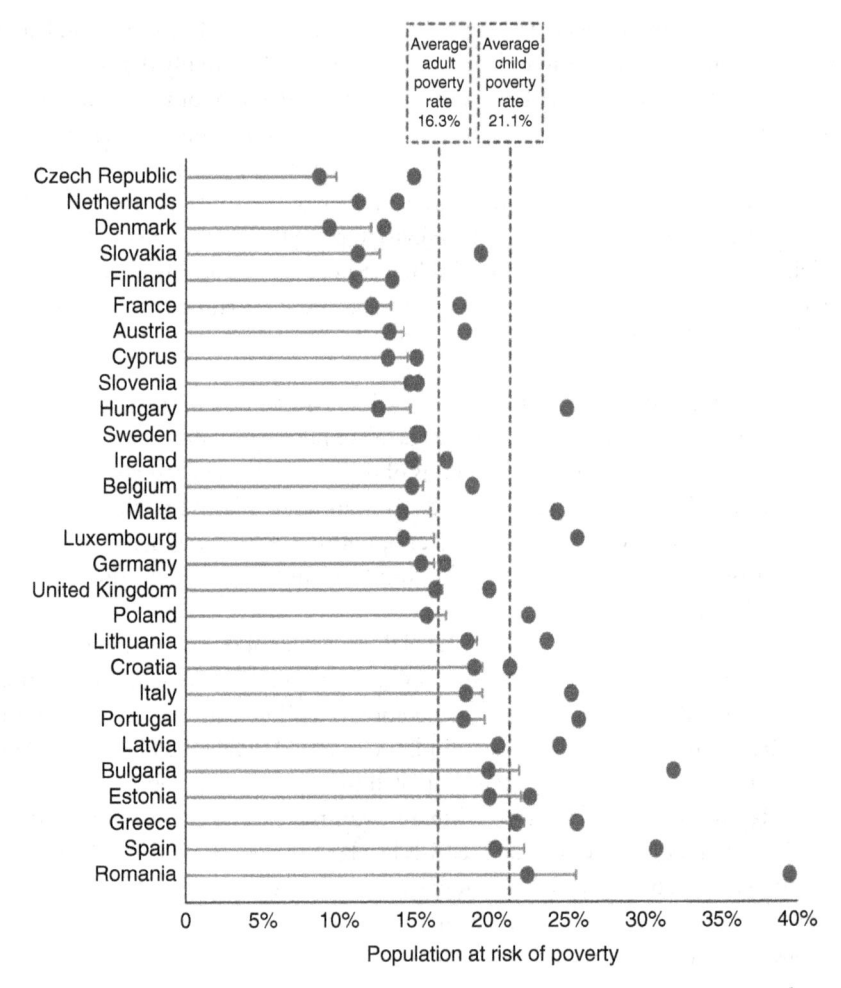

FIGURE 5.1 Percentage of population at risk of poverty in the European Union, by age group, 2014
Source: Eurostat (2016) via UNICEF (2016).

Some examples are academic difficulties and high school dropout (Reardon, 2011; Youngblade et al., 2007), behavioral and emotional problems (McLoyd, 1997), and a greater likelihood of living in poverty as adults (Vartanian, 1999), as well as smoking, teen pregnancy, and crime (Carneiro, Crawford, & Goodman, 2007). In addition, youth living in poverty are more likely than middle- or upper-class youth to take part in antisocial behaviors (Moore & Glei, 1995). One explanation for this could be experienced trauma due to poverty that can have a negative effect on social skills development in children (Wilkinson, 2016). Insufficient social skills development is negatively associated with developing positive peer and teacher relationships, self-control (Tarullo, Obradovic, & Gunnar, 2009), and educational performance (Tremblay et al., 2005). Thus, there is ample evidence that the poverty of children and young people is a serious concern for psychosocial development. Some youths with low resources have demonstrated an increased prevalence of physical and psychological symptoms as well as increased risk of depression as young adults that may be partly due to their exposure to and the impact of bullying victimization (Due, Damsgaard, Lund, & Holstein, 2009a; Due, Lynch, Holstein, & Modvig, 2003). However, most studies on the determinants or consequences of school bullying do not consider students' poverty in their analyses (Due et al., 2009b).

Poverty and bullying. *School bullying* is a relational phenomenon that takes place in a social context (Salmivalli, 2010). This means that contextual factors such as school characteristics are essential in explaining bullying behavior (Bradshaw, Sawyer, & O'Brennan, 2009; Cook, Williams, Guerra, Kim, & Sadek, 2010). Some studies have found that youth from low socioeconomic status (SES) schools report more bullying (e.g., Bradshaw et al., 2009; Whitney & Smith, 1993), and a more recent meta-analysis showed that SES was weakly related to bullying roles (Tippett & Wolke, 2014). These authors found that bullies and victims were more likely to come from low SES households, whereas bullies and victims were less likely to come from high SES backgrounds. Other studies have found that underprivileged youth report having fewer friends (Olsson, 2007; Sletten, 2010), receive fewer friendship nominations from school peers (Hjalmarsson & Mood, 2015), and are at a higher risk of social isolation in the school class (Hjalmarsson & Mood, 2015). Students with few friends, especially those with no friends in school, are more likely to be victimized (Juvonen & Graham, 2014). In addition, studies on poverty propose that economic inability to participate in common or expected activities or consumption causes feelings of shame and inadequacy that can lead to social withdrawal (e.g., Townsend, 1979).

Peers might also stigmatize adolescents from poorer backgrounds. Several qualitative studies have found that young adolescents believe that bullying happens because the victim deviates from group norms (e.g., Thornberg, 2011; Thornberg & Knutsen, 2011). Youth from deprived homes – i.e., homes of inadequate structure, amenities, and space in relation to the numbers of users, believe it is important to appear non-deprived so that they will not be seen as dissimilar to their peers (Attree, 2006; Ridge, 2011). Lacking economic resources could result in perceptions of deviance, but being poorer than peers may result in deviation from group norms in other dimensions such as being seen as different based on "wrong" or out-of-fashion clothing (e.g., Frisén et al., 2008), and youth who cannot partake in expected activities or consumption may be seen by peers as "boring, cheap or weird" (Fernqvist, 2013, p. 79).

An early study found that schoolchildren from low-income families were twice as likely as other children to be excluded in school, and the association remained statistically significant after controlling for ethnicity, family structure, and gender (Patterson et al., 1990; Patterson et al., 1991). More recently, a study on Swedish adolescents found that adolescents who were unable to participate in activities with peers for economic reasons were at higher risk of victimization (Hjalmarsson, 2018). Poor households and the experience of economic and material deprivation of children and youth are associated with internalizing symptoms and self-rated health (Plenty & Mood, 2016). *Self-rated health* is defined as the response to a single question framed as "How in general would you rate your health – poor, fair, good, very good or excellent?" (Benyamini, 2011). Self-rated health is the most frequently used, validated, single-item indicator of health status in social science research that independently predicts sickness and mortality (Idler & Benyamini, 1997). Internalizing problems (e.g., anxiety, insecurity in social interactions, and social withdrawal) are important risk factors for victimization (Juvonen & Graham, 2014; Reijntjes et al., 2010).

Another reason for their increased risk of becoming bullies may be that many children who bully have been victims of adverse childhood experiences and have thus witnessed family violence, addictions, lack of attachment to parents, neglect, and poor modeling. They may have problems making friends because of poor social skills due to their experiences (Wilkinson, 2016). Youth who rarely experience empathic relationships can develop problems demonstrating empathy and risk engaging in hostile behaviors toward others. They are sometimes depressed and display anxiety and, as a result, may feel rejected and see bullying as the only way to bring together a group of peers around them. However, despite all these findings, SES does not seem to offer much direction for targeted intervention to reduce the adverse effects of bullying (Tippett & Wolke, 2014).

Implications. Stimulating a positive school climate may be favorable (Bosworth & Judkins, 2014). A meta-analysis (Tippett & Wolke, 2014) found that children and youth from homes with economic challenges had greater odds of being victimized even if effects were small. In addition, Tippett and Wolke (2014) pointed out that socioeconomic backgrounds were conceptualized in many different ways, and when they were measured as household wealth, associations were stronger. Some examples are Due et al. (2009b), who found that lower household wealth was associated with more victimization in children and young adolescents in thirty-five countries, and Chaux and Castellanos (2015), who found that youth with lower household wealth in fifth and ninth grade in Colombia were at a higher risk of victimization.

On the other hand, the associations were weaker when using measures of parental education or occupation (e.g., Lemstra et al., 2012; Nordhagen et al., 2005). For instance, family structure, immigration background, and parental health or unemployment could also play a role. With regard to immigration background, studies in the Swedish context have found mixed results. Hjern et al. (2013) found that first-generation immigrant students had a higher overall risk of victimization, while Plenty and Jonsson (2017) did not. Yet both studies found the immigrant density of the school/school class was significant, demonstrating a complex pattern of links. For example, besides victimization, there are links to multiple aspects of social exclusion that are more subtle or even implicit (Plenty & Jonsson, 2017). In addition, we do not fully understand the underlying mechanisms that explain the links between immigrant children and victimization. Language, behavioral or cultural competencies, hierarchies related to social or economic resources, parental unemployment, and the likelihood of social exclusion of immigrants by other immigrant youth may all be associated with health problems or internalizing symptoms among youth (Hjern et al., 2013; Melchior et al., 2010; Plenty & Jonsson, 2017; Reiss, 2013).

Based on studies that indicate poverty has a strong negative impact on youth development, it is crucial to detect factors that might lessen these harmful effects. To understand the impact of deprivation on bullying behavior within a school, it is crucial to take into account not only the degree of school deprivation but also the individual child's experiences with deprivation. One way to understand how poverty affects the well-being of youth is self-determination theory (SDT; Deci & Ryan, 2017), which posits that the needs for autonomy, competence, and relatedness define critical psychological satisfactions essential for the healthy development of self when taking part in the world within and around one's self (Deci & Ryan, 2017). Studies have found that a substantial share of the variance in health-related outcomes can be accounted for by the three basic need satisfactions (González, Swanson, Lynch, & Williams, 2016). These needs – the need for autonomy, the need for competence, and the need for relatedness – are said to be as essential for optimal psychological functioning as water, food, and shelter are for our physical health (Deci & Ryan, 2017). The *need for autonomy* is defined as individuals' desire to behave in line with their own interests, to make their own choices, to express their feelings freely, and to initiate their own actions. The need for autonomy is about volition, and should not be equated with independence (Ryan, 1995). Independent people are not influenced by others and stick to their own agenda, but people who have satisfied the need for autonomy may volitionally follow the requests of others as long as they feel psychologically free in endorsing these requests (Van den Broeck, Vansteenkiste, De Witte, Soenens, & Lens, 2010).

The *need for competence* refers to an individual's sense of being effective and having a sense of mastery (Ryan & Deci, 2017). When people are allowed to engage in challenging tasks so as to develop their skills and when they can adapt to complex and changing environments, their need for competence is satisfied. Finally, the *need for relatedness* entails the wish to have caring bonds and positive alliances with others (Baumeister & Leary, 1995; Deci & Ryan, 2000). The need for relatedness refers to one's need to feel connected to others and to care and to be cared for.

With regard to poverty, it has been found that basic need satisfaction mediates the associations between perceived SES, household income, the degree of the environment's socioeconomic inequality, and self-reported health and wellness (Di Domenico & Fournier, 2014). Thus, there is evidence that economic factors, such as living in poverty, are associated with lower satisfaction of needs for personal autonomy, relatedness to others, and competence, and the lack of need satisfaction may likely be an important factor that explains negative outcomes (e.g., poorer health, lower well-being, emotional exhaustion, and lower vitality).

Furthermore, evidence suggests it is particularly destructive when people see themselves as low status and internalize it as their own fault. Thwarting of psychological needs is intensified when individuals view their lower social status as reflective of who they are (Jackson, Richman, LaBelle, Lempereur, & Twenge, 2015). Stereotypes and stigma in society are important factors that contribute to this internalization process (Deci & Ryan, 2017).

POLICY SUGGESTIONS

Not all children and youth growing up in poverty engage in antisocial behaviors or are struck by the negative effects outlined in this chapter (Ronald & Rand, 2018). Identifying and understanding the resilience factors against poverty is a way to promote the well-being of disadvantaged youth. *Psychological resilience* is the ability to cope with a crisis and to return to precrisis status quickly; it can be seen, in physical terms, as the ability of an object to spring back into its original form after suffering the application of pressure (Judge, 2005). Children with fewer resources have been shown to exhibit resilience traits in some situations. For example, social skills resilience at preschool have been related to higher kindergarten social skills, mathematics resilience has been related to lower behavior problems and higher mathematics and literacy in kindergarten, and literacy resilience has been related to higher mathematics and literacy (see, e.g., Judge, 2005; Masten, 2011). Therefore, as we can see, early indicators of resilience carry out into successive school grades and can protect children from some of the negative effects of poverty. However, resilience comes from a range of factors, such as personal traits, childrearing techniques, and actual training received on this subject. Therefore, it would be useful to invest in resilience training for children with fewer resources in order to protect them effectively from the negative implications of poverty and to allow them and their families, with the right help, to improve their conditions.

Governments need to invest more in poverty reduction if we are to stop the sequence of the effects of poverty amongst children and youth, as those cycles have detrimental consequences for most youth. Poverty puts a pressure on healthcare, education, and the criminal justice system in which the poor are disproportionally represented. For example, governments could increase their investment in early childhood education and develop a universal program for children with fewer resources that may help reduce the stigma attached to poverty, decrease the achievement gap, improve social relations between peers from different backgrounds, diminish the risk of involvement in bullying, and reduce overall social costs (Cunha, Heckman, Lochner, & Masterov, 2006). It would furthermore be very helpful if governments and municipalities made sure to invest in good schools in poor neighborhoods. Additionally, social protection mechanisms (e.g., pensions, cash transfers, etc.) can be an effective approach to reducing vulnerability to poverty and can strengthen families' capability of caring for children and overcoming barriers to accessing vital services (UNICEF, 2016).

Cash transfer programs cannot, on their own, lift most households above the monetary poverty threshold because of their small size (UNICEF, 2016). Structural poverty requires long-term interventions that ensure improved physical and human capital. Thus, even if cash transfer programs help beneficiary households become relatively less poor, such households remain vulnerable and require improvements in the quality of the supply of education and healthcare, in particular (Stampini & Tornarolli, 2012). However, they can make a difference in reducing the effects of poverty and bolstering families and economies. Cash transfers inject more money into individual households, strengthen local markets, and create various social benefits accompanying poverty reduction. As households spend the transfers they receive, the impact of these transfers is multiplied in the local economy and these benefits are transmitted to other members of society (UNICEF, 2016), such as when a villager uses the transfer to purchase goods or services from another villager, directly influencing the economy by providing a need that is met by someone whose finances are increased by servicing said need. If, for example, the provider of services is a shopkeeper, the fact that the transaction increased his or her finances might lead him or her to purchase more stock to sell, thus helping a third individual increase his or her finances. As you can see, the effects of a single cash transfer go far beyond the hands of the receiver.

Cash transfers have also been proven to have an impact on reducing child marriage and child labor and on the educational disadvantages that these practices entail (UNESCO, 2015; UNICEF, 2016). It has been shown that cash transfers can alleviate the financial pressure that sometimes forces families to give their children up for work or marriage. For example, a cash transfer program could help families with providing for their children's education, thus reducing the need for other children in the family to work so as to help sustain their siblings' studies. Although addressing these issues is a challenge that requires action in multiple sectors, cash transfers can play a role in alleviating some of the financial pressures that force children into work or marriage and out of school.

Finally, as a call to action, and in line with the 2030 UN Sustainable Development Goals as cited by UNICEF (2016), this chapter concludes with a set of principles to guide more equity-focused policy planning and interventions. These broad principles include: (a) gathering more information about who is being left behind and why, so as to gain a clearer picture of the extent of the issue; (b) improving integration to tackle multiple dimensions of deprivation, so as to guarantee that people receive the right kind of help in all the dimensions that are lacking; (c) fueling innovation to reach the hardest-to-reach children, using creativity and problem-solving skills to get help where it needs to go; (d) increasing investment in equity-focused programs, so as to ensure that everyone is receiving the right kind of help; and (e) fostering involvement by communities and citizens around the world, so as to have more hands in the field and so that everyone may contribute their particular knowledge to the cause.

REFERENCES

Ackerman, B. P., Brown, E. D., & Izard, C. E. (2004). The relations between persistent poverty and contextual risk and children's behavior in elementary school. *Developmental Psychology, 40*, 367–377.

Ackerman, B. P., Izard, C. E., Kobak, R., Brown, E. D., & Smith, C. (2007). Relation between reading problems and internalizing behavior in school for preadolescent children from economically disadvantaged families. *Child Development, 78*(2), 581–596.

Attree, P. (2006). The social costs of child poverty: A systematic review of the qualitative evidence. *Children & Society, 20*(1), 54–66.

Baumeister, R. F., & Leary, M. R. (1995). The need to belong: Desire for interpersonal attachments as a fundamental human motivation. *Psychological Bulletin, 117*(3), 497.

Benyamini, Y. (2011). Why does self-rated health predict mortality? An update on current knowledge and a research agenda for psychologists. *Psychology & Health, 26*, 1407–1413.

Black, M., & Krishnakumar, A. (1998). Children in low-income, urban settings: Interventions to promote mental health and well-being. *American Psychologist, 53*, 635–646.

Bosworth, K., & Judkins, M. (2014). Tapping into the power of school climate to prevent bullying: One application of schoolwide positive behavior interventions and supports. *Theory into Practice, 53*(4), 300–307.

Bradley, R. H., & Corwyn, R. F. (2002). Socioeconomic status and child development. *Annual Review of Psychology, 53*, 371–399.

Bradshaw, C. P., Sawyer, A. L., & O'Brennan, L. M. (2009). A social disorganization perspective on bullying-related attitudes and behaviors: The influence of school context. *American Journal of Community Psychology, 43*(3–4), 204–220.

Bronfenbrenner, U. (1979). *The ecology of human development.* Cambridge, MA: Harvard University Press.

Carneiro, P., Crawford, C., & Goodman, A. (2007). The impact of early cognitive and non-cognitive skills on later outcomes. https://discovery.ucl.ac.uk/id/eprint/16164/1/16164.pdf.

Chaux, E., & Castellanos, M. (2015). Money and age in schools: Bullying and power imbalances. *Aggressive Behavior, 41*(3), 280–293.

Coleman, J. (1990). *The foundations of social theory.* Cambridge, MA: Harvard University Press.

Conger, R. D., & Conger, K. J. (2002). Resilience in Midwestern families: Selected findings from the first decade of a prospective, longitudinal study. *Journal of Marriage and Family, 64*(2), 361–373.

Conger, R. D., & Donnellan, M. B. (2007). An interactionist perspective on the socioeconomic context of human development. *Annual Review of Psychology, 58*, 175–199. doi:10.1146/annurev.psych.58.110405.085551.

Cook, C. R., Williams, K. R., Guerra, N. G., Kim, T. E., & Sadek, S. (2010). Predictors of bullying and victimization in childhood and adolescence: A meta-analytic investigation. *School Psychology Quarterly, 25*, 65–83.

Cook, J. T., Frank, D. A., Levenson, S. M., et al. (2006). Child food insecurity increases risks posed by household food insecurity to young children's health. *Journal of Nutrition*, 136(4), 1073–1076.
Cunha, F., Heckman, J. J., Lochner, L., & Masterov, D. V. (2006). Interpreting the evidence on life cycle skill formation. In E. Hanushek & F. Welch (eds.), *Handbook of the Economics of Education, Vol. 1* (pp. 697–812). Amsterdam: Elsevier.
Deci, E. L., & Ryan, R. M. (2017). *Self-determination theory: Basic psychological needs in motivation, development, and wellness*. New York: Guilford.
Deci, E. L., & Ryan, R. M. (2000). The "what" and "why" of goal pursuits: Human needs and the self-determination of behavior. *Psychological Inquiry*, 11(4), 227–268.
Di Domenico, S. I., & Fournier, M. A. (2014). Socioeconomic status, income inequality, and health complaints: A basic psychological needs perspective. *Social Indicators Research*, 119(3), 1679–1697.
Due, P., Damsgaard, M. T., Lund, R., & Holstein, B. E. (2009a). Is bullying equally harmful for rich and poor children? A study of bullying and depression from age 15 to 27. *European Journal of Public Health*, 19(5), 464–469.
Due, P., Lynch, J., Holstein, B. E., & Modvig, J. (2003). Socioeconomic health inequalities among a nationally representative sample of Danish adolescents: The role of different types of social relations. *Journal of Epidemical Community Health*, 57, 692–698.
Due, P., Merlo, J., Harel-Fisch, Y., et al. (2009b). Socioeconomic inequality in exposure to bullying during adolescence: A comparative, cross-sectional, multilevel study in 35 countries. *American Journal of Public Health*, 99(5), 907–914.
Engle, P. L., & Black, M. M. (2008). The effect of poverty on child development and educational outcomes. *Annals of the New York Academy of Science*, 1136, 234–256. doi:10.1196/annals.1425.023.
Entwisle, D., Alexander, K., & Olson, L. (2005). First grade and educational attainment by age 22: A new story. *American Journal of Sociology*, 110, 1458–1502.
Fernqvist, S. (2013). En erfarenhet rikare?: En kvalitativ studie av barns strategier och barnfattigdomens villkor i välfärdsstaten (Doctoral dissertation). Acta Universitatis Upsaliensis. www.diva-portal.org/smash/record.jsf?pid=diva2%3A571574&dswid=238.
Fink, E., Patalay, P., Sharpe, H., & Wolpert, M. (2018). Child- and school-level predictors of children's bullying behavior: A multilevel analysis in 648 primary schools. *Journal of Educational Psychology*, 110, 17–26.
Frisén, A., Holmqvist, K., & Oscarsson, D. (2008). 13-year-olds' perception of bullying: Definitions, reasons for victimisation and experience of adults' response. *Educational Studies*, 34(2), 105–117.
González, M. G., Swanson, D. P., Lynch, M., & Williams, G. C. (2016). Testing satisfaction of basic psychological needs as a mediator of the relationship between socioeconomic status and physical and mental health. *Journal of Health Psychology*, 21(6), 972–982.
Hart, S. L. (2007). *Capitalism at the crossroads: Aligning business, earth, and humanity*. Upper Saddle River, NJ: Pearson Prentice Hall.
Hjalmarsson, S. (2018). Poor kids? Economic resources and adverse peer relations in a nationally representative sample of Swedish adolescents. *Journal of Youth and Adolescence*, 47(1), 88–104.
Hjalmarsson, S., & Mood, C. (2015). Do poorer youth have fewer friends? The role of household and child economic resources in adolescent school-class friendships. *Children and Youth Services Review*, 57, 201–211.

Hjern, A., Rajmil, L., Bergström, M., et al. (2013). Migrant density and well-being: A national school survey of 15-year-olds in Sweden. *European Journal of Public Health*, 23(5), 823–828.

Idler, E. L., & Benyamini, Y. (1997). Self-rated health and mortality: A review of twenty-seven community studies. *Journal of Health and Social Behavior*, 38, 21–37.

Jackson, B., Richman, L., LaBelle, O., Lempereur, M., & Twenge, J. (2015). Experimental evidence that low social status is most toxic to well-being when internalized. *Self and Identity*, 14(2), 157–172.

Judge, S. (2005). Resilient and vulnerable at-risk children: Protective factors affecting early school competence. *Journal of Children and Poverty*, 11(2), 149–168.

Juvonen, J., & Graham, S. (2014). Bullying in schools: The power of bullies and the plight of victims. *Annual Review of Psychology*, 65, 159–185.

Kudamatsu, M. (2012). Has democratization reduced infant mortality in sub-Saharan Africa? Evidence from micro data. *Journal of the European Economic Association*, 10, 1294–1317.

Lemstra, M. E., Nielsen, G., Rogers, M. R., Thompson, A. T., & Moraros, J. S. (2012). Risk indicators and outcomes associated with bullying in youth aged 9–15 years. *Canadian Journal of Public Health*, 103(1), 9–13.

Leventhal, T., & Brooks-Gunn, J. (2000). The neighborhoods they live in: The effects of residence on child and adolescent outcomes. *Psychological Bulletin*, 126, 309–337.

Ma, X. (2002). Bullying in middle school: Individual and school characteristics of victims and offenders. *School Effectiveness and School Improvement*, 13, 63–89.

Masten, A. S. (2011). Resilience in children threatened by extreme adversity: Frameworks for research, practice, and translational synergy. *Development and Psychopathology*, 23(2), 493–506.

McLoyd, V. C. (1997). The impact of poverty and low socioeconomic status on the socio-emotional functioning of African-American children and adolescents: Mediating effects. In R. D. Taylor & M. Wang (eds.), *Social and emotional adjustment and family relations in ethnic minority families* (pp. 7–34). Mahwah, NJ: Erlbaum.

Melchior, M., Chastang, J. F., Walburg, V., Arseneault, L., Galéra, C., & Fombonne, E. (2010). Family income and youths' symptoms of depression and anxiety: A longitudinal study of the French GAZEL youth cohort. *Depression and Anxiety*, 27(12), 1095–1103.

Moore, K. A., & Glei, D. (1995). Taking the plunge an examination of positive youth development. *Journal of Adolescent Research*, 10, 15–40.

Murnane, R. J. (2007). Improving the education of children living in poverty. *Future of Children*, 17, 795–810.

Nordhagen, R., Nielsen, A., Stigum, H., & Köhler, L. (2005). Parental reported bullying among Nordic children: A population-based study. *Child: Care, Health and Development*, 31(6), 693–701.

Olsson, E. (2007). The economic side of social relations: Household poverty, adolescents' own resources and peer relations. *European Sociological Review*, 23(4), 471–485.

Parker, S., Greer, S., & Zuckerman, B. (1988). Double jeopardy: The impact of poverty on early child development. *Pediatric Clinics of North America*, 35(6), 1227–1240.

Patterson, C. J., Kupersmidt, J. B., & Vaden, N. A. (1990). Income level, gender, ethnicity, and household composition as predictors of children's school-based competence. *Child Development*, 61(2), 485–494.

Patterson, C. J., Vaden, N. A., Griesler, P. C., & Kupersmidt, J. B. (1991). Income level, gender, ethnicity, and household composition as predictors of children's peer companionship outside of school. *Journal of Applied Developmental Psychology*, 12(4), 447–465.

Plenty, S., & Jonsson, J. O. (2017). Social exclusion among peers: The role of immigrant status and classroom immigrant density. *Journal of Youth and Adolescence, 46*(6), 1275–1288.

Plenty, S., & Mood, C. (2016). Money, peers and parents: Social and economic aspects of inequality in youth wellbeing. *Journal of Youth and Adolescence, 45*(7), 1294–1308.

Poverty (n.d.). In *Merriam-Webster's online dictionary* (11th ed.). Retrieved from: www.merriam-webster.com/dictionary/poverty.

Reardon, S. F. (2011). The widening academic achievement gap between the rich and the poor: New evidence and possible explanations. In R. Munane & G. Duncan (eds.), *Whither opportunity? Rising inequality and the uncertain life chances of low income children* (91–116). New York: Russell Sage Foundation Press.

Reijntjes, A., Kamphuis, J. H., Prinzie, P., & Telch, M. J. (2010). Peer victimization and internalizing problems in children: A meta-analysis of longitudinal studies. *Child Abuse & Neglect, 34*(4), 244–252.

Reiss, F. (2013). Socioeconomic inequalities and mental health problems in children and adolescents: A systematic review. *Social Science & Medicine, 90*, 24–31.

Ridge, T. (2011). The everyday costs of poverty in childhood: A review of qualitative research exploring the lives and experiences of low-income children in the UK. *Children & Society, 25*(1), 73–84.

Ronald, L. S., & Rand, D. R. (2018). Life-course contingencies in the development of adolescent antisocial behavior: A matching law approach. In T. Thornberry (ed.), *Developmental theories of crime and delinquency* (pp. 55–100). New York: Routledge.

Ryan, R. M. (1995). Psychological needs and the facilitation of integrative processes. *Journal of Personality, 63*(3), 397–427.

Salmivalli, C. (2010). Bullying and the peer group: A review. *Aggression and Violent Behavior, 15*, 112–120.

Sletten, M. A. (2010). Social costs of poverty: Leisure time socializing and the subjective experience of social isolation among 13–16-year-old Norwegians. *Journal of Youth Studies, 13*(3), 291–315.

Stampini, M., & Tornarolli, L. (2012). The growth of conditional cash transfers in Latin America and the Caribbean: Did they go too far? (No. 49). IZA Policy Paper.

Tarullo, A. R., Obradovic, J., & Gunnar, M. R. (2009). *Self-control and the developing brain.* Washington, DC: Zero to Three.

Tippett, N., & Wolke, D. (2014). Socioeconomic status and bullying: A meta-analysis. *American Journal of Public Health, 104*(6), e48–e59.

Tremblay, R. E., Hartup, W. W., & Archer, J. (eds.). (2005). *Developmental origins of aggression.* New York: Guilford.

Thornberg, R. (2011). "She's weird!" The social construction of bullying in school: A review of qualitative research. *Children & Society, 25*(4), 258–267.

Thornberg, R., & Knutsen, S. (2011). Teenagers' explanations of bullying. *Child & Youth Care Forum, 40*(3), 177–192.

Townsend, P. (1979). *Poverty in the United Kingdom: A survey of household resources and standards of living.* Berkeley: University of California Press.

United Nations Educational Scientific and Cultural Organization (UNESCO) (2017, November 26). Poverty. Retrieved from: www.unesco.org/new/en/social-and-human-sciences/themes/international-migration/glossary/poverty/.

UNESCO Institute for Statistics and United Nation Children's Fund (2015). *Fixing the broken promise of education for all: Findings from the Global Initiative on Out-of-School Children.* Montreal: UNESCO-UIS.

United Nations Children Fund (UNICEF) (2016). *The state of the world's children 2016: A fair chance for every child* (Research Report No. 37). Retrieved from: www.unicef.org/publica tions/index_91711.html.

Van den Broeck, A., Vansteenkiste, M., De Witte, H., Soenens, B., & Lens, W. (2010). Capturing autonomy, competence, and relatedness at work: Construction and initial validation of the Work-Related Basic Need Satisfaction Scale. *Journal of Occupational and Organizational Psychology, 83*(4), 981–1002.

Vartanian, T. P. (1999). Adolescent neighborhood effects on labor market and economic outcomes. *Social Service Review, 73,* 142–167.

Whitney, I., & Smith, P. K. (1993). A survey of the nature and extent of bullying in junior/middle and secondary schools. *Educational Research, 35*(1), 3–25.

Wilkinson, I. G. (2016), Why some children come to school with "baggage": The effects of trauma due to poverty, attachment disruption and disconnection on social skills and relationships. *Canadian Journal of Family and Youth, 8*(1), 173–203.

Woolcock, M. (2014). *Engaging with fragile and conflict-affected states.* Helsinki: World Institute for Development and Economic Research.

World Bank. (2011). *World Development Report 2011: Conflict, security, and development.* World Bank. © World Bank. Retrieved from: https://openknowledge.worldbank.org/han dle/10986/4389 License: CC BY 3.0 IGO.

Youngblade, L. M., Theokas, C., Schulenberg, J., Curry, L., Huang, I. C., & Novak, M. (2007). Risk and promotive factors in families, schools, and communities: A contextual model of positive youth development in adolescence. *Pediatrics, 119,* S47–S53.

6

Educational Access for Women and Girls As a Social Justice Issue

Ghana As a Case Study

Lynn Pasquerella and Dawn Michele Whitehead

INTRODUCTION

Recent studies show that many women around the globe remain far outside the circle of equality, most particularly when it comes to access to education. This finding is highlighted in the latest Global Gender Gap Index, issued by the World Economic Forum in October 2017 (Leopold, Ratcheva, & Zahidi, 2017). The index, tracking gender-based disparities among 144 countries, measures the size of the gender gap between male and female populations in four specific areas: economic participation and opportunity, political empowerment, health and survival, and educational opportunities. In 2017, only 27 out of these 144 countries had fully closed the gap on educational attainment (Leopold et al., 2017).

Saadia Zahidi, head of the Women Leaders and Gender Parity program at the World Economic Forum, has stated, "Both within countries and between countries are two distinct tracks to economic gender equality, with education serving as the accelerator. For countries that provide this basic investment, women's integration in the workforce is the next frontier of change. For those that haven't invested in women's education, addressing this obstacle is critical to women's lives as well as the strength of economies" (Cann, 2013).

"Education ... as the accelerator." Zahidi confirms what we already know: education for women is the engine for achieving economic stability, independence, self-respect, and influence. Study after study has concluded that when girls and women are educated, everyone thrives: families as well as nations. Economic prosperity, as well as personal well-being, is enhanced. Still, as the numbers show, too many girls around the globe are not being educated or, even worse, are being denied an education.

Consider these sobering facts. Of the 750 million people in the world who are illiterate, two-thirds of them are female (UNESCO, 2017). In fact, worldwide, more than half of the population of women over age fifteen cannot read or write. Two-thirds of the world's children who receive less than four years of education are girls, and 15 million girls will never attend school. Globally, 130 million girls aged six to seventeen are denied access to schools (World Bank, 2017).

Grim statistics such as these, while certainly revealing, provide only part of the story, of course. Personal histories offer an even more compelling portrait of what happens when women and girls are denied education. On October 9, 2012, while riding a bus on her way to school in the Swat Valley of Pakistan, Malala Yousafzai was shot on the left side of her forehead by members of the Taliban. The bullet entered her left eye socket and traveled through her shoulder. Malala's wounds were grievous, and many thought she would die. She did not. Thanks to quick medical care and a strong will, she slowly recovered (Yousafzai & Lamb, 2013).

Malala knew why she had been shot. The Taliban had targeted the fifteen-year-old for assassination because she spoke out when schools started to close in the Swat Valley. Five years before, the Taliban had blasted more than 400 schools in Malala's region, forcing many schools to shut their doors or go underground. Following the attacks, the Taliban issued a formal ban on education for girls – a proscription affecting more than 50,000 girls, including Malala (Yousafzai & Lamb, 2013).

It was only after girls' schools began closing that Malala fully realized how important education was to her. Something had been stolen from her, she said, something that rightfully belonged to every girl. "We are human beings," she reminded us, "and this is part of our human nature: that we don't learn the importance of anything until it's snatched from our hands. . . . When we were stopped from going to school, it was at that time I realized education was very important" (*The Daily Show*, 2013). At first, Malala thought the Pakistani government would defend her right to go to school, but she realized she could not wait for politicians. As young as she was, she had to stand up for her rights. "I asked myself," she confessed, "why am I waiting for someone else? The government? The Army to help me? Why someone else? Why don't I raise my voice?" (*The Daily Show*, 2013). She did raise her voice and the Taliban tried to silence her with a gun. Malala realized that fear pulled the trigger. The Taliban was afraid, she said, that once women were educated, they would become more powerful. Even a fifteen-year-old girl. Perhaps especially a fifteen-year-old girl.

Nine months after the shooting, while still recovering from her wounds, Malala Yousafzai spoke out again – this time on her sixteenth birthday to a special assembly of the United Nations. "Bullets cannot silence us," she maintained. "Let us pick up our books and our pens. They are our most important weapons. One child, one teacher, one book and one pen can change the world. Education is the only solution" (Yousafzai, Speech to the United Nations, 2013).

United Nations Secretary-General Ban Ki-moon confirmed what most of the world had come to realize: "The terrorists showed what frightens them the most," he said. "A girl with a book" (Ki-moon, 2013). When the Taliban attempted to assassinate Malala Yousafzai, they were attacking not only the idea of an educated young woman; they also were attacking the idea of enlightenment, progress, and equality. Is the image of an educated young woman so persistently revolutionary that it continues to threaten those who cling to the past? Was the violence of the Taliban against Malala and girls everywhere nothing less than an attempt to extinguish the future and the light of change?

The story of Malala's great courage, not surprisingly, has captured the imagination of the world. The overwhelming support she has garnered is striking and demonstrates how important defending girls' rights is to much of the world. Support for Malala has drawn attention to the global inequities of education, and also to the benefits society reaps when girls go to school:

> Girls with higher levels of education are less likely to get married at an early age. Indeed, if all girls had a primary education, there would be 14% fewer child marriages.
> If all girls had a secondary education, there would be two-thirds fewer child marriages.
> Educated girls are healthier girls and their health benefits flow to the next generation. Hence, the UNESCO Institute for Statistics reports that educated women are less likely to be die in childbirth. Moreover, if all women had a primary education, 1.7 million children would be saved from malnutrition (UNESCO, 2013).

Educating girls means decreasing their exclusion from the labor market and their marginalization by forcing them into unpaid or low-paying work. Studies have shown that a girl with an extra year of education can earn 20 percent more as an adult (World Vision International, 2013). That enhanced income can help break the cycle of poverty that disproportionately affects women around the world. Educating women and bringing them into the labor market also spurs a country's economic growth.

These statistics and others like them underscore that we must look at the importance of educating girls not solely as a gender issue, but also as a development issue. Researchers have determined that investing in girls and their education is the surest way to spur international development. The inverse is also true: not educating girls and young women sends a nation's development into a tailspin. Quite clearly, women's education is good for families, nations, and the prosperity and well-being of the world. Klaus Schwab, founder and executive chairperson of the World Economic Forum, has argued that "countries ... need to start thinking about human capital very differently – including how they integrate women into leadership roles. This shift in mindset and practice is not a goal for the future, it is an imperative today" (Cann, 2013).

CASE OF GHANA

This chapter focuses on Ghana as a case study in promoting women's empowerment through educational resources. Ghana is in West Africa along the Atlantic Ocean and bordered by Togo, Ivory Coast, and Burkina Faso. With just over 29 million people living across ten regions, Ghana's population is diverse with about seventy-five ethnic groups and about eighty-one languages (Owu-Ewie, 2017). Ghana was the first nation on the African continent to gain independence in 1957, and an expansion of education was one of the first priorities of the Nkrumah government. While education has expanded over the years, a gap remains between educational access and completion for males and females, and this case study examines the historical legacy and attempts to overcome this gap so as to provide girls and women with this human right.

HISTORY OF EDUCATION IN GHANA

Although informal education was a part of the Ghanaian cultural fabric before contact with Europeans, the presence of missionaries and colonial officers contributed to the development of formal education in Ghana in the eighteenth century and further expansion in the nineteenth century (Darkwah, 2010; Nortey, 2017). The development of schools followed the travels of these Europeans along the coast and then through the hinterland in Ghana with the latest developments in the northern part of the country. As a result, a limited number of schools were established in the north, and schools were ultimately set up there about 100 years later than in the rest of the country (Darkwah, 2010).

From 1919 to 1927, the colonial government provided financial assistance to church missionary organizations to expand access to formal schooling (Akyeampong, 2011), and they were guided by Governor Guggisberg's sixteen principles. Principle 4 was equal educational opportunities for boys and girls (McWilliam & Kwamena-Poh, 1975). Despite the policy and guiding principles, in the colonial period, boys were favored when it came to access to schooling (Darkwah, 2010), much like they were in formation of schools in Great Britain. While boys were educated to become clerks, teachers, and new professionals, the few girls fortunate enough to gain access – only about 10 percent of students – were trained in order to enhance their preparation for wifely duties for this new class of men in Ghana (Graham, 1971).

Given this type of education that privileged a small sector of children in the pre-independence era, primarily boys persisted. However, the Accelerated Development Plan (ADP), implemented in 1951, was an initial effort to expand education by offering unrestricted, tuition-free, compulsory schooling (Akyeampong, 2009, 2011; Nortey, 2017), with a goal of universal primary schooling within fifteen years (Akyeampong, 2009). As a result of the ADP, the number of schools increased from 1,081 in 1951 to 3,372 in 1952 (Nortey, 2017).

After independence, the quest for education for all became even more important in the efforts to prepare citizens for the new country, and the Education Act of 1961 continued to expand free and compulsory education by establishing more schools and new teacher training colleges so as to address the lack of qualified teachers. The act abolished tuition fees for schooling at public primary, middle, and special schools, but parents were still responsible for paying for books, stationery, and other materials (Akyeampong, 2011). In a demonstration of the government's commitment to education, fines were threatened for parents who did not send their children to school, although they were never actually enforced (Nortey, 2017). The value of education was clear. While the expansion of education was vast, most of it occurred in the southern and central parts of Ghana, which offered much more infrastructure and a greater foundation for schools and healthcare due to the longer contact with missionaries and the colonial government. Many more boys than girls were still enrolled in school, and children in southern Ghana enjoyed greater access to education than children in the northern part of the country. This gap persisted for years because the north did not experience the same rate of development of infrastructure, healthcare, and education as the south. The north was also much more isolated from contact with Europeans (Akyeampong, 2009).

Following the initial efforts to expand schooling in the early postindependence years, many policies and programs were implemented that were meant to increase educational access in Ghana, including attempts targeting girls over the next five decades. The 1987 Education Reform expanded access to schools and sought to improve quality. The structure of schools also changed, and the number of years of pre-tertiary education was reduced to twelve with nine years of basic education (primary and junior secondary school) and three years of senior secondary school. The Basic Education Certificate Examination, which was the gateway exam into senior secondary school, was also introduced (Nortey, 2017). This reform effort improved participation for girls and boys, but the gap in attendance persisted (Akyeampong, 2011; Donkor & Justice, 2016).

The 1992 constitution included education as a human right (Akyeampong, 2009). No discrimination due to gender was to be allowed, and equality before the law was mandated. The constitution also referenced the possible provision of special policies in order to address gender imbalances (Ghana Statistical Service, 2014), indicating the challenge that the country was facing with inequitable access to schools.

In 1995, the Free Compulsory Universal Basic Education (FCUBE) program was introduced. This included primary and junior secondary school and offered tuition-free, compulsory schooling for all school-aged children (Akyeampong, 2011; Nortey, 2017). Slow, steady growth resulted from this policy, but it didn't reduce many other school-related costs – user fees, uniforms, and school-related materials were still needed (Akyeampong, 2009) – limiting the policy's impact on girls' education. This reflected the influence of international donors, such as the World Bank and the International Monetary Fund (IMF), which encouraged developing countries to expand access primary education until 100 percent enrollment rates were achieved. Many donors also offered funding to support an expansion of primary schooling through different initiatives (Nortey, 2017).

The Education Strategic Plan (ESP) for 2003–2015 also had the goal of education for all and contained several references to educating girls and women. The plan addressed skills training for females and the importance of programs to raise awareness about the relevance of female education, the value of gender-friendly

TABLE 6.1 *Ghanaian educational structure*

	Basic Education	Second Cycle	Tertiary
Components	2 years of kindergarten	3 years of senior high school, vocational, technical, business, and/or agricultural school	University, polytechnic, or teacher training college
	6 years of primary		
	3 years of junior high school		
Examination Option	Basic Education Certificate examination	West African Secondary School Certificate examination	Certificate, diploma, degree
Required	Yes	No	No

Data from Nortey (2017); table created by the authors

environments, and identification of ways for girls to enhance their participation in schooling – district scholarships, counseling, and guidance programs for support – and encouragement for females to take up traditionally male-dominated subjects such as mathematics, science, and technology (Ministry of Education, 2003).

In 2004, the Education White Paper on Education Reforms built on the ESP 2003–2015, with an emphasis on providing high-quality, free basic education for all, more inclusive and appropriate secondary education (Camfed Ghana, 2012), and an expansion of basic education to include two years of preprimary education (Camfed Ghana, 2012; Nortey, 2017). See Table 6.1.

As the demand for schooling continued to grow, and the burden of the associated costs of schooling persisted, the Capitation Grant was introduced (Akyeampong, 2011). In 2004, the effort to abolish all costs associated with basic education led to a pilot program for the Capitation Grants, implemented in forty deprived districts. An allocation of 2.5–3.5 Ghanaian cedis (approximately 1.30–1.82 US dollars) was available for each male and female student (Akyeampong, 2011; Nortey, 2017). The funds could be used for teaching and learning materials, payment for school and extracurricular activities, and transportation costs (Nortey, 2017). After the pilot year, enrollment increased by 15 percent in the forty districts. The Capitation Grants were expanded nationwide in 2005, with a goal of improving teaching and learning, providing support to more students, and ensuring school infrastructure costs and sports and culture expenses were not levied on parents. By the 2007 academic year, basic school enrollment increased by 17 percent, and there was a positive impact in deprived areas. By 2011, there appeared to be a 2.2 percent increase – when controlling for dropouts and overage enrollment (Akyeampong, 2011).

The elimination of all fees allowed parents to send their children to school without fear of retribution if they could not pay extra fees (Donkor & Justice, 2016; Nortey, 2017). The funding allocation was based on gross enrollment rates and performance of students in basic schools (Nortey, 2017). Some argue that this contributed to a narrowing of the gender gap in terms of access to primary schools in Ghana (Donkor & Justice, 2016) because no additional fees, such as user fees or fees for related materials, were needed to support girls' attendance. These fees had previously been identified as a barrier to girls' attendance in schools.

The 2005 Ghana School Feeding Program (GSFP) provided students with a daily, hot, nutritious meal at basic schools in the poorest areas of Ghana (Atta & Manu, 2015) with the goal of increasing attendance and retention at the primary level (Wolf, McCoy, & Godfrey, 2016). Sustainability presented a challenge for this program due to the need to obtain the necessary financial support, and the need to identify the neediest schools as priorities (Wolf et al., 2016).

CURRENT EDUCATIONAL SITUATION FOR GIRLS IN GHANA

Due to the gender gap, in 1996, the Girls' Education Unit (GEU) was established in the Ministry of Education under the Basic Education Division (Atta & Manu, 2015). The GEU's charge is to ensure girls have access to a safe, welcoming school, teachers who understand their needs, and a chance to reach their potential, graduate, and become productive members of Ghanaian society (Asiegbor et al., 2018). As a coordinating unit, the GEU increases awareness of initiatives, encourages community participation, and offers training for educational leaders while also providing monitoring and evaluation for work done at all levels. Each district education office has representatives, and the GEU has also provided scholarship and food provisions, especially in the northern regions (Nortey, 2017). This unit seeks to increase the literacy levels for women, net enrollment rates at all levels, and representation of women in the teaching ranks at all levels. See Tables 6.2, 6.3, 6.4, 6.5, 6.6, and 6.7.

Despite policy efforts, the establishment of the GEU, and other educational programs, gender gaps persist in access, enrollment, transition, achievement, and

TABLE 6.2 *Literacy levels*

	Women	Men
2000	49.8% Literate 50.2% Illiterate	66.4% Literate 33.6% Illiterate
2010	65.3% Literate 34.7% Illiterate	78.3% Literate 21.7% Illiterate

Data from Ghana Statistical Service (2014); table created by the authors completion. While gains have been made for girls (Donkor & Justice, 2016), the gap between boys and girls at the primary level has narrowed the most. The rates are approaching gender parity (Atta & Manu, 2015). However, at the higher levels of schooling, a gap continues between the genders, and it remains highest at the tertiary level (Darkwah, 2010). This impacts access to careers for Ghanaian women (see Table 6.3).

TABLE 6.3 *2016 net enrollment rates (number of students in the theoretical age group for each level in % of total population in the age group)*

	Primary	Secondary	Tertiary
Total	86.17	52.67	16.07
Female	87.01	52.68	13.37
Male	85.37	52.66	18.65

Data from UNESCO (2017); table created by the authors

TABLE 6.4 *Teaching staff in primary schools in 2010/2011*

	Public	Private
Total	94,927	29,432
Female	37,003	8,648
Male	57,924	20,784

Data from Ghana Statistical Service (2014); table created by the authors

TABLE 6.5 *Teaching staff in senior high schools in 2010/2011*

	Public	Private
Total	24,293	3,288
Female	5,095	370
Male	19,198	2,918

Data from Ghana Statistical Service (2014); table created by the authors

TABLE 6.6 *Teaching staff in technical and vocational schools in 2010/2011*

	Public	Private
Total	2,723	1,443
Female	737	599
Male	1,986	844

Data from Ghana Statistical Service (2014); table created by the authors

TABLE 6.7 *Full-time academic staff at public universities in 2009/2010*

	Women	Men
University of Ghana	199	644
KNUST	88	639
University of Education	59	379
University for Development Studies	45	238
University of Mines and Technology	50	362
University of Cape Coast	447	2329

Data from Ghana Statistical Service (2014); table created by the authors

Due to past gender inequity, school staffing has an even larger gender gap with males in the majority of teaching positions from primary school through the tertiary levels. Years of inequitable access to schooling are reflected in the reality that few women have persisted in the secondary or tertiary levels where they would be positioned to enter the teaching ranks. If women are unable to last through the tertiary level, they are unable to even become candidates for teaching. However, with progress at the primary and secondary levels, intentional programming seeking to raise the number of women entering and completing tertiary education can be increased in this next generation.

Why haven't girls persisted across educational levels in Ghana? The reasons are similar to those on an international scale, but some factors are specific to Ghana. These barriers are sociocultural, school-related, and connected to public perceptions of education for women. Some of the sociocultural factors are deeply rooted in tradition. For instance, early marriage and/or betrothal of girls ends the educational experience for some girls in Ghana. Over the years, the rates of child marriage have decreased, but it remains an issue in some communities. As a result of the intersection with poverty and the need for the promised dowry or its equivalent (Atta & Manu, 2015; Donkor & Justice, 2016), some fathers may offer their daughters in marriage at an early age. There is sometimes a flawed perception that the more years in school a girl has completed, the fewer children she will have (Atta & Manu, 2015), and this also causes some future husbands or parents to pull girls out of school. For families who anticipate their daughters' eventual marriage, they realize their daughters will leave the family, so there is also hesitancy to invest financially in the education of girls. The idea here is that this would be a *wasted* investment (Atta & Manu, 2015). Boys, on the other hand, will not leave the family and will continue to invest in it. This male privilege encourages some parents to invest in the education of boys over that of girls when a choice must be made (Atta & Manu, 2015; Donkor & Justice, 2016).

While the Ghana Labor Decree of 1967 makes it illegal for children under the age of fifteen to be employed, except for undefined *light* work (Atta & Manu, 2015;

Camfed Ghana, 2012), about 20 percent of Ghanaian children work while attending school (Wolf et al., 2016). Many children engage in labor inside and outside the home, which has the potential to interfere with schooling. For girls, household chores have been a barrier to full participation in school. They are often more responsible for household chores – to lighten their mother's load – and typically start work at an earlier age than their male counterparts (Atta & Manu, 2015). Some children are fostered with family members in different towns or cities, and this has a negative impact on girls' education, as they are responsible for household duties and possibly childcare, which is a priority over their own schooling (Darkwah, 2010).

Girls who may gain access to school at times also suffer from absenteeism given some of the aforementioned factors – household chores, a family emergency, or other issues. Absenteeism is a serious problem for girls in Ghana, and it interferes with their ability to successfully complete their education (Wolf et al., 2016).

Negative perceptions can be associated with educating girls, especially in rural communities and in the northern part of Ghana. Some in these areas hold onto the idea of traditional roles for girls, and subsequently don't see the value of educating a girl if she is going to marry, have children, and remain in the home (Atta & Manu, 2015; Donkor & Justice, 2016). Many also fear that higher education has the potential to damage women's moral lives (Donkor & Justice, 2016), as an educated woman may challenge her husband and could be influenced by external ideas about traditional roles of women, which could result in a disruption in the "normal" ways of life for women.

School-related factors that hinder girls' participation in schooling are sexual harassment, lack of female teachers as role models (Atta & Manu, 2015), lack of safe transportation to and from school, and concerns about health and hygiene. Girls have been subjected to sexual harassment and/or violence by male teachers and classmates. Some girls have been threatened with failure, humiliation, and other harsh treatment if they didn't comply with sexual advances by a teacher. These types of advances also have an impact on the performance of female students who may revert to being very quiet, and some may avoid going to school. The fear of this type of harassment is also a reason that some parents are hesitant to send their girls to school. These incidents are often underreported (Atta & Manu, 2015), like in many other countries, based on the data that have been collected.

An understated connection exists between sanitary care and schooling. Infrastructure constraints hinder girls who are menstruating from coming to school. A lack of private latrines, water, and sanitary supplies contributes to absenteeism and even dropping out for some girls (Dolan, Ryus, Dopson, Montgomery, & Scott, 2013).

Finally, the lack of female teachers at all levels discourages girls' participation in schooling and their everyday performance. Having a female teacher does have an impact on access, retention, and achievement for girls. Girls' enrollment is positively associated with the percentage of female teachers in Ghana and in many other lower- and lower-middle-income countries (Atta & Manu, 2015).

EFFORTS TO ENHANCE PARTICIPATION BY GIRLS

In attempts to ensure girls have access to education in Ghana, a number of programs have been implemented in concert with the GEU and as stand-alone projects. These programs have advanced the opportunities for girls and brought them one step closer to educational empowerment. Incentives, such as scholarships and stipends, which have been used to cover the costs of uniforms, school fees, and other associated expenses, have been particularly effective in supporting girls' attendance and completion at the senior high school level. These types of programs are not as sustainable as others because once the funding ends, there may not be another sponsor to provide support for the students. Reduced costs for transportation and/or boarding facilities have also been an incentive to shift the cost burden from parents; they also enhance the safety of girls. Engaging the community with a campaign that highlights the real value for education of girls is another critical effort to encourage greater access and participation of girls. Finally, strategic recruitment and training of female teachers, assistant teachers, and other educators also has a positive impact on girls' participation in schooling (Camfed Ghana, 2012).

Individual schools have created girls' clubs that are interactive, school-based programs where girls come together to learn about reproductive health, rights of children, time management, and vocations that promote economic independence. These programs help girls navigate some of the challenges that often result in dropping out and provide them with opportunities to lead and take ownership of activities and projects (Asiegbor et al., 2018). The Role Model Outreach program is another opportunity for girls to engage with professional women in their own communities. Here role models come to the schools or to community meetings that the girls attend with their parents and speak with the girls about their own life stories as well as how they attained educational and professional success (Asiegbor et al., 2018).

However, these programs can present challenges. If a district doesn't have funding to provide support, the programs can be short-lived and lack sustainability. Programs also take place outside of class hours, and if the girls are needed at home for chores or live a great distance from school and need to walk home early in order to avoid walking in the dark, they may not be able to participate. If the role models do not live in the community, it is difficult to develop a relationship beyond the formal interaction during the sessions, which can also limit the impact of such role models (Asiegbor et al., 2018).

THE CONNECTION BETWEEN FORMAL EDUCATION AND THE WORKFORCE

Once girls and women do successfully complete their education, they will have a more equitable chance to participate in the formal economy, which is where they will be able to make a living wage. Women in Ghana have a very limited presence in the formal economy, and this is directly related to the historical lack of access to formal education. Participants in the formal economy have the potential to earn a higher income and have more job security than laborers in the informal economy (Darkwah, 2010). In 2011, 86 percent of women who worked worked in the informal sector, while 4 percent were employed in the formal public sector, and 6 percent were employed in the formal private sector. Women have encountered resistance when entering these spaces (Camfed, 2012), which is indicated by their slow growth in the areas and by the persistence of the gender gap. It is not surprising that women dominate the informal economy.

In 2009, 6.3 percent of Ghanaian men had completed postsecondary education while only 2.6 percent of Ghanaian women had. There were almost three times the number of men with postsecondary degrees as women (Darkwah, 2010), and these men had greater access into this formal sector. As Table 6.2 notes, the literacy rates for women have increased significantly, and this is also critical. Even women who would like to study vocational training must take the Vocational Technical Institute Qualifying Exam, so they must be able to read and write so as to participate in the formal economy for hairdressing, and they must have access to funds in order to purchase a dryer, mirrors, chairs, and water (Darkwah, 2010). This comes from postsecondary education and access to resources. Therefore, formal education is the key to obtaining positions in the formal economy (Darkwah, 2010).

In order to reach postsecondary education, Ghanaian women need to enroll and complete senior high school in higher numbers. In recent years, there has been a desire to transform senior high school education so as to include the skills that youth need in the world of work. Educators are making efforts to connect skills with employment across the African continent and in Ghana. So far, employers have not been too pleased with the skills that graduates are bringing to the workplace. Students need to work independently, solve problems, and demonstrate creativity (Akyeampong, 2014). Many women are already displaying these skills in the marketplace, where they are dominant. With greater access to and participation in secondary school, they will have an opportunity to apply these skills in the school setting and be prepared academically for tertiary education and, subsequently, the formal economy.

Until women gain equal access to postsecondary opportunities, they may continue to be relegated to the less secure informal economy.

CONCLUDING THOUGHTS

There is an urgent need today to expand educational opportunities for girls and young women around the world. This is not just a matter of simply building more schools, making sure more girls are in classrooms, or increasing a nation's gross national product. We also need to think about the deeper issues of why we educate girls and women. We need mentors and role models for young women so as to show that learning adds dignity to a life, opens the mind to possibilities, and helps a woman control her own destiny. We also need books and educational materials reflecting that women have the capacity to doing anything and have done everything. Texts should end the erasure of women and all people who live on the margins of history. Education for young women must not reinforce the intractable stereotype of women as passive onlookers who sit quietly while the world spins. Education must encourage young women to be bold, assertive, resilient, and forward-thinking.

Regrettably, misogyny remains virulent in some places in the world today, where the idea of women's influence is so threatening that girls are murdered because they are viewed as "trouble." In their award-winning book *Half the Sky*, Sheryl WuDunn and Nicholas Kristof tell the stories behind the mind-boggling statistic that "more girls have been killed in the last fifty years, precisely because they were girls, than men were killed in all the battles of the twentieth century" (Kristof & WuDunn, 2010, p. xvii). Just as slavery was the central moral challenge of the nineteenth century, and the battle against totalitarianism was the major challenge of the twentieth, the authors maintain, "in this century, the paramount moral challenge will be the struggle for gender equality around the world" (Kristof & WuDunn, 2010, p. xvii).

Taking up this challenge is daunting. Women need to be empowered through measures to increase social, economic, and political equity that will in turn bolster access to fundamental human rights. As we know from the civil rights movement in the United States, passing laws is not enough in the face of overriding cultural, social, and political forces that make exercising these rights impossible. To promote women's leadership and political participation, to strengthen women's economic capacity, and to stem violence against women, we must turn to education. It is incumbent upon all of us involved in education to exert pressure on those who deny access to education for women. We need to overturn those economic structures that reinforce a division of labor in which women and girls spend up to six hours a day gathering water and firewood. We must prevent girls from being subject to harassment from both classmates and teachers because of a sexism that is too frequently reinforced by school officials. This is not mere rhetoric or a plank in the platform of a specious political equity. It is a matter of social justice. It is an issue of human rights. Investing in girls will change the world.

REFERENCES

Akyeampong, K. (2009). Revisiting free compulsory universal basic education (FCUBE) in Ghana. *Comparative Education*, 45(2), 175–195.

Akyeampong, K. (2011). (Re)Assessing the impact of school Capitation Grants on education access in Ghana. Consortium for Educational Access, Transitions and Equity, Research Monograph 71.

Akyeampong, K. (2014). Reconceptualized life skills in secondary education in the African context: Lessons learnt from reforms in Ghana. *International Review of Education*, 60(2), 217–234.

Asiegbor, I. K., Dakeh, M., Hayibor, F., et al. (2018). Promoting gender equality in Ghana through girls' clubs and role model outreach. United Nations Girls' Education Initiative. Retrieved from www.goodpracticefund.org/documents/Adaklu-UNGEI-Final.pdf.

Atta, G., & Manu, J. (2015). Ghana school feeding program: A retrospective review. *International Journal of Innovative Research and Development*, 4(8), 402–410.

Camfed Ghana (2012). What works in girls' education in Ghana: A critical review of the Ghanaian and international literature. Ministry of Education and the Girls' Education Unit. Retrieved from www.ungei.org/files/What_Works_in_Girls_Education_in_Ghana.pdf.

Cann, O. (2013, October 25). The global gender gap report 2013: Increased political participation helps narrow global gender gap in 2013. Retrieved from https://reliefweb.int/report/world/global-gender-gap-report-2013.

The Daily Show (2013, October 18). Extended interview with Malala Yousafzai.[Video]. Retrieved from www.amara.org/en/videos/ywQDmibRdFiB/en/577415/802426.

Darkwah, A. K. (2010). Education: Pathway to empowerment for Ghanaian women? *IDS Bulletin*, 41(2), 28–36.

Dolan, C. S., Ryus, D. R., Dopson, S., Montgomery, P., & Scott, L. (2013). A blind spot in girls' education: Menarche and its webs of exclusion in Ghana. *Journal of International Development*, 26(5), 643–657.

Donkor, A. K., & Justice, D. K (2016). Girls' education in science: The challenges in northern Ghana. *Journal of Education & Social Policy*, 3(1), 82–96.

Ghana Statistical Service (2014). *Women and men in Ghana: A statistical compendium 2014*. Accra: Statistical Service.

Global Gender Gap Index (2013). Retrieved from www.weforum.org/docs/WEF_GenderGap_Report_2013.pdf.

Graham, C. K. (1971). *The history of education in Ghana from the earliest times to the declaration of independence*. Oxford: Routledge.

Ki-moon, Ban. (2013, April 5). Secretary-General Ban Ki-moon talks to Malala. [Web blog post]. Retrieved from www.blogs.un.org.

Kristof, N. D., & WuDunn, S. (2010). *Half the sky: Turning oppression into opportunity for women worldwide*. New York: Vintage Books.

Leopold, T. A., Ratcheva, V., & Zahidi, S. (2017). *The global gender gap report 2017*. Geneva: World Economic Forum.

McWilliam, H. O. A., & Kwamena-Poh, M. A. (1975). *The development of education in Ghana*. London: Longman.

Ministry of Education (2003). *Education Strategic Plan 2003 to 2015: Volume 1 policies, targets and strategies*. Accra: Government of Ghana.

Nortey, M. A. N. (2017). An assessment of Ghana's effective implementation of gender equality in education-MDG3. University of Ghana master of arts dissertation. Legon, University of Ghana.

Owu-Ewie, C. (2017). Language, education and linguistic human rights in Ghana. *Journal of the Humanities*, 28(2), 151–172.

UNESCO (2013, October). Education for all global monitoring report. Retrieved from www.en.unesco.org/gem-report/sites/gem-report/files/girls-factsheet-en.pdf.

UNESCO (2017, January 9). International literacy day 2017. Retrieved from www.uis.unesco.org/en/news/international-literacy-day-2017.

UNESCO (n.d.). Ghana [Data File]. Retrieved from http://uis.unesco.org/country/GH.

Wolf, S., McCoy, D. C., & Godfry, E. B. (2016). Barriers to school attendance and gender inequailty: Empirical evidence from a sample of Ghanaian school children. *Research and in Comparative and International Education*, 11(2), 178–193.

World Bank (2017, September 25). Girls' education. Retrieved from www.worldbank.org/en/topic/girlseducation.

World Vision International (2013). 10 facts about girls' education. Retrieved from www.wvi.org/girl-rising/10-facts-about-girls-education.

Yousafzai, M. (2013, July 12). Speech to the United Nations. [Video]. Retrieved from www.amara.org/en/videos/ywQDmibRdFiB/en/577415/802426.

Yousafzai, M., & Lamb, C. (2013). *I am Malala: The girl who stood up for education and was shot by the Taliban*. London: Orion Books.

7

The Youngest Victims

Children and Young People Affected by War

James Garbarino, Amy E. Governale, and Danielle Nesi

Manuel T. started his life in the war zone of El Salvador during the period of violent political repression that dominated events there in the 1970s.[1] *The war grew out of local conditions – a leftist uprising against the political elite who governed ruthlessly on behalf of the small group of families who owned most of the land and held the country's wealth. The war continued as long as it did because of global politics; El Salvador had become a pawn in the Cold War, with the United States supporting the government and the Soviet Union backing the rebels. Growing up in a war zone infected every aspect of Manuel's life, with many long-term consequences. Manuel's father went to prison for a murder that grew out of his role in a death squad. With his father gone and the family's financial status desperate, his mother "abandoned" him to seek work in the United States. After Manuel's grandfather was murdered in front of him, his mother returned to get him and bring him to the United States. There he moved into the dark world of the MS-13 gang, and was eventually deported back to El Salvador, where the war was over but the combatants continued to fight as "security forces" and "gangs" (most notably MS-13). The rest of Manuel's story is a tale of brutality, murder, and sexual assault that has resulted in him receiving a death sentence. It's hard to know what Manuel would have become had he grown up in peace. We do know that growing up in a war zone poisoned him psychologically.*

In 1989, the United Nation's Convention on the Rights of the Child declared, "[state parties] shall take all feasible measures to ensure protection and care of children who are affected by an armed conflict" (p. 11). In addition to attempting to secure the welfare of children in armed conflict, the Convention went on to ban the recruitment and deployment of children during war. Despite the vast majority of sovereign nations signing and ratifying this agreement, this treaty, unfortunately, has not prevented children and youth from witnessing, becoming victims of, or participating in political, ethnic, religious, and cultural violence across the past three decades. For example, it is estimated tens of thousands of children serve in armed militant groups, with an additional 2 million children killed and 6 million becoming permanently disfigured as a result of modern warfare (Grusovin, Makome, Nayak, Nicolai, & Verhey, 2009).

In recognition of the abuses and tragedies that befall the nearly 250 million children currently living in countries affected by armed conflict (UNICEF, 2016), this chapter summarizes the direct developmental and psychological consequences of exposure to warfare and political violence. We also emphasize the indirect implications of growing up in a culture of violence and fear – including indirect traumatization and socially toxic messaging that often coincide with modern warfare.

Because warfare permeates so many contexts within a community or country, one of the theories most commonly used to explain the impact of political violence on childhood development is Urie Bronfenbrenner's (1979) social-ecological theory (Cummings, Merrilees, Taylor, & Mondi, 2017). The social-ecological theory states that the dynamic and reciprocal environments that a person experiences shape human development (Bronfenbrenner & Morris, 1998). This begins with individuals' own biology and personal characteristics and their microsystems (direct environments in which a child lives and interacts). In instances of political violence, it is easy to see how microsystems may be disrupted or endanger a child's well-being. For example, fighting may destroy the home or community spaces that children previously frequented, daily life may become strained as caregivers deal with their own traumas, and normal routines such as going to school or the grocery store may no longer be considered safe or may be restricted by parents (Qouta, Punamäki, & El-Sarraj, 2008). Furthermore, children's mesosystems (connections of microsystems), may be disrupted in times of crises. Teachers, neighbors, or relatives may be closer, or lived with, in refugee camps. Areas like religious buildings may start to serve different purposes, such as becoming shelters offering food and schooling. In addition, children's personal characteristics may buffer or worsen the impact of trauma. Beyond gender and age – discussed later in this chapter – children with higher levels of self-agency, acculturation skills, or "hardiness/resilience" may not suffer the same psychological impacts as a result of political violence exposure compared to children who do not possess such attributes (Masten & Narayan, 2012).

Moving beyond microsystems, there is still a possibility of psychological or traumatic consequences even if children do not directly experience environments that are impacted by political violence or warfare. Children's immediate environments are disrupted by secondary stressors, such as poverty, displacement, or familial strain, that negatively impact daily functioning. For example, if caregivers' workplaces become disrupted or lost, children's home life may be negatively impacted, which in turn is correlated with more internalizing symptoms and post-traumatic stress symptoms (PTSS; Comer et al., 2010). Thus, children may experience psychological or traumatic consequences through indirect exposure to violence associated with war or armed conflict.

Secondhand trauma may be passed down through generations. A caregiver's exposure to political violence in the past has been shown to negatively impact children's mental health, even when the conflict has been long resolved. Examples of the transmission of trauma from one generation to the next, commonly referred to as intergenerational trauma, can been seen throughout history in the descendants of Holocaust survivors (Danieli, 1998), American Indians (Brave Heart & DeBruyn, 1998), and combat veterans (see review by Dekel & Goldblatt, 2008). Various mechanisms have been proposed to explain this phenomenon, ranging from psychodynamic perspectives that emphasize children's unconscious absorption of repressed and unresolved parental traumas (e.g., Rowland-Klein & Dunlop, 1998), to biological explanations that focus on genetically based predispositions or vulnerabilities created from neurological change stemming from traumatic exposure (Yehuda, 1999). Other theories focus on the family system itself, suggesting that family dynamics and familial dysfunction are the root of difficulties experienced by children of trauma survivors (Rosenheck & Fontana, 1998). For example, children may develop maladaptive thinking and/or behaviors as a direct result of exposure to parents' psychopathology, such as when children view parents' hypervigilance and then subsequently come to perceive the world as dangerous, leading to the development of anxiety, or children may develop maladaptive thinking and behaviors through dysfunctional relationships with their parents, not from their parents' trauma-related psychopathology directly (Schwartz, Dohrenwend, & Levav, 1994). For example, a parent with a history of trauma may struggle with being emotionally responsive to a child's needs, which can lead to problems such as emotional dysregulation.

Additionally, violent images or depictions of conflict can desensitize children to violence or create secondhand trauma or anxiety (Joshi & O'Donnell, 2003). On a macro level, the environment of a country, which includes culture, laws, and social norms, is also disrupted during warfare. These macrosystems can shift to become distrustful or suspicious of outsiders or perceived enemies of the state, leading to new security laws that might restrict the freedom or the movement of families, and communities and states may be formed, destroyed, or devastated. Changing landscapes may confuse young children and fundamentally alter life as they have known it.

A direct implication of this ecological perspective is the fact that rarely if ever does a single influence determine the course of a child's life, for better or for worse. Whether these influences are negative – "risk factors" – or positive – "developmental assets" – it is extremely rare that a single influence is decisive. Rather, it is the accumulation of risk factors and the counterbalancing by developmental assets that determines whether an environment will lead to social toxicity or robustness. Thus, the goal of this chapter is to provide a broad overview of the impact of warfare and political violence on children who directly experience conflict, as well as the indirect impact of growing up in cultures that experience fighting but where children do not directly witness the violence. We end with suggestions for policy makers and practitioners on how to promote healthy development for youth who may be particularly vulnerable to the impacts of warfare.

DIRECT EFFECTS OF WARFARE AND POLITICAL VIOLENCE

Modern diplomacy has shifted armed conflict from occurring between territories or countries to now taking place within a country (Marshall & Elzinga-Marshall, 2017). This means children from all over the world have witnessed or been affected by warfare and political violence not at their borders but within divided communities. Fortunately, after a disaster (such as exposure to systematic or random political violence), between 60 percent and 80 percent of children are likely to recover naturally and emerge without major psychopathology or violent lifestyles (e.g., Hoven et al., 2005; Thabet & Thabet, 2015). For example, during the thirty-year conflict between Protestants/Separatists and Catholics/Loyalists in Northern Ireland, Northern Irish children did not significantly differ from European children in terms of depression (Cairns, 1996), anxiety (McWhirter, 1984), or self-esteem (Granleese, Turner, & Trew, 1989), despite being exposed to the worst violence in Europe at the time. In the United States, using a nationally representative sample, parents reported just over a third of children showed trouble concentrating, sleep problems, irritability, or avoidance of the topic or of distressing thoughts immediately after the September 11 terrorist attacks (Schuster et al., 2001), with 22 percent of New York City schoolchildren seeking mental health counseling in the months following the attack (Stuber et al., 2002).

Decades of developmental research related to stress and internalizing symptoms have shown the children most likely to suffer serious and long-term mental health, behavioral, or emotional problems from their encounters with traumatic events are the 20 percent of children who experience those events and are emotionally vulnerable, who have accumulated risk factors, or who have been directly impacted from events such as personal injury or the injury or death of a loved one (Joshi & O'Donnell, 2003; Sameroff, Bartko, Baldwin, Baldwin, & Seifer, 1998). Children who come from families with high levels of family conflict, divorce, or parental depression or stress during instances of political violence are more likely to report post-traumatic stress symptoms (PTSS) following the attack. For example, parental distress, including children who witnessed their parents crying or reported impaired communication with parents, is one of the most consistent predictors of later PTSS in children following exposure to political violence (Chemtob et al., 2010; Fairbrother, Stuber, Galea, Fleischman, & Pfefferbaum, 2003; Gil-Rivas, Silver, Holman, McIntosh, & Poulin, 2007; Hagan, 2005; Otto et al., 2007; Stuber et al., 2002; Wilson, Lengua, Meltzoff, & Smith, 2010). This is consistent with social-ecological theory, which states children's immediate environments, such as a stable home life and normal routines, are the most influential and important contexts in shaping healthy developmental outcomes.

Children are aware of and terrified by terror attacks and armed conflict just as adults are. However, the individual risk factors associated with children who develop acute or long-term psychopathological symptoms as a result of exposure to traumatic events have shown mixed results. On one hand, research has suggested that children under the age of twelve, who depend on support systems that nurture and shape their daily lives but lack the cognitive resources to make sense of political or cultural violence, are especially susceptible to the effects of trauma (Cummings et al., 2011). For example, short-term effects following exposure to trauma within younger children typically include trouble sleeping, separation anxiety or clinging behavior, or trouble concentrating, although these are likely to dissipate over time (Cummings et al., 2017; Joshi & O'Donnell, 2003). For school-aged children, traumatic symptoms as a result of political violence exposure may manifest as regressive behaviors such as fear of being alone, aggression or hyperarousal, trouble concentrating, or anxiety (Gurwitch, Pfefferbaum, & Leftwich, 2002). On the other hand, research examining cognitive development and understanding of political violence suggests older youth, who understand the realities of armed conflict, may have more difficulties blocking out intrusive thoughts (Masten & Narayan, 2012). Older children's advanced autonomy, cognitive maturity, and responsibilities may mean they feel compelled to participate in violence, and with reduced parental monitoring they may be more exposed to traumatic violent events, which in turn correlates with developing PTSS (Barber, 2008; Macksoud & Aber, 1996). Youth may display externalizing behaviors such as aggression, risk-taking, or substance use (Schiff & Fang, 2014; Schiff et al., 2012). Additionally, older children who participate in armed conflict may be met with greater family and community distrust and stigmatization. Such marginalization was associated with increase depressive and internalizing symptoms (Betancourt et al., 2010).

Similar to findings regarding age and exposure, there is also inconsistent evidence regarding gender and PTSS, with males often being exposed to more violence but females reporting higher levels of traumatic symptoms (APA, 2017). While the literature has shown that girls are more likely to report higher levels of fear following an attack or an instance of violence than boys, when using more indirect measures of fear (like unconscious projections onto a picture), boys report higher levels of fear, and more severe PTSS (Greenbaum, Erlich, & Toubiana, 1993; Laufer & Solomon, 2006) suggesting that fear in boys is more internalized.

Overall, more research is needed so as to fully understand how the exposure to armed conflict impacts youth. Critics have argued that models that assume a direct relationship between exposure to war-related violence and later mental health problems are too narrow in their focus and have failed to capture the complex, overlapping pathways that determine how organized violence disrupts or shapes a child's life (Miller & Rasmussen, 2010). It is unclear how variables within political violence (such as the type, duration, frequency of exposure, and proximity to events) mediate the development of social, emotional, cognitive, and psychological issues among children who are exposed to armed conflict (Barber, 2008, 2013; Cairns, 1996; Cummings et al., 2017; Dubow, Huesmann, & Boxer, 2009). Variability in the methodologies and instruments used to measure symptoms (Betancourt et al., 2012) secondary to political violence further complicates the synthesis of evidence.

INDIRECT EFFECTS AND SOCIALLY TOXIC MESSAGES

Beyond directly witnessing violence, children can also internalize the cultural messaging surrounding armed political conflicts can also affect psychological and behavioral outcomes. For example, children who view political hardship as ideologically or spiritually meaningful may show resilience against some of the negative effects of violence exposure (Wright, Masten, & Narayan, 2012). This coping strategy was shown to protect against the development of internalizing problems among Israeli youth (Punamäki, 1996), and the youth who joined the African National Congress Youth League (aka the "Young Lions") in South Africa during the apartheid era. Joining this political movement, which fought to bring democracy through strikes and walkouts, seemed to buffer the impact of the government's violence against people of color (Slone, Kaminer, & Durrheim, 2002).

The worst situation for youth seems to be when they are given information about the threat in such a way that both their fears and their inability for action increase. Children who internalize the event and use it as a basis for peace or social justice show empowerment rather than pessimism while children with a sense of fear and a feeling of helplessness after learning of the threat of violence seem to have worse outcomes (Punamäki, Qouta, & El-Sarraj, 2001). This is particularly concerning regarding media or internet exposure that children may access with little to none adult supervision. Research following the Oklahoma City bombing found that the majority of television watched was related to the bombing, and children who watched more television coverage of the attack reported more distressing thoughts and PTSS (Pfefferbaum et al., 2001). Because of the growing ubiquity of social media and the Internet to spread not just violent images but also messages of hate or discrimination, more research is needed into how youth internalize the potentially socially toxic messages that proliferate during times of armed conflict.

Social toxicity refers to the extent to which the social environment is psychologically poisonous. A socially toxic environment contains serious threats to the development of identity, competence, moral reasoning, trust, hope, and the other features of personality and ideology that are the building blocks for success in school, family, work, and the community. What social and cultural poisons are psychologically equivalent to lead and smoke in the air, PCBs in the water, and pesticides in the food chain? We can see social toxicity in the values, practices, and institutions that breed feelings of racism and misogyny, fear about the world, feelings of rejection by adults inside and outside the family, exposure to traumatic images and experiences, absence of adult supervision, and/or inadequate exposure to positive adult role models. These feelings and experiences arise from being embedded in a shallow materialist culture, being surrounded with negative and degrading media messages, and being deprived of relationships with sources that provide role models of character within a school, the neighborhood, and the larger community. Here we consider elements of social toxicity (i.e., misogyny and sexualization or exploitation) that are especially relevant to the well-being and development of young children in situations of warfare and political violence.

Misogyny

The messages that young boys and young girls receive about their inherent worth, value, and abilities are staggeringly different. Across the world, misogyny is demonstrated in clear differences between selective abortions, school graduation rates, the frequency of forced marriages, physical and sexual violence, and power differentials in gender roles between male and female children. Although the United States has reached "gender parity" (i.e., girls and boys have equal literacy and school attendance rates), that is not to say that children in the United States are not exposed to misogynist messages. Indeed, 50 percent of respondents in a representative survey of US adults endorsed the statement "women are not qualified to hold high-power positions in companies or government" (Pew Research Center, 2015).

Refugee children who come to a classroom as a result of fleeing war or other humanitarian crises may be from cultures that devalue girls' education and autonomy. Female students may be at greater risk to experience psychological distress that disrupts academic or social functioning when crises occur in the immediate community. Studies of both domestic and international disasters have found that on average, female gender is a significant predictor of developing PTSS in children (Furr, Comer, Edmunds, & Kendall, 2010). Even in studies of exposure to disasters and political violence in the United States, elementary school-aged girls are more likely to report being upset (Lengua, Long, Smith, & Meltzoff, 2005), despite reporting higher levels of social support from parents following traumatic events (Vernberg La Greca, Silverman, & Prinstein, 1996).

Why would girls show more symptoms of trauma even after receiving parental support? On one hand, genetics or hormone levels might impact girls' level of anxiety, depression, or internalizing symptoms (Tolin & Foa, 2006; Yehuda, 1999). On the other hand, this may be partly related to differences in parenting and behavioral expectations that reinforce messages for girls to be more sensitive or anxious than boys. For example, parents who repeatedly ask their girls about their feelings might increase their children's rumination and prevent them from returning to normal routines. Studies conducted during the two-decades-long conflict between British Loyalist Protestants and independence-seeking Catholics in Northern Ireland (also called "The Troubles") demonstrated just this effect: girls were more likely to report internalizing symptoms of anxiety or fearfulness whereas boys were more likely to report externalizing problems (e.g., Cummings et al., 2011; Granleese et al., 1989). In decades of debate, researchers have examined to what extent the grades of low-achieving students are influenced by low expectations and a lack of attention from teachers (Jussim & Harber, 2005). These "self-fulfilling prophecies" can act in similar ways following traumatic events – in trying to be sensitive to students' needs, adults may actually be reinforcing and strengthening gender stereotypes.

Sexualization and Sexual Exploitation

Early objectification promotes messages that children offer little value beyond their physical bodies. Young girls are inundated with images in mass media that show thin, overly sexualized women (APA, 2007; Durham, 2010). Girls have higher levels of internalization of these messages compared to boys, and are more likely to report lower body satisfaction and self-esteem as a result (Dohnt & Tiggemann, 2006; Murnen, Smolak, Mills, & Good, 2003; Starr & Ferguson, 2012). Sexualization reinforces cultural ideals that tie self-worth to standards of physical attractiveness, and ultimately prevents children from obtaining developmentally appropriate information about sexuality.

It is the responsibility of adults to protect children from adult sexual experiences and to ensure that children are off-limits to adults sexually (Garbarino, 1994). Although the majority of studies regarding sexual exploitation are carried out among adolescents, this does not mean that young children are not at risk before, during, and after crises. Because young children rely heavily on caregivers, especially in the wake of disasters, victims are unlikely and unwilling to disclose sexual abuse out of fear of retribution or removal from their homes (Rafferty, 2013; UNICEF, 2013). Children are also likely to become separated from their families during emergencies, and are at an increased vulnerability to sexual abuse or exploitation from outside perpetrators (UNICEF, 2014).

The stigma of sexual abuse and the isolation that exploited children experience make it difficult for educators to identify and protect these children. Children may feel too ashamed to admit these abuses have occurred or may fear backlash from their abuser. Risk factors for abuse include previous abuse (McClanahan, McClelland, Abram, & Teplin, 1999), low-income and/or high-crime neighborhood residence (Cecchet & Thoburn, 2014; Twill, Green, & Traylor, 2010; Rafferty, 2008), and few adult connections (i.e., youth in foster care or homeless or runaway youth; Fong & Cardoso, 2010; Wilson & Butler, 2014).

Political violence is an ongoing phenomenon in Middle Eastern countries and therefore provides a unique view of how exposure to chronic, repeated acts of political violence impacts youth and their development. While exposure to single-instance attacks that occur during acts of terrorism is of growing concern, a second major concern in the research literature is understanding how prolonged exposure to conflict impacts development compared to single-instance exposure (Barber, 2013), and how generalizable effects across individual conflicts truly are (Cairns, 1996). Studies of the impact of prolonged conflict on child and adolescent development often show increased likelihood of internalizing (such as anxiety or depression) or externalizing (such as aggression or acting out) symptoms. For example, studies of Palestinian children have demonstrated higher rates of PTSS and sleep disturbance and reemergence of PTSS during periods of heightened violence compared to Israeli children who experience relatively minor exposure (Miller-Graff & Cummings, 2017). Additionally, use of substances like alcohol and other consciousness-altering drugs is sometimes suggested to increase as a coping mechanism for stress (Schiff, Zweig, Benbenishty, & Hasin, 2007). Furthermore, studies of prolonged political violence exposure demonstrate, on average, greatest impact among youth who are most vulnerable, particularly those living in low-income communities or those with high levels of exposure to community violence. For example, a study of Israeli teenagers found that the greatest increase in alcohol consumption was among those with the closest physical and psychological proximity to terrorist attacks (Schiff et al., 2007).

Regardless of single or prolonged exposure, trauma symptoms do not necessarily dissipate in the days following an attack. Resiliency is an ongoing process that varies across individuals, but can be transient and mutable over time depending on different factors. In countries such as South Africa and Northern Ireland, continued inequality and segregation have led to secondhand trauma in the newest generation of children and adolescents. Poverty, experiences of discrimination, and a lack of access to education and healthcare has led some children to further endorse violence as a means to gain a better life.

Given the broad, disruptive nature of political conflict, it is striking that some children seem resilient to the impacts of trauma. How is it that some children will not show long-term symptoms of anxiety or developmental disruption? Children's experiences will be filtered through their most immediate environment, such as the impact the event has on their family functioning. Children who report high levels of parental supervision, strong parent–child relationships, and security within their communities are less likely to report any PTSS even after direct exposure to political violence. However, this relation also shows bidirectional effects between parents and children. Children's signs of stress may lead to more strained parenting conditions. Parents may then exhibit more difficulty and stress in their own functioning, which may impair their parenting ability and worsen their children's functioning. Support for this view is found in a study of parents of distressed children after the September 11 attacks (Phillips, Featherman, & Liu, 2004), in which these parents reported more vulnerabilities and stronger feelings of threat one year later compared to parents of non-distressed children

Further, when trauma becomes chronic, its effects can manifest in ways that at first glance appear paradoxical – namely, less rather than more overt distress. A study of Israeli children subjected to repeated shelling from Lebanon found that these children appeared no more anxious than kids living in similar communities far enough from the border that they never experienced shelling (Bat-Zion & Levy-Shiff, 1993). The best explanation for this is that for the children living near the border, chronic shelling became a way of life, and they engaged in a process of adaptation (or *habituation*, to use a term psychologists prefer). Of course, this process of adaptation itself can mask deeper existential issues of meaningfulness as well as confidence in the future and trust in adults. In countries with ongoing violence, such as Israel and Palestine, some children show signs of habituation, with others reporting more substance use as a means to cope. Therefore, it is vital to examine and assist not just children who show symptoms of anxiety or trauma, but those who seem resilient as well.

Implications and Recommendations

After what seems like a senseless attack, everyone is left with a feeling of "now what?" If you are a parent, or work or interact with children, you should keep a few things in mind. The vast majority of children will recover naturally as their lives and the environment return to normal. Disruptions to normal family life (such as not eating dinner together, or witnessing parents crying) can impede children's healing, which is why children who were already facing disruptions pre-disaster have a much harder time coping. Following this, note that children mirror adults. Adults who are calm in their thoughts and actions and positive about the future will transmit these messages to their children. Remember to be emotionally responsive and sensitive when talking to children, and to dispel unfounded rumors. At the same time, children can see the world differently than adults – and it is important to shield them from the most violent images of destruction. They are more likely to feel personally connected to the attack, to feel personally threatened, and to see the situation in black and white. If they hear demonizing statements about a particular group after the attack, and do not have any opportunity for positive interactions that facilitate understanding, they are more likely to internalize fear, distrust, or hatred for that group. In highly segregated countries and communities like South Africa and Northern Ireland this is especially true.

Just as the public health response to physical toxins introduced during disasters includes removing and replacing any contaminated materials, so teachers and caregivers can provide "antidotes" to socially toxic messages in the form of developmental assets. Research has clearly demonstrated that those who are already dealing with other stressors are at the greatest risk for PTSS. Thus, it is crucial again to point out that socially toxic messages are the most damaging for children who are already vulnerable from the impact of risk factors such as poverty, abuse, or exploitation (Cummings et al., 2017; Shaw, 2003).

Unfortunately, low-income communities often are hit hardest and left the most devastated during warfare. For example, the Flint, Michigan, water crisis impacted the physical health of citizens by introducing elevated levels of *E. coli* bacteria, pollutants, and lead (a neurotoxin in large doses) into the drinking water. When tested, children from disadvantaged areas or neighborhoods with high levels of minority populations had the most elevated levels of lead in their blood (Hanna-Attisha, LaChance, Sadler, & Schnepp, 2016). These children, the researchers noted, already had a higher likelihood of exposure to lead poisoning due to poor nutrition and concentrated poverty, resulting in older and lower-quality housing (Hanna-Attisha et al., 2016). Like physical toxicity, social toxicity can be fatal – in the form of suicide, homicide, drug-related, and other lifestyle-related preventable deaths. But mostly it results in diminished "humanity" in the lives of children and youth by virtue of leading them to live in a state of degradation, whether they know it or not. It is the antithesis of what positive psychology aspires to foster in kids – and in their parents, teachers, and neighbors.

Social norms surrounding the emotional sensitivity of young girls not only lead to psychological distress but also permit the emotional distress of boys to go overlooked. Educators can promote the developmental asset of empowerment through activities in which all students have an opportunity to express their feelings, strategies for moving forward, and ways to contribute or give back to the community. Additionally, be sure to provide opportunities for all students to participate and respond with precise comments about each student's participation in order to validate them.

An antidote to socially toxic messages of sexual exploitation comes in the form of boundaries and expectations. This developmental asset reinforces the need for safety within children's homes and the proper expectations and relationships between children and adults. Being aware that sexual exploitation is possible in the wake of disasters, especially for students with weak connections to others, is an important first step in identifying which children may be at risk. Another activity that children can use to process traumatic events includes narrative books or activities such as Garbarino's "Let Talk about Violence." This coloring book is geared toward young children and gives them an opportunity to write about their lives and to form a meaningful narrative around their experiences in a creative way.

Children who do not act in gender-typical ways are at greater risk from bullying at school and physical abuse at home. Activities that promote the developmental asset of support might include team-building, cooperation, or empathy-building activities. Further, you can work with your school to set up safe, low-cost childcare for parents who feel torn between going back to work in order to provide for their children and wanting to make sure their children are taken care of (Peek & Fothergill, 2009). This can minimize some of the stress parents feel at home.

Clearly, growing up in societies where racism and discrimination are prevalent can have serious negative consequences for youth; however, not all youth who experience the same level of racial discrimination experience the same level of adverse consequences due to this exposure (Neblett et al., 2008). Particularly, research has shown that highly positive racial experience in influential adults appears to have a buffering effect that reduces the negative impacts of racism (Neblett et al., 2008). Thus, activities that emphasize racial pride, positive self-worth, and egalitarian values, as well as discussion of the racial barriers youth of color will likely encounter, will reinforce the development asset of positive identity.

CONCLUSION

Social toxicity in the wake of disasters can have long-term, compounding negative effects on young children. While a growing literature has examined the broad impact of disasters on development and how teachers can respond (e.g., Szente, 2016), more research is needed so as to determine how the individual characteristics of children, their families, and their teachers may interact in a community or society that is reeling from crises. However, any steps taken to reduce messages of rejection and instead promote the development of character will allow children not to just be resilient but to thrive later.

Note

1. The case study has been de-identified to protect confidentiality.

REFERENCES

American Psychological Association (APA) (2007). Report of the APA Task Force on the Sexualization of Girls. Retrieved from www.apa.org/pi/women/programs/girls/report-summary.pdf.

American Psychological Association (APA) (2017). *APA Handbook of trauma psychology, Volume 1.* Washington, DC: American Psychological Association.

Barber, B. K. (2008). Contrasting portraits of war: Youths' varied experiences with political violence in Bosnia and Palestine. *International Journal of Behavioral Development, 32,* 298–309.

Barber, B. K. (2013). Annual research review: The experience of youth with political conflict – challenging notions of resilience and encouraging research refinement. *Journal of Child Psychology and Psychiatry, 54,* 461–473. doi:10.1111/jcpp.12056

Bat-Zion, N., & Levy-Shiff, R. (1993). Children in war: Stress and coping reactions under the threat of Scud missile attacks and the effect of proximity. In L. Leavitt & N. Fox (eds.), *The psychological effects of war and violence on children* (pp. 143–161). Hillsdale, NJ: Lawrence Erlbaum.

Betancourt, T. S., Agnew-Blais, J., Gillman, S. E., Williams, D. R., & Ellis, B. H. (2010). Past horrors, present struggles: The role of stigma in the association between war experiences and psychosocial adjustment among former child soldiers in Sierra Leone. *Social Science Medicine, 70*, 17–26. doi:10.1016/j.socscimed.2009.09.038

Betancourt, T. S., Borisova, I., Williams, T. P., et al. (2012). Psychosocial adjustment and mental health in former child soldiers: A systematic review of the literature and recommendations for future research. *Journal of Child Psychology and Psychiatry, 54*, 17–36, doi:10.1111/j.1469.-7610.2012.02620.x

Brave Heart, M., & DeBruyn, L. (1998). The American Indian holocaust: Healing historical unresolved grief. *American Indian and Alaska Native Mental Health Research, 8*, 60–82.

Bronfenbrenner, U. (1979). *The ecology of human development: Experiments by design and nature.* Cambridge, MA: Harvard University Press.

Bronfenbrenner, U., & Morris, P. A. (1998). The ecology of developmental processes. In W. Damon & R. M. Lerner (eds.), *Handbook of child psychology: Theoretical models of human development* (pp. 993–1028). Hoboken, NJ: John Wiley.

Cairns, E. (1996). *Children and political violence.* Malden, UK: Blackwell Publishing.

Cecchet, S. J., & Thoburn, J. (2014). The psychological experience of child and adolescent sex trafficking in the United States: Trauma and resilience in survivors. *Psychological Trauma: Theory, Research, Practice, and Policy, 6*, 482–493. doi:10.1037/a0035763

Chemtob, C. M., Nomura, Y., Rajendran, K., et al. (2010). Impact of maternal post-traumatic stress disorder and depression following exposure to the September 11 attacks on preschool children's behavior. *Child Development, 81*, 1129–1141. doi:10.1111/j.1467-8624.2010.01458.x

Comer, J. S., Fan, B., Duarte, C. S., et al. (2010). Attack-related life disruption and child psychopathology in New York City public schoolchildren 6 months post-9/11. *Journal of Clinical Child & Adolescent Psychology, 39*, 460–469. doi:10.1080/15374416.2010.486314

Cummings, E. M., Merrilees, C. E., Schermerhorn, A. C., et al. (2011). Longitudinal pathways between political violence and child adjustment: The role of emotional security about the community in Northern Ireland. *Journal of Abnormal Child Psychology, 39*, 213–224. doi:10.1007/s10802-010-9457-3

Cummings, E. M., Merrilees, C. E., Taylor, L. K., & Mondi, C. F. (2017). Developmental and social-ecological perspectives on children, political violence, and armed conflict. *Development and Psychopathology, 29*, 1–10. doi:10.1017/S0954579416001061

Danieli, Y. (1998). Introduction: History and conceptual foundations. In Y. Danieli (ed.), *International handbook of multigenerational legacies of trauma* (pp. 1–13). New York: Plenum Press.

Dekel, R., & Goldblatt, H. (2008). Is there intergenerational transmission of trauma? The case of combat veterans' children. *American Journal of Orthopsychiatry, 78*(3), 281–289. https://doi-org.ez.lib.jjay.cuny.edu/10.1037/a0013955.

Dohnt, H., & Tiggemann, M. (2006). The contribution of peer and media influences to the development of body satisfaction and self-esteem in young girls: A prospective study. *Developmental Psychology, 42*, 929–936. doi:10.1037/0012-1649.42.5.92

Dubow, E. F., Huesmann, L. R., & Boxer, P. (2009). A social-cognitive-ecological framework for understanding the impact of exposure to persistent ethnic-political violence on children's psychosocial adjustment. *Clinical Child and Family Psychology Review, 12*, 113–126. doi:10.1007/s10567-009-0050-7

Durham, M. G. (2010). *The Lolita effect: The media sexualization of young girls and five keys to fixing it.* New York: Overlook Press.

Fairbrother, G., Stuber, J., Galea, S., Fleischman, A. R., & Pfefferbaum, B. (2003). Post-traumatic stress reactions in New York City children after the September 11, 2001, terrorist attacks. *Ambulatory Pediatrics, 3*, 304–311. doi:10.1367/1539-4409(2003)003<0304:psriny>2.0.CO;2

Fong, R., & Cardoso, J. B. (2010). Child human trafficking victims: Challenges for the child welfare system. *Evaluation and Program Planning*, 33, 311–316. doi:10.1016/j.evalprogplan.2009.06.018

Furr, J. M., Comer, J. S., Edmunds, J. M., & Kendall, P. C. (2010). Disasters and youth: A meta-analytic examination of posttraumatic stress. *Journal of Consulting and Clinical Psychology*, 78, 765–780. doi:10.1037/a0021482

Garbarino, J. (1994). *Raising children in a socially toxic environment*. San Francisco, CA: Jossey-Bass.

Gil-Rivas, V., Silver, R. C., Holman, E. A., McIntosh, D. N., & Poulin, M. (2007). Parental response and adolescent adjustment to the September 11, 2001 terrorist attacks. *Journal of Traumatic Stress*, 20, 1063–1068. doi:10.1002/jts.20277

Granleese, J., Turner, I., & Trew, K. (1989). Teachers' and boys' and girls' perceptions of competence in the primary school: The importance of physical competence. *British Journal of Educational Psychology*, 59, 31–37. doi:10.1111/j.2044-8279.1989.tb03073.x

Greenbaum, C. W., Erlich, C., & Toubiana, Y. H. (1993). Settler children and the Gulf War. In L. Leavitt & N. Fox (eds.), *The psychological effects of war and violence on children* (pp. 109–130). Hillsdale, NJ: Lawrence Erlbaum.

Grusovin, K., Makome, A., Nayak, B., Nicolai, S., & Verhey, B. (2009). *Machel study 10-year strategic review: Children and conflict in a changing world*. United Nations report. New York: United Nations Children's Fund.

Gurwitch, R. H., Pfefferbaum, B., & Leftwich, M. J. T. (2002). The impact of terrorism on children: Considerations for a new era. *Journal of Trauma Practice*, 1, 101–124. doi:10.1300/J189v01n03_06

Hagan, J. F. (2005). Psychosocial implications of disaster or terrorism on children: A guide for the pediatrician. *Pediatrics*, 116, 787–795. doi:10.1542/peds.2005-1498

Hanna-Attisha, M., LaChance, J., Sadler, R. C., & Schnepp, A. C. (2016). Elevated blood lead levels in children associated with the Flint drinking water crisis: A spatial analysis of risk and public health response. *American Journal of Public Health*, 106, 283–290. doi:10.2105/AJPH.2015.303003

Hoven, C. W., Duarte, C. S., Lucas, C. P., et al. (2005). Psychopathology among New York City public school children 6 months after September 11. *Archives of General Psychiatry*, 62, 545–551. doi:10.1001/archpsyc.62.5.545

Joshi, P. T., & O'Donnell, D. A. (2003). Consequences of child exposure to war and terrorism. *Clinical Child and Family Psychology Review*, 6, 275–292. doi:1096-4037/03/1200-0275/0

Jussim, L., & Harber, K. D. (2005). Teacher expectations and self-fulfilling prophecies: Knowns and unknowns, resolved and unresolved controversies. *Personality and Social Psychology Review*, 9, 131–155. doi:10.1207/s15327957pspr0902_3

Laufer, A., & Solomon, Z. (2006). Post-traumatic symptoms and post-traumatic growth among Israeli youth exposed to terror incidents. *Journal of Social and Clinical Psychology*, 25(4), 429–447. doi:10.1521/jscp.2006.25.4.429

Lengua, L. J., Long, A. C., Smith, K. I., & Meltzoff, A. N. (2005). Pre-attack symptomatology and temperament as predictors of children's responses to the September 11 terrorist attacks. *Journal of Child Psychology and Psychiatry*, 46, 631–645. doi:10.1111/j.1469-7610.2004.00378.x

Macksoud, M. S., & Aber, J. L. (1996). The war experiences and psychosocial development of children in Lebanon. *Child Development*, 67, 70–88.

Marshall, M. G., & Elzinga-Marshall, G. (2017). *Global report 2017: Conflict, governance and state fragility*. Center for Systemic Peace. Retrieved from www.systemicpeace.org/vlibrary/GlobalReport2017.pdf.

Masten, A. S., & Narayan, A. J. (2012). Child development in the context of disaster, war, and terrorism: Pathways of risk and resilience. *Annual Review of Psychology, 63*, 227–257. doi:10.1146/annurev-psych-120710-100356

McClanahan, S. F., McClelland, G. M., Abram, K. M., & Teplin, L. A. (1999). Pathways into prostitution among female jail detainees and their implications for mental health services. *Psychiatric Services, 50*, 1606–1613. doi:10.1176/ps.50.12.1606

McWhirter, L. (1984). Is getting caught in a riot more stressful for children than seeing a scary film or moving to a new school? Paper presented at the annual conference of the Northern Irish Branch of the BPS, Port Ballintrae, Northern Ireland.

Merrilees, C. E., Cairns, E., Taylor, L. K., et al. (2013). Social identity and youth aggressive and delinquent behaviors in a context of political violence. *Political Psychology, 34*, 695–711. doi:10.1111/pops.12030

Miller, K. E., & Rasmussen, A. (2010). War exposure, daily stressors, and mental health in conflict and post-conflict settings: Bridging the divide between trauma-focused and psychosocial frameworks. *Social Science & Medicine, 70*, 7–16. doi:10.1016/j.socscimed.2009.09.029

Miller-Graff, L., & Cummings, E. M. (2017). The Israeli–Palestinian conflict: Effects on youth adjustment, available interventions, and future research directions. *Developmental Review, 43*, 1–47. doi:10.1016/j.dr.2016.10.001

Murnen, S. K., Smolak, L., Mills, J. A., & Good, L. (2003). Thin, sexy women and strong, muscular men: Grade-school children's responses to objectified images of women and men. *Sex Roles, 49*, 427–437. doi:10.1023/A:1025868320206

Neblett, E. W., White, R. L., Ford, K. R., et al. (2008). Patterns of racial socialization and psychological adjustment: Can parental communications about race reduce the impact of racial discrimination? *Journal of Research on Adolescence, 18*(3), 477–515.

Otto, M. W., Henin, A., Hirshfeld-Becker, D. R., et al. (2007). Post-traumatic stress disorder symptoms following media exposure to tragic events: Impact of 9/11 on children at risk for anxiety disorders. *Journal of Anxiety Disorders, 21*, 888–902. doi:10.1016/j.janxdis.2006.10.008

Peek, L., & Fothergill, A. (2009). Using focus groups: Lessons from studying daycare centers, 9/11, and Hurricane Katrina. *Qualitative Research, 9*, 31–59. doi:10.1177/1468794108098029

Pew Research Center (2015). Women and leadership: Public says women are equally qualified, but barriers persist. Pew Research Center. Retrieved from www.pewsocialtrends.org/2015/01/14/women-and-leadership/.

Pfefferbaum, B., Nixon, S. J., Tivis, R. D., et al. (2001). Television exposure in children after a terrorist incident. *Psychiatry, 64*, 202–211. doi:10.1521/psyc.64.3.202.18462

Phillips, D., Featherman, D. L., & Liu, J. (2004). Children as an evocative influence on adults' reactions to terrorism. *Applied Developmental Science, 8*, 195–210. doi:10.1207/s1532480xads0804_3

Punamäki, R. L. (1996). Can ideological commitment protect children's psychosocial well-being in situations of political violence? *Child Development, 67*, 55–69. doi:10.1111/j.1467-8624.1996.tb01719.x

Punamäki, R., Qouta, S., & El-Sarraj, E. (2001). Resiliency factors predicting adjustment after political violence among Palestinian children. *International Journal of Behavioral Development, 25*, 256–267.

Qouta, S., Punamäki, R. L., & El-Sarraj, E. (2008). Child development and family mental health in war and military violence: The Palestinian experience. *International Journal of Behavioral Development, 32*, 310–321. doi:10/1177/0165025408090973

Rafferty, Y. (2008). The impact of trafficking on children: Psychological and social policy perspectives. *Child Development Perspectives, 2*, 13–18. doi:10.1111/j.1750-8606.2008.00035.x

Rafferty, Y. (2013). Child trafficking and commercial sexual exploitation: A review of promising prevention policies and programs. *American Journal of Orthopsychiatry, 83*, 559–575. doi:10.1111/ajop.12056

Rosenheck, R., & Fontana, A. (1998). Warrior fathers and warrior sons: Intergenerational aspects of trauma. In Y. Danieli (ed.), *International handbook of multigenerational legacies of trauma* (pp. 225–242). New York: Plenum Press.

Rowland-Klein, D., & Dunlop, R. (1998). The transmission of trauma across generations: Identification with parental trauma in children of Holocaust survivors. *Australian and New Zealand Journal of Psychiatry, 32*(3), 358–369.

Sameroff, A. J., Bartko, W. T., Baldwin, A., Baldwin, C., & Seifer, R. (1998). Family and social influences on the development of child competence. In M. Lewis & C. Feiring (eds.), *Families, risk, and competence* (pp. 161–185). Mahwah, NJ: Lawrence Erlbaum.

Schiff, M., & Fang, L. (2014). Adolescent substance use in Israel: The roles of exposure to political traumas and posttraumatic stress symptoms. *Psychology of Addictive Behaviors, 28*, 453–463.

Schiff, M., Pat-Horenczyk, R., Benbenishty, R., et al. (2012). High school students' posttraumatic symptoms, substance abuse and involvement in violence in the aftermath of war. *Social Science & Medicine, 75*, 1321–1328. doi:10.1016/j.socscimed.2012.05.010

Schiff, M., Zweig, H. H., Benbenishty, R., & Hasin, D. S. (2007). Exposure to terrorism and Israeli youths' cigarette, alcohol, and cannabis use. *American Journal of Public Health, 97*, 1852–1858. doi:10.2105/AJPH.2006.090514

Schuster, M. A., Stein, B. D., Jaycox, L. H., et al. (2001). A national survey of stress reactions after the September 11, 2001, terrorist attacks. *New England Journal of Medicine, 345*, 1507–1512. doi:10.1056/NEJM200111153452024

Schwartz, S., Dohrenwend, B., & Levav, I. (1994). Nongenetic familial transmission of psychiatric disorders? Evidence from children of Holocaust survivors. *Journal of Health and Social Behavior, 35*, 385–402. doi:jstor.org/stable/2137216

Shaw, J. A. (2003). Children exposed to war/terrorism. *Clinical Child and Family Psychology Review, 6*, 237–246.

Slone, M., Kaminer, D., & Durrheim, K. (2002). The contributions of political life events to psychological distress among South African adolescents. *Political Psychology, 21*(3), 465–487.

Slone, M., Lavi, I., Ozer, E. J., & Pollak, A. (2017). The Israeli–Palestinian conflict: Meta-analysis of exposure and outcome relations for children of the region. *Children and Youth Services Review, 74*, 50–61. doi:10.1016/j.childyouth.2017.01.019

Starr, C. R., & Ferguson, G. M. (2012). Sexy dolls, sexy grade-schoolers? Media & maternal influences on young girls' self-sexualization, *Sex Roles, 67*(463), 463–476. doi:10.1007/s11199-012-0183-x

Stuber, J., Fairbrother, G., Galea, S., et al. (2002). Determinants of counseling for children in Manhattan after the September 11 attacks. *Psychiatric Services, 53*, 815–822. doi:10.1176/appi.ps.53.7.815

Szente, J. (2016). Assisting children caught in disasters: Resources and suggestions for practitioners. *Early Childhood Education Journal, 44*, 201–207. doi:10.1007/s10643-015-0709-2

Thabet, A. A., & Thabet, S. (2015). Trauma, PTSD, anxiety, and resilience in Palestinian children in the Gaza strip. *British Journal of Education, Society & Behavioural Science, 11*, 1–13. doi:10.973/BJESBS/2015/19101

Tolin, D. F., & Foa, E. B. (2006). Sex differences in trauma and posttraumatic stress disorder: A quantitative review of 25 years of research. *Psychological Bulletin, 132*(6), 959–992. doi:10.1037/0033-2909.132.6.959

Twill, S. E., Green, D. M., & Traylor, A. (2010). A descriptive study on sexually exploited children in residential treatment. *Child & Youth Care Forum, 39*, 187–199. doi:10.1007/s10566-010-9098-2

UNICEF (2013). Minimum standards for child protection in humanitarian action. UNICEF Child Protection Working Group. Retrieved from www.cpaor.net/sites/default/files/cp/CP-Minimum-Standards-English-2013.pdf.

UNICEF (2014). Girls' education and gender equality. Retrieved from www.unicef.org/education/bege_70640.html.

UNICEF (2016). The state of the world's children 2016: A fair chance for every child. Retrieved from www.unicef.org/publications/index_91711.html.

Vernberg, E. M., La Greca, A. M., Silverman, W. K., & Prinstein, M. J. (1996). Prediction of posttraumatic stress symptoms in children after Hurricane Andrew. *Journal of Abnormal Psychology, 105*, 237–248. doi:10.1037/0021-843X.105.2.237

Wilson, A. C., Lengua, L. J., Meltzoff, A. N., & Smith, K. A. (2010). Parenting and temperament prior to September 11, 2001, and parenting specific to 9/11 as predictors of children's posttraumatic stress symptoms following 9/11. *Journal of Clinical Child & Adolescent Psychology, 39*(4), 445–459. doi:10.1080/ 15374416.2010.486317

Wilson, B., & Butler, L. D. (2014). Running a gauntlet: A review of victimization and violence in the pre-entry, post-entry, and peri-/post- exit periods of commercial sexual exploitation. *Psychological Trauma: Theory, Research, Practice, and Policy, 6*, 494–504. doi:10.1037/a0032977

Wright, M. O. D., Masten, A. S., & Narayan, A. J. (2013). Resilience processes in development: Four waves of research on positive adaptation in the context of adversity. In S. Goldstein & R. Brooks (eds.), *Handbook of resilience in children* (pp. 15–37). Boston, MA: Springer.

Yehuda, R. (1999). Biological factors associated with susceptibility to posttraumatic stress disorder. *Canadian Journal of Psychiatry, 44*, 34–39. doi:10.1177/070674379904400104

8

Lesbian, Gay, Bisexual, Transgender, and Queer Youth and Social Justice

Susan W. Jones, Aradhana Bela Sood, Nancy Bearss, and Caroline S. Clauss-Ehlers

INTRODUCTION

According to the criminalization data updated by the Human Rights Campaign (HRC) as of January 2019, lesbian, gay, bisexual, transgender, and queer (LGBTQ) behavior is criminalized in sixty-nine countries around the world (HRC, 2019). In ten countries, LGBTQ behavior is punishable by death. In Nigeria, Lithuania, and Russia, anti-propaganda laws inhibit any advocacy for LGBTQ rights. Most of these countries are located in the global south, where the majority of the world's children ages ten to twenty-four reside. Although actual prevalence of LGBTQ children throughout the world is not known due to this discrimination, we do know that violence, a lack of legal protection, economic hardship, the lack of access to competent healthcare, and self-stigma occur (Keifer & Arshad, 2016).

In 2011, the United Nations submitted a report requested by the United Nations Human Rights Council under resolution 17/19 to the High Commissioner for Human Rights. The Council under this resolution requested the High Commissioner to "commission a study documenting discriminatory laws and practices and acts of violence against individuals based on their sexual orientation and gender identity, and how international human rights law can be used to end violence and related human rights violations based on sexual orientation and gender identity" (United Nations General Assembly, 2011, p. 1).

In this study, titled *Discriminatory Laws and Practices and Acts of Violence against Individuals Based on Their Sexual Orientation and Gender Identity*, reports of violations against LGBTQ individuals around the world were documented that include killings, rape, physical attack, and torture. The right to assemble, freedom of expression, and freedom from discrimination in employment, healthcare, and education were reportedly actively denied to LGBTQ individuals. The Universal Declaration of Human Rights states that "all human beings are born free and equal in dignity and rights." The denial of these rights to LGBTQ individuals has been, and continues to be, a violation of basic human rights.

An extension of this basic human right is the right and freedom to healthy sexual development. In some countries and regions, this basic right is actively denied. Human sexuality is a dynamic characteristic, heavily influenced by cultural and biological factors. The repression of this development leads to the many deleterious outcomes we see among LGBTQ children, such as increased rates of suicide, depression, economic hardship, and social isolation (Connolly, Zervos, Barone, Johnson, & Joseph, 2016; Russell & Fish, 2016).

Gender identity is formed as early as age three with gender constancy established by age five or six. A transgender child will identify as the opposite of their phenotypic gender and may be attracted to either males or females independent of their gender constancy. In an environment of repression and hardship, these children are particularly at risk for harm and abuse. Sexual attraction does not develop until preadolescence, at the onset of puberty. This can be as early as nine or ten years of age, when children are still in the early grades of school.

Discrimination against LGBTQ youth can begin as early as fifth grade in children who later identify as sexual minorities and may take the form of bullying (Schuster et al., 2015). The development of intimacy begins the realization of same-sex attraction, and some LGBTQ youth realize that they are not heterosexual. In cultures where heterosexuality is not only dominant but also enforced, this is a very precarious time for LGBTQ youth. By middle childhood, a young child can make social comparisons and form an abstract concept of himself or herself. The gender roles young people will adapt as they further age are heavily influenced by the intense socialization they have received in their early development. If repression of these gender roles occurs, youth are at high risk for true identity crises, self-harm, and morbidity (Kuhl & Martino, 2018).

CURRENT STATUS OF DISCRIMINATION AFFECTING LGBTQ YOUTH IN THE UNITED STATES

In January 2018, the US federal government created the Conscience and Religious Freedom division at the Department of Health and Human Services (DHHS) under which healthcare workers are allowed to object to participating in abortions, sterilizations, or other procedures related to reproduction. These laws have been in place since the Bush administration, but were narrowed in scope during the Obama presidency. The DHHS also proposed a rule entitled Protecting Statutory Conscience Rights in Health Care, which could increase the list of services that healthcare providers could decline to perform. The rule specifically cites abortion, sterilization, physician-assisted suicide, and advanced directives, but also allows for a wide interpretation of treatments that are counter to a healthcare provider's conscience or religion. Under this regulation, an agency or individual can cite religious convictions so as to refuse to treat or participate in the treatment of a patient that may include moral objections to gender identity or sexual orientation.

Title IX (US Department of Justice, 2013) prohibits sexual discrimination in any federally funded education program or activity. From 2014 through 2016, the US Department of Education specified that transgender students are also protected from gender discrimination under Title IX. By 2017, however, the federal government had rolled back Title IX protections that allowed transgender students to use bathrooms and locker rooms corresponding to their identified gender.

Twenty-one states, two territories, and the District of Columbia have laws that explicitly prohibit discrimination based on sexual orientation and gender identity. Additional protections are provided per state. On the federal level, in 2019, transgender individuals were excluded from military service, a pullback from previous legislation. Legal protection for businesses, healthcare providers, and others exists if religion is cited as a reason to refuse to serve LGBTQ people.

These recent changes in federal law have prompted reactions. The Trevor Project, a youth suicide hotline for LGBTQ youth, experienced a spike in calls from transgender youths in the twenty-four hours following the Twitter announcement of the ban on transgender military service. Contacts to The Trevor Project surged 116 percent in the two days after the 2016 presidential election (see www.thetrevorproject.org/).

In addition to the impact of laws affecting LGBTQ youth, there is clear evidence of the effect of this prejudice on the well-being of communities. Sexual minorities living in communities with high levels of prejudice died twelve years earlier than those living in supportive communities (Hatzenbuehler et al., 2014). Lesbian, gay, bisexual, transgender, and queer youth were more likely to attempt suicide in counties with greater antigay stigma (Hatzenbuehler et al., 2011). Lesbian, gay, bisexual, transgender, and queer youth, compared to heterosexual youth, struggle with a higher incidence of diseases and healthcare disparities because of physicians untrained to meet the unique needs of this group (Hafeez, Zeshan, Tahir, Jahan, & Naveed, 2017).

Health risks are evident in the United States for LGBTQ youth. Research shows, for instance, that gay and lesbian youth reported greater likelihood of having been treated for HIV in comparison to their heterosexual counterparts (Rew, Whittaker, Taylor-Seehafer, & Smith, 2005). This type of data is amplified by other research that shows clinical healthcare providers providing sexual healthcare services to LGBTQ youth may lack cultural competence (Knight, Shoveller, Carson, & Contreras-Whitney, 2014). Lesbian, gay, bisexual, transgender, and queer youth often lack comfort in developing a trusting relationship with their healthcare provider, which poses barriers to education, screening, or interventions to optimize health and prevent chronic disease (Hafeez et al., 2017).

Minority stress describes the excess anxiety that impacts individuals from a social minority group that is unique, chronic, and socially based (Meyer, 2003). Studies across several decades have examined a minority stress model applied to lesbians, gay men, and bisexuals, and consistently found poor mental and physical health outcomes in these groups (Baams, Grossman, & Russell, 2015; Brooks, 1981; Fergusson, Horwood, & Beautrais, 1999; Meyer, 1995). Extrapolating that to transgender individuals revealed similar prejudice, discrimination, and victimization.

One-half of mental illnesses have their onset during adolescence (Kessler et al., 2007; Paus, Keshavan, & Giedd, 2008). The higher prevalence of mental illness among LGBTQ youth is well documented. In a recent review of mental health in LGBTQ youth, Russell and Fish (2016) summarized both national and international studies supporting elevated rates of emotional distress, substance use, abuse, and dependence, symptoms related to mood and anxiety disorders, self-harm, suicidal ideation, and suicidal behavior in LGBTQ youth compared to heterosexual youth. The 2017 Youth Risk Behavior Surveillance summary showed an increase in both suicidal thoughts and plans, and a fourfold higher rate of suicide attempts in LGBTQ adolescents in comparison to heterosexual adolescents (Kann et al., 2018). A two- to threefold increase in the risk of depression, anxiety disorders, suicidal thoughts and attempts, self-harm, and inpatient and outpatient mental health treatment was found in a cohort of 180 transgender individuals compared to a cisgender control group (Reisner et al., 2015).

Lesbian, gay, bisexual, transgender, and queer youth have a higher risk of unsafe sexual behaviors at an earlier age than their non-sexual-minority peers (Cochran, Stewart, Ginzler, & Cauce, 2002; Tyler, 2013). This is related to bullying and physical and sexual abuse as well as to increased risk of depression, suicidal behaviors, and substance abuse stemming from family rejection (Fergusson et al., 1999; Reisner et al., 2015; Russell & Fish, 2016). Sexual minority youth are overly represented among homeless adolescents (Choi, Wilson, Shelton, & Gates, 2015), who are more prone to current major depressive episodes, post-traumatic stress disorder (PTSD), suicidal ideation, and suicide attempts (Keuroghlian, Shtasel, & Bassuk, 2014), and are also at higher risk to be in locked psychiatric facilities (Noell & Ochs, 2001). As a cause of their homelessness, 46 percent cited family rejection of their sexual orientation or gender identity, 50 percent were forced out by parents, and 33 percent were physically, emotionally, or sexually abused at home. Youth who have been rejected by their families tend to live in public places and risk associating with strangers (Rice et al., 2013).

One of the most obvious examples of social injustice in the United States affecting LGBTQ youth is conversion therapy (CT). Conversion therapy is also known as reparative therapy, and has been defined as "a range of dangerous and discredited practices that falsely claim to change a person's sexual orientation or gender identity or expression" (HRC, 2019). In 2009, the American Psychological Association (APA) Task Force on Appropriate Therapeutic Responses to Sexual Orientation published a report on research published in peer-reviewed journals that was focused on sexual orientation change efforts (SOCEs).

The Task Force's review covered journal articles from 1960 to 2007. Interestingly, the Task Force found that "most studies in this area were conducted before 1981, and only a few studies have been conducted in the last 10 years" (APA, 2009, p. 2). Further, the Task Force found that existing studies had "serious methodological problems" (p. 2). Between 1969 and 1978, only one study included a control group that compared those who received treatment with those who did not (Tanner, 1974). From 1999 to 2007, the Task Force found, "none of the recent research (1999–2007) meets methodological standards that permit conclusions regarding efficacy or safety" (p. 2). While the Task Force acknowledges some high-quality qualitative studies on individuals who have gone through SOCEs, these qualitative studies aren't evidence to indicate whether SOCEs are safe and effective. The Task Force concluded that "efforts to change sexual orientation are unlikely to be successful and involve some risk of harm, contrary to the claims of SOCE practitioners and advocates" (APA, 2009, p. v).

An estimated 350,000 LGBTQ adults had CT as adolescents. Sixteen thousand LGBTQ individuals, ages thirteen to seventeen, will receive CT from licensed healthcare professionals before they reach the age of eighteen in the thirty-two states that don't currently ban the practice, and an estimated 57,000 youth ages thirteen to seventeen across all states will receive CT from religious or spiritual advisors before they reach the age of eighteen (Mallory, Brown, & Conron, 2019). Although talk therapy is the most commonly used technique, some CT practitioners have also used aversion techniques such as inducing nausea, vomiting, or paralysis, electric shocks, or snapping an elastic band on the wrist to deter patients from contemplating same-sex attraction. Other techniques involve changing thought patterns by reframing desires, redirecting thoughts, or using hypnosis.

The following professional and scientific organizations have come together "to express professional and scientific consensus on the impropriety, inefficacy, and detriments of practices that seek to change a person's sexual orientation or gender identity, commonly referred to as 'conversion therapy'" (www.hrc.org/resources/the-lies-and-dangers-of-reparative-therapy). These include the American Academy of Child and Adolescent Psychiatry, the American Academy of Pediatrics, the American Association for Marriage and Family Therapy, the American College of Physicians, the American Counseling Association, the American Medical Association, the American Psychiatric Association, the American Psychological Association, the American Psychoanalytic Association, the American School Counselor Association, the American School Health Association, the National Association of Social Workers, the Pan American Health Organization, the Just the Facts Coalition, and the World Psychiatric Association. Indeed this practice should be outlawed throughout the world.

GLOBAL REFORM EFFORTS

As a result of the aforementioned report commissioned by the United Nations in 2011 in order to address discrimination against LGBTQ individuals, the High Commissioner recommends that Member States:

(a) Investigate promptly all reported killings and other serious incidents of violence perpetrated against individuals because of their actual or perceived sexual orientation or gender identity, whether carried out in public or in private by State or non-State actors, and hold perpetrators accountable, and establish systems for the recording and reporting of such incidents;

(b) Take measures to prevent torture and other forms of cruel, inhuman or degrading treatment on grounds of sexual orientation and gender identity, to investigate thoroughly all reported incidents of torture and ill-treatment, and to prosecute and hold accountable those responsible;

(c) Ensure that no one fleeing persecution on grounds of sexual orientation or gender identity is returned to a territory where his or her life or freedom would be threatened, and that asylum laws and policies recognize that persecution on account of one's sexual orientation or gender identity may be a valid basis for an asylum claim;

(d) Repeal laws used to criminalize individuals on grounds of homosexuality for engaging in consensual same-sex sexual conduct, and harmonize the age of consent for heterosexual and homosexual conduct; ensure that other criminal laws are not used to harass or detain people based on their sexuality or gender identity and expression, and abolish the death penalty for offenses involving consensual sexual relations;

(e) Enact comprehensive anti-discrimination legislation that includes discrimination on grounds of sexual orientation and gender identity among prohibited grounds and recognizes intersecting forms of discrimination; ensure that combating discrimination on grounds of sexual orientation and gender identity is included in the mandates of national human rights institutions;

(f) Ensure that individuals can exercise their rights to freedom of expression, association and peaceful assembly in safety without discrimination on grounds of sexual orientation and gender identity;

(g) Implement appropriate sensitization and training programs for police, prison officers, border guards, immigration officers and other law enforcement personnel, and support public information campaigns to counter homophobia and transphobia among the general public and targeted anti-homophobia campaigns in schools;

(h) Facilitate legal recognition of the preferred gender of transgender persons and establish arrangements to permit relevant identity documents to be reissued reflecting preferred gender and name, without infringements of other human rights (United Nations General Assembly, 2011, pp. 24–25).

The High Commissioner also recommends that the UN Human Rights Council:

(a) Keep regularly informed and updated on incidents of violence and discrimination linked to sexual orientation and gender identity;

(b) Encourage existing special procedures to continue to investigate and report on human rights violations affecting individuals on the basis of sexual orientation or gender identity within the context of their specific mandates (United Nations General Assembly, 2011, p. 25).

In addition to this proclamation and due to international advocacy by LGBTQ groups, several legislative cases have occurred of reversal of this discrimination

(Keifer & Arshad, 2016). Table 8.1 presents a timeline of recent reversals of discrimination in Nepal, Argentina, Bangladesh, Africa, South Africa, India, Mozambique, Malta, Chile, Colombia, and Pakistan.

TABLE 8.1 *Timeline of recent legislative cases of reversals of LGBTQ discrimination by country/region*

Year	Country/Region	Legislative Case of Reversal of LGBTQ Discrimination
2011	Nepal	• The 2011 Nepal census is the first ever to include a third gender category where people can indicate a gender other than female or male.
2012	Argentina	• Some of the most liberal rules in the world on changing gender are put in place, allowing people to alter their gender on official documents without first having to receive a psychiatric diagnosis or surgery.
2013	Bangladesh	• *Hijra* is formally recognized as a third gender by the Bangladeshi government.
2014	Africa	• The African Commission of Human and People's Rights passes a resolution condemning violence and human rights violations against the LGBTQ community. • The Organization of American States approves its seventh resolution on human rights, sexual orientation, and gender.
2014	South Africa	• The National Task Force on Gender and Sexual Orientation–Based Violence is established.
2015	India	• India's Supreme Court takes proactive action, recognizing transgender people as a legal third gender and granting transgender Indians status as an official minority requiring protection from discrimination.
2015	Mozambique	• Same-sex relationships are decriminalized, which revises the colonial penal code dating back to 1886.
2015	Malta	• Malta becomes one of two countries in the world with a directive on intersex rights. • In April 2015, Malta becomes the first country to prohibit "normalization" surgeries on intersex children by law.
2016	Chile	• The government of Chile announces a directive on intersex rights whereby the Ministry of Health issued guidance to stop "normalization" surgeries on intersex children.
2016	Colombia	• Colombia's Constitutional Court voted in favor of legal marriage equality.
2018	Pakistan	• The Transgender Persons Protection of Rights Act is passed. • This act gives transgender citizens core rights. • It prohibits discrimination in schools, when receiving medical care, on public transport, and at work. • It gives transgender people the right to vote and run for office. • It allows people to choose their identity. • It allows the chosen identity to be included on documents.

DISCRIMINATORY LAWS AND PRACTICES AND ACTS OF VIOLENCE AGAINST INDIVIDUALS BASED ON THEIR SEXUAL ORIENTATION AND GENDER IDENTITY

Active social media efforts have also been implemented in order to reverse discrimination against LGBTQ individuals worldwide. Most notable of these is the United Nations' Free and Equal public information campaign launched in July 2013 by the Office of the United Nations High Commissioner for Human Rights (OHCHR; see www.unfe.org). Free and Equal aims at "promoting equal rights and fair treatment" among LGBTQ individuals. As of 2017, Free and Equal reached 2.4 billion social media feeds around the world. Several of its campaign videos – including a popular Bollywood-themed clip "The Welcome" – rank among the most watched videos ever produced by the United Nations. National Free and Equal events have been organized in almost thirty countries, with visible support from the United Nations and from political, community, and religious leaders, as well as from celebrities in all regions of the world (see www.unfe.org/).

Global human rights organizations, such as Amnesty International and Human Rights Watch, now include LGBTQ rights in their platforms. In addition, OutRight Action International (https://outrightinternational.org/) and the International Lesbian, Gay, Bisexual, Trans and Intersex Association (https://ilga.org/) exist specifically to promote the rights of LGBTQ peoples and to advocate for justice around the world.

In 2013, the Gay, Lesbian and Straight Education Network (GLSEN) met with the United Nations Educational, Scientific and Cultural Organization (UNESCO) in order to address homophobic and transphobic prejudice and violence in schools (Kosciw & Pizmony-Levy, 2013). This international workgroup gathered to focus on "where would we like to be?" and "how will we get there?"

When asked "where would we like to be?" 86 percent of the group voted to establish evidence-based advocacy and 70 percent of the group prioritized sharing resources and best practices. More than 50 percent of the group wanted to have international accountability on LGBTQ issues and inclusive educational policies. Changing public opinion and secular state education for a pluralistic society were voted on as high priorities by less than 30 percent of the group. This reflects a clear shift to accountability and the promotion of facts and evidence-based practices from changing opinions or attitudes (Kosciw & Pizmony-Levy, 2013, p. 5). When asked how to achieve these goals, 74 percent of the group voted to develop LGBTQ education resource hubs and 71 percent voted to map funding opportunities. Policy research was voted on as a priority by 53 percent of the group (Kosciw & Pizmony-Levy, 2013, p. 6).

Clearly, the major focus for both the global and the educational communities is to raise awareness of discrimination against LGBTQ youth and individuals. As with many cases of repression, breaking the silence in an honest, truthful manner is the first step to justice. Discussions of this workgroup included how to work in hostile environments, the role of networking, and specific school-based educational efforts.

In addition to advocacy and awareness so as to promote justice for LGBTQ individuals, international efforts to combat bullying have grown. The International Bullying Prevention Association (IBPA) was founded in 2003 and focuses specifically on anti-bullying efforts (see https://ibpaworld.org/about/our-mission/). The IBPA is structured around four guiding principles:

- Ethical training practices
- Ethical conduct toward practices and performance
- Ethical conduct toward professional colleagues
- Ethical conduct toward community

In addition, many countries have adapted anti-bullying efforts for their school curricula. Every state in the United States has an anti-bullying law or policy, and many school districts have established anti-bullying policies. The Centers for Disease Control and Prevention (CDC) has guidelines and recommendations (www.stopbullying.gov/) that outline how school districts can best adhere to these policies. This includes evidence-based studies that confirm the value of anti-bullying efforts.

School-based anti-bullying efforts are needed given the increased prevalence of bullying experienced by LGBTQ youth (Kann et al., 2018). For instance, the Youth Risk Behavior Surveillance – United States 2017 survey (Kann et al., 2018) found that gay, lesbian, and bisexual students were more likely to be bullied in school than their heterosexual counterparts. The survey found that 33 percent of gay, lesbian, and bisexual students were bullied on school grounds in comparison to 17.1 percent of heterosexual youth. At a prevalence rate of 24.3 percent, students who reported what the authors present as a "being not sure" category about their sexual orientation were also more likely to be bullied at school in comparison to heterosexual peers.

Gay, lesbian, bisexual, and not sure students were also more likely to be cyber-bullied in comparison to their heterosexual peers. For instance, 27.1 percent of gay, lesbian, and bisexual students and 22 percent of not sure students reported being electronically bullied. For heterosexual students, the prevalence rate was 13.3 percent (Kann et al., 2018).

We might assume that the answers to these questions influenced responses to the statement of "did not go to school because of safety concerns" (Kann et al., 2018, p. 19). This question focused on whether a student had not gone to school because they didn't feel safe for a minimum of one day up to thirty days prior to taking the survey. Similar to the aforementioned data, 10 percent of gay, lesbian, and bisexual students and 10.7 percent of not sure students missed at least one day because they didn't feel safe going to school. The prevalence rate for heterosexual students was

6.1 percent. In addition to safety implications, these data also have academic implications given the importance of school attendance for academic achievement (Maxwell, 2016).

The current research indicates that short-term, incidental approaches often do not work when addressing bullying (Skiba, 2008). The entire school climate needs to change so as to be more tolerant and accepting. Zero tolerance, individual counseling, and peer mediation do not often reduce bullying (see Misdirections in Prevention Fact Sheet, www.stopbullying.gov/). While existing research has suggested some promising avenues for bullying prevention and intervention, it is important to note that more research is needed to identify the efficacy and impact of anti-bullying programs: "Considerable work is still needed for its successful translation into effective practice and policy" (Bradshaw, 2015, p. 325).

Some scholars have taken a public health approach to bullying, stating that "schools adopt the three-tiered public health model when aiming to prevent bullying and other emotional and behavioral problems" (Bradshaw, 2015, p. 325). In the multitiered model, programs are universal in that their components involve almost all youth in the school setting rather than a select few. Many such programs are preventative in nature. Universal anti-bullying prevention often focuses on "improving school climate, shifting the norms about bullying, and targeting bystander behavior" (Bradshaw, 2015, p, 325). In addition, LGBTQ staff should be accepted and validated in this process. Too often the rights of LGBTQ adults in school systems are compromised, giving a mixed message to young people seeking justice.

One of the most effective anti-bullying programs was implemented in Finland. Kuisaamista Vastaan (Against Bullying) (KiVa) is an evidence-based anti-bullying program developed in the University of Turku, Finland, with funding from the Ministry of Education and Culture. It has been evaluated and shown to reduce bullying in schools (www.kivaprogram.net/). KiVa uses a schoolwide approach that focuses on classroom and parent training and teaching to enhance empathy, self-efficacy, and the anti-bullying attitudes of *onlookers*. This model has shown evidence of effectiveness in reducing self- and peer-reported victimization and self-reported bullying (Kärnä et al., 2011). Over the two decades since the school shootings in Columbine, Colorado, we have learned that support does need to occur for victims and perpetrators of violence, but it also needs to occur in a larger social context – the rest of society and school climates need to develop if we are to see healthy development occur in our children. Two centers were established in the United States in 1995 to address school mental health. These centers continue to be valuable resources for schools wanting to address school climate. The National Center for School Mental Health (http://csmh.umaryland.edu/) at the University of Maryland and the National Center for Mental Health in Schools at the University of California, Los Angeles (http://smhp.psych.ucla.edu/) were created to provide support, technical training, and evidence-based support in order to improve mental health in schools and enhance school climate. Their work has been invaluable in promoting lasting, evidence-based school climate changes. School districts need only take advantage of the resources available through these publicly funded centers.

Gay and Straight Alliances (GSA) are also available for every school district to enhance this integration of social justice in schools, at both the secondary and college levels. The National Association of GSA Networks, consisting of at least 3,500 GSA clubs across the country, strategizes for both racial and gender justice (https://gsanetwork.org/). Gay and Straight Alliances work with students on leadership development and activism through training, national workshops, and networking to teach young people skills to promote justice and equality. Gay and Straight Alliances prioritize building alliances across all lines, including sexual orientation, gender identity, race, and class. They work to build creative and productive coalitions. As is seen with the anti-bullying movement, the success of reversing prejudice against LGBTQ children is to work to build social justice overall, not to victimize or demonize.

Since 1985, GLAAD has been "working to shape the narrative and provoke dialogue that leads to cultural change. The Gay and Lesbian Alliance Against Defamation protects all that has been accomplished and creates a world where everyone can live the life they love" (www.glaad.org). GLAAD has been instrumental in creating a productive dialogue through the use of media and an ongoing conversation. Since 2014, GLAAD has conducted a Harris poll to judge the acceptance of Americans of LGBTQ individuals (GLAAD, 2018). In 2017, GLAAD documented as many as 20 percent of millennials (e.g., young people who became adults around the time of the 21st century such as close to the year 2000) identifying as LGBTQ. In 2018, the annual report stated:

> Each year, the Accelerating Acceptance report showed positive momentum. Year over year, Americans said they were more comfortable with LGBTQ people and more supportive of LGBTQ issues. These results paralleled historic steps in LGBTQ visibility in our culture as well as the passage of marriage equality nationwide and other pro-LGBTQ legal wins. This year, the acceptance pendulum abruptly stopped and swung in the opposite direction. More non-LGBTQ adults responded that they were "very" or "somewhat" uncomfortable around LGBTQ people in select scenarios. The decline is paired with a significant increase in LGBTQ people reporting discrimination because of sexual orientation or gender identity (GLAAD, 2018)

The executive summary of the 2018 report added:

> This change can be seen as a dangerous repercussion in the tenor of discourse and experience over the last year. 2017 brought heightened rhetoric toward marginalized communities to the forefront of American culture. Policies and headlines ran that were anti-LGBTQ including the President's proposed ban on transgender people entering the U.S. military, confirmation of a Supreme Court justice opposed to marriage equality, and the passage of a state law in Mississippi which allows

businesses to legally deny service to LGBTQ families. LGBTQ people fell victims to violence in Chechnya, Egypt, [and] Indonesia, and the U.S. mourned the death of at least 26 transgender women. LGBTQ visibility slipped in news and entertainment media – Americans can no longer see LGBTQ stories that change hearts and minds with the same frequency (GLAAD, 2018, Accelerating Acceptance Executive Summary).

Clearly the rise in conservatism across the world has led to enhanced isolation, violence, and discrimination against LGBTQ and other diverse communities. This puts all of our children at risk.

One of the oldest and most productive organizations promoting social justice for LGBTQ children at the grassroots level has been PFLAG (formerly Parents, Families and Friends of Lesbians and Gays) (https://pflag.org/). PFLAG was established in 1973 after the act of a mother publicly supporting her gay son. PFLAG is the nation's largest family and ally organization. In addition to supporting international chapters, PFLAG has 400 chapters and 200,000 supporters crossing multiple generations of American families in major urban centers, small cities, and rural areas in all fifty states, the District of Columbia, and Puerto Rico. This broad grassroots organization supports chapter development, school and scholarship programs, legislative efforts, and advocacy. It is a valuable resource for any community wanting to promote justice and equality for LGBTQ youth.

CONCLUSION

Since the Stonewall Uprising fifty years ago, the rights of LGBTQ individuals have made incredible strides. We have addressed child development and have provided support for young children and youth who are struggling with issues of gender identity. We have evidence of the biological nature of sexual identity that allows us to celebrate LGBTQ behavior instead of calling it an illness. We have legalized marriage for same-sex couples allowing equal rights to LGBTQ parents and their children. We have broken the silence worldwide of the discrimination that exists and have supportive active organizations and the United Nations (after 2011) supporting LGBTQ rights.

As with many public health efforts and issues of justice, this is only the beginning. We need to be vigilant in this dangerous time to continue to support these grassroots efforts, both domestically and internationally, to make sure our schools have a climate that is supportive and nondiscriminatory, and to actively block legislation, both domestically and internationally, that discriminates against anyone because of who they may choose to love or be. The true measure of any country is the manner in which it treats its children. Each country owes its youngest members a healthy sexual development and the ability to love in a manner that is true to self.

REFERENCES

American Psychological Association (2009). Report of the American Psychological Association Task Force on Appropriate Therapeutic Responses to Sexual Orientation. Task Force on Appropriate Therapeutic Responses to Sexual Orientation. Available at www.apa.org/pi/lgbc/publications/therapeutic-resp.html.

Baams, L., Grossman, A. H., & Russell, S. T. (2015). Minority stress and mechanisms of risk for depression and suicidal ideation among lesbian, gay, and bisexual youth. *Developmental Psychology*, 51(5), 688–696.

Bradshaw, C. P. (2015). Translating research to practice in bullying prevention. *American Psychologist*, 70(4), 322–332. Available at http://dx.doi.org/10.1037/a0039114. Accessed on February 2, 2020.

Brooks, V. (1981). *Minority stress and lesbian women*. Lexington, MA: Lexington Books.

Centers for Disease Control and Prevention (2015). 2015 Youth Risk Behavior Survey. Available at www.cdc.gov/yrbss. Accessed on April 28, 2018.

Choi, S., Wilson, B., Shelton, J., & Gates, G. (2015). *Serving our youth 2015: The needs and experiences of lesbian, gay, bisexual, transgender, and questioning youth experiencing homelessness*. Los Angeles, CA: Williams Institute at UCLA School of Law.

Cochran, B. N., Stewart, A. J., Ginzler, J. A., & Cauce, A. M. (2002). Challenges faced by homeless sexual minorities: Comparison of gay, lesbian, bisexual, and transgender homeless adolescents with their heterosexual counterparts. *American Journal of Public Health*, 92(5), 773–777. Available at https://doi.org/10.2105/AJPH.92.5.773.

Connolly, M. D., Zervos, M. J., Barone, C. J., Johnson, C. C., & Joseph, C. L. M. (2016). The mental health of transgender youth: Advances in understanding. *Adolescent Health*, 59(5), 489–495.

D'Augelli, A. R., Grossman, A. H., Starks, M. T., & Sinclair, K. O. (2010). Factors associated with parents' knowledge of gay, lesbian, and bisexual youths' sexual orientation. *Journal of GLBT Family Studies*, 6(2), 178–198. Available at https://doi.org/10.1080/15504281003705410.

Fergusson, D., Horwood, L., & Beautrais, A. (1999). Is sexual orientation related to mental health problems and suicidality in young people? *Archives of General Psychiatry*, 56(10), 876–880. doi:10.1001/archpsyc.56.10.876

Gallup (2018). Gay and lesbian rights. Available at https://news.gallup.com/poll/1651/gay-lesbian-rights.aspx.

Gay and Lesbian Alliance Against Defamation (2018). Accelerating acceptance. Available at www.glaad.org/publications/accelerating-acceptance-2018.

Hafeez, H., Zeshan, M., Tahir, M., Jahan, N., & Naveed, S. (2017). Health care disparities among lesbian, gay, bisexual, and transgender youth: A literature review. *Cureus*, 9(4). doi:10.7759/cureus.1184

Hatzenbuehler, M. L. (2011). The social environment and suicide attempts in lesbian, gay, and bisexual youth. *Pediatrics*, 127(5), 896–903. Available at https://doi.org/10.1542/peds.2010-3020.

Hatzenbuehler, M. L., Bellatorre, A., Lee, Y., et al. (2014). Structural stigma and all-cause mortality in sexual minority populations. *Social Science & Medicine*, 103, 33–41.

Human Rights Campaign (HRC) (2019). Criminalization around the world. Available at https://assets2.hrc.org/files/assets/resources/Criminalization-Map-042315.pdf?_ga=2.7155 2915.1621276977.1558541375-391074718.1558541375.

International Lesbian and Gay Association (2006, January). ECOSOC dismisses two LGBT organizations without fair hearing! Available at www.ilga.org/news_results.asp?LanguageID=1&FileID=741&FileCategory=1&Zone.

Kann, L., McManus, T., Harris, W. A., et al. (2017). Youth Risk Behavior Surveillance – United States. MMWR Surveill Summ 2018; 67(No. SS–24–28).

Kärnä, A., Voeten, M., Little T., et al. (2011, January/February). A large-scale evaluation of the KiVa Antibullying Program: Grades 4–6. *Child Development*, 82(1), 311–330.

Katz-Wise, S. L., Rosario, M., & Tsappis, M. (2016). Lesbian, gay, bisexual, and transgender youth and family acceptance. *Pediatric Clinics of North America*, 63(6), 1011–1025. Available at https://doi.org/10.1016/j.pcl.2016.07.005.

Keifer, M. A., & Arshad, U. (2016). *Lesbian, gay, bisexual, and transgender (LGBT) youth in the global south.* Washington, DC: Advocates for Youth.

Keith, Katie. (2016, March 30). 15 States and DC now prohibit transgender insurance exclusions. [Blog post]. Available at http://chirblog.org/15-states-and-dc-nowprohibit-transgender-insurance-exclusions/

Kessler, R. C., Ammiger, G. P., Aguilar-Gaxiola, S., et al. (2007). Age of onset of mental disorders: A recent review of the literature. *Current Opinion in Psychiatry*, 20(4), 359–364.

Keuroghlian, A. S., Shtasel, D., & Bassuk, E. L. (2014). Out on the street: A public health and policy agenda for lesbian, gay, bisexual, and transgender youth who are homeless. *American Journal of Orthopsychiatry*, 84(1), 66–72. Available at https://doi.org/10.1037/h0098852.

Knight, R. E., Shoveller, J. A., Carson, A. M., & Contreras-Whitney, J. G. (2014). Examining clinicians' experiences providing sexual health services for LGBTQ youth: Considering social and structural determinants of health in clinical practice. *Health Education Research*, 29(4), 662–670. Available at https://doi.org/10.1093/her/cyt116.

Kosciw, J. G., Greytak, E. A., Zongrone, A. D., Clark, C. M., & Truong, N. L. (2018). *The 2017 National School Climate Survey: The experiences of lesbian, gay, bisexual, transgender, and queer youth in our nation's schools.* New York: Gay, Lesbian, and Straight Education Network.

Kosciw, J. G., & Pizmony-Levy, O. (2013). *Fostering a global dialogue about LGBT youth and schools: Proceedings from a meeting of the global network combating homophobic and transphobic prejudice and violence in schools sponsored by GLSEN & UNESCO.* New York: Gay, Lesbian, and Straight Education Network.

Kuhl, D., & Martino, W. (2018). "Sissy" boys and the pathologization of gender nonconformity. In S. Talburt (ed.), *Youth sexualities: Public feelings and contemporary cultural politics* (vol. 1, pp. 31–60). Santa Barbara, CA: Praeger.

Mallory, C., Brown, T. N. T., & Conron, K. J. (2019, June). Conversion therapy and LGBT youth: Update. Brief. Williams Institute, UCLA School of Law. Available at https://williamsinstitute.law.ucla.edu/wp-content/uploads/Conversion-Therapy-LGBT-Youth-Update-June-2019.pdf.

Marx, R. A., & Kettrey, H. H. (2016). Gay–straight alliances are associated with lower levels of school-based victimization of LGBTQ+ youth: A systematic review and meta-analysis. *Journal of Youth and Adolescence*, 45(7), 1269–1282. Available at https://doi.org/10.1007/s10964-016-0501-7.

Maxwell, L. E. (2016). School building condition, social climate, student attendance and academic achievement: A mediation model. *Journal of Environmental Psychology*, 46, 206–216.

Meyer, I. (1995). Minority stress and mental health in gay men. *Journal of Health and Social Behavior*, 36, 38–56.

Meyer, I. (2003). Prejudice, social stress, and mental health in lesbian, gay, and bisexual populations: Conceptual issues and research evidence. *Psychological Bulletin*, 129(5), 674–697.

Movement Advancement Project. Equality maps: State non-discrimination laws. Available at www.lgbtmap.org/equality-maps/non_discrimination_laws. Accessed July 2019.

Noell, J., & Ochs, L. (2001). Relationship of sexual orientation to substance use, suicidal ideation, suicide attempts, and other factors in a population of homeless adolescents. *Journal of Adolescent Health*, 29(1), 31–36.

Paus, T., Keshavan, M., & Giedd, J. N. (2008). Why do many psychiatric disorders emerge during adolescence? *Nature Reviews Neuroscience*, 9(12), 947–957. Available at https://doi.org/10.1038/nrn2513.

Raifman, J., Moscoe, E., Austin, S. B., & McConnell, M. (2017). Difference-in-differences analysis of the association between state same-sex marriage policies and adolescent suicide attempts. *JAMA Pediatrics*, 171(4), 350. Available at https://doi.org/10.1001/jamapediatrics.2016.4529.

Reisner, S., Vetters, R., Leclerc, M., et al. (2015). Mental health of transgender youth in care at an adolescent urban community health center: A matched retrospective cohort study. *Journal of Adolescent Health*, 56(3), 274–279. doi:10.1016/j.jadohealth.2014.10.264

Rew, L., Whittaker, T. A., Taylor-Seehafer, M. A., & Smith, L. R. (2005). Sexual health risks and protective resources in gay, lesbian, bisexual, and heterosexual homeless youth. *Journal for Specialists in Pediatric Nursing*, 10(1), 11–19. Available at https://doi.org/10.1111/j.1088-145X.2005.00003.x.

Rice, E., Barman-Adhikari, A., Rhoades, H., et al. (2013). Homelessness experiences, sexual orientation, and sexual risk taking among high school students in Los Angeles. *Journal of Adolescent Health*, 52(6), 773–778. Available at https://doi.org/10.1016/j.jadohealth.2012.11.011.

Russell, S., & Fish, J. (2016). Mental health in lesbian, gay, bisexual, and transgender (LGBT) youth. *Annual Review of Clinical Psychology*, 12(1), 465–487. doi:10.1146/annurev-clinpsy-021815-093153

Schuster, M., Bogart, L., Klein, D., et al. (2015). A longitudinal study of bullying of sexual-minority youth. *New England Journal of Medicine*, 372(19), 1872–1874. doi:10.1056/nejmc1413064

Skiba, R. (2008). Are zero tolerance policies effective in the schools? An evidentiary review and recommendations. *American Psychologist*, 63(9), 852–862.

Stevens, J., Gomez-Lobo, V., & Pine-Twaddell, E. (2015). Insurance coverage of puberty blocker therapies for transgender youth. *Pediatrics*, 136(6), 1029–1031. doi:10.1542/peds.2015-2849

Tankard, M. E., & Paluck, E. L. (2017). The effect of a Supreme Court decision regarding gay marriage on social norms and personal attitudes. *Psychological Science*, 28(9), 1334–1344. Available at https://doi-org.proxy.library.vcu.edu/10.1177/0956797617709594.

Tanner, B. A. (1974). A comparison of automated aversive conditioning and a waiting list control in the modification of homosexual behavior in males. *Behavior Therapy*, 5, 29–32.

The Trevor Project (2016, November). Crisis contacts from youth to The Trevor Project surge immediately following the election [Blog post]. Available at www.thetrevorproject.org/trvr_press/crisis-contacts-from-youth-to-the-trevorproject-surge-immediately-following-the-election/#sm.0000la9pozt31epusk12n95w7dest.

Tyler, K. A. (2013). Homeless youths' HIV risk behaviors with strangers: Investigating the importance of social networks. *Archives of Sexual Behavior*, 42(8), 1583–1591. Available at https://doi.org/10.1007/s10508-013-0091-3.

United Nations (n.d.). Free and Equal. Available at www.unfe.org/.

United Nations General Assembly (2011, November 17). Document A/HRC/19/41. Available at www.un.org/en/ga/search/view_doc.asp?symbol=A/HRC/19/41.

US Department of Justice. (2013). Title IX of the Education Amendments of 1972. Archived from the original on November 4, 2013. Retrieved November 12, 2013. Available at www.justice.gov/crt/title-ix-education-amendments-1972.

9

Social Justice for Child Immigrants

Shawn S. Sidhu and Balkozar S. Adam

INTRODUCTION

Give me your tired, your poor, your huddled masses yearning to breathe free.

Emma Lazarus, "The New Colossus," November 2, 1883. Placed on the Statue of Liberty in New York City in 1903 (National Park Service)

I will remember that I remain a member of society, with special obligations to all my fellow human beings, those of sound mind and body as well as the infirm.

Hippocratic Oath (Lasagna, 1964)

Though deportation is not technically a criminal proceeding, it visits a great hardship on the individual and deprives him of the right to stay and live and work in this land of freedom. . . . That deportation is a penalty – at times a most serious one – cannot be doubted. Meticulous care must be exercised lest the procedure by which he is deprived of that liberty not meet the essential standards of fairness.

Supreme Court Justice Murphy in *Bridges* v. *Wixon* (1945)

In this chapter, we discuss the ways in which child and adolescent immigrant populations have suffered social injustices, psychosocial adversity, and barriers to accessing basic services in the United States. This population is divided into two groups. The first refers to children who are fleeing torture and persecution in other countries and are seeking political asylum in the United States. The second group encompasses the children of undocumented immigrants currently residing within the United States.

Case Example of Both Domestic and International Trauma

Alejandra is a seven-year-old female who was born in the United States, where she lived with both of her biological parents until the age of two. Her parents then separated, and her mother returned to their native country of El Salvador so that she could raise Alejandra with more family support. However, shortly after moving back to El Salvador, the family realized that the level of gang violence had escalated significantly since they had lived there. Alejandra's mother also began dating a boyfriend who was nice initially, but later became possessive, controlling, violent, and abusive, and who ultimately threatened to kill Alejandra's mother on multiple occasions. Fearing for her life and the life of her child, Alejandra's mother decided to journey back to the United States when Alejandra was six. The family initially traveled to Mexico, where they attempted to apply for humanitarian relief. After six months, no relief had come, and they were running out of money. In desperation, Alejandra and her mother crossed the US–Mexico border by a low-lying river and the border patrol discovered them shortly thereafter. The next day, Alejandra was forcibly separated from her mother with little notice or explanation, and the following day, Alejandra was flown to a shelter more than 1,000 miles away, where she was amidst strangers. After a month at the shelter, Alejandra was reunited with her biological father, who remained in the United States while her mother stayed in detention. On interview, Alejandra meets full criteria for post-traumatic stress disorder (PTSD), and endorses severe depression and accompanying hallucinations and "strange" thinking. Despite living in considerable distress, she has not received any treatment because her biological father is not educated about mental health conditions, and because her family avoids contact with those in authority in the United States for fear of deportation. Alejandra does go to school and is a stellar student who wants to become a doctor when she grows up. She cries several nights a week, "sick with worry" about her mother being "all alone in jail."[1]

Evidence suggests that both children fleeing persecution and children of undocumented immigrant parents are at considerable risk for social injustice (Adam, 2017; Henderson & Baily, 2013; Loo, Sidhu, & Larroque, 2015; Sidhu, 2017a, 2017b; Sidhu & Boodoo, 2017; Sidhu & Song, 2019). They face an increased risk of negative educational, psychological, and social outcomes at a higher rate than their peers, in part due to discrimination, among other causes (Brown, 2015).

This chapter defines the scope of the social injustice experienced by special immigrant children and adolescent populations.

SCOPE OF CHILD AND ADOLESCENT IMMIGRANTS FLEEING PERSECUTION

According to the United Nations High Commissioner for Refugees (UNHCR), 65.6 million people were displaced by persecution, conflict, violence, and human rights violations in 2017. That is more than the 50 million people displaced during World War II (UNHCR, 2018b). We are currently experiencing the highest levels of displacement in our global history. Consider these statistics: 10 million individuals are "stateless" after having been denied access to their country of birth and to basic rights such as education, healthcare, and employment. At least half of the 22.5 million refugees in the world are under eighteen, and 50 million children were uprooted worldwide in 2016 with a 450 percent increase from 2010 to 2016 in unaccompanied minors worldwide (UNICEF, 2017).

While the global statistics on refugee populations are quite striking, a number of specific regions deserve mention. Approximately 12 million Syrians alone have been displaced since the beginning of the Syrian civil war in 2011 (UNHCR, 2016), 76 percent of whom are women and children (Yuruk, 2013). Similarly, 87 percent of South Sudanese refugees are women and children (UNHCR, 2016). Last, the Northern Triangle of Central America (Honduras, El Salvador, and Guatemala) has quickly become one of the most dangerous places in the world, where there are more gang and cartel members than military and police officials (UNODC, 2012). According to the United Nations Office of Drugs and Crime (UNODC), in 2013, Honduras led the world in murders per capita, followed closely by Belize at third, El Salvador at fourth, and Guatemala at fifth (UNODC, 2013). The number of unaccompanied minors in the United States from the Northern Triangle countries has increased from an average of fewer than 3,000 per year between 2009 and 2011, to an average of 42,000 per year between 2014 and 2016 (Meyer, Margesson, Seelke, & Taft-Morales, 2016), with 87 percent of children from El Salvador reporting fleeing violence from criminal actors or abuse in the home (UNHCR, 2018a).

Social Justice Issues in Refugee Populations (Including Mental Health)

Immigrants fleeing persecution are at significant risk for social injustice and must overcome considerable barriers while transitioning to a completely new country and culture. Barriers for asylum-seeking immigrants are mostly at the legal and due process levels, while barriers for those granted refugee status include poverty and a lack of economic opportunity, mental health issues, language, a lack of social support, and difficulty with cultural assimilation.

CASE EXAMPLE HIGHLIGHTING CULTURE ASSIMILATION ISSUES

Mariam is a seventeen-year-old Somalian Muslim refugee who emigrated to the United States six months after living at a refugee camp for three years. When she started going to school, her classmates made fun of her, calling her "stupid," "weird," and "smelly," saying "she can't think right," and making pejorative references to her as "Eww, the African" and telling her to "go back home." After becoming suicidal, she was admitted to the hospital. She had previous episodes of aggressive behavior at school and at home, where she had hit her siblings and yelled at boys. While no specific trigger was identified, the school counselor noted she had problems dealing with men.[2]

Asylum-seeking immigrants are guaranteed specific due process protections and legal rights through a number of international treaties (United Nations General Assembly Resolution 429 [V], 1950; United Nations Treaty Collection, 1967; Sidhu & Boodoo, 2017). According to these treaties, which the United States has signed as a full participating member, immigrants fleeing persecution are protected from refoulement (forceful deportation), discrimination, and penalization.

Non-refoulement states no government "shall expel or return a refugee against his or her will, in any manner whatsoever, to a territory where he or she fears threats to life or freedom." Non-discrimination requires "provisions to be applied without discrimination as to race, religion or country of origin," or "to sex, age, disability, sexuality, or other prohibited grounds of discrimination." Last, non-penalization states asylum-seeking individuals "should not be penalized for their illegal entry or stay ... the seeking of asylum can require refugees to breach immigration rules" (United Nations General Assembly Resolution 429 [V], 1950).

Non-refoulement Infractions

Immigrants fleeing persecution must be informed by US Customs and Border Protection (CBP) officers of their right to seek asylum. They must be given paperwork in their native language in order to apply for asylum, with the support of a translator if necessary. They are then to be transferred to a US asylum officer, who will conduct a credible fear interview and determine if their case meets criteria for a hearing with a federal immigration judge (Mehta, 2015; Sidhu & Boodoo, 2017; USCIRF, 2007; Wadhia, 2014). An estimated 15–40 percent of asylum seekers report being deported without seeing an asylum officer or having a fair hearing, even though they expressed a clear fear of persecution (Mehta, 2015; USCIRF, 2007). In half of these cases, the immigrants were not informed about their right to apply for asylum, and CBP officers had not mentioned these fears in their paperwork. In 72 percent of these cases, detainees were not given an opportunity to review their sworn statements, which is required (USCIRF, 2007). The majority of those surveyed reported being given forms only in English, which they could not read and did not understand verbally, and some said they felt pressured to sign the forms without a translator, interpreter, or officer who spoke their language (Mehta, 2015).

There are allegations of asylum-seeking immigrants being abused by US officers. A report from the American Immigration Council claims that some individuals fleeing torture and persecution are dissuaded from seeking asylum. Still others report being berated, yelled at, harassed, and threatened with separation from their families or long detentions if they even applied for asylum (Campos & Friedland, 2014).

Despite the aforementioned non-refoulement clause, many individuals are being returned to the very places where their life is in incredible danger. In addition, evidence suggest that this can result in catastrophic consequences for those immigrants who are genuinely fleeing torture and persecution. One study from January 2014 to September 2015 showed that the murder rate of US deportees to Central America has "dramatically increased," with at least eighty-three people reported murdered within a year of their return (Magana-Salgado, 2016). Others have reported being raped, kidnapped, exploited, and sex-trafficked shortly after deportation from the United States (Mehta, 2015).

Non-penalization Infractions

Despite the aforementioned non-penalization clause, multiple sources have confirmed that asylum-seeking immigrants are detained in US prisons or detention camps for months or years while awaiting their hearings (Campos & Friedland, 2014; Cole, 2002; Kalhan, 2010; Mehta, 2015; Wadhia, 2014). Individuals meeting criteria for a credible fear interview wait an average of 111 days in detention, while the law technically requires that such interviews be conducted and a final decision reached within 10 days (Mehta, 2015). There has been a massive expansion of immigration detention, from a total of 65,000 immigrants detained in 1994 to 360,000 detained in 2016 (Detention Watch Network). Supreme Court cases *Wong Wing v. United States* (1896) (cited), *Carlson v. Landon* (1952) (cited), and *Zadvydas v. Davis* (2001) (cited) have all unequivocally held that preventatively detaining individuals without a known flight risk or a specific and known danger to the community is a violation of their due process rights. In the words of Justice Kennedy in *Zadvydas v. Davis*, "Both removable and inadmissible aliens are entitled to be free from detention. . . . Where detention is incident to removal, the detention cannot be justified. . . . This accords with international views on the detention of refugees and asylum seekers." Despite these clear guidelines by the US Supreme Court, the executive branch of the federal government has considerable authority over immigration policy, which may at times differ from the aforementioned Supreme Court precedent.

Nondiscrimination Infractions

The nondiscrimination clause states that asylum-seeking immigrants should not be denied entry on the basis of race, religion, or country of origin. However, Executive Orders 13769 and 13780 effectively ban entry to the United States for citizens from six Muslim-majority countries, and suspended the US Refugee Program for at least four months (Sidhu, 2017a). Despite 12 million Syrians being displaced in the Syrian civil war, and despite some of the worst war crimes in decades – including the use of chemical weapons on innocent children – the United States granted asylum to only eleven individuals from January 2018 to April 2018 (Amos, 2018).

The shutting of the proverbial door to refugees and asylum seekers is not limited to Syrians. Although the US Customs and Immigration Services saw a 600 percent increase in credible fear reports at the US–Mexico Border – from 5,000 in 2008 to 37,000 in 2013 – the number of individuals granted asylum after presenting to the border over that time remained flat at 10,000 per year (Campos & Friedland, 2014).

The US Office of Refugee Resettlement and local nonprofit, grassroots, and/or charitable organizations assist refugees in transitioning from alien status and extended detention to legal life in the United States. Such assistance is typically time-limited and very basic, and may include start-up funding, housing, links to employment and education, and medical services. For some refugees, this is insufficient, with refugees who are older at the time of resettlement experiencing lower levels of education, language difficulties, high unemployment, high welfare utilization, and low earnings compared to matched controls (Evans & Fitzgerald, 2017). Some of these outcomes, such as unemployment, do improve with increased time in the country but typically do not catch up to US-born peers.

According to the World Health Organization (WHO), refugees suffer from major mental illnesses such as major depressive disorder, PTSD, and psychosis at double the rate of non-refugees. According to a recent study published by the German Federal Chamber of Psychotherapists from 2015 to 2016, more than 50 percent of refugees were "showing signs of mental illness" after migration. The same study found 25 percent met clinical criteria for major depressive disorder, PTSD, or anxiety (Hunter, 2016). Another German study (Ullmann et al., 2015) found that almost half of refugees surveyed met criteria for PTSD.

Mental illness is a significant risk factor for poverty, unemployment, and increased morbidity and mortality (WHO, 2012). Individuals with mental illness have decreased access to equitable healthcare, housing, jobs, and social support compared to peers without mental illness.

SCOPE OF THE DOMESTIC IMMIGRATION PROBLEM

The population of immigrants in the United States has grown at a rapid rate over the past thirty years and is currently near historic levels. In 2015, 46.6 million immigrants lived in the United States – approximately 13.4 percent of the population. That is nearly triple the immigrant population of 1970, which was 4.7 percent (Lopez & Bialik, 2017). In 2014, 25.4 percent of children younger than eighteen were either first- or second-generation immigrants, up from 17.5 percent in 1994 (Child Trends Data Bank, 2014). That same year, at least 4.7 million US-born children lived with an undocumented parent, according to the PEW Research Center (Passel & Cohn, 2016). More than 1 million children are estimated to be living in the United States who were born elsewhere, according to the most recent Pew data. Seven to nine percent of all children born in the United States between 2003 and 2014 had at least one undocumented parent.

Deferred Action for Childhood Arrivals (DACA) is a presidential executive order signed into effect by President Barack Obama in 2014 (American Immigration Council, 2017). As of September 4, 2017, the total number of individuals granted DACA in the United States was approximately 800,000 (USCIS, 2017).

SOCIAL JUSTICE ISSUES IN CHILDREN OF UNDOCUMENTED IMMIGRANTS

Children of undocumented immigrant parents are at risk for many of the same negative outcomes as their parents. They may face poverty, discrimination, parental stress affecting the parent–child relationship, and unreported domestic violence (American Psychological Association, 2012). They also experience decreased access to adequate housing, healthcare, and education (see references cited later in this chapter). Overall, they are more likely to suffer from mental health issues (Henderson & Baily, 2013). A recent study of 900 undocumented adults who were arrested at their workplace found that 500 children were affected by the arrest, and that 66 percent of those children were under the age of five (Chaudry et al., 2010). Immediate effects of the arrests included loss of childcare, dramatic loss of income, reluctance to go to agencies in order to obtain emergency assistance, and difficulty obtaining basic needs for children such as food, diapers, formula, and clothing. In the weeks and months that followed, the remaining caregivers experienced social isolation, depressive symptoms, and suicidal ideation, while long-term changes in children included anxiety, depression, and PTSD (Chaudry et al., 2010).

Case Example Highlighting the Impact of Immigration Stress

Diyana was a fourteen-year-old Arab female admitted to an inpatient unit after drinking toilet bowl cleaner in a suicide attempt. She was a ninth grader, living with her mother, siblings, and new stepfather. They were recent refugees from Iraq living in public housing. She made friends with the kids in the neighborhood and started self-medicating with drugs for her depression. Her family could not recognize the warning signs for substance use, and because of the stigma did not get her help right away. Diyana talked about having a lot of stress in her life. Her eighteen-year-old sister had just gotten married and moved to a different state. Her mother also had recently married a new immigrant from a different culture, and was two months pregnant. She was struggling with no longer being the baby of the family. She started spending more time with her friends because, she stated, her family wasn't there for her anymore.[3]

These children are already more likely than their peers to suffer from poverty. Undocumented immigrants are often paid below legal minimum wage (Bernhardt et al., 2009), meaning their children are at higher risk for food insecurity and poor health. This is in part because undocumented immigrants are ineligible for public assistance programs such as welfare. Poverty has been correlated to negative cognitive and emotional outcomes in low-income children (Johnson, Kalil, & Dunifon, 2010; Yoshikawa, Godfrey, & Rivera, 2008).

Undocumented immigrants also are ineligible for housing assistance. This ineligibility increases the likelihood of overcrowding in the home, which has been correlated to low academic achievement, high blood pressure, and increased behavior problems at school in children (Evans et al., 1998). Forty percent of undocumented farmworker households report more than one adult per room and lower rates of washers and dryers than their rural counterparts (Early et al., 2006).

Low-income undocumented immigrant families have been covered by health insurance at increasingly lower rates since 1996 (Kalil & Ziol-Guest, 2009; Kaushal & Kaestner, 2005; Lurie, 2008). It comes as little surprise that Ortega, Fang, and Perez (2007) found lower rates of healthcare utilization and continuity of care in undocumented immigrant families. Even though US-born children of undocumented immigrants may be eligible for many services, undocumented immigrants are less likely to be aware of or fully understand eligibility requirements of community programs and healthcare services than matched peers (Capps, Ku, & Fix, 2002; Shields & Behrman, 2004; Yu et al., 2005). The result in many cases is that children in immigrant families may not receive the basic resources they need.

In a study by Ortega et al. (2009), the children of Mexican undocumented parents had higher developmental risk (as measured by language, health, and socioemotional domains) than the children of US-born White parents. Specifically, the children of Mexican parents reported lower reading and math skills at school entry than other ethnic groups matched for poverty and for immigrant and minority status (Crosnoe, 2007; Fuller et al., 2009; Han, 2006). Similarly, undocumented immigrants were less likely than other ethnic groups to send their children to preschool (Crosnoe, 2006; Hernandez, Denton, & Macartney, 2008; Kalil & Crosnoe, 2009; Magnuson, Lahaie, & Waldfogel, 2006; Matthews & Ewan, 2006). For example, the children of Mexican and Central American immigrants ages three to five show much lower rates of preschool enrollment (Matthews & Ewan, 2006), even though parental preferences for preschool are not lower among these ethnic groups (Garcia & Jensen, 2007). Preschool has been demonstrated to be of significant benefit to low-income children's cognitive development (Gormley et al., 2005).

Preliminary research demonstrates that experiences of parental deportation are linked to future emotional and behavioral problems, including substance abuse, unemployment, and interpersonal difficulties with family members (Brabeck, Lykes, & Hunter, 2014; Zuniga & Hamann, 2006).

A qualitative study on the children of undocumented parents by Gulbas et al. (2014) found that more than half of the children sampled were directly affected by parental deportation or detention, and 30 percent of the children met criteria for probable depression. That is dramatically higher than the national child and adolescent average of 1–3 percent (Angold & Costello, 2001). The study reports that the children of undocumented Mexican immigrants in general experience stress in the form of an inability to communicate with friends, negative perceptions of their parents' home country, financial struggles, loss of supportive school networks, relations with parent(s), and violence. In this study, undocumented children affected by parental deportation reported a greater burden of stressors than those not affected by parental deportation, although both groups reported considerable hardship. Those who experienced parental deportation reported it as a major life trauma, which either generated or exacerbated these stressors.

Family members of children who experienced the arrest of at least one parent reported behavioral changes in most children, including difficulty with sleep and appetite, excessive crying, increased fear, increased aggression, and withdrawn behavior in older youth, frequently persisting past six months. Children who experience multiple immigration-related stressors, such as parental deportation, immigration raids, or detention are at increased risk for the development of depression, anxiety, and PTSD (American Psychological Association, 2012; Perez-Foster, 2001). Additionally, children of undocumented parents in the United States suffer from a greater burden of anxiety and depression, attention problems, social withdrawal, and rule-breaking behaviors (Allen, Cisneros, & Tellez, 2013; Dreby, 2014; Suarez-Orozco, Hee Jin, & Ha, 2010; Suarez-Orozco et al., 2011). Even when children experience the loss of a parent under voluntary or desired circumstances, they are still at greater risk for anxiety and depression than non-separated children (Suarez-Orozco et al., 2011).

Parents report that their own vulnerability to deportation affects their emotional adjustment, their ability to support their children financially, their relationships with their children, and their children's emotional well-being and school performance (Brabeck & Xu, 2010). Parental stress can impact the socioemotional development of children through parenting practices that are less warm or more harsh (Yoshikawa, 2011).

CONCLUSION

Children of undocumented immigrant parents and children who have come to the United States to flee torture and persecution in their home countries are at risk of increased mental health issues and socioeconomic and psychosocial problems, as well as medical and physical challenges. These children face discrimination, social injustice, and even increased morbidity and mortality. In 2017 alone, the United Nations reports, conflict and war created more than 60 million refugees escaping persecution, violence, and human rights violations. Research shows that refugees are twice as likely to experience mental illness.

Children of undocumented immigrants and those who were unaccompanied when they entered the United States face similar challenges. They are more likely to have mental health problems and less likely to access care. In addition, these children live their daily lives in limbo. The threat of deportation hangs over their families. A large percentage of these children have witnessed their parents' arrest, which wreaks a different kind of havoc in their lives. They lose their caregiver and financial supporter, and must struggle with poverty, depression, and PTSD.

While a range of legislative actions and executive orders have been enacted to address the legal status of both populations, little has been done to address the significant mental, social, and economic challenges these children face. The social injustices extend beyond the immediate adversities these children encounter. With each passing year, refugee children and children of undocumented immigrant parents confront additional difficulties that lead to long-term negative outcomes.

RECOMMENDATIONS

With the unprecedented number of refugees, undocumented minors, and stateless individuals who face mounting mental health challenges and ongoing social injustice, it behooves those individuals who interact with this population as clinicians, administrators, and agency personnel to extend support, including treatment when needed. These children have overcome countless barriers before, during, and after migration. They have endured numerous traumas and have been victimized again and again. When they finally arrive to the United States, they often struggle with poverty, lack of mental healthcare services, language barriers, acculturation stress, and little or no social support. The children and youth may also face discrimination, educational, and developmental difficulties and decreased access to healthcare and the negative effects of the family stress. Some children may demonstrate behavior changes, including difficulty with sleep and appetite, excessive crying, increased fear, and increased aggression, as well as withdrawn behavior.

The time-limited assistance offered by the US Office of Refugee Resettlement, as well as the well-meaning but minimal aid provided by other charitable organizations, is insufficient in addressing all their needs. Therefore, those coming in contact with these children and families should be educated about the various risk factors, barriers to care, and impact of social injustice on the mental health of refugees, undocumented minors, and stateless children, especially in the current political climate. In addition, we need to address their specific cultural needs by providing culturally sensitive care. Immigrants fleeing torture and persecution can also benefit from trauma-focused systems of care that minimize re-traumatization, and treatment modalities that focus on the transgenerational elements of trauma by working with the entire family to improve internal supports, communication, and healing. We can also learn how to perform asylum evaluations and advocate for them in the legal and the educational systems to help them overcome their traumas and achieve their goals. We can refer patients and families to community organizations that can assist them with housing, educational and legal support, and social services. Last, we also must collaborate with other providers, institutions, and agencies while using our voices to advocate for families who fear retaliation.

Notes

1. Elements of this case have been de-identified such that the patient's identity would not be compromised.
2. Elements of this case have been de-identified such that the patient's identity would not be compromised.
3. Elements of this case have been de-identified such that the patient's identity would not be compromised.

REFERENCES

Adam, B. (2017). Treating refugees from Syria and beyond: A moral and professional responsibility. *Journal of the American Academy of Child and Adolescent Psychiatry*, 56(10), 803–804.

Allen, B., Cisneros, E. M., & Tellez, A. (2013). The children left behind: The impact of parental deportation on mental health. *Journal of Child and Family Studies*, 24(2), 386–392. doi:10.1007/s10826-013-9848-5

American Immigration Council (2017). The Dream Act, DACA, and other policies designed to protect Dreamers. An official report of the American Immigration Council. Accessed September 6, 2019. Available at: www.americanimmigrationcouncil.org/research/dream-act-daca-and-other-policies-designed-protect-dreamers.

American Psychological Association (2012). Crossroads: The psychology of immigration in the new century. APA Presidential Task Force on Immigration. Accessed September 6, 2019. Available at: www.apa.org/topics/immigration/immigration-report.pdf.

Amos, D. (2018). The U.S. has accepted only 11 Syrian refugees this year. National Public Radio. Accessed September 6, 2019. Available at: www.npr.org/sections/parallels/2018/04/12/602022877/the-u-s-has-welcomed-only-11-syrian-refugees-this-year.

Angold, A., & Costello, E. J. (2001). The epidemiology of depression in children and adolescents. In I. M. Goodyer (ed.), *The depressed child and adolescent* (vol. 2, pp. 143–178). Cambridge: Cambridge University Press.

Bernhardt, A., Milkman, R., Theodore N, et al. (2009). *Broken laws, unprotected workers: Violations of employment and labor laws in America's cities*. New York: National Employment Law Project.

Brabeck, K., Lykes, M. B., & Hunter, C. (2014). The psychosocial impact of detention and deportation on U.S. migrant children and families. *American Journal of Orthopsychiatry*, 84, 496–505.

Brabeck, K., & Xu, Q. (2010). The impact of detention and deportation on Latino immigrant children and families: A quantitative exploration. *Hispanic Journal of Behavioral Science*, 32(3), 341–361.

Bridges v. Wixon, 326 U.S. 135 (1945).

Brown, C. S. (2015). The educational, psychological, and social impact of discrimination on the immigrant child. An official report of the National center on Immigrant Integration Policy and the Migration Policy Institute. Accessed September 6, 2019. Available at: www.migrationpolicy.org/sites/default/files/publications/FCD-Brown-FINALWEB.pdf.

Campos, S., & Friedland, J. (2014). Mexican and Central American asylum and credible fear claims: Background and context. A special report of the American Immigration Council. Washington, DC. Accessed September 6, 2019. Available at: www.americanimmigration council.org/sites/default/files/research/asylum_and_credible_fear_claims_final_0.pdf.

Capps, R., Ku, L., & Fix, M. (2002). *How immigrants are faring: Preliminary evidence from Los Angeles and New York City*. Washington, DC: Urban Institute.
Carlson v. Landon, 342 U.S. 524 (1952).
Chaudry, A., Capps, R., Pedroza, J., et al. (2010). *Facing our future: Children in the aftermath of immigration enforcement*. Washington, DC: Urban Institute.
Child Trends Data Bank (2014). Immigrant children: Indicators of child and youth well-being. An official report of Child Trends Data Bank. Bethesda, MD. Accessed September 6, 2019. Available at: www.childtrends.org/wp-content/uploads/2013/07/110_Immigrant_Children.pdf.
Cole, D. (2002). In aid of removal: Due process limits on immigration detention. *Emory Law Journal*, 51, 1003–1039.
Crosnoe, R. (2006). *Mexican roots, American schools: Helping Mexican immigrant children succeed*. Palo Alto, CA: Stanford University Press.
Crosnoe, R. (2007). Early child care and the school readiness of children from Mexican immigrant families. *International Migration Review*, 41, 152–181.
Detention Watch Network (Part of the International Detention Coalition). Immigration detention 101. Accessed September 6, 2019. Available at: www.detentionwatchnetwork.org/issues/detention–101.
Dreby, J. (2014). US immigration policy and family separation: The consequences for children's well-being. *Social Science and Medicine*, 132, 245–251.
Early, J., Davis, S. W., Quandt, S. A., et al. (2006). Housing characteristics of farmworker families in North Carolina. *Journal of Immigrant and Minority Health*, 8, 173–184.
Evans, G. W., Lepore, S. J., Shejwal, B. R., et al. (1998). Chronic residential crowding and children's well being: An ecological perspective. *Child Development*, 69, 1514–1523.
Evans, W. N., & Fitzgerald, D. (2017). The economic and social outcomes of refugees in the United States: Evidence from the ACS. An official report of the National Bureau of Economic Research. Accessed September 6, 2019. Available at: www.nber.org/papers/w23498.pdf.
Fuller, B., Bridges, M., Bein, E., et al. (2009). The health and cognitive growth of Latino toddlers: At risk or immigrant paradox? *Maternal and Child Health Journal*, 13, 755–768.
Garcia, E., & Jensen, B. (2007). Helping young Hispanic learners. *Educational Leadership*, 64(6), 34–39.
Gormley, W. T., Gayer, T., Phillips, D. A., et al. (2005). The effects of universal pre-K on children's cognitive development. *Developmental Psychology*, 41, 872–884.
Gulbas, I. E., Zayas, L. H., Yoon, H., et al. (2014). Deportation experiences and depression among U.S. citizen children with undocumented Mexican parents. *Child Care, Health, and Development*, 42(2), 220–230.
Han, W. (2006). Academic achievements of children in immigrant families. *Educational Research and Reviews*, 1, 286–318.
Henderson, S. W., & Baily, C. D. R. (2013). Parental deportation, families, and mental health. *Journal of the American Academy of Child and Adolescent Psychiatry*, 52, 451–453.
Hernandez, D., Denton, S., & Macartney, S. E. (2008). Children in immigrant families: Looking to America's future. *Social Policy Reports of the Society for Research in Child Development*, 22(3), 1–22.
Hunter, P. (2016). The refugee crisis challenges national healthcare systems. EMBO Press. Accessed September 6, 2019. Available at: www.embopress.org/doi/10.15252/embr.201642171.
Johnson, R. C., Kalil, A., & Dunifon, R. (2010). *Mother's work and children's lives: Low-income families after welfare reform*. Kalamazoo, MI: W. E. Upjohn Institute for Employment Research.

Kalhan, A. (2010). Rethinking immigration detention. *Columbia Law Review Sidebar*, 110, 42–58.

Kalil, A., & Crosnoe, R. (2009). Two generations of educational progress in Latin American immigrant families in the U.S.: A conceptual framework for a new policy context. In E. Grigorenko & R. Takanishi (eds.), *Immigration, diversity, and education* (pp. 188–204). New York: Routledge.

Kalil, A., & Ziol-Guest, K. (2009). Welfare reform and health among the children of immigrants. In J. Ziliak (ed.), *Welfare reform and its long-term consequences for America's poor* (pp. 308–336). Cambridge, UK: Cambridge University Press.

Kaushal, N., & Kaestner, R. (2005). Welfare reform and health insurance of immigrants. *Health Services Research*, 40, 697–722.

Lasagna, L. (1964). Hippocratic Oath: Modern version. WGBH Educational Foundation for PBS and NOVA Online. Published November 7, 2001. Accessed September 6, 2019. Available at: www.pbs.org/wgbh/nova/body/hippocratic-oath-today.html.

Loo, D., Sidhu, S., & Larroque, C. (2015). Detainment of Central American child refugees sheds light on a global humanitarian crisis. *AACAP News*, 46(2), 77–78.

Lopez, G., & Bialik, K. (2017). Key findings about U.S. Immigrants. Pew Research Center: Fact Tank. Accessed September 6, 2019. Available at: www.pewresearch.org/fact-tank/2017/05/03/key-findings-about-u-s-immigrants/.

Lurie, I. (2008). Welfare reform and the decline in health-insurance coverage of children and non-permanent residents. *Journal of Health Economics*, 27, 786–793.

Magana-Salgado, J. (2016). Relief not raids: Temporary protected status for El Salvador, Guatemala, and Honduras. An official report by the Immigrant Legal Resource Center. San Francisco, CA. Accessed September 6, 2019. Available at: www.ilrc.org/relief-not-raids-temporary-protected-status-el-salvador-guatemala-honduras.

Magnuson, K., Lahaie, C., & Waldfogel, J. (2006). Preschool and school readiness of children of immigrants. *Social Science Quarterly*, 87, 1241–1262.

Matthews, H., & Ewan, D. (2006). *Reaching all children? Understanding early care and education participation among immigrant families*. Washington, DC: Center for Law and Social Policy.

Mehta, S. (2015). American exile: Rapid deportations that bypass the courtroom. An official report of the American Civil Liberties Union. Accessed September 6, 2019. Available at: www.aclu.org/report/american-exile-rapid-deportations-bypass-courtroom/.

Meyer, P. J., Margesson, R., Seelke, C. R., & Taft-Morales, M. (2016). Unaccompanied children from Central America: Foreign policy considerations. An official report of the Congressional Research Service. Accessed September 6, 2019. Available at: https://fas.org/sgp/crs/homesec/R43702.pdf.

National Park Service. "The New Colossus." Statue of Liberty. Updated January 31, 2018. Accessed September 6, 2019. Available at: www.nps.gov/stli/learn/historyculture/colossus.htm.

Ortega, A. N., Fang, H., & Perez, V. (2007). Health care access, use of services, and experiences among undocumented Mexicans and other Latinos. *Archives of Internal Medicine*, 167, 2354–2360.

Ortega, A. N., Horwitz, S. M., Fang, H., et al. (2009). Documentation status and parental concerns about development in young US children of Mexican origin. *Academic Pediatrics*, 9, 278–282.

Passel, J. S., & Cohn, D. (2016). Number of babies born to unauthorized immigrants in U.S. continues to decline. Pew Research Center: Fact Tank. Accessed September 6, 2019. Available at: www.pewresearch.org/fact-tank/2016/10/26/number-of-babies-born-to-unauthorized-immigrants-in-u-s-continues-to-decline/.

Perez-Foster, R. (2001). When immigration is trauma: Guidelines for the individual and family clinician. *American Journal of Orthopsychiatry*, 71, 153–170.

Shields, M. K., & Behrman, R. E. (2004). Children of immigrant families: Analysis and recommendations. *Future of Children*, 14(2), 4–16.

Sidhu, S. (2017a). Haunted souls: Tales of immigrant children torn from their parents in America. *AACAP News*, 48(5), 219–221.

Sidhu, S. (2017b). Impact of recent executive actions on minority youth and families. *Journal of the American Academy of Child and Adolescent Psychiatry*, 56(10), 805–807. PMID: 28942800

Sidhu, S., & Boodoo, R. (2017). Domestic case law and legal precedent relating to the rights of asylum-seeking undocumented immigrants. *Journal of the American Academy of Psychiatry and the Law*, 45(3), 365–373. PMID: 28939736

Sidhu, S., & Song, S. (2019). Growing up with an undocumented parent in America: Psychosocial adversity in domestically residing immigrant children. *Journal of the American Academy of Child and Adolescent Psychiatry*, 58(10), 933–935. doi:https://doi.org/10.1016/j.jaac.2019.05.032

Suarez-Orozco, C., Hee Jin, B., & Ha, Y. K. (2010). I felt like my heart was staying behind: Psychological implications of family separations and reunifications for immigrant youth. *Journal of Adolescent Research*, 25, 222–257.

Suarez-Orozco, C., Yoshikawa, H., Teranishi R, et al. (2011). Growing up in the shadows: The developmental implications of unauthorized status. *Harvard Educational Review*, 81, 438–473.

Ullmann, E., Barthel, A., Tache, S., et al. (2015).Emotional and psychological trauma in refugees arriving in Germany in 2015. *Molecular Psychiatry*, 20, 1483–1484.

UNICEF (2017). Five-fold increase in number of refugee and migrant children traveling alone since 2010. United Nations International Children's Emergency Fund (UNICEF). Accessed September 6, 2019. Available at: www.unicef.org/media/media_95997.html.

United Nations General Assembly Resolution 429 (V) of 14 December 1950. Text of the 1951 Convention Related to the Status of Refugees. Text of the 1967 Protocol Relating to the Status of Refugees. Resolution 2189 (XXI) Adopted by the United Nations General Assembly. Geneva: Office of the United Nations High Commissioner for Refugees. Accessed September 6, 2019. Available at: www.unhcr.org/en-us/3b66c2aa10/.

United Nations High Commissioner for Refugees (2018a). Children on the run. An official report of the United Nations High Commissioner for Refugees. Accessed September 6, 2019. Available at: www.unhcr.org/56fc266f4.html.

United Nations High Commissioner for Refugees (2018b). Figures at a glance. UN Refugee Agency. Accessed September 6, 2019. Available at: www.unhcr.org/en-us/figures-at-a-glance.html.

United Nations High Commissioner for Refugees (2017). Global trends: Forced displacement in 2016. UN Refugee Agency. Accessed September 6, 2019. Available at: www.unhcr.org/en-us/statistics/unhcrstats/5943e8a34/global-trends-forced-displacement-2016.html.

United Nations Office on Drugs and Crime (UNODC) (2012). Transnational organized crime in Central America and the Caribbean: A threat assessment. An official publication of the United Nations Office on Drugs and Crime. Vienna, Austria. Accessed September 6, 2019. Available at: www.unodc.org/documents/data-and-analysis/Studies/TOC_Central_America_and_the_Caribbean_english.pdf.

United Nations Office on Drugs and Crime (UNODC) (2013). Global study on homicide: Trends, contexts, data. Vienna, Austria. Accessed September 6, 2019. Available at: www.unodc.org/documents/gsh/pdfs/2014_GLOBAL_HOMICIDE_BOOK_web.pdf.

United Nations Treaty Collection (UNTC) (1967). Chapter V: Refugees and stateless persons. Section 5: Protocol relating to the status of refugees. New York: UNTC, Accessed September 6, 2019. Available at: https://treaties.un.org/pages/ViewDetails.aspx?src=TREATY&mtdsg_no=V-5&chapter=5&clang=_en/.

US Citizenship and Immigration Services (USCIS) (2018). Immigration and citizenship data. DACA: Population data as of September 4, 2017. Accessed September 6 2019. Available at: www.uscis.gov/tools/reports-studies/immigration-forms-data.

US Commission on International Religious Freedom (USCIRF) (2007). Expedited removal report card: 2 years later. Based on original report on asylum seekers in expedited removal (2005), Vols. I and II. An official report of the United States Commission on International Religious Freedom. Washington, DC: USCIRF. Accessed September 6, 2019. Available at: www.uscirf.gov/sites/default/files/resources/stories/pdf/scorecard_final.pdf.

Wadhia, S. S. (2014). The rise of speed deportation and the role of discretion. *Columbia Journal of Race & Law*, 5, 1–27.

Wong Wing v. United States, 163 U.S. 228 (1896).

World Health Organization (WHO) (2012). Risks to mental health: An overview of vulnerabilities and risk factors. Accessed September 6, 2019. Available at: www.who.int/mental_health/mhgap/risks_to_mental_health_EN_27_08_12.pdf.

Yoshikawa, H. (2011). *Immigrants raising citizens: Undocumented parents and their young children*. New York: Russell Sage Foundation.

Yoshikawa, H., Godfrey, E. B., & Rivera, A. C. (2008). Access to institutional resources as a measure of social exclusion: Relations with family process and cognitive development in the context of immigration. *New Directions in Child and Adolescent Development*, 121, 73–96.

Yu, S. M., Huang, Z. J., Schwalberg, R. H., et al. (2005). Parental awareness of health and community resources among immigrant families. *Maternal and Child Health Journal*, 9, 27–34.

Yuruk, B. (2013). 76% of Syrian refugees women, children: UNHCR. United Nations High Commissioner for Refugees: The UN Refugee Agency. Operational Data Portal. Accessed September 6, 2019. Available at: https://data2.unhcr.org/en/news/13033.

Zadvydas v. Davis, 533 U.S. 678 (2001).

Zuniga, V., & Hamann, E. T. (2006). Going home? Schooling in Mexico of transitional children. *CONfines (Mexico)*, 4, 41–57.

10

Social Justice for Children and Young People with Disabilities

Elizabeth H. Jensen and Judith R. Harrison

INTRODUCTION

The role of education in promoting social justice theories and principles has grown exponentially in the United States since the middle of the 1980s (Connor, 2013). Many groups of people, including those with disabilities, have fought for social justice and have gained greater access to societal rights, including educational opportunities within schools and universities (Connor, 2013). In this chapter, the concept of social justice and how it relates to children and young people with disabilities is discussed within an educational context. Consensus statements and federal mandates that guide the educational system within the United States are described from an educational perspective as are mental health issues that face our children and young people with disabilities. Implications for practice are considered.

ROOTS OF SOCIAL JUSTICE

Social justice is a complex and multifaceted concept, which is often understood differently across various platforms, environments, and professions. Defining social justice is particularly difficult due to the conflicting dimensions and ideological perspectives of the varying stakeholders involved (Reisch & Garvin, 2016). Social justice is rooted in our early history when human societies first emerged. The premise of social justice has been found as early as 400 BC in ancient Greece, when Plato, Socrates, and Aristotle all played a role in molding the concept. In *The Republic*, Plato argued "that an ideal state would rest on the following four virtues: wisdom, justice, courage, and moderation" (as cited in Zajda, Majhanovich, & Rust, 2006, p. 9). Socrates posed the idea that a social system should ensure the good for the city-state, as well as for the citizens within (Griffiths, 1998). Aristotle built on this concept in the *Rhetoric* and concluded that social justice "is the justice that includes the law but which goes beyond it. The distinction [is] between justice as following legal rules, and the wider sense of justice as the right distribution of benefits in a society ('distributive justice')" (as cited in Griffiths, 1998, p. 179).

Aristotle's influence can be further seen in the writings of recent theorists. When Thomas Aquinas wrote that "justice is a certain rectitude of mind whereby a man does what he ought to do in the circumstances confronting him," he espoused that justice is an internal sense of duty where a man does what is appropriate in an effort to help others (as cited in Zajda et al., 2006, p. 9). Early philosophers thought about the individual and collective needs of society and how they can be addressed, identifying the tenets of a just society and the behaviors of just individuals (Kretchmar, 2013). John Rawls, an American political philosopher and one of the most cited writers on this subject, wrote A *Theory of Justice* (1971/1999), in which he argues that the way to contemplate the principles of justice would be to ask what principles we would agree to if we were in the same position of equality (Sandel, 2009). Specifically, Rawls contends that social justice involves the following:

> For us the primary subject of justice is the basic structure of society, or more exactly, the way in which the major social institutions distribute fundamental rights and duties and determine the division of advantages from social cooperation. . . . The major institutions define men's rights and duties and influence their life prospects, what they can expect to be and how well they can hope to do. (pp. 6–7)

This principle can be applied more broadly to the general structure of society, which is intended to govern by justice and to regulate the assignment of rights and duties, as well as the distribution of social and economic advantages (Reisch & Gavin, 2016). Social justice, as Rawls defines it, "is an abstraction which is humanistic in essence" (Zajda et al., 2006, p. 11).

One pivotal factor in attaining social justice is the general consensus that society is operating in a "fair" way, in which individuals are enabled as much freedom as possible, given their role within society (Zajda et al., 2006). As a result, social justice can be achieved only through the cooperative efforts of those individuals within the society, "who in their own self-interest, accept the current norms of morality as the price of membership in the community" (Zajda et al., 2006, p. 11).

More recently, social justice has been discussed and written about in the context of modern education in the United States. Policy makers have addressed issues of social justice in areas such as gender equality and desegregation in an effort to achieve equivalence for individuals and for society (Kretchmar, 2013). Although social justice in education has been written about and studied extensively by educators and researchers, there appears to be such an increased use of the term "social justice" that it has led to a "diffusion of meaning that threatens to make the concept of social justice ineffective and difficult to document through empirical research" (Connor, 2013, p. 113).

As such, we acknowledge the critical continuing debate regarding the true meaning of "social justice" in education (e.g., Enslin, 2006; Gewirtz, 2006; Griffiths, 1998) and the differences of opinion about what constitutes it. This debate over the meaning of social justice and how it can best be achieved ultimately contributes to the instability and discontinuity within the field (Kretchmar, 2013). Gewirtz (2006), drawing from principles of postmodernism, writes, "it is not possible to resolve the question of what counts as justice in education at a purely abstract level, and ... what counts as justice can only be properly understood within specific contexts of interpretation and enactment" (cited in Kretchmar, 2013, p. 2). This is, in part, due to seeing justice as a multidimensional concept, and can be interpreted differently depending on who is seeking it and their perspective (Kretchmar, 2013). Neito and Bode (2007) offer a different description and describe social justice education as "a philosophy, an approach, and actions that embody treating all people with fairness, respect, dignity, and generosity" (cited in Connor, 2013, p. 113). Enslin states that "justice is relational rather than static and is concerned with action and process" (2006, p. 58). Additionally, Dover defines social justice education "as the conscious and reflexive blend of content and process intended to enhance equity across multiple social identity groups (i.e., race, class, gender, sexual orientation, ability), foster critical perspectives, and promote social action" (2009, p. 508). Similarly, social justice can be interpreted as that which "is concerned with basic human rights that all people are entitled to regardless of conditions of economic disparity or of class, gender, race, ethnicity, citizenship, religion, age, sexual orientation, disability or health" (Zajda et al., 2006, p. 11). The key is that social justice is actionable and concerned with promoting fairness across all domains, regardless of class or social group. As such, action is a necessary component to promoting equality within the constructs of schools and educational systems; however, partnerships with those who make the laws and distribute the advantages from social cooperation are also a prime factor. As Zajda et al. state:

> The principle of providing quality education for all, in view of the presently widening gap of wealth, power, income, SES [socioeconomic status] disadvantage and inequity between the rich and the poor locally and globally continues to remain a myth. To solve the inequalities requires an ideological and radical policy shift in current models of governance, and an authentic and equal partnership between the state, multinational corporations, policy-makers and educators, all working together towards the eradication of inequality and poverty locally and globally – for the common good of humanity. (2006, p. 14)

WORLDWIDE CONSENSUS OF EDUCATION AS A CIVIL RIGHT FOR ALL CHILDREN AND ADOLESCENTS

Social justice for individuals with disabilities has been a focus across the world for at least two decades. In 1994, at the World Conference on Special Needs Education: Access and Quality, ninety-two governments and twenty-five international organizations drafted and adopted the Salamanca Statement and Framework for Action on Special Needs Education (UNESCO, 1994), which promotes the inclusion of all students with disabilities in educational settings. In addition, all countries and organizations proclaimed a commitment to develop policies and programs in order to increase the inclusion of students with disabilities. More recently, the passage of an inclusive agenda in the United Nations Millennium Development Goals reaffirms that inclusive education is a civil right for all students (UN, 2013).

FEDERAL EDUCATION MANDATES AND SOCIAL JUSTICE

As previously discussed, social justice requires more than policy and discussion; it requires action so as to guarantee the necessary education for all, regardless of class, race, and disability. Historically, individuals with disabilities have experienced injustice and unfair and sometimes cruel treatment, and they have been denied rights allowed to individuals without disabilities. As recently as half a century ago, children and adolescents with disabilities were excluded from compulsory education in the United States and often were not allowed to attend schools. Since that time, three federal US mandates have guided the education of students at risk of and with disabilities and required action on the part of educators.

In 1965, the Elementary and Secondary Education Act (ESEA), a general education mandate, was passed in order to provide additional federal funds to public education in the United States and to combat the effects of poverty on children with a directive for equal access to education. The ESEA has been reauthorized seven times, with the last reauthorization in 2015 as the Every Student Succeeds Act (ESSA). Each reauthorization has seen an increasing focus on the attainment of education for all students. The ESSA includes the requirement for college and career readiness standards with regulations for schools that receive federal funding and a strong focus on assessment, accountability, and school improvement. Specifically, the law holds schools and teachers accountable for the education of all students, including those with disabilities. Schools are required to conduct grade-level districtwide testing with a large majority of students within their student population, including those with disabilities. Students with significant cognitive disabilities are the only students allowed to take an alternative test (ESSA, 2015). In addition, scores are disaggregated and reported separately for students with disabilities, those who are economically disadvantaged, and those who are English language learners. Specific accommodations are allowed so as to ensure the test measures what it is intended to measure and not the effects of the student's disability. The purpose of these regulations is to reduce performance gaps between students with and without disabilities and their typically developing peers, to assure that all students are expected to master grade-level standards, and that schools are held accountable for the progress of all, including those with disabilities. As such, the ESEA is a general education mandate with a focus on ensuring social justice for all students with a focus on equal educational opportunities through access to equitable curriculum.

In 1973, Section 504 of the Vocational Rehabilitation Act, a civil rights law, was passed in order to eliminate discrimination based on disability in any program receiving federal financial assistance. Students may be considered for accommodation under Section 504 if they have any disabling condition that can be documented as "interfering with a student's learning process" (Baumberger & Harper, 2007, p. 9). Section 504 defines a person with a disability as an individual who (a) has a "physical or mental impairment that substantially limits one or more major life activities including learning and behavior" and (b) "has a record of having such an impairment or being regarded as having such an impairment" (42 U.S. Code § 12102). Through Section 504, students are provided classroom and assessment accommodations designed to "level the playing field" between those with and without disabilities in order to assure that students with disabilities have the same opportunity as their typically developing peers. Section 504 is considered a general education mandate with no federal funding and is enforced by the US Office of Civil Rights (OCR).

The law considered most relevant to individuals with disabilities was first passed in 1975 as P.L. 94–142, the Education for all Handicapped Children Act (EHA). The EHA, a special education mandate intended to ensure that all students with disabilities have a right to a free appropriate public education (FAPE), denied schools the opportunity to forbid any student from attending publicly funded schools. The EHA has been reauthorized eight times with the most recent reauthorization in 2004 as the Individuals with Disabilities Education Improvement Act (IDEIA). The IDEIA (2004) mandates a FAPE to students with disabilities with specifically designed instruction in order to meet students' individual learning needs in the least restrictive environment (LRE). The IDEIA (2004) is a special education law and provides some funding to states for the education of individuals with disabilities. The IDEIA mandates that students with disabilities be provided a FAPE in the LRE and encourages the education of students with disabilities alongside their typically developing peers; however, the exact setting in which services are provided to students with disabilities is determined by a multidisciplinary team based on individual student needs. According to federal regulations:

> To the maximum extent appropriate, children with disabilities, including children in public or private institutions or other care facilities, are educated with children who are not disabled, and ... special classes, separate schooling, or other removal of children with disabilities from the regular educational environment occurs only when the nature or severity of the disability is such that education in regular classes with supplementary aids and services cannot be achieved satisfactorily. (34 CRF 300.114(a)(2))

Each of these mandates was passed into law in order to assure the civil rights of children and adolescents who could otherwise be at risk of being denied a socially just education on the basis of individual and environmental conditions. Conditions such as living in impoverished circumstances or having a disability plague young people, and such students are in need of federally mandated protection. At face value, this issue seems very clear. All individuals have a right to an equal education. However, the reality is that socially just education is a multifaceted and complex phenomenon and exists in the context of defining and assuring fair and just access to an education that meets the individual needs of students with disabilities while avoiding social exclusion, over- or underrepresentation of specific minority groups, and bullying.

CONTINUING ISSUES OF SOCIAL JUSTICE

Educational Access

At the most basic level, children with disabilities, along with all children, have a right to an education. As previously mentioned, students with disabilities were not always given the opportunity to attend school. As such, social justice, with respect to educational access and attainment, goes a step further so as to ensure that students with disabilities have the opportunity to receive an education that is equivalent to that of individuals without disabilities. The opportunity to receive an education is paramount, as currently, the high school dropout rate for students with disabilities is more than 38 percent, compared to 11 percent of the general population in high school (Baumberger & Harper, 2007). Thus, the IDEIA guarantees a FAPE in the LRE. The mandate of the LRE and education with nondisabled peers is entrenched in strong and passionate feelings regarding social injustices. Some experts fervently contend that any placement other than full inclusion in the general education setting is "segregation" and is less than socially just. These individuals argue that inclusion is a fundamental right that can be facilitated through teacher training and environmental and social adaptations (Lamport, Graves, & Ward, 2012). Sapon-Shevin writes, "inclusion is not about disability, nor is it only about schools" (2003, p. 26). Inclusion is about social justice and advocating for the right of all children to be included in the general education settings at all times. In addition, those who support only full inclusion believe that students in less inclusive settings cannot be taught the attitudes, values, and skills required to live in the adult world (Salend, 2016). As a result, students with disabilities should always receive services and supports in the general education setting so as to increase their ability to form friendships with a diverse group and become more accepting of individual differences (Jorgensen, McSheehan, & Sonnenmeier, 2007). The overarching message of these discussions is the contention that those taught in general education settings fare better than those taught in special education environments and removing students with disabilities is a social injustice (Blanchett, Mumford, & Beachum, 2005).

Others argue that without specialized and individualized education, students with disabilities are denied a socially just education. They contend that placing students in inclusive settings before the students are prepared to meet the demands of that setting and without concentrated instruction to meet their needs is an injustice (Anastasiou & Kauffman, 2011). Kauffman and Badar write, "a focus on anything other than instruction undercuts the legal and moral rights of students with disabilities to an appropriate education and fails to produce substantive social justice" (2014, p. 13). Those opposed to only inclusionary practices find the feasibility of general education teachers teaching some students with disabilities unlikely.

Social Exclusion

The negative impact of placement in self-contained or resource class settings is purported to be especially salient for students with learning disabilities (LD). The number of children identified with LD continues to increase annually, with approximately 2.9 million youth in the United States receiving special support in school environments (Baumberger & Harper, 2007). Learning disabilities can negatively affect a child's school performance, behavior in the classroom and/or at home, educational attainment and goals, career aspirations, self-esteem, socialization, motivations, and everyday daily living activities. Moreover, youth with disabilities may find themselves separated from the general population and learning apart from their peers. National data indicate 43 percent of students with an intellectual disability, 28 percent of students with multiple disabilities, and 57 percent of students with autism spend 40 percent of their day in general education classes (Carter et al., 2016). The separation from their peers potentially has an impact on their interactions with classmates, academic engagement, social participation, and number of friendships due to the isolated nature of their specialized learning instruction (Salend & Duhaney, 1999).

On the other hand, the negative impact of placing students with severe disabilities in general education settings with intensive individualized assistance has raised concerns regarding the quality and benefits of the inclusive setting (Carter et al., 2016). Data show that more than 411,000 full-time special education staff members work with students between the ages of six and twenty-one on a one-to-one basis weekly. This support may be provided within the general education classroom and may be the primary or exclusive source of assistance. Support from staff members may hinder interactions between students with disabilities and their peers, due to the close proximity of an adult (Carter et al., 2016). To address the negative effects of having an adult in constant close proximity, some studies have supported a peer support arrangement, where students with disabilities work with their peers in the general education classroom. This approach fosters greater social and academic benefits for students with disabilities due to more frequent communication with their peers, relationship opportunities in the general education classroom, and increased participation in classroom activities (Carter et al., 2016). However, questions remain regarding the quality of instruction in general education settings for this population.

Aside from exclusion within the school day, students with disabilities also contend with exclusion in other educational environments, such as after-school extracurricular activities and transportation around school. As per research, a significant number of youth with disabilities in middle and high school are not accessing or deriving benefits from after-school participation and have a limited involvement (Carter et al., 2010; Simeonsson, Carlson, Huntington, McMillen, & Brent, 2001). This is problematic and goes against the direction of IDEIA (2004), as it specifically instructs the individualized education program (IEP) teams to consider the support and services students with disabilities require so as to "participate in extracurricular and other nonacademic activities" (Carter et al., 2010, p. 275). Extracurricular activities help students learn and develop life skills, such as time management and problem-solving, and social skills, such as cooperation and conflict resolution. In addition, students involved in extracurricular activities develop self-confidence and self-discipline and have increased opportunities to earn college admission and scholarships (Miller, Jensen, & Clauss-Ehlers, 2010). However, in a study conducted by Powers et al. (2005), researchers reviewed the IEPs of approximately 400 transition-age youth with disabilities and found only 11.3 percent of the IEPs included any notation regarding adolescent involvement in extracurricular activities. This limited number is particularly discouraging due to the notion that participation in extracurricular activities is a recommended component of dropout-prevention mechanisms for youth with behavioral challenges (Carter, Swedeen, Moss, & Pesko, 2010).

Involvement in extracurricular activities is important as it provides students a platform for exploring other interests and developing additional strengths (e.g., working on a school newspaper, debate club, student government). The membership in extracurricular activities also increases the opportunities for peer relationships, fosters a sense of school pride and belonging within the school community, and helps develop social and daily life skills (Carter et al., 2010).

A number of reasons may contribute to the low participation rate of youth with disabilities in extracurricular activities, including but not limited to barriers extrapolating from a lack of awareness, opportunities, and a support system within the educational arena. For example, students may spend a majority of their time in self-contained settings and are not aware of the opportunities to get involved within their school. Moreover, teachers and educators may believe these students lack the needed social skills to participate successfully and thus do not include these students or extend an invitation to join such clubs. Research reports that teachers often indicate a lack of knowledge and strategies to successfully and confidently support students with disabilities in these inclusive extracurricular settings, thereby creating a continuous and endemic cycle (Carter et al., 2010). Further, parents may be unaware of the availability of such activities or their importance. In addition, extracurricular activities can require resources that parents do not have, such as the cost of materials and/or transportation (White, Hill, Kemp, McRae, & Young, 2012). As such, although the fight for social justice has been predominantly fought on the academic battleground, these other areas also affect children's overall well-being and deserve attention and advocacy.

Transportation for youth with disabilities is a necessary component of the education system and has the potential to decrease the probability of equitable access for students with disabilities; however, this area has received limited attention in the research. The IDEIA (2004) includes travel to and from school, as well as around school, as necessary parts of the LRE. Research suggests that access and transportation requirements for students with disabilities should be equivalent to those without disabilities, thus enabling the same school day start and finish times (Graham, Keys, McMahon, & Brubacher, 2014). Additionally, transportation problems have been associated with an increased rate of school stressors, lower rates of school involvement, and higher rates of anxiety, depression, and aggression (Graham et al., 2014). The inadequacy of transportation options and difficulty moving around the school environment leads to low involvement in school activities and social participation. As a result, such transportation issues are key elements to consider in relation to the inclusion of students with disabilities.

Disproportional Representation in Special Education

Another area of concern that speaks to social injustice for individuals with disabilities is the disproportional representation in special education. For the past four decades, it has been an accepted fact established through research that students from specific ethnic/racial groups are disproportionally represented in high-incidence disability categories (e.g., mild cognitive disabilities, learning disabilities, or emotional and behavioral disorders). According to the National Association of Bilingual Education (2002), "disproportionality" is defined as the over- or underrepresentation of a demographic group in gifted or special education compared to the overall student population. Situations of such disproportionality date back to 1968, when Dunn revealed data suggesting that African American students were overrepresented in the category of mild mental retardation (i.e., mild cognitive disabilities). Similarly, Mercer (1973) found that Mexican American students were overrepresented in the same category. For this reason, in 1971, the Supreme Court ruled in the case of *Larry P. v. Riles* that students could not be identified as "educably mentally retarded" based simply on scores from IQ tests. The finding was established on the evidence of potential bias in IQ tests and the need for more than one source of information. Although methodology for determining special education eligibility changed across the nation after 1971, overrepresentation continued and continues today.

Overrepresentation of students of color in special education is an issue of equity and social justice. It means that some students are receiving services who do not need them and other students who need such services are not receiving them. Moreover, students who are receiving unnecessary services are likely being denied educational opportunities. For example, an IEP team determined that the best placement for a student eligible for special education with a learning disability was a resource classroom. If that student did not have a learning disability, then modifications being made to the general education curriculum in the student's IEP would inadvertently disallow access to the general education curriculum. As educators, we must question the explanations for this perpetual cycle of inequity. Some contend that it is a complex phenomenon with historical racial hierarchies as the foundation. Connor writes, "notions of differing racial intelligences became perpetuated by many interlocking historical forces stretching over time, reifying the correlation between race and ability as a fact" (2017, p. 227). According to Connor, after the ruling in *Brown v. Board of Education* (1954), in which public schools in the United States were desegregated, the number of students served by special education in the categories of intellectual and behavioral disabilities increased. Partially in response to this, the trend toward educating students with disabilities in general education settings with supports and services flourished; however, African American students continued to be placed in more restrictive special education settings (Parrish, 2002). In order to avoid this social injustice, as previously discussed, some contend that full inclusion of all students with disabilities is the only acceptable placement (Frattura & Capper, 2007; Theoharris, 2009). On the other hand, some special education experts believe that placement of students identified with special needs in inclusive settings without consideration to needed supports and services is an injustice (Kauffman & Badar, 2014). Special education is not a place; it is the process of providing supports and services for students with disabilities in order to allow them to receive educational benefit. As such, it is important that special education decisions are individualized, based on student needs and empirical evidence. Placement decisions should be based on the needs of the student without compromising rigorous education or minimizing expectations for the child. We agree that to reduce inequitable services, teachers must learn to work against racism and toward ableism, reflect on their own biases and beliefs, consider the individual characteristics of the students in their classes and use those differences to inform their teaching practices, carefully consider referrals to special education, and support appropriate inclusive education (Connor, 2017). In addition, policies beyond teacher control, including federal- and state-level mandates, must be reconsidered. However, we acknowledge that this is a simplistic view. Reducing the disproportional placement of students of color in special education is not a simple task and requires systemic, philosophical, and societal change.

OVERREPRESENTATION IN EXCLUSIONARY DISCIPLINE

In addition to being overrepresented in special education settings and services, male students of color with disabilities have been historically overrepresented in exclusionary disciplinary practices (Christle, Nelson, & Jolivette, 2004). Specifically, they have been suspended or expelled at a greater rate than students of color without disabilities (Christle et al., 2004; USDOE, 2014). The US Department of Education (2014) reports that students with disabilities are twice as likely to be suspended as their typically developing peers. Unfortunately, students who are most excluded from school for disciplinary reasons are those who struggle academically and socially, avoid school as much as possible, and do not feel a strong connection with the school.

Students who are expelled or suspended are being denied the right to an equitable educational opportunity when compared to those who are not suspended. Students already at risk of school failure lose valuable instructional time (Brown, 2007). In some instances, students are not allowed to be in a school setting of any kind or receive instruction in any form. In other instances, students are assigned to disciplinary alternative settings. Some schools allow students to get their work and complete it independently while others do not. Still others may reduce the academic grade of the student as part of the punishment. However, the exposure to quality, effective instructional time in these settings is doubtful.

Further, students who are suspended once are likely to be suspended numerous times, increasing the amount of classroom instruction missed (Brown, 2007). Other time associated with the disciplinary action is missed from school, such as time lost in administrative procedures to transfer students from one setting to another (Brown, 2007). This is especially detrimental to the population of students frequently excluded from school, as they are known to be at risk of school failure prior to the exclusion. Missed instructional time and opportunities to learn leads to lack of academic engagement and achievement, failing classes, being retained in a grade, and underdeveloped academic skills (Arcia, 2006; Brown, 2007).

Excluding students from schools that are designed to be environments for students to grow, not only academically, but also socially, denies them the right to positive role models and academic buffers to negative life experiences. Expulsion can lead students to believe that adults are not concerned with their well-being (Brown, 2007) and decreases the opportunity for positive adult relationships. Confounding the issue, school staff have been found to perceive minority parents as powerless to prevent their children from being expelled (Bowditch, 1993). These educator and student beliefs are supported by the fact that students of color receive more severe discipline than their white peers for the same behaviors (Skiba et al., 2011). Students who receive numerous office discipline referrals are known to have more negative attitudes and school dispositions and lower rates of school bonding than students with lower levels (Hawkins, Guo, Hill, Battin-Pearson, & Abbott, 2001; Toldson, McGee, & Lemmons, 2013). This is unfortunate, as "positive student–teacher relationships" is a known factor that increases academic engagement and resiliency in the face of adversity (Sointu, Savolainen, Lappalainen, & Lambert, 2017).

Beyond the lack of learning and negative social and emotional experiences, excluding students from the opportunity to learn – a social injustice with no known positive effects on behavior (Raffaele-Mendez & Knoff, 2003; Tobin, Sugai, & Colvin, 1996) – is associated with numerous high-stakes negative consequences (Brown, 2007). Students who are not in school are at increased risk for drug use and abuse, sexual and illegal activity, juvenile justice involvement, and academic failure (Christle et al., 2004; Fabelo et al., 2011; Morrison, Anthony, Storino, & Dillon, 2001). Further, students who are suspended from school are at increased risk of dropping out of school altogether (Balfanz, Byrnes, & Fox, 2013).

The cost of these negative consequences is felt not only by the students but also by the students' families and by society as a whole. In a study (Parker, Paget, Ford, & Gwernan-Jones, 2016) of parent perceptions of exclusionary discipline practices with children ages five to twelve years old, parents reported an array of complex feelings and concerns regarding themselves and their children. For example, parents reported feeling out of control and in disbelief that their children were expelled for the exact behaviors for which they needed help. Additionally, parents reported that exclusion was a journey that started with a misbehavior, a "seed," that continued to grow throughout the children's school experience, becoming more punishing and less helpful. This spiraling experience can have a detrimental impact on children. Students who are frequently excluded from schools for disciplinary infractions are more likely to drop out of school and in turn are more likely to earn less money than high school and college graduates and contribute less to society (Toldson et al., 2013). Further, students who drop out of high school prior to graduation are eight times more likely to be incarcerated than those who graduate from high school (Christle, Jolivette, & Nelson, 2005).

Bullying

Another form of social injustice faced by individuals with disabilities in schools is bullying. The complexity of bullying involves a myriad of components that leaves researchers and experts in debate regarding a plethora of issues, such as what defines "bullying," how to effectively describe the bully, victim, and bully-victim, predictive and protective factors, federal and state laws, the impact on mental health issues (e.g., depression, self-esteem, anxiety), and best practices for intervention (Rose, Simpson, & Moss, 2015). The term "bully-victim" refers to youth with disabilities who engage in perpetration (e.g., bully role) as a result of their own victimization or as a function of their disability (Rose, Simpson, & Preast, 2016). Recently, experts and policy makers have focused on bullying due to the recognized and notable health concerns it poses for school-aged youth. Research provides evidence to suggest students with disabilities are disproportionately involved in the bullying dynamic (Rose et al., 2016). Bullying is defined as "a form of aggressive behavior that is intentional, repetitive, and causing harm, distress or discomfort to someone else" (Maiano, Aime, Salvas, Morin, & Normand, 2016, p. 182). Bullying implies a power imbalance where a bully acts negatively toward a victim who cannot defend himself or herself (Maiano et al., 2016). Bullying can be direct (e.g., physical, verbal) or indirect (e.g., exclusion, social isolation, lying, spreading rumors) and also encompasses cyberbullying (e.g., Facebook posts, emails).

Studies indicate that students with disabilities can be up to one and a half times more likely to report victimization than the national average (Rose et al., 2016). A study conducted by Blake, Lund, Zhou, Kwok, and Benz (2012) found that, in grades one through ten, 24.5 percent of elementary school students, 34.1 percent of middle schoolers, and 26.6 percent of high school students with disabilities reported victimization. Research on the prevalence rates of bullying perpetration and victimization among youth with disabilities demonstrates that youth with various types of disabilities are at a greater risk of being bullied than their peers without disabilities (Maiano et al., 2016). Rose, Stormont, et al. (2015) suggest that victimization rates may vary depending on the disability and educational setting. For example, some research has found that youth with intellectual disabilities and emotional/behavioral disorders experience a higher rate of victimization in more restrictive settings (Rose, Stormont, et al., 2015). Other studies suggest that students with disabilities are disproportionately represented in the bullying dynamic as either a perpetrator, victim, or bully-victim (Rose & Gage, 2017). Students may experience different forms of victimization, ranging from physical and verbal victimization to social exclusion and cyber victimization. Students victimized by bullies often exhibit adverse student outcomes, such as "school avoidance, decreased academic performance, anxiety, suicidal ideation, depressive symptoms, and low self-esteem" (Rose, Simpson, & Moss, 2015, p. 517). Scholars purport students with learning disabilities experience higher rates of depression than their peers who do not have disabilities (Mishna, 2003).

Due to the overrepresentation of students with disabilities who are involved in the bullying cycle, it is imperative to understand the predictive and protective factors for this population (Rose, Simpson, & Moss, 2015). Studies have found that the most distinguishable predictors for bullying involvement for students with disabilities are lack of social and communication skills (Rose, Monda-Amaya, & Espelage, 2011). The lack of social and interpersonal skills may contribute to an increase in social exclusion that may subsequently predict an increase in bullying and victimization. As a result, it is likely that the diagnosis of a "disability does not place a student at escalated risk; it is more likely that the characteristics associated with the disability serve as risk factors" (Rose, Simpson, & Moss, 2015, p. 529).

It is important to consider the purpose of special education and the services it should offer to aid in the development of academic, social, and behavioral skills. It is critical for IEP teams and special education providers to make an increased effort "to reduce the discrepancy between youth with and without disabilities by prioritizing functional and behavioral skill acquisition in the IEP" (Rose & Gage, 2017, p. 310).

Experts suggest the most effective methods to decrease bullying involvement among youth with disabilities are direct interventions concentrating on communication and social skills (Rose & Espelage, 2012; Rose & Gage, 2017; Rose et al., 2011).

IMPLICATIONS

Social justice as a construct aims to answer the question "how can we contribute to the creation of a more equitable, respectful, and just society for everyone?" (Zajda et al., 2006, p. 13). When viewed through the lens of an educational context, one must consider if the school environment fosters an unequal distribution of economic, social, or educational capital to any one group of students. If there is an unequal division, it can be assumed one group may be gaining an advantage over another group. Advocating for social justice for students with disabilities is a complex and multifaceted issue; however, the prior sections of this chapter demonstrate many arenas in which students with disabilities are treated unjustly. As such, implications emerge in the areas of policy and advocacy, the meaning of social justice in school settings for individual students through engagement, family involvement and collaboration, and strategies to increase the just treatment of students with disabilities. Various intervention and prevention approaches can be applied and have proved promising for youth and young people with disabilities, but continued advocacy and research is still needed in this area.

Advocacy and Policy

Advocates for social justice must become aware of the vast range of unique challenges, differences, and needs of the students they support. Those working in the educational environment are expected to advocate for and successfully serve students from varying backgrounds, working for a socially just education for all. As such, they must reflect on and consider the many arenas in which it appears students with disabilities may not be treated in a socially just fashion. Educators can begin by viewing students' strengths and challenges, instead of "handicaps," and acknowledge the range of limitations inherent in all students. Educators may also simultaneously reframe limitations as "differences." This highlights the myriad of differences people encompass and brings to the fore a discussion of how unique differences can connect and unite people (Holt, Bowlby, & Lea, 2017) as opposed to segregating and punishing for differences.

The research purports that, across student differences (i.e., race, sex, religion, or language), students "benefit socially and academically in heterogeneous, integrated settings" (Capper & Young, 2014, pp. 162–163). Based on this knowledge, scholars and social advocates must be aware of empirical support when developing persuasive arguments for how and when segregated programs can hinder children's educational opportunities. As demonstrated here, segregation is more than simply an educational environment. Students with disabilities are frequently segregated through classroom settings, social situations, extracurricular activities, disciplinary actions, and unjust treatment by peers. Although the education of students with disabilities has come a long way in the past half-century, more work is needed.

Student Engagement

When working with students with disabilities, research has highlighted the importance of engaging and empowering students in every aspect of their own lives. In addition to advocating for youth with disabilities, it is the responsibility of educators to teach them to advocate for themselves. It is not for educators to determine what is best for youth with disabilities, but it is their responsibility to allow and to teach them to explore all of their options. This includes having conversations regarding individual interests, goals, future plans, and skill sets. When youth struggle to articulate their needs and concerns, we encourage adults to provide extra support and assistance, and to make decisions with the input of the student. The IEP meeting offers a platform for involving students, parents, and other stakeholders in discussing students' current needs and future plans (Carter et al., 2010). Involving students and engaging them in the IEP empowers them and enables them to verbalize their desires. As such, talking with students about their goals during school, life after graduation, or personal interests allows them to provide valuable information needed to facilitate dialogue crucial for advocacy. The process of "identifying activities, gathering needed information, setting goals for participation, taking initiative, advocating for needed supports, and problem-solving challenges can provide students with a meaningful opportunity to practice valuable self-determination skills across all settings" (Carter et al., 2010, p. 278). Additionally, connecting their experiences in the academic disciplines with practical real-life situations can help students gain awareness of their interests, aptitudes, and career options. Social justice for youth with disabilities is possible only through a concerted effort between students and professionals.

Family Involvement

In addition to communicating with the youth, collaborating with parents/guardians and garnering their involvement is an integral component of advocating for social justice. Parental support bolsters students in their development, social engagement, and relationships with professional staff and peers (Carter et al., 2010). As a result, educators must make a conscious effort to engage and support parents in their involvement. At the most basic level, educators must inform parents/guardians about meetings, student progress, and school activities, so as to promote communication and collaboration. Ideally, these conversations allow professionals an opportunity to hear concerns from parents, as well as to provide a vehicle through which to address them. It is also important to understand the viewpoint of parents and be cognizant of feelings. For instance, parents may have differing views of what type of educational setting might best reflect their children's needs (Fish, 2006). Further, we encourage educators to be gentle and protective of their relationships with parents. To assure parents involvement, parents must feel valued, comfortable, and not overwhelmed by the educational process.

Collaboration

As the African proverb claims, "it takes a village to raise a child." The same mind-set can be applied to the academic environment. Youth with disabilities often need an entire support system consisting of special and general education teachers, professional support staff and aides, IEP planning teams, extracurricular advisors, and higher administration in order to achieve their goals. This network of varying professionals is a crucial aspect in the success and achievement youth will be able to attain. Moreover, collaboration and communication across the network facilitates an exchange of ideas and has the capacity to prompt discussions to address how children's needs may be best met. If a problem arises in one element of education, the network of professionals can be alerted so that support and assistance can be provided.

Strategies

The issues of social justice explored in this chapter are only words without concrete, actionable strategies to address the areas of injustice so as to increase the likelihood that: (a) individuals within the education system will advocate for students with disabilities and policies that support an equitable education for all students; (b) students with disabilities will engage successfully and fully in the academic environment; (c) families will feel comfortable and confident in educational settings and believe that they have a true voice in the decision-making process; and (d) collaboration will occur between everyone in the "village."

At the national level, we encourage educators to become advocates for students by engaging directly in policy activism. As educators, we often "admire problems" and complain about policies placed upon us. In fact, it appears that many educators have not explored methods of using their voice to shape policy. In the words of Rita Pearson (n.d.), "We listen to policy that doesn't make sense and we teach anyway." However, as those on the front lines, educators must make their voices heard. To make this leap, educators are encouraged to reach out to national organizations and to request training and guidance so they can become effective advocates at the national level. Educators can find such training from the Council for Exceptional Children (CEC), a leader in advocating for special education legislation. The Children and Youth Action Network (CAN) is an organization of volunteers within the CEC that aims to "advance policy affecting students with disabilities and gifts and talents" (CEC, n.d.). Each summer, the CEC provides advocacy training for educators at the Special Education Legislative Summit in Alexandria, Virginia.

Similarly, educators are encouraged to advocate at the school level for programs known to increase student engagement and feelings of belonging at school. The challenges described in this chapter make clear that students with disabilities need adult champions in their schools. Mentoring programs provide a structured vehicle for reaching out to students. Mentoring programs have decades of support to increase the likelihood that students will become engaged in schools (see DuBois, Holloway, Valentine, & Cooper, 2002, for review).

In one example, Check and Connect (C&C) is a structured mentoring program that utilizes a problem-solving strategy to increase student performance (Christenson, Sinclair, Thurlow, & Evelo, 1999). Through the program, an adult "checks" on student progress in areas known to contribute to student performance (e.g., attendance, grades, or tardiness) and "connects" with students in regular mentoring sessions. This connection involves problem-solving around areas of need and building student capacity to address those needs (Christenson et al., 1999). At the heart of mentoring is the ability of the mentor to build quality relationships with students. Educators must be attuned to the needs and perceptions of students with disabilities in relation to students' sense of social justice. Mentoring programs, such as C&C, are ideal vehicles to facilitate this process.

Experts contend that educators must reflect on their own environments and practices to increase parent engagement. It is important that educators ensure that parents feel welcome in schools and address the barriers to parent involvement. Known barriers include language, work schedules, childcare, and a sense of disenfranchisement (Smith, Wohlstetter, Kuzin, & DePedro, 2011). Simple strategies are available to address language, work schedules, and childcare. For example, we must include interpreters in our involvement with parents and schedule activities and meetings at times more convenient (e.g., evenings) for those involved. When feasible, providing childcare after hours and in evenings may assist parents who may otherwise not be able to find or afford childcare.

Decreasing feelings of disenfranchisement is a more complex barrier to address. Helping parents feel part of the school involves reflecting on practices that alienate them. For example, parents might feel less than welcomed by staff in reception areas in schools (Lucas, 2015). Additionally, parents might have difficulties when scheduling appointments to meet with teachers and other issues such as non-responsiveness from educators, discomfort when educators have asked them to sit in child-sized seats, use of educational jargon, and educators' failure to truly listen to parental suggestions (Lucas, 2015). When parents have had their own negative school experiences when they were children, it may be difficult to convey to them the importance of becoming engaged in their children's education. Educators are encouraged to reflect and problem-solve when these issues arise.

True collaboration among all members of the "village" can range from team-based decision-making within the school context to more extensive involvement of all community partners and wraparound services. Wraparound services frequently include interventions provided by social workers, psychologists, mentors and counselors, juvenile justice services, and social services. Positive behavioral interventions and supports (PBIS), a multitiered system of prevention of behavioral challenges, includes wraparound services to address the needs of students with complex behavioral issues (Eber, 2008). Collaboration is essential to assure social justice for individuals with disabilities.

CONCLUSION

In conclusion, given the challenges and implications identified, those who care about social justice are encouraged to become better informed and more aware of the central tenets that encompass the academic environment. An agreed-upon understanding of what social justice means should be unambiguous, anchoring the foundation on which policies, practices, and procedures are predicated. If educators and advocates for social justice understand these aspects, they will make greater gains toward creating a more inclusive community focused on providing just outcomes for all students, including those with disabilities. Schools and educators within the educational context are encouraged to utilize innovative ways to meet the needs of the young people they aim to support and to be forever cautious of intentional and unintentional breaches in social justice (Cooney, Jahoda, Gumley, & Knott, 2006).

REFERENCES

Anastasiou, D., & Kauffman, J. M. (2011). A social constructionist approach to disability: Implications for special education. *Exceptional Children*, 77(3), 367–384.

Arcia, E. (2006). Achievement and enrollment status of suspended students: Outcomes in a large, multicultural school district. *Education and Urban Society*, 38, 359–369.

Balfanz, R., Byrnes, V., & Fox, J. (2013). Sent home and put off-track: The antecedents, disproportionalities, and consequences of being suspended in the ninth grade. Paper presented at Closing the School Discipline Gap: Research to Practice, Washington, DC. Retrieved from www.civilrightsproject.ucla.edu/resources/projects/center-for-civil-rights-remedies/school-to-prison-folder/state-reports/sent-home-and-put-off-track-the-antecedents-disproportionalities-and-consequences-of-being-suspended-in-the-ninth-grade.

Baumberger, J., & Harper, R. E. (2007). *Assisting students with disabilities*. Thousand Oaks, CA: Corwin Press.

Blake, J. J., Lund, E. M., Zhou, Q., Kwok, O., & Benz, M. R. (2012). National prevalence rates of bullying victimization among students with disabilities in the United States. *School Psychology Quarterly*, 27, 210–222.

Blanchett, W. J., Mumford, V., & Beachum, F. (2005). Urban school failure and disproportionality in a post-Brown era: Benign neglect of the constitutional rights of students of color. *Remedial and Special Education*, 26(2), 70–81.

Bowditch, C. (1993). Getting rid of troublemakers: High school disciplinary procedures and the production of dropouts. *Social Problems, 40*, 493–507.

Brown, C. P. (2007). Examining the streams of a retention policy to understand the politics of high stakes reform. *Education Policy Analysis Archives, 15*(9), 1–28.

Capper, C. A., & Young, M. D. (2014). Ironies and limitations of educational leadership for social justice: A call to social justice educators. *Theory into Practice, 53*, 158–164. doi:10.1080/00405841

Carter, E. W., Asmus, J., Moss, C., et al. (2016). Randomized evaluation of peer support arrangements to support the inclusion of high school students with severe disabilities. *Exceptional Children, 82*, 209–233. doi:10.1177/0014402915598780

Carter, E. W., Swedeen, B., Moss, C. K., & Pesko, M. (2010). "What are you doing after school?" Promoting extracurricular involvement for transition-age youth with disabilities. *Intervention and School and Clinic, 45*, 275–283. doi:10.1177/1053451209359077

Christenson, S. L., Sinclair, M. F., Thurlow, M. L., & Evelo, D. (1999). Promoting student engagement with school using the Check & Connect model. *Australian Journal of Guidance and Counseling, 9*, 169–184.

Christle, C. A., Jolivette, K., & Nelson, C. M. (2005). Breaking the school to prison pipeline: Identifying school risk and protective factors for youth delinquency. *Exceptionality, 13*, 69–88.

Christle, C. A., Nelson, C. M., & Jolivette, K. (2004). School characteristics related to the use of suspension. *Education and Treatment of Children, 27*, 509–526.

Connor, D. J. (2013). Social justice in education for students with disabilities. In L. Florian (ed.), *The SAGE Handbook of Special Education: Two Volume Set* (pp. 111–128). Thousand Oaks, CA: Sage. doi:10.4135/9781446282236

Connor, D. J. (2017). Who is responsible for the racialized practices evident within (special) education and what can be done to change them? *Theory into Practice, 56*(3), 226–233. doi:10.1080/00405841.2017.1336034

Cooney, G., Jahoda, A., Gumley, A., & Knott, F. (2006). Young people with intellectual disabilities attending mainstream and segregated schooling: Perceived stigma, social comparison and future aspirations. *Journal of Intellectual Disability Research, 50*, 432–444. doi:10.1111/j.1365-2788.2006.00789.x

Council for Exception Children (CEC) (n.d.). Children and Youth Action Network (CAN). Retrieved from www.cec.sped.org/Policy-and-Advocacy/Children-and-Youth-Action-Network.

Dover, A. G. (2009). Teaching for social justice and K-12 student outcomes: A conceptual framework and research review. *Equity & Excellence in Education, 42*, 506–524. doi:10.1080/10665680903196339

DuBois, D. L., Holloway, B. E., Valentine, J. C., & Cooper, H. (2002). Effectiveness of mentoring programs for youth: A meta-analytic review. *American Journal of Community Psychology, 30*, 157–197. doi:10.1023/ A:1014628810714

Dunn, L. (1968). Special education for mildly retarded: Is much of it justifiable? *Exceptional Children, 35*, 5–22.

Eber, L. (2008). Wraparound: A key component of school-wide systems of positive behavior supports. In E. J. Bruns & J. S. Walker (eds.), *The resource guide to wraparound*. Portland, OR: National Wraparound Initiative, Research and Training Center for Family Support and Children's Mental Health.

Enslin, P. (2006). Democracy, social justice and education: Feminist strategies in a globalizing world. *Educational Philosophy and Theory, 38*, 57–67.

Every Student Succeeds Act (ESSA) of 2015, Pub. L. No. 114–95 § 114 Stat. 1177 (2015–2016).

Fabelo, T., Thompson, M. D., Plotkin, M., et al. (2011). *Breaking schools' rules: A statewide study of how school discipline relates to students' success and juvenile justice involvement* (pp. 1–124). College Station, TX: Public Policy Research Institute.

Fish, W. W. (2006). Perceptions of parents of students with autism towards the IEP meeting: A case study of one family support group chapter. *Education, 127*(1), 56–68.

Frattura, E. M., & Capper, C. A. (2007). *Leading for social justice: Transforming schools for all learners.* Thousand Oaks, CA: Corwin Press.

Gewirtz, S. (2006). Towards a contextualized analysis of social justice in education. *Educational Philosophy and Theory, 38*(1), 69–81. doi:10.1111/j.1469-5812.2006.00175.x

Graham, B. C., Keys, C. B., McMahon, S. D., & Brubacher, M. R. (2014). Transportation challenges for urban students with disabilities: Parent perspectives. *Journal of Prevention and Intervention in the Community, 42*, 45–57. doi:10.1080/10852352.2014.855058

Griffiths, M. (1998). Towards a theoretical framework for understanding social justice in educational practice. *Educational Philosophy and Theory, 30*, 175–192.

Hawkins, J. D., Guo, J., Hill, K. G., Battin-Pearson, S., & Abbott, R. (2001). Long-term effects of the Seattle Social Development intervention on school bonding trajectories. *Applied Developmental Science, 5*, 225–236.

Holt, L., Bowlby, S., & Lea, J. (2017). "Everyone knows me ... I sort of like move about": The friendships and encounters of young people with special educational needs in different school settings. *Environment and Planning, 49*, 1361–1378.

Individuals with Disabilities Education Improvement Act (IDEIA). 20 U.S. Code § 1400 (2004).

Jorgensen, C. M., McSheehan, M., & Sonnenmeier, R. (2007). Presumed competence reflected in the educational programs of students with IDD before and after the Beyond Access professional development intervention. *Journal of Intellectual and Developmental Disabilities, 32*(4), 248–262.

Kauffman, J. M., & Badar, J. (2014). Instruction, not inclusion, should be the central issue in special education: An alternative view from the USA. *Journal of International Special Needs Education, 17*(1), 13–20.

Kretchmar, J. (2013). Social justice in education. *Research Starters: Education*, 1–7. Retrieved from http://connection.ebscohost.com/c/essays/27577654/social-justice-education.

Lamport, M. A., Graves, L., & Ward, A. (2012). Special needs students in inclusive classrooms: The impact of social interactions on educational outcomes for learners with emotional and behavioural disabilities. *European Journal of Business and Social Sciences, 1*(5), 54–69.

Lucas, B. (2015). 10 ways in which schools alienate parents. Retrieved from www.tes.com/news/10-ways-which-schools-alienate-parents.

Maiano, C., Aime, A., Salvas, M. C., Morin, A., & Normand, C. L. (2016). Prevalence and correlates of bullying perpetration and victimization among school-aged youth with intellectual disabilities: A systemic review. *Research in Developmental Disabilities, 49*, 181–195.

Mercer, J. (1973). *Labeling the mentally retarded.* Berkeley: University of California Press.

Miller, L., Jensen, E., & Clauss-Ehlers, C. S. (2010, April). The influence of extracurricular activities on student achievement: Why school counselors should encourage students to get involved. Presentation at the 2010 New Jersey Counseling Association Conference, Somerset, NJ.

Mishna, F. (2003). Learning disabilities and bullying: Double jeopardy. *Journal of Learning, 4*, 336–347.

Morrison, G. M., Anthony, S., Storino, M., & Dillon, C. (2001). An examination of the disciplinary histories and the individual and educational characteristics of students who

participate in an in-school suspension program. *Education & Treatment of Children*, 24(3), 276–293.
National Association for Bilingual Education (NABE). (2002). *Determining appropriate referrals of English language learners to special education: A self-assessment guide for principals*. Arlington, VA: Council for Exceptional Children.
Neito, S., & Bode, P. (2007). *Affirming diversity: The sociopolitical context of multicultural education*. Boston, MA: Allyn and Bacon
Parker, C., Pagat, A., Ford, T., & Gwernan-Jones, R. (2016). "He was excluded for the kind of behavior that we thought he needed support with … " A qualitative analysis of the experiences and perspectives of parents whose children have been excluded from school. *Emotional and Behavioural Difficulties*, 21, 133–151.
Parrish, T. (2002). Racial disparities in the identification, funding, and provision of special education. In D. J. Losen & G. Orfield (eds.), *Racial inequality in special education* (pp. 15–37). Cambridge, MA: Harvard Education Press.
Pearson, R. (n.d.). Every kid needs a champion. TED Talk. Retrieved from www.ted.com/talks/rita_pierson_every_kid_needs_a_champion/discussion?utm_medi#t–414767.
Powers, K. M., Gil-Kashiwabara, E., Geenan, S. J., et al. (2005). Mandates and effective transition planning practices reflected in IEPs. *Career Development for Exceptional Individuals*, 28, 47–59.
Raffaele-Mendez, L. M., & Knoff, H. M. (2003). Who gets suspended from school and why: A demographic analysis of schools and disciplinary infractions in a large school district. *Education and Treatment of Children*, 26, 30–51.
Rawls, J. (1971/1999). *A theory of justice*. Harvard, MA: Harvard University Press.
Reisch, M., & Garvin, C. D. (2016). *Social work and social justice: Concepts, challenges, and strategies*. Oxford: Oxford University Press.
Rose, C. A., & Espelage, D. L. (2012). Risk and protective factors associated with the bullying involvement of students with emotional and behavioral disorders. *Behavioral Disorders*, 37, 133–148.
Rose, C. A., & Gage, N. A. (2017). Exploring the involvement of bullying among students with disabilities over time. *Exceptional Children*, 83, 298–314. doi:10.1177/0014402916667587
Rose, C. A., Monda-Amaya, L. E., & Espelage, D. L. (2011). Bullying perpetration and victimization in special education: A review of the literature. *Remedial and Special Education*, 32, 114–130.
Rose, C. A., Simpson, C. G., & Moss, A. (2015). The bullying dynamic: Prevalence of involvement among a large-scale sample of middle and high school youth with and without disabilities. *Psychology in the Schools*, 52, 515–531.
Rose, C. A., Simpson, C. G., & Preast, J. L. (2016). Exploring psychosocial predictors of bullying involvement for students with disabilities. *Remedial and Special Education*, 37, 308–317. doi:10.1177/0741932516629219
Rose, C. A., Stormont, M., Wang, Z., et al. (2015). Bullying and students with disabilities: Examination of disability status and educational placement. *School Psychology Review*, 44, 425–444. doi:10.17105/spr-15-0080.1
Salend, S. J. (2016). *Creating inclusive classrooms: Effective, differentiated and reflective practices* (8th ed.). Columbus, OH: Pearson.
Salend, S. J., & Duhaney, L. M. G. (1999). The impact of inclusion on students with and without disabilities and their educators. *Remedial and Special Education*, 20, 114–126.
Sandel, M. (2009). *Justice: What's the right thing to do?* New York: Farrar, Straus and Giroux.
Sapon-Shevin, M. (2003). Inclusion: A matter of social justice. *Educational Leadership*, 61(2), 25–29.

Simeonsson, R. J., Carlson, D., Huntington, G. S., McMillen, J. S., & Brent, J. L. (2001). Students with disabilities: A national survey of participation in school activities. *Disability and Rehabilitation, 23*, 49–63.

Skiba, R. J., Horner, R. H., Chung, C., et al. (2011). Race is not neutral: A national investigation of African American and Latino disproportionality in school discipline. *School Psychology Review, 40*(1), 85–107.

Smith, J., Wohlstetter, P., Kuzin, C. A., & DePedro, K. (2011). Parent involvement in urban charter schools: New strategies for increasing participation. *School Community Journal, 21*(1), 71–94. Retrieved from www.schoolcommunitynetwork.org/SCJ.aspx.

Sointu, E. T., Savolainen, H., Lappalainen, K., & Lambert, M. C. (2017). Longitudinal associations of student–teacher relationships and behavioural and emotional strengths on academic achievement. *Educational Psychology, 37*(4), 457–467. doi:10.1080/01443410.2016.1165796

Theoharris, G. (2009). *The school leaders our children deserve: Seven keys to equity, social justice, and school reform.* New York: Teachers College Press.

Tobin, T., Sugai, G., & Colvin, G. (1996). Patterns in middle school discipline records. *Journal of Emotional and Behavioral Disorders, 4*, 82–94.

Toldson, I. A., McGee, T., & Lemmons, B. P. (2013). Reducing suspension among academically disengaged black males. The Civil Rights Project. Retrieved from www.civilrightsproject.ucla.edu/resources/projects/center-for-civil-rights-remedies/school-to-prison-folder/state-reports/copy3_of_dignity-disparity-and-desistance-effective-restorative-justice-strategies-to-plug-the-201cschool-to-prison-pipeline.

United Nations (UN) (2013). The millennium development goals. Retrieved from www.un.org/millenniumgoals/pdf/report-2013/mdg-report-2013-english.pdf.

United Nations Educational, Scientific and Cultural Organization (UNESCO) (1994). The Salamanca Statement and Framework for Action on Special Needs Education. Retrieved from http://unesdoc.unesco.org/images/0009/000984/098427eo.pdf.

US Department of Education (USDOE) (2014). *Civil rights data collection data snapshot: School discipline* (Issue Brief No. 1). Retrieved from www.ocrdata.ed.gov/Downloads/CRDC-School-Discipline-Snapshot.pdf.

White, M., Hill, I., Kemp, S., MacRae, J., & Young, L. (2012). Poverty and education: A teacher's perspective – Summary of the findings of the focus group research. Retrieved from www.bctf.ca/PovertyResearch.aspx.

Zajda, J., Majhanovich, S., & Rust, V. (2006). Introduction: Education and social justice. *Review of Education, 52*, 9–22. doi:10.1007/s11159-005-5614-2

11

Critical School Mental Health Praxis (CrSMHP)

A Framework for Change

Jennifer Ulie-Wells, Katherine Richardson Bruna, and Carrie Romo

INTRODUCTION

The question of how to address the toxicity of racism in the lives of youth has been part of the historical development of the fields of education and mental healthcare. While research and federal mental healthcare initiatives show that equity is intended to be a priority in school policy and practice, gaps remain in how we understand the intersection of racial marginalization and mental health. In particular, there is a lack of research from a critical perspective. This perspective asserts that schools mirror a social system built on an ideology of White supremacy. Following this assertion, it is assumed that school systems may perpetuate racial trauma for students of color. For this reason, the critical perspective holds, teachers who demonstrate culturally responsive identities through their practice have important roles to play in counteracting racial trauma and promoting the mental health of students of color.

In this chapter, we extend sorely needed attention to dismantling oppressive systems from critical race theory (CRT) with the intervention strategies of relational cultural theory (RCT) in order to propose a new framework for understanding cultural competence at the intersection of racism and mental health. Critical School Mental Health Praxis (CrSMHP) is different than many frameworks throughout school mental healthcare as it uses a critical lens to challenge models of resiliency that put the onus on the victim to overcome circumstances instead of targeting the root cause of the traumas – oppressive social systems and their perpetuation in schools through praxis. Freire (1972) provides one of the most thought-provoking definitions of praxis. "It is only when the oppressed become involved in the organized struggle for their liberation that they begin to believe in themselves. This discovery cannot be purely intellectual but must involve action; nor can it be limited to mere activism, but must include serious reflection; only then will it be a praxis" (Freire, 1972, p. 15).

We extend Freire's conception to include a coalition-based approach to praxis in which individuals whose social locations provide privilege have important roles to play in liberatory struggle. As women education professionals at differing points in our respective careers of advocacy for minoritized youth, we describe in this chapter an approach to mental health inspired by Freire's ideas. Our Critical School Mental Health Praxis (CrSMHP) combines the goals of critical thinking, self-reflection, and connected relationships toward the development of a culturally conscious school climate that can prepare young people to engage in their own praxis as agents of institutional and individual change in society.

Our hope with CrSMHP is to increase conversations and action within school mental healthcare by challenging the traditional frameworks and raising the focus on the intersection of race and school mental health. For instance, scholars are paying closer attention to using trauma-sensitive frameworks in schools based on the adverse childhood experiences (ACEs) work from the mid-1990s (Felitti et al., 1998), but often absent is the inclusion of racism as a trauma, specifically when it is perpetuated within schools. We begin this journey with a discussion on school and race, specifically focusing on the racial battle fatigue felt by students of color, which directly deteriorates their mental health. Then we offer a brief history of equity and school mental health from the mid-twentieth century to the present. We continue by setting the foundation for CRT and RCT before we conclude by proposing the CrSMHP framework. In proposing CrSMHP, we intend to suggest specific recommendations for professionals as a method for improving the mental wellness of underserved and underrepresented populations.

SCHOOL AND RACE

An abundance of research argues that perceived discrimination, racism (Masko, 2005), and stigma increase negative mental health outcomes (Brown, 2003, 2008; Cokley, Hall-Clark, & Hicks, 2011; Guzman, Goto, & Wei, 2016; McGee & Stovall, 2015). These negative outcomes may include experiences of anxiety, depression, and suicidal ideation (Guzman et al., 2016). Overt and covert racism is associated with traumatic responses ranging from hypervigilance and vulnerability reflecting a constant state of fear due to racial identity (Daniel, 2000; Jernigan & Daniel, 2011; Truong & Museus, 2012). Some researchers resist popularized understandings of resiliency that stress its "heroic" nature as "the capability of individuals to cope successfully in the face of significant change, adversity, or risk" (Greene & Conrad, 2002, p. 37). McGee and Stovall assert that the tone of resiliency thinking is to make victims responsible for surviving the very situations that threaten their well-being. These scholars emphasize that the emotional and psychological stress result not in resiliency but in "racial battle fatigue," the physical and emotional exhaustion caused by systemic and everyday racism (McGee & Stovall, 2015, p. 495). Youth of color struggle and tire against school structures established as part of racial hierarchization in which an ideology of White supremacy is perpetuated through curricula, instruction, assessment, and family outreach.

Masko (2005) provides an example of the "racial battles" youth of color experience in schools. She captures the stories students tell about teachers' and administrators' (non)reactions, as primary or secondary witnesses, to their accounts of racism. Similarly, Langhout (2005) offers additional instances in her research of how the negative stereotypes held by school personnel about students of color lead to inappropriate disciplinary sanctions and, as a result, to student resistance. These situations cause students to feel disrespected by teachers, create a sense of racial unfairness, and result in negative social and academic outcomes (Jernigan & Daniel, 2011). When school personnel fail to protect children from feeling emotionally and physically unsafe, they further damage children's personal and intellectual growth (Masko, 2005). Students who are not direct victims but who witness racism against other students are just as vulnerable to this damage (Jernigan & Daniel, 2011, p. 131). Students may perceive a lack of response or an inappropriate response as a microaggression (Jernigan, 2009; Jernigan & Daniel, 2011). Psychologist Dr. Chester Pierce coined the term *microaggression* in the 1970s in order to denote the "small" yet constant, persistent incidents of discrimination toward a marginalized group (Pierce, 1970) such as a White woman tightly grasping her purse as she walks by a Black man. As Jernigan and Daniel write, "The compounding effects of microaggressions over time have the potential for particularly negative consequences because of their frequency and often lack of explicit validation from others" (Jernigan & Daniel, 2011, pp. 130–131). In this way, to ignore the importance of cultural competence in the professionalization of educators is a continuation of White supremacy as a form of systemic oppression. For this reason, educators need to do more work at the intersection of racism and school mental health (McGee & Stovall, 2015) so as to understand how best to prepare teachers and administrators who can, in the "racial battle" of schools, serve on the side of students. This implies rethinking the relationship between the mental healthcare and schooling systems and what we consider the knowledge, skills, and dispositions required for entry into the career of teaching.

A BRIEF HISTORY OF EQUITY AND SCHOOL MENTAL HEALTH IN THE UNITED STATES

While scholars and researchers have given some attention to improving the current mental healthcare system, they have taken limited to no legislative action focused on understanding the system as oppressive. Neither have they made efforts to dismantle it so as to build a new one that can ensure equitable outcomes for all students. In the 1950s, for example, awareness grew in the United States that all students need access to school mental health support (Courtney, 1951), but existing laws did not protect racially or culturally marginalized populations or provide benefits toward mental healthcare (US Department of Health and Human Services [USDHHS], 2001). This led, in the 1960s, to researcher George Albee's fierce stance on the importance of eliminating racism, sexism, and homophobia as a way to prevent mental illness (Albee, 1968, 2005; Albee & Fryer, 2003). Short of Albee's goal of eliminating oppressive forces, the 1980s saw an upsurge in attention to providing "quality services, independent of the socioeconomic or ethnic groups being served" (Stroul & Friedman, 1986, p. 24). By the late 1990s, Adelman and Taylor were returning to Albee's stance, recognizing the importance of addressing the social-environmental challenges students face such as language, income, mobility barriers, gangs, and violence (Adelman & Taylor, 1998, p. 135). Throughout the 1990s and 2000s researchers paid increased attention to making sure all students had access to resources (Barrett, Eber, & Weist, 2013), including having a diverse group of stakeholders on action teams (Tashman et al., 2000). Systemic racism prevents all students from having equity in education. Even with mandated legislation, further research is needed in order to better understand how to dismantle racism in schools as well as how to prevent schools from perpetuating its traumas.

Despite these advances toward equity in school mental health, we have yet to heed Albee's call for a systemic approach, one that takes the elimination of oppressive forces such as racism as the most fundamental step in prevention. The aim to transform the underlying structure for liberatory purposes rather than just to reform the existing one is what separates critical from liberal approaches to social change (McLaren, 1994). The critical multiculturalist or "resistance" view is that, without explicit intervention, schools reproduce the dominant ideologies in society that are at the heart of injustice. Only through a critical pedagogy that provides opportunities for individuals, students, and school professionals alike to examine the values, assumptions, and interests embodied in taken-for-grant bodies of knowledge, representations of identity, and repertoires of practice will we be able to deconstruct, in order to reconstruct, the meaning systems from which these ideologies derive. Short of a critical pedagogical approach, schools, even while purporting to advance equity, will not achieve genuine change unless our very understandings of the categories used to label students and the sources of difference and disparity associated with those categories are targeted for intervention and interruption. Resiliency models that focus only on the victim's ability to overcome the situation, rather than responding to the racism that may be at the core of the trauma, are indicative of these liberal multicultural approaches. In 2017, the American Psychological Association (APA) adopted new multicultural guidelines that recognize sociocultural contexts that influence resiliency. These guidelines assert that psychologists need to recognize and understand that inequities create barriers to resiliency, and they provide more evidence that action toward dismantling systemic injustice is critical (APA, 2017). The CrSMHP model, because of its focus on deconstructing oppressive forces and reconstructing liberatory ones in their place, provides a transformative orientation for the equity work that Albee began fifty years ago.

CRITICAL RACE THEORY

Albee's interest in oppressive structures preceded the emergence of critical race theory (CRT). Critical race theory emerged in US legal studies in the mid-1970s as a way to spur urgency for racial justice (Ladson-Billings, 1998). Critical race theory is best understood as a set of ideas that expose the hidden and traditional ways that racism is inherent in systems and institutions (Sleeter, 2012). Within the CRT literature, these systems are defined as White supremacist systems in the sense that, historically, the United States is based on racially biased policies and legislation designed to benefit the dominant White culture (Stovall, 2016). By the early 1990s, CRT had made its way into several disciplines, including education. The tenets of CRT initially identified by Bell (1980) and popularized in education by scholars such as Gloria Ladson-Billings (1998) and Delgado and Stefancic (2001) include assertions about the social construction, normalization, interest convergence, intersectionality, and counter-narratives. Critical race theory scholars acknowledge and believe that race is not scientifically valid but was socially constructed in order to maintain a hierarchy in which whiteness and white supremacy control the upper crust of society (Bell, 1980). Critical race theory posits that racism is not only the overt behaviors of a person but that it has been intentionally normalized as part of the fabric of the United States, while interest convergence suggests that any progress toward racial justice occurs only to the benefit of white people (Bell, 1980; Ladson-Billings, 2013). *Intersectionality* was coined by critical legal theorist Kimberlé Crenshaw, and it postulates that human beings have identities that are oppressed and privileged within society and that those identities intersect in complex ways so as to create our lived experiences (Crenshaw, 1991; Sensoy & DiAngelo, 2017). As a strategy to challenge oppressive and generational discourse, counter-narratives are the stories told by racially minoritized people exposing and allowing others to understand the complexity and pervasiveness of racism (Delgado & Stefancic, 2001). In summary, we assert that each of these CRT tenets has implications for transforming school mental health:

1. Critical race theory scholars do not believe in race as a scientifically valid idea; they adhere strongly, however, to the social validity of race as a tool used to establish and maintain a hierarchy of white supremacy (Bell, 1980).
2. The social construction of race and racism is a normalized and intentional identity-formation process in the United States (Ladson-Billings, 2013).
3. White people will only converge on matters of racial justice if it is in their best interest (Bell, 1980; Ladson-Billings, 2013).
4. Intersectionality names the complex ways that forces of oppression intersect with those of privilege to create our unique lived experiences (Crenshaw, 1991; Sensoy & DiAngelo, 2017).
5. Critical race theory suggests that racially marginalized people must themselves provide a counter-narrative that exposes, in new ways, the racism that infiltrates their everyday lives (Delgado & Stefancic, 2001).

If CRT's approach to racial justice is to highlight the institutional systems through which oppression is reproduced for liberation, relational cultural theory's (RCT) approach is complementary. Relational cultural theory highlights the role of human development and self-expansion in building relationships. It helps us think about the kinds of relational networks required to nurture the individual agency required for institutional change.

RELATIONAL CULTURAL THEORY

Relational cultural theory approaches social justice through the intentional professionalization of individuals who engage in critical self-reflection on a journey to be effective advocates and allies for institutional change. Pioneered in the 1970s, RCT focuses on the quality of interpersonal relationships, recognizing that healthy relatedness and connectedness are essential to healthy development (Miller, 1976). Lenz defines RCT as "a contemporary psychodynamic framework for understanding human development based on the assumption that individuals' happiness and well-being are a product of the degree to which they participate in growth-fostering relationships" (Lenz, 2016, p. 415).

Relational cultural theory's inherently feminist theoretical framework provided its own counter-narrative to male-centered paradigms of knowledge-as-rationality. It was a response to the absence of research understanding knowledge-as-relationality; RCT sought to highlight how relational experiences contribute to mental wellness (Comstock et al., 2008; Miller, 1976). Relational cultural theory contradicted the traditional counseling ideology of the time that valued independence and autonomy as markers for mental maturity and emotional health (Comstock et al., 2008; Miller, 1976), arguing instead that growth develops through human connection rather than separation (Duffey & Trepal, 2016; Jordan, 2001). The importance of connection to personal growth is clear in the seven tenets of RCT as proposed by Jordan:

1. People grow through and toward relationship throughout the lifespan,
2. Movement toward mutuality rather than separation characterizes mature functioning,
3. Relationship differentiation and elaboration characterize growth,
4. Mutual empathy and mutual empowerment are at the core of growth-fostering relationships,
5. Authenticity is necessary for real engagement and full participation in growth-fostering relationships,
6. In growth-fostering relationships, all people contribute and grow or benefit,
7. One of the goals of development from a relational perspective is the development of increased relational competence and capacities over the life span (Jordan, 2000, p. 1005).

That RCT centers these tenets as part of mental healthcare practice is thought to lead to an increased sense of zest (energy and vitality) in a relationship; a greater understanding of self, other, and the relationship; an enhanced sense of worth; increased productivity; and a desire for more connection (Comstock et al., 2008, p. 282). In this way, RCT theorists argue, reciprocal empathetic and growth-fostering relationships help individuals transform and heal (Jordan, 2001). The RCT approach grounded in these tenets provides opportunities for therapists to increase their cultural awareness by hearing the stories and worldviews of their clients; it encourages the offering of an empathic response while also exploring different life experiences and opportunities (Comstock et al., 2008).

While RCT was designed as a therapist-client framework, it has implications as a teacher-student framework. Studies using RCT in academic settings have revealed that the RCT tenets have improved teacher-student partnerships (Liang, Tracy, Kenny, Brogan, & Gatha, 2010; Schwartz & Holloway, 2012). In taking up CRT's call for sociopolitical consciousness about the social construction and normalization of race and racism, RCT offers a reflexive framework through which a focus on cultural competence emerges as important to the interplay of therapist-client/teacher-student knowledge, attitudes and beliefs, behavioral dispositions, and possible intervention strategies (Sue, 2006). Sociocultural contexts influence bicultural relationships between teacher and student (APA, 2017). The intention of extending RCT into the school realm is not to transform teachers into therapists, but rather to expand the repertoire of teachers to embody core RCT concepts, therefore potentially improving mental health outcomes for students. When the amount of time children spend in school is considered, there are implications that an RCT-oriented instructional environment can contribute to their mental wellness. The challenge becomes folding RCT's emphasis on self-change into CRT's emphasis on societal change; the question is how we can infuse into a system established on the foundation of racial hierarchy and whiteness policies and practices that intend, through radical connection, to dismantle the very racial privilege they provide and protect.

RESISTING RESILIENCY WITH CRITICAL RACE THEORY AND RELATIONAL CULTURAL THEORY

From a critical perspective, resilience does not adequately allow for identification and interrogation of the systemic oppression created in schools. The idea celebrates the reforming of the individual in adaptation to institutional limitations. Together, CRT – with its focus on institutional transformation – and RCT – with its focus on individual transformation – challenge the resiliency model. They resist placing responsibility on the individual alone to overcome the oppressive situation and instead give focused attention to the actual problem, a social system established on racial hierarchization and a self wounded by disconnected relationships within that system that reproduce the construction and normalization of race. This shift away from the lone individual to the institution and the relationships it construes in perpetuation allows for consideration of the generational nature of "racial battle fatigue" (McGee & Stovall, 2015, p. 495). A critique of resiliency also provides an opportunity to resist the quantification that accompanies the meritocratic celebration of a survivor's "grit" (Duckworth, Peterson, Matthews, & Kelly, 2007). When the focus for change is on the oppressive forces of the institution and the way relationships may reproduce those forces, it necessarily shifts the question away from "how resilient" a person is. This keeps attention concentrated on the cause of racial oppression, not its symptom. The tenets of CRT and RCT, formalized into the new Critical School Mental Health Praxis (CrSMHP) framework, can guide future efforts at the intersection of educational equity and school mental health.

MOVING FORWARD WITH CRITICAL SCHOOL MENTAL HEALTH PRAXIS

Critical School Mental Health Praxis (CrSMHP) combines the critical lens of CRT and RCT toward dismantling oppressive institutional and relational systems. Critical School Mental Health Praxis recognizes that transformation is required on both fronts if students of color are to thrive. As CRT stresses, it is not enough to build positive interpersonal relationships when youth of color still have to experience discriminatory policies and practices. It is impossible for a person to recover from wounds of racial battle fatigue when the system is set on racial stratification, making it critical for professionals to acknowledge how they contribute to oppression. Adults must commit to intensive self-reflection regarding the stereotypes, biases, and expectations that influence their ability to build genuinely healthy relationships with students. Figure 11.1 illustrates how overlapping and complementary tenets of CRT and RCT interact as part of CrSMHP and outlines recommendations that arise out of the new framework.

Addressing equity and school mental health through the new CrSMHP framework highlights three areas in need of attention:

Tenet 1: A critical lens is needed to address the root cause of ongoing systemic oppression reproduced through the policies of institutions and the practices of individuals working within them.

Tenet 2: Intensive professional and personal self-reflection is needed to challenge stereotypes, biases, and expectations that influence the ability to build connected relationships with students.

Tenet 3: Connected relationships between students and teachers create a culturally conscious school climate that can prepare young people to be agents of institutional and individual change in their society.

From each tenet, connect emerging recommendations so as to align school mental healthcare efforts with a culturally conscious lens.

Critical School Mental Health Praxis (CrSMHP)

Critical Race Theory (CRT)	Relational Cultural Theory (RCT)
Critical framework with feminist influences	
Seeks to balance power dynamics	
Increases cultural awareness by hearing stories, beliefs, and worldviews from youth through counter-storytelling	Increases cultural awareness by hearing stories, beliefs, and worldviews from youth through empathetic response
Increases social justice education and praxis to make professionals agents of change	
Argues that racial inequities contribute to mental health demise	Argues that relational disconnection contributes to mental health demise
Centers on dismantling oppressive systems that create ongoing racial traumas for the marginalized population	Does not center on dismantling oppressive systems but rather focuses on increasing cultural competence
Does not provide explicit direction for building culturally competent relationships	Centers on building culturally competent relationships that genuinely seek to understand the identity experiences of students

CrSMHP Tenets

Tenet 1: A critical lens is needed to address the root cause of ongoing systemic oppression reproduced through the policies of institutions and the practices of individuals working within them.

Tenet 2: Intensive professional and personal self-reflection is needed to challenge stereotypes, biases, and expectations that influence the ability to build connected relationships with students.

Tenet 3: Connected relationships between students and teachers create a culturally conscious school climate that can prepare young people to be agents of institutional and individual change in their society.

CrSMHP Recommendations

Recommendation 1: Renovate teacher preparation programs
  a. Recruit and maintain high-quality teachers representing diverse populations
  b. Require intensive training by highly qualified, culturally competent faculty emphasizing critical reflection praxis on top of basic required diversity courses
  c. Provide highly effective culturally competent mentors and models
  d. Redesign classroom management classes so as to build relationships and develop culturally conscious classroom climates
  e. Offer mandatory coursework in school mental health, including topics in traumas for marginalized populations

Recommendation 2: Overhaul school systems
  a. Stakeholders and leadership need to reevaluate policies, procedures, curricula, and assessments
  b. Engage and innovate models for teaching that allow students to participate in applicable hands-on learning
  c. Gather ongoing input from students, families, and community members
  d. Ongoing intensive critical training
  e. Abolish expectation for teachers to remain neutral in the face of injustice

FIGURE 11.1 (cont.)

Recommendation 3: Legislation
    a. Mandate greater time for educators to participate in training regarding race, culture, intersectionality, and their impact on mental health
    b. Develop a system of accountability in order to support and require culturally competence educational reform
Recommendation 4: Research
    a. Increase research specifically focusing on how schools impact racial and cultural diverse student mental health using a critical lens
    b. Invite persons with racially and culturally diverse backgrounds to research conversations and studies regarding school mental health

FIGURE 11.1 Critical School Mental Health Praxis Framework (CrSMHP)

CRITICAL SCHOOL MENTAL HEALTH PRAXIS RECOMMENDATIONS

Critical School Mental Health Praxis maximizes the efforts of CRT and RCT with the intention of expanding efforts to improve equity in school mental healthcare by dismantling the cause of the trauma for underserved and underrepresented youth. While CRT emphasizes the importance of teachers as agents of change through activism (Taylor, Gillborn, & Ladson-Billings, 2009), CrSMHP challenges us to develop a systemic way to prepare teachers and encourage school systems to advocate underserved and underrepresented students. To further the work of CrSMHP four primary recommendations emerge as next steps: (1) renovate teacher preparation programs; (2) overhaul school systems; (3) enact equity legislation; and (4) expand research.

Recommendation 1: Renovate Teacher Preparation Programs

Recruit and Maintain High-Quality Teachers Representing Diverse Populations

Evidence supports that students perform better when they have teachers who are racially similar to themselves (Egalite & Kisida, 2018). In US K–12 classrooms, 82 percent of teachers are white, yet by 2024 more than 53 percent of students will be students of color (US Department of Education, 2016). This cultural "mismatch" can have a negative impact on classroom relationships (McAllister & Irvine, 2000; Rothenberg, 1997). Students benefit when schools consider racial and cultural diversity as an asset in hiring practices.

Require Intensive Training by Highly Qualified, Culturally Competent Faculty Emphasizing Critical Reflection Praxis on Top of Basic Required Diversity Courses

Teachers have an obligation to dismantle racism in schools (Ladson-Billings, 2018). It is not enough in preservice preparation programs to help students know that injustice occurs; they need to know how to actively work to disrupt it. Absent in most teacher education programs are classes that teach future teachers to think critically about race, including how to reflect on and engage in discussions about race. These courses generally teach a low-risk version of cultural competence that does not engage teachers in challenging reflection about their own stereotypes and biases. This leaves teachers unprepared to address race in classrooms and dismantle racism within their schools.

Educators would benefit from training in cultural humility. *Cultural humility* is defined as a "lifelong process of self-reflection, self-critique, continual assessment of power imbalances, and the development of mutually respectful relationships and partnerships" (Gallardo, 2014, p. 3; as cited in APA, 2017, p. 21 APA, 2017) that empowers educators to decrease the injustices within educational systems.

Provide Highly Effective Culturally Competent Mentors and Models

The Interstate Teacher Assessment and Support Consortium (InTASC) teaching standards have a specific guideline regarding "diversity": "The teacher uses understanding of individual differences and diverse cultures and communities to ensure inclusive learning environments that enable each learner to meet high standards" (Council of Chief State School Officers, 2011, p. 11). While this is a well-intended standard, without intentionality toward a critical approach the audience is by and large White teachers being held accountable by unprepared White administrators and White preservice students being held accountable by untrained White higher education faculty. Without a critical understanding of race and Whiteness, these teachers risk a shallow understanding of diversity and culture.

Redesign Classroom Management Classes to Build Relationships and Develop Culturally Conscious Classroom Climates

Many times classroom climate development and relationship-building are folded into preservice teacher program courses focused on classroom management. The course title, classroom management, sends the message that maintaining power and control is important to success and children need to be managed. Additionally, teacher preparation programs are not adequately preparing educators to work with diverse populations (Alismail, 2016), making it more challenging to build relationships and create culturally conscious classrooms. While preservice programs may offer attention to the importance of relationship-building or creating a student-centered climate, they often neglect a critical lens that helps teachers better understand and address the injustices being perpetuated in American classrooms. Critical School Mental Health Praxis proposes teaching educators how to create a critical climate based on shared power through intensive relationship-building. Within the redesign, classroom management classes need to be shaped into a course(s) focusing on culturally competent relationship-building and developing culturally conscious classroom climates rather than how to control and have power over youth.

Offer Mandatory Coursework in School Mental Health Including Topics in Traumas for Underserved/Underrepresented Populations

According to the 2015–2016 National Teacher and Principal Survey, 74 percent of teachers indicated they had preservice instruction on classroom management techniques, 70 percent had instruction on students with special needs, and 64 percent had coursework on working with students from diverse economic backgrounds, while 38 percent were prepared to work with limited-English proficient or English-language learners (Taie & Goldring, 2017). As of this publication there is no national requirement for school mental health training, though, according to the American Foundation of Suicide Prevention (AFSP), eleven states require annual suicide prevention training, two of those included trauma training, and zero specified training on trauma for underrepresented/underserved populations (State Laws, 2017). The Centers for Disease Control (CDC) (2018) indicates that 20 percent of all children live with a mental health disorder that can interfere with their progress at school. Educators would benefit from school mental health training that informs them of these dynamics and outlines their roles and responsibilities.

Recommendation 2: Overhaul School Systems

Stakeholders and Leadership Need to Reevaluate Policies, Procedures, Curricula, and Assessments

All students benefit from learning with a robust and diverse curriculum. Ample research supports efforts to move to culturally rich curricula as a means of creating critical climates (Ladson-Billings, 1998, 2018). Privileged children need access to accurate history and critical conversations toward the dismantling of racist systems (Swalwell, 2013). Social justice education gives attention to oppressive policies, including discipline, that create racial traumas for students of color.

School systems need to access experts in cultural competence in order to evaluate system policies and make swift changes. Timeliness is valuable when considering the short- and long-term impact on students of color at the hands of oppressive systems. Action plans intended to last for three to five years mean that for three to five years, students of color will still be subjected to racial traumas with consequences for a lifetime.

Engage in Innovative Models for Teaching That Allow Students to Engage in Applicable Hands-On Learning

Linda Darling-Hammond asserts in her book *The Flat World and Education* that underserved students find greatest success engaging in innovative models for education that allow them to interact with applicable, hands-on learning opportunities. She argues that many schools need a massive redesign so as to take them from the early twentieth-century framework they continue to operate within and to make them highly effective for today (Darling-Hammond, 2015). Approaches to curricula, instruction, and assessment, such as Ambitious Science Teaching (Windschitl, Thompson, & Braaten, 2018), provide a clear outline for such redesign. These approaches center students' inherent capacity to be agents of their own development and to build teaching and learning activities around meaningful interests generated from their own lives. Principles and practices oriented to authentic problem-posing, drawing on students' ideas, scaffolding for cognitive growth, and establishing discursive communities oriented to "thinking about thinking" can be applied in multidisciplinary ways so as to engage youth who are otherwise approached with low academic expectations. In general, the shift Darling-Hammond calls for, one that turns away from propositional modes of knowledge toward performative modes of knowledge, aligns with broader assertions that the primary goal of education in democratic societies should be, for all students, humanizing and soul-enhancing (Richardson Bruna, 2016).

Gather Ongoing Input from Students, Families, and Community Members

Critical race theory and relational cultural theory both assert that voice through storytelling is critical to increasing understanding of marginalized groups (Jordan, 2000; Taylor et al., 2009). Critical School Mental Health Praxis states that increased voice also contributes to shared power between schools, youth, families, and the community. Hart (1992) provides a model that promotes student engagement using eight tiers that range from full adult control and manipulation through youth and adults sharing decision-making.

Evidence shows that creating meaningful two-way partnerships with families and communities improves academic outcomes, attendance, and student behavior (González & Jackson, 2013). In order to minimize barriers for families that may feel unheard, Cook, Shah, Brodsky, and Morizio recommend that schools facilitate community dialogues and intergroup conversations where individuals from different racial, ethnic, and cultural groups meet to talk openly in a safe and structured environment about personal experiences with race and discuss ways to address race relations in the community (Cook, Shah, Brodsky, & Morizio, 2017, pp. 10–11). These opportunities strengthen and develop relationships between schools, families, and communities.

Provide and Engage in Ongoing Intensive Critical Training

It is arguably impossible to meet the needs of racially and culturally diverse students without first acknowledging that schools can be oppressive for students of color.

Understanding that not all students are afforded the same experiences in schools is a first step in teachers developing authentic and empathetic relationships with their students. The next step is to create spaces that give students opportunities to have a voice and to be heard. Teachers are encouraged to work in systems that support advocacy without being fearful of getting in trouble for challenging dominant systems. Many educators join the field so as to make a difference for children. One challenge to teachers is learning to be vulnerable and willing to be challenged by students and other staff. Without willingness for change, teachers will perpetuate a system that continues to protect White dominant culture while risking traumatizing students and staff in the process.

Abolish the Expectation for Teachers to Remain Neutral in the Face of Injustice

Education is built on an expectation that teachers remain neutral in their professional capacities. Critical School Mental Health Praxis contends that neutrality is dangerous and damaging to underrepresented students in an unjust system. School systems need to actively engage in dialogue and encourage a climate that not only teaches but also expects educators to challenge systems and each other in the best interest of the students.

Recommendation 3: Legislation

Mandate Greater Time for Educators in Training Regarding Race, Culture, Intersectionality, and Their Impact on Mental Health

As mentioned earlier in this chapter, 20 percent of students have a mental illness (CDC, 2018), but students of color also suffer from racial battle fatigue as they attempt to navigate oppressive systems that result in the erosion of their mental wellness.

Develop a System of Accountability in Order to Support and Require Culturally Responsive Educational Reform

One of the most challenging issues in education is enacting quality funded legislation. Education mirrors the oppressive policies and laws of the government. Schools, educators, and students would benefit from legislation requiring and funding educators to spend greater amounts of time in training regarding race, culture, intersectionality, and their impact on mental health. So as to maintain rigorous expectations for cultural competence that will improve students' mental wellness, legislators are encouraged to develop a system of accountability in order to support and require culturally competence educational reform. Considering the short- and long-term impact of trauma on children, this issue needs to be addressed with immediate attention.

Recommendation 4: Research

Increase Research Specifically Focused on How Schools Impact the Mental Health of Diverse Student Groups Using a Critical Lens

Using a critical lens can be challenging, because it pushes the field into uncomfortable territory. Education and mental healthcare are driven with "happiness" in mind, but in fields that are predominantly White, we have to continue to ask ourselves "whose happiness?" Using a critical lens in research is an opportunity to create more authentic work toward meeting the needs of marginalized populations.

Ensure Racially and Culturally Diverse Representation in Conversations about School Mental Health Research and Ongoing Studies

In a scholarly field, intentional planning needs to include a wide variety of representation at places of decision-making so as to increase voices and to deepen, challenge, and enhance the much-needed work to improve school mental health for all students.

CONCLUSION

Critical School Mental Health Praxis looks to scholars to use a critical lens to expand and increase research that specifically focuses on how schools have impact racially and culturally diverse students' mental health. Without acknowledging injustice and putting more attention toward strategies to dismantle oppressive systems, students will continue to experience racial and cultural trauma. Given a predominance of researchers across mental healthcare and education fields who represent a White dominant culture, it's important to have targeted efforts to increase persons with racially and culturally diverse backgrounds engaging in school mental health research and related conversations.

As the diversity in our country and its schools continues to increase, we need a new approach to teacher preparation and development that places the onus on our own professional responsibility, not students' personal resilience, to ensure equitable access to the opportunities we have historically proclaimed as open to all, but protected in fact for the few. We need to work harder and quicker to prepare our educational systems to receive, accept, and empower students exactly as they are. We can all learn from taking time to listen, understand, and acknowledge how we interpret the world around us, especially from our youth. Their voices and stories are powerful road maps, but we cannot hear them if we do not listen.

REFERENCES

Adelman, H. S., & Taylor, L. (1998). Reframing mental health in schools and expanding school reform. *Educational Psychologist*, 33(4), 135–152.

Albee, G. W. (1968). Conceptual models and manpower requirements in psychology. *American Psychologist*, 23(5), 317.

Albee, G. W. (2005). Call to revolution in the prevention of emotional disorders. *Ethical Human Sciences and Services*, 7(1), 37–44.

Albee, G. W., & Fryer, D. M. (2003). Praxis: Towards a public health psychology. *Journal of Community & Applied Social Psychology*, 13(1), 71–75.

Alismail, H. A. (2016). Multicultural education: Teachers' perceptions and preparation. *Journal of Education and Practice*, 7(11), 139–146.

American Psychological Association (APA) (2017). *Multicultural guidelines: An ecological approach to context, identity, and intersectionality*. Washington, DC: American Psychological Association. Retrieved from www.apa.org/about/policy/multicultural-guidelines.pdf.

Barrett, S., Eber, L., & Weist, M. D. (2013). *Advancing education effectiveness: An interconnected systems framework for positive behavioral interventions and supports (PBIS) and school mental health*. Center for Positive Behavioral Interventions and Supports (funded by the Office of Special Education Programs, US Department of Education). Eugene: University of Oregon Press.

Bell, D. (1980). *Brown v. Board of Education* and the interest-convergence dilemma. *Harvard Law Review*, 93(3), 518–533.

Brown, T. N. (2003). Critical race theory speaks to the sociology of mental health: Mental health problems produced by racial stratification. *Journal of Health and Social Behavior*, 44(3), 292–301.

Brown, T. N. (2008). Race, racism, and mental health: Elaboration of critical race theory's contribution to the sociology of mental health. *Contemporary Justice Review*, 11(1), 53–62. Retrieved from https://doi.org/10.1080/10282580701850405.

Centers for Disease Control (CDC) (2018, March 14). Children's mental health. Retrieved from www.cdc.gov/childrensmentalhealth/basics.html.

Cokley, K., Hall-Clark, B., & Hicks, D. (2011). Ethnic minority-majority status and mental health: The mediating role of perceived discrimination. *Journal of Mental Health Counseling*, 33(3), 243–263.

Comstock, D. L., Hammer, T. R., Strentzsch, J., et al. (2008). Relational-cultural theory: A framework for bridging relational, multicultural, and social justice competencies. *Journal of Counseling & Development*, 86(3), 279–287. Retrieved from https://doi.org/10.1002/j.1556-6678.2008.tb00510.

Cook, A. L., Shah, A., Brodsky, L., & Morizio, L. J. (2017). Strengthening school-family-community engagement through community dialogues. *Journal for Social Action in Counseling & Psychology*, 9(1), 1–29.

Council of Chief State School Officers (2011). *Interstate Teacher Assessment and Support Consortium (InTASC) model core teaching standards: A resource for state dialogue*. Washington, DC: Council of Chief State School Officers.

Courtney, D. (1951). Clinical psychology in public schools. *Journal of Clinical Psychology*, 7(2), 171–175.

Crenshaw, K. (1991). Mapping the margins: Identity politics, intersectionality, and violence against women. *Stanford Law Review*, 43(6), 1241–1299.

Daniel, J. H. (2000). *The courage to hear: African American women's memories of racial trauma. Psychotherapy with African American women: Innovations in psychodynamic perspective and practice*. New York: Guilford Press.

Darling-Hammond, L. (2015). *The flat world and education: How America's commitment to equity will determine our future*. New York: Teachers College Press.

Delgado, R., & Stefancic, J. (2001). *Critical race theory: An introduction*. New York: New York University Press.

Duckworth, A. L., Peterson, C., Matthews, M. D., & Kelly, D. R. (2007). Grit: Perseverance and passion for long-term goals. *Journal of Personality and Social Psychology*, 92(6), 1087.

Duffey, T., & Trepal, H. (2016). Introduction to the special section on relational-cultural theory. *Journal of Counseling & Development*, 94(4), 379–382.

Egalite, A. J., & Kisida, B. (2018). The effects of teacher match on students' academic perceptions and attitudes. *Educational Evaluation and Policy Analysis*, 40(1), 59–81.

Felitti, V. J., Anda, R. F., Nordenberg, D., et al. (1998). Relationship of childhood abuse and household dysfunction to many of the leading causes of death in adults: The adverse childhood experiences (ACE) study. *American Journal of Preventive Medicine*, 14(4), 245–258.

Freire, P. (1972). *Pedagogy of the oppressed*. Translated by Myra Bergman Ramos (published in English 1970). New York: Bloomsbury.

Gallardo, M. E. (2014). *Developing cultural humility: Embracing race, privilege and power*. Thousand Oaks, CA: Sage.

González, R. L., & Jackson, C. L. (2013). Engaging with parents: The relationship between school engagement efforts, social class, and learning. *School Effectiveness and School Improvement*, 24(3), 316–335.

Greene, R. R., & Conrad, A. P. (2002). Basic assumptions and terms. In R. R. Greene (ed.), *Resiliency: An Integrated Approach to Practice, Policy, and Research* (pp. 29–62). Washington, DC: NASW Press.

Guzman, L., Goto, S. G., & Wei, K. (2016). Self-control depletion in predominantly white institutions: Intra and intergroup variability in the relations among stigma sensitivity, mental health, and academic motivation. *Journal of Social and Clinical Psychology*, 35 (9), 754–780. Retrieved from https://doi.org/http://dx.doi.org/101521jscp2016359754.

Hart, R. (1992).*Children's participation*. Florence, Italy: UNICEF International Child Development Centre.

Jernigan, M. M. (2009).Using a Sankofa intervention to influence black girls' racial identity development and school-related experiences. *Dissertation Abstracts International Section A: Humanities and Social Sciences*, 70(2-A), 472.

Jernigan, M. M., & Daniel, J. H. (2011). Racial trauma in the lives of black children and adolescents: Challenges and clinical implications. *Journal of Child & Adolescent Trauma*, 4 (2), 123–141. doi:10.1080/19361521.2011.574678

Jordan, J. V. (2000). The role of mutual empathy in relational/cultural therapy. *In Session: Psychotherapy in Practice*, 56(8), 1005–1016.

Jordan, J. V. (2001). A relational-cultural model: Healing through mutual empathy. *Bulletin of the Menninger Clinic*, 65(1: Special issue), 92–103.

Ladson-Billings, G. (1998). Just what is critical race theory and what's it doing in a nice field like education? *International Journal of Qualitative Studies in Education*, 11(1), 7–24.

Ladson-Billings, G. (2013). Critical race theory: What it is not! In M. Lynn & A. D. Dixson (eds.), *Handbook of Critical Race Theory in Education*. Retrieved from www.routledgehandbooks.com/doi/10.4324/9780203155721.ch3.

Ladson-Billings, G. (2018). The social funding of race: The role of schooling. *Peabody Journal of Education*, 93(1), 90–105.

Langhout, R. D. (2005). Acts of resistance: Student (in)visibility. *Culture & Psychology*, 11(2), 123–158.

Lenz, A. S. (2016). Relational-cultural theory: Fostering the growth of a paradigm through empirical research. *Journal of Counseling & Development*, 94(4), 415–428. doi:10.1002/jcad.12100

Liang, B., Tracy, A. J., Kenny, M. E., Brogan, D., & Gatha, R. (2010). The relational health indices for youth: An examination of reliability and validity aspects. *Measurement & Evaluation in Counseling & Development*, 42(4), 255–274. Retrieved from http://10.0.4.153/0748175609354596.

Masko, A. L. (2005). I think about it all the time: A 12-year-old girl's internal crisis with racism and the effects on her mental health. *Urban Review*, 37(4), 329–350.

McAllister, G., & Irvine, J. J. (2000). Cross cultural competency and multicultural teacher education. *Review of Educational Research*, 70(1), 3–24.

McGee, E. O., & Stovall, D. (2015). Reimagining critical race theory in education: Mental health, healing, and the pathway to liberatory praxis. *Educational Theory*, 65(5), 491–511.

McLaren, P. L. (1994). *Revolutionary multiculturalism*. Boulder, CO: Westview Press.

Miller, J. B. (1976). *Toward a new psychology of women*. Boston, MA: Beacon.

Pierce, C. (1970). Offensive mechanisms. In F. B. Barbour (ed.), *The black seventies* (pp. 265–282). Boston, MA: Porter Sargent Publisher.

Richardson Bruna, K. (2016). A struggle for the soul: Reversing the odd alchemy of science education and research. *Mind, Culture, & Activity*, 2(3), 259–269.

Rothenberg, J. J. (1997). Preparing white teachers for urban schools: A compendium of research. Paper presented at the annual meeting of the American Educational Research Association, Chicago (ERIC Document Reproduction Service No. ED407455).

Schwartz, H. L., & Holloway, E. L. (2012). Partners in learning: A grounded theory study of relational practice between master's students and professors. *Mentoring & Tutoring: Partnership in Learning*, 20(1), 115–135.

Sensoy, O., & DiAngelo, R. (2017). *Is everyone really equal? An introduction to key concepts in social justice education*. New York: Teachers College Press.

Sleeter, C. (2012). Critical race theory in education. *Encyclopedia of Diversity in Education*. Retrieved from http://christinesleeter.org/wp-content/uploads/2015/07/Critical-Race-Theory-and-Education-Encyclopedia-of-Diversity-in-Education.pdf.

State Laws: Suicide Prevention in Schools (K–12) (Issue brief). (June 2). Retrieved from American Foundation on Suicide Prevention website: https://afsp.org/wp-content/uploads/2016/04/Suicide-Prevention-in-Schools-Issue-Brief-1.pdf.

Stovall, D. (2016). Out of adolescence and into adulthood: Critical race theory, retrenchment, and the imperative of praxis. *Urban Education*, 51(3), 274–286.

Stroul, B., & Friedman, R. M. (1986). *A system of care for children and adolescents with severe emotional disturbances*. Washington, DC: Georgetown University Center for Child Development, National Technical Assistance Center for Children's Mental Health.

Sue, S. (2006). Cultural competency: From philosophy to research and practice. *Journal of Community Psychology*, 34, 237–245. doi:10.1002/jcop.20095

Swalwell, K. M. (2013). *Educating activist allies: Social justice pedagogy with the suburban and urban elite*. New York: Routledge.

Taie, S., & Goldring, R. (2017). *Characteristics of public elementary and secondary school teachers in the United States: Results from the 2015–16 National Teacher and Principal Survey First Look* (NCES 2017–072). US Department of Education. Washington, DC:

National Center for Education Statistics. Retrieved from https://nces.ed.gov/pubsearch/pubsinfo.asp?pubid=2017072.

Tashman, N. A., Weist, M. D., Acosta, O., et al. (2000). Toward the integration of prevention research and expanded school mental health programs. *Children's services: Social policy, research & practice*, 3(2), 97–115.

Taylor, E., Gillborn, D., & Ladson-Billings, G. (2009). *Foundations of critical race theory in education*. New York: Routledge.

Truong, K., & Museus, S. (2012). Responding to racism and racial trauma in doctoral study: An inventory for coping and mediating relationships. *Harvard Educational Review*, 82(2), 226–254.

US Department of Education takes action to deliver equity for students with disabilities. (2016, February 23). Retrieved from www.ed.gov/news/press-releases/us-department-education-takes-action-deliver-equity-students-disabilities.

US Department of Health and Human Services (USDHHS) (2001). *Mental health: Culture, race, and ethnicity – A supplement to mental health: A report of the Surgeon General*. Rockville, MD: US Department of Health and Human Services, Public Health Service, Office of the Surgeon General.

Windschitl, M., Thompson, J. J., & Braaten, M. L. (2018). *Ambitious science teaching*. Cambridge, MA: Harvard Education Press.

12

Family-School Partnerships within Tiered Systems of Support to Increase Access, Improve Equity, and Promote Positive Outcomes for All Children and Families

S. Andrew Garbacz, Christopher H. Vatland, Laura Kern, Nathaniel P. von der Embse, Tanya Novotnak, Devon R. Minch, and Mark D. Weist

INTRODUCTION

Emotional and behavioral problems and academic deficits in childhood have serious implications for public health (Dodge, Greenberg, Malone, & Conduct Problems Prevention Research Group, 2008). Unfortunately, many children do not receive the necessary evidence-based interventions (Dodge et al., 2008), and families from diverse racial and ethnic backgrounds are disproportionately impacted (Skiba et al., 2014). As such, students may be subject to practices that do not consider their cultural norms. Implementing scoped and sequenced family-school partnership approaches within a tiered, school-based framework can improve access to evidence-based interventions (Garbacz, Herman, Thompson, & Reinke, 2017). In the sections that follow, we review social justice, international policy, relevant theory, and conceptual frameworks in order to integrate social justice and cultural responsiveness into family-school partnerships in tiered systems.

SOCIAL JUSTICE THROUGH A POLICY PERSPECTIVE

Social justice has been a central tenet within many helping professions. Over the past fifteen years, social justice advocacy and research have increased within education and psychology (Shriberg, Wynne, Briggs, Bartucci, & Lombardo, 2011). Fundamental to these efforts is the overarching goal and guiding belief that all children and youth have rights and opportunities that are protected in their school communities and that the cultures and beliefs of families and their related influence on school practices should be considered. As such, professional, educational, and mental healthcare (e.g., psychology, social work, counseling) organizations have sought to codify social justice principles within formal operating guidelines. For example, the National Association of School Psychologists (NASP) has incorporated social justice as one of its five strategic priorities, and it defines social justice as:

a process and a goal that requires action. School psychologists work to ensure the protection of the educational rights, opportunities, and well-being of all children, especially those whose voices have been muted, identities obscured, or needs ignored. Social justice requires promoting non-discriminatory practices and the empowerment of families and communities. School psychologists enact social justice through culturally-responsive professional practice and advocacy to create schools, communities, and systems that ensure equity and fairness for all children and youth (NASP, 2017, para. 4).

Collective efforts across service professions have led to a changing understanding that social justice is an active rather than passive process, and one that is best accomplished at the systems level (American Counseling Association, 2014). As a result, many professions are grappling with how to apply the goals and values of a social justice orientation to practice.

Additionally, social justice efforts are supported by seminal laws that provide a foundation for social justice principles in education. For example, in the United States, the Individuals with Disabilities Education Act (IDEA) (2004) has substantially broadened the scope of educational practice and solidified the legal right to a free and appropriate public education in the least restrictive environment for students with various disabilities. This law was a catalyst for significant research and advocacy on topics such as children's rights, nondiscriminatory assessment, and systems change (Hart & Prasse, 1991). Additional laws protect students with disabilities in the US school system, including laws prohibiting discrimination while improving access to instruction and facilities (e.g., Americans with Disabilities Act; Section 504 of the Rehabilitation Act of 1973). Additionally, US laws encourage schools to use a tiered system of intervention in order to identify students with disabilities and increase access to education for all students (e.g., IDEA, 2004). All of these legal mandates support tenets of social justice against discrimination while encouraging inclusion of students with disabilities in school settings. Many of these laws also promote parental involvement as a key component, such as through the establishment of protected procedures so as to ensure parental participation.

Internationally, the United Nations Convention on the Rights of the Child (United Nations General Assembly, 1989) created policy that influenced how social justice is conceptualized and acted upon within education around the world. The Convention, ratified by 193 of 195 nations, delineates universal expectations for the development and treatment of children. The themes of the Convention underscore respect for children's dignity, promotion of physical and mental health, and social, spiritual, and moral development (Miller, Colebrook, & Ellis, 2014). Moreover, the Convention recognizes the role of parents and families, including differences among family cultural values, as fundamental to child development. Articles 4 and 18 in the Convention address the role of society in ensuring support for families in order to protect child rights such as encouraging access to high-quality educational opportunities. Articles 28 and 29 demonstrate how education is a means by which children fulfill their potential and obtain human rights and freedoms (Miller et al., 2014). These articles can serve as important guides for practitioners to ensure their work is guided by principles of social justice.

Another policy of the United Nations, the Convention of Rights of Persons with Disabilities, was ratified in 2006 by 175 countries (excluding the United States) and consists of an international treaty that supports fundamental rights and freedoms of persons with ongoing physical, mental, intellectual, or sensory disabilities (United Nations General Assembly, 2006, Article 1). The Convention is guided by several key principles, ranging from respect for human dignity and freedom from discrimination to accessibility and inclusion (United Nations General Assembly, 2006).

Article 24 focuses specifically on education (United Nations General Assembly, 2006) and recognizes the rights of persons with disabilities to an inclusive education that promotes individuals' dignity and self-worth and allows them to develop to their full potential. Overall, this article promotes education as a means to participate in society through inclusive, free general education, reasonable accommodations, and individualized support.

Considered together, these laws and guidance from the UN Convention can serve as important guides for practitioners. Themes from US laws that intersect with the UN Conventions on the rights of children with and without disabilities identify the importance of inclusive education that balances the dignity of the individual with the right to participate in society. The role of the family is also emphasized as vital to both the procedural and substantive goals of law and policy, informing social justice priorities at the systems level. Finally, a systems perspective is encouraged that incorporates a tiered system of delivery so individuals receive support congruent with their strengths and needs.

Even with legal protections in place, disproportionate practices still occur in schools. For example, the US Office of Civil Rights reports that African Americans are more likely to be suspended; Black male students comprised 8 percent of the total enrolled students but 25 percent of students who received an out-of-school suspension and 23 percent of students who were expelled (Civil Rights Data Collection, 2018). Additionally, as African American students are more likely to be identified for special education compared to students of other ethnic backgrounds, IDEA (2004) has called for states to monitor and alter policy when disproportionality is discovered (Posney, 2007). Many of these inequitable practices are not direct but may reflect an implicit bias that occurs when personal cultural responses and perspectives influence decisions at vulnerable decision points (Implicit Bias, 2018). To fully consider social justice as a goal in education, more needs to be done to consider the background and culture of the families that are part of the school communities.

THEORETICAL JUSTIFICATION

Laws and conventions from the international community promote education for all and position families and other key stakeholders as vital in children's development, but more is needed to address existing problems. Theories that blend mental health and education perspectives provide a helpful orientation for identifying effective prevention and intervention strategies for children (Dishion & Stormshak, 2007). Primary theoretical support for connecting families and school personnel in partnership emanates from ecological systems theory (Bronfenbrenner, 1979) and critical race theory (Ladson-Billings & Tate, 1995). Whereas ecological systems theory identifies key systems of child development (Bronfenbrenner, 1979), critical race theory describes race as a core element of educational systems (Ladson-Billings & Tate, 1995). Ecological systems theory identifies concentric systems that influence child development. Microsystems are the most proximal and reflect the primary settings in which a child develops, such as home and school. The mesosystem reflects interactions among microsystems. For example, the mesosystem describes processes, such as school–home communication or parent–teacher collaboration, to develop individualized support plans for children. Moving further out from the center, the exosystem includes social services, neighborhood activities, and local policies. These systems describe individuals and settings that impact child development. Thus, child development does not simply reflect an additive effect of home, school, neighborhood, and social services, neither is it enough to say that systems interact to support child development; rather, it is important to attend to the fit across individuals and settings (Richman, Bowen, & Woolley, 2004).

Critical race theory (CRT) (Ladson-Billings & Tate, 1995) holds that racism is a permanent feature of society and implicates educational systems in creating racial inequality. Ladson-Billings and Tate (1995) note that just as civil rights litigation did not end race-based segregation of US schools, multiculturalist approaches are inadequate to bring about equitable educational outcomes. Critical race theory holds that racial power structures and property rights associated with race intersect in schools and continue to determine social and educational inequities along racial lines (Ladson-Billings & Tate, 1995). For example, curriculum that presents only the dominant cultural perspective may be less accessible to minority students and promote incongruence across home and school. Based on critical race theory, social change occurs when people in communities voice their realities and experiences and when educators integrate their perspectives in educational systems, such as modifying school expectations to align with parent expectations (Ladson-Billings, 1998). Thus, socially just family-school partnerships must invite and merge the perspectives of students and families who identify as racial minorities.

CORE CHARACTERISTICS OF FAMILY-SCHOOL PARTNERSHIPS

Grounded in ecological systems theory, *family-school partnerships* refer to behaviors families and educators exhibit in order to collaborate with each other and coordinate activities across home and school so to promote positive social behavior, academic learning and achievement, and well-being (Christenson & Sheridan, 2001). Thus, family-school partnerships are child-centered and encourage active family participation. For example, families and educators may collaborate to improve cultural responsiveness in schoolwide systems. Alternatively, families and educators may meet to develop a plan to improve a child's behavior at recess. Effective communication is central to family-school partnerships. The extent to which families and educators can coordinate and collaborate to strengthen shared plans relies on effective, back-and-forth communication.

In their seminal book, Christenson and Sheridan (2001) identify three conditions that support family-school partnerships: approach, atmosphere, and attitudes. Each of the three conditions supports actions families, educators, and other key stakeholders take to promote positive outcomes for children. Families often wait for educators to initiate contact (Davies, 1991). Thus, the impetus is on the school to define expectations for family-school partnerships and create clear roles for families and educators within the partnership (Dishion, 2011). School administrators can communicate role expectations for families and educators at the beginning of each school year using multiple methods (e.g., Facebook announcement, newsletter) and reinforce those messages throughout the school year by (a) including families on school teams, (b) giving families a voice in school decisions, (c) seeking and integrating family and educator feedback about school practices (e.g., through surveys), and (d) supporting families as they work with their children to promote social development and academic achievement. This approach uses partnerships as an anchor so school initiatives and programs reflect the beliefs and expectations of the school community.

A school's atmosphere goes beyond the appearance of school buildings; *atmosphere* also refers to the relational process and communication patterns in schools. In family-school partnerships, the emphasis is on proactive, positive outreach, trusting and authentic relationships, and a welcoming and supportive atmosphere that promotes inclusion of families in the school community (Christenson & Sheridan, 2001; Dishion, 2011). The nature of school outreach and communication must be differentiated so all families can access support and engage as a full partner. For example, whereas one family may see an announcement about parent–teacher conferences on a website, another family may benefit from a text message from a teacher.

Attitudes families and educators hold about the other party influence the approach each party takes and the atmosphere surrounding their shared work. It can be helpful for families and educators to take stock of their attitudes in order to identify attitudes they hold and how those views may influence their work together. For example, educators and families can complete a survey about their attitudes toward partnering, which can be used to target interventions (Christenson & Sheridan, 2001). If survey findings suggest a disconnect between families and educators in their attitudes about partnering, focus groups could be held to identify targets for action.

The approach, atmosphere, and attitudes toward family-school partnerships in a school can be measured through questionnaires before addressing each condition and again after conditions have been addressed so as to determine progress in each area (Christenson & Sheridan, 2001). These conditions promote the ideals of social justice by empowering families and allowing full participation in the educational process. In this way, the rights of all parties are reflected in school operating procedures. In the sections that follow, we describe a systems-level, tiered approach to family-school partnerships, focused on establishing conditions to family-school partnerships, promoting equity, and improving positive outcomes for children. Specific elements of family-school partnerships that embrace social justice and span programs and initiatives that we review in this chapter include: (a) parents and educators partnering on school teams and making decisions together, (b) parents and educators working together to extend core features of school programs to the home setting, and (c) parents and educators using communication pathways so that contact can be initiated by any party and messages can flow in both directions (Garbacz, 2019).

TIERED SYSTEMS OF SUPPORT IN EDUCATION

Many schools throughout the world have adopted tiered systems of support in order to systematically and proactively address students' academic and behavioral needs (McIntosh & Goodman, 2016). Multitiered systems of support (MTSS), a concept that has its roots in a prevention-based public health model (World Health Organization, 2004), includes three tiers of support that can be matched to individual students based on need so as to address academics and behaviors (Horner, Sugai, & Anderson, 2010). At the universal level, a public health model includes primary prevention (Tier 1) strategies to support all individuals. Those who require more intensive intervention also receive secondary prevention (Tier 2), leaving a small percentage who receive an additional tier of interventions, tertiary prevention (Tier 3). Each of these tiers of intervention involves coordinated schoolwide prevention efforts with an emphasis on monitoring and evaluation with data-based decision-making, professional development that focuses on evidence-based practices, and a team-based process to drive implementation (Hawken, Vincent, & Shumann, 2008; Sugai & Horner, 2006).

One example of an MTSS framework is positive behavioral interventions and supports (PBIS) – an applied scientific approach with key elements focused on effective teams, data-based decision-making, and evidence-based practices and implementation support toward systems-level prevention that promotes a positive school climate, minimizes challenging behavior, and improves the likelihood of academic success (Sugai & Horner, 2002; Walker et al., 1996). Approaches within MTSS such as PBIS have been applied in school settings (Sugai et al., 2000), family homes (Dunlap et al., 2017), and alternative community settings such as juvenile justice and residential programs (Swain-Bradway, Swoszowski, Boden, & Sprague, 2013). Early childhood programs have also embraced MTSS (Fox, Dunlap, Hemmeter, Joseph, & Strain, 2003) through the development of program-wide positive behavior support and the pyramid model. The pyramid model outlines a systematic, multitiered approach to proactive behavior intervention, social-emotional support, and learning that is reflective of the unique structure of early childhood programs (Fox, Carta, Strain, Dunlap, & Hemmeter, 2010). The pyramid model and PBIS have been adapted for use across a number of countries, with careful attention to alignment with cultural norms (e.g., Hurley, Saini, Warren, & Carberry, 2012) and governmental guidelines and mandates (e.g., McIntosh, Bennett, & Price, 2011).

In school environments, primary prevention or Tier 1 focuses on prevention for all students in all school settings. This typically includes clear schoolwide expectations and an acknowledgment system used to promote desired behavior. In addition, systemic features that enable consistent support to all students include data collection and data-based decision-making to align supports with student needs and characteristics (Office of Special Education Programs [OSEP] Technical Assistance Center on Positive Behavioral Interventions and Supports, 2017). Family members collaboratively develop expectations and acknowledgment systems with school teams.

Secondary prevention in a schoolwide framework (Tier 2) focuses on additional supports for students for whom primary prevention (Tier 1) is not sufficient; for example, for students contending with conditions of risk or demonstrating early social, emotional, or behavioral problems. Tier 2 approaches might include additional instructional supports, academic and behavioral contract systems, mentoring programs, and modular academic or social skills programs that can augment Tier 1 practices to target specific student needs (McIntosh, Campbell, Carter, & Rossetto Dickey, 2009). Families provide input on monitoring systems for academics or behavior, which can include regular home–school communication.

Tertiary prevention (Tier 3) typically includes about 5 percent of students who benefit from additional individualized academic, social, behavior, or mental health support that cannot be adequately addressed with Tiers 1 and 2 (Ingram, Lewis-Palmer, & Sugai, 2005; McIntosh, Chard, Boland, & Horner, 2006). Examples of Tier 3 supports include function-based behavior intervention planning and individualized supports for academic needs. For example, for a student who is physically aggressive with peers, a Tier 3 team would collect data about factors that lead to aggressive behavior. The team might identify that inadequate expectations, lack of adult attention for appropriate behavior, and deficits in problem-solving skills occasion aggressive behavior. The team would use that information to develop tailored support, build problem-solving skills, and promote appropriate behavior.

Families and other key stakeholders in children's lives (e.g., community mental healthcare providers, case managers) can contribute to developing and implementing an MTSS framework. Family engagement is defined within MTSS as bidirectional, in that families and stakeholders receive information about their children, but also have a voice regarding practices as they apply to all children across tiers within the education environment (Garbacz, McIntosh, Vatland, Minch, & Eagle,

2018; Weist, Garbacz, Lane, & Kincaid, 2017). Such approaches encourage a back-and-forth sharing of information so that families and other stakeholders collaborate with school personnel to design effective practices in schools while facilitating the adoption of complementary practices in non-school settings (e.g., home- and community-based supports; Weist et al., 2017).

CULTURAL RESPONSIVENESS

Central to family-school partnerships is integrating information about the experiences of minority students and families in tiered, culturally responsive systems of support. *Cultural responsiveness* refers to incorporating the cultural expertise and norms of minority students and their families into curricula and instruction, school activities, and support services (Peek Crockett & Esparza Brown, 2009). Research on school disciplinary practices provides clear evidence that racial bias continues to affect students of color, who are disciplined more often for subjective behaviors such as defiance (Girvan, Gion, McIntosh, & Smolkowski, 2017), and disciplined more often using exclusionary practices such as out-of-school suspension and expulsion (Skiba et al., 2014). Preventing such systematic discrimination of minoritized youth and families in education requires strengthening cultural responsiveness in multitiered school systems, as reviewed in the next section.

CULTURALLY RESPONSIVE FAMILY-SCHOOL PARTNERSHIP SYSTEMS AND PRACTICES

Based on theory and existing family-school partnership models, we identify culturally responsive family-school partnership systems and practices aligned with a tiered system of support. In this section, we examine Tier 1, Tier 2, and Tier 3 approaches. Modifying malleable school features such as policies and procedures by embedding family-school partnerships can promote equity and mitigate prejudice against minority students and families. Leverson and colleagues (2016) suggest that positive school cultures that explicitly reflect values and beliefs within the school community include five components: identity exploration and awareness, opportunities for voice, a supportive environment, recognition that students' behavior is learned and may be appropriate in some situations, and the use of data for equity (e.g., regularly disaggregating disciplinary data by race to monitor for patterns that may be discriminatory). We infuse Leverson and colleagues' suggestions within the family-school partnership systems and practices that follow.

Readiness. A first step in readying a school system for working with families is to take stock of attitudes and approaches to partnering in the school community. School faculty, staff, and families can complete brief surveys about their attitudes and current approaches to working with families (Christenson & Sheridan, 2001). Approaches for ongoing assessment to explore and integrate minoritized group identities, cultures, values, and expectations include conducting focus groups with families in order to assess community values, beliefs, and expectations. The survey and focus group data are used to tailor the school's approach to partnering with families and may have implications for how schoolwide tiered frameworks are implemented. For example, if families report they do not receive information about school programs sent home with their children, alternative communication methods can be used, such as social media posts or email. Giving voice to minoritized students, families, and community members and honoring community values and expectations helps to create a positive and supportive school culture (Leverson et al., 2016). In the next section, we provide examples of these approaches.

Tier 1. We identify several Tier 1 approaches schools can use to enhance family-school partnerships in their systems and practices. The Tier 1 approaches we emphasize include (a) collaborating with families on school teams and in decision-making, (b) using data for equity, and (c) communicating effectively with families.

Engaging families on school teams and in decision-making. Engaging families (including family representatives and advocates) as members of schoolwide problem-solving teams can support a climate of collaboration and advance the notion that the school is a community space shared by all its members. School faculty may not be accustomed to working with families on school teams and parents may have little experience serving on school teams and partnering with faculty. It may be useful for school faculty to receive technical assistance from a family-school partnership organization about creating an equitable role for families on school teams and supporting parents as partners. Such approaches could take stock of beliefs about family-school partnerships and describe how family-school partnerships benefit students. Similarly, parents may need some support to engage as full partners. School personnel may offer training and support for parents. Finally, schools might target their invitations and proactive outreach to families of diverse backgrounds and nondominant cultures.

Using data for equity. School leadership teams can promote equity by regularly examining disciplinary data disaggregated by racial/ethnic status, and data on student outcomes and implementation fidelity (Leverson et al., 2016). Disaggregated data may be used to examine trends in disproportionality and to identify targets for intervention, such as key situations (e.g., specific behaviors, locations) or disciplinary policies (e.g., office disciplinary referrals, suspensions). Data on student outcomes may also be shared with stakeholders for input and considered as the basis for modifying systemic factors before intervening at the individual student level, and school teams can solicit input from families and other stakeholders about schoolwide practices so as to promote multiple viewpoints and equitable systematic practices.

Communicating effectively with families. Effective communication is an essential feature of family-school partnerships as it underlies all interactions families and educators share (Christenson & Sheridan, 2001). To promote family-school partnering, communication is proactive, frequent, varied, positive, and multidirectional (Dishion et al., 2003; Sheridan, Rispoli, & Holmes, 2013). Since many families wait for schools to initiate contact, proactive communication is essential (Christenson & Reschly, 2010). In addition, particularly with families who have children with academic or behavior concerns, their past interactions with school personnel may have been characterized by the school reporting concerns with their children. Rearranging communication patterns to focus on proactive and positive communication can facilitate family engagement and give families access to evidence-based parenting information (Stormshak, Dishion, Light, & Yasui, 2005). Communication can also lead to an enhanced understanding of assumptions that are made about family lived experiences, which influence interactions and might unintentionally promote racial inequities (Barajas-Lopez & Isimaru, 2016). A school team could assess family preferences for communication and use that information to target strategies that are aligned with family preferences.

Tier 2. At Tiers 2 and 3, school personnel act as agents for social justice when they explicitly consider macrosystem and mesosystem factors that affect minoritized students and families (Li & Vazquez-Nuttall, 2009). For instance, practitioners may consider how student behavior (and perceptions of student behavior) are affected by factors in the macro-level social-ecological context, such as racial prejudice and discrimination, and the validity of psychometric assessment for a student's cultural background (Li & Vazquez-Nuttall, 2009). At the level of the mesosystem, academic and behavioral expectations for students may differ between home and school settings, and this misalignment can sometimes be interpreted as a problem within the children (Li & Vazquez-Nuttall, 2009). Two Tier 2 approaches include collaborating with families to develop behavior change plans and group skills training. Smolkowski and colleagues (2017) outline an approach for collaborating with families in Tier 2 behavior change plans that provide support for students across the day, based on check-in/check-out (Crone, Hawken, & Horner, 2010). Consonant with Smolkowski and colleagues, school personnel create Tier 2 behavior change plans with families and integrate opportunities to review data and evaluate progress with families, which can occur through in-person meetings, home–school notes, and an electronic data dashboard. Another approach to Tier 2 student support is group-based skills training. One example of a group skills training is the Coping Power Program (CPP). In CPP, group leaders facilitate a series of sessions for children with disruptive behavior in order to promote skills such as perspective taking, problem solving, and emotion regulation (Lochman, Wells, & Lenhart, 2008). Group leaders facilitate regular communication with parents and teachers. In addition, parents are invited to attend the group sessions and leaders may also hold separate parent meetings to collaborate with families.

Tier 3. At Tier 3, the emphasis is on partnering with families to address specific concerns at home and in school. The Family Check-Up (FCU) (Dishion & Stormshak, 2007) and Conjoint Behavioral Consultation (CBC) (Sheridan & Kratochwill, 2008) are two approaches that facilitate strengths-based, collaborative meetings to collect data, set goals, develop and implement plans, and evaluate progress. The FCU is a three-session tailored approach to assessment and treatment. As a family-centered approach, the FCU may be conducted only with families or integrated school personnel and other stakeholders. The CBC is a family-school partnership approach to individualized assessment, goal-setting, intervention planning and implementation, and evaluation. In the CBC, parents, teachers, and other key stakeholders participate with a consultant in approximately three or four structured meetings in order to identify a specific behavior of concern at home and/or school to address through collecting and examining data, setting goals, creating a function- and evidence-based intervention plan, supporting cross-setting implementation, and evaluating outcomes. Thus, the CBC can be helpful for creating shared goals and expectations that effectively give voice to minoritized communities. The CBC improves child behavior and the parent-teacher relationship (Sheridan et al., 2012). In fact, the parent-teacher relationship has been identified as a mediator in child behavior improvements. To improve cultural responsiveness at Tier 3, contextual factors and social acceptability can drive theoretically sound adaptations to interventions (Lau, 2006). In the CBC, consultants talk with families at the beginning of the process about their culture, beliefs, values, and expectations, and then integrate that information throughout the collaborative process. In addition, strong objectivity can be used to create space for the narratives of marginalized families, which can lead to identifying alternative strategies that may be more effective than those that are embedded in a majority culture (Henning-Stout & Meyers, 2000).

INTEGRATING CULTURALLY RESPONSIVE FAMILY-SCHOOL PARTNERSHIPS IN TIERED SYSTEMS

Additionally, several existing models might be used in tiered systems that provide parenting support and bridge the home-school connection. We review a family intervention model (the FCU and the Parent Management Training-Oregon Model) and the Positive Parenting Program (Triple P). We chose these approaches due to their (a) theoretical alignment with this chapter and (b) applications across contexts.

The family intervention model was developed by scholars in Oregon, in the United States, as an ecological, family-centered approach to intervention and treatment grounded in a developmental cascade model that is responsive to family and child needs (Dishion et al., 2016). The FCU was designed to support intact families experiencing some risk, but who may change with minimal support (Dishion & Stormshak, 2007). The FCU begins with an initial interview during which background information about family strengths and needs is gathered. Next, an ecological assessment is conducted. After assessment data are collected, a family consultant facilitates a strengths-based feedback session where families can see assessment data displayed in a family-friendly manner. Family consultants use motivational interviewing strategies to support families and motivate change. Some families engage in treatment based on their needs and motivation to change. Several randomized controlled trials have shown effects of the FCU on child and family outcomes, such as substance use (Dishion, Nelson, & Kavanagh, 2003), antisocial behavior (Stormshak et al., 2011), and family conflict (Smith et al., 2014).

The Parent Management Training–Oregon Model (PMTO) is a set of evidence-based interventions used to support families with young children and adolescents and to prevent and address a variety of concerns (e.g., academic, externalizing; Dishion et al., 2016). The PMTO is strengths-based and PMTO therapists work directly with parents who serve as the primary interventionists/change agents. The PMTO can be delivered in individual or group sessions. Like the FCU, several outcomes studies show empirical support for the PMTO on family and child outcomes, such as parenting practices (Forgatch, DeGarmo, & Beldavs, 2005) and child behavior (Martinez & Forgatch, 2001). The FCU and the PMTO share a focus on supporting and partnering with parents and motivating change (Dishion et al., 2016) rather than using didactic teaching.

The PMTO has been adapted for a variety of contexts in the United States and around the world. Implementation sites have launched in Norway, Mexico, and the Netherlands with a pilot program in northern Uganda (Dishion et al., 2016; Forgatch, Patterson, & Gewirtz, 2013). In addition, the PMTO has been adapted across contexts, such as for military families and Latino immigrant families. Using a cultural process model, Domenech Rodríguez, Baumann, and Schwartz (2011) demonstrate an adaptation of the PMTO for Latino families. Domenech Rodríguez and colleagues describe several adaptations, such as metaphors, content, concepts, treatment goals, and procedures.

In Norway, the PMTO has been integrated in schools' tiered support framework, Positive Behavior, Interactions, and Learning Environment in School (PALS) (Arnesen, Ogden, & Sørlie, 2006). In PALS, universal, targeted, and indicated supports are embedded in school settings and linked to children's needs. Over a three-year period, PALS is introduced to families and implemented in school settings. In the third year, the PMTO is offered as an individualized support for families of high-risk children (Dishion et al., 2016).

Originating in Australia, Triple P integrates family engagement into an MTSS framework and has been applied across contexts. Triple P provides a range of education and supports for families (Sanders, Kirby, Tellegen, & Day, 2014). At the primary prevention level, Triple P provides families with a series of parenting sessions. To address secondary prevention, Triple P has been adapted for use for children of different ages and with various concerns (Hoath & Sanders, 2002). Triple P also offers classes tailored to address the needs and concerns of specific subsets of families (e.g., families in rural settings; Morawska & Sanders, 2006) and has offered different modalities, including a web interface. Triple P has been adapted for use in a variety of contexts, including at least sixteen different countries (Nowak & Heinrichs, 2008), as well as with different ethnic populations in Australia (Matsumoto, Sofronoff, & Sanders, 2007).

CONCLUSION

Social justice, international policy, and cultural responsiveness can be integrated with family-school partnerships in tiered systems of support in order to promote positive and equitable academic, social, and behavior outcomes for children. Several examples of aligning and integrating family-school partnerships with tiered systems exist in several countries, including Mexico, Norway, and the United States. Using theoretical frameworks, conceptual models, and empirical findings, we have described several characteristics of effective culturally responsive family-school partnership approaches that align with a tiered system of support, promote equal opportunities and rights, and guard against discrimination, intentional or implicit. Tiered approaches that use CRT and a systems perspective can promote social justice and be adapted across contexts.

Note

[*] The research reported here was supported by the Institute of Education Sciences, US Department of Education, through grant R324B160043 to the University of Wisconsin–Madison. The opinions expressed are those of the authors and do not represent views of the Institute or the US Department of Education. Correspondence concerning this chapter should be addressed to S. Andrew Garbacz, Department of Educational Psychology, University of Wisconsin–Madison, 1025 West Johnson Street, Madison, Wisconsin 53706. Email: sgarbacz@wisc.edu.

REFERENCES

American Counseling Association (2014). Code of ethics. Retrieved from www.counseling.org/resources/aca-code-of-ethics.pdf.

Americans with Disabilities Act of 1990, 42 U.S.C. § 12101 et seq.

Arnesen, A., Ogden, T., & Sørlie, M.-A. (2006). *Positiv atferd og støttende loringsmiljø I skolen* [*Positive behavior and support learning environments in school*]. Oslo: Universitets-forlaget.

Barajas-López, F., & Ishimaru, A. M. (2016). "Darles el lugar": A place for nondominant family knowing in educational equity. *Urban Education*, 55(1), 38–65.

Barret, S., Eber, L., & Weist (2013). *Advancing education effectiveness: Interconnecting school mental health and school-wide positive behavior support*. Eugene: University of Oregon Press.

Batsche, G., Elliott, J., Graden, J. L., et al. (2005). *Response to intervention: Policy considerations and implementation.* Alexandria, VA: National Association of State Directors of Special Education.

Bronfenbrenner, U. (1979). Contexts of child rearing. *American Psychologist,* 34(10), 844–850.

Christenson, S. L., & Reschly, A. R. (2010). Preface. In S. L. Christenson & A. L. Reschly (eds.), *Handbook of school-family partnerships* (pp. xiii–xvii). New York: Routledge.

Christenson, S. L., & Sheridan, S. M. (2001). *Schools and families: Creating essential connections for learning.* New York: Guilford Press.

Civil Rights Data Collection (2018). 2015–16 Civil Rights Data Collection: School climate and safety issue brief. US Department of Education. Retrieved from www2.ed.gov/about/offices/list/ocr/docs/school-climate-and-safety.pdf

Crone, D. A., Hawken, L. S., & Horner, R. H. (2010). *Responding to problem behavior in schools: The Behavior Education Program* (2nd ed.) New York: Guilford Press.

Davies, D. (1991). Schools reaching out: Family, school, and community partnerships for student success. *Phi Delta Kappan,* 72(5), 376–382.

Dishion, T. J. (2011). Promoting academic competence and behavioral health in public schools: A strategy of systemic concatenation of empirically based intervention principles. *School Psychology Review,* 40(4), 590–597.

Dishion, T. J., Forgatch, M., Chamberlain, P., & Pelham, W. E., III (2016). The Oregon model of behavior family therapy: From intervention design to promoting large-scale system change. *Behavior Therapy,* 47(6), 812–837.

Dishion, T. J., Nelson, S. E., &Kavanagh, K. (2003). The Family Check-Up with high-risk young adolescents: Preventing early-onset substance use by parent monitoring. *Behavior Therapy,* 34(4), 553–571.

Dishion, T. J., & Stormshak, E. A. (2007). *Intervening in children's lives: An ecological, family-centered approach to mental health care.* Washington, DC: American Psychological Association.

Dodge, K. A., Greenberg, M. T., Malone, P. S., & Conduct Problems Prevention Research Group (2008). Testing an idealized dynamic cascade model of the development of serious violence in adolescence. *Child Development,* 79(6), 1907–1927.

Domenech Rodríguez, M. M., Baumann, A. A., & Schwartz, A. L. (2011). Cultural adaptation of an evidence-based intervention: From theory to practice in a Latino/a community context. *American Journal of Community Psychology,* 47 (1–2), 170–186.

Dunlap, G., Strain, P. S., Lee, J. K., et al. (2017). *Prevent teach reinforce for families.* Baltimore, MD: Paul H. Brookes.

Forgatch, M. S., DeGarmo, D. S., & Beldavs, Z. (2005). An efficacious theory-based intervention for stepfamilies. *Behavior Therapy,* 36(4), 357–365.

Forgatch, M. S., Patterson, G. R., & Gewirtz, A. H. (2013). Looking forward: The promise of widespread implementation of parent training programs. *Perspectives on Psychological Science,* 8(6), 682–694.

Fox, L., Carta, J., Strain, P. S., Dunlap, G., & Hemmeter, M. L. (2010). Response to intervention and the pyramid model. *Infants & Young Children,* 23(1), 3–13.

Fox, L., Dunlap, G., Hemmeter, M. L., Joseph, G. E., & Strain, P. S. (2003). The teaching pyramid: A model for supporting social competence and preventing challenging behavior in young children. *Young Children,* 58(4), 48–52.

Garbacz, S. A. (2019). Enhancing family engagement in schoolwide positive behavioral interventions and supports. *Intervention in School and Clinic,* 54(4), 195–203.

Garbacz, S. A., Herman, K. C., Thompson, A. M., & Reinke, W. M. (2017). Family engagement in education and intervention: Implementation and evaluation to maximize family, school, and student outcomes. *Journal of School Psychology,* 62(1), 1–10.

Garbacz, S. A., McIntosh, K., Vatland, C., Minch, D., & Eagle, J. W. (2018). Identifying and examining school approaches to family engagement within schoolwide positive behavioral interventions and supports. *Journal of Positive Behavior Interventions*, 20(3), 127–137.

Girvan, E. J., Gion, C., McIntosh, K., & Smolkowski, K. (2017). The relative contribution of subjective office referrals to racial disproportionality in school discipline. *School Psychology Quarterly*, 32(3), 392–404.

Harding, S. (1991). *Whose science? Whose knowledge? Thinking from women's lives*. Ithaca, NY: Cornell University Press.

Hart, S. N., & Prasse, D. P. (1991). Theme editors' comments: Children's rights and education. *School Psychology Review*, 20(3), 344.

Hawken, L. S., Vincent, C. G., & Schumann, J. (2008). Response to intervention for social behavior: Challenges and opportunities. *Journal of Emotional and Behavioral Disorders*, 16(4), 213–225.

Henning-Stout, M., & Meyers, J. (2000). Consultation and human diversity: First things first. *School Psychology Review*, 29(3), 419–425.

Hoath, F. E., & Sanders, M. R. (2002). A feasibility study of Enhanced Group Triple P – Positive Parenting Program for parents of children with attention-deficit/hyperactivity disorder. *Behaviour Change*, 19(4), 191–206.

Horner, R. H., Sugai, G., & Anderson, C. M. (2010). Examining the evidence base for schoolwide positive behavior support. *Focus on Exceptional Children*, 42(8), 1–14.

Hurley, J. J., Saini, S., Warren, R. A., & Carberry, A. J. (2012). Use of the pyramid model for supporting preschool refugees. *Early Child Development and Care*, 183(1),75–91.

Implicit Bias (2018). Part II: Addressing disproportionality in discipline: A prospective look at culturally responsive positive behavior intervention and supports. *Communique*, 46, 20–21. Retrieved from http://ezproxy.lib.usf.edu/login?url=http://search.ebscohost.com/login.aspx?direct=true&db=edsgao&AN=edsgcl.541397284&site=eds-live.

Individuals with Disabilities Act, 20 U.S.C. §§ Section 1414 *et seq.* (2006 & Supp. V. 2011).

Ingram, K., Lewis-Palmer, T., & Sugai, G. (2005). Function-based intervention planning: Comparing the effectiveness of FBA function-based and non-function-based intervention plans. *Journal of Positive Behavior Interventions*, 7(4), 224–236.

Koegel, L. K. E., Koegel, R. L., & Dunlap, G. E. (1996). *Positive behavioral support: Including people with difficult behavior in the community*. Baltimore, MD: Paul H Brookes.

Ladson-Billings, G. (1998). Just what is critical race theory and what's it doing in a nice field like education? *International Journal of Qualitative Studies in Education*, 11(1), 7–24.

Ladson-Billings, G., & Tate, W. F. (1995). Toward a critical race theory of education. *Teachers College Record*, 97(1), 47–68.

Lau, A. S. (2006). Making the case for selective and directed cultural adaptations of evidence-based treatments: Examples form parent training. *Clinical Psychology: Science and Practice*, 13(4), 295–310.

Leverson, M., Smith, K., McIntosh, K., et al. (2016). *PBIS cultural responsiveness field guide: Resources for trainers and coaches*. Eugene: University of Oregon Press.

Li, C., & Vazquez-Nuttall, E. (2009). School consultants as agents of social justice for multicultural children and families. *Journal of Educational and Psychological Consultation*, 19(1), 26–44.

Lochman, J. E., Wells, K. C., & Lenhart, L. A. (2008). *Coping power child group program: Facilitator guide*. New York: Oxford University Press.

Martinez, C. R., & Forgatch, M. S. (2001). Preventing problems with boys' noncompliance: Effects of a parent training intervention for divorcing mothers. *Journal of Consulting and Clinical Psychology*, 69(3), 416–428.

Matsumoto, Y., Sofronoff, K., & Sanders, M. R. (2007). The efficacy and acceptability of the Triple P-Positive Parenting Program with Japanese parents. *Behaviour Change*, 24(4), 205–218.

McIntosh, K., Bennett, J. L., & Price, K. (2011). Evaluation of social and academic effects of school-wide positive behaviour support in a Canadian school district. *Exceptionality Education International*, 21(1), 46–60.

McIntosh, K., Campbell, A. L., Carter, D. R., & Rossetto Dickey, C. (2009). Differential effects of a tier two behavior intervention based on function of problem behavior. *Journal of Positive Behavior Interventions*, 11(2), 82–93.

McIntosh, K., Chard, D. J., Boland, J. B., & Horner, R. H. (2006). Demonstration of combined efforts in school-wide academic and behavioral systems and incidence of reading and behavior challenges in early elementary grades. *Journal of Positive Behavior Interventions*, 8 (3), 146–154.

McIntosh, K., & Goodman, S. (2016). *Integrated multi-tiered systems of support: Blending RTI and PBIS*. New York: Guilford Publications.

Miller, G. E., Colebrook, J., & Ellis, B. R. (2014). Advocating for the rights of the child through family-school collaboration. *Journal of Educational and Psychological Consultation*, 24(1), 10–27.

Morawska, A., & Sanders, M. R. (2006). Self-directed behavioural family intervention. *International Journal of Behavioral Consultation and Therapy*, 2(3), 141–149.

National Association of School Psychologists (NASP) (2017). *Adoption of social justice definition*. Bethesda, MD: National Association of School Psychologists.

Nowak, C., & Heinrichs, N. (2008). A comprehensive meta-analysis of Triple P-Positive Parenting Program using hierarchical linear modeling: Effectiveness and moderating variables. *Clinical Child and Family Psychology Review*, 11(3), 114–144.

O'Connell, M. E., Boat, T., & Warner, K. E. (2009). *Committee on the prevention of mental disorders and substance abuse among children, youth, and young adults: Research advances and promising interventions*. Washington, DC: National Academies Press.

Office of Special Education Programs (OSEP) Technical Assistance Center on Positive Behavioral Interventions and Supports (2017). Positive behavioral interventions and supports. Retrieved from www.pbis.org.

Peek Crockett, D., & Esparza Brown, J. (2009). Multicultural practices and response to intervention. In J. M. Jones (ed.), *The psychology of multiculturalism in the schools: A primer for practice, training, and research* (pp. 117–138). Bethesda, MD: National Association of School Psychologists.

Posney, A. (2007). OSEP memorandum 07-09 to state directors of special education on disproportionality or racial and ethnic groups in special education. Retrieved from www2.ed.gov/policy/speced/guid/idea/letters/2007-2/osep0709disproportionality2q2007.pdf.

Richman, J. M., Bowen, G. L., & Woolley, M. E. (2004). School failure: An eco-interactional developmental perspective. In M. W. Fraser (ed.), *Risk and resilience in childhood: An ecological perspective* (pp. 133–160). Washington, DC: NASW Press.

Sanders, M. R., Kirby, J. N., Tellegen, C. L., & Day, J. J. (2014). The Triple P-Positive Parenting Program: A systematic review and meta-analysis of a multi-level system of parenting support. *Clinical Psychology Review*, 34(4), 337–357.

Section 504 of the Rehabilitation Act of 1973, 29 U.S.C. § 701 et seq.

Sheridan, S. M., Bovaird, J. A., Glover, T. A., et al. (2012). A randomized controlled trial examining the effects of conjoint behavioral consultation and the mediating role of the parent-teacher relationship. *School Psychology Review*, 41(1), 23–46.

Sheridan, S. M., & Kratochwill, T. R. (2008). *Conjoint behavioral consultation: Promoting family-school connections and interventions* (2nd ed.). New York: Springer.

Sheridan, S. M., Rispoli, K., & Holmes, S. R. (2013). Treatment integrity in conjoint behavioral consultation: Conceptualizing active ingredients and potential pathways of influence. In L. Sanetti & T. Kratochwill (eds.), *Treatment integrity: A foundation for evidence based practice in applied psychology* (pp. 255–278). Washington, DC: American Psychological Association.

Shriberg, D., Wynne, M. E., Briggs, A., Bartucci, G., & Lombardo, A. C. (2011). School psychologists' perspectives on social justice. *School Psychology Forum, 5*(2), 37–53.

Skiba, R. J., Chung, C. G., Trachok, M., et al. (2014). Parsing disciplinary disproportionality: Contributions of infraction, student, and school characteristics to out-of-school suspension and expulsion. *American Educational Research Journal, 51* (4), 640–670.

Smith, J. D., Dishion, T. J., Shaw, D. S., et al. (2014). Coercive family process and early-onset conduct problems from age 2 to school entry. *Development and Psychopathology, 26*(4), 917–932.

Smolkowski, K., Seeley, J. R., Gau, J. M., et al. (2017). Effectiveness evaluation of the positive family support intervention: A three-tiered public health delivery model for middle schools. *Journal of School Psychology, 61*(1), 103–125.

Stormshak, E. A., Connell, A. M., Véronneau, M. H., et al. (2011). An ecological approach to promoting early adolescent mental health and social adaptation: Family centered intervention in public middle schools. *Child Development, 82*(1), 209–225.

Stormshak, E. A., Dishion, T. J., Light, J., & Yasui, M. (2005). Implementing family-centered interventions within the public middle school: Linking service delivery to change in student problem behavior. *Journal of Abnormal Child Psychology, 33*(6), 723–733.

Sugai, G., & Horner, R. H. (2002). The evolution of discipline practices: School-wide positive behavior supports. *Child & Family Behavior Therapy, 24*(1–2), 23–50.

Sugai, G., & Horner, R. H. (2006). A promising approach for expanding and sustaining school-wide positive behavior support. *School Psychology Review, 35*(2), 245–259.

Sugai, G., Horner, R. H., Dunlap, G., et al. (2000). Applying positive behavior support and functional behavioral assessment in schools. *Journal of Positive Behavior Interventions, 2*(3), 131–143.

Swain-Bradway, J., Swoszowski, N. C., Boden, L. J., & Sprague, J. R. (2013). Voices from the field: Stakeholder Perspectives on PBIS implementation in alternative education settings. *Education and Treatment of Children, 36*(3), 31–46.

United Nations General Assembly (1989, November 17). *Adoption of a Convention on the Rights of the Child.* New York: United Nations General Assembly.

United Nations General Assembly (2006, December 13). UN Convention on the Rights of Persons with Disabilities. Articles 1, 2, & 24.

Walker, H. M., Horner, R. H., Sugai, G., et al. (1996). Integrated approaches to preventing antisocial behavior patterns among school-age children and youth. *Journal of Emotional and Behavioral Disorders, 4*(4), 193–256.

Weist, M. D., Garbacz, S. A., Lane, K. L., & Kincaid, D. (2017). *Aligning and integrating family engagement in positive behavioral interventions and supports (PBIS): Concepts and strategies for families and schools in key contexts.* Center for Positive Behavioral Interventions and Supports (funded by the Office of Special Education Programs, US Department of Education). Eugene: University of Oregon Press.

World Health Organization (2004). *Prevention of mental disorders: Effective interventions and policy options.* Geneva: World Health Organization.

13

Social Justice and School Discipline

Schoolwide Positive Behavioral Interventions and Supports (SWPBIS)

Jessica Swain-Bradway, Satish Moorthy, and Milaney Leverson

INTRODUCTION

Exclusionary discipline practices in the US public school system have a historic, disproportionate, negative impact on Black and Hispanic American youth, in particular those receiving special education services. Use and overuse of exclusionary discipline limit students' ability to access academic and social success. Because the high risk of suspension is not equally distributed to all students, but is predictably related to race and ethnicity, at its root, exclusionary discipline is a civil and human rights issue (Losen & Gillespie, 2012; Noguera, 2003). Beginning in the mid-twentieth century, social justice movements internationally and in the United States were based on declarations, laws, and policies prioritizing individual rights and protections so as to preserve the dignity of the person (UN Declaration of Human Rights, 1948, Article 26). This movement served as an important means to achieve and sustain civil and political as well as economic, social, and cultural rights of individuals (Monshipouri & Welch, 2001).

This chapter provides a broad context for these civil, disability, and human rights-based movements, including the precedent for full inclusion of African American students and students with special needs in the US public school system. Next this chapter details the evidence for a lack of equitable disciplinary systems and practices, and how state and federal policies are responding by addressing equity through changes in policies. This chapter then moves to a treatment of equity beyond policy and describes how schoolwide positive behavioral interventions and supports (SWPBIS) can address this multifaceted social issue.

Schoolwide positive behavioral interventions and supports (SWPBIS) is an empirically valid systems approach to reducing exclusionary discipline (Bradshaw, Waasdorp, & Leaf, 2012; Horner et al., 2009). More than twenty years of evidence document discipline, academic, and organizational improvements related to SWPBIS (Horner, Sugai, & Lewis, 2007).

This chapter also provides evidence of the overall impact of SWPBIS on student outcomes related to discipline, with a focus on recent adaptations to SWPBIS to explicitly address disciplinary equity. Examples from state education agencies implementing SWPBIS specifically in order to ameliorate disciplinary gaps between student ethnicity groups are included. These state exemplars provide early evidence of the potential for SWPBIS to positively affect rates of disciplinary disproportionality for ethnic minority student populations, in particular African American males. This chapter closes with suggestions for future direction so as to achieve and sustain more equitable outcomes for all students.

SOCIAL JUSTICE AND SCHOOL DISCIPLINE

Justice in Education: Universal Declaration of Human Rights

Internationally, the roots of modern social justice in education largely stemmed from a response to the atrocities of World War II and from nations' desire to outline and protect fundamental rights for all persons, ranging from civil and political rights, to economic, social, health and well-being, educational, and cultural rights (United Nations, 1948 Universal Declaration of Human Rights). Supported by the establishment of the United Nations (UN) through its 1945 charter, the preamble of the 1948 Universal Declaration of Human Rights begins with an acknowledgment that a "recognition of the inherent dignity and of the equal and inalienable rights of all members of the human family is the foundation of freedom, justice and peace in the world" (p. 1).

Recognizing foundational human experiences and the need for equitable access to education, the Declaration of Human Rights explicitly asserts: (1) Everyone has the right to education. (2) Education shall be free, at least in the elementary and fundamental stages. (3) Elementary education shall be compulsory. (4) Education shall be directed to the full development of the human personality, and to the strengthening of respect for human rights and fundamental freedoms (Article 26).

Precedent for Inclusion

Not long after the 1948 Declaration of Human Rights, a landmark court case established a firm foothold for social justice in education in the United States. *Brown v. Board of Education of Topeka* was decided on May 17, 1954, through a unanimous US Supreme Court decision. The court determined that racial segregation in public schools violates the Fourteenth Amendment to the US Constitution, prohibiting states from denying equal protection of the laws to any person (Warren, 1954). The decision established the inherent inequality of separate educational facilities for White and Black students, thus rejecting the "separate but equal" doctrine advanced by the Supreme Court in *Plessy v. Ferguson* (Ferguson, 1896). Although the 1954 decision strictly applied only to public schools, it implied that segregation was not permissible in other public facilities, making clear that regardless of race, gender, or disability, individuals have a right to a public education (Esteves & Rao, 2008).

This firm reiteration of the individual protections afforded to all US citizens by the Fourteenth Amendment established a precedent for equal access to education for all students, thereby leading the way for the establishment of the Education of All Handicapped Children Act (EHA) (1975), renamed in 1990 as the Individuals with Disabilities Education Act (IDEA). The Individuals with Disabilities Education Act required access to a free, appropriate public education in the least restrictive environment for all children with disabilities. International actions at this same time, stemming from the UN Convention on the Rights of the Child, extended the Declaration of Human Rights (Article 26), explicitly recognizing unique educational needs for children with disabilities, and stated that education must be designed to ensure that children with disabilities have access to and receive comprehensive supports conducive to their achieving the fullest possible social integration and individual development (United Nations, Convention on the Rights of the Child, Article 23, 1989). The international evolution of social justice in education, with parallel movements in the United States, was clearly aimed at increasing access to or inclusion in education for all children, as represented by the UN Convention on the Rights of the Child.

Beyond Inclusion to Quality

While the EHA focused on access to educational programs for students with disabilities, it did not address the degree of educational opportunity (Yell & Drasgow, 1999). The first special education case to test the limits of "appropriate" was heard by the Supreme Court in the case of *Board of Education of the Hendrick Hudson Central School District v. Rowley* (*Board v. Rowley*) (1982). *Board v. Rowley* interpreted congressional intent in requiring that public schools provide a free appropriate public education (FAPE) to students with disabilities under the IDEA. The narrow *Board v. Rowley* decision ruled that the EHA does not mandate that supportive services provided for students with special needs help the students achieve their full potential as learners; it is sufficient to show that the students are benefiting from instruction (Powell, 1981).

Since *Board v. Rowley*, a series of Supreme Court cases has continued to refine the idea of "appropriate" as an articulation of the extent to which a school must go in educating children, in part based on the individual educational requirements of students with special needs (Yell & Drasgow, 2000).

A more recent court case in the United States, *Endrew v. Douglas County*, advanced the application of social justice beyond simple educational access to educational quality. In the Supreme Court's ruling in favor of a higher standard of education for children with disabilities, Chief Justice John G. Roberts Jr. delivered the opinion for a unanimous court, which stated that children's "educational program must be appropriately ambitious in light of [their] circumstances" (*Endrew v. Douglas County*, No. 15–827, 2017, p. 3). Roberts quoted from the *Rowley* decision: "Every child should have the chance to meet challenging objectives. When all is said and done, a student offered an educational program providing 'merely more than de minimis' progress from year to year can hardly be said to have been offered an education at all" (*Rowley*, 458 U.S., at 179, 102 S.Ct. 3034, quoted at *Endrew v. Douglas County*, No. 15–827, 2017, p. 3).

Lack of Equity in School Discipline

Despite the international declarations and the US federal legislation mandating educational access and quality, the disciplinary practice of excluding students from the school environment through out-of-school suspension (OSS) continues to rise in the United States (Losen & Martinez, 2013). This has been a consistent trend since the early 1970s, especially for children of color and students with special needs (Losen & Martinez, 2013). It is also well documented that suspension from school or the classroom significantly increases the likelihood of dropping out, even after controlling for other factors that also increase dropout rates (Balfanz, Byrnes, & Fox, 2015). Removing students from instruction as a disciplinary practice is harmful in terms of increased risk for dropping out (Balfanz et al., 2015) and future incarceration (Rosenbaum, 2018; Rumberger & Losen, 2016).

This negative effect of exclusionary discipline has a disproportionately negative impact on subpopulations of US public schools. Black students have a 30 percent risk of suspensions, almost twice the 16 percent rate for their White peers (Rumberger & Losen, 2016). Black students also have higher rates of exclusionary discipline than their White peers for the *same* infraction (Skiba et al., 2011). Exclusionary discipline rates for students with a special education classification are almost twice those for their nondisabled peers (Losen, 2018). The intersection of ethnicity and disability increases the risk of exclusionary discipline even more: Black students with disabilities experience approximately seventy-seven more days of lost instruction due to exclusionary discipline than their White counterparts with disabilities, a gap that has increased in at least twenty-eight states since 2015–2016 (Losen, 2018).

The difference in days of lost instruction translates into substantial inequities in the opportunity to learn due to persistent inequitable disciplinary practices. Black students in general and especially those with disabilities do not have the same access to educational opportunities or instructional hours as their White and nondisabled peers (Losen, 2018). The problems of exclusionary punishment, with its negative, immediate, and long-term disparate impacts on Black students, reiterate that the current and historical disciplinary trend in the United States is a social justice issue and a violation of students' civil rights.

Addressing Equity through Policy

While inequity persists in the educational system, it has not persisted without garnering attention from federal and state departments of education. In 2011, the

US Department of Education (DOE) and the US Department of Justice (DOJ) launched the Supportive School Discipline Initiative in order to coordinate federal efforts to reform school disciplinary practices. In January 2014, the DOE released a resource package with a variety of informational materials designed to support state and local efforts to improve school climate and discipline. The package included a "Dear Colleague" letter, published jointly by the DOE and the DOJ, that explicitly raised concerns around and warned against intentional racial discrimination. The letter also stated that schools unlawfully discriminate even "if a policy is neutral on its face – meaning that the policy itself does not mention race – and is administered in an even handed manner but has a disparate impact, i.e., a disproportionate and unjustified effect on students of a particular race" (Lhamon, 2014, p. 8; Steinberg & Lacoe, 2017). Following this letter, the White House issued "The Continuing Need to Rethink Discipline" (US Office of the Press Secretary, 2016), a comprehensive report with recommendations for reshaping school discipline so as to foster safe, supportive, and productive learning environments. The recommendations were in alignment with a 2014 Council of State Governments report supporting the use of alternatives to suspension as a way to reduce disproportionate exclusion of students of color (Morgan, Salomon, Plotkin, & Cohen, 2014).

Individual states are taking increased legislative action limiting the use of suspension and expulsion. In 2012 in California, Assembly Bill 420 eliminated willful defiance or disruption of school activities as a reason to expel students. It also prevented administrators from using that reason to issue suspensions to K–3 students. The willful defiance category had come under scrutiny in California because it had been disproportionately used statewide to discipline Black students and, in some districts, Latino students. In 2012–2013, African Americans made up about 6 percent of total California public school enrollment, but accounted for 19 percent of suspensions for defiance. According to a 2014 survey of 500 district superintendents conducted by the School Superintendents Association (www.aasa.org), 84 percent of respondents reported that their districts had updated their code of conduct within the previous three years, and as of the 2015–2016 school year, 23 of the 100 largest US school districts reported policy reforms requiring nonpunitive discipline strategies and/or limiting exclusionary disciplinary suspensions (Steinberg & Lacoe, 2017).

In December 2016, final regulations under Part B of the IDEA were released. These regulations were aimed at promoting equity by targeting widespread disparities in the treatment of students of color with disabilities, and specifically addressed a number of issues related to significant disproportionality in the identification, placement, and discipline of students with disabilities based on race or ethnicity (US Department of Education, 2016). In order to address these inequities, the IDEA requires states to identify districts with "significant disproportionality" in special education – that is, when districts identify, place in more restrictive settings, or discipline children from any racial or ethnic group at markedly higher rates than their peers. The regulation was designed to develop a uniform methodology for states to use in identifying disproportionality and to take steps to address it. In 2016 and 2017, sixteen different states enacted legislation directly related to suspension and expulsion (Education Commission of the States, 2018). However, the explicit federal commitment to address disciplinary disproportionality has not been met with linear progress since 2016. In 2018, over concerns that the US Department of Education would rescind the accountability components included in the 2016 IDEA regulations, the National Association of State Directors of Special Education (NASDSE) urged the federal government to implement the regulations without delay. Despite the wavering federal regulations, state-level stakeholders, education policy makers, research groups, and civil rights advocates continue to work to support and provide evidence for reducing school inequalities by addressing disciplinary disproportionality.

From Policy to Practice

Joint recommendations from the Center for Civil Rights Remedies at the Civil Rights Project, and the Charles Hamilton Houston Institute for Race & Justice provide guidelines to impact high and disproportionate rates of exclusionary discipline (Losen, 2018). These recommendations are pulled directly from a 2018 brief authored by Losen, *Disabling Punishment: The Need for Remedies to the Disparate Loss of Instruction Experienced by Black Students with Disabilities*, and include suggestions for data use, policy revision, professional development, and reallocation of resources.

Data use includes (a) identifying districts that have problematic racial and disability disparities in discipline, (b) engaging state-level administrators in supporting districts to conduct root-cause analyses, and (c) using multiple sources of data, including school climate surveys, behavior incident reports, and other monitoring to ensure that school reforms are improving the learning conditions. Policy revision includes revising codes of conduct and other disciplinary practices in order to reduce the use of removal from the classroom, except as a measure of last resort, and to provide safeguards to ensure that implementation of the changes does not implicate safety. Professional development requires staff training for evidence-based intervention programs that have shown to reduce disparate loss of instructional time. Resource reallocation consists of actionable steps, including (a) redirecting IDEA funds toward affecting a remedy, (b) setting aside the resources needed for leadership and staff training, (c) dedicating resources to evaluating reform efforts, and (d) investing in the infrastructure necessary for the timely collection and public reporting of accurate data on discipline at the district and school levels, including disaggregating the days of lost instruction for all subgroups.

A FRAMEWORK FOR REFORMING DISCIPLINE: SCHOOLWIDE POSITIVE BEHAVIORAL INTERVENTIONS AND SUPPORTS

Schoolwide positive behavioral interventions and supports (SWPBIS) has been identified as a viable, evidence-based alternative to suspension to manage behavior and reflects the recommendations by Losen (2018). Grounded in behavioral psychology, SWPBIS is an implementation framework for maximizing the selection and use of evidence-based prevention and intervention practices along a multitiered continuum that supports the academic, social, emotional, and behavioral competence of all students (Horner et al., 2009). It is a direct response to "zero-tolerance" exclusionary discipline and explicitly includes systems to support adults in the school to consistently and accurately deliver strategies matched to students' needs in opposition to excluding students from school. The National Positive Behavioral Interventions and Supports (PBIS) Technical Assistance Center is funded by the US Office of Special Education Programs (OSEP). The Technical Assistance Center has developed blueprints for implementation, as well as fidelity measures and metrics for evaluating impact on student outcomes (Algozzine et al., 2010).

The SWPBIS framework includes four elements considered in all decisions related to supporting academic and social outcomes for students: (1) Data: what information is needed to improve decision-making? (2) Outcomes: what do students need to do for academic and behavioral success? (3) Practices: what can students experience to support their academic and behavioral success, e.g., teaching, prompting, and recognizing expected social behaviors? (4) Systems: what can educators experience to support their use of evidence-based academic and behavioral practices, e.g., school leadership teams, data-based decision-making, continuous professional development and coaching? (OSEP National Technical Assistance Center on PBIS, 2018). As described by the Technical Assistance Center, the multitiered "continuum" is comprised of carefully selected, evidence-based practices at three different levels of support. Specific practices are matched both to the level of support needed and to the local cultural context. Tiers of support are described in the Technical Assistance Center's Implementation Blueprint (Lewis, Barrett, Sugai, & Horner, 2010) and can be summarized as follows:

- Tier 1: Universal practices are experienced by all students and educators across all settings in order to establish a predictable, consistent, positive, and safe climate.
- Tier 2: Targeted practices are designed for groups of students who need more structure, feedback, instruction, and support than Tier 1 alone.
- Tier 3: Indicated practices are more intense and individualized so as to meet the challenges of students who need more than Tiers 1 and 2 alone.

SWPBIS Evidence of Impact

Research on SWPBIS documents robust, persistently positive outcomes for students, teachers, and other school community stakeholders, and it is explicitly included in the 2015 Every Student Succeeds Act (ESSA), the reauthorization of the fifty-year-old

Elementary and Secondary Education Act (ESEA). Evidence from experimental and quasi-experimental studies on SWPBIS are summarized by evaluation summary by Horner and colleagues (2015) and include: (a) reductions in major disciplinary infractions, antisocial behavior, and substance abuse; (b) reductions in aggressive behavior and improvements in emotional regulation and academic engagement and achievement; (c) improvements in perceptions of organizational health and school safety; (d) reductions in teacher- and student-reported bullying behavior and victimization; (e) improvements in perceptions of school climate; and (f) reductions in teacher turnover (Horner et al., 2015; OSEP National Technical Assistance Center on PBIS, 2018).

In addition to the aforementioned findings from research studies, state and regional PBIS networks have provided evidence of the impact of SWPBIS on vulnerable students, including students presenting with disabilities and in special education (Illinois PBIS Network, 2014), and students of color (Wisconsin RTI Network, 2016). Earlier research on the impact of SWPBIS on the disciplinary gap between Black and White students showed that while schools implementing SWPBIS may reduce overall exclusionary discipline for all students, Black and White alike, it did not necessarily reduce the disciplinary gap (Tobin, Horner, Vincent, & Swain-Bradway, 2013). Case studies published in 2016 and 2018 have shown that schools implementing SWPBIS decreased discipline disparities over time (Betters-Bubon, Brunner, & Kansteiner, 2016; McIntosh, Ellwood, McCall, & Girvan, 2018). Moreover, an examination of nationwide data showed decreased ethnic disproportionality for SWPBIS at fidelity compared to national averages (McIntosh, Gion, & Bastable, 2018).

SWPBIS to Address Disciplinary Disproportionality: The 5-Point Intervention Approach for Enhancing Equity in School Discipline

While the empirical basis for the impact of SWPBIS on enhancing social discipline in education by reducing disciplinary disproportionality is in the early stages, the Technical Assistance Center is publishing growing guidance. This guidance operationalizes the previously described, overarching suggestions from the Center for Civil Rights Remedies at the Civil Rights Project, the Charles Hamilton Houston Institute for Race & Justice, and the ESSA (2015). Using SWPBIS as the foundation for intervention, McIntosh, Girvan, Horner, Smolkowski, and Sugai (2014) have developed the 5-Point Intervention Approach for Enhancing Equity in School Discipline. The 5-Point Intervention includes: (1) collect, use, and report disaggregated discipline data; (2) implement a behavior framework that is preventive, multitiered, and culturally responsive; (3) use engaging instruction to reduce the opportunity (achievement) gap; (4) develop policies with accountability for disciplinary equity; and (5) teach adults strategies for neutralizing implicit bias in discipline decisions.

These five points reflect emerging knowledge about two forms of bias: implicit bias and explicit bias (McIntosh et al., 2014). Explicit bias is a purposeful discrimination against others that perpetuates inequities, and as a conscious act, should be addressed directly through policy (Pettigrew & Tropp, 2006). Implicit bias is an unconscious form of discrimination with unintended discriminatory impact that originates from an overreliance on stereotypes. A promising way to reduce the discriminatory impact of implicit bias is to identify specific situations where biased decisions are more likely to occur, referred to as *vulnerable decision points*, and to utilize concrete teaching practices and systems accountability so as to ensure more equitable or just disciplinary practices (Green et al., 2015). The following sections describe these five components, followed by student outcomes and impact data from states utilizing them.

Collect, use, and report disaggregated discipline data. Schools, districts, and states must examine their disciplinary data, disaggregated by ethnicity, to identify specific situations in which inequities are strongest as well as situations with equity in decision-making, and implement interventions tailored to enhance equity in those situations (McIntosh, Ellwood, et al., 2018). These data serve as the baseline for social inequities in discipline, as well as progress in monitoring and accountability metrics for improvement over time.

Implement a behavior framework that is preventive, multitiered, and culturally responsive. The focus of SWPBIS on instructional, problem-solving approaches to keep students in the classroom and engaged in learning is a key feature to reducing disproportionate disciplinary practices. The foundational practice embedded in SWPBIS – establishing a clear, consistent, and positive social culture by identifying and teaching clear expectations for behavior – can reduce ambiguity for both students and adults and ensure all stakeholders understand expected behaviors. Educators invested in reducing disciplinary disproportionality need to guarantee that the school culture is "contextually fit" or reflects the larger culture of the entire community.

When SWPBIS is deeply connected to the context of the host setting, it is representative and reflective of the students', families', and communities' values and beliefs. This contextual fit, then, is one way to ensure that school systems are culturally responsive. Gloria Ladson-Billings coined the term *cultural relevance* as a way of describing teaching that "empowers students intellectually, socially, emotionally, and politically by using culture to impart knowledge, skills, and attitudes" (Ladson-Billings, 1992, p. 382). Culturally responsive practices include holding high expectations for all students; using students' cultures and experiences to enhance their learning; providing all students with access to effective instruction and adequate resources for learning (Klingner et al., 2005); recognizing the importance of culture; and incorporating cultural elements (e.g., characteristics, experiences, and perspectives) into interpersonal interactions to facilitate more effective relationships (Gay, 2002).

Efforts such as these must include a distinct focus on student, family, and community engagement in order to be effective (Ladson-Billings, 1995). Without this broad reach for engagement, efforts and systemic supports will likely "fit" the decision makers who enact them, rather than enhancing the outcomes of those meant to benefit from them, the students.

Use engaging instruction to reduce the opportunity (achievement) gap. The strategies suggested to create engaging instruction stem from research on direct instruction (Archer & Hughes, 2011) and acknowledge the well-documented relation between academic achievement and problem behavior (McIntosh, Sadler, & Brown, 2012) as well as the opportunity gap between students of color and their White peers (Gregory, 2010). Each student must have access to effective instruction as a foundation for reducing disproportionality, including the following strategies: (a) use explicit instruction (Hattie, 2012), (b) build and prime background knowledge (Al-faki & Siddiek, 2013), (c) increase opportunities to respond (Armendariz & Umbreit, 1999), and (d) provide performance feedback (Chaparro, Nese, & McIntosh, 2015; Hattie, 2009). Using these instructional strategies has been shown to decrease the disparate outcomes between White and Black students (Chaparro, Helton, & Sadler, 2016).

Develop policies with accountability for disciplinary equity. More important than an explicit commitment to equity is for policies to establish clear steps and accountability in order to achieve equity (Devine, Forscher, Austin, & Cox, 2012; Petersen & Togstad, 2006).

Policies should reflect: (1) specific commitment to equity, (2) family engagement and partnership in policy development and refinement, (3) focus on implementing positive, proactive behavior support practices, (4) clearly stated, objective discipline procedures, (5) removal or reduction of exclusionary practices, (6) discipline systems with instructional alternatives to exclusion, and (7) procedures with accountability for equitable student outcomes.

Teach adults strategies for neutralizing implicit bias in discipline decisions. Smolkowski and colleagues (2016) have documented specific situations in schools in which implicit bias is more likely to influence decision-making, referred to as *vulnerable decision points* (VDPs). Researchers have identified two elements of decision points that make them vulnerable: (a) the situation itself (e.g., the inherent subjectivity in classifying defiance vs. smoking), and (b) the teacher's state in that moment (e.g., fatigued as opposed to focused) (Smolkowski, Girvan, McIntosh, Nese, & Horner, 2016).

To mitigate the impact of VDPs, McIntosh, Ellwood, and colleagues (2018) suggest it may be effective to provide training to school personnel to identify situations in which their decisions may be vulnerable to bias (e.g., fatigue, subjective behavior, unfamiliar student), and at the schoolwide- or districtwide-level, use of disaggregated discipline data by ethnicity and student behavior may help decision makers identify these patterns of vulnerable decision points (McIntosh, Ellwood, et al., 2018). Mendoza, Gollwitzer, and Amodio (2010) suggest that implementation intentions, short "if-then" statements, are most effective for reducing the expression of implicit stereotypes, for example: ***If** a student is disrespectful,* **then** *handle it after class.*

Early Evidence for the 5-Point Intervention Approach

Researchers continue to document evidence of the potential impact of various components of the 5-Point Intervention. Chaparro and colleagues (2015) document the relationship of engaging instructional strategies and reductions in the achievement gap between White and Latino students on meeting state testing standards (Chaparro et al., 2015). In a separate study, McIntosh, Ellwood, and colleagues (2018) record a consistent decrease in discipline disproportionality over time, in conjunction with the use of data guidelines for identifying, and neutralizing routines for vulnerable decision points. In their 2018 study, across three years, office discipline referral rates for Black students reduced from 0.5 office referrals per 100 students per day to 0.2 office referrals per 100 students per day.

Several US states have adopted larger-scale implementation of the 5-Point Intervention. Michigan's Integrated Behavior and Learning Support Initiative (MIBLSI) is engaged in an equity pilot that utilizes the Technical Assistance Center's five-point multicomponent approach to prevent and reduce disproportionality in schools. Early results are promising as overall averages for suspensions decreased with substantial reduction in the gaps between White and Black students' rates of exclusionary discipline. The MIBLSI team examined risk ratios for suspensions in order to determine the relative risk for an OSS by Black students compared to their White peers. Risk ratios represent the likelihood of the outcome (e.g., ODRs) for one group in relation to a comparison group.

Risk ratios are calculated by dividing the risk index of the group of interest by the risk index of a comparison group. The comparison group most commonly used is White students, but others, such as the risk index for all other groups, are sometimes used. A risk ratio of 1.0 shows that the risk for the two groups is equal, whereas a risk ratio greater than 1.0 is indicative of overrepresentation, and a risk ratio less than 1.0 is indicative of underrepresentation (Boneshefski & Runge, 2014). The MIBLSI team documented that in the pilot schools, the risk ratio for Black students reduced by 25 percent from September to February between the 2016–2017 and 2017–2018 school years (Payno-Simmons & Hill, 2018). More rigorous evaluations are under way and will be reported in early 2020.

The Wisconsin Department of Public Instruction (WI-DPI) (www.wisconsinrti center.org) has documented compelling reductions in both academic and disciplinary outcomes between White and Black students. The WI-DPI has implemented a statewide multilevel system of support (MLSS) that includes the SWPBIS five-point intervention approach. Wisconsin was early in the statewide adoption of several of the five-point interventions and has manualized the training and technical support related to SWPBIS that is focused on reducing disciplinary disproportionality. The investment of statewide resources included ensuring that school personnel were trained in engaging instructional practices and building a statewide discipline and academic database that allows for disaggregating disciplinary data by ethnicity. Some of these efforts predated and contributed to the full development of the National Technical Assistance Center's 5-Point Intervention Approach.

This early adoption has been widely beneficial to all students in the state. As documented in the 2015–2016 and 2016–2017 Wisconsin statewide PBIS annual reports, schools implementing the five-point intervention recorded an overall lower percentage of suspensions for all students compared to schools not implementing SWPBIS, in addition to lowering the average suspension rate from 10.77 percent to 4.05 percent for all students. The overall rate of suspensions for Black students saw a significant change, from 16.05 percent to 8.06 percent: Wilks' $\lambda = 0.50$, $F(1,64) = 65.22$, $p < 0.001$, $\eta^2 = 0.51$.

Wisconsin schools documenting the highest levels of SWPBIS fidelity experienced an average reduction in OSSs for Black students from 23 percent (2008–2009) to 7.29 percent (2015–2016), representing a 71 percent reduction in the discipline gap between Black and White students in this cohort. In addition to disciplinary impact, schools implementing the five-point approach saw an increase in reading benchmarks with Black and Hispanic students. In reading, 11.78 percent more Black students met or exceeded state benchmarks, with 10.44 percent more Hispanic students meeting or exceeding reading benchmarks (Swain-Bradway, Gulbrandson, Galston, & McIntosh, 2019).

A secondary measure of benefit to Wisconsin's efforts was gains in administrative time for school leaders and in instructional time for students related to reduced OSS rates. Overall, the reductions in suspension were equivalent to an increase of 10,525 school days for all students represented in the fidelity cohort. For Black students, this represented a savings of 8,366 instructional days, and for Hispanic students, 1,103 days. These recouped instructional days represent a "reinvestment" of $536,320.56 and $70,710.20, respectively (Wisconsin RTI Network, 2016). More rigorous statistical analyses of the changes in discipline data are currently under way to determine the extent and sustainability of the positive impact of this approach over time.

FUTURE DIRECTION

While the trajectory of US education legislation related to dismantling inequitable access through school discipline reform is promising, substantial work lies ahead. The 2016 ESSA accountability regulations related to disproportionate discipline may be more crucial than ever, as the field of education sees increasing evidence for the potential of SWPBIS, as part of a five-point intervention, to enhance equity. The early descriptive data are promising, but more research into SWPBIS and equitable disciplinary outcomes, including gains in instructional days, is necessary. The potential of the five-point intervention to enhance equity bears broad replication in randomized controlled trials, and should the research continue to reflect improved disciplinary outcomes for students, by decreasing the disciplinary gap, the approach should be: (a) legislatively cemented within state education policies, (b) established as core components of teacher and administrative training and licensure programs, and (c) developed fully into school accountability metrics.

Recognizing foundational human dignity and the need for equitable access to education as articulated by the UN Declaration of Human Rights (1948), the SWPBIS five-point intervention to establish more equitable school outcomes has early evidence that all students can access education, if we are intentional, and use research and evidence-based approaches to disciplinary obstacles to instruction. Persistent inequitable disciplinary practice is at its core a social justice issue and should be dismantled using legislative, systemic, and strategic policy means.

REFERENCES

Al-faki, I. M., & Siddiek, A. G (2013). The role of background knowledge in enhancing reading comprehension. *World Journal of English Language*, 3(4), 42–66.

Algozzine, B., Horner, R. H., Sugai, G., et al. (2010). *Evaluation blueprint for school-wide positive behavior support*. Eugene, OR: National Technical Assistance Center on Positive Behavior Interventions and Support.

Archer, A. L., & Hughes, C. A. (2011). *Explicit instruction: Effective and efficient teaching*. New York: Guilford Press.

Armendariz, F., & Umbreit, J. (1999). Using active responding to reduce disruptive behavior in a general education classroom. *Journal of Positive Behavior Interventions*, 1, 152–158.

Balfanz, R., Byrnes, V., & Fox, J. H. (2015). Sent home and put off track. Closing the school discipline gap: Equitable remedies for excessive exclusion, 17–30. http://digitalcommons.library.tmc.edu/childrenatrisk/vol5/iss2/13

Betters-Bubon, J., Brunner, T., & Kansteiner, A. (2016). Success for all? The role of the school counselor in creating and sustaining culturally responsive positive behavior interventions and supports programs. *Professional Counselor*, 6(3), 263–277. https://files.eric.ed.gov/fulltext/EJ1115904.pdf

Biglan, A. (1995). Translating what we know about the context of anti-social behavior into a lower prevalence of such behavior. *Journal of Applied Behavior Analysis*, 28, 479–492.

Bishaw, A., & Fontenot, K. (2012). Poverty: 2010 and 2011. American community survey briefs US Census. www2.census.gov/library/publications/2012/acs/acsbr11-01.pdf

Boneshefski, M. J., & Runge, T. J. (2014). Addressing disproportionate discipline practices within a school-wide positive behavioral interventions and supports framework: A practical guide for calculating and using disproportionality rates. *Journal of Positive Behavior Interventions*, 16(3), 149–158.

Bradshaw, C., Waasdorp, T., & Leaf, P. (2012). Examining the variation in the impact of school-wide positive behavioral interventions and supports. *Pediatrics*, 10(5), 1136–1145.

Chaparro, E. A., Helton, S., & Sadler, C. A. (2016). Oregon Effective Behavioral and Instructional Support Systems initiative: Implementation from district and state level perspectives. In K. McIntosh & S. Goodman (eds.), *Multi-tiered systems of support: Integrating academic RTI and school-wide PBIS* (pp. 267–286). New York: Guilford.

Chaparro, E. A., Nese, R. N. T., & McIntosh, K. (2015). Examples of engaging instruction to increase equity in education. Eugene, OR: Center on Positive Behavioral Interventions and Supports. University of Oregon. www.pbis.org/resource/examples-of-engaging-instruction-to-increase-equity-in-education.

Colvin, G., Sugai, G., Good, R., & Lee, Y-Y. (1987). Using active supervision and precorrection to improve transition behaviors in an elementary school. *Education & Treatment of Children, 20,* 209–222.

Devine, P. G., Forscher, P. S., Austin, A. J., & Cox, W. T. L. (2012). Long-term reduction in implicit race bias: A prejudice habit-breaking intervention. *Journal of Experimental Social Psychology, 48,* 1267–1278.

Dunlosky, J., Rawson, K. A., Marsh, E. J., Nathan, M. J., & Willingham, D. T. (2013). Improving students' learning with effective learning techniques: Promising directions from cognitive and educational psychology. *Psychological Science in the Public Interest, 14,* 4–58.

Ferguson, P. V. (1896). 163 US 537 (1896). Jurisdiction: United States of America, Supreme Court Date of Decision, 18.

Fuchs, D., Fuchs, L. S., Mathes, P. G., & Simmons, D. C. (1997). Peer-assisted learning strategies: Making classrooms more responsive to diversity. *American Educational Research Journal, 34,* 174–206.

Education Commission of the States (2018). Policy snapshot: Suspension and expulsion. www.ecs.org/wp-content/uploads/Suspension_and_Expulsion.pdf.

Endrew F. v. Douglas County School District, 798 F. 3d 1329 (10th Cir. 2015). www.supremecourt.gov/opinions/16pdf/15-827_0pm1.pdf.

Esteves, K. J., & Rao, S. (2008). The evolution of special education. *Principal, 88*(2), 1. www.naesp.org/sites/default/files/resources/1/Principal/2008/N-Oweb2.pdf.

Gay, G. (2002). Preparing for culturally responsive teaching. *Journal of Teacher Education, 53* (2), 106–116.

Green, A. L., Nese, R. N. T., McIntosh, K., et al. (2015). Key elements of policies to address disproportionality within SWPBIS: A guide for district and school teams. OSEP Technical Assistance Center on Positive Behavioral Interventions and Supports. www.pbis.org.

Gregory, A., Skiba, R. J., & Noguera, P. A. (2010). The achievement gap and the discipline gap: Two sides of the same coin? *Educational Researcher, 39*(1), 59–68. https://pdfs.semanticscholar.org/5e29/3a4598fece049e2e33b1254dd46d73106780.pdf.

Hattie, J. (2012). *Visible learning for teachers: Maximizing impact on learning.* New York: Routledge.

Hattie, J., & Timperley, H. (2007). The power of feedback. *Review of Educational Research, 77,* 81–112.

Haydon, T., Mancil, G., & Van Loan, C. (2009). Using opportunities to respond in a general education classroom: A case study. *Education & Treatment of Children, 32,* 267–278.

Horner, R. H., & Sugai, G. (2015). School-wide PBIS: An example of applied behavior analysis implemented at a scale of social importance. *Behavior Analysis in Practice, 8*(1), 80–85. doi:10.1007/s40617-015-0045-4

Horner, R., Sugai, G., Smolkowski, K., et al. (2009). A randomized control trial of school-wide positive behavior support in elementary schools. *Journal of Positive Behavior Interventions, 11*(3), 113–144.

Hunt, P., Farron-Davis, F., Beckstead, S., Curtis, D., & Goetz, L. (1994). Evaluating the effects of placement of students with severe disabilities in general education versus special classes. *Journal of the Association for Persons with Severe Handicaps, 19*(3), 200–214.

Illinois PBIS Network (2014, May). Quarterly report.
Individuals with Disabilities Education Act, 20 U.S.C. §§ 1400 et seq. (2006 & Supp. V. 2011).
Johnson, P. (1982). Effects on reading comprehension of building background knowledge. *TESOL Quarterly*, 16, 503–516.
Klingner, J. K., Artiles, A. J., Kozleski, E., et al. (2005). Addressing the disproportionate representation of culturally and linguistically diverse students in special education through culturally responsive educational systems. *Education Policy Analysis Archives*, 13(38), 1–40.
Ladson-Billings, G. (1992). Liberatory consequences of literacy: A case of culturally relevant instruction for African American students. *Journal of Negro Education*, 61(3), 378–391.
Ladson-Billings, G. (1995). Toward a theory of culturally relevant pedagogy. *American Educational Research Journal*, 32(3), 465–491.
Lai, C. K., Hoffman, K. M., Nosek, B. A., & Greenwald, A. G. (2013). Reducing implicit prejudice. *Social and Personality Psychology Compass*, 7, 315–330.
Lewis, T. J., Barrett, S., Sugai, G., & Horner, R. H. (2010). *Blueprint for school-wide positive behavior support training and professional development*. Eugene, OR: National Technical Assistance Center on Positive Behavior Interventions and Support.
Lhamon, C. E. (2014). United States Department of Education Office for Civil Rights, Dear Colleague Letter, October 1, 2014. www2.ed.gov/about/offices/list/ocr/letters/colleague-resourcecomp-201410.pdf.
Losen, D. (2018). Disabling punishment: The need for remedies to the disparate loss of instruction experienced by Black students with disabilities. The Center for Civil Rights Remedies at the Civil Rights Project. www.schooldisciplinedata.org/ccrr/docs/disabling-punishment-report.pdf
Losen, D., & Gillespie, J. (2012). Opportunities suspended: The disparate impact of disciplinary exclusion from school. Civil Rights Project/Proyecto Derechos Civiles. https://eric.ed.gov/?id=ED534178
McIntosh, K., Ellwood, K., McCall, L., & Girvan, E. J. (2018). Using discipline data within a PBIS framework to enhance equity in school discipline. *Intervention in School and Clinic*, 53, 146–152.
McIntosh, K., Gion, C., & Bastable, E. (2018). Do schools implementing SWPBIS have decreased racial and ethnic disproportionality in school discipline? OSEP Technical Assistance Center on Positive Behavioral Interventions and Supports.
McIntosh, K., Girvan, E. J., Horner, R. H., Smolkowski, K., & Sugai, G. (2014). Recommendations for addressing discipline disproportionality in education. OSEP Technical Assistance Center on Positive Behavior Intervention and Supports.
McIntosh, K., Girvan, E. J., Horner, R. H., Smolkowski, K., & Sugai, G. (2018). A 5-point intervention approach for enhancing equity in school discipline. OSEP Technical Assistance Center on Positive Behavioral Interventions and Supports.
McIntosh, K., Sadler, C., & Brown, J. A. (2012). Kindergarten reading skill level and change as risk factors for chronic problem behavior. *Journal of Positive Behavior Interventions*, 14(1), 17–28. www.researchgate.net/profile/Jacqueline_Brown9/publication/233942516_Kindergarten_Reading_Skill_Level_and_Change_as_Risk_Factors_for_Chronic_Problem_Behavior/links/5508aa540cf2d7a2812ae83f.pdf
Mendoza, S. A., Gollwitzer, P. M., & Amodio, D. M. (2010). Reducing the expression of implicit stereotypes: Reflexive control through implementation intentions. *Personality and Social Psychology Bulletin*, 36, 512–523. doi:10.1177/0146167210362789
Monshipouri, M., & Welch, C. E. (2001). The search for international human rights and justice: Coming to terms with the new global realities. *Human Rights Quarterly*, 23(2), 370–401.

Morgan, E., Salomon, N., Plotkin, M., & Cohen, R. (2014). *The school discipline consensus report: Strategies from the field to keep students engaged in school and out of the juvenile justice system.* New York: Council of State Governments Justice Center.

Noguera, P. A. (2003). Schools, prisons, and social implications of punishment: Rethinking disciplinary practices. *Theory into Practice, 42*(4), 341–350.

OSEP National Technical Assistance Center on PBIS (2018). Brief introduction and frequently asked questions about PBIS. www.pbis.org/school/swpbis-for-beginners/pbis-faqs

Payno-Simmons, R., & Hill, B. (2019). *Practices for systematically reducing disproportionality in discipline.* Washington, DC: Association for Positive Behavior Supports. www.apbs.org/sites/default/files/conference-2016/presentations/a4-payno-simmons_hill-apbs-2019.pdf

Petersen, T., & Togstad, T. (2006). Getting the offer: Sex discrimination in hiring. *Research in Social Stratification and Mobility, 24,* 239–257.

Pettigrew, T. F., & Tropp, L. R. (2006). A meta-analytic test of intergroup contact theory. *Journal of Personality and Social Psychology, 90,* 751–783.

Powell Jr., L. F. (1981). *Board of Education of the Hendrick Hudson Central School District, Westchester County v. Rowley.* www.supremecourt.gov/opinions/16pdf/15-827_opm1.pdf.

Reddy, L. A., Fabiano, G. A., Dudek, C. M., & Hsu, L. (2013). Instructional and behavior management practices implemented by elementary and general education teachers. *Journal of School Psychology, 51,* 683–700.

Rosenbaum, J. (2018). Educational and criminal justice outcomes 12 years after school suspension. *Youth & Society, 1-33,* Sage Publications. https://doi.org/10.1177/0044118X17752208.

Rosenshine, B. (1995). Advances in research on instruction. *Journal of Educational Research, 88,* 262–268.

Rowe, D., & Rayford, L (1987). Activating background knowledge in reading comprehension assessment. *Reading Research Quarterly, 22,* 160–176.

Rumberger, R. W., & Losen, D. J. (2016). The high cost of harsh discipline and its disparate impact. Civil Rights Project/Proyecto Derechos Civiles. https://escholarship.org/uc/item/85m2m6sj

Simmons, D. C., Fuchs, L. S., Fuchs, D., Mathes, P., & Hodge, J. P. (1995). Effects of explicit teaching and peer tutoring on the reading-achievement of learning-disabled and low-performing students in regular classrooms. *Elementary School Journal, 95,* 387–408.

Skiba, R. J., Horner, R. H., Chung, C., et al. (2011). Race is not neutral: A national investigation of African American and Latino disproportionality in school discipline. *School Psychology Review, 40,* 85–107.

Smolkowski, K., Girvan, E. J., McIntosh, K., Nese, R. N. T., & Horner, R. H. (2016). Vulnerable decision points in school discipline: Comparison of discipline for African American compared to White students in elementary schools. *Behavioral Disorders, 41,* 178–195.

Stein, M., Carnine, D., & Dixon, R. (1998). Direct instruction: Integrating curriculum design and effective teaching practice. *Intervention in School and Clinic, 33,* 227–234.

Steinberg, M. P., & Lacoe, J. (2017). What do we know about school discipline reform? *Education Next, 17*(1), 44–53.

Swain-Bradway, J., Gulbrandson, K., Galston, A., & McIntosh, K. (2019). Do Wisconsin schools implementing an integrated academic and behavior support framework improve equity in academic and school discipline outcomes? Technical Assistance Center on

Positive Behavioral Interventions and Supports. www.pbis.org/resource/do-wisconsin-schools-implementing-an-integrated-academic-and-behavior-support-framework-improve-equity-in-academic-and-school-discipline-outcomes

Tobin, T., Horner, R. H., Vincent, C. G., & Swain-Bradway, J. (2013). If discipline referral rates for the school as a whole are reduced, will rates for students with disabilities also be reduced? www.pbis.org/common/cms/files/pbisresources/Evalu_Brief_revised_IEP_ODR_Nov25.pdf

United States (1975). Public Law 94–142: Education for All Handicapped Children Act of 1975. Washington, DC: US Government Printing Office.

US Department of Education (2016). Fact Sheet: Equity in IDEA. www.ed.gov/news/press-releases/fact-sheet-equity-idea

US Department of Education (2015). Elementary and Secondary Education Act of 1965, as amended by the Every Student Succeeds Act of 2015. Pub. L. 89–10. https://legcounsel.house.gov/Comps/Elementary%20And%20Secondary%20Education%20Act%20Of%201965.pdf

US Office of the Press Secretary (2016). White House Report: The continuing need to rethink discipline. https://obamawhitehouse.archives.gov/the-press-office/ 2016/12/09/white-house-report-continuing-need-rethink-discipline

Warren, C. J. E. (1954). *Brown v. Board of Education*. United States Reports, 347(1954), 483. www.law.cornell.edu/supremecourt/text/347/483

Wehmeyer, M. L., Lattin, D. L., Lapp-Rincker, G., & Agran, M. (2003). Access to the general curriculum of middle school students with mental retardation: An observational study. *Remedial and Special Education*, 24(5), 262–272. https://kuscholarworks.ku.edu/bitstream/handle/1808/5904/AGC6_AGC%20of%20Middle%20School.pdf?sequence=1

Wisconsin RTI Network (2016). Annual report. www.wisconsinrticenter.org/assets/Annual-Report-15-16-web.pdf

Yell, M. L., & Drasgow, E. (1999). A legal analysis of inclusion. *Preventing School Failure: Alternative Education for Children and Youth*, 43(3), 118–123.

Yell, M. L., & Drasgow, E. (2000). Litigating a free appropriate public education: The Lovaas hearings and cases. *Journal of Special Education*, 33(4), 205–214.

14

Understanding Body Respect As a Social Justice Issue for Young People

Sigrún Daníelsdóttir

INTRODUCTION

For more than half a century, research has documented pervasive social stigma toward higher-weight youth (Puhl & King, 2013; Puhl & Latner, 2007). Weight stigma has been found in nearly every aspect of children's lives – in school, peer relations, the media, and even their own homes (Puhl & Latner, 2007). Being the target of weight-based prejudice and discrimination has serious and long-lasting consequences for children's health, emotional well-being, and future prosperity (Puhl & Latner, 2007). While higher-weight children and adolescents undeniably bear the brunt of societal weight stigma, youth across the weight spectrum are negatively affected by a culture that idealizes thinness and condemns fatness (e.g., Eisenberg, Neumark-Sztainer, & Story, 2003; Jendrzyca & Warschburger, 2016; Zuba & Warschburger, 2018). Body image and eating concerns, fear of fatness, weight-related teasing, and bullying are prevalent among youth and underscore the need for sociocultural change in values and views around body size (Eisenberg et al., 2003; Neumark-Sztainer, Paxton, Hannan, Haines, & Story, 2006; Wertheim & Paxton, 2011). This chapter explores the prevalence and presentation of weight bias in youth and the consequences of growing up in an environment that does not respect body diversity. It considers important intersections of weight, health, and social justice, and concludes with a case example of structural efforts to promote body respect and equality.

WEIGHT-RELATED INJUSTICE AMONG YOUTH

Weight bias refers to prevailing negative views and beliefs about higher-weight people where larger bodies are associated with stereotypes such as being lazy, ugly, stupid, unhappy, insecure, incompetent, and undisciplined (Puhl & Brownell, 2001; Puhl & Heuer, 2009; Robinson, Bacon, & O'Reilly, 1993). The literature on weight stigma was launched by a pioneering study in the early 1960s that aimed to examine cultural uniformity among children. In the study, children were asked to rank pictures of youth who were fat or who had disabilities, facial anomalies, or no stigmatized condition, in terms of how well they liked each picture (Richardson, Goodman, Hastorf, & Dornbusch, 1961). The researchers found a strong aversion to fatness among the children, with the picture of the fat child consistently ranked lowest – a finding that was subsequently confirmed in several studies involving both children and adults across different socioeconomic strata and ethnic backgrounds (see Latner & Stunkard, 2003, for review).

Sixty years later, Latner and Stunkard (2003) replicated Richardson and colleagues' original study in order to examine whether children's attitudes about weight had changed over the decades. Significant milestones had been reached during that time in terms of civil rights – for example, women's liberation, LGBTI+ rights, and racial justice – which might be expected to translate into more accepting views around body diversity. In addition, higher weight had become more common among youth (Fryar, Carroll, & Ogden, 2016), which might also have fostered greater acceptance and normalization of larger bodies. The researchers discovered, however, that not only was the picture of the fat child still liked least of all, it was significantly *less* liked than in the 1961 study. Thus, during a time when major cultural shifts had taken place in terms of social justice, weight stigma had intensified among children. A corresponding increase in weight bias has since been reported in adult studies as well (Andreyeva, Puhl, & Brownell, 2008; Tomiyama et al., 2015).

THE PRESENTATION OF WEIGHT BIAS IN CHILDHOOD

Weight bias may be particularly salient in youth. When Latner, Stunkard, and Wilson (2005) tested the same picture-ranking conditions with an adult sample, they found that, compared to adults, children had even more negative views of their higher-weight peers. Since then, numerous studies have reported anti-fat sentiments among children as young as three years old (e.g., Spiel, Paxton, & Yager, 2012; Su & Di Santo, 2012). Preschool children have consistently demonstrated anti-fat bias, as evidenced by a tendency to associate a story's villain more readily with a larger figure, attribute more negative and fewer positive characteristics to pictures of heavier children, and indicate less preference for them as playmates (e.g., Damiano, Gregg, et al., 2015; Meers, Koball, Wagner Oehlhof, Laurene, & Musher-Eizenman, 2011; Spiel et al., 2012). In an attempt to examine just how early these attitudes are formed, Ruffman, O'Brien, Taumoepeau, Latner, and Hunter (2016) used a preferential looking paradigm with infants and toddlers so as to detect the emergence of anti-fat bias. They found that while infants preferred looking at fat figures, toddlers tended to prefer smaller sizes, and this relationship corresponded with their mothers' anti-fat attitudes.

In line with a social learning perspective, anti-fat attitudes have been shown to increase with age and are firmly established by age four (Damiano, Gregg, et al., 2015; Spiel et al., 2012, 2016). In elementary school, studies find that children endorse strong negative stereotypes of their higher-weight peers, regardless of their own age, gender, or body weight (Latner & Schwartz, 2005; Puhl & Latner, 2007; Tiggemann & Anesbury, 2000). Higher-weight youth are less likely to be selected as friends (Kihm, 2014; Smolak, 2011) and by adolescence they are more likely to be peripheral to social networks than their lower-weight peers (Strauss & Pollack, 2003). As with adults, children's beliefs about the controllability of body weight are positively associated with the strength of anti-fat bias. An Australian study among children in the fourth through sixth grades found consistent anti-fat stereotyping among the children and a universal belief that fatness was largely under volitional control (Tiggemann & Anesbury, 2000). In another study, where eight- to twelve-year-old children were presented with a vignette on teasing and name-calling, the children not only identified their higher-weight peers as more likely victims of such treatment but suggested weight control as an effective strategy to avoid it (Nabors et al., 2011). Such "victim blaming" has been widely documented in the literature as prevalent and positively associated with the strength of anti-fat bias (Puhl, Latner, O'Brien, Luedicke, Daníelsdóttir, Forhan et al., 2015; Teachman, Gapinski, Brownell, Rawlins, & Jeyaram, 2003).

Numerous studies also confirm that higher-weight youth are frequent targets of teasing and bullying (for review, see Puhl & King, 2013; Puhl & Latner, 2007). In fact, fatness has been identified across multinational samples as the *most common* reason for teasing and bullying, by a substantial margin over bullying based on race, ethnicity, sexual orientation, and religion (Puhl, Latner, O'Brien, Luedicke, Forhan, & Daníelsdóttir, 2015). Similar findings were reported in a large study among more than 5,000 teachers and education support professionals, who found weight-related bullying to be most problematic among students (Bradshaw, Waasdorp, O'Brennan, & Gulemetova, 2013). Another study examining adolescents' own perceptions of weight-based victimization found that 84 percent of students had witnessed a higher-weight peer being teased and at least two-thirds had observed them being ignored, avoided, or excluded from social activities, or having negative rumors spread about them (Puhl, Luedicke, & Heuer, 2011). Most students had also witnessed verbal threats, teasing during physical activities, and physical harassment toward their higher-weight peers.

Qualitative studies among adolescents with personal experiences of weight stigmatization also identify the school as the most common setting in which stigmatization takes place, followed by the home (Neumark-Sztainer, 2011). As much as 60 percent of higher-weight youth report weight-related teasing by a family member, and critical comments about weight are common (Neumark-Sztainer et al., 2010; Neumark-Sztainer, Falkner, Story, Perry, & Hannan, 2002). A recent meta-analysis found that such family teasing and criticism was significantly associated with poorer self-perception and with dysfunctional eating among children and adolescents (Gillison, Lorenc, Sleddens, Williams, & Atkinson, 2016). Finally, in a study involving more than 300 higher-weight adults examining their lifetime experiences of weight stigma, nearly one in five identified childhood as the period of their worst stigma experience, with parents, siblings, or other family members as perpetrators in 23 percent of the cases (Puhl, Moss-Racusin, Schwartz, & Brownell, 2008). Together, the studies illustrate that for many higher-weight youth, there may be little refuge where they can expect to be safe from weight-based stigmatization.

SOCIOCULTURAL INFLUENCES OF WEIGHT STIGMA

Children acquire the unwritten rules, norms, and values of their surroundings – including biases and stereotypes – through socialization early in life (Brown & Lepore, 1995). While parents appear to play an important role in the development of weight-related attitudes among children (Damiano, Gregg, et al., 2015; Spiel et al., 2016; Tatangelo, McCabe, Mellor, & Mealey, 2016), peer and media influences are also significant (Damiano, Paxton, Wertheim, McLean, & Gregg, 2015; Puhl & Latner, 2007). Weight bias appears frequently in children's media with a recent content analysis of popular children's films revealing that most (70 percent) contained anti-fat bias, such as "fat jokes" and negative comments about weight (Throop et al., 2014). A study analyzing weight-related connotations in animated cartoons also found a marked difference in the way thinner and fatter characters were depicted in terms of intelligence, physical attractiveness, and the display of prosocial and antisocial behaviors (Klein & Shiffman, 2005). In all instances, positive attributes were linked to thinness and negative to fatness. Even emotional states, such as being happy, energetic, and loving, were more often seen among thinner cartoon characters than heavier ones (Klein & Shiffman, 2005).

This is echoed in mainstream adult culture, where weight bias is commonplace in both news and entertainment media (e.g., Ata & Thompson, 2010; Himes & Thompson, 2007; Puhl, Peterson, DePierre, & Luedicke, 2013). An analysis of more than 1,000 characters from popular television shows found that higher-weight characters were consistently presented in a negative manner (Greenberg, Eastin, Hofschire, Lachlan, & Brownell, 2003). Fat male characters were more often presented as unemployed and were less likely to have friends, go on dates, or be sexually active than thinner males. They were also more frequently shown to be eating and were less likely to be considered attractive or intelligent. Larger female characters were also less likely to be considered attractive and more rarely seen in romantic situations, but were twice as likely to be the object of humor than thinner female characters (Greenberg et al., 2003). Fouts and Burggraf (2000) even detected a linear correlation between female characters' body size in television sitcoms and negative comments from male co-stars, with audience laughter significantly associated with such derogatory remarks. In this way, the authors conclude, the media plays a powerful role in affirming and perpetuating body shaming and weight prejudice through vicarious modeling and reinforcement (Fouts & Burggraf, 2000).

THE WAR AGAINST OBESITY

Another important consideration regarding the prejudice and discrimination faced by higher-weight youth is the fact that today's children are being raised in the era of the "obesity epidemic," when rejection of fatness may be seen as not only socially acceptable but also healthy and responsible. Health authorities worldwide have condemned higher body weight and officially waged war against it for more than two decades (World Health Organization, 1997). During this time, higher-weight youth have been heavily and publicly stigmatized with disparaging images in mainstream media, alarmist predictions about their future, and accusatory discourse toward parents for "letting it happen" (Boero, 2009; Gard & Wright, 2005; Puhl Peterson, DePierre, & Luedicke, 2013; Saguy & Almeling, 2008).

There is ample evidence to suggest that the war against obesity has served to increase and socially sanction weight-related stigma. News reports on obesity consistently uphold a negative depiction of fat people, with content analyses of the images that accompany stories about obesity from major news websites, such as CNN.com and CBSnews.com, revealing that fat individuals are presented in a degrading and dehumanizing manner in the majority of cases (Heuer, McClure, & Puhl, 2011; Puhl, Peterson, DePierre, & Luedicke, 2013). Compared to thinner individuals, higher-weight people are more likely to be portrayed without a head or a face, to be partly naked or dressed in ill-fitting clothing, or to be reduced to an isolated body part, such as a protruding belly (Puhl, Peterson, DePierre, & Luedicke, 2013). They are also more likely to be shown eating unhealthy foods and engaging in sedentary behavior, thus reinforcing the stereotype of fat people as lazy gluttons. Even more disturbing is the fact that researchers find a higher ratio of stigmatizing images of children than adults, with a staggering 77 percent of higher-weight youth presented in a disparaging manner in online news media (Puhl, Peterson, DePierre, & Luedicke, 2013).

It is not only the visual presentation of higher-weight individuals in the media that raises concern but the content as well. In their review of the literature, Ata and Thompson (2010) found that the media tend to present a biased view where personal control over body weight is emphasized and individuals are blamed for their size. This view has been strongly associated with weight prejudice among both children and adults (e.g., Puhl, Latner, O'Brien, Luedicke, Daníelsdóttir, Forhan, et al., 2015; Tiggemann & Anesbury, 2000) and confirmed by experimental studies to clearly elicit anti-fat bias (McClure, Puhl, & Heuer, 2011; Saguy, Frederick, & Gruys, 2014; Teachman et al., 2003). For example, Saguy and colleagues (2014) examined the influence of different news framings of obesity on weight-related attitudes across five experimental studies. Participants were assigned either to a control condition or to read a news report portraying obesity as a public health crisis, a report suggesting that obesity may not be as much of a problem as previously thought, or an article on weight discrimination. They found that, compared to a control condition, the framing of higher weight as a public health crisis significantly increased the expression of anti-fat prejudice, leading the authors to conclude that news reports on the "obesity epidemic" may indeed activate prejudice.

CONSEQUENCES OF WEIGHT STIGMA

Weight stigma has been shown to have serious and long-lasting consequences with adverse outcomes including depression, anxiety, low self-esteem, body dissatisfaction, maladaptive eating behaviors, physical inactivity, poor academic performance, and increased risk for self-harm and suicidal behavior (see Puhl & King, 2013, for review). A recent longitudinal study among adolescents found that body discrimination significantly increases the risk of self-harm, suicide ideation, and suicide attempts after controlling for sociodemographic factors, body mass index (BMI), and depressive symptoms (Sutin, Robinson, Daly, & Terracciano, 2018). Weight stigma also negatively impacts a young person's future and prosperity through discrimination in education and employment. In a large longitudinal study among more than 3,000 children, an increase in BMI from fifth to eighth grade was significantly associated with a worsening of teacher perception of academic abilities for both boys and girls after adjusting for standardized test scores (Kenney, Gortmaker, Davison, & Austin, 2015). Burmeister, Kiefner, Carels, and Musher-Eizenman (2013) also found that higher-weight applicants to graduate university programs were significantly less likely to receive postinterview offers than lower-weight applicants, a relationship that proved to be stronger for females. In employment, weight bias and discrimination have been shown to operate across all domains, from hiring to placement, wages, advancement opportunities, and likelihood of discharge (for review, see Puhl & Heuer, 2009).

While youth at the higher end of the weight spectrum are most seriously and systematically affected by weight stigma, all children are harmed by a culture that fails to respect body diversity. Body image concerns are prevalent among youth, especially in in adolescence, with an increased risk for mental health problems such as eating disorders and depression (Neumark-Sztainer et al., 2006; Stice, Hayward, Cameron, Killen, & Taylor, 2000; Stice & Shaw, 2002). Children across weight trajectories report being teased for being "fat" (Jendrzyca & Warschburger, 2016), and weight-related teasing in youth is associated with low body satisfaction, low self-esteem, depressive symptoms, suicide ideation, and attempting suicide regardless of weight status (Eisenberg et al., 2003). The internalization of weight bias; that is, applying anti-fat bias and stereotypes to oneself, has also been observed in children and adolescents across the weight spectrum (Zuba & Warschburger, 2018) and is associated with eating pathology, body dissatisfaction, low self-esteem, and symptoms of anxiety and depression, even among leaner individuals (Pearl & Puhl, 2014; Schvey & White, 2015).

Children do not have to experience weight stigma and rejection personally in order to reap the negative effects of such injustice. As previously noted, today's youth regularly witness other people being body shamed and stigmatized, if not in their immediate surroundings, such as in school, then most definitely in the media. This may cultivate feelings of body shame and fear of fatness through vicarious punishment, especially among youth who perceive their bodies to be similar to those subjected to social reprimand (Fouts & Burggraf, 2000; Seligman & Bechtoldt Baldacci, 2005). In societies rampant with publicly sanctioned weight stigma, the well-being of all children is compromised with those at the higher end of the weight spectrum particularly vulnerable to negative outcomes.

WEIGHT AS A SOCIAL JUSTICE ISSUE

Despite overwhelming evidence that higher-weight youth are exposed to multiple forms of stigma and discrimination from an early age, and that weight bias threatens youth well-being across weight trajectories, there is still little recognition of weight stigma as a form of social injustice in the lives of children. Unlike other marginalized identities that are seen as deserving of social protection from systemized injustice, higher weight is often considered primarily in terms of individual responsibility, medical pathology, and public health threat (Boero, 2007; O'Hara & Taylor, 2018; Saguy & Riley, 2005). Indeed, weight prejudice is widely framed in the literature as a "social consequence of obesity" (e.g., Ferraro & Kelley-Moore, 2003; Gibson et al., 2017; Puhl, Heuer, & Brownell, 2010; Sahoo et al., 2015). In comparison with other subordinate identities, this would be akin to framing misogyny as a consequence of being female or racism as a social consequence of having darker skin. Similarly, negative body image and emotional difficulties among higher-weight youth are routinely framed as "psychological consequences of obesity" (e.g., Gibson et al., 2017; Harriger & Thompson, 2012; Rankin et al., 2016) rather than the consequence of growing up in a weight-stigmatizing environment.

The medicalization of obesity and the framing of the "obesity epidemic" play an important part in this regard, as Nutter and colleagues have noted. "[The 'obesity epidemic' discourse] is problematic, as the ongoing discussion of large bodies as an 'epidemic,' 'infection' or a 'plague' leaves no room for the acceptance of natural body diversity. By being complicit with this discourse of the obesity epidemic researchers have asserted that large bodies will continue to be excluded, marginalized, and regarded as immoral" (Nutter et al., 2016, p. 4). Greenhalgh similarly criticizes medical and public health models for portraying fat people, if not as lazy and out of control, then as abnormal or diseased: "medical fat-talk and its messages are ubiquitous, subtly or not so subtly informing cultural ideas about weight. The fat-talk of the physician is complemented and amplified by fat-talk coming from other segments of society (aesthetic, moral, and so on)" (Greenhalgh, 2016, p. 549). Indeed, Saguy and Riley suggest that by refusing to recognize fatness as a part of human diversity "medical arguments about the health risks of obesity have been effectively used to stymie political arguments about rights for fat individuals" (Saguy & Riley, 2005, p. 871). Thus, many see moving toward social justice as requiring a paradigm shift in current approaches to health and well-being (e.g., Bombak, 2014; LaMarre & Daníelsdóttir, 2019; O'Hara & Taylor, 2018; Tylka et al., 2014).

SOCIAL JUSTICE-INFORMED APPROACHES TO HEALTH

In response to the stigma and harm associated with the fight against fatness, scholars and healthcare professionals have increasingly looked toward alternative means of promoting health that avoid the stigmatization or pathologizing of larger bodies (e.g., Bombak, 2014; Burgard, 2009; Tylka et al., 2014). One such approach is Health at Every Size® (see Figure 14.1), which focuses on increasing health-promoting behaviors, improving access to non-stigmatizing healthcare, and respecting the diversity of body sizes while rejecting the idealization or pathologizing of certain bodies (Association for Size Diversity and Health, n.d.). Evidence has shown that health can be improved in the absence of weight loss (e.g., Pedersen & Saltin, 2015; Tylka et al., 2014), illustrating that weight does not need to be the target for amelioration or the measure of success in health-promoting efforts. Indeed, weight-neutral approaches produce similar benefits in biomedical and psychological health despite little or no weight change (see Tylka et al., 2014, for review).

Research suggests that weight-neutral approaches are more in accordance with social justice than dominant weight-centered approaches. In a series of experimental studies, Frederick, Saguy, and Gruys (2016) invited participants to read news articles where fatness was presented through the lens of either a public health crisis, personal responsibility, Health at Every Size (HAES), or fat rights. The results showed that presenting higher weight as a personal failing or public health crisis elicited more anti-fat prejudice and willingness to discriminate against fat people, whereas the HAES and fat rights frames significantly reduced willingness to discriminate on the basis of weight. However, only participants exposed to fat rights expressed fewer anti-fat attitudes and a willingness to celebrate size diversity, emphasizing that fat rights as human rights need to be front and center in the pursuit of body respect and equality.

A SOCIALLY JUST FUTURE FOR ALL YOUTH

Recently, Nutter, Russell-Mayhew, Arthur, and Ellard (2018) positioned weight bias as a form of social oppression in terms of three social justice perspectives – distributive, procedural, and ecological. In their review, they detail the systemic injustice higher-weight people face regarding fair access to resources, power, and opportunities, lack of voice and agency with regard to policies and actions that affect them, and lack of influence over the social conditions that determine their status.

Health at Every Size (HAES)®: A Model Using a Weight-Inclusive Approach

DEFINITION

A model to support the health of people *across the weight spectrum* that challenges the current cultural oppression of higher-weight people. Specifically, the model seeks to end (1) the stigmatizing of health problems (healthism), and (2) weight-based discrimination, bias, and iatrogenic practices within health care and other health-related industries, as well as other areas of life. The model acknowledges that weight is not a behavior or personal choice; that normal human bodies come in a wide range of weights; and seeks alternatives to the overwhelmingly futile and harmful practice of pursuing weight loss.

PRINCIPLES

1. Do no harm
2. Create practices and environments that are sustainable
3. Keep a process focus rather than end-goals; day-to-day quality of life
4. Incorporate evidence in designing interventions where there is evidence
5. Include all bodies & lived experiences; a norm of diversity
6. Increase access, opportunity, freedom, and social justice
7. Given that health is multi-dimensional, maintain a holistic focus
8. Trust that people (and bodies!) move toward greater health given access and opportunity

APPLIED TO POLICY
Provide environments that give access to all the things that support the well-being of human bodies of all sizes

WITHIN HEALTH CARE
Provide health interventions that give benefit to people at any size, without discrimination or bias

IN PERSONAL LIFE
Provide yourself with the features of life you find sustainable, within the context of your life, that support your well-being

EXAMPLES
Recess for all ages, abilities and sizes
Living wages to provide time for self-care
Nourishing, affordable, & accessible food
An end to weight discrimination in schools, insurance, workplaces, housing, etc.
Regulation of weight loss advertising
Support for communities & social networks
Community involvement in making policy
Medical research and education in health needs of higher-weight people
Redress of structural racism and inequality

EXAMPLES
Medical education on "best practices" for providing health care to higher-weight people
Assist patients in developing long-term health practices rather than pursuing weight loss
End BMI-based treatment decisions
Require >5 yrs of maintenance/outcomes for all participants in weight-change interventions and benefits for the majority before use
Base practice on the lived experiences of patients: *listen and learn*
Defend the therapeutic relationship

EXAMPLES
Re-connect with your body's cues to make decisions about what you need now
Find playful and/or purposeful motives for moving that are not tied to weight loss goals
When hurt, direct your anger to the person who hurt you rather than blaming your body
Look for direct ways to improve life and health that do not require a thinner body
Find others who are opting out of weight cycling and developing sustainable practices
Know your worth is not based on health

FIGURE 14.1 A Health at Every Size (HAES) model for health promotion (Tylka et al., 2014)

Clearly, in order for children of all sizes to obtain equal opportunities to grow and flourish, perspectives that position higher weight as inherently diseased and defective must recede. In particular, it seems, discourse stemming from authoritative social agents, such as science, medicine, and the media, needs to be better informed by social justice and respect for body size diversity. Requirements to do no harm are imperative in public health, as interventions and messages designed to reach masses of people must be free of harmful effects in order to be justified. As such, a public health agenda that does not welcome body diversity is incompatible with social justice.

Shifting the focus from weight to health does not need to be difficult or complicated, and the public seems to more positively receive such approaches. In a survey among more than 1,000 adults examining public appraisal of different health messages, participants responded most favorably to messages that promoted healthy behaviors without any reference to weight or obesity (Puhl, Peterson, & Luedicke, 2013). A similar preference for weight-neutral language emerged in a Canadian report where members of the community were invited to discuss feasible action to promote healthy weight in children. The proposal to turn away from a weight-centric discourse toward a focus on healthy living was voted the most popular idea in an online forum (Public Health Agency of Canada, 2011). Also, in an analysis of policy options for implementing weight-neutral approaches in public health, O'Reilly and Sixsmith (2012) found that the adoption of weight-neutral language in public health messages received the most positive rating among stakeholders in terms of effectiveness, public acceptance, political feasibility, and likelihood of reducing weight bias. Thus, while eliminating weight-based injustice calls for more prolonged and multidimensional undertakings, this highlights that simple, low-cost action can indeed make a difference. Turning away from a negative weight-centered focus in public discourse contributes to a landscape where weight shaming and stigmatization are no longer seen as normative or valid.

Such a development has been observed in Iceland in recent years with a growing awareness of the responsibility to avoid weight stigmatization in public health and for authorities to be leaders in promoting body respect and equality. The Icelandic Directorate of Health is a government agency that, among its many responsibilities, manages large-scale, universal health-promoting efforts such as "Health-Promoting Schools" and "Health-Promoting Communities" (World Health Organization, n.d.). In this work, the Directorate maintains a strong emphasis on body respect and reducing harm associated with negative body image, body shaming, weight-related teasing, and bullying. Specifically, the Directorate's Guidelines for Health-Promoting Schools, in place in all of Iceland's upper secondary schools, half of primary schools, and a growing number of preschools, contain distinct clauses about the school's role in promoting healthy body image, focusing on health rather than weight in the school's health-promoting efforts, having effective anti-bullying strategies in place, and developing a positive school ethos that celebrates body diversity as part of human diversity.

In 2016, a major milestone for body respect was reached when the capitol city of Iceland, Reykjavik, issued a new human rights policy that included body type and build as a protected class. This marked the first time an Icelandic authority acknowledged body size as part of human rights. The policy frames body discrimination as a form of social injustice and delineates the city's responsibilities in addressing it as a public authority, as an employer, and as a service provider. For example, the policy prohibits weight discrimination in the city's workplaces and requires that efforts be made "to create a constructive atmosphere in City workplaces, free of stereotypes, prejudice and discrimination in connection with body build, appearance and body type" (Reykjavik City, 2016, p. 9). As a public authority, Reykjavik shall take care to "prevent the City's activities from encouraging negative attitudes, stereotypes, prejudices or discrimination in connection with build, appearance or body type" (Reykjavik City, 2016, p. 9). For youth, the policy addresses weight- and appearance-related teasing and bullying and requires that schools and recreational centers take effective action against it. It asserts:

> Body types and appearances should be discussed in a positive and unprejudiced manner. Teachers and personnel in schools, recreational centers and other activities involving children and youth shall make human diversity visible in their work, e.g. in the selection of instructional and leisure materials. Instructional or leisure materials presenting negative stereotypes with regard to body build, height or appearance shall be avoided. (Reykjavik City, 2016, p. 9)

Last, the policy requires that "school administrators and other persons responsible for school and recreational activities under the City's auspices shall see to it that health promotion efforts are free of negative messages regarding build, appearance or body type, as it is important for children and youth to feel they are welcome and respected on their own premises" (Reykjavik City, 2016, p. 10).

Indeed, a welcoming environment for body diversity is imperative for all children to feel included as valued members of their society. Toward this end, weight stigma must be recognized as a form of social injustice and actions taken to confront it in all segments of society. The right to feel safe, respected and at home in one's body should be regarded among the most fundamental of children's rights.

REFERENCES

Andreyeva, T., Puhl, R. M., & Brownell, K. D. (2008). Changes in perceived weight discrimination among Americans, 1995–1996 through 2004–2006. *Obesity*, 16, 1129–1134.

Association for Size Diversity and Health (n.d.). The Health at Every Size® approach. www.sizediversityandhealth.org/images/uploaded/ASDAH%20HAES%20Principles.pdf. Retrieved on October 17, 2018.

Ata, R. N., & Thompson, J. K. (2010). Weight bias in the media: A review of recent research. *Obesity Facts*, 3, 41–46.

Boero, N. (2007). All the news that's fat to print: The American "obesity epidemic" and the media. *Qualitative Sociology*, 30, 41–60.

Boero, N. (2009). Fat kids, working moms, and the "epidemic of obesity": Race, class, and mother blame. In E. Rothblum & S. Solovay (eds.), *The fat studies reader* (pp. 113–119). New York: New York University Press.

Bombak, A. (2014). Obesity, Health at Every Size and public health policy. *American Journal of Public Health, 104*, e60–e67.
Bradshaw, C. P., Waasdorp, T. E., O'Brennan, L. M., & Gulemetova, M. (2013). Teachers' and education support professionals' perspectives on bullying and prevention: Findings from a national education association study. *School Psychology Review, 42*, 280–297.
Brown, R., & Lepore, L. (1995). Prejudice. In A. S. R. Manstead & M. Hewstone (eds.), *The Blackwell encyclopedia of social psychology* (pp. 450–455). Oxford: Blackwell Publishers.
Burgard, D. (2009). What is "Health at Every Size?" In E. Rothblum & S. Solovay (eds.), *The fat studies reader* (pp. 42–53). New York: New York University Press.
Burmeister, J. M., Kiefner, A. E., Carels, R. A., & Musher-Eizenman, D. R. (2013). Weight bias in graduate school admissions. *Obesity, 21*, 918–920.
Damiano, S. R., Gregg, K. J., Spiel, E. C., et al. (2015). Relationships between body size attitudes and body image of 4-year-old boys and girls, and attitudes of their fathers and mothers. *Journal of Eating Disorders, 3*, 16.
Damiano, S., Paxton, S. J., Wertheim, E. H., McLean, S. A., & Gregg, K. J. (2015). Dietary restraint of 5-year-old girls: Associations with internalization of the thin ideal and maternal, media, and peer influences. *International Journal of Eating Disorders, 48*, 1166–1169.
Eisenberg, M. E., Neumark-Sztainer, D., & Story, M. (2003). Associations of weight-based teasing and emotional well-being among adolescents. *Archives of Pediatrics and Adolescent Medicine, 157*, 733–738.
Ferraro, K. F., & Kelley-Moore, J. A. (2003). Cumulative disadvantage and health: Long-term consequences of obesity? *American Sociological Review, 68*, 707–729.
Fouts, G., & Burggraf, K. (2000). Television situation comedies: Female weight, male negative comments, and audience reactions. *Sex Roles, 42*, 925–932.
Frederick, D. A., Saguy, A. C., & Gruys, K. (2016). Culture, health, and bigotry: How exposure to cultural accounts of fatness shape attitudes about health risk, health policies, and weight-based prejudice. *Social Science & Medicine, 165*, 271–279.
Fryar, C. D., Carroll, M. D., & Ogden, C. L. (2016). Prevalence of overweight and obesity among children and adolescents aged 2–19 years: United States, 1963–1965 through 2013–2014. Hyattsville, MD: National Center for Health Statistics.
Gard, M., & Wright, J. (2005). *The obesity epidemic: Science, morality and ideology.* New York: Routledge.
Gibson, L. Y., Allen, K. L., Davis, E., et al. (2017). The psychosocial burden of childhood overweight and obesity: Evidence for persisting difficulties in boys and girls. *European Journal of Pediatrics, 176*, 925–933.
Gillison, F. B., Lorenc, A. B., Sleddens, E. F. C., Williams, S. L., & Atkinson, L. (2016). Can it be harmful for parents to talk to their child about their weight? A meta-analysis. *Preventive Medicine, 93*, 135–146.
Greenberg, B. S., Eastin, M., Hofschire, L., Lachlan, K., & Brownell, K. D. (2003). Portrayals of overweight and obese individuals on commercial television. *American Journal of Public Health, 93*, 1342–1348.
Greenhalgh, S. (2016). Disordered eating/eating disorder: Hidden perils of the nation's fight against fat. *Medical Anthropology Quarterly, 30*, 545–562.
Harriger, J. A., & Thompson, J. K. (2012). Psychological consequences of obesity: Weight bias and body image in overweight and obese youth. *International Review of Psychiatry, 24*, 247–253.
Heuer, C. A., McClure, K. J., & Puhl, R. M. (2011). Obesity stigma in online news: A visual content analysis. *Journal of Health Communication, 0*, 1–12.
Himes, S. M., & Thompson, J. K. (2007). Fat stigmatization in television shows and movies: A content analysis. *Obesity, 15*, 712–718.

Jendrzyca, A., & Warschburger, P. (2016). Weight stigma and eating behaviours in elementary school children: A prospective population-based study. *Appetite*, 102, 51–59.

Kenney, E. L., Gortmaker, S. L., Davison, K. K., & Bryn Austin, S. (2015). The academic penalty for gaining weight: A longitudinal, change-in-change analysis of BMI and perceived academic ability in middle school students. *International Journal of Obesity*, 39, 1408–1413.

Kihm, H. S. (2014). The Friendship Study: An examination of weight-based stigmatization during elementary and middle school years. *Journal of Family and Consumer Sciences*, 106, 37–44.

Klein, H., & Shiffman, K. S. (2005). Thin is "in" and stout is "out": What animated cartoons tell viewers about body weight. *Eating and Weight Disorders*, 10, 107–116.

LaMarre, A., & Daníelsdóttir, S. (2019). Health at Every Size: A social justice-informed approach to embodiment. In T. Tyka & N. Piran (eds.), *Handbook of positive body image and embodiment: Constructs, protective factors, and interventions* (pp. 300–311). Oxford: Oxford University Press.

Latner, J. D., & Schwartz, M. B. (2005). Weight bias in a child's world. In K. D. Brownell, R. M. Puhl, M. B. Schwartz, & L. Rudd (eds.), *Weight bias: Nature, consequences, and remedies* (pp. 54–67). New York: Guilford Press.

Latner, J. D., & Stunkard, A. J. (2003). Getting worse: The stigmatization of obese children. *Obesity Research*, 11, 452–456.

Latner, J. D., Stunkard, A. J., & Wilson, G. T. (2005). Stigmatized students: Age, sex, and ethnicity effects in the stigmatization of obesity. *Obesity*, 13, 1226–1231.

McClure, K. J., Puhl, R. M., & Heuer, C. A. (2011). Obesity in the news: Do photographic images of obese persons influence antifat attitudes? *Journal of Health Communication*, 16, 359–371.

Meers, M. R., Koball, A. M., Wagner Oehlhof, M., Laurene, K. R., & Musher-Eizenman, D. R. (2011). Assessing anti-fat bias in preschoolers: A comparison of a computer generated line-drawn figure array and photographic figure array. *Body Image*, 8, 293–296.

Nabors, L., Thomas, M., Vaughn, L., et al. (2011). Children's attitudes about an overweight or non-overweight weight victim. *Journal of Developmental and Physical Disabilities*, 23, 87–98.

Neumark-Sztainer, D. (2011). Obesity and body image in youth. In T. F. Cash & L. Smolak (eds.), *Body image: A handbook of science, practice, and prevention* (2nd edition) (pp. 180–188). New York: Guilford Press.

Neumark-Sztainer, D., Bauer, K. W., Friend, S., et al. (2010). Family weight talk and dieting: How much do they matter for body dissatisfaction and disordered eating behaviors in adolescent girls? *Journal of Adolescent Health*, 47, 270–276.

Neumark-Sztainer, D., Falkner, N., Story, M., Perry, C., & Hannan, P. J. (2002). Weight-teasing among adolescents: Correlations with weight status and disordered eating behaviors. *International Journal of Obesity*, 26, 123–131.

Neumark-Sztainer, D., Paxton, S. J., Hannan, P. J., Haines, J., & Story, M. (2006). Does body satisfaction matter? Five-year longitudinal associations between body satisfaction and health behaviors in adolescent females and males. *Journal of Adolescent Health*, 39, 244–251.

Nutter, S., Russell-Mayhew, S., Alberga, A. S., et al. (2016). Positioning of weight bias: Moving towards social justice. *Journal of Obesity*, 1–10.

Nutter, S., Russell-Mayhew, S., Arthur, N., & Ellard, J. H. (2018). Weigh bias as a social justice issue: A call for dialogue. *Canadian Psychology*, 59, 89–99.

O'Hara, L., & Taylor, J. (2018). What's wrong with the "war on obesity"? A narrative review of the weight-centered health paradigm and development of the 3C framework to build critical competency for a paradigm shift. *SAGE Open*. 1-28. doi:10.1177/2158244018772888

O'Reilly, C., & Sixsmith, J. (2012). From theory to policy and practice: Reducing harms associated with the weight-centered paradigm. *Fat Studies*, 1, 97–113.

Pearl, R. L., & Puhl, R. M. (2014). Measuring internalized weight attitudes across body weight categories: Validation of the modified Weight Bias Internalization Scale. *Body Image*, 11, 89–92.

Pedersen, B. K., & Saltin, B. (2015). Exercise as medicine: Evidence for prescribing exercise as therapy in 26 different chronic diseases. *Scandinavian Journal of Medicine & Science in Sports*, 25, 1–72.

Public Health Agency of Canada (2011). Our health, our future: A national dialogue on healthy weights dialogue report. www.canada.ca/en/public-health/services/health-promotion/healthy-living/health-future-national-dialogue-healthy-weights-dialogue-report.html. Retrieved on October 29, 2018.

Puhl, R. M., Andreyeva, T., & Brownell, K. D. (2008). Perceptions of weight discrimination: Prevalence and comparison to race and gender discrimination in America. *International Journal of Obesity*, 32, 992–1000.

Puhl, R. M., & Brownell, K. D. (2001). Bias, discrimination, and obesity. *Obesity Research*, 9, 788–805.

Puhl, R. M., & Heuer, C. A. (2009). The stigma of obesity: A review and update. *Obesity*, 17, 941–964.

Puhl, R. M., Heuer, C. A., & Brownell, K. D. (2010). Stigma and social consequences of obesity. In P. G. Kopelman, I. D. Caterson, & W. H. Dietz (eds.), *Clinical obesity in adults and children* (3rd edition) (pp. 25–40). Hoboken, NJ: Wiley-Blackwell.

Puhl, R. M., & King, K. M. (2013). Weight discrimination and bullying. *Best Practice & Research: Clinical Endocrinology & Metabolism*, 27, 117–127.

Puhl, R. M., & Latner, J. D. (2007). Stigma, obesity, and the health of the nation's children. *Psychological Bulletin*, 133, 557–580.

Puhl, R. M., Latner, J. D., O'Brien, K. O., Luedicke, J., Daníelsdóttir, S., & Forhan, M. (2015). A multinational examination of weight bias: Predictors of anti-fat attitudes across four countries. *International Journal of Obesity*, 39, 1166–1173.

Puhl, R. M., Latner, J. D., O'Brien, K. O., Luedicke, J., Daníelsdóttir, S., & Salas, X. R. (2015). Potential policies and laws to prohibit weight discrimination: Public views from 4 countries. *Milbank Quarterly*, 93, 691–673.

Puhl, R. M., Latner, J. D., O'Brien, K. O., Luedicke, J., Forhan, M., & Daníelsdóttir, S. (2015). Cross-national perspectives about weight-based bullying in youth: Nature, extent and remedies. *Pediatric Obesity*, 11, 241–250.

Puhl, R. M., Luedicke, J., & Heuer, C. A. (2011). Weight-based victimization toward overweight adolescents: Observations and reactions of peers. *Journal of School Health*, 81, 696–703.

Puhl, R. M., Moss-Racusin, C. A., Schwartz, M. B., & Brownell, K. D. (2008). Weight stigmatization and bias reduction: Perspectives of overweight and obese adults. *Health Education Research*, 23, 347–358.

Puhl, R. M., Peterson, J. L., DePierre, J. A., & Luedicke, J. (2013). Headless, hungry, and unhealthy: A video content analysis of obese persons portrayed in online news. *Journal of Health Communication*, 18, 686–702.

Puhl, R., Peterson, J. L., & Luedicke, J. (2013). Fighting obesity or obese persons? Public perceptions of obesity-related health messages. *International Journal of Obesity*, 37, 774–782.

Rankin, J., Matthews, L., Cobley, S., et al. (2016). Psychological consequences of childhood obesity: Psychiatric comorbidity and prevention. *Adolescent Health, Medicine & Therapeutics*, 7, 125–146.

Reykjavik City (2016). The City of Reykjavik's human rights policy. https://reykjavik.is/en/city-of-reykjaviks-human-rights-policy. Retrieved on October 30, 2018.

Richardson, S. A., Goodman, N., Hastorf, A. H., & Dornbusch, S. M. (1961). Cultural uniformity in reaction to physical disabilities. *American Sociological Review*, 26, 241–247.

Robinson, B. E., Bacon, J. G., & O'Reilly, J. (1993). Fat phobia: Measuring, understanding, and changing anti-fat attitudes. *International Journal of Eating Disorders*, 14, 467–480.

Ruffman, T., O'Brien, K. S., Taumoepeau, M., Latner, J. D., & Hunter, J. A. (2016). Toddlers' bias to look at average versus obese figures relates to maternal anti-fat prejudice. *Journal of Experimental Child Psychology*, 142, 195–202.

Saguy, A. C., & Almeling, R. (2008). Fat in the fire? Science, the news media, and the "obesity epidemic." *Sociological Forum*, 23, 53–83.

Saguy, A. C., Frederick, D., & Gruys, K. (2014). Reporting risk, producing prejudice: How news reporting on obesity shapes attitudes about health risk, policy, and prejudice. *Social Science & Medicine*, 111, 125–133.

Saguy, A. C., & Riley, K. W. (2005). Weighing both sides: Morality, mortality, and framing contests over obesity. *Journal of Health Politics, Policy and Law*, 30, 869–921.

Sahoo, K., Sahoo, B., Choudhury, A. K., et al. (2015). Childhood obesity: Causes and consequences. *Journal of Family Medicine and Primary Care*, 4, 187–192.

Schvey, N. A., & White, M. A. (2015). The internalization of weight bias is associated with severe eating pathology among lean individuals. *Eating Behaviors*, 17, 1–5.

Seligman, L. D., & Bechtoldt Baldacci, H. (2005). Vicarious punishment. In M. Hersen, J. Rosqvist, A. M. Gross, R. S. Drabman, G. Sugai, & R. Horner (eds.), *Encyclopedia of behavior modification and cognitive behavior therapy* (pp. 1085–1086). Thousand Oaks, CA: Sage Publications.

Smolak, L. (2011). Body image development in childhood. In T. F. Cash & L. Smolak (eds.), *Body image: A handbook of science, practice, and prevention* (2nd edition) (pp. 65–73). New York: Guilford Press.

Spiel, E. C., Paxton, S. J., & Yager, Z. (2012). Weight attitudes in 3- to 5-year-old children: Age differences and cross-sectional predictors. *Body Image*, 9, 524–527.

Spiel, E. C., Rodgers, R. F., Paxton, S. J., et al. (2016). "He's got his father's bias": Parental influence on weight bias in young children. *British Journal of Developmental Psychology*, 34, 198–211.

Stice, E., Hayward, C., Cameron, R. P., Killen, J. D., & Taylor, C. B. (2000). Body image and eating disturbances predict onset of depression among female adolescents. *Journal of Abnormal Psychology*, 109, 438–444.

Stice, E. & Shaw, H. E. (2002). Role of body dissatisfaction in the onset and maintenance of eating pathology: A synthesis of research findings. *Journal of Psychosomatic Research*, 53, 985–993.

Strauss, R. S., & Pollack, H. A. (2003). Social marginalization of overweight children. *Archives of Pediatrics & Adolescent Medicine*, 57, 746–752.

Su, W., & Di Santo, A. (2012). Preschool children's perceptions of overweight peers. *Journal of Early Childhood Research*, 1, 19–31.

Sutin, A. R., Robinson, E., Daly, M., & Terracciano, A. (2018). Perceived body discrimination and intentional self-harm and suicidal behavior in adolescence. *Childhood Obesity*. doi:10.1089/chi.2018.0096

Tatangelo, G., McCabe, M., Mellor, D., & Mealey, A. (2016). A systematic review of body dissatisfaction and sociocultural messages related to the body among preschool children. *Body Image*, 18, 86–95.

Teachman, B. A., Gapinski, K. D., Brownell, K. D., Rawlins, M., & Jeyaram, S. (2003). Demonstrations of implicit antifat bias: The impact of providing causal information and evoking empathy. *Health Psychology*, 22, 68–78.

Throop, E. M., Skinner, A. C., Perrin, A. J., et al. (2014). Pass the popcorn: "Obesogenic" behaviors and stigma in children's movies. *Obesity*, 22, 1694–1700.

Tiggemann, M., & Anesbury, T. (2000). Negative stereotyping of obesity in children: The role of controllability beliefs. *Journal of Applied Social Psychology*, 30, 1977–1993.

Tomiyama, A. J., Finch, L. E., Belsky, A. C. I., et al. (2015). Weight bias in 2001 versus 2013: Contradictory attitudes among obesity researchers and health professionals. *Obesity*, 23, 46–53.

Tylka, T. L., Annunziato, R., Burgard, D., et al. (2014). The weight-inclusive vs. weight-normative approach to health: Evaluating the evidence for prioritizing well-being over weight loss. *Journal of Obesity*, 1–18. doi:10.1155/2014/983495

Wertheim, E. H., & Paxton, S. J. (2011). Body image development in adolescent girls. In T. F. Cash & L. Smolak (eds.), *Body image: A handbook of science, practice, and prevention* (2nd edition) (pp. 76–92). New York: Guilford Press.

World Health Organization (1997). *Obesity: Preventing and managing the global epidemic.* Geneva: World Health Organization.

World Health Organization (n.d.). Health promoting schools. www.who.int/health-topics/health-promoting-schools Retrieved on October 30, 2018.

Zuba, A., & Warschburger, P. (2018). Weight bias internalization across weight categories among school-aged children: Validation of the Weight Bias Internalization Scale for Children. *Body Image*, 25, 56–65.

PART III

Regional and Country Case Studies on Social Justice for Youth

15

The Need for Bridging the Gap between the Academy and Public Services in Brazil

Two Case Reports

Cristina de Andrade Varanda, Fernanda Dreux Miranda Fernandes, and Cibelle Albuquerque de la Higuera Amato

BRAZIL: PARAMETERS IN EDUCATION

According to the latest census carried out by the Instituto Brasileiro de Geografia e Estatística (Brazilian Institute of Geography and Statistics) (IBGE) (2010), Brazil had a total of 190,732,694 inhabitants in 2010, 60,849,269 of which were children and adolescents with ages from zero to seventeen. The United Nations' (UN) current estimate for Brazil's population is 209.288 million (UN, 2017), making Brazil the fifth most populated country in the world following China, India, the United States of America, and Indonesia. Twenty-two percent of the Brazilian estimated population is composed of children from zero to fourteen years of age.

Important social factors put children at risk of having difficulties in fully developing such as discrimination, isolation, socioeconomic disadvantage, and a lack of access to support services. Race discrimination is one of the most unjust or undermining forms of violence that is perceived by children and adolescents in Brazil. The Regional Center of Studies for the Development in the Society of Information in Brazil (see Cetic.br) has investigated the use of the Internet among children and adolescents in order to identify new areas of investigation, improve methodological procedures, and obtain reliable data on the risks and opportunities generated by children's use of information and communications technology (ICT). According to this research, Internet users between the ages of nine and seventeen years have seen someone being discriminated against on the Internet. Twenty-four percent of Brazilian children and adolescents have witnessed discrimination based on skin color, followed by 16 percent who have witnessed discrimination based on physical appearance, 13 percent based on gender issues, 10 percent based on religion, and 8 percent based on economic status (CGI.br, 2017).

In Brazil, more than half of all children and adolescents are Afro-descendants and more than a third of the 821,000 Brazilian Indians are children (IBGE, 2010). These statistics are based on how families self-classify when completing the census. Language and geographical region also play a role in identification.

The country has made progress regarding the guarantee of rights and duties of children and adolescents, but millions still need adequate conditions in order to fully develop. In 2010, 37 percent of White Brazilian children and adolescents lived in poverty in comparison to 61 percent of children and adolescents of color living in the same condition (IBGE, 2010).

Access to support services such as healthcare and education is necessary so as to guarantee proper conditions for child and adolescent development. Damasceno et al. (2016) conducted a literature review from 2002 to 2012 that analyzed scientific knowledge with regard to the orientation of Brazilian basic care services in primary healthcare that focused on child health. Primary care services in Brazil face financial, structural, and organizational difficulties. Given these difficulties, parents whose children need care tend to look for emergency services in hospitals in order to fulfill their needs. This relates in part to a lack of structure and procedure in service systems – a system issue that interferes with parental and system ability to plan for ongoing medical care outside of the emergency care setting. Different regions and contexts in Brazil have experienced various results. The authors conclude that Brazilian primary healthcare services should consider specific needs and characteristics for child care (Damasceno et al., 2016). Currently there is a scarcity in the presence and scope of essential basic care services for Brazilian children.

Regarding access to education, the focus of discussion in the present chapter, protective factors related to education may prevent children from risks or hazards, and may promote social and emotional competence. Positive school climate, sense of belonging and connectedness between family and school, opportunity for participation in a range of activities, and academic achievement are important protective factors that support children's development and help reduce the risk of mental health difficulties (Commonwealth of Australia, 2008). As such, access to education may not only guarantee the acquisition of abilities and competence for children to be integrated in their social environment and become participative citizens in the future; it may also foster healthy social and emotional development.

The World Conference on Special Needs Education: Access and Quality held in Spain in 1994 brought together senior education officials, administrators, policy makers, specialists, representatives of the United Nations and the Specialized Agencies, and other international governmental organizations to discuss policy shifts necessary to promote the approach of inclusive education for all. The conference adopted the Salamanca Statement and Framework for Action on Principles, Policy, and Practice in Special Needs Education (UNESCO, 1994). Discussions at the conference were guided by the principle of inclusion, recognition of the need to work toward having institutions that include everybody, and supporting different learning styles.

The Salamanca Statement (UNESCO, 1994), the product of that discussion, reaffirmed the right to education of every individual, as enshrined in the 1948 Universal Declaration of Human Rights (UN General Assembly, 1948). As a result, the need to improve access to education for children with special needs was acknowledged (UNESCO, 1994). Although Brazil was one of the countries that supported this resolution, actual changes were not introduced in education until more than a decade later, and they are still in process. In April 2007, the president of Brazil issued a decree that aimed to guarantee the access and permanence of people with special needs in regular classes within the school system, ensuring the educational inclusion of those with special needs in public schools (Brazil Ministry of Education, 2007).

The Ministry of Education in Brazil defines children with special needs as children with disabilities, global developmental disorders, and gifted children and adolescents (Brazil Ministry of Education, 2016). The fifth edition of the *Diagnostic and Statistical Manual of Mental Disorders* (DSM-V) (American Psychiatric Association, 2013) defines global developmental disorders as a category that pertains to children under the age of five. This category is used when a child doesn't accomplish developmental milestones that are expected for his or her age. For children above the age of five, the DSM-V refers to neurodevelopmental disorders as including intellectual challenges, communication disorders, autism disorder, attention deficit hyperactivity disorder, specific learning disorders, and motor disorders.

Law 9394 was approved in Brazil on December 20, 1996, creating a foundation of national education that included providing special educational services to students with physical disabilities, sensory disabilities, and psychological and pedagogical disorders (Brazil Ministry of Education, 1996). Law 12796 was passed on April 4, 2013, and altered Law 9394 with regard to education for children with special needs. This law established a free special educational service for students with special needs, including children with sensory and/or intellectual deficits, behavior disorders, or mobility impairments, as well as highly gifted children. These services were to be transversal to every level and modality, meaning that they should include all children, regardless of their level of development or type of impairment, in all educational levels, and preferably available in the regular teaching system (Brazil Ministry of Education, 2013).

In 2013, the IBGE published the main socioeconomic indicators for Brazil, based on the National Research by Domicile Sampling (IBGE, 2015). According to this research, in 2013, the percentage of school-age children who were out of school was only 7 percent in comparison to 19.6 percent of children who were out of school in 1990. Even though these data demonstrate fewer children being out of school, the 7 percent figure means that more than 3 million children were out of school in 2013 (IBGE, 2015). It is important to point out that these data do not include further information with regard to how long the children were out of school or the reasons they were not in attendance; it may be that they either dropped out of school or were never enrolled in the first place.

Regarding the rights of children with physical, sensory, psychological, and pedagogical needs to attend regular classes, in 1998, approximately 200,000 children with these needs attended a basic education school program, with 13 percent attending regular classes (Brazil Ministry of Education, 2015). Brazilian basic education comprises nine years of study, from the first to the ninth grade, before high school. Although regular classes are not intended to offer specialized teaching for children with special needs, in 2014, 900,000 children with special needs enrolled in basic education schools and 79 percent enrolled in regular classes (Brazil Ministry of Education, 2015).

Autism spectrum disorder (ASD) is a developmental disorder where children demonstrate deficits in communication and social interaction and present patterns of repetitive behavior and restricted interests. Students with ASD have been included in the educational system mostly in regular classrooms and without the necessary support for the children and their teachers (Fernandes, Amato, Defense-Netrval, & Molini-Avejonas, 2014). An epidemiological study of autism in Brazil identified a prevalence rate of 0.3 percent among seven- to twelve-year-old children in a typical town in southeast Brazil (Paula, Ribeiro, Fombonne, & Mercadante, 2011). In 2015, 27,931,210 typically developing children enrolled in the Brazilian educational system and 49,438 children with ASD. In 2016, 27,691,478 typically developing children enrolled in the educational system and 66,910 children with ASD (Instituto Nacional de Estudos e Pesquisas Educacionais [National Institute for Study and Research on Education] [INEP], 2016). This prevalence requires that children with autism have specialized attention in their schooling process (Oliveira & Paula, 2012). For this reason, it is important to identify and promote a level of awareness among parents, teachers, policy makers, and the population in general regarding autism spectrum characteristics.

Fernandes, Amato, Defense-Netrval, and Molini-Avejonas (2014) investigated the services provided by the Brazilian healthcare and educational systems to persons with ASD and realized many challenges still need to be addressed. Concerning the educational system, the inclusion of children with ASD in regular schools demands support and training for teachers who may be unprepared and overloaded – a national policy regarding this issue is missing.

BARRIERS TO SOCIAL JUSTICE FOR YOUNG PEOPLE

In many countries, efforts to promote social justice in general rarely take children and adolescents into account, as stated by a recent United Nations report (2017). As such, many barriers interfere with child and adolescent development. Social justice depends upon a range of multiple factors, one of the most important being the implementation of social policies that guarantee equal opportunities for children and adolescents to have an adequate quality of life, including physical and psychological well-being, and social and emotional school support.

With regard to public policy implementation, efforts are needed to consider specific needs and challenges for specific groups or communities. At the same time, evidence-based knowledge should be considered to act on those problems and difficulties. The investigation of a group or community's needs and difficulties ought to be part of scientific research as a first step toward understanding if a particular kind of experiment or action can bring positive results to a community.

Nonetheless, there can be a gap between what is produced academically and the data and information policy makers rely on when designing and proposing the implementation of a new social policy. In these situations, the participation of the community in advocacy processes regarding minority rights (such as, for example, the efforts by the American Speech-Language-Hearing Association [ASHA] regarding persons with communication disorders in the United States or the Brazilian Association of Autism [ABRA] – in Brazil) may be reflected in laws and resolutions.

One reason for this gap is that academic knowledge may not be available for politicians in a way that information can be clearly understood. Further, such academic knowledge may not seem applicable in natural and real environments. This is why experimental research should be encouraged and supported in natural environments, such as schools, hospitals, and communities. Moreover, the knowledge produced as the result of such research should be easily accessed and understood by all involved: policy makers, community members, parents, children, adolescents, and other researchers.

For this purpose, some researchers have been working on "translational science" or "translational research" that involves "translating knowledge or evidence into action" (Pearson, Jordan, & Munn, 2012, p. 1). This effort began with a focus on healthcare services and currently also embodies school, family, and community environments (Pina-Oliveira, Germani, & Chiesa, 2014). Regarding children and adolescents, translational science is vital for providing useful and evidence-based knowledge for parents, teachers, policy makers, and healthcare professionals regarding how to deal with problems or difficulties that make children vulnerable in a majority of countries (Bakan, 2009; Pillay & Kathard, 2015).

An important international effort toward the dissemination of information regarding the health and educational needs of persons is the *World Report on Disability* published by the World Health Organization (WHO) (2011). There are clearly challenges to the implementation of the report's main recommendation of equal opportunities for persons with and without disabilities (WHO, 2011). The identification of underserved populations in a country such as Brazil is a task that must be taken with consistency, creativity, and fierceness. Fernandes and Behlau (2012) point to the need of culturally appropriate data-gathering instruments because the simple translation or adaptation of tests and other tools may be insufficient or even inadequate in the Brazilian context. Further, parameters determined for one language rarely are applicable to other languages. Instruments for the diagnosis of language disorders in children require extreme caution with respect to cultural factors even when they are just based on nonverbal prompts (Hyter & Salas-Provence, 2018).

Another challenge for professionals around the globe is the routine use of the *International Classification of Functioning, Disability and Health* (WHO, 2007). The proposal of merging the ICF-CY (children and youth) with the main ICF in 2012 changed some parameters that were just starting to become more familiar to professionals and services in Brazil. The World Health Organization also suggests that the identification of intervention priorities and the optimization of the use of resources could benefit from adequate functional analysis, as proposed in the *World Report on Disability* (WHO, 2011). On the same path, the identification of social and environmental barriers is essential to improve the focus of healthcare and education programs directed toward children and adolescents in situations of social, educational, and health risk.

RESEARCH GUIDING THE SUGGESTION OF PUBLIC POLICIES FOR TYPICALLY DEVELOPING CHILDREN AND CHILDREN WITH AUTISM: TWO CASE REPORTS

Bridging the gap between what academics produce in research as a basis for healthcare and educational intervention among children and adolescents is an important tool to build capacity for justice efforts that advocate for children and young people. Considering issues regarding the intervention services provided to persons with ASD, research conducted in 2014 in the Brazilian city of São Paulo aimed to determine the profile of the population with ASD receiving healthcare and educational services (Defense-Netrval, 2014). Data collected indicated that speech-language services were available to 64 percent of the sample (i.e., 854 children and adolescents) with an average of one speech-language pathologist (SLP) providing one weekly therapy session to an average of eighteen persons with ASD.

This research allowed for a determination of the profile of services provided to persons with ASD and of their clients, indicating the characterization of the treatment and the population. However, the research could not provide adequate criteria for the evaluation of the service offered, mainly because of the difficulties associated with obtaining collaboration with governmental agencies or the institutions that were contacted. It is important to mention that these data refer to São Paulo, which is an important city in Brazil and one of the most developed regions in Latin America (Defense-Netrval, 2014).

The Maria Cecilia Souto Vidigal Foundation is a Brazilian family foundation whose mission is to generate and disseminate knowledge on early child development (e.g., the period that goes from pregnancy to six years of age) and seeks to help guarantee the full development of Brazilian children (www.fmcsv.org.br/en-US/). This foundation engages in actions articulated with public and private sectors and with the scientific community and civil society to generate and disseminate knowledge to develop and refine resources that contribute to improved child development. A focus of the Maria Cecilia Souto Vidigal Foundation is to invest in research that can have an important impact on the elaboration and implementation of public policies on children's development in Brazil. The São Paulo Research Foundation (FAPESP), an independent public foundation whose mission is to foster research as well as scientific and technological development, together with the Maria Cecilia Souto Vidigal Foundation, has had an agreement since 2010 to support research projects focused on children's development.

Brazil Country Case Study 1

The first case report refers to research developed in 2014 and 2015 by five researchers at Universidade de São Paulo and Universidade Paulista, two of them authors of the present chapter. This research project focused on the investigation and intervention in language development and behavioral problems among four-year-old preschoolers to prevent future social and academic problems. The research took place in four municipal preschools in Santos city (Varanda, Mendes, Aulicino, Campina, & Fernandes, 2015a; Varanda, Mendes, Campina, Aulicino, & Fernandes, 2015b; Varanda et al., 2016, 2017).

The aim of the study was to provide early access and intervention in language and behavioral problems of children in regular schools, thus providing data so as to inform educational public policy in the city where the study was conducted. Assuming that children use play to process emotions and interact with adults and peers, Brazilian preschoolers were assessed with regard to language and behavior. They engaged in an intervention for three months that involved guided play activities and multi-touch tablet applications by a team of speech therapists, psychologists, and psychopedagogues (i.e., educators with special training on the study of how people learn with regard to student outcomes, the instructional process, individual differences in learning, gifted learners, and learning disabilities – including the social, emotional, and cognitive processes involved in learning).

The study was designed as a pretest-posttest model with 178 subjects, 90 girls and 88 boys, who were divided into control (N = 94) and experimental groups (N = 84), with an average age of 3.7 years. In the pretest phase, preschoolers were tested in receptive vocabulary through the Auditory Vocabulary Test (TvAud) (Capovilla, Negrão, & Damázio, 2011); in expressive vocabulary, they were tested through the Expressive Vocabulary Test (TvExp) (Capovilla et al., 2011) and the Language Development Survey (LDS) (Achenbach & Rescorla, 2000; Silvares, Rocha, & Linhares, 2010). They were also tested in auditory processing through the Simplified Assessment of the Auditory Processing (ASPA) (Pereira & Schochat, 1997). Regarding behavior, the children's parents answered the Child Behavior Checklist (CBCL) that is applicable for children from one and a half to five years of age (Achenbach & Rescorla, 2000; Silvares et al., 2010) and identifies problem behavior in children.

The activities aimed to enhance intrapersonal and interpersonal skills and language abilities involving auditory perception, localization, memory, attention, and identification of rhymes, alliteration, syllable segmentation, manipulation, synthesis, and word awareness. Shared book reading for refining communicative skills and adaptability (i.e., adjusting one's emotions and behaviors to changing situations) was one of the strategies used.

Findings indicated that the research participants improved their performance in all tests with a significant difference in performance of behavioral and language tests in the posttest phase. The authors conclude that early identification of communication disorders and behavioral difficulties, and the development of continuing education actions for teachers, can be a way of dealing with socioeconomic inequalities in developing countries such as Brazil (Varanda et al., 2017). For this reason, the results of this research corroborated the idea that healthcare professionals such as language pathologists and psychologists could work in a school setting in Brazil in a preventative way, an important finding given this is currently not done in Brazil.

Concerning the importance of translating these academic results and research into accessible language for teachers, professionals, and parents, a website was created to provide such data and information. The website includes downloadable material for parents to guide them regarding ways to promote language development and manage problem behavior (see https://lingcomp.wixsite.com/lingcomp). In addition to available downloadable material, the website presents the design and results of this research (Varanda et al., 2015a, 2015b, 2016, 2017).

Finally, it is important to note that there were efforts in Brazil to minimize the gap between what is produced academically and the use of research results by policy makers and the population regarding the inclusion of children with special needs. In this particular study, results were presented to municipal policy makers to offer them the possibility of using the data to propose a new educational policy. However, the presentation of scientific data to politicians seems to be not enough to bridge this gap as can be noted by the time lag between scientific data and the legal resolutions regarding people with special needs (Brazil Ministry of Education, 2007; Ministério da Saúde, Brasil, 2014). The need to rely on scientific research for the implementation of public policies should be an issue of concern and debate among politicians and civil society.

Brazil Country Case Study 2

The second case report addresses this issue with a focus on the need to minimize the gap between academics and politicians regarding the inclusion of children with autism. A large research study was conducted by three researchers, two of them authors of the present chapter, to investigate people's knowledge about the autism spectrum (Amato, Varanda, Fernandes, & Molini-Avejonas, 2017). The aim of this research was to identify the level of knowledge and information about autism in the general population, with the idea that the study's findings could support decision-making processes about intervention proposals geared toward children and adolescents with autism.

An online questionnaire with fifty-seven questions divided into five domains was made available. The questions focused on personal data: how participants had access to the issue of autism (i.e., questions sought to determine if participants already had some contact with the topic of autism such as having a family member diagnosed with ASD, being a professional working with individuals with ASD, having heard about ASD in the media, having studied the subject, among other options); participants' concept of autism (i.e., signs, symptoms, and etiology); knowledge of autism symptoms; and how participants understood what professionals designated to assist children with autism should be doing to provide support.

Questionnaires were answered by a total of 4,282 respondents who lived in the five large regions of Brazil. Most of the participants were mothers, followed by teachers. The analysis of results considers the hypothesis that although most of the participants answered that they know what autism is, this knowledge is based on lay beliefs and not on scientifically based information. This perspective is fundamental since disinformation is one of the main factors for discrimination and prejudice. The results of the study point to great sociodemographic diversity, which reflects the sociocultural diversity present in Brazil. It is necessary to ensure that all children have equal access to quality and timely diagnosis. Information and awareness are important tools for social justice and healthcare professionals should be sensitive enough to distinguish cultural differences from disorders. This reality must be taken into account when proposing intervention programs directed for young people with autism spectrum disorders (Amato et al., 2017).

One of the major issues regarding providing adequate services to the Brazilian population is the quality of professional education and training among healthcare professionals. Opportunities for hands-on training and supervised practice must be carefully considered to build professional abilities such as independent thinking, creativity, and criticism. At the same time, patients receiving the services are to be protected by the trainee guaranteeing close follow-up and supervision by an experienced professional. This strategy is frequently used in areas such as psychology, speech-language pathology, physical therapy, and other healthcare professions where the interaction between clinician and patient is fundamental to the development of professional competence. Usually high-quality services are provided by school clinics and hospitals because they count on experienced and qualified professionals, teachers, and researchers as supervisors and mentors for the students.

The need for organized and easily available data also makes these settings appropriate for research that will provide evidence to improve professional practice. In this way, a virtuous cycle is established: appropriate practice training that demands access to updated scientific data leads to high-quality services, which then promotes the development of good research that can be used in public services. Given that in many developed countries most of the research is financed by public resources, the gap between society and science may be bridged by efficient and collaborative work between universities and public services by supporting research that will be useful in solving immediate problems and responding meaningfully to various situations, such as the experiences of children and young people (Fernandes et al., 2014).

REFERENCES

Achenbach, T., & Rescorla, L. (2000). *Manual for the ASEBA preschool forms & profiles*. Burlington: University of Vermont Research Center for Children, Youth & Families.

Amato, C. L. H., Varanda, C. A., Fernandes, F. D. M., & Molini-Avejonas, D. R. (2017). Information to improve awareness, contribution to evidence-based practice. What does the Brazilian population know about autism? *Proceedings of the 25th European Congress of Psychiatry*, 41, S122–S122. doi:10.1016/j.eurpsy.2017.01.1918

American Psychiatric Association (2013). *Diagnostic and statistical manual of mental disorders* (5th ed.). Arlington, VA: American Psychiatric Association.

Bakan, M. (2009). Measuring happiness in the twenty-first century: Ethnomusicology, evidence-based research, and the new science of autism. *Ethnomusicology*, 53(3), 510–518. Retrieved from www.jstor.org/stable/25653090.

Brasil Ministério da Saúde. Secretaria de Atenção à Saúde. Departamento de Ações Programáticas Estratégicas. Diretrizes de Atenção à Reabilitação da Pessoa com Transtornos do Espectro do Autismo (TEA) / Ministério da Saúde, Secretaria de Atenção à Saúde, Departamento de Ações Programáticas Estratégicas. – Brasília: Ministério da Saúde (2014). Retrieved from http://bvsms.saude.gov.br/bvs/publicacoes/diretrizes_aten cao_reabilitacao_pessoa_autismo.pdf

Brazil Ministry of Education (1996). Law No. 9394 of December 20, 1996. Retrieved from www.planalto.gov.br/Ccivil_03/leis/L9394.htm.

Brazil Ministry of Education (2007). Decree No. 6024 of April 24, 2007. Addresses the implementation of the Plan of Goals "All for Education." Retrieved from www.planalto .gov.br/ccivil_03/_ato2007-2010/2007/decreto/d6094.htm.

Brazil Ministry of Education (2013). Law No. 12796 of April 4, 2013. Altered Law No. 9394 of December 20, 1996. Retrieved from www.planalto.gov.br/ccivil_03/_Ato2011-2014/2013/Lei/ L12796.htm#art1.

Brazil Ministry of Education (2016). Decree No. 243, of April 15, 2016. Establishes the criteria for the functioning, assessment and supervision of public and private institutions which provide care for students with deficiencies, pervasive development disorder and gifted students. Retrieved from http://portal.mec.gov.br/index.php?option=com_docman&view=downloa d&alias=39501-5maio-port-243-mec-pdf&category_slug=maio-2016-pdf&Itemid=30192.

Brazil Ministry of Education, Portal Brasil (2015). Dados do censo escolar indicam aumento de matrícula de alunos com deficiência [Data from the school census indicate an increase of enrollments of students with deficiencies]. Retrieved from www.brasil.gov.br/educacao/ 2015/03/dados-do-censo-escolar-indicam-aumento-de-matriculas-de-alunos-com-deficiencia.

Capovilla, F. C., Negrão, V. B., & Damázio, M. (2011). *Teste de vocabulário auditivo e teste de vocabulário expressivo: Validado e normatizado para o desenvolvimento da compreensão e da* produção da fala dos 18 meses aos 6 anos. [Auditory vocabulary test and expressive vocabulary test: Validated and normalized for the development of comprehension and production of speech from 18 months to 6 years of age]. São Paulo: Memnon.

Comitê Gestor da Internet no Brasil (CGI.br) (2017). Pesquisa sobre o uso da Internet por crianças e adolescentes no Brasil – TIC Kids Online Brasil 2016 [Survey on Internet use by children and adolescents in Brazil – TIC Kids Online Brazil 2016]. São Paulo: CGI.br. Retrieved from http://cetic.br/media/docs/publicacoes/2/TIC_KIDS_ONLINE_2016_LivroEletronico.

Commonwealth of Australia (2008). Risk and protective factors: The primary years. Department of Health, KidsMatter. Retrieved from www.kidsmatter.edu.au/mental-health-matters/mental-health-basics-promoting-mental-health/risk-and-protective-factors.

Damasceno, S. S., Nóbrega, V. M., Coutinho, S. E. D., et al. (2016). Saúde da criança no Brasil: Orientação da rede básica à atenção primária à saúde [Children's health in Brazil: Orienting basic network to primary healthcare]. *Ciência & Saúde Coletiva*, 21(9), 2961–2973. doi:10.1590/1413-81232015219.25002015

Defense-Netrval, D. A. (2014). Proposta de modelo de indicadores de qualidade para o atendimento oferecido aos indivíduos autistas na cidade de São Paulo [A model of quality indicators for the service provided to subjects with autism in the city of São Paulo] (Doctoral thesis, Faculdade de Medicina, Universidade de São Paulo, Brazil). Retrieved from www.teses.usp.br/teses/disponiveis/5/5162/tde . . . /DanielleAzariasDefenseNetrval.pdf.

Fernandes, F. D. M, Amato, C. A. H., Defense-Netrval, D. A., & Molini-Avejonas, D. R. (2014). Speech-language intervention for children with autism spectrum disorder in Brazil. *Topics in Language Disorders*, 34(2), 155–167. doi:10.1097/TLD.0000000000000011

Fernandes, F. D. M., & Behlau, M. (2012). Implications of the *World Report on Disability* for responding to communication disorders in Brazil. *International Journal of Speech-Language Pathology*, 15, 113–117. doi:10.3109/17549507.2012.731435

Hyter, Y. D., & Salas-Provence, M. S. (2018). *Culturally responsive practices in speech-language and hearing sciences*. San Diego, CA: Plural +Plus.

Instituto Brasileiro de Geografia e Estatística (IBGE) (2010). Censo demográfico 2010 [Demographic census 2010]. Rio de Janeiro: IBGE. Retrieved from www.ibge.gov.br.

Instituto Brasileiro de Geografia e Estatística (IBGE) (2015). Pesquisa nacional por amostra de domicílios: síntese de indicadores 2013 [National Research by Domicile Sampling: Indicators' synthesis 2013]. Retrieved from ww2.ibge.gov.br/home/estatistica/populacao/trabalhoerendimento/pnad2013/default.shtm.

Instituto Nacional de Estudos e Pesquisas Educacionais (INEP) (2015). Sinopse estatística da educação básica [Statistical summary of basic education]. Retrieved from http://download.inep.gov.br/informacoes_estatisticas/sinopses_estatisticas/sinopses_educacao_basica/sinopse_estatistica_educacao_basica_2015.zip.

Instituto Nacional de Estudos e Pesquisas Educacionais (INEP) (2016). Sinopse estatística da educação básica [Statistical summary of basic education]. Retrieved from http://download.inep.gov.br/informacoes_estatisticas/sinopses_estatisticas/sinopses_educacao_basica/sinopse_estatistica_educacao_basica_2016.zip.

Oliveira, J., & Paula, C. S. (2012). Estado da arte sobre inclusão escolar de alunos com transtornos do espectro do autismo no Brasil [The state of art of school inclusion of students with autistic spectrum disorder in Brazil]. *Cadernos de Pós- graduação em Distúrbios do Desenvolvimento*, 12(1), 53–65. Retrieved from www.mackenzie.br/fileadmin/Graduacao/CCBS/Pos-Graduacao/Docs/Cadernos/Volume_12/20_vol_12/Artigo6.pdf.

Paula, C., Ribeiro, S., Fombonne, E., & Mercadante, M. (2011). Brief report: Prevalence of pervasive developmental disorder in Brazil. A pilot study. *Journal of Autism and Developmental Disorders*, 41(12), 1738–1742. doi:10.1007/s10803-011-1200-6

Pearson, A., Jordan, Z., & Munn, Z. (2012). Translational science and evidence-based healthcare: A clarification and reconceptualization of how knowledge is generated and used in healthcare. *Nursing Research and Practice*, Article ID 792519. doi:10.1155/2012/792519

Pereira, L. D., & Schochat, E. (1997). *Processamento auditivo central: Manual de avaliação* [*Central auditory processing: Assessment manual*]. São Paulo: Editora Lovise.

Pillay, M., & Kathard, H. (2015). Decolonising health professionals' education: Audiology and speech therapy in South Africa. *African Journal of Rhetoric: Transitions and Transformative Rhetoric, 17*, 193–227.

Pina-Oliveira, A. A., Germani, A. C. C. G., & Chiesa, A. M. (2014). Potencialidades e limitações do acervo digital em um programa de promoção do desenvolvimento infantil. [Potentialities and limitations of a digital repository on a program to promote early childhood development]. *Revista Eletrônica de Comunicação, Informação & Inovação em Saúde, 8*(3), 413–424. doi:10.3395/reciis.v8i3.913.pt

Silvares, E. F. M., Rocha, M. M., & Linhares, M. B. M. (2010). Inventário de Comportamentos de Crianças entre 1 1/2–5 anos (CBCL/1½-5). Versão brasileira do Child Behavior Checklist for ages 1 1/2–5 [Child Behavior Checklist for ages 1 1/2–5 (CBCL/1 1/2–5). Brazilian version of the Child Behavior Checklist for ages 1 1/2–5]. Unpublished manuscript, Department of Psychology, Institute of Psychology, University of São Paulo, Brazil.

UNESCO (1994). *The Salamanca Statement and Framework for Action on Special Needs Education*. Adopted by the World Conference on Special Needs Education: Access and Quality. Salamanca, Spain, June 7–10. Retrieved from http://unesdoc.unesco.org/images/0009/000984/098427eo.pdf.

United Nations (2017). World population prospects: The 2017 revision, key findings and advance tables. Working Paper No. ESA/P/WP/248. Department of Economic and Social Affairs, Population Division. Retrieved from https://esa.un.org/unpd/wpp/publications/Files/WPP2017_KeyFindings.pdf.

UN General Assembly (1948). Universal Declaration of Human Rights (217 [III] A). Paris. Retrieved from www.un.org/en/universal-declaration-human-rights/.

Varanda, C. A., Mendes, E. C. C. S., Aulicino, M. G. G. M. C., Campina, N. N., & Fernandes, F. D. M. (2015a). Identificação precoce de déficits de linguagem e dificuldades comportamentais para intervenção psicoeducativa como política pública de educação. [Early identification of language deficits and behavioral difficulties for psychoeducational intervention as a public educational policy]. Retrieved from http://lingcomp.wixsite.com/lingcomp/about1-c1x1t.

Varanda, C. A., Mendes, E. C., Aulicino, M. G. G. M. C., et al. (2017). Enhancement of language abilities and behavioral repertoire through guided play activities and multitouch tablet applications. Proceedings of the 15th European Congress of Psychology, 2017, Amsterdam, 157. Retrieved from https://etouches-appfiles.s3.amazonaws.com/html_file_up loads/11b1c4ac7df1af5d68c6a0fb9be8f57c_20170623WednesdayJuly12Oral.pdf?response-content-disposition=inline%3Bfilename%3D%2220170623%20Wednesday%20July%2012%20Oral.pdf%22&response-content-type=application%2Fpdf&AWSAccessKeyId=AKIAJC6CRYNXDRDHQCUQ&Expires=1521397232&Signature=6ATneQFol5fj3kPDFvqeDp1UILs%3D.

Varanda, C. A., Mendes, E. C. C. S., Campina, N. N., et al. (2015b). The relation of externalizing behavior and central auditory processing deficits in 4-year-old children. *Psychology, 6*, 1589–1593. doi:0.4236/psych.2015.613156

Varanda, C. A., Mendes, E. C. C. S., Campina, N. N., et al. (2016). Early identification of language and behavioral deficits for psycho-educational intervention as a public policy. In *Proceedings of the 24th European Congress of Psychiatry, 2016, Madrid. European Psychiatry: Journal of the European Psychiatric Association*. Paris: Elsevier Masson SAS, 33, S544–S544. doi:10.1016/j.eurpsy.2016.01.1594

World Health Organization (WHO) (2007). International classification of functioning, disability and health: Children & youth version : ICF-CY. Retrieved from http://apps.who.int/iris/bitstream/10665/43737/1/9789241547321_eng.pdf.

World Health Organization (WHO) (2011). *World report on disability*. Retrieved from www.who.int/disabilities/world_report/2011/report.pdf.

16

The Education of Migrant Children in China's Cities

Donghui Zhang and Tanja Sargent

INTRODUCTION

Contemporary global society is characterized by increasing flows of people, giving rise to complex issues in human rights and social welfare. The internal migration that has taken place in China in the past four decades has resulted in social justice issues that are both unique to the Chinese context and comparable to the experience of other countries who are the receivers of large numbers of external migrants. The rapid increase in China's internal migration began in the 1980s when economic reforms opened up employment opportunities in urban areas, which both demanded and attracted labor from rural villages. Issues in social welfare for the migrant population emerged as a result of China's household registration system (*hukou*), which grants benefits based on local residency. In this chapter, we provide an overview of the Chinese rural migrant populations and the restrictions they face in Chinese cities, and describe the ways in which migrant children suffer discrimination and disadvantage as a result of the *hukou*, as well as other forms of social and cultural marginalization.

THE HISTORICAL AND POLICY CONTEXT OF MIGRANT EDUCATION IN CHINA

China's unprecedented growth of economically driven rural-to-urban migration has been considered "history's largest labor flow" (Wang & Zuo, 1999, p. 276). The migrant population increased exponentially from 6 million in 1982 to 221 million in 2010, almost 16.5 percent of the total Chinese population (National Bureau of Statistics of China, 2011), of which 74 percent are rural migrants with limited education who engage in unskilled/semiskilled occupations (National Bureau of Statistics of China, 2011). The latest estimate of the migrant population is that it reached 247 million (18 percent of the total population in China) by 2015 (Office of the Floating Population, 2016). Please see Figure 16.1.

According to official estimates, the number of children under the age of seventeen who migrate with their parents increased from 19.82 million in 2000 to 35.81 million in 2010, of whom 80 percent (28.77 million) came from rural

Education of Migrant Children in China's Cities 261

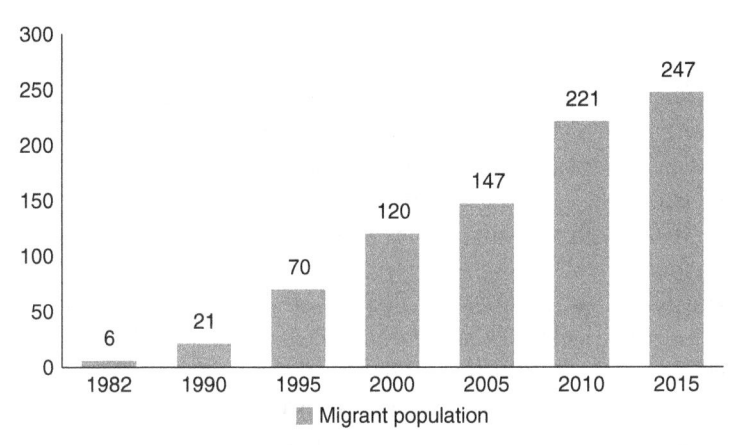

FIGURE 16.1 Increase in the migrant population in China (1982–2015) (Millions)
Source: National Bureau of Statistics of China, www.stats.gov.cn/, and Office of the Floating Population (2016)

areas. At the same time, 61.02 million children were left behind in rural areas by their migrant parents in 2010 (All-China Women's Federation, 2013). The migrant children are largely concentrated in big cities along the east coast, with Beijing, Shanghai, and Guangzhou being the three top destination cities where parents labor in jobs with long working hours and low pay. In Beijing, the capital of China and one of the largest metropolises attracting migrant laborers, the latest report of migrant children was 687,000 out of a total of 8.2 million migrants in 2016 (Yang, 2017).

Rural–urban migrants face a series of institutional barriers and are excluded from various social benefits in the host cities due to the *hukou* in China, which the Chinese central government established in the 1950s in order to control population flow in the planned economy (Chen, 2006). The *hukou* has played two important roles in Chinese society. First, it serves as an important governing lever for allocating social resources. Under the *hukou* system, people are entitled to social welfare services such as education, employment, housing, and medical services only in their official place of registration. Given its importance in social life, the *hukou* became a fixed status for each Chinese citizen and would pass on from parents to children, except in certain limited conditions, such as obtaining a government job. Second, the *hukou* is generally classified into two types: rural *hukou* and urban *hukou*. In 1957, the State Council stipulated a series of policies that forbade people with rural *hukou* to flow "blindly" to towns or cities in order to ensure social stability and to protect employment opportunities for urban residents. As a result, a rural–urban dualistic social structure emerged in China, with social resources largely concentrated in urban areas and rural *hukou* holders contained in the farmlands (Chen, 2006; Wu & Treiman, 2004).

Since the 1980s, the Chinese government has loosened regulations of population flow due to economic reforms and the consequent increasing demand for labor in the cities (Chen, 2006). However, the *hukou* system remained in effect and migrant workers were hired as temporary laborers by urban employers and retained rural *hukou* in their place of origin. Lacking the status of permanent residents in the cities, they were effectively second-class citizens in their workplaces and were excluded from social benefits that urban residents were entitled to, including access to public education for their children.

On January 21, 1995, an article entitled "Where Do the Migrant Children Go to School?" was published by *China Education Daily*, the most influential newspaper on education in China, bringing public attention to migrant children's access to schooling in cities (Li, 1995). According to the 1986 Compulsory Education Law, all children were to go to neighborhood schools in their place of household registration (Office of Legal Affairs, Ministry of Education, 2010). As a result, public schools closed their doors to migrant children, who had to resort to self-funded, makeshift schools (*dagong zidi xuexiao*) set up by migrant workers or parents in the outskirts of the city (Han, 2004). The number of privately run migrant schools expanded quickly and became the main schooling option for migrant children before 2000. In Beijing, for example, it was reported that more than 200 migrant schools had been established, with student enrollment of 90,000 in 2010 (Zhao, Wang, & Liu, 2015; 21st Century Educational Research Institute and New Citizens Program, 2017).

Because of their low fees and the absence of government funding, conditions in the migrant schools were grave, with dilapidated classrooms, poor facilities, underqualified teachers, and a below-standard curriculum. The unsatisfactory conditions of these schools were documented and their legitimacy was debated among educators and policy makers. While some scholars regarded the migrant children's schools as "self-help" and "solve-it-yourself" endeavors when there was no alternative, others condemned the segregation of migrant children in such low-quality schools and called for equal "citizenship" rights of the migrant population with the local people (Han, 2004; L. Wang, 2008). Moreover, as these schools had not been inspected or approved by education departments, they were often in danger of being shut down or forced to move to another locale further away from the city center. According to a report, twenty-four migrant schools were shut down in Beijing in 2011 (J. Wang, 2011).

With the growing visibility of migrant children, their access to urban public schools was increasingly put on policy makers' agendas. Since the 1990s, the Chinese central government has repeatedly urged city and provincial governments to redirect public resources to the migrants in their localities. In 1996, the State Education Commission (now the Ministry of Education) issued the Regulations on the Schooling of School-Age Children and Juveniles of the Floating Population in Cities and Towns, which stated that (1) urban public schools had an obligation to enroll children whose families had acquired local residence permits; (2) urban public schools were allowed to enroll migrant children on the condition that they paid a sum of "borrow-study" (*jiedu*) nonresident fees. However, the reality was that very few migrant families were eligible to obtain local residence permits and most were unable to afford the exorbitant nonresident fees that public schools would charge them. In 1998, the Provisional Regulations on Schooling for Migrant Children and Juveniles were announced by the State Education Commission and the Ministry of Public Security, stipulating that the governments of the home city and the host city should take joint responsibility for migrant children's schooling, with the home city governments controlling the number of outflowing migrant children and the destination governments controlling the number of incoming migrant children. These policies started to pay attention to the welfare of migrant children, yet still treated them as outsiders and did nothing to improve their access to the urban school systems.

The main policy breakthrough came in 2001, when the central government issued its Decisions on Basic Education Reform and Development (State Council of the People's Republic of China, 2001), which formed the basis for the most important school access policy for migrant children, popularly known as the "Two Primaries" policy. The Two Primaries policy stipulated that "the education of migrant children in the compulsory education period (grades 1–9) be the primary responsibility of the destination government rather than the origin government and that of the public schools rather than private schools" (State Council of the People's Republic of China, 2003). This policy, jointly issued by the Ministry of Education, the State Public Sectors Reform Commission, the Ministry of Public Security, the Ministry of Finance, the State Development and Reform Commission, and the Ministry of Labor and Social Security, and forwarded by the State Council of the People's Republic of China, for the first time provided legal support for migrant children's entitlements and rights to access urban public schools.

Following the Two Primaries policy, a series of "equal treatment" policies was issued with regard to migrant children's educational rights vis-à-vis local children. In these policy documents, "equal treatment between the local students and the migrant students" (Article 4) in terms of school participation, awards, and extracurricular activities, as well as tuition and fees, was more clearly specified (State Council of the People's Republic of China, 2003). In 2006, the Revised Compulsory Education Law of China was passed, which removed all tuition charges for Chinese children, including migrant children, during the nine-year compulsory education period (National People's Congress of the People's Republic of China, 2006). As a result of these accommodating policies issued by the central government, 9.3 million rural migrant children enrolled in urban primary schools (grades 1–6) nationwide, making up more than one-third of the total student population in these schools, and 3.5 million migrant students in middle schools (grades 7–9) nationwide, or 24 percent of the total student population in urban middle schools in 2014 (Yang, 2017).

PERSISTENT BARRIERS TO SOCIAL JUSTICE FOR MIGRANT CHILDREN IN CHINA

The growing number of migrant children in Chinese urban cities has drawn considerable attention from scholars across different disciplines, both domestically and outside of China (e.g., Luo, Zeng, & Zhong, 2015; Ming, 2014; Wang & Gao, 2010; Xiong, 2015; Zhang & Luo, 2016). Since the Two Primaries policy, migrant students have obtained legal rights to access public schools in the cities. However, the policy did not translate into the reality of school access overnight. Earlier reports found that migrant children showed lower enrollment rates and far higher dropout rates: 6.9 percent of migrant children had never attended school, and 2.4 percent dropped out before completing the mandatory years of schooling. Furthermore, many migrant children attending school were older than the usual age; 47 percent of migrant children started school older than age six, the age of school entry specified by Chinese education law (Project Team of Educational Development and Research at the Chinese National Institute of Education Research, 2007). More recent studies have pointed out that migrant children face various kinds of institutional barriers in urban schooling and suffer from widespread social stigma and discrimination, which prevents them from successfully integrating into the host cities (Wang & Gao, 2010; Zhang & Luo, 2016).

Although the Two Primaries policy urged local governments and schools to accommodate the educational needs of migrant students, it relied upon top-down directives and didn't provide financial resources to the host cities or schools (Liu, Liu, & Yu, 2017). Therefore, the implementation of the policy has depended on both the willingness and the resources of destination cities and local schools in receiving migrant children. In response, municipal governments and local school districts have issued further detailed requirements for those eligible to enter public schools. The gatekeepers for school access vary from city to city and from school to school, depending on the actual circumstances and contexts. Major barriers that lead to a denial of social justice for migrant children can be found in the following four aspects: documentation requirements, entrance examinations, ongoing stigmatization, discrimination, and marginalization, and high school as a bottleneck (Xiong, 2015; Zhang & Luo, 2016).

Documentation

In most cities, migrant families have to produce at least five certificates – namely, proof of temporary residence, a work contract, a sublease, proof of only one child, and proof of no caregivers in the home city – before they are eligible for urban school admission (Lei & Wang, 2012). A significant number of migrant children's families cannot provide these five certificates, and this is especially difficult for the most disadvantaged groups. A large number of migrant workers (such as peddlers) are employed seasonally or informally and thus do not have an employment permit, let alone the ability to pay for social insurance. Due to the high cost of urban housing, migrant families also tend to live in makeshift accommodations and thus cannot provide an apartment lease or proof of property ownership. Therefore, many migrant children continue to be excluded from the public education system for failing to secure the prerequisite certificates required by local governments. In general, the more disadvantaged a migrant family is, the smaller the chance that their children can attend an urban public school, especially in big cities with a large migrant population. Beijing is a case in point. In 2014, the municipal government of Beijing set a total population limit of 23 million by 2020 and clearly expressed reluctance to receive migrants unless they work in the fields "needed" per city development plans (Ming, 2014). Accordingly, its regulations concerning documentation for school access have become increasingly strict in recent years and are particularly unfavorable to migrant children from the lowest social rung.

Entrance Examinations

In spite of the efforts to eliminate entrance examinations by the upper-level educational administrations, it is common practice for good public schools in Chinese cities to evaluate students' school readiness with paper and/or oral tests before admission. Migrant children are usually disadvantaged when competing with their urban peers during such evaluations. As good public schools often have more than enough student applicants, migrant children have to enter the less attractive "weak schools" in the urban school hierarchy (Luo et al., 2015; Shi, 2017). As more urban students manage to get into "good" public schools, weak schools with less favorable reputations in Chinese cities tend to have a predominant proportion of migrant students, some as high as 80 percent (Luo et al., 2015).

Local governments generally require public schools to prioritize the admission of local students and to enroll migrant children only if there is space after local students' needs are met. Schools with high teaching standards are very popular for local students and thus do not have any extra space for migrant children. Furthermore, in schools that recruit migrant students, fewer local students enroll, so that these schools gradually come to contain only migrant students. This situation somewhat mirrors the discrimination against Black children that occurred in the United States during integration in the 1960s and 1970s (Massey & Denton, 1993). The only local students who remain in schools with migrant children are those who cannot attend other schools because their families either cannot afford the school choice fees or cannot provide transportation to and from such relatively distant schools. In this context, equal educational opportunities and conditions between migrant and local children have not been truly achieved.

Discrimination and Marginalization

While access continues to be a dominant concern among both researchers and policy makers (Yang, 2017; Yuan, 2015), the schooling experiences of migrant children after they enter urban schools have received increasing attention in recent years. Although "equal treatment between migrant children and local children" was emphasized in the policy document, actual school practice is largely determined by the micro-level interactions between different school actors in specific school contexts. Zhang and Luo (2016) found that migrant children were subjected to social and cultural exclusion in urban school settings. Due to the huge gap between rural migrant children and local urban children in terms of institutional rights, socioeconomic status, and academic performance, migrant children are often targets of discrimination and prejudice. In schools with a predominantly migrant student population, teachers tend to use a watered-down curriculum and hold low expectations for migrant students' future. They attribute their school failures to students' migrant status and lack of parental support (Shi, 2017). The morale in these weak schools is typically low both among the teachers and among the migrant students. A "counter-school culture" has been found among the migrant students, similar to the one found among the working-class "lads" described by Willis (1981), who defy school authorities and challenge teachers with misconduct and disobedience and a lack of effort in their studies (Xiong, 2015).

In schools where migrant children are in the minority, however, the migrant children suffer in different ways as their cultural markers, such as accents, speech codes, dress, tastes, and mannerisms, easily set them apart from their more sophisticated local peers (Kwong, 2011). In these schools, migrant children have reported difficulties in school performance, loneliness, anxiety, and a sense of inferiority (Shi, 2017; Wang & Gao, 2010). For fear of rejection by their "superior" urban peers, they prefer to socialize with fellow migrant children and develop a pan-migrant identity as a protective cover (Ming, 2014). While such a group-based identity helps them combat a sense of inferiority, it forestalls intergroup contact and prevents the migrant children from interacting with the more advantaged urban students, leading to further marginalization in the urban school system (Zhang, 2018).

Educational Ceiling: No Access to Urban High Schools

As the Chinese Compulsory Education Law defines compulsory education as nine years of schooling, excluding high school (grades 10–12 in China), high school is not mandatory but rather an individual's free choice. Hence local governments are not required to take legal responsibility for migrant children's education beyond the ninth grade under the Two Primaries policy. Lacking a local *hukou* in the cities, the migrant children have to return to their parents' place of origin, *laojia*, in order to attend high school and take the college entrance examination, which varies from province to province. Exclusion from high school in the cities has a significant impact on students' school life, especially for those children who have college aspirations. With restricted future schooling options in the host cities, migrant children find no point in attending urban middle schools, and start to migrate back to their hometowns during middle school in order to perform well on the high school entrance examination and get into a good high school in the *laojia* (Li, 2015). It's a hard decision as the migrant families might have settled down in the cities and feel unwilling to give up their present jobs. Moreover, for the migrant children born or raised in the cities, the *laojia* might have become a distant memory or a totally unfamiliar place (Ming, 2014). They neither speak the dialect nor are they familiar with the rural/regional culture. In cases in which the parents cannot return, the migrant children either attend boarding schools in the *laojia* or are entrusted to relatives as temporary caregivers, causing the children to endure family separation and become "left-behind children." As an alternative, some children choose to stay close to their families, give up the dream of college, and enroll in a vocational high school. However, the option of vocational high school attendance is not an appealing one as it does not lead to social mobility and implies a blue-collar position in the job market.

THE NEW CITIZENS PROGRAM

From an economic perspective, migrant workers contribute to the economic development of cities, and therefore their children are entitled to enjoy public educational resources. The most pressing issues facing migrant children in China today are, first, the persistent barriers to primary and middle school attendance, including obtaining documentation and screening in entrance examinations; and, second, restrictions to access post-compulsory education in the host cities, i.e., lacking the right to access urban high schools and to take the college entrance examination off-site.

At a deeper level, the social tensions between the locals and the nonlocals should be acknowledged as an obstacle to building capacity benefiting the migrant student population. The underlying rationale behind the current restrictive school policy is local protectionism and a prevalent social attitude that views rural migrants as outsiders instead of an integral part of the cities as a result of the long-standing rural–urban dualistic social structures in Chinese society.

As an educational solution, the Two Primaries policy requires public schools in host cities to shoulder the responsibilities for migrant children's schooling, while neglecting the power relations and hierarchies embedded in the larger social and economic circumstances in which public schools are situated. Therefore, it can only protect migrant children's educational rights partially and temporarily, yet leaves the *hukou*-based social injustice intact. Further policies that address rural–urban inequalities are needed in order to guarantee equal educational opportunities for migrant children in cities.

Should urban public schools admit unconditionally all migrant children coming to their doors? Or should host governments subsidize migrant schools so as to make them better suited for migrant children? No easy answer can be found to these questions and it is unrealistic to expect school access for migrant children to be solved in a short time. Complex social, political, financial, and cultural factors have to be taken into consideration – such as the political environment, population pressures in host cities, the capacity of urban schools, and cities' long-term development plans – which, if not dealt with properly, will lead to social turmoil and unexpected consequences.

In spite of political obstacles and pressures from locals, some provincial and municipal governments have adopted effective measures to benefit migrant students. For example, following the Ministry of Education's August 2012 call for an off-site college entrance examination for nonlocals, several provinces, one after another, announced plans to reform their own off-site college examination policies. The province of Shandong was the first to announce that starting from 2014, all students who completed their entire high school education locally would be allowed to take its local college entrance examination. Several cities, such as Shijiazhuang and Wuxi, have opened their high schools to migrant children. The municipalities of Tianjin and Shanghai have opened their vocational schools to migrant students and entitled them to compete for scholarships equally with local students, on the condition that they study in local schools for two consecutive years or longer.

Nongovernmental organizations can play an important role in helping migrant students to grow and achieve success. The New Citizens Program is an example. Established in August 2007 by the South Capital Foundation with the vision to provide every migrant child with an "equitable, excellent, and suitable education," it aims to set up New Citizens Schools for migrant children who cannot access public schools. As the school name demonstrates, these schools are different from the elite private schools that cater to middle-class children aspiring to academic excellence. Instead, with the motto of "Empowerment, Equity, Trust, Respect," these schools emphasize migrant children's social development and consider it their major task to cultivate them into "New Citizens" who will eventually fit into Chinese urban society. While it is debatable whether such schools reflect a deficit view of migrant children, the New Citizens Program has been influential in mobilizing social resources from enterprises, businesses, and the public so as to participate in the common cause of migrant children's education. In the past five to ten years, the New Citizens Program has established 293 schools nationally.[1]

The New Citizens Program also supports and develops various community projects serving migrant students, in terms of moral and academic tutoring, health-care and growth, career guidance, lifestyles, and social interactions. For example, it recruited and organized volunteer teams to manage small libraries within low-income migrant communities in order to "provide sustainable educational and cultural service" to the migrant children who face cultural deprivation in these communities. It created forums and salons for teachers from migrant schools so that they can exchange ideas, learn about the newest educational technology, and engage in professional development. In 2015, the New Citizens Program supported 337 teachers from eleven cities in China with a total of 258,548 RMB (renminbi, the currency of China) in developing curriculum and activities targeted at migrant children, covering subjects such as language, science, society, art, and physical education, and benefiting 93,800 children altogether. These activities brought public attention to the teachers serving in migrant schools, who were not formally recognized as teachers by the educational administration.

The New Citizens Program also supports research and advocacy on behalf of migrant children's welfare. From 2014 to 2016, it drafted annual research-based blue book reports on migrant children, which provided detailed information about the demographics of migrant children, traced school access policies across different cities, and made policy recommendations. These reports, different from the official reports that largely treated migrant children as one single group, helped to raise public awareness about the heterogeneity of the migrant population and their disadvantaged situations.

The aforementioned example indicates that individuals, organizations, and governments can work together to enhance social justice for migrant children in China. Although institutional barriers persist in the dualistic social structure of contemporary Chinese society that cannot be removed in the short term, the education of migrant children can still be improved with continued and concerted efforts by policy makers, educators, urban local residents, and the society at large. In return, access to quality education for migrant children will contribute to welfare in the society as a whole as these children grow up to become responsible community members who join the labor market in host cities.

Note

1. The data source for the New Citizens Program here and later in this chapter comes from its official website: www.xingongmin.org.cn.

REFERENCES

All-China Women's Federation (2013). *The research report of left-behind children and migrant children in Rural China*. Chongqing: Southwest China Normal University Press.

Beijing Office of the Sixth Census (2011). An analysis of school-age children from outside Beijing: The sixth national census data. Accessed June 2, 2019. Available at: http://news.ifeng.com/main land/detail_2011_08/17/8459554_0.shtml.

Beijing Office of the Sixth Census (2013). Tabulation of the 2010 population census of Beijing Municipality. Accessed June 2, 2018. Available at: http://tjj.beijing.gov.cn/tjnj/rkpc-2010/indexch.htm.

Chen, J. (2006). China's household registration system reform and rural–urban population flow [Zhongguo huji zhidu gaige he chengxiang renkou qianyi]. In F. Cai & N. Bai (eds.), *The labor flow in China's transformation period* [Zhongguo zhuangui shiqi de laodongli liudong]. Beijing: Social Sciences Literature Press.

Department of Development and Planning, Ministry of Education (2017). *Educational statistics: Yearbook of China 2016*. Beijing: China Statistics Press.

Duan, C., Lv, L., & Zou, X. (2013). Major challenges for China's floating population and policy suggestions: An analysis of the 2010 population census data [Dangqian woguo liudong renkou mianlin de zhuyao wenti he duice]. *Population Research* [Renkou Yanjiu], 37(2), 17–24.

Han, J. (2004). Survey report on the state of compulsory education among migrant children in Beijing. *Chinese Education and Society*, 37(5), 29–55.

Kwong, J. (2011). Education and identity: The marginalisation of migrant youths in Beijing. *Journal of Youth Studies*, 14(8), 871–883.

Lei, W., & Wang, C. (2012). On the legitimacy of school access gatekeepers for rural migrant children [Nongmingong suiqian zinv ruxue menkan de helixing yanjiu]. *Research in Educational Development* [Jiaoyu fazhan yanjiu], 10, 7–13 (in Chinese).

Li, J. (1995, January 21). Where do the migrant children go to school? An exploration of rural migrant children's education [Liudong de haizi nar shangxue – liudong renkou zinv jiaoyu tantao]. *China Education Daily* [Zhongguo jiaoyu bao].

Li, M. (2015). *Citizenship education and migrant youth in China: Pathways to the urban underclass*. New York: Routledge.

Liu, S., Liu, F., & Yu, Y. (2017). Educational equality in China: Analysing educational policies for migrant children in Beijing. *Educational Studies*, 43(2), 210–230. doi:10.1080/03055698.2016.1248904

Luo, Y., Zeng, R., & Zhong, J. (2015). An examination of distributional justice and relational justice in the education of migrant children in China. *Peking University Education Review*, 13(4), 146–167.

Massey, D. S., & Denton, N. A. (1993). *American apartheid: Segregation and the making of the underclass*. Cambridge, MA: Harvard University Press.

Ming, H. H. (2014). *The education of migrant children and China's future: The urban left-behind*. New York: Routledge.

National Bureau of Statistics of China. (2011). Gazette on major figures of the 1% sampling of the 2010 population census [2010 nianquanguo 1% renkouchouyangdiaochazhuyaoshujugongbao]. Accessed June 2, 2019. Available at: www.stats.gov.cn/tjgb/rkpcgb/qgrkpcgb/t20110428_402722232html.

National People's Congress of the People's Republic of China (2006). The Revised Compulsory Education Law. Accessed June 2, 2018. Available at: www.gov.cn/flfg/2006-06/30/content_323302.htm中华人民共和国义务教育法

Office of Legal Affairs, Ministry of Education (2010). *A compilation of education laws, policies, and regulations in the People's Republic of China* [Zhonghuarenmingonghe- guojiaoyufalvfaguiguizhanghuibian]. Shanghai: East China Normal University Press.

Office of the Floating Population, National Health and Family Planning Commission (2016). *Report on the floating population in China*. Beijing: China Population Press (in Chinese).

Project Team of Educational Development and Research at the Chinese National Institute of Educational Research (2007). Compulsory education for rural migrant workers' children in

China [Zhongguo jincheng wugong jiuye nongmin zinv yiwu jiaoyu yanjiu]. *Journal of Central China Normal University, Humanities and Social Sciences Edition* [*Huazhong shifan daxue xuebao, renwen shehui kexue ban*], 2, 129–134.

Shi, Q. (2017). *Migrant children's educational process and its stratification function* [*Nongmingong zinv de jiaoyu guocheng yu shehui fenceng gongneng*]. Beijing: Social Sciences Archives Press (in Chinese).

State Council of the People's Republic of China (2001). Decisions on basic education reform and development. Accessed June 2, 2018. Available at: www.edu.cn/20010907/3000665.shtml 国务院关于基础教育改革与发展的决定.

State Council of the People's Republic of China (2003). Notice on how to work well with children of peasant workers and provide compulsory education. Accessed June 2, 2018. Available at: www.gov.cn/zwgk/2005-08/14/content_22464.htm 关于进一步做好进城务工就业农民子女义务教育工作意见的通知.

State Council of the People's Republic of China (2006). Suggestions on resolving problems of migrant workers. Accessed June 2, 2018. Available at: www.gov.cn/jrzg/2006-03/27/content_237644.htm 国务院关于解决农民工问题的若干意见.

State Council of the People's Republic of China (2012). Suggestions on entrance examination opportunities for migrant children after receiving compulsory education locally. Accessed June 2. 2018. Available at: www.gov.cn/zwgk/2012-08/31/content_2214566.htm 关于做好进城务工人员随迁子女接义务教育后在当地参加升学考试工作的意见.

State Education Commission (1996). Act regarding the education of school-age children and youth of the floating population in cities and towns (tentative). Accessed June 2, 2018. Available at: www.lawxp.com/statute/s1049977.html 城镇流动人口中适龄儿童、少年就学办法(试行).

State Education Commission and Ministry of Public Security (1998). Provisional regulations on schooling for migrant children and juveniles. Accessed June 2, 2018. Available at: http://old.moe.gov.cn//publicfiles/business/htmlfiles/moe/moe_621/200409/3192.html 流动儿童少年就学暂行办法.

Wang, F., & Zuo, X. (1999). Inside China's cities: Institutional barriers and opportunities for urban migrants. *American Economic Review*, 89(2), 276–280.

Wang, J. (2011). The closing of 24 unlicensed migrant schools in Beijing: No dropout guaranteed by BMCE. Accessed June 2, 2018. Available at: http://news.ifeng.com/mainland/detail_2011_08/17/8459554_0.shtml.

Wang, L. (2008). The marginality of migrant children in the urban Chinese educational system. *British Journal of Sociology of Education*, 29(6), 691–703. doi:10.1080/01425690802423361

Wang, Y., & Gao, Y. (2010). *Social integration between the migrant peasants' children and urban citizens*. Beijing: Social Sciences Archives Press.

Willis, P. (1981). *Learning to labor: How working class kids get working class jobs*. New York: Columbia University Press.

Wu, X., & Treiman, D. J. (2004). The household registration system and social stratification in China: 1955–1996. *Demography*, 41(2), 363–384.

Xiong, Y. (2015). The broken ladder: Why education provides no upward mobility for migrant children in China. *China Quarterly*, 221, 161–184. doi:10.1017/S0305741015000016

Yang, D. (ed.) (2017). *Migrant children bluebook: The 2016 report on the education and development of migrant children in China*. Beijing: Social Sciences Archives Press.

Yuan, G. (2015). An analysis of the "Two Primaries" policy [*Liangweizhu zhengce yuanze fenxi*]. *China Agricultural University Journal, Social Sciences Edition* [*Zhongguo nongye daxue xuebao shehui kexue ban*], 32(1), 51–54 (in Chinese).

Zhang, D. (2018). The rural–urban divide, intergroup relations and social identity formation of rural migrant children in a Chinese urban school. *International Studies in Sociology of Education*, 27(1), 60–77.

Zhang, D. & Luo, Y. (2016). Social exclusion and the hidden curriculum: The schooling experiences of Chinese rural migrant children in an urban public school. *British Journal of Educational Studies*, 64(2), 215–234.

Zhao, X., Wang, R., & Liu, F. (2015). The status of migrant schools in Beijing. *Primary School Science*, 1 (in Chinese).

17

Inequalities in Healthcare for Children and Adolescents in Colombia

Erwin H. Hernandez-Rincon and Yahira Rossini Guzmán-Sabogal

REGION/COUNTRY PARAMETERS

As a population group, children and adolescents experience multiple risks and vulnerabilities, and progress in this area must be recognized as a fundamental objective for advancing the welfare and development of any society or country (Presidencia de la República de Colombia, 2013; Torres & Orozco, 2013). Likewise, in order to ensure that this population group reaches its potential, multiple actors – including families, schools, communities, healthcare services, and decision makers or politicians in a given area – must intervene in a timely manner and give priority to this issue (Neves, Cabral, & Silveira, 2013; Sousa & Erdmann, 2012).

The healthcare sector is among the sectors that should consider how it approaches children and adolescents since health is a complex dimension that depends upon multiple factors (López, 2005). This is so much so that the Organización Mundial de la Salud (OMS) defines health as incorporating physical, mental, and social dimensions (OMS, 2014). From this it follows that health depends upon political, social, economic, and cultural factors and contexts, among other things, and that we need an approach that not only includes the healthcare sector and hospitals, but that also involves various sectors and agents (Alcantará, 2008; López, 2005). In the case of children and adolescents, this should include at least home, school, public spaces, and healthcare services (Presidencia de la República de Colombia, 2013).

According to an article published by the *Revista Colombiana de Psiquiatría* (*Colombian Journal of Psychiatry*), risk factors for emotional problems and suicidal behaviors have become an attention marker in public health for early detection and prevention. In Colombia, the general rate of death by suicide is 4.7–6 per 100,000 inhabitants, according to the year, with said behaviors starting as early as five years old. The average age of death for males and females is 36.4 and 27.7 years old, respectively. Among the male group there were more young adults (41.6 percent), while among the female group there were more adolescents (38.5 percent). This rate is lower than that reported in the United States and some European countries (Cardona-Arango, Medina-Pérez, & Cardona-Duque, 2016).

For adolescents, a shortage of coping strategies and low self-perception of one's abilities to handle stressful situations are associated with suicidal thoughts and attempts at self-harm. Indeed, some children and adolescents assert that they experience rapid relief of tension after a self-harm episode (Rodríguez Navarrete, 2016).

On the other hand, the Americas region constitutes the most inequitable area in the world, reflected in differences in its population's living and social conditions, as well as the presence of barriers that prevent access to healthcare services, including mental healthcare services, in the most vulnerable populations (Linares & López, 2008). As a consequence of these inequalities, countries in the region have marked differences, for example, in terms of infant mortality – between 2008 and 2010, Cuba's infant mortality rate was 5 per 1,000 live births (LB) and that of Chile was 7 per 1,000 LB, as opposed to Haiti with 64 per 1,000 LB or Bolivia with 40 per 1,000 LB. Differences also arise in terms of maternal mortality and life expectancy (Cardona, Acosta, & Bertone, 2013).

BARRIERS TO SOCIAL JUSTICE FOR YOUNG PEOPLE THE SITUATION IN COLOMBIA

Colombia is located in Latin America and had a population of 50 million inhabitants as of 2018 (Departamento Administrativo Nacional de Estadística [DANE] de Colombia, 2018). With respect to its epidemiological profile, and like many other countries in the world, Colombia has advanced toward a predominance of chronic disease (Bernal, Forero, Villamil, & Pino, 2012). However, as a consequence of the country's particular circumstances (Eslava, 1993) and the inequality of conditions found there – indeed, it is considered one of the most inequitable countries in the world (Banco Mundial, 2018; Organisation for Economic Co-operation and Development [OECD], 2017) – in Colombia chronic diseases have emerged, as have infectious diseases and malnutrition, and the latter disproportionately affect the younger population (Bernal et al., 2012). In addition, the country has suffered armed conflict during the past fifty years, and the risks that this presents for the population are substantial (Gaitán, 2016; Urrego, 2015). Mental healthcare coverage is not sufficient for the population's needs in the described context.

In this regard, the Colombian healthcare system favors a model based on illness and treatment (rather than prevention), is centered on the hospital (rather than on the family and community), is based on specialists (rather than on primary care physicians and the basic healthcare team), and falls under a free market theory model (where economic interests outweigh health). Consequently, this model has benefited commercial more than collective interests, in addition to mostly focusing on the allocation of economic resources to healthcare services (WHO, 2008a).

All of these factors generate inequalities in financing and access to healthcare services (Agudelo, Cardona, Ortega, & Robledo, 2011; Starfield, 2011). Thus, the Colombian healthcare system prioritizes its healthcare services component over other determinants that explain the influence on common diseases and the maintenance of health, especially in a population as diverse and with as much inequality as found in Colombia (Lalonde, 1981, 2002; MacDougall, 2007).

However, in Colombia, recent healthcare regulation contemplates the importance of addressing these factors through a comprehensive care approach (see Table 17.1). In addition, this regulation considers children and adolescents as a vulnerable group that requires preferential and differential attention, allowing for comprehensive care action and addressing social determinants of health (Ministerio de Salud y Protección Social, 2011, 2012, 2015, 2016).

TABLE 17.1 *Recent healthcare regulations in Colombia, 2011–2021 (public information, compiled by authors based on recent Colombian health regulations [2012–2021])*

Recent regulation on healthcare in Colombia, 2011–2021
1. **Law 1438 from 2011**   a. Considers that the healthcare system in Colombia should be based on public health and primary healthcare   b. Establishes the system's priorities, including the prevalence and incidence of maternal, perinatal, and infant morbidity and mortality, the incidence of diseases with public health interest, the incidence of chronic noncommunicable diseases and high-cost precursors, the incidence of prevalent communicable diseases, and effective access to healthcare
2. **Ten-Year Public Health Plan, 2012–2021**   a. Returns to the principles of primary care and defines public health orientation for the coming years   b. Defines Colombia's vulnerable populations, including children and adolescents, ethnic groups, people with disabilities, the elderly, and victims of armed conflict   c. Determines eight priority dimensions (which are transversal with regard to the vulnerable populations): environmental health, social coexistence and mental health, Food and nutrition security, sexuality and sexual and reproductive rights, healthy lifestyles and communicable diseases, public health in emergencies and disasters, healthy lifestyles and noncommunicable conditions, health and work environments
3. **Law 1751 from 2015**   a. Considers healthcare a fundamental right   b. Establishes that, in order to achieve this fundamental right, Colombia must pay close attention to it and address the social determinants involved   c. Views children and adolescents as a differential population
4. **Modelo Integral de Atención en Salud (MIAS) (Integral Model of Healthcare)**   a. Sets its core strategies as primary care, a focus on care, risk management, and a difference approach   b. Prioritizes a family and community health approach   c. Defines the self-care actions that individuals are expected to undertake, the actions oriented toward promoting individual welfare and development in the environments in which people develop, as well as prevention interventions, diagnosis, treatment, rehabilitation, and palliative care

In Colombia, the Presidency of the Republic considers children a priority with the formulation of a strategy in 2013 called "From Zero to Always," which promotes an approach during the first years of life within the home, educational, health, and public environments, where we are all responsible for this population group (Presidencia de la República de Colombia, 2013). In this sense, in addition to parents and family members, other actors should contribute to children's integral development and care, including professionals dedicated to healthcare and family sectors, as well as healthcare services and governmental institutions (Neves et al., 2013; Sousa & Erdmann, 2012).

REBUILDING CAPACITY
EQUALITY IN HEALTH

Equality in health can be defined as "giving each person their due" according to their circumstances so as to improve their health conditions and resolve health problems in the population (Martínez, 2007). In contrast, inequality in health is considered "the presence of systematic health differences between groups from different social spheres" (Braveman & Gruskin, 2003, p. 254). Indeed, studies have shown that the worse off a population group's socioeconomic situation is, the worse off its health status is, and inequalities in health are more evident in vulnerable groups with greater social disadvantages, such as the poor, women, children, members of underrepresented racial/ethnic groups, and victims of conflict (Braveman & Gruskin, 2003; Tapia, 2013).

Thus, in order to reduce and address these inequalities in health, the World Health Organization (WHO) convened the Commission on Social Determinants of Health (CSDH) from 2005 to 2008 with the aim of reviewing different models that explain increasing health inequalities among the population, as well as analyzing social conditions related to globalization, healthcare services, gender, environment, and childhood development that may lead to health inequalities around the world (OMS, 2008b; Public Health Agency of Canada [PHAC], 2011; WHO, 2008; Villar, 2011). This effort produced action recommendations based on the CSDH (see Table 17.2), chief among which is that some guarantee of equality is required from the first years of life onward in order to achieve adequate living conditions (OMS, 2008b; WHO, 2008).

In Colombia, the Ten-Year Public Health Plan, 2012–2021 has deemed the equality approach in healthcare and social determinants of health (SDH) necessary for achieving the fundamental right to health and the reduction of health inequalities in the population.

PROGRAMMATIC EXAMPLES
INEQUALITIES IN HEALTH AMONG CHILDREN AND ADOLESCENTS IN COLOMBIA

Children and adolescents are considered among the most vulnerable population groups in Colombia (Ministerio de Salud y Protección Social, 2012; Presidencia de

TABLE 17.2 *Recommendations from the World Health Organization (WHO) for actions regarding social determinants of health (SDH) (authors' elaboration based on a document from the WHO Commission on Social Determinants of Health, "Closing the Health Inequalities Gap" (OMS, 2008; WHO, 2008b)*

Action areas for the reduction of health inequalities

1. Improve daily living conditions
   a. Equality from the beginning
   b. Healthy environments
   c. Employment and decent work
   d. Social protection throughout life
   e. Universal healthcare
2. Challenging the unequal distribution of power, money, and resources
   a. Health equity in policies, systems, and programs
   b. Equitable financing
   c. Market responsibility
   d. Gender equality
   e. Political emancipation: integration and the possibility of expressing oneself
   f. Effective global governance
3. Measurement and analysis of the problem

la República de Colombia, 2013) because of the conditions of inequality they present. To start with, like many countries in the world, Colombia has marked differences between social conditions and individual health outcomes. This is due in part to poverty, especially in the rural and most remote areas of the country in which, for example, there is a greater proportion of childhood malnutrition compared to the rest of the country (Lissbrant, 2015; Ministerio de Salud y Protección Social, 2018a). These social differences affect Colombia's main health indicators. While, on the whole, infant mortality has decreased from 27 per 1,000 LB in 1990 to 14 per 1,000 LB in 2015, mortality is still one and a half times higher in rural areas, in low socioeconomic strata, and in populations with low education levels (Jaramillo, 2016). In the same way, differences are also found in populations with different cultural and ethnic backgrounds; greater infant malnutrition and higher infant mortality have been documented in territorial zones inhabited by indigenous and Afro-descendant populations. In 2016, for example, 40 percent of these cases occurred in the states of Guajira, Vichada, and Chocó (Osorio, Bolancé, & Madise, 2014; Osorio, Romero, Bonilla, & Aguado, 2018).

Likewise, another consequence of health inequality among Colombia's youngest population is reflected in its epidemiological profile since, although acute respiratory disease (ARD) is the main reason for visits to the emergency room among the child population, differences in infant and child mortality rates occur by region and socioeconomic stratum. Acute respiratory disease corresponds with a group of illnesses that occur in the respiratory tract and are caused by viruses and bacteria. Most

ARDs are mild, like the common cold, although a small percentage can worsen into otitis, sinusitis, or pneumonia. Acute respiratory diseases are the most frequent infection in the world and, in Colombia, they represent a significant part of public healthcare; a similar situation occurs in cases of acute diarrheal disease (ADD). In addition, regarding how nutritional issues are tracked, children who are overweight and obese and children who are malnourished are counted in the same population. For example, some places in Bogotá include overweight and obese populations, while other sectors include children suffering from malnutrition; in the same sense, overweight and obese populations are on the rise in regions like Bogotá, while children are dying from malnutrition in other regions like Chocó and Guajira (Ministerio de Salud y Protección Social, 2018b). The latter are mainly found in the most vulnerable areas of the country. This demonstrates the variability of the country's epidemiological profile and represents an additional significant challenge when providing healthcare services (Bernal et al., 2012; Ramos, 2012).

On the other hand, the violence that has occurred over the past fifty years is a relevant public health problem since it has generated an increase in homicides, population displacement, and drug trafficking, among other things. All of this has affected neighboring populations and has limited the state's capacity to provide social programs (health, employment, and education) and humanitarian aid to those most in need (Franco, 2003).

In addition, Colombia's armed conflict has had various consequences for children and adolescents; from 1992 to 1999, violence was particularly associated with drug trafficking in some areas of the country, which generated an increase in assaults and homicides. This situation especially had an impact on adolescents given their limited sources of employment and economic resources (Duque, Montoya, & Restrepo, 2013). Between 2015 and 2017, Save the Children ranked Colombia as the country with the third highest homicide rate among adolescents in the world. Homicide accounted for 51 percent of deaths among adolescents age ten to nineteen. For example, in 2017 alone, 715 children between ages zero and eighteen were victims of homicide (Save the Children, 2018b).

In addition, armed conflict, a consequence of forced migration, has mainly affected women, children, and the country's indigenous population since, in addition to increasing socioeconomic problems, forced migration has increased homicides, mental health problems, and human rights violations. Faced with this situation, some children born as migrants require greater physical aid, including both basic and mental health support, in order to return to normal conditions (Shultz et al., 2014). Forced displacement corresponds with people being forced to flee their homes because of armed conflict. According to Save the Children (2018a), forced displacement has affected 7 million Colombians, among whom 2 million are children. Save the Children (2018a) notes that displacement puts children and adolescents at increased risk for physical, sexual, and psychological abuse, homicide, and human trafficking.

In addition to the aforementioned risks, according to the Centro Nacional de Memoria Histórica (National Center for Historical Memory) (2017), in Colombia, guerrillas (69 percent) and paramilitaries have recruited children and adolescents as combatants. To date, there is no exact record of the number of children and adolescents recruited, but of 16,879 registered cases in 2016, 40 percent were recruited through persuasion on the part of armed groups (Centro Nacional de Memoria Histórica, 2017).

RESOURCES

The context is fundamental for reducing a population's social inequalities since this context directly affects the health of children and adolescents. Therefore, so as to improve health outcomes among this population group and reduce social inequalities, health conditions, education, social networks, and socioeconomic status must be improved (Osorio et al., 2018). In order to address children and adolescents' main problems and healthcare needs, we must rely on an approach that includes the greatest possible number of actors, including decision makers who favor the formulation and implementation of public policies focused on reducing inequalities in this population's health outcomes (Bolduc & Grand, 2007). Likewise, resolving health inequalities for children and adolescents should not be left to the healthcare sector alone, but should also include sectors like education, the economy, recreation, and social and community leaders, among others (Neves et al., 2013; WHO, 2000).

On the other hand, advancing comprehensive healthcare for children and adolescents requires that healthcare professionals recognize the complexity of the health and disease process, as well as that of public health, health promotion, the primary care approach in health, SDH, and the influence of context for recognizing and approaching this population's health problems, and its diverse epidemiological characteristics. These problems range from infectious diseases, malnutrition, obesity, chronic diseases, mental health problems, and the influence of social conditions on children and adolescents' health outcomes (López, 2005; Ministerio de Salud y Protección Social, 2018a).

For example, the issue of suicide risk is currently addressed in schools, universities, and with parents in campaigns that for now are only developed when an event or suspicion occurs, with the additional availability of helplines and the possibility of assessment from the point of view of psychology, pediatrics, family medicine, general medicine, and general and child psychiatry. Additionally, professionals who normally work with adolescents and see their initial and general mental health problems have received training with the mental health GAP (mhGAP) strategy (OMS, 2011a). The mhGAP strategy is defined as an action program to overcome mental health gaps, and addresses the principal neurological and substance abuse disorders at the level of nonspecialized healthcare (WHO, 2011).

Furthermore, so as to guarantee comprehensive care for children and adolescents, a variety of authors recommend the primary healthcare (PHC) approach (WHO, 1978) and the integrated management of childhood illness (IMCI) (Díaz, 2012). These approaches allow us to consider the specific condition of children and adolescents in vulnerable situations within the framework of each country's particularities and to achieve universal healthcare access and coverage (Cassiani, 2014; OPS, 2014). The implementation of PHC has improved health indicators in many countries; it has helped reduce low birth weight, infant mortality, mortality due to cardiovascular disease, and general mortality, as well as improved the distribution of resources, the insurance process, and government-sponsored healthcare services, increasing families and populations' positive perception of healthcare services, as well as contributing to the improvement of colon, breast, cervical, and skin cancer programs (Somocurcio, 2013).

Thus, Colombia's primary care strategy, which has been in place since 2011, is constituted as a strategy that integrates the needs of the population, the system's response, and available resources. Communities have proven this integration to be a fundamental component for the participatory resolution of the population's health problems and needs, especially with regard to the most vulnerable groups (Hernandez et al., 2017).

Finally, the situation in Colombia is an opportunity to guarantee equality in healthcare for children and adolescents – first, because this population group is considered fundamental for the country (Presidencia de la República de Colombia, 2013); second, because children and adolescents have been prioritized in recent healthcare regulations in order to guarantee their fundamental right to healthcare access without barriers (Ministerio de Salud y Protección Social, 2011, 2012, 2015, 2016); and third, and finally, because the country recently signed a peace agreement (Gaitán, 2016).

This peace agreement, signed in 2016 between the Colombian government and the Fuerzas Armadas Revolucionarias de Colombia (Revolutionary Armed Forces of Colombia) (FARC) guerrillas, supposes the end of almost fifty years of armed conflict. The members of the country's main guerrilla group committed to laying down arms, reintegrating their population, and helping the victims of the conflict (Alto Comisionado para la Paz, 2016).

For children and adolescent victims of the conflict, as well as for other victims in the country, the signing of this agreement supposes a restoration of the rights of children and the elimination of the risks resulting from war, including the opportunity of return to their places of origin, access to education, food, healthcare, play, recreation, and the possibility of living in peace, among other opportunities (Save the Children, 2019). The peace agreement allows children and adolescents to disengage from the ranks of guerrillas and signifies the definitive suspension of armed groups' efforts to recruit them (Alto Comisionado para la Paz, 2017).

The country's social features, its diverse epidemiological profile, and the current challenge of peace in Colombia leads to the conclusion that healthcare professionals, institutions that train healthcare professionals and service providers, and decision makers must reorient their approach to the needs of the country in the post-conflict era (Bolduc & Grand, 2007). They can be a bridge between the healthcare system and vulnerable communities that have suffered the effects of war. Colombia must be able to address new challenges, such as those related to mental health issues and to healthcare for children and adolescents, to guarantee stable and lasting peace, and to contribute to health equality in the country (Gaitán, 2016; Insuasty & Borja, 2016).

REFERENCES

Agudelo, C., Cardona, J., Ortega, J., & Robledo, R. (2011). Sistema de salud en Colombia: 20 años de logros y problemas. *Ciência & Saúde Coletiva*, 16(6), 2817–2828.

Alcantará, G. (2008). La definición de salud de la Organización Mundial de la Salud y la interdisciplinariedad. *Sapiens*, 9(1), 93–107.

Alto Comisionado para la Paz (2016). Acuerdo final para la terminación del conflicto y la construcción de una paz estable y duradera. Bogotá: Retrieved from www.altocomisiona doparalapaz.gov.co/procesos-y-conversaciones/Documentos%20compartidos/24–11-2016 NuevoAcuerdoFinal.pdf.

Banco Mundial. (2018). Índice de Gini. World Bank: Washington, DC: Retrieved from https://datos.bancomundial.org/indicador/SI.POV.GINI?view=map.

Bernal, O., Forero, J., Villamil, M., & Pino, R. (2012). Disponibilidad de datos y perfil de morbilidad en Colombia. *Revista Panamericana Salud Pública*, 31(3), 181–187.

Bolduc, N., & Grand, P. (2007). Towards unity for health: Lessons for health development in Canada. *Education for Health*, 20(1), 1–12.

Braveman, P., & Gruskin, S. (2003). Defining equity in health. *Journal of Epidemiology and Community Health*, 57, 254–258.

Cardona, S., Acosta, L., & Bertone, C. (2013). Inequidades en salud entre países de Latinoamércia y el Caribe (2005–2010). *Gaceta Sanitaria*, 27(4), 292–297.

Cardona-Arango, D., Medina-Pérez, O., & Cardona-Duque, D. (2016). Caracterización del suicidio en Colombia, 2000–2010. *Revista Colombiana de Psiquiatría*, 45(3), 170–177.

Cassiani, S. H. B. (2014). Estrategia para el acceso universal a la salud y la cobertura universal de salud y la contribución de las Redes Internacionales de Enfermería. *Revista Latino-Americano Enfermagem*, 22(6), 891–892.

Centro Nacional de Memoria Histórica (2017). Una guerra sin edad. Informe nacional de reclutamiento y utilización de niños, niñas y adolescentes en el conflicto armado colombiano. Bogotá. Retrieved from www.centrodememoriahistorica.gov.co/descargas/informes-accesibles/una-guerra-sin-edad_accesible.pdf.

Departamento Administrativo Nacional de Estadística (DANE) de Colombia (2018). Población de Colombia a hoy. Retrieved from www.dane.gov.co/.

Díaz, M. (2012). Introducción del *Manual de enfermedades prevalentes de la infancia en la enseñanza de enfermería*. *Revista Cubana Enfermería*, 28(2), 118–124.

Duque, L., Montoya, N., & Restrepo, A. (2013). Aggressors and resilient youths in Medellin, Colombia: The need for the paradigm shift in order to overcome violence. *Cad Saúúe Pública*, 29(11), 2208–2216.

Eslava, J. (1993). Climatología y diversidad climática de Colombia. *Revista de la Academia Colombiana de Ciencias Exactas, 18*(71), 507–538.

Franco, S. (2003). A social-medical approach to violence in Colombia. *American Journal of Public Health, 93*(12), 2032–2036.

Gaitán, H. (2016). La paz en Colombia: Una oportunidad para la construcción de un país más justo. *Revista Colombiana de Obstetricia y Ginecología, 67*(3), 181–183.

Hernandez, E., Lamus, F., Carratala, C., et al. (2017). Building community capacity in leadership for primary health care in Colombia. *MEDICC Review, 19*(2–3), 65–70.

Insuasty, A., & Borja, E. (2016). El papel de la comunidad universitaria en el pos-acuerdo o pos-conflicto en Colombia. *Agora Universidad de San Buenaventura, 16*(2), 373–376.

Jaramillo, M. (2016). Encuesta nacional de demografía y salud. Bogotá: ENDS – Profamilia Retrieved from https://hera.ugr.es/tesisugr/26329748.pdf.

Lalonde, M. (1981). A new perspective on the health of Canadians: A working document. Ottawa: Public Health Agency of Canada. Retrieved from www.phac-aspc.gc.ca/ph-sp/pdf/perspect-eng.pdf.

Lalonde, M. (2002). New perspective on the health of Canadians: 28 years later. *Revista Panamericana de Salud Pública, 12*(3), 149–152.

Linares, N., & López, O. (2008). La equidad en salud: Propuestas conceptuales, aspectos críticos y perspectivas desde el campo de la salud colectiva. *Medicina Social, 3*(3), 247–259.

Lissbrant, S. (2015). Food and nutritional security in the Caribbean region: Consequences of malnutrition and good practices as solutions. *Investigación y Desarrollo, 23*(29), 117–138.

López, E. (2005). Hacia una nueva salud pública en Latinoamérica. *Atención Primaria, 36*(6), 336–338.

MacDougall, H. (2007). Reinventing public health: A new perspective on the health of Canadians and its international impact. *Journal of Epidemiology and Community Health, 61*(11), 955–959.

Marca País Colombia (2013). Un país pluriétnico y multicultural. Bogotá: Marca País Colombia Retrieved from www.colombia.co/asi-es-colombia/colombia-un-pais-plurietnico-y-multicultural.html.

Marmot, M., Pellegrini, A., Vega, J., Solar, O., & Fortune, K. (2013). Acción con respecto a los determinantes social de la salud en las Américas. *Revista Panamericana Salud Pública, 34*(6), 382–384.

Martínez, S. (2007). Equidad y situación de salud. *Revista Cubana Salud Pública, 33*(3), 1–8.

Ministerio de Salud y Protección Social (2011). Ley 1438. Bogotá. Retrieved from www.minsalud.gov.co/Normatividad/LEY%201438%20DE%202011.pdf.

Ministerio de Salud y Protección Social (2012). Plan Decenal de Salud Pública, 2012–2021. Bogotá. Retrieved from www.minsalud.gov.co/Documentos%20y%20Publicaciones/Plan%20Decenal%20-%20Documento%20en%20consulta%20para%20aprobaci%C3%B3n.pdf.

Ministerio de Salud y Protección Social (2015). Ley 1751. Bogotá. Retrieved from www.minsalud.gov.co/Normatividad_Nuevo/Ley%201751%20de%202015.pdf.

Ministerio de Salud y Protección Social (2016). Resolución 429 de 2016. Bogotá. Retrieved from www.minsalud.gov.co/Normatividad_Nuevo/Resoluci%c3%b3n%200429%20de%202016.pdf.

Ministerio de Salud y Protección Social (2018a). Análisis de Situación de Salud (ASIS) Colombia, 2017. Bogotá. Retrieved from www.minsalud.gov.co/sites/rid/Lists/BibliotecaDigital/RIDE/VS/ED/PSP/asis-nacional-2017.pdf.

Ministerio de Salud y Protección Social (2018b). Infecciones respiratorias agudas (IRA). Bogotá. Retrieved from www.minsalud.gov.co/salud/Paginas/Infecciones-Respiratorias-Agudas-(IRA).aspx.

Montes, C. (2008). La violencia en Colombia: Análisis histórico del homicidio en la segunda mitad del Siglo XX. *Revista Criminalidad*, 50(1), 73–84.

Neves, E., Cabral, I., & Silveira, A. (2013). La red familiar de niños con necesidades especialies de salud: Implicaciones para la enfermería. *Revista Latino-Americana de Enfermagem*, 21(2), 562–570.

Organisation for Economic Co-operation and Development (OECD) (2017). OECD Economic Surveys: Colombia. Paris. Retrieved from www.oecd.org/eco/surveys/Colombia-2017-OECD-economic-survey-overview.pdf.

Organización Mundial de la Salud (OMS) (2008a). Informe sobre la salud en el mundo 2008: La atención primaria de salud, más necesaria que nunca. Geneva. Retrieved from www1.paho.org/hq/dmdocuments/2010/APS_Informe_sobre_Salud_en_el_mundo-2008_resumen.pdf.

Organización Mundial de la Salud (OMS) (2008b). Subsanar las desigualdades en una generación. Alcanzar la equidad sanitaria actuando sobre los determinantes sociales. Geneva. Retrieved from http://apps.who.int/iris/bitstream/10665/44084/1/9789243563701_spa.pdf.

Organización Mundial de la Salud (OMS) (2011a). Guía de intervención mhGAP. Geneva. Retrieved from https://apps.who.int/iris/bitstream/handle/10665/44498/9789243548067_spa.pdf?sequence=1.

Organización Mundial de la Salud (OMS) (2011b). *Guía de intervención para los trastornos mentales, neurológicos y por uso de sustancias*. Geneva: Organización Mundial de la Salud.

Organización Mundial de la Salud (OMS) (2014). Documentos básicos: Organización Mundial de la Salud. 48th ed. Retrieved from http://apps.who.int/gb/bd/PDF/bd48/basic-documents-48th-edition-sp.pdf#page=7.

Organización Panamericana de la Salud (OPS) (2014). *Estrategia para el acceso universal a la salud y la cobertura universal de salud*. Washington, DC: Organización Panamericana de la Salud.

Osorio, A., Bolancé, C., & Madise, N. (2014). Community socioeconomic context and its influence on intermediary determinants of child health: Evidence from Colombia. *Journal of Biosocial Science*, 47(2015), 1–27.

Osorio, A., Romero, G., Bonilla, H., & Aguado, L. (2018). Contexto socioeconómico de la comunidad y desnutrición crónica infantil en Colombia. *Revista de Saúde Pública*, 52(73), 1–12.

Presidencia de la República de Colombia (2013). Estrategia de atención integral a la primera infancia. Fundamentos políticos, técnicos y de gestión. Bogotá. Retrieved from www.deceroasiempre.gov.co/QuienesSomos/Documents/Fundamentos-politicos-tecnicos-gestion-de-cero-a-siempre.pdf.

Public Health Agency of Canada (PHAC) (2011). What determines health? Ottawa: Public Health Agency of Canada. Retrieved from www.phac-aspc.gc.ca/ph-sp/determinants/index-eng.php.

Ramos, E. (2012). Transición epidemiológica en Colombia: De las enfermedades infecciosas a las no trasmisibles. *Revista Ciencias Biomédicas*, 3(2), 282–290.

Rodríguez Navarrete, J. (2016). Comportamiento del suicidio. Colombia 2016. In I. N. Forenses (ed.), *Datos para la vida* (pp. 402–436). Bogotá: Instituto Nacional de Medicina Legal y Ciencias Forenses.

Save the Children (2018a). Migración y desplazamiento de niños y niñas en América Latina y el Caribe. London: Save the Children. Retrieved from www.savethechildren.org.co/sites/savethechildren.org.co/files/resources/Migracion.pdf.

Save the Children (2018b). Violencia contra adolescentes en América Latina y el Caribe. London: Save the Children. Retrieved from www.savethechildren.org.co/sites/savethechildren.org.co/files/resources/Violencia%20en%20adolescentes.pdf.

Save the Children (2019). Alto a la guerra contra la niñez. London: Save the Children. Retrieved from www.savethechildren.org.co/sites/savethechildren.org.co/files/resources/Alto%20a%20la%20guerra%20contra%20la%20ninez%20compreso.pdf.

Shultz, J., Rose, D., Espinel, Z., et al. (2014). Internally displaced "victims of armed conflict" in Colombia: The trajectory and trauma signature of forced migration. *Current Psychiatry Reports*, 16(10), 475–501.

Somocurcio, J. (2013). La atención primaria de la salud. *Revista Peruana de Medicina Experimental y Salud Pública*, 30(2), 171–172.

Sousa, F., & Erdmann, A. (2012). Qualifying child care in primary health care. *Revista Brasileira de Enfermagem*, 65(5), 795–802.

Starfield, B. (2011). Politics, primary healthcare and health: Was Virchow right? *Journal of Epidemiology and Community Health*, 65, 653–655.

Tapia, J. (2013). Crecimiento económico e inequidades en salud. *Revista Peruana de Medicina Experimental y Salud Pública*, 30(4), 657–664.

Torres, N., & Orozco, C. (2013). Colombia y sus compromisos con la primera infancia. *Revista PALOBRA*, 12(12), 236–249.

Urrego, D. (2015). Conflicto armado en Colombia y misión médica: Narrativas médicas como memorias de supervivencia. *Revista de la Facultad de Medicina*, 63(3), 377–388.

Villar, M. (2011). Factores determinantes de la salud: Importancia de la prevención. *Acta médica peruana*, 28(4), 237–341.

World Health Organization (WHO) (1978). Declaration of Alma-Ata. Adopted at the International Conference on Primary Health Care. World Health Organization (WHO), Alma Ata. Retrieved from www.paho.org/hq/index.php?option=com_docman&task=doc_view&gid=19004&Itemid=2518.

World Health Organization (WHO) (2000). *Towards unity for Health: Challenges and opportunities for partnership in health development. A working paper*. Geneva: World Health Organization.

World Health Organization (WHO) (2008). Social determinants of health. Geneva: World Health Organization. Retrieved from www.who.int/social_determinants/en/.

World Health Organization (WHO) (2011). Guía de intervención mhGAP para los trastornos mentales, neurológicos y por uso de sustancias en el nivel de atención de la salud no especializada. Geneva: Organización Mundial de la Salud. https://apps.who.int/iris/handle/10665/44498

18

Learning for Psychology via the Cuban Program of Care for People Affected by the Chernobyl Accident: 1990–2011

Alexis Lorenzo Ruiz

INTRODUCTION

Disaster situations can cause great loss of human life and substantial material damage to the economies of the countries in which they occur.* In the case of Latin American countries, observers have marked historical and cultural reasons to be concerned given the risk factors and vulnerabilities demonstrated in that region. Explicit assessment had its peak during 1990–2000, a period known as the International Decade for the Reduction of Natural Disasters (IDRND) (UNODRR, 2000). At present, with the increase in disaster situations worldwide and their growing impact, it is impossible to deny or minimize the participation of psychological science in disaster preparedness and response.

One way to understand the increased magnitude of disasters is to highlight their growing economic cost. Economic damage caused by disasters has tripled in the past forty years. According to estimates reached during the 1960s, disasters cost the world 40 billion US dollars. In the 1970s and 1980s, that cost rose to $70 billion and $120 billion, respectively. Estimates for this past decade (i.e., the second decade of the twenty-first century) far exceed these previous costs and their impact (United Nations Development Programme [UNDP], 2014). For instance, an in-depth study carried out by the United Nations Office for Disaster Risk Reduction (UNISDR) in 2016 found that economic losses from disasters such as earthquakes, tsunamis, cyclones, and flooding reached an average of $250–300 billion per year (see United Nations University and Institute for Environment and Human Security [UNU-EHS], 2016).

Following this growing trend, the United Nations' (UN) 2016 World Risk Report (UNU-EHS, 2016) indicates 31.1 million new cases of internal displacement caused by conflicts, violence, and disasters. The UN reports that in 2016, a person fled his or her home every three seconds due to war and violence (as cited in *The Guardian*, n.d.). In 2017 and the first half of 2018, worldwide disaster situations continued to occur with equal frequency and with increasing impact and repercussions of all kinds (International Federation of Red Cross and Red Crescent Societies, 2018).

Taking these realities into account, this chapter focuses on an experience that occurred several years ago. However, given the number of disasters we currently experience globally, this past disaster remains fully valid, and has greater relevance based on the global data described earlier. In the pages that follow, best practices with regard to professional response to disaster are presented as well as reflections of a theoretical-methodological nature. Lessons learned with regard to working in disaster situations are introduced.

DEFINING DISASTER

Disaster can be defined as an event or series of major events that seriously affects the basic structures and normal functioning of a society, community, or territory, causing damage or a loss of material goods and human lives. This loss includes a resulting lack of a societal infrastructure as well as a lack of essential services/ livelihoods on a scale beyond the normal capacity of those involved to deal with the disaster without outside help (Cohen, 1999a, 1999b; Cohen & Ahearn, 1980; Noji, 2000; Sauchay, 2009; Seaman, 1984). This chapter takes a psychological, holistic, and integrative social approach to disaster situations. Interrelationships between psychology and disasters are considered. Chapter objectives include:

1. Describe the creation and development of the Cuban Children of Chernobyl Program.
2. Determine the role of psychology in this program.
3. Value the learning from and for psychological science via this professional experience.

Cuban Children of Chernobyl Program (see www.sld.cu/sitios/chernobil/)

In the wake of the Chernobyl accident on April 26, 1986, until the year 1990, when the Union of Soviet Socialist Republics (USSR) still existed, state healthcare programs were being developed in response to the crisis. Most of these were developed in the areas of greatest contamination and in those cities that had been evacuated. The vast majority of people affected by the Chernobyl accident were from places adjacent to the central electro-nuclear (CEN) plant of Chernobyl and other territories (e.g., Ukraine, Belarus, West Russia). These areas were also most affected by the radioactive contamination of the rains and winds associated with polluted clouds during and after the reactor's explosion. In the years after the worst nuclear accident in history, new scientific findings have suggested that the effects of the Chernobyl explosion were underestimated. The nuclear accident of Chernobyl has been considered, due to its magnitude, the greatest technological catastrophe of humanity (United Nations Scientific Committee on the Effects of Atomic Radiation [UNSCEAR], 2000).

CAUSES OF THE CHERNOBYL ACCIDENT

The explosion in the fourth reactor of the Chernobyl nuclear power plant occurred due to overheating and human error. According to the Nuclear Energy Institute (NEI), the Chernobyl reactor differed from reactors in the United States due to its being a *reaktor bolshoy moshchnosty kanalny* (RBMK), "designed to produce both plutonium and electric power, [and] were very different from standard commercial designs and employed a unique combination of a graphite moderator and water coolant. The reactors were highly unstable at low power due to control rod design and 'positive void coefficient,' factors that accelerated the nuclear chain reaction and power output if the reactors lost cooling water" (NEI, 2019).

The morning of the explosion, operators at the plant ran things at low power and without communication to those involved with procedural safety measures (NEI, 2019). As such, nuclear security and protection regulations were not complied with. The lack of communication, involvement of personnel involved with safety procedures, and RBMK instability when operating at low power all came together to contribute to the intense power surge that increased heat levels to the point that pressure tubes with fuel started to burst (NEI, 2019).

A steam explosion was caused when the hot fuel mixed with water – leading to the top of the reactor being blown off. This led to more tubes breaking, which caused a second explosion that left the reactor core open to the environment (NEI, 2019). The burning fire from the explosion continued for ten days. The Chernobyl plant, in contrast to other plants, did not have a protective structure around it that would prevent radioactive materials from being released into the environment should such a crisis occur.

At the time of the Chernobyl explosion, there was also little knowledge about ionizing radiation. While in several countries accidents with radioactive substances had already occurred, these tended to be local in character (e.g., the Three Mile Island accident) and many took place in military and/or strategic installations (e.g., SL-1 in 1961, nuclear-powered submarine accidents that occurred from 1961 to 1985). Likewise, the world only imagined the occurrence of a possible large-scale nuclear confrontation between the Warsaw Pact and NATO military blocs. The knowledge of scientists was therefore limited. The only experience of a massive population affected by radiation was the atomic bombings to the Japanese cities of Hiroshima and Nagasaki in 1945.

In these latter cases, radiological damage was associated with large doses of radiation in a short period of time. In Chernobyl, something different happened. The Chernobyl phenomenon related to low doses of radiation over a long period of time. The following paragraphs show how, in the territories linked to the consequences of these disasters, an ongoing effect lingers – even though many years and several generations of people have passed.

MAJOR CONSEQUENCES OF THE CHERNOBYL DISASTER

During the years after the Chernobyl disaster, thyroid cancer and its social and psychological impact were considered among the explosion's most negative consequences. Children with health problems associated with the consequences of Chernobyl exceeded 4 million in the territory of Ukraine. Among these consequences, the author must also highlight the post-disaster collapse of socialism in these countries, a phenomenon known as "The Second Disaster." Here the stress and psycho-traumatic character of the psychosocial impact multiplies and deepens in its multiple manifestations (IAEA-TECDOC-958, 1997; Pergamenchik et al., 1989; Yakovenko, 1998). The specific psychological and social aspects of accidents and disasters associated with radiation can be summarized as follows:

- Lack of familiarity with radiological events. This leads to difficulty making predictions.
- The duration of events and their interrelationship with possible psychological effects, e.g., the speed of events in these disasters.
- Risks to sensory perception and its mismatch with objective reality, because radiation is not perceived through the sense organs, as in most disasters.
- The peculiarities of the organization faced with a radiological emergency (Gallego, Gil, & Ortego, 1996; Helou & Benicio da Costa Neto, 1995; IAEA-TECDOC-958, 1997; Quarentelli, 1991; Lifton, 1967; Lorenzo Ruiz, 1997, 2000, 2006; Lorenzo Ruiz et al., 1997; Pergamenchik et al., 1989; Vasconcelos, 1992; Yakovenko, 1998).

Gallego and colleagues (1996) talk about responding to two differing groups affected by the consequences of the Chernobyl accident: (a) responding to the "direct" group, such as understanding the experiences of people living with the effects of radioactivity; and (b) responding to the "indirect" group that is not sensitive to radioactivity. The following are considered to be true "direct" effects of the consequences of the Chernobyl accident:

- Increase in cancer rates and thyroid pathologies.
- Modifications in the morbidity of the usual diseases of these populations.
- Post-disaster psychological and social impact.

THE BIRTH OF THE CUBAN CHILDREN OF CHERNOBYL PROGRAM

In January 1990, the president of the Soviet Union, Mikhail Gorbachev, addressed the UN General Assembly with a request for urgent help to meet the growing demands of medical assistance to those affected by the Chernobyl disaster. Cuba was among the countries that immediately agreed to provide humanitarian aid. Cuba continued to provide such humanitarian aid over the next decades and even during the most difficult moments of the 1990s economic crisis. Hence, as of March 29, 1990, Cuba organized the specialized medical care program known internationally as the Children of Chernobyl Program. In Cuba, the Children of Chernobyl Program could be carried out for the following reasons: a commitment to principles of humanism and internationalism (Castro, Melluish, & Lorenzo, 2014); health being considered a priority in Cuban society; the presence of a national healthcare system organized and prepared to respond immediately to any contingency; and the valuable role of the Cuban physician and family nurse within the medical system.

The tasks of the Children of Chernobyl Program were threefold. First, the program aimed to provide medical care to children/adolescents and accompanying adults/family members coming to Cuba from areas affected by the Chernobyl accident. Second, the program sought to compare the main biopsychosocial conditions of the child/adolescent population and the accompanying adults/family members from areas affected by the Chernobyl accident during their stay in Cuba. A third program task was to highlight the state of integral health among this population (Dotres Martínez et al., 1995).

Hence, from 1990 to 2011 in the city of Tarará in the eastern part of Havana, more than 25,000 children and their adult relatives from Ukraine, Belarus, and Russia were served. Under the program, people from Moldova (four patients) and Armenia (eleven patients) also received medical care. The experience gained running the program provided preparation to advise and provide medical assistance to other people affected by radiation. Such was the case, for instance, of the fifty-three Brazilian patients affected by the manipulation of a radioactive source of Cesium-137 in the city of Goiânia, Brazil (Dotres Martínez et al., 1995; Lorenzo Ruiz, 1997, 2000, 2001, 2006, 2009a, 2009b; Lorenzo Ruiz et al., 1997).

Several goals were outlined in the Children of Chernobyl Program. The first goal was to provide specialized medical attention. This included laboratory analysis, a thorough study of the thyroid gland, and consultations with all the necessary specialties. A second goal was to provide specialized stomatological care due to the high rate of dental caries, especially in the first years of the program. These are still significant today and require intense promotion, prevention, and education. A third goal was to provide specialized psychological and social care. Finally, a fourth goal was the evaluation of possible radioactive contamination via physical dosimetries (e.g., specialized cytogenetic studies to assess the dosage of radiation received), including receiving a forecast assessment for the next seventy years of life (García & Medina, 2001).These goals were organized through an algorithm that can be synthesized as follows:

1. Selection and previous classification of patients and companions in Ukraine and other territories of the former Soviet Union. This process was executed jointly by

a Cuban-Ukrainian healthcare team. Initial documentation was prepared regarding patient health problems and strategies to be followed for each case in Cuba.
2. Organizing the stay in Cuba, whose center was in the Tarará Sanitarium. Here primary and secondary healthcare levels were combined as per the Cuban model of the family doctor and nurse (Márquéz, Soberats, & Galván, 2011; Alvarez Sintes, 2001a, 2001b).
3. At the end of the stay in Cuba, a final document was prepared that spelled out the necessary specialized medical recommendations to be carried out upon the patient's return to the country of origin.
4. Upon return to the country of origin, ongoing future monitoring of cases was carried out in four ways. First, in most cases, ongoing and future monitoring involved the healthcare system in the patient's own territory of residence. Second, monitoring also occurred via a Cuban medical team in the capital city of Ukraine, Kiev. A third aspect of monitoring was carried out in the Yevpatoriya International Children's Medical Center (see www.rada.com.ua/eng/catalog/10544/; e.g., "Druzhba/Amistad") by a Cuban multidisciplinary team. This team included specialists in comprehensive general medicine, pediatrics, endocrinology, hematology, dermatology, health psychology, and translation, working together with Ukrainian specialists. A fourth aspect of monitoring occurred among those patients who returned to Havana for medical care (Dotres Martínez et al., 1995; García & Medina, 2001; Lorenzo Ruiz, 1997, 2000, 2001).

THE ROLE OF PSYCHOLOGY IN THE CHILDREN OF CHERNOBYL PROGRAM

The following describes the role of psychology in the Cuban Children of Chernobyl Program in 1990. Due to the specificity and particularities of the psychological aspects of this program, the paragraphs that follow first describe how this field of knowledge (e.g., responding to disasters) has evolved both in general and in relation to the Chernobyl accident. This is followed with a specific focus on a description of the psychological program of care organized in Cuba.

Unlike other medical specialties and the different disciplines linked to the Cuban Children of Chernobyl Program, psychological science in the area of disaster response, both within Cuba and across the world, was in the early stages of development. Therefore, scientific society and the international community had very limited recognition about the psychological science of understanding disasters. For instance, it is now almost incredible to recognize that in the year 1990, when the Children of Chernobyl Program began, the team only had access to one book in the national library of Cuba – Cohen and Ahearn's *Handbook for Mental Health Care of Disaster Victims* (1980).

Only later and already into the first five to ten years of its work was the team able to expand access to specialized literature. This occurred via participation in conferences/congresses and through academic exchanges with Latin American, European, and North American professionals. Through this process we learned about other important thematic publications (Albuquerque, 1992; Beristain, 1999; Campuzano, 1997; Cohen, 1999a, 1999b; Gallego et al., 1996; Lazarus & Folkman, 1986; Lima, 1992; Lima & Lozano, 1989; Riso, 1996; Robles Sánchez, 2002; Rodríguez Marín, 1994; Seaman, 1984). We combined this self-learning process with the rereading of Cuban research that served as an orientation (Grau Abalo et al., 1993; Guevara Váldez et al., 2002; Zaldívar, Vega, & Perara, 2004).

After the year 2000, little by little, the team began to perceive work on the psychological understanding of disasters not as something strange or unknown, but as a new area of professional practice with work emerging from researchers and professionals in psychology and psychiatry dedicated to the subject (Araya, 2000; Benyakar, 2006; Mitchell & Everly, 1997; Noji, 2000; Valero, 2014). Following the chronological developments for the field, one could say that the psychology of disasters as a field gradually developed from an idea of being "mystical" to the reconceptualization and revaluation of this area from a scientific perspective (Lorenzo Ruiz, 1997, 2006, 2009a, 2009b, 2017a, 2017b). Building on a chronology of the field, the following paragraphs address these questions:

- How did Cuba contribute to the psychology of disasters?
- What is the specific role of psychology and the psychological team in the Children of Chernobyl Program?
- Has the experience of the Children of Chernobyl Program made a contribution? How will this program continue to be developed in Cuba?

In 1990, the team worked to organize the Program for Psychological and Social Care. To describe this work it's important to understand the context of psychological science in Cuba. Cuba's history of psychological science started in 1969 within the national healthcare system and was disseminated in most spheres of current Cuban society. The general objective of psychological and social care in the Children of Chernobyl Program was to evaluate the system of psychological intervention that Cuba provided to people affected by Chernobyl. This evaluation took into account variables related to the disaster itself as well as those derived from personal characteristics such as adaptability. Along with this overall goal, the following specific objectives were implemented:

- Estimate the improvement in mental health during the stay in Cuba, as well as satisfaction with the services received;
- Determine characteristics of the internal (subjective) picture of diseases;
- Identify and quantify primary influencing factors in the psychosocial adaptation of children and families affected by the Chernobyl disaster;
- Design and implement a system of evidence-based psychological interventions that not only facilitate psychosocial adaptation to the Cuban environment but

also promote a more effective readaptation to the child's/family's environment of origin.

This psychological attention aspired to promote a range of benefits for the children and families affected by the Chernobyl disaster.

With regard to contributions to psychological knowledge, it was thought that research could explore the impact of such a disaster and the diverse ways it damages health and the environment. On a practical level, it was thought that the information learned from working with the children of Chernobyl would provide insight into the effectiveness of medical-psychological-social systems of care whose goal was to minimize damage produced by the disaster and provide preparation for living one's future life.

For these reasons, the new independent Psychology Service was organized in the city of Tarará, under the direct supervision of the Provincial Group in the City of Havana and the National Psychology Department of the Ministry of Public Health. The Psychology Service was responsible for designing a comprehensive system of psychological interventions that addressed environmental, educational, cultural, and recreational domains. The Psychology Service also provided transmission of knowledge, support skills, and psychosocial intervention to medical, paramedical, and general services personnel. Interventions incorporated individual and group techniques related to family, school, work, and interpersonal or other conflicts. Psychoeducational interventions focused on the concerns of the children and families affected by the Chernobyl disaster, in addition to organizing a health education program (Lorenzo Ruiz, 1997, 2000, 2006, 2017a). The activities of specialized psychological care following this line of thought were as follows:

- *Initial psychological evaluation.* The initial psychological evaluation was usually done in the first seven to ten days of a child's/family's stay in Cuba. An individual, group, and family psychosocial interview method was used for this assessment. Here Cuban family doctors and nurses collaborated with the Ukrainian accompanying adult staff (e.g., relatives, doctors, and educators). In this way, the initial psychosocial symptoms of greater or lesser extent become known and were shared in initial diagnostic impressions.
- *Establish psychosocial action strategies.* After the initial evaluation, the team worked to establish psychosocial action strategies. Here the team focused on different ways to provide psychological attention to those affected by the disaster. To provide more attention, especially when there were large numbers of children/families with whom the team was working (e.g., at times this number was 1,000), we would stratify interventions into three domains: interventions for children under seven years, interventions for children between seven and seventeen years, and interventions for adults.
- *Definition of studies and psychological treatments available in Cuba.* With children under seven years of age, a global psychological assessment of

psychomotor, language, and social development was performed. If disorders and alterations were detected, a stimulation and training program was implemented that involved a multi- and interdisciplinary approach. Among schoolchildren, adolescents, young people, and other cases as needed, intellectual capacity was evaluated, as well as identity development, emotional state, and areas of conflict. In all cases, the team evaluated the psychological and social impact of the Chernobyl disaster. Psychodiagnostic evaluations were carried out with two groups of instruments: the first included those already established and recognized by the specialized literature; and the second, those that our working team designed and validated as necessary.

- *Organization of multidisciplinary consultations and specialized assessments.* Children and families were referred to various specialists as needed. Consultation and referral was made to specialists that included child and adolescent psychiatry, general psychiatry for adults, neurology, psychopedagogy, and speech therapy, among others. In each of the cases, the referral/referral criteria and subsequent follow-up were determined individually and when multi- and interdisciplinary care was needed.
- *Design, piloting, implementation, and evaluation of psychological and social programs.* Implementation and evaluation of programs was marked by the specificity of interventions as well as the short time in which to implement them given a child's/family's limited duration of stay in Cuba to receive specialized medical-psychosocial rehabilitative care.

PROGRAM EVALUATION

An evaluation of psychological and social programs that worked with the Children of Chernobyl Program has shown that, since 1990, the Psychology Service provided outreach and solutions to multiple situations via the application of professional tools and knowledge. In addition, the psychological and social approach that was taken supported collaboration between and among multi- and interdisciplinary teams. This was a new framework for intervention that was unprecedented in the country.

Evaluation also revealed that the psychosocial assessment and diagnostic instruments designed for the Children of Chernobyl Program proved to be adequate, reliable, and valid. The reliability and validity of the program was reflected in a significant decrease in symptoms when comparing initial psychosocial presentations when children/families first started the program to final evaluation results at time of discharge. Such changes included addressing issues such as high levels of anxiety and depression, feeling overwhelmed, inadequate coping styles, lack of awareness and assessment about the disease process, lack of information about disasters and related psychological impact, and pessimism with regard to having a sense of control of one's future destiny.

A move toward recovery emerged from the Children of Chernobyl Program as a result of the stay in Cuba and the services received there. Program participants tended to provide satisfactory evaluations because the program was in accordance with initial hopes and expectations (Vasileva, 2004). Results obtained by our work team coincided with those of other specialists and were ratified in joint studies conducted in Ukraine (Lorenzo Ruiz et al., 1999; Shestopalova et al., 1998; Yakovenko, 1998). Hence, the program's psychological and social services facilitated an ability to adapt to one's situation and provided resources to restructure future capacity for psychosocial rehabilitation in the home environment, despite this affected population not having a previous culture of specialized psychological care.

SYNTHESIS OF PROGRAM RESULTS

Since the start of the Children of Chernobyl Program we can say that research and intervention aimed at populations and communities affected by disasters is now a reality. Much of this work has provided an emphasis on prevention, promotion, preparation, education, and training among communities and institutions with greater risk and vulnerability.

The approach taken by the Children of Chernobyl Program was to empower children and families and minimize the loss of human lives. Based on the integration of all these experiences, it has been possible to form a working methodology of psychological science in disaster situations. The experience and results of the work carried out from 1990 to 2011 via the Cuban Children of Chernobyl Program confirm what was stated earlier – e.g., the multidisciplinary approach of the program served to build a professional network that addressed the needs of children and their families (Betancourt, 2013).

Although this program was implemented many years ago, events at this juncture of the twenty-first century help us analyze international experiences and consider how emergencies and disasters can lead to variable psychosocial reactions. Given the global scope of disasters, it becomes impossible to ignore the role of culture among nations affected by disasters (Lorenzo Ruiz, 1997, 2000, 2001, 2006a, 2006b; Valero, 2014). Here it's important to define a new psychological and social formation that the author calls "cultural historical training." This concept can be explained in terms of understanding how specific cultural nuances impact a culture's reactions to and interpretation of emergencies and disasters. For instance, for some nations a certain type of emergency or disaster may be perceived as "unexpected" while for others it may be considered "usual." It is with the second case that the affected populations (and response teams) can face greater challenges related to being psychologically and socially prepared to deal with extreme situations and events (Castro et al., 2014; Lorenzo Ruiz, 1997, 2000, 2001).

The systems and programs of preparation that include prevention, promotion, and training with regard to psychological and social impact are vital for the "before" aspect of the disaster. This implies that communities need to develop individual-group-institutional-community-social levels of support and training so as to be responsive to disasters before they occur. Preparedness prior to the disaster can address all potential factors through a process of psychological and social preparation that systematizes adaptive responses.

The team's preparedness response process involves analyzing five variables and the interrelations between them: the disaster, those affected by the disaster, communities, pattern of response, and programs/action protocols (Lorenzo Ruiz, 2006, 2009a, 2009b). This approach is in contrast to the more common trend of responding or intervening *after* a disaster occurs. Practical-instrumental learning for the psychology field, based on our work with the Children of Chernobyl Program, is to consider psychosocial support as the central axis of disaster intervention. Table 18.1 presents a chronological timeline of the development of a Cuban psychology of disaster response.

These experiences, initiated with the Chernobyl program, demonstrate that a central activity in disaster response must always be psychological and include social preparation. Those studying in pre- and postgraduate programs in Cuba learn about this approach to disaster response preparedness (Lorenzo Ruiz, 2017a). This approach should be incorporated into the legal framework of each country where a system of protection/civil defense measures is established. In Cuba, this area is governed by Directive No. 1 of the President of the National Defense Council (2010). Hence, the learning in Cuba from the Children of Chernobyl Program was reflected in a document known as the "Guidelines for Mental Health in Emergencies and Disasters in Cuba." This is considered the methodological basis for the preparation and implementation of Indication No. 20 of the Minister of Public Health of Cuba, signed on September 30, 2008 (Ruíz et al., 2012). Its implementation in different situations has been evaluated as favorable, adequate, and necessary (Sánchez Gil et al., 2014).

Finally, the role of psychology in emergencies and disasters can be expressed as follows:

- Emergencies and disasters are undeniably a reality of everyday life in Cuba and in the Latin America region.
- Scientific understanding does not necessarily advance along with media dissemination of the impact and consequence of emergencies and disasters. A lack of perception and acceptance remains of the role of psychological and social factors in disaster response.
- It's important for responders to understand risk/vulnerability factors versus protective factors that have an impact on human resilience.
- The disciplinary approach prevails (e.g., single disciplines responding to disasters on their own), rather than multi- and transdisciplinary approaches

TABLE 18.1 *Timeline of the development of a Cuban psychology of disaster response*

1990–1992	Initial systematization of scientific and psychological experience on disaster response in Cuba and internationally
1992–1993	Organize a national reference center focused on psychological support/disaster preparation in disasters (CRNAPPD), together with the Cuban National Society of the Red Cross (SNCRC) (Foyo Ceballos, 2000)
1993	Recognition and affiliation of the CRNAPPD with the International Psychological Support Center of the International Federation of the Red Cross and Red Crescent (IFRC), based in Copenhagen, Denmark
1993–1998	Redesign and gradual implementation of specialized programs on disaster response in Cuban communities and other areas
1998–2000	Dissemination of the Children of Chernobyl Program at major levels and scales throughout the country, coordinated by the SNCRC and with the cooperation of the National Group and Cuban Society of Psychology
2001–2011	Integration of disaster-response-related activities coordinated collectively by the National Groups of Psychology, Psychiatry and Childhood Psychiatry, Cuban Societies of Psychology and Psychiatry, and in the Advisory Council of the Latin American Center for Disaster Medicine (CLAMED) (www.sld.cu/sitios/desastres/)
2002	Organization of the Latin American Federation of Psychology in Emergencies and Disasters (FLAPED)
2006	Development of the Latin American Network of Psychology in Emergencies and Disasters (RedLAPED) (http://psicologiaenemergencias.blogspot.com/)
2009	Development of the Spanish Society of Psychology Applied to Disasters, Emergencies and Emergencies (Sociedad Española de Psicología Aplicada a Desastres Urgencias y Emergencias [SEPADEM])
2011–2018	Consolidation and improvement of theoretical, practical, and instrumental learning with regard to disaster response

(e.g., working across disciplines to address and respond to disaster situations), to the detriment of integrating psychological and social understanding with other professions engaged in disaster and emergency response.
- The role of psychology in emergencies and disasters needs to be recognized among universities, training facilities, and institutions charged with disaster response.
- Individual, family, institutional, and above all, community preparation and mitigation programs should be developed in a way that incorporates an understanding of psychological and social factors.
- Collaborative research is encouraged to provide more information about psychology in emergencies and disasters (Alves, Lacerda, & Legal, 2012; Figueroa & Marín, 2016; Figueroa, Marín, & González, 2010; Galindo, 2010; Lorenzo Ruiz, 2017a, 2017b; Mattedi, 2008; Pineda & López, 2010).

CONCLUSION

By way of closure – and reminder – disasters never warn in enough time, neither is it easy to control their effects. Therefore, this chapter's central conclusion is associated with the hope that psychology and society can and should be better prepared psychologically and socially for each moment of the disaster reduction cycle. The discipline of psychology needs to know and understand how to handle the complexities of disasters. Psychology as a field is encouraged to continue to generate new knowledge to respond to the growing impact and resulting consequences of disasters occurring across the globe.

Note

* The author recognizes the scientific value of results obtained by the Russian-Ukrainian and Belarusian specialists, first in the specialized institutes and hospitals in Moscow, Kiev, and Minsk. This was where some of the first victims, firefighters, and other responders who were in action to put down the fire caused by the explosion of the fourth reactor of the central electro-nuclear (CEN) plant were treated (Yakovenko, 1998).

REFERENCES

Albuquerque, A. (1992). Tratamiento del estrés postraumático en excombatientes. In E. Echeburrúa (ed.), *Avances en el tratamiento psicológico de los trastornos de ansiedad* (pp. 171–187). Madrid: Ediciones Pirámide.

Alves, R. B., Lacerda, M. A. D. C., & Legal, E. J. (2012). A atuação do psicólogo diante dos desastres naturais: Uma revisão. *Psicologia em estudo*, 17(2), 307–315.

Alvarez Sintes, R. (2001a). *Temas de medicina general integral: Volumen II Principales afecciones del individuo en los contextos familiar y social.* La Habana: Editorial Ciencias Médicas.

Alvarez Sintes, R. (2001b). *Temas de medicina general integral: Volumen II Salud y medicina.* La Habana: Editorial Ciencias Médicas.

American Psychiatric Association (1995). *Diagnostic and Statistical Manual, 4th Edition (DSM-IV).* Washington, DC: American Psychiatric Association.

Anguelova, M. V. (2004). Evaluación de la satisfacción con la estancia en Cuba en los damnificados de Chernóbil. Manuscrito, Universidad de Médicas de La Habana, Cuba.

Araya, C. (2001). *Psicología de la Emergencia*, Ed. Kartel, 7ma edn. Santiago: PSICOPREV.

Benyakar, M. (2006). *Lo disruptivo: Amenazas individuales y colectivas: El psiquismo ante guerras, terrorismos y catástrofes sociales.* Buenos Aires: Argentina Editorial Biblos.

Beristain, C. (1999). *Catástrofes y ayuda de emergencia y reconstruir el tejido social.* Barcelona: Icaria Editorial.

Betancourt, J. A. (2013). Modelo transdisciplinario para la investigación en salud pública. *Revista Panamericana de Salud Pública*, 34(5), 359–363.

Calviño, M. (2000). *Orientación psicológica: Esquema referencial de alternativa múltiple.* La Habana: Editorial Científico-Técnica.

Campuzano, M. (1997). *Psicología para casos de desastre.* Ciudad de México: Editorial Pax.

Castro, M., Melluish, S., & Lorenzo, A. (2014). Cuban internationalism: An alternative form of globalization. *International Review of Psychiatry*, 26(5), 595–601.

Cohen, R. E. (1999a). *Salud mental para víctimas de desastres: Guía para instructores*. Ciudad de México: El Manual Moderno.
Cohen, R. E. (1999b). *Salud mental para víctimas de desastres: Manual para trabajadores*. Ciudad de México: El Manual Moderno.
Cohen, R. E., & Ahearn, F. L. (1980). *Handbook for mental health care of disaster victims*. Baltimore, MD: Johns Hopkins University Press.
Directiva No. 1 del Presidente del Consejo de Defensa Nacional de la República de Cuba. Estado Mayor Nacional de la Defensa Civil (2010).
Dotres Martínez, C., Grandío Zequeira, O., & Llanes Pérez, R. L. (1995). Programa para la atención integral a niños expuestos a la contaminación ambiental por sustancias radiactivas. *Revista Cubana de Pediatría*, 67(1).
Figueroa, R., & Marín, H. (2016). Desafíos que enfrenta Latinoamérica en salud mental en emergencias y desastres. Retrieved from www.sochped.cl/noticias/prioridades-para-la-proteccion-de-la-salud-mental-despues-de-desastres-en-latinoamerica-y-el-caribe.
Figueroa, R. A., Marín, H., & González, M. (2010). Apoyo psicológico en desastres: Propuesta de un modelo de atención basado en revisiones sistemáticas y metaanálisis. *Revista médica de Chile*, 138(2), 143–151.
Foyo Ceballos, L., Huergo Silverio, V., & Peraza Fernández, J. (2000). *Manual del Facilitador*. La Habana: Editado por la Sociedad Nacional de la Cruz Roja Cubana.
Galindo, E. (2010). Intervención de los psicólogos de la UNAM Iztacala después de los sismos de 1985 en México. Ciudad de México: AMAPSI Editorial. Retrieved from https://dspace.uevora.pt/rdpc/bitstream/10174/13116/1/Galindo%20(2010)%20Intervencion-de-psicologos-de-la-UNAM-sismos1985.pdf.
Gallego, E., Gil, E., & Ortego, P. (1996). Las consecuencias radiologicas del accidente de Chernobil. Balance a los diez a os. *Revista de la Sociedad Nuclear Española*, 29–38.
Garcia, O., & Medina, J. (2001). Medical and research results in the Cuban Chernobyl programme. *International Journal of Radiation Medicine*, 3(1–2), 44.
Grau Abalo, J., Martín, M., & Portero, D. (1993). Resultados de las investigaciones Cubanas efectuadas sobre la base del enfoque personal. *Revista Interamericana de Psicología*, 27(1), 37–58.
The Guardian (n.d.). One person forced to flee their home every three seconds by war and violence. Retrieved from www.theguardian.com/global-development/2017/jun/19/one-person-forced-to-flee-their-home-every-three-seconds-by-war-and-violence.
Guevara Váldez, J. J., Zaldívar Pérez, D., &. Roca Perara, M. A. (1997). *Reflexiones sobre el Estrés*. Brasil: Rosthill, Artes Gráficas.
Helou, Z., & Benicio da Costa Neto, S. (1995). *Cesio: Consecuencias psicosocciais do Accidente de Goiania*. Estado do Goias, Brasil: Editora U.F.G.
IAEA-TECDOC-958 (1997). *Biomedical studies conducted in Cuba of children from areas of the former USSR affected by the radiological consequences of the Chernobyl accident*. Vienna: International Atomic Energy Agency. Retrieved from https://scholar.google.com.cu/scholar?q=IAEA-TECDOC-958+1997&hl=es&as_sdt=0&as_vis=1&oi=scholart.
International Federation of Red Cross and Red Crescent Societies (2018). World Disasters Report 2018. Retrieved from https://media.ifrc.org/ifrc/world-disaster-report-2018/.
Lazarus, R. S., & Folkman, S. (1986). *Estrés y procesos cognitivos*. Barcelona: Martínez Roca.
Lifton, R. J. (1967). *Death in life: Survivors of Hiroshima*. Los Angeles: S and S Enterprises.
Lima, B. (1992). La atención comunitaria en salud mental en víctimas de desastres. In *Temas de salud mental*. Levav I (edit.) (pp. 218–236). Washington, DC: Organización Panamericana de la Salud.

Lima, B., & Lozano, J. (1989). Atención en salud mental para víctimas de desastres. In B. Lima & M. Gaviria (eds.), *Desastres. Consecuencias psicosociales de los desastres: La experiencia latinoamericana*. Programa de Cooperación Internacional en Salud Mental Simón Bolívar. Retrieved from http://helid.digicollection.org/en/d/Jph30/6.2.6.html.

Lorenzo Ruiz, A. (1997). La psicología de la salud y su rol en las situaciones de desastre. Antecedentes, resultados y perspectivas. Manuscrito, Instituto Superior de Ciencias Médicas de La Habana.

Lorenzo Ruiz, A. (2006a). La psicología en el programa cubano de atención a personas afectadas por el accidente de Chernobil. In *La monografía "Hacer y pensar La Psicología"* (pp. 129–156). Compilación y prólogo Ana María del Rosario Asebey y Manuel Calviño. La Habana: Editorial Caminos.

Lorenzo Ruiz, A. (2009a). *Lecciones aprendidas en la organización de programas de ayuda e intervención psicológica para las situaciones de emergencias y desastres en Cuba*. La Habana: Editorial de Ciencias Médicas (ECIMED) y Centro Latinoamericano de Medicina de Desastres (CLAMED). Retrieved from www.scribd.com/document/292147887/lecciones-desastres.

Lorenzo Ruiz, A. (2017a). Psicología en emergencias y desastres: Contextualización y principales perspectivas para Cuba y América Latina / Psychology in emergencies and disasters: Contextualization and main perspectives for Cuba and Latin America. *Problems of Extreme and Crisis Psychology*, 15–34.

Lorenzo Ruiz, A. (2017b). Psicología en emergencias y desastres: Realidades cambiantes y demandas por innovaciones científico-tecnológicas para su desarollo en Latinoamericana. *Memorias electrónicas IV Internacional y IX Nacional Congreso de Innovaciones en Psiclogía y Salud Mental*, 13–16, 34–45. Retrieved from www.uptc.edu.co/eventos/2017/sf/esf_021.

Lorenzo Ruiz, A. (2000). Psychological base of international rehabilitation programs for people who had suffered after the biggest critical incident. Manuscript, National University of Internal Affairs Ukraine, Kharkov.

Lorenzo Ruiz, A. (2001). Psychological cultural legacy of Chernobyl: 15 years after disaster. *Journal Bulletin of Physiotherapy and Resortoly*, 7(1), 120–124.

Lorenzo Ruiz, A. (2006b). Reflexiones sobre la evolución del quehacer psicológico en el tema de emergencias y desastres. Análisis de la experiencia en Cuba. *Cuadernos de Crisis*, 2(5), 7–37.

Lorenzo Ruiz, A. (2009b). *Regularidades psicológicas y sociales imprescindibles a conocerse por parte del personal e instituciones vinculados a las situaciones de desastres*, 74–82. See http://avv.gov.ua/news.php?newsID=39. In Матеріали міжнародної науково-практичної конференції (Україна, м. Харків, 18 листопада 2009 року). – Х.: Академія внутрішніх військ МВС України, 2009.

Lorenzo Ruiz, A., Gómez Martínez, C., Ventura Velázquez, R. E., & Mesa Ridel, G. (2012). Lineamientos para la salud mental en emergencias y desastres en Cuba. Indicación No. 20 del Ministro de Salud Pública de Cuba. La Habana, Cuba. In *"Salud y Desastres." Experiencia Cubana*. Colectivo de Autores. Editora Científica Lic. Yraida Rodríguez Luís. Editorial de Ciencias Médicas (ECIMED) y Centro Latinoamericano de Medicina de Desastres (CLAMED). La Habana, Cuba. Tomo V. 2012. Retrieved from www.bvs.sld.cu/libros/salud_desastre_v/cap_01.pdf.

Lorenzo Ruiz, A., Lovelle, R. P., Amargós, G., et al. (1997). *Psychological study of the children from the areas affected by the nuclear accident in Chernobyl who were treated in Cuba*. Vienna: International Atomic Energy Agency, pp. 69–89.

Lorenzo Ruiz, A., Martínez C. G., Velázquez, R. E. V., & Ridel, G. M. (2012). *Lineamientos para la salud mental en emergencias y desastres en Cuba*. La Habana:

Editorial de Ciencias Médicas (ECIMED) y Centro Latinoamericano de Medicina de Desastres (CLAMED).

Márquéz, M., Soberats, F. J. S., & Galván, P. A. (2011). *Medicina general. Medicina familiar: Experiencia internacional y enfoque cubano*. La Habana: Editorial Ciencias Médicas.

Mattedi, M. A. (2008). The psychology approach on the issue of disasters: A challenge for vocational and cognitive psychology. *Psicologia Ciência e Profissão, 28*(1), 162–173.

Mitchell, J. T., & Everly, G. S., Jr. (1997). *Critical Incident Stress Debriefing (CISD): An operations manual for the prevention of traumatic stress among emergency services and disaster workers*. Ellicott City, MD: Chevron Publishing.

Noji, E. K. (2000). *Impacto de los desastres en la salud pública*. Washington, DC: Pan American Health Organization.

Nuclear Energy Institute (NEI) (2019, May). Chernobyl accident and its consequences. Retrieved from www.nei.org/resources/fact-sheets/chernobyl-accident-and-its-consequences.

Nuñez, A. (2010). *Haití. Un sueño por la vida*. La Habana: Editorial Pablo de la Torriente.

Pergamenchik, L. A., Lorenzo Ruiz, A., Forinder, U., et al. (1989). *The critical incidents and the human's psychological problems*. Monograph edited by the Institute of Education in Belarus, Minsk. *Psychological Aspects of Disasters*. Edited by R. Gist & B. N. Y. Lubin.

Pineda, C., & López, W. (2010). Post-disaster psychological attention: More than a "stay calm." A review of intervention strategic models. *Terapia Psicológic, 28*(2), 155–160.

Quarentelli, E. L. (1991). *Radiation disasters: Similarities and differences from others disasters*. Elsevier.

Riso, W. (1996). *La terapia cognitivo informacional. Crítica a las terapias tradicionales e implicaciones clínicas*. Medellín: Ediciones Gráficas.

Robles Sánchez, J. I., & Medina Amor, J. L. (2002). *Intervención psicológica en las catástrofes*. Madrid: Editorial Síntesis.

Rodriguez-Marín, J. (1994). Health psychology. *Applied Psychology: An International Review, 43*(2), 213–230.

Sánchez Gil, Y. Y., Lorenzo Ruiz, A., Mesa Ridel, G., Del Huerto Marimón, M. E., & Sauchay Romero, L. (2015). *Propuesta metodológica para el Postgrado Internacional en Salud y Desastres. Centro Latinoamericano de Medicina de Desastres*. La Habana: Editorial de Ciencias Médicas (ECIMED) y Centro Latinoamericano de Medicina de Desastres (CLAMED).

Sánchez Gil, Y. Y., Ruiz, A. L., Velázquez, R. E. V., Gómez, C. M., & Estévez, J. B. (2014). Estrategia de implementación de los lineamientos sobre la salud mental en situaciones de desastres en Cuba. *Salud y desastres. Experiencias cubanas, 8*, 69–76.

Sauchay Romero, L. (2009). Reflexiones sobre definiciones de desastre. In *"Salud y Desastres." Experiencia Cubana*. Colectivo de Autores. Editora Científica Lic. Yraida Rodríguez Luís. Editorial de Ciencias Médicas (ECIMED) y Centro Latinoamericano de Medicina de Desastres (CLAMED). La Habana, Cuba. Tomo I. Octubre del 2009. pp. 271–279. Retrived from www.bvs.sld.cu/libros/salud_desastre_i/.

Seaman, J. (1984). *Epidemiología de desastre naturales*. Ciudad de México: Editorial Harla.

Shestopalova, L. F., Lorenzo Ruiz, A., Timchenko, A. V., & Kristemko, V. E. (1998). *El debriefing como método de corrección psicológica a los trastornos estresantes post-traumáticos: Folleto instructivo metodológico*. Kharkov: Universidad Nacional del Ministerio del Interior de Ucrania.

United Nations Development Programme (UNDP) (2014). *Human development report 2014. Sustaining human progress: Reducing vulnerabilities and building resilience*. New York: United Nations Development Programme.

United Nations Office for Disaster Risk Reduction (UNODRR) (2000). Campaña de las Naciones Unidas sobre la reducción de desastres en el 2000. Retrieved from www.unisdr.org.

United Nations Scientific Committee on the Effects of Atomic Radiation (UNSCEAR) (2000) Annex J. *Exposures and effects of the Chernobyl accident.*

United Nations University and Institute for Environment and Human Security (UNU-EHS) (2016). World risk report. United Nations University and Institute for Environment and Human Security in cooperation with the University of Stuttgart.

Valero, S. (2014). Psicologia en emergencias y desastres una nueva especialidad. Retrieved from www.monografias.com/trabajos10/emde/emde.shtml.

Vasconcelos, L. A. (1992). Algumas características da readaptação de sobreviventes da bomba atômica em Hiroshima. *Psicologia: Teoria e Pesquisa,* 8(1), 113–122.

Vasileva, A. M. (2004). Evaluación de la satisfacción con la estancia en Cuba en los damnificados de Chernóbil. Trabajo para Optar por el Título científico de Master en Ciencias Especialista en Psicología de la Salud. Facultad de Ciencias Médicas "Gral. Calixto García Iñiguez" de la Universidad Médica de La Habana, Cuba, noviembre del 2004.

Yakovenko, S. I. (1998). The theory and practice of psychological help to people who suffered after disasters (on the example of the Chernobyl disaster). Manuscript, G. S. Kostyuk's Institute of Psychology Academy of the Pedagogical Sciences of Ukraine, Kiev.

Zaldívar, D., Vega, R., & Perara, M. A. R. (2004). *Psicoterapia General.* La Habana: Editorial Félix Varela.

19

Learning from the Perspectives of At-Risk Resilient Ethiopian Students

How School-Based Resilience Arises from Connectedness, Competence, and Contribution

Maura Mulloy

INTRODUCTION

Ethiopia has one of the lowest school completion rates in the world. This chapter offers a fresh understanding of this key social justice issue by examining the firsthand experiences of two twelfth grade students in Addis Ababa, Ethiopia, enrolled in a scholarship program designed to promote secondary school completion for high-need students. Using a resilience lens, this chapter illuminates a framework of program-based supports and relationships that empowered these students to achieve educational success despite serious adversity in their lives. By listening to the compelling voices of these students as they describe the essential components of their educational success, we can arrive at a more intuitive understanding of the ingredients necessary to improve school completion in vulnerable populations around the world.

In this chapter, we learn how students' embeddedness in this network counterbalanced the risk factors in their lives, and led them to achieve beyond the bounds of what they previously perceived as possible. We study how their sense of connectedness to this caring and supportive community, along with the confidence they developed within a culture that encouraged high expectations and built upon their strengths, motivated them to channel their talents and successes into career and life goals that centered around contributing to their communities and their country at large, and to boosting others' capacities to realize their dreams.

A BRIEF HISTORY OF ETHIOPIA AND ITS DEMOGRAPHICS

A landlocked country in the eastern horn of Africa, Ethiopia is the only African nation never colonized – a fact in which its citizens with their rich culture take great pride. The second half of the twentieth century witnessed tumultuous upheavals in the country, from the overthrow of the monarchy in 1974 to decades of repressive socialist and democratically elected (at least in name) regimes. In 2018, Ethiopians elected a progressive prime minister who plans to usher in widespread political, economic, and educational reforms in order to help Ethiopia's citizens keep pace in one of Africa's fastest-growing manufacturing economies.

Ethiopia is roughly twice the size of France, with a population swiftly approaching 100,000,000 and 45 percent of its citizens under the age of fourteen. More than 80 percent of the country's population – comprised of dozens of varied ethnic groups and languages – lives in rural areas, although ever-increasing numbers flock to Ethiopia's capital of Addis Ababa seeking greater economic opportunity. The nation's rapid population growth, combined with environmental degradation exacerbated by climate change, overtaxes its ability to provide sufficient food for its citizens and worsens the poverty that grips most of its populace. Ethiopia has long relied on foreign governments to supplement its food capacity and to provide economic, educational, health, and humanitarian aid for its citizens.

EDUCATION AS A KEY SOCIAL JUSTICE ISSUE

Ethiopia's primary school enrollment (66 percent) and adult literacy (41.5 percent) rates are some of the lowest in the world, with primary school completion rates dipping much lower (Pereznieto & Jones, 2006). Although government efforts combined with Millennial Development Goals across Africa have prioritized expanding access to primary schools, less attention has been given to keeping students in the educational pipeline or to improving the quality of education. Many government schools suffer from low teacher–student ratios, outdated curricula and textbooks, aging buildings, and lack of access to technology and other resources (Pereznieto & Jones, 2006).

Poverty is a key barrier to education, especially for girls and students in rural areas (UNESCO, 2012). Girls are far more likely to drop out of school early, with only 41 percent making it to the last grade of primary school, and only 18 percent attaining literacy by adulthood (Pereznieto & Jones, 2006). Sociocultural factors, including an emphasis on traditional roles for women, stigma around girls' education, and early marriage and teen-age pregnancy, combine to limit girls' access to and completion of schooling (Pereznieto & Jones, 2006). In more rural regions of the country, the distance from school, high cost of school supplies and uniforms, and cost to families in terms of lost work capacity make it far less likely that students will attend school on a regular basis, much less continue to pursue their educational path through secondary school and beyond (Woldehanna, Mekonnen, & Jones, 2009).

Education is the surest route out of poverty, and parents' education level (and particularly mothers' educational attainment) is a strong predictor of their children's educational achievement (UNESCO, 2012). If Ethiopia's intergenerational cycle of low educational achievement is not interrupted, younger generations will continue to struggle in a country affected deeply by overpopulation, environmental degradation, climate change, and insufficient resources. This makes education a key social justice issue for Ethiopia, worth exploring in depth in order to determine how best to support the 50 million young Ethiopians who carry the future of their country on their slight yet strong shoulders.

THE VOICES OF AT-RISK ETHIOPIAN STUDENTS

Education policy initiatives and programs must draw upon stakeholders' perspectives and firsthand expertise so as to be most effective (USAID Education Strategy, 2011). This section highlights firsthand perspectives on issues that hinder or improve access to education, as illuminated by the experiences of two twelfth grade students in Ethiopia who are enrolled in a school program that aims to promote high school completion and college acceptance for high-risk students. Through these compelling students' voices, we hear the challenges they face, as well as explore the program-based supports that empowered them to overcome barriers and to successfully pursue higher education.

By drawing lessons from high-need students whose voices are not often heard and yet whose lives are most intimately affected by these challenges or supports, we might better understand how to structure policy initiatives and programs to promote students' achievement despite adversity. The spotlighting of these Ethiopian students' experiences also addresses the expressed need in the literature for more contextualized understandings of resilience processes in high-need schools (Clauss-Éhlers, 2004; Waxman, Gray, & Padron, 2003), as well as for social justice efforts that "take children into account" (UNICEF). Please note that the names of the students and organizations have been changed in order to protect the students' confidentiality, and that other key identifiers have been altered.

INTRODUCTION TO THE STUDENTS AND TO THE SCHOOL PROGRAM

Students accepted within the Ethiopian Students' Scholarship Foundation's (ESSF) scholarship program fit the conditions of "resilience" generally set forth by researchers: exposure to serious risk or adversity as well as evidence of positive adaptation despite that adversity. The ESSF, a UK sponsorship program operating in Addis Ababa, was founded with the specific mission to provide excellent educational opportunities for underprivileged yet academically motivated and strong students in Ethiopia, thus empowering them with the skills to help transform their country's future (www.ethiopianeducationfoundation.org).

The ESSF aims to accomplish this goal by providing underprivileged students four years of access to one of Addis Ababa's leading secondary schools, along with residential living as needed, in order to remove excess educational barriers and empower them to go on to university. Approximately twenty "severely underprivileged yet motivated and academically promising" students are selected for the program each year, after passing through a competitive selection process consisting of math and English exams, school transcript analysis, and an interview. According to the school's website, the program has educated more than 220 students over a twelve-year span, with 100 of its students currently at university.

METHODOLOGY

Qualitative research methods, with an emphasis on semi-structured interview protocols organized around themes of resilience and motivation, were utilized so as to illuminate the challenges that hindered these students' access to and completion of schooling, as well as the program-based supports that empowered them to surmount these barriers and continue moving toward fulfilling their educational and career potential. The researcher, an educational psychologist living in Ethiopia while writing a book on school-based resilience (Mulloy, 2014), had formed a volunteer consulting relationship with the ESSF, and had inquired with staff about conducting informal interviews with a few students considered especially "resilient" in terms of demonstrating educational and social-emotional success despite adversity. The purpose of the interviews was to gather interested senior students' perspectives about school program and residential supports that boosted their capacity for school success despite adversity, in order to inform the researcher's understanding of cross-cultural issues around school-based resilience as well as to inform the ESSF's continued development of social-emotional supports to boost students' academic resilience.

The ESSF's on-site manager recommended two senior students who had faced "great adversity" and who had "excelled academically" during their time at the school. These two students were first informed by the manager that they had been nominated to share their stories of resilience and then asked if they would like to participate. They were told that their participation was entirely voluntary and would have no bearing on their school performance in any way. After soliciting their initial agreement through the on-site manager, the researcher then met with each student in the residential common area, and again asked for their consent to participate via recruitment letters that explained the goals of the informal interview, the process of informed consent, and the nature of their voluntary participation. In addition to reading through the recruitment letter with the students, the researcher informed them orally that their vital first-person perspectives would be used to inform the researcher's writings on school-based resilience, as well as to inform the ESSF's efforts to weave in greater supports for students' success and well-being. These students were identified as age eighteen by the organization (due to age estimates and A-level schooling attainment), with the caveat that birth records and exact proof of age can be difficult to determine in this high-need population.

Both students expressed enthusiasm about being able to share their stories of resilience and pride in having been selected to do so. Completed transcripts were shared with the two students via email, and their consent was again sought (and granted) via email to share their perspectives both with the ESSF in the researcher's volunteer consultant capacity, and in the researcher's published writings on school-based resilience. Again, both students in their emails displayed eagerness at giving their accounts and the hope that they might one day see their stories in print.

Data collection and analysis proceeded according to grounded theory methods that involve gathering data from real-life contexts, coding it into meaningful categories, and ultimately coalescing these coded categories into a framework that explains the real-life phenomenon under investigation (Glaser & Strauss, 1967) – in this case, how school-based supports and relationships empowered high-risk Ethiopian students to successfully complete their schooling.

Before moving into an examination of how the school wove in supports that reduced barriers and boosted achievement, it may be helpful to summarize these students' life situations and states of mind upon arrival into the program.

Hagare.[1] A twelfth grader, Hagare was among the first students accepted into the ESSF program. Orphaned at a young age due to her parents' death from HIV-AIDS, she lived with an extended family member who abused and neglected her.

> *My uncle wanted me to move out – he said I caused my parents to die. He insulted me, told me I cannot study – he would splash water on me and my books. When I was twelve he locked the house while it was raining and I slept on the veranda. If I had a mother and father, none of that would have happened to me. I had no helper at all, no one that was there for me.*

When Hagare was in the eighth grade, the ESSF directors visited her school in order to solicit nominations for potential students. Hagare applied, was accepted, and soon thereafter moved into the residential hostel. She described her time in the program as a process of building trust and opening up to new expectations of what she could accomplish, ones that were quite at odds with her uncle's predictions:

> *My uncle said I'd be trash, I'd be someone on the road, I'd be a street girl, a bitch, pregnant at fifteen* (smiles ruefully). *The directors say I'll be a doctor.*

She smiled through tears as she explained the impact the program, and especially living in residence while attending school, has had on her life:

> *Living in ESSF is the thing that changed my life, the thing that made me feel like I will be so, so much better than what I am. Living in ESSF, having all these people around me who I feel care for me, especially I know the responsibilities that I had. Getting all the responsibilities off my shoulders and feeling free. I want to learn, I want to be somebody in the future.*

These reflections offer a glimpse at some of the key programmatic factors responsible for her success – a reduction in the responsibilities she faced so that she could feel free to pursue her dreams, and a network of caring and supportive people who expressed belief in her capacity to develop to her full potential.

Alemu.[2] Alemu, another twelfth grader, came from quite a different living situation – yet one that posed challenges to higher educational pursuits all the same. One of five siblings, he lived with his mother and stepfather and attended a government school that he described as:

> a difficult place to study, but my family couldn't afford to pay money for a nice school and pay for everything. In our country, most of the schools are government schools that are not providing library books, laboratories.

Like Hagare, he told how the ESSF directors had come to his school asking for teachers to select "top students" to apply to the program. With pride, he talked of how he competed that year with approximately 100 other students for twenty-five to thirty slots, and passed. Although he initially felt "kind of afraid – I was that person who's not informed about the world," he soon felt a shift.

> Now it's completely changed. I'm very happy, I'm so confident now. At the beginning I was scared. It's not only academically that I've changed. By sharing things, talking with friends, by discussing, I started building my confidence. I have many friends and many experiences with them – we shared many things like how to live life, how to manage, how to get good things where good things are found. ... I have visited my old friends, they are the same. But I think I have changed a lot.

In Alemu's reflection, we hear how his school-based and programmatic experiences boosted not only his academics but also his sense of well-being. Through his deeply honed connections with motivated students and supportive staff, he internalized a sense of confidence and happiness that helped to transform his life.

SCHOOL-BASED RESILIENCE PROCESSES

Let us begin to look more closely at the means by which this scholarship program achieved such transformations. The next sections illuminate how student participants perceived that the school laid the foundation for dynamic resilience processes by reducing their exposure to risk as well as by boosting their sense of connectedness to staff and school peers who highly value education, building their sense of confidence, and empowering them to use their talents to contribute to their communities and to live purposeful and fulfilling lives.

How the School Program Addressed Barriers and Reduced Students' Exposure to Risk. Because interactive resilience processes develop out of a positive counterbalance of protective factors versus risk factors in one's life (Winfield, 1994), the first step toward enhancing a person's resilience is to reduce the risk in their environment. Through granting students free access to a high-performing private school and housing them in a residential hostel that took care of basic needs and allowed them to focus their energies on studying, the school addressed key financial and even family risk factors that might otherwise have hindered students' educational success.

For example, Hagare's move into the hostel reduced educational barriers that included living with an abusive relative who actively undermined her schooling aspirations, as well as financial insecurity that likely would have made it impossible for her to continue her schooling past the eighth grade.

> They would give me a chance since my uncle wouldn't help me. The directors told me I'd be in a special school – a top school in the country and that everything is possible here. They told me that I will get everything I need, that the residential compound was so safe. I was so excited about the school, I was so excited because I became independent of my uncle.

This removal of barriers was essential to building Hagare's sense of safety and her readiness to open up to new opportunities and relationships that could help her move forward with her education. Similarly, Alemu described how the opportunity both to attend private school and to live in a hostel allowed him and others to focus more fully on their education and to open up to new possibilities in life.

> In our school, it's a private school where the directors were really interested to give this big opportunity to have everything. Most students living here came from difficult family backgrounds. For example, most students were working and learning [before coming here]. We got this chance to have more time and to get our human basic needs met. We get an allowance per month. Right now our work is only to study. You are free here. The only thing you have to do is reading, eating, and personal hygiene. It's so comfortable living here.

The ESSF thus reduced financial barriers for at-risk students through free education at a private secondary school, as well as providing residential living that met the students' basic needs and freed them to focus on studying. An additional benefit of residential living included the greater level of connectedness to peers who were similarly motivated to succeed – an important resilience support that is fleshed out in the following sections.

How the School Program Wove in Key Supports: Caring Connections Combined with High Expectations. In the following quotations, we read how the scholarship program fostered students' sense of connectedness to staff members and to each other, and developed a culture supportive of achievement.

Creating a Supportive School Culture. From their very first exposure to the directors and to the scholarship program and residence, students were welcomed into a community – a place where they could be surrounded by people who cared for them and who believed in their capacity.

> Even when we met for the first time, they were so open, saying welcome. We were like kids but they were respecting us. They told us to say whatever to them, whatever difficulty you can come to us. They were very open.

In addition to these welcoming messages that conveyed staff members' openness to hearing students' needs, the program structured many opportunities for bonding throughout students' days.

> We are eating together, living, studying. We celebrate holidays together, there was a party to help us bond. During TV programs we sit together and have a bond. We eat together in the dining room. We are living peaceful, like brothers and sisters. We are becoming more and more family.

Both the messages and the many opportunities for bonding helped students feel more comfortable in opening up and building trust with members of the school community. This greater sense of trust and openness laid a key foundation for further growth, especially as students were embedded within a community of caring people who helped them overcome challenges and who believed in their capacity to achieve great things.

Trust and Connectedness Lay the Foundation for Academic Achievement. Students' interactions with supportive staff created a sense of trust and connectedness that laid a key foundation for academic growth. For example, Hagare's experience of school staff members caring for her during a time of illness went a long way toward helping her becoming more trusting and open within the school community.

> I have a problem in my heart, and the doctor told me it was a psychological defect because I have a lot of stress. Sue [the hostel manager] was so worried, and told me she's here for me and she wanted to help me. I didn't trust her at first. If I'm sick, she cares a lot. Since the sickness was psychological, she told me a lot of things about her life. She's so open with me – she's more like my friend than my manager. I could trust her.

This greater sense of trust, developed through many expressions of caring, helped Hagare to feel more comfortable in reaching out for help during times of need – a key factor in becoming more resilient to life's challenges (Stanton-Salazar & Spina, 2000).

> All of them care for me. Especially Alec, he was writing me emails many times. When he was here he was talking to me about my problems. He said he would help me and not to worry about my future. I feel so comfortable, he was writing for me. Even when my sponsor didn't reply, I felt sad or neglected but I wrote Alec. When I got sick, he was so worried. He said he'd help me and I didn't have to worry about anything else. He was so happy with my grades when I scored straight A's. If people are happy for you, that's what we call caring.

Students learned to become comfortable in reaching out to others for support in times of need.

> I turn to people who are more experienced than me, like a teacher or director. Or like a psychiatrist, these people can help me. I don't want to stay in difficulty. When I say something of what I feel inside, it may be easier to deal with. I believe that. Because it's good to share with somebody, your family or your friends. They may have a solution.

By developing relationships that went the extra mile to provide students with both emotional and academic support, staff members created a sense of connectedness that buffered the challenges students faced and that laid the foundation for resilient development and academic success – as is further described in the following sections.

Students Manifest This "Culture of Care" by Caring for Each Other. Students spoke of how they absorbed and began to replicate these welcoming messages and supportive day-to-day interactions, thus perpetuating the schoolwide culture of community and respect.

> I learned these behaviors from them [the directors]. They were so open, respectful of us. I have to be more open and respectful, honest like that.

Alemu shared an example of how he took a shy student under his wing and, through his consistent care, helped him to blossom into a confident young man.

> The directors asked me to help one student – he wasn't talking with anyone. I tried talking with him to tell jokes and stories, and he became more social, more confident. For five months, I'm doing the same thing. They assigned me to change him, to be his best friend, to help him by being close at breakfast, lunch, dinnertime. Now he's confident.

Galvanized by their capacity to use their strengths to create positive change in their community, the students feel more empowered to share their unique talents in ways that strengthen their connection to the community.

> Even the directors were really surprised at our commitment and our community. We were singing, sharing our culture. We are so close. We are like family.

Most important for students' educational success, their sense of connectedness to motivated peers and to staff who believed in their capabilities played a key role in motivating them to strive for excellence.

Connection to – and Help-Seeking from – Academically Supportive Peers. Just as they have learned to be open with and seek help from supportive staff members, so too did students begin to feel more comfortable reaching out to each other for academic and emotional support.

> I have many friends at school, and three of them are attending school in America, and they know how much I am responsible, honest. They are finding me a scholarship, I am on the way. I took the TOEFL two weeks ago because the school has requirements – high school transcript, TOEFL, immunization card – to go there and attend and have [an] international degree.

This connectedness within an academically supportive network of peers enhanced students' exposure to educational opportunities and helped them internalize behaviors that built upon their personal resilience.

> One of the top students before – he was my roommate – he's now a medicine student. I follow him, I was asking him how to be good, the process of my life.

As recipients of help and support from both staff and fellow students, students spoke of internalizing behaviors that empowered them to perpetuate this supportive climate, and imbued them with confidence in their capacity to create positive change in their community.

High Expectations Linked with Goals to Help Others. Immersed in a culture of high expectations, students are challenged to use their talents to be a force for good in the lives of others.

> They gave me the award [for academics and behavior] and I felt a power, a force to help more people. That was special for me – it built my confidence and made me feel more interested to be a friend for those who are not confident and don't shine – to help them change their behavior to be like me and to be a nice man. That was special for me.

This experience bolstered Alemu's confidence, and deepened his desire to help others transform their lives in positive ways. These high expectations and imbuing of responsibility also deepened the students' sense of being connected within caring relationships and helped them internalize beliefs and behaviors that bolstered their future resilience and success.

> The directors always told me they were appreciating me. It makes me more respectful, honest, responsible – even in the future – because they always expected so much of me. I have a close relationship with them because they give me a lot of responsibilities.

Similarly, Hagare spoke of her sense of pride and confidence that developed from staff members' encouragement, especially from one with whom she felt particularly close and connected:

> They told me that I'm good and that I can be somebody who I want to be. Alec told me he will be my patient and I will be his doctor. When he says that, it feels as though I am a doctor right then – I feel too happy.

Students explained that these expressed high expectations demonstrated to students that staff cared enough about them to believe in their capabilities and imbued them with a greater self-confidence and motivation to achieve.

Expectations to Become Role Models for Their Communities. These high expectations were often explicitly tied to the students using their talents and strengths to help others, whether in their time in the scholarship program or in their future careers. Alemu spoke of how the expectations he heard from respected staff emphasized his becoming a role model within the scholarship program's community and beyond:

> The directors and managers, they expect to see me after I complete my degree to help people. They expect from me to be honest, a role model, to teach the new students.

Similarly, Hagare spoke of the staff's high expectations for her – specifically that she become a role model in both academics and behavior and that she channel her yearnings into a successful career in which she could help others.

> They expect a lot. They want me to be a role model by outshining, by having a good score, by having good behavior. In the future they want to see me be successful in any field I want to be. Since I said I want to be a doctor so many times, they want me to be a good doctor.

These expressed expectations – that students should tap into their inner strengths and talents in ways that empower them to become leaders who contribute to the larger society – had a great impact upon students, as described in what follows.

Students' Internalized Desire to Help Others and to Contribute to Their Communities. Both students spoke passionately of how they want to channel their educational success into careers that empower them to be of help others. For example, Hagare reflected on how her career goals arose out of her own deepest challenges and on how she yearned to use her talents to help other children avoid the pain of losing their parents.

> I want to be a doctor and help people. My parents died of HIV-AIDS, and I don't want anyone to lose their parents. I want to cure HIV-AIDS. It's like my enemy. It took everything I had. My confidence, happiness, love. I want to help people who are suffering from HIV. I want to help those children who lost their parents. Maybe I will build a house for them. If God says. Helping people who are where you were may make you feel comfortable. So I will do that. I have strong determination.

Similarly, Alemu's conceptualization of personal success involves having a positive impact on his family and on his country through using his talents to make a tangible contribution.

> My dream is to get an international degree and to get a good chance to get a job to change my family and to contribute to my country. I believe as a human being I have to contribute something to this world. At least for my country. Our country

doesn't have educated people. We have resources but we are not using our resources in the proper way. I have a dream to change our country, to contribute something.

Students' expressed desires to use their talents to help others seem a natural outgrowth of their embeddedness within a community that went above and beyond to provide help and encouragement to them.

THE BLOSSOMING "3 CS" PROCESS OF SCHOOL-BASED RESILIENCE AND MOTIVATION: OUT OF <u>C</u>ONNECTION FLOWS <u>C</u>ONFIDENCE AND A DESIRE TO <u>C</u>ONTRIBUTE TO THE LIVES OF OTHERS

Students' experiences at the ESSF connected them to a safety net of adults and peers who comforted and encouraged them to persist despite hurdles, imbued them with a sense of confidence in their capabilities, and motivated them to excel to their potential and to contribute of themselves to the larger community.

They help me, they change my life, trying to make me a good person. I will sacrifice myself for a good mission. Even if there is a difficult situation I will sacrifice for a good thing.

Their yearning to contribute of themselves to the larger community is indelibly interwoven with the encouragement they received from personal relationships formed during their time at the ESSF, and so the positive cycle of helping others continues to widen, rippling out through larger and larger communities.

I'm only thinking to be successful and to change my family's life and as a human being to contribute something to this world. When someone gives you something, you feel like giving for something, which is very important. I'm always dreaming to be kind, generous. They provide many things for us to be good and to change our lives. They are my role models.

Just as staff have been role models for the student, so do the students desire to become role models for others in their community.

I am someone who wants to learn, and be successful, and dreams a lot. I don't want to die being unknown. I want everyone to know me, how I passed all these challenges, how I became successful. I want to be a role model for those who think they cannot do things because of difficult times.

Moreover, just as these students have been helped, so do they desire to help others. This desire to help others also imbues the students with a sense of purpose that empowers them to live up to their highest potential.

Before ESSF, I had no helper. I got someone to help me. I think I have to help someone else. Since they were helping me, I have to help others who have lost their parents. They [at the ESSF] changed the perceptions of life for me. I thought I was alone and that I had no one. I thought I would be doing labor to survive. They helped me to think

> about my future and to feel that there is a better life, and to feel that I could be important for my society. Maybe one day everyone needs me, needs my help, needs my attention. I feel like I am living.

Even more powerfully, Hagare spoke of how her firsthand knowledge of what it means to be Ethiopian, and of the needs of her country's citizens, strengthened her capacity to make a positive contribution in the lives of her country's people.

> I am Ethiopian, and the directors are not. They want to help us – they don't know anything about us, but they think we have a good future. I can help a lot because I understand my people.

In summary, students became more motivated to strive for success because the scholarship program helped them to see not only how their talents and interests could influence the careers that they chose for themselves but also how they could use their talents to make a positive contribution to their communities, thus imbuing their lives with a greater sense of meaning and purpose – and helping them grow to their highest potential as human beings.

CONCLUSIONS

Researchers consistently note that school environments that are caring and supportive, set high expectations, and solicit student participation and voice can nurture students' resilience (Benard, 2004; Henderson & Milstein, 2003). Therein lays the foundation for the dynamic interactive processes of school-based resilience: the ESSF provided a safe space where students learned to let down their barriers, build their sense of connectedness to supportive members of the scholarship community, be exposed to messages and experiences that developed their sense of confidence in their capacities, and learned to draw upon their inner strengths and talents to craft purposeful educational and life goals that empowered them to contribute deeply of themselves to their communities.

From a social justice perspective, we can see that the ESSF's interwoven school-based and residential supports enabled these students to transcend schooling barriers related to poverty and disease, from being orphaned by AIDS to feeling pressured to quit school early so as to provide the family with financial support. By selecting high-need and high-potential students to participate in a combined residential and academic program, the ESSF addressed their basic living and safety needs and surrounded them with a community of other high-achieving students and supportive staff members, thus empowering them to overcome an array of risk factors and strive to fulfill their educational potential.

Notes

1. The case has been de-identified to protect confidentiality.
2. The case has been de-identified to protect confidentiality.

REFERENCES

Benard, B. (2004). *Resiliency: What we have learned*. San Francisco: WestEd.

Clauss-Ehlers, C. S. (2004). Re-inventing resilience: A model of "culturally-focused resilient adaptation." In C. S. Clauss-Ehlers & M. D. Weist (eds.), *Community planning to foster resilience in children* (pp. 27–44). New York: Kluwer Academic Publishers.

Glaser, B. G., & Strauss, A. L. (1967). *The discovery of grounded theory*. New York: Aldine de Gruyter.

Henderson, N., & Milstein, M. (2003). *Resiliency in schools: Making it happen for students and educators*. Thousand Oaks, CA: Corwin Press.

Mulloy, M. (2014). *Resilience-building schools for at-risk youth: Developing the social, emotional, and motivational foundations of academic success*. Kingston, NJ: Civic Research Institute.

Pereznieto, P., & Jones, N. (2006). *Educational choices in Ethiopia: What determines whether poor children go to school?* Open access publication. Oxford: Oxford University Press. www.researchgate.net/publication/46432079_Educational_Choices_in_Ethiopia_what_determines_whether_poor_children_go_to_school

Stanton-Salazar, R. D., & Spina, S. U. (2000). The network orientations of highly resilient urban minority youth. *Urban Review: Issues and Ideas in Public Education*, 32(3), 227–261.

UNESCO (2012). Global partnership for girls' and women's education: One year on (2011–2012). Ethiopia Fact Sheet. Retrieved on June 15, 2018, from www.unesco.org/eri/cp/fact sheets_ed/ET_EDFactSheet.pdf.

UNICEF. About the Convention on the Rights of the Child. Retrieved on February 4, 2020, from www.unicef.ca/en/policy-advocacy-for-children/about-the-convention-on-the-rights-of-the-child.

USAID Education Strategy (2011). Opportunity through learning. Retrieved on June 15, 2018, from www.usaid.gov/sites/default/files/documents/1865/USAID_Education_Strategy.pdf.

Waxman, H. C., Gray, J. P., & Padron, Y. N. (2003). Review of research on educational resilience. Center for Research on Education, Diversity, & Excellence. Research Reports. Retrieved on February 23, 2008, from http://repositories.cdlib.org/crede/rsrchrpts/rr_11/.

Winfield, L. (1994). Developing resilience in urban youth. *Urban monograph series*. Oak Brook, IL: North Central Regional Educational Laboratory.

Woldehanna, T., Mekonnen, A., & Jones, N. (2009). Education choices in Ethiopia. *Ethiopian Journal of Economics*, 17(1), 43–80.

20

Social Justice for Children and Young People

A Qualitative Case Study of India

Rajeev Seth, Riti Chandrashekhar, Shubhangi Kansal, and Vijayluxmi Bose

INTRODUCTION

India is home to the largest child population in the world, with almost 39 per cent out of its 1.2 billion total population children under the age of eighteen years (Childline, 2018). Given the large number of children and the adverse socio-economic circumstances, abuse, neglect and violence against children are major child rights violations and widely prevalent public health problems (Seth, 2014; Srivastava, 2012). The urban underprivileged, internally displaced street children, child labourers and rural children are susceptible to insufficient education, ill health and poor sanitation (Seth, 2014; Srivastava, 2012). Underprivileged and marginalized children continue to suffer from denial of child rights, protection and social justice.

India has the largest number of child labourers in the world today. The 2011 national census of India found the total number of child labourers, aged five to fourteen, to be at 4.35 million (Niekerk, Srivastava & Seth, 2013). The numbers for out-of-school children put out by different official sources in India show wide variations, between 6 million and 20 million (Centre for Policy Research, 2018). These children do not go to school and have little or no time to play. Many do not receive proper nutrition or care. They may work in hazardous environments, as forms of child labour or be inducted into illicit activities including drugs, trafficking and commercial sexual exploitation. Despite legislation, the prevalence of child marriage is estimated to be as high as 29 per cent amongst girls in backward districts of India (Young Lives, 2018). In addition, children in difficult circumstances such as children affected by disasters, those in conflict zones, those with HIV/AIDS, and those with disabilities and mental health disorders face major challenges in their attempts to access social justice. These underprivileged children are invisible, voiceless and ignorant about the rights and entitlements enshrined in the Indian constitution.

This chapter is divided into the following sections:

- Constitution of India and policy framework
- India's approach to the protection of child rights

- India case studies and case analysis
- Discussion
- Challenges and opportunities
- Recommendations

CONSTITUTION OF INDIA AND POLICY FRAMEWORK

The constitution of India guarantees fundamental rights to all children and empowers the state to make special provision for children. The directive principles of state policies specifically guide the states in securing children from abuse and giving them equal opportunities and facilities in which to develop in a holistic manner in conditions characterized by freedom, dignity and social justice (National Portal of India, 2018a). India accepted the obligations of the United Nations Convention on the Rights of the Child (UNCRC) in 1992 (UNICEF, 2018). Article 19 of the UNCRC underscores the rights of children to be free from all forms of violence (Child Rights International Network, 2018). Policies for children in India have been formulated in consonance with the UNCRC. The National Policy for Children was adopted by the government of India in 2013 and the National Plan of Action for Children followed in 2016 (Ministry of Women and Child Development, 2018; Press Information Bureau, Government of India, 2018). The National Policy for Children adheres to the constitutional mandate and guiding principles of the UNCRC and identifies the rights of children in four key priority areas – namely survival, development, protection, and participation. The newly launched National Nutrition Mission (POSHAN Abhiyaan) complements the Integrated Child Development Scheme that provides free-of-cost midday meals through day care centres for children under six years called *anganwadis* (POSHAN Abhiyaan, 2018).

INDIA'S APPROACH TO THE PROTECTION OF CHILD RIGHTS

The Ministry of Women and Child Development, Government of India is the apex body for the administration of the rules, regulations, and laws relating to women and children (Ministry of Women and Child Development, Government of India, 2018). The National Commission for Protection of Child Rights (NCPCR) was constituted in 2007 (Government of India, 2018). The Ministry of Social Justice and Empowerment is responsible for welfare, social justice, and the empowerment of disadvantaged and marginalized sections of society, including scheduled castes (SC), other backward classes (OBC), the disabled, the elderly and the victims of drug abuse (The Quint, 2018a).

In the past two decades, the government of India has taken several steps towards overtly advancing children's rights (Government of India, 2018; UNICEF, 2017). These include the formation of the National Commission for Protection of Child

Rights (2005), the National Policy for Children (2013) and the National Plan of Action for Children (2016), and legislation such as the Right to Education Bill (2009), the Protection of Children from Sexual Offences (POCSO) Act 2012, and the amendment to the Juvenile Justice Act (2015) to protect, promote, and defend child rights. The Child Labour Prohibition and Regulation Act was amended in 2016 and eased child labour restrictions (UNICEF India, 2018). These government institutions are required to converge and work together; however, significant gaps occur between government policies, legislation, and implementation at the grassroots level (HAQ, 2016). The political will to bring about change is often reflected in the financial planning inherent in India's budget document. However, analysis of the budget shows an alarming decline in the percentage allocation of the Budget for Children (BfC) over the years (HAQ, 2018a). Recent analysis of the Union BfC for 2018–2019 revealed that over a period of seven consecutive financial years the BfC has decreased from 4.76 per cent of the total Union Budget to 3.24 per cent of the total Union Budget. Child education was allocated the highest percentage of the Union Budget (2.25 per cent) followed by child development (0.82 per cent), child health (0.13 per cent), and child protection (0.05 per cent). In India, the central budget allocation for child protection has never reached even 50 paisa (half a rupee) out of every 100 rupees pledged for child protection. This grave resource challenge calls for a re-examination of increasing the BfC as a component of the Union Budget of India (HAQ, 2018a).

THE INDIA CASE STUDIES

Bal Umang Drishya Sanstha (BUDS) (www.budsngo.org) is an Indian registered non-profit organization formed with the objective of advancing the well-being, education, health, and welfare of children in India without distinction on the basis of caste, class, gender, ethnicity, religion, rural/urban background, or physical or mental disability (BUDS, 2018). The BUDS organization is involved in the delivery of public healthcare, prevention of violence against children, realization of children's rights and protection, advocacy, research, and comprehensive rehabilitation of orphans and vulnerable children.

Bal Umang Drishya Sanstha operates a mobile healthcare van initiative in order to reach out to several marginalized communities of India on the basis of three principles (3Ps): prevention of disease, prompt treatment, and promotion of health. The BUDS medical professionals come across a variety of cases of child abuse, neglect and exploitation. This study elaborates on two model cases BUDS staff encountered during the course of community healthcare outreach programmes.

CASE STUDIES: RATIONALE AND METHODOLOGY

The BUDS physicians and medical social workers are often the first point of contact for abused and exploited children. In such cases taking history often includes descriptions of home situations. The professionals maintain confidentiality and adhere to the best interests of the children. Interviewing children and youth requires a sensitive and ethnographic approach rather than direct questioning that might cause discomfort and evasion. Prior to conducting the case interviews, in these two model cases, informed consent was taken from the participants. Since the BUDS team is accepted by the community, we conducted a participative, exploratory case analysis so as to gain a better understanding of violations of child rights and social injustice. This narration was then translated from Hindi to English and back-checked for translational integrity. Names have been changed in order to protect identities. The verbatim description was then written as two case studies.

The qualitative cases are based on in-depth interviews wherein the medical professionals asked the respondents to narrate their stories episodically and in chronological order over multiple visits. These cases are stories of survivors in their own words. No time restrictions or analytical frameworks were used; neither was there a structured questionnaire. As mentioned, names have been changed so as to protect identities.

Robust narrative analysis can also be used to support a theory by showing how it plays out in real life (Sage, 2017). The cases that have been analysed may be termed paradigmatic cases since they exemplify certain overarching principles or help illustrate patterns that may be common. We use these case studies to emphasize the need for a paradigm shift towards a child-centric, empathic process of programme planning and an efficient and equitable delivery system.

THE CASE FOR SOCIAL JUSTICE FOR CHILDREN

Case Study 1 Salmi's Aspirations

Salmi (name changed) is now a twenty-nine-year-old woman. Salmi is the youngest of three sisters and was born in a village in Assam.[1] Salmi's mother was sexually abused, robbed, and abandoned by Salmi's biological father under the pretext that she could not produce a male child for him. Salmi and her sisters always wanted to help their mother financially and did odd jobs in order to assist her. Salmi managed to complete primary education. Salmi's oldest sister got married when Salmi was an infant. Most of her childhood was spent with her mother and middle sister.

Salmi was thirteen when she persuaded her mother to take her sibling and herself to Arunachal Pradesh – a neighbouring state – so as to meet with their married sister. Salmi's mother was approached by a family for her elder sister's hand in marriage, but the groom's family wanted a younger bride. Hence, Salmi found herself married to a twenty-six-year-old with promises that Salmi could pursue her studies as a married woman.

'They lied through their teeth and we bought it,' said Salmi during the interview. Salmi soon realized that she was a child bride married to an unemployed alcoholic adult. Although it was a physically abusive relationship, she kept her troubles to herself. When Salmi became pregnant at fourteen years of age, her in-laws forced her to abort her pregnancy since her husband was unemployed. After the abortion, Salmi's struggle for survival began. She managed to set up a local grocery store, worked really hard to understand the market, and failed a couple of times before she gained financial stability. As her earnings grew, so did the demands from her alcoholic husband.

As a child of sixteen years Salmi gave birth to her son, and she was abandoned by her husband when her newborn was only twenty-two days old. Salmi still did not lose hope; she was subsidized by her mother who sent her food supplies and money, and she learned to manage financially. 'I can't believe how I managed those days. I guess that it just was my survival instincts that kept me going,' she said during the interview.

Eleven years passed in this manner; Salmi educated her son and took care of his needs. At this juncture her in-laws deluded her by saying that they wanted to bring up their grandson. Even though she would regret her decision in years to come, she decided to go to Delhi, leaving her son in their care, and she joined a childcare institution (CCI) as a caregiver. She said, 'I wanted to make a difference in someone's life. It was never about the money; I just wanted to try making life better for my son so I thought that coming to Delhi would be a good choice.'

She later found out that her in-laws had brainwashed her son, telling him that his mother – Salmi – had moved on in life and married again in Delhi. This fabric of lies and the consequent trust deficit caused emotional and mental distress; she often felt suicidal: 'Sometimes when I am alone I look at the fan and think about hanging myself to death. It feels like the more I try the more I fail. I have been on my own for too long. I just wish I had someone in my life who would understand how I felt.'

CASE ANALYSIS

Salmi's mother was abused, robbed, and abandoned by Salmi's biological father under the pretext that she could not produce a male child for him. Desertion on this flimsy but common excuse is a form of abuse that is punishable by law and defined as 'torture, both mental and physical' (Indian Penal Code, Section 498) (Law Commission of India, 1971). Preference for sons is a big issue in most sections of Indian society; the birth of a girl is a cause of distress. It is also a form of gender-based violence (Esquivel & Kaufmann, 2017).

Salmi's childhood was spent in poverty. The problem of poverty is intricately linked to illiteracy, ignorance, neglect, abuse, exploitation, and violence in Salmi's case. The provision of social and economic justice in adverse circumstances needs urgent attention by policy makers.

Child marriage: UNICEF defines 'child marriage as a violation of child rights, and [it] has a negative impact on physical growth, health, mental and emotional development, and education opportunities' (Esquivel & Kaufmann, 2017 pp. 470–487; Young Lives, 2018, pp. 1–13). India has high rates of child marriage amongst women. According to the National Family Health Survey (NHFS) (2015–2016), child marriage has declined in India among women twenty to twenty-four years old, from 47.4 per cent to 26.8 per cent (International Institute for Population Sciences, 2016; Young Lives, 2018). The government of India enacted the Prohibition of Child Marriage Act (PCMA) 2006 and appointed child marriage prohibition officers in order to prevent child marriage. The role of medical professionals in preventing and ending child marriage is likewise crucial (Seth et al., 2018). Child marriage is indeed a major public health problem, not just a sociolegal issue. It is a risk factor for violence against girls and it can lead to death during childbirth and to non-fatal pregnancy-related complications, low birth weight, and infant mortality (Seth et al., 2018). India health indices are unlikely to improve unless child marriage is prevented (Godha, Hotchkiss & Gage, 2013; Salvi, 2009). Medical professionals can be trained to identify potential cases of child marriage and make prompt referrals to multidisciplinary teams and legal services.

Abandoning the family home in order to seek better economic opportunities in metropolitan cities is becoming a common reason for massive rural-to-urban migration. Migrant adolescents and youth can afford only the cheapest accommodation in municipal resettlement colonies and urban slums, where provision of civic amenities is appalling. Although Salmi could sustain herself, she may not have earned sufficiently or felt secure enough to bring her infant son to Delhi. This gave rise to a gamut of social and psychological problems that separated a mother from her son.

The promise of equality guaranteed to every citizen in the constitution is poorly implemented, especially with respect to migrant, displaced, and marginalized populations. Rights to education, healthcare, dignity of labour, and access to the full complement of basic rights and services should be urgently provided through efficient government schemes and integrated into provisions of economic and social justice. Despite all the government skills-building programmes and the promises of women's empowerment, the government schemes were inaccessible to Salmi. 'I had three wishes. I wanted to wear a *lehenga-choli* [a gathered skirt and a blouse], I wanted to travel in an airplane, and I wanted to get a chance to wear a pair of jeans with a t-shirt. I am twenty-eight years old now and I have managed to earn enough to make all my three wishes come true. All by myself.'

Case Study 2 Nitin, Now an Inspiring Young Adult

Jatin was born in September 1994 in Bodh Gaya, a village in the north-eastern Indian state of Bihar, as the eldest of three siblings. Today we know him as Nitin (name changed) because of an administrative error that changed his name to Nitin, changed his date of birth and gave him a new legal identity.[1]

When Nitin was about three years old his mother passed away due to a complicated pregnancy. He was left with his two young siblings and an unstable and alcoholic father who was unable to cope with the changed circumstances. Nitin's father gave his little daughter Malini to another family. Nitin couldn't handle two successive losses, and his early relationship with his father was damaged. The four-year-old Nitin and his two-year-old brother had to fend for themselves. The big Patna railway station became their playground.

'I just wish I could remember her face. I remember her swollen stomach and she loved singing; over the years I would sometimes hum this unfamiliar song which reminded me of her and when I searched for the song, I realized it was a folk song of the village I belonged to.'

Nitin and his brother realized that the primary source of income for their playmate's family was beggary. Hence, they also started begging outside temples and stations. They also realized that there was money in rag-picking and collecting discarded and lost items. The brothers started commuting in the local trains to scrounge for leftover food, lost money and sundry articles that could be exchanged for money.

'People used to ask us if we were lost or separated from our parents, but we always remained aloof, because we were scared they would kidnap us or worse we would get caught in illegal organ trafficking.'

The brothers accidentally boarded a train which took them to the New Delhi railway station about 1,000 miles away from their hometown. At the railway platform, they were found by a social worker who took them to the closest CCI. A CCI as defined under the Juvenile Justice Act of India 2015 refers to a children's home, open shelter, observation home, special home, place of safety, specialized adoption agency or a fit facility. These CCIs are recognized under the act for providing care and protection to children who are in need of such services (*Gazette of India*, 2016).

'I remember one night while we were sleeping on the train platform, a man came and tried to sleep next to my brother and cover him with his blanket. The rage I felt then still surprises me.'

Initially, they tried to run away from this CCI, but realized that life could be simpler if they stayed there. Nitin's brother (who was just three years old at the time) ran away from the CCI, leaving Nitin in despair. Nitin's best friend was sexually abused by one of the CCI staff. They were forced to work in the fields for barely INR.1,400 (equivalent to twenty dollars a month). Nevertheless, Nitin built up his courage, and with the support of a few friends, decided to run away from that CCI.

'We had less than two dollars; I and my two friends hitchhiked [and] reached another NGO [non-governmental organization]. I still feel the rejection when they told us they had no place for boys who ran away; after sleeping on the roads for a few weeks, some policemen helped us.'

By chance, Nitin found a new CCI that changed his life completely. It was at this CCI that Nitin accidentally got a new identity. With the birth date changed, on paper he was now two years older and his name was changed from Jatin to Nitin. He stayed at the CCI for most of his teenage life and completed his schooling – driven by the hope that he could be reunited with his family.

'These years were the toughest. I was severely depressed and could barely take care of myself, and I used to help people cheat in exams for money; even then monetary happiness was not enough. The only goal was to find my brother and go back home in search for my father and little sister.'

It is evident that Nitin's emotional and mental health was compromised due to adverse childhood experiences. After he received a bachelor of commerce degree he eventually became an accounts manager. Subsequently he reunited with his younger brother, whom he now supports.

'If I could live my life again, I would change nothing. I am who I am because of what I faced, and yes I sometimes feel the big question of what if? Maybe if everything was fine I would have followed the same path as my father and would have become a contract killer or alcoholic.'

Nitin's story is that of resilience over adverse childhood experiences. Nitin's grit, courage and perseverance helped him survive in difficult circumstances.

CASE ANALYSIS

Given his dysfunctional family, Nitin was at risk for maltreatment as a child due to several social, cultural and economic factors. His father's alcoholism and intimate partner violence followed by his abandonment led to severe neglect and violence in early childhood. Although the Child Welfare Committee (CWC) and the child teleline were available, no agency reached out to him for prevention and anticipatory guidance. Realizing child rights and social justice requires additional education, human resource development, training and allocation of multidisciplinary professionals (Seth et al., 2018). In developing countries such as India, with its adverse socio-economic situation and large population base, child abuse and neglect is a serious, widely prevalent public health problem. Poverty, illiteracy, ignorance and poor access to healthcare lead to considerable pressure on families, particularly in the middle-to-lower income groups, and consequently to low availability of resources for the care of children (Seth, 2014).

Nitin's father gave his little daughter Malini away. Extreme poverty and neglect lead to these social injustices. Bringing access to justice to the poor, illiterate and underprivileged is a multilayered challenge that involves many players. The problems of child abuse and neglect in India need serious and wider consideration, particularly among the underprivileged rural and urban communities, where child protection systems are not developed or do not reach. There is also an urgent need to develop and train human resources in diverse professional fields. The combined convergence of these trained professionals and multidisciplinary child protection systems can contribute to comprehensive healthcare, protection, development, treatment, social reintegration and rehabilitation of abused and neglected children.

Nitin and his younger brother took to working as street children. The compulsion to survive amidst poverty and adverse circumstances forced the two small children to work as street children. From a rights-based perspective, there can be no excuse for the existence of child labour. Child labour is a serious violation of the fundamental rights of children (UNICEF India, 2018; US Department of Labor's Bureau of International Labor Affairs, 2011). It deprives children of their childhood, their potential and their dignity, and that is harmful to their physical and mental development.

Both brothers were in childcare institutions (CCI). For migrants and street children, access to care can be provided by drop-in centres (DIC), night shelters and CCI support. Healthcare should become an integral part of rehabilitation through education, mobile healthcare clinics and immunization drives. The Juvenile Justice (Care and Protection) Act 2000 (amended in 2015) is the primary legal framework for juvenile justice in India (*Gazette of India*, 2016). It establishes a framework for both children in need of care and protection (CNCP) and children in conflict of law (CCL). Children in need of care and protection and reports of child abuse are heard by the Child Welfare Committee (CWC), which has a chairperson and four other members of whom at least one is a woman and at least one is an expert in children's issues. The CCL are handled by juvenile justice boards (JJBs), which have a metropolitan or judicial magistrate and two social workers, where one of the workers must be a woman.

Sibling separation and sexual abuse in CCI. Children are vulnerable to physical, sexual and emotional abuse and exploitation. This situation becomes acute in institutions where they have no one to confide in or turn to for anticipatory guidance. Anticipatory guidance means measures taken towards primary prevention of child maltreatment. Physicians can integrate personal space/body safety information in a developmentally appropriate manner into every annual health maintenance assessment in children from as early as three years of age. Close supervision of institutional facilities (children's homes, shelters homes, hostels etc.) is essential. A child protection policy should be in place for all staff and workers in such facilities.

Medical professionals could periodically visit these facilities with local officials and report on their conditions to the media, which can also play an educative and informative role.

DISCUSSION

This chapter describes the lives of two adults who were neglected and abused as children and analyses them from the children's rights and social justice perspectives. Set in the Indian scenario, both these cases are different and culturally diverse. The first case is of a girl who grew up in poverty and was subjected to abuse, exploitation and gender-based violence through a forced child marriage; the other case is of a boy who was born in a poor family where he was abused, neglected and exploited as a street child labourer till he was rehabilitated in a CCI. Both of these cases reveal the dark realities of a child protection system in urgent need of revamping and updating in the face of adverse childhood experiences (Centers for Disease Control and Prevention, 2018).

It is important to note that both Salmi and Nitin became internally displaced persons (IDP). At the end of 2017, some 40 million people were internally displaced globally and one third of them were children (United Nations High Commissioner for Refugees, 2018). Amongst them, street children comprise a large segment of IDP in developing countries (Nath, Shannon, Georgiades, Sword & Raina, 2016). The UN describes four types of street children: (a) children at risk; (b) children on the street, 'home based', who spend a portion of the day on the street, but have some family support; (c) children of the street, 'street-based' children who spend most days and nights on the streets with minimal family support; and (d) abandoned children. Both of our respondents fell under the category of children of the street. The goal of the state should be to reduce the vulnerability of children and youth living and working on the streets through a continuum of services which address their education, physical and psychological health, life skills, vocational development and access to social justice.

The Juvenile Justice Act (2015) contains provisions to provide for care and protection (a) to vulnerable children and (b) to children in conflict with law (*Gazette of India*, 2016). Knowledge of the law was absent in both our respondents. It was only an accident that Nitin was taken to a CCI and that Salmi got a job at a CCI. These trust deficits and access gaps may be filled in by civil society and policy makers.

Child sexual abuse, assault, commercial sexual exploitation, child marriage and child labour are major public health problems in India. Data on sexual abuse are often under-reported. The 2007 National Study on Child Abuse documented extraordinarily high rates of sexual abuse among children and youth. Of the more than 12,000 children surveyed 50.8 per cent were subjected to various forms of sexual abuse (Ministry of Women and Child Development, 2007). The Protection of

Children from Sexual Offences (POCSO) Act 2012 specifically addresses the offences committed against children (Seth & Srivastava, 2017). It mandates reporting of child abuse by multidisciplinary professionals. However, weak reporting mechanisms and management in care homes and schools make these crimes go undetected. Children carry the burden of such experiences into adulthood, leading to many mental health problems.

Both the young respondents encountered several adverse childhood experiences that impacted their development. The adverse childhood experiences (ACE) epidemiological study has established powerful relationships between child maltreatment and adverse, long-lasting health effects in adult life (Centers for Disease Control and Prevention, 2018). It is quite probable that in the near future, both these respondents might require mental health resources so as to attend to their needs (Dong et al., 2004). Our cases have shown immense resilience in moving forward despite adverse experiences. Demonstrating equity and access to healthcare, including mental healthcare, is always a challenge in the lives of street and displaced children.

CHALLENGES AND OPPORTUNITIES

There is an urgent need to develop holistic, comprehensive community services linked to programmes that realize children's rights to education, development, healthcare, protection and access to social justice. The operation of various government-sponsored schemes is seldom uniform. It is always a challenge to see effective coordination and convergence of various schemes and programmes by various ministries and agencies in charge of their implementation. It is difficult to expect the illiterates, internally displaced children and migrants to understand which government scheme is likely to benefit them. The paperwork and often the behaviour of officials they have to deal with are daunting. There are laws, but there is unequal access to legal resources. Delays in the justice system, inequities and the dysfunctional child protection system create an atmosphere of social injustice.

As multidisciplinary professionals, whether we work in the area of clinical research, public healthcare or policy, we encounter issues of children's rights on a daily basis, as is evident from these two cases of Salmi and Nitin. Children's rights are fundamental to our practice, yet they are by no means always acknowledged, respected or protected. Professionals working with and for children need to have knowledge of UN children's rights, become guardians of children's rights, support children's rights in all settings and become effective social justice advocates for children and their families.

Multidisciplinary professionals have to manifest their efforts to address child protection and child maltreatment issues. Some states have made strides in that direction (e.g., signing memorandums of understanding for umbrella schemes like Ayushman Bharat [2018]) and are giving the marginalized their entitlements;

however, this needs to be ensured by the professionals who administer and implement these schemes (HAQ, 2018b). The case studies featured in this chapter demonstrate that some deprived children and adolescents get benefits and improve the quality of their lives, if their condition is brought to the attention of social workers, community-based organizations, religious groups and philanthropists. But for many who do not come into contact with agencies that help children there is an ongoing struggle for survival and justice.

WAYS FORWARD AND RECOMMENDATIONS

Social justice is integral to the management and efficient delivery of all child-serving programmes – whether healthcare, food and nutrition, sanitation, child-friendly spaces (*anganwadis*), midday meals, education, development or protection. Neglect of national child policy and action plans incurs huge costs for both individuals and society (Raman, et al., 2017). Recently, the World Health Organization (2018) released INSPIRE, a package of seven evidence-based strategies to prevent violence against children which are anchored in the UNCRC (World Health Organization, 2018). It is an essential tool to help achieve sustainable development goals that target poverty, health, education, gender equality, safe environment and social justice (United Nations, 2018).

Medical professional societies, paediatricians and mental health and community medicine professionals will need to focus on addressing social determinants of health. Proactive and sustained/evidence-based advocacy with government, civil societies and especially professional bodies can bring about changes in the macro-environment, provide 'teeth' to law enforcement and eventually help children and young people find their rightful place in society. Every underprivileged child who is uprooted – even those within their own borders – deserves to be protected and enjoy the full complement of children's rights and social justice.

Note

1. The participants approached for this study were informed that they would be interviewed focusing on their personal experiences during their childhood. They were given consent forms and told that their participation in the study was completely voluntary. The participants were also informed that their names would be changed in the study to keep their identities anonymous. Since both the participants were in their twenties, consent forms were signed.
The consent forms signed by the participants were approved by the Institutional Review Board of Bal Umang Drishya Sanstha (BUDS). During the interviews the names of the participants were not noted. Instead the timestamp and the location of the interview were noted. This enabled us to ensure that the two accounts were kept confidential. While compiling the interviews of the participants, the names were changed to Salmi and Nitin.

REFERENCES

Bal Umang Drishya Santha (2018, March 21). About us. Retrieved from Bal Umang Drishya Sanstha: www.buds.in/about.asp.

Centers for Disease Control and Prevention (2018, March 12). Adverse childhood experiences (ACEs). Retrieved from Centers for Disease Control and Prevention: www.cdc.gov/violenceprevention/childabuseandneglect/acestudy/index.html?CDC_AA_refVal=https%3A%2F%2Fwww.cdc.gov%2Fviolenceprevention%2Facestudy%2Findex.html.

Centre for Policy Research (2018, July 20). Retrieved from Centre for Policy Research: www.cprindia.org/news/understanding-out-school-children-oosc-india-numbers-and-causes.

Childline 1098 (2018, May 15). CHILD Protection & Child Rights II. Child in India. Retrieved from Childline 1098: www.childlineindia.org.in/child-in-india.htm.

Child Rights International Network (2018, April 2). Article 19: Protection from abuse and neglect. Retrieved from Child Rights International Network: https://archive.crin.org/en/home/rights/convention/articles/article-19-protection-abuse-and-neglect.

Dong, M., Giles, W. H., Felitti, V. J. et al. (2004). Insights into causal pathways for ischemic heart disease: Adverse childhood experiences study. *PubMed*, 110(13), 1761–1766.

Esquivel, V., & Kaufmann, A. (2017). *Gender dimensions of violent urban contexts: Bridging the gaps in theory and policy*. New Delhi: Know Violence in Childhood.

Gazette of India (2016, January 12). The Juvenile Justice Act of India. Retrieved from Ministry of Women and Child Development: http://uphome.gov.in/writereaddata/Portal/Images/j-j-act.PDF.

Godha, D., Hotchkiss, D. & Gage, A. J. (2013). Association between child marriage and reproductive health outcomes and service utilization: A multi-country study from South Asia. *Journal of Adolescent Health*, 52(5), 552–558.

Government of India (2018, February 11). National Commission for Protection of Child Rights. Retrieved from National Commission for Protection of Child Rights: http://ncpcr.gov.in/.

HAQ (2016). *Budget for Children 2016–2017 not even halfway through its demographic dividend*. New Delhi: HAQ Centre for Child Rights.

HAQ (2018a, May 1). Budget for Children. Retrieved from HAQ Centre for Child Rights: http://haqcrc.org/our-work/governance/budget-for-children/.

HAQ (2018b). *Budget for Children in #NewIndia*. New Delhi: HAQ Centre for Child Rights.

HAQ (2019, January 14). Home. Retrieved from HAQ Centre for Child Rights: http://haqcrc.org/.

International Institute for Population Sciences (2016). *National Family Health Survey (NFHS-4)*. Mumbai: Ministry of Health and Family Welfare.

Law Commission of India (1971). *Indian penal code*. New Delhi: Government of India.

Ministry of Women and Child Development (2007). *Study on child abuse: India 2007*. New Delhi: Government of India.

Ministry of Women and Child Development (2018). *National Plan of Action for Children, 2016: Putting the last child first*. New Delhi: Government of India.

Ministry of Women and Child Development, Government of India (2018). *India: Third and fourth combined periodic report on the Convention on the Rights of the Child*. New Delhi: Government of India.

Nath, R., Shannon, H., Georgiades, K., Sword, W. & Raina, P. (2016). The impact of drop-in centers on the health of street children in New Delhi, India: A cross-sectional study. *Child Abuse and Neglect*, 62, 122–131.

National Portal of India (2018a, May 2). Constitution of India. Retrieved from National Portal of India: www.india.gov.in/my-government/constitution-india.

National Portal of India (2018b, October 22). POSHAN Abhiyaan. Retrieved from National Portal of India: www.india.gov.in/spotlight/poshan-abhiyaan-pms-overarching-scheme-holistic-nourishment.

Niekerk, J. V., Srivastava, R. N., & Seth, R. (2013). *Child abuse and neglect challenges and opportunities*. New Delhi: Jaypee Brothers Medical Publishers.

POSHAN Abhiyaan (2018, March 22). Ministry of Women and Child Development. Retrieved from POSHAN Abhiyaan: https://icds-wcd.nic.in/nnm/home.htm.

Press Information Bureau, Government of India (2018, January 12). National Policy for Children 2012. Retrieved from Press Information Bureau, Government of India: http://pib.nic.in/newsite/erelease.aspx?relid=94782.

The Quint (2018a, June 12). What does the law say about Scheduled Castes, Scheduled Tribes, and Other Backward Classes? Retrieved from The Quint: www.thequint.com/explainers/scheduled-caste-scheduled-tribe-obc-ebc-sc-st-prevention-of-atrocities-act-explainer#gs.kZMfoDlr.

The Quint (2018b, June 12). Who are the Scheduled Castes, Scheduled Tribes, OBCs and EBCs? Retrieved from The Quint: www.thequint.com/explainers/scheduled-caste-scheduled-tribe-obc-ebc-sc-st-prevention-of-atrocities-act-explainer#gs.kZMfoDlr.

Raman, S., Kadir, A., Seth, R. et al. (2017). Violence against children of the world: Burden, consequences and recommendations for action. *Pakistan Pediatric Journal*, 30–54.

Sage (2017). *Narrative analysis*. New Delhi: Sage.

Salvi, V. (2009). Child marriage in India: A tradition with alarming implications. *Lancet*, 373 (9678) 1826–1827.

Seth, R. (2014). Child abuse and neglect in India. *Indian Journal of Pediatrics*, 82(8), 82–88.

Seth, R., & Srivastava, R. N. (2017). Child Sexual Abuse: Management and Prevention, and Protection of Children from Sexual Offences (POCSO) Act. *Indian Pediatrics*, 54(11), 949–953.

Seth, R., Bose, V., Qaiyum, Y. et al. (2018). Social determinant of child marriage in rural India. *Ochsner Journal*, 18(4), 390–394.

Srivastava, R. N. (2012). Child abuse and neglect: Asia Pacific Conference and the Delhi Declaration. *Indian Pediatrics*, 49(1), 11–12.

United Nations (2018, May 31). Sustainable development goals. Retrieved from United Nations Sustainable Development Goals: https://sustainabledevelopment.un.org/?menu=1300.

United Nations High Commissioner for Refugees (2018, February 16). Internally displaced people. Retrieved from UNHCR, the UN Refugee Agency: www.unhcr.org/internally-displaced-people.html.

UNICEF (2017). *UNICEF annual report 2017*. New York: UNICEF.

UNICEF (2018, March 5). Convention on the Rights of the Child. Retrieved from UNICEF: www.unicef.org/crc/.

UNICEF India (2018, June 15). Child labour in India. Retrieved from UNICEF India: http://unicef.in/whatwedo/21/child-labour.

US Department of Labor's Bureau of International Labor Affairs (2011). *Findings on the worst forms of child labor*. New York: US Department of Labor's Bureau of International Labor Affairs.

World Health Organization (2018). *INSPIRE: Seven strategies for ending violence against children*. Luxembourg: World Health Organization.

Young Lives (2018, June 15). Launch of analysis of child marriage in India based on the 2011 census. Retrieved from Young Live: www.younglives-india.org/news/launch-analysis-child-marriage-india-based-2011-census.

LIST OF TERMS

- HAQ: HAQ is not an abbreviation but instead the Urdu equivalent of the word 'right' (HAQ, 2019).
- Other Backward Classes: 'Communities that have been historically marginalized in India, and continue to face oppression and social, economic and educational isolation but do not fall into the Scheduled Castes or Scheduled Tribes list, fall into the Other Backward Classes category' (The Quint, 2018b).
- POSHAN Abhiyaan: 'Prime Minister's [of India] overarching scheme for holistic nourishment' (National Portal of India, 2018b).
- Scheduled Caste: 'Scheduled castes are sub-communities within the framework of the Hindu caste system who have historically faced deprivation, oppression and extreme social isolation in India on account of their perceived low status' (The Quint, 2018b).
- Scheduled Tribe: 'Scheduled tribes are classified as marginalized communities on the basis of geographical isolation' (The Quint, 2018b).

SUGGESTED MATERIAL FOR READING

- Juvenile Justice Act of India 2015 (JJ Act of India, 2015), available at http://uphome.gov.in/writereaddata/Portal/Images/j-j-act.PDF
- Protection of Children from Sexual Offenses Act (POCSO Act), available at http://wcd.nic.in/sites/default/files/childprotection31072012.pdf
- Union Budget 2018–2019 Budget for Children in #NewIndia (HAQ Report), available at http://haqcrc.org/wp-content/uploads/2018/02/haq-budget-for-children-2018-19.pdf
- The Prohibition of Child Marriage Act 2006 (PCMA), available at http://legislative.gov.in/sites/default/files/A2007-06.pdf
- The Dowry Prohibition Act 1961, available at http://bombayhighcourt.nic.in/libweb/actc/1961.28.pdf

21

Israel

Features of Injustice in the Context of Educational Opportunities

Audrey Addi-Raccah and Moshe Israelashvili

INTRODUCTION

On a personal level, the existence of social justice is a major prerequisite for the emergence of feelings of control and personal management. On a societal level, social justice is a natural right for all society members as well as a prerequisite for building a stable democracy. Social justice can be and should be implemented along several domains, such as (1) *distributive justice* – i.e., each one gets his/her share in accordance with one's right, as defined by the accepted rule of justice; (2) *procedural justice* – i.e., the rules are equally applied once goods are allocated; and (3) *affirmative (corrective) justice* – i.e., each one gets equal treatment once complaining about injustice (Myyry & Helkama, 2002; Tyler, 2006).

The current chapter presents aspects of social justice in Israel. Assuming that education is a major component in approaching personal and community well-being, the discussion focuses especially on several aspects of affirmative justice, as implemented in the context of achieving equal educational opportunities. Following a short description of Israel's natural and human landscapes, a detailed analysis of the educational opportunities and challenges that Israeli society encounters in pursuing social justice is presented. To conclude, several interventions of different scales to promote social justice among children in Israel are outlined and analyzed.

THE STATE OF ISRAEL

Twice a year Israel's sky is covered by millions of birds flying in flocks from Europe in autumn and back to Europe in spring, searching for better weather. This relatively minor aspect of Israel's life represents a major component in explaining its past and present situation – i.e., Israel's geographical location. Lying on the coast of the Mediterranean Sea, in between Europe (to its north), Asia (to its east), and Africa (to its south), and part of the Middle East, the land of Israel has always been and is currently an attractive focal point for conquerors, merchants, and travelers. In addition, as Israel is "The Holy Land" for three major religions (i.e., Judaism,

Christianity, and Islam), one can easily comprehend why Israel is so frequently mentioned in history books as well as in current news broadcasts.

The state of Israel is small, equal in size to the US state of New Jersey; however, its landscape is considerably diverse, from mountains covered with winter snow in the north to the Dead Sea and the Negev Desert in the south. In parallel, Israel's human landscape is very rich and diverse. The (modern) state of Israel was established seventy years ago, following the Holocaust and the passing of a United Nations (UN) General Assembly resolution. The state identified itself both as a democracy and as "the home for all Jewish people." As a result, since its establishment, Jews from all over the world see Israel as their destination and immigrate to it almost on a daily basis. Many of them do so in search for personal security as Jews and/or for the possibility of practicing Jewish life daily (e.g., having kosher food). However, alongside the Jewish people live the Israeli Arab citizens, some of them living in mixed-residential areas and others in their homogeneous cities and villages throughout the country. Currently, Israel's population is composed of almost 9 million people, of which 75 percent are Jews, and the remainder comprise Muslims (17.7 percent), Christians (2 percent), Druze (1.5 percent), and others (4 percent).

Several important facts about Israel should be mentioned. To begin with, since its establishment, Israel has been in a continual armed conflict with several of its neighboring states (e.g., Syria). Hence, most Jewish and some non-Jewish citizens (males and females) are obligated to serve in the Israel Defense Forces (three years for males and two years for females), followed by approximately twenty years of reserve service. During their military service, soldiers and their families are comprehensively supported in accordance with their needs, including massive support in resocialization after completion of their military service. Thus, those who do not serve in the military receive much less support, if any at all, in their transition into adulthood. By Israeli law, two groups of people are not required to enlist – Ultra-Orthodox Jews and most Muslim Arabs. Notably, these two groups are also those with lower socioeconomic status (SES) in Israel (see later in this chapter).

Another important factor is that Israel's economy is among one of the world's fastest growing. For the past twenty years, its gross domestic product (GDP) has continually been increasing while its unemployment rate has been declining, reaching a record low (currently about 4.8 percent). One of the major factors that promote Israel's economic growth is found in its strongly developed high-technology (high-tech) industry, leading it to be titled as a "Start-Up Nation" (Senor & Singer, 2009). Likewise, a key driving force behind the development of Israel's high-tech industry is the Israel Defense Forces, which challenges its personnel and supports various civilian scientific advancements in pursuit of finding new solutions to its constant and changing security needs.

Moreover, in comparison to other countries affiliated with the Organisation for Economic Co-operation and Development (OECD), Israel has a high rate of inequality (Gini index = 0.371) (Swirski, Konor-Attias, & Zelinger, 2015). A major reason for this is that Israel's prominent high-tech industry provides extremely high salaries to its leading workers. This has implications for gender and ethnic inequality as more men than women are employed in the high-tech industry. One of the reasons for women's lower occupation rate in the high-tech industry refers to Israeli female high school students' preference to study in "intensive programs" such as mathematics or other science-related subjects. Hence, although women's employment rate in Israel is one of the highest among OECD nations, women's underrepresentation in the high-tech industry leads to their monthly income being lower in comparison to that of men.

The ethnic gap is confounded with differences in religion or religiosity, as the average salaries among the secular Jewish population, whose orientation is to study science and computation, tend to be higher compared to those of the Ultra-Orthodox Jews, who prefer to pursue a life of religious studies, as well as compared to those of the non-Jewish populations, whose representation in related academic studies is lower (see later in this chapter).

The ethnic-religious gap in salaries is prominent when focusing on poverty rates. According to a recent OECD report, poverty rates among Israel's population are relatively high, especially among the Arab population, with 8 percent of the Jewish and 28 percent of the Arab population reporting (OECD, 2018) feelings of poverty. However, these rates may be misleading, as Ultra-Orthodox Jews in Israel define their preliminary economic expectations differently (i.e., de-evaluate material achievements).

Last, the average level of education in Israel is higher than in other developed and undeveloped nations. Yet the rate of people who attend higher education is changing from one subgroup to another, with recent improvements between the two groups – i.e., the non-Jewish and the Ultra-Orthodox Jewish populations.

SOCIAL JUSTICE IN ISRAEL

Since Israel's establishment, the topic of social justice has been a major issue of concern among Israel's governments and citizens for several reasons. First, the clear bias of Judaism and Jewish history toward helping the poor and (socially/physically) disabled is not only well documented (Zohar, 1998), but also well practiced. Importantly, up to now, support for those in need has been supplied by numerous nongovernmental organizations (NGOs) (Feldman, Strier, & Schmid, 2016) and individuals (Malchi & Ben-Porat, 2018). This is true especially in times of crisis (Kulik, 2017). Second, as Israel is a society that is largely composed of former immigrants, issues related to societal gaps and social justice have always been the responsibility of Israel's government and its society's daily routines. For example, Israeli society is still greatly occupied by the need to support the relatively recent (about twenty years) wave of Jewish immigrants who came from Ethiopia. Third, Israel's diverse population and varied cultural roots make reaching a consensus (either political or social) on almost any topic that relates to social justice a real challenge (see

Factor, Castilo, & Rattner, 2014; Walzer, 1983). Fourth, due to the continual armed conflict between Israel and some of its neighbors, especially with Palestinians, many national and international organizations intensively advocate the need to strive for (more) social justice (Omer, 2013). Finally, people in Israel feel much more involved and care for their state in comparison to citizens of other nations, and hence are also more reactive to occurrences of social injustice (Shavit, Lahav, & Shahrabani, 2014).

These characteristics of Israeli society are only a few of the reasons why the topic of social justice is constantly and publicly discussed among the Israeli population. Interestingly, most Israelis are relatively tolerant to the high levels of income differences and attribute inequality to external causes (Sabbagh, Powell, & Vanhuysse, 2007). One explanation suggested for this difference between high sensitivity and relative tolerance to social injustice in Israel refers to Larsen's (2016) discussion on narratives of modernity. According to Larsen, based on the 2009 International Social Survey Program (ISSP), which includes thirty-eight countries, three "narratives of modernity" account for differences in people's acceptance of income differences: (a) the "tunnel effect" – i.e., perceptions of generational mobility; (b) the "procedural justice effect" – i.e., perceived fairness in the process of getting ahead; and (c) the "middle-class effect" – i.e., perceptions of the social structure of society and of oneself as related to the middle class. In other words, the more people in a given nation perceive their nation as enabling generational mobility, having a fair process of getting ahead, and having a large middle class (to which one belongs), the more tolerant they will be of ("temporary") income differences. Based on the 2009 ISSP (http://w.issp.org/about-issp/), Larsen shows that people in Israel are among the more tolerant of income differences out of thirty-eight countries included in the study.

Israel's youth cannot escape and usually do not want to ignore public debates regarding various aspects of social justice, especially once a question of security versus human rights emerges (e.g., when it comes to dealing with a young adult suicide bomber) (Ward, 2018). In addition, naturally, they are exposed to "normative" events of injustice, such as in the school context or with their peer group (e.g., Dar & Resh, 2003; Israelashvili, 1997; Sabbagh, Resh, Mor, & Vanhuysse, 2006). Finally, many feel injustice in terms of their living conditions (e.g., poverty), social rejection (e.g., immigrants), ethnicity (e.g., Arabs), religiosity (e.g., Ultra-Orthodox Jews), gender and/or sexual orientation, etc. For these reasons, a considerable number of Israeli children, Jews and non-Jews, may feel injustice that would lower their feeling of control over their life and especially over their future (Resh & Sabbagh, 2014).

Notably, in light of the accumulating data regarding the impact of education on well-being (e.g., Clark, Flèche, Layard, Powdthavee, & Ward, 2018), promoting social justice within the school context seems to be the most promising act for further improving Israeli children's future well-being. Hence, what follows is a more detailed analysis of the problem of social injustice in the context of Israel's educational system, followed by several examples of potential ways to bridge educational gaps.

EDUCATIONAL INEQUALITY IN ISRAEL

The educational system in Israel is subdivided into sectors based on cultural-social and political differentiations. Generally speaking, the educational system is composed of four prominent sectors segregated by nationhood ethnicity (Jewish, Arab), level and type of religiosity (i.e., within Hebrew education: secular, state-religious, and Ultra-Orthodox; within Arab education: state [usually Muslim] and private [usually Christian]), and K–12 educational settings. Indeed, few schools have students of various demographic (e.g., religion, ethnicity) backgrounds study together. In addition, due to economic-based segregations among and within communities (Addi-Raccah, Grinshtain, & Bahak, 2015; Milgrom, 2015), there are also SES differences in students' educational opportunities between sectors and schools within each sector. These differences are a major challenge to the Israeli educational system (Bar-Haim, Blank, & Sahvit, 2013). An illustration of this issue emerges once focusing on students' achievements in mathematics.

An Illustration of Educational Inequality in Israel

Focusing on students' achievements in mathematics is important for several reasons. (1) It acts as the base for other science, technology, engineering, and math (STEM) fields, which are considered important for societies' future development and sustaining high-tech innovations. Indeed, mathematics is a prominent subject in the Israeli school curriculum. Furthermore, recently the Israeli minister of education promoted a program to pursue an increase in the number of students who study in the most advanced classes ("five math units"). (2) In Israel, math is a prerequisite for university enrollment. Taking five math units gives students a greater advantage when enrolling in university. (3) Studying higher levels of math carries some benefit in the labor market as it relates with prestigious employment and higher income rewards (Kimhi & Horovitz, 2015). Thus, analyzing achievements in math would enable a bird's-eye view of the major challenges that the Israeli educational system encounters at its different levels, all the way to higher education.

ELEMENTARY SCHOOL ACHIEVEMENTS

In elementary schools, at the fifth and eighth grade levels, students are tested in low-stakes standardized tests (i.e., standardized tests aim to identify learning problems or inform instructional adjustments) in language (Hebrew, Arabic, English as a foreign language), science, and mathematics. Exploring students' achievements indicates a difference between the various educational sectors alongside consistent socioeconomic gaps within each sector. These findings are shown in Figure 21.1.

Figure 21.1 shows that students in the Jewish sector have higher mathematic achievements in comparison to those in the Arab sector. The differences between

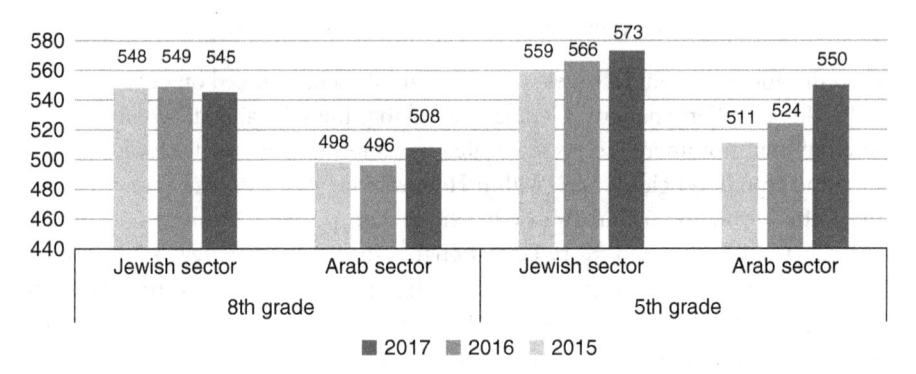

```
580 ─────────────────────────── 573 ──────────────────
          548  549  545                559  566
560 ─────                                              550
540 ─                                           524
520 ─                    508             511
500 ─              498  496
480 ─
460 ─
440 ─
        Jewish sector   Arab sector   Jewish sector   Arab sector
             8th grade                      5th grade
                        ■ 2017  ■ 2016  ■ 2015
```

FIGURE 21.1 Average of achievements in mathematics in the fifth and eighth grades by sector and year
Source: National Authority for Measurement and Evaluation in Education (RAMA), 2017b.

the two sectors are greater in the eighth grade than in the fifth. However, over the years there has been an increase in fifth grade students' achievements, particularly in the Arab sector, while among eighth graders the sectorial gap remains stable. Addressing SES differences, Figure 21.2 shows that for both sectors among eighth graders, the gap between high- and low-SES schools is greater than among fifth graders. However, within each grade level the gap between high- and low-SES schools appears to be greater for the Jewish sector in comparison to the Arab sector.

Figure 21.2 also indicates differences between Jewish and Arab schools in students' achievements, once SES is taken into account. First, within each SES school, the differences between the sectors are much smaller than those presented in Figure 21.1. Second, the largest sectorial differences seem to exist at the fifth grade in high-SES schools (e.g., 588 compared to 560 for 2017); smaller differences between the sectors were found in low-SES schools (e.g., 541 compared to 536 for 2017) or in eighth grade. These data indicate that a large portion of the sectorial differences is related to SES differences. Thus, generally speaking, it seems that factors related to SES may be more prominent in explaining differences in students' achievements in math than factors that are related to students' sectorial relatedness. The differences in Arab versus Jewish students' achievements in math seemed smaller within each school's SES level than the differences between low- and high-SES schools in each educational sector. Yet further multilevel analyses of existing data files are still needed in order to provide further support for this notion.

HIGH SCHOOL ACHIEVEMENTS

The Israeli educational system is characterized by widespread high school completion and a relatively low dropout rate. While the OECD's average

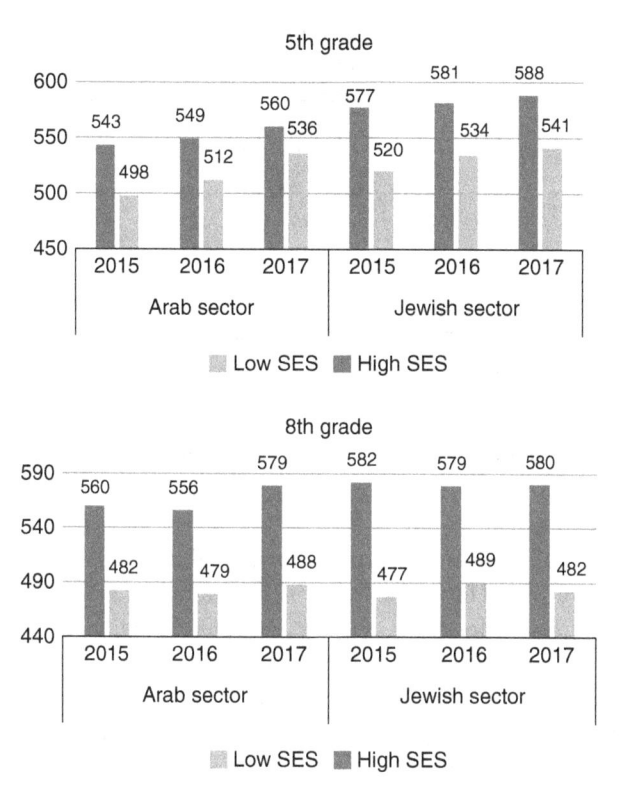

FIGURE 21.2 Students' achievements in math by years, school SES, and grade level
Source: RAMA, 2017b.

rate of youth aged fourteen to seventeen enrolled in schools is 84 percent (OECD, 2012), in Israel this rate is 96 percent and 92 percent in Jewish and Arab schools, respectively (Blass, 2017). Yet the more significant indications of educational achievements are not the dropout rates but rather the achievements in the matriculation exams, which are mainly administered at the end of high school.[1] The Israeli educational system intensively challenges its students and teachers to pursue a successful matriculation diploma. Moreover, in higher institutions in Israel, the matriculation diploma is a prerequisite for application. Notably, many researchers argue that matriculation exams serve as a mechanism for social stratification and maintaining educational inequality (e.g., Ayalon & Shavit, 2004). Generally speaking, about 55 percent of annual twelfth graders cohorts achieve a matriculation diploma. Yet, in spite of the constant and long-term efforts of the Ministry of Education, major sectorial and socioeconomic differences still exist (Table 21.1), indicating a higher rate of students in the Jewish sector, compared to students in the Arab sector, who finally earn a matriculation diploma. However, these differences are smaller

TABLE 21.1 *Eligibility for a matriculation diploma and advanced math level, by school SES and sector (percentages, 2015)*

	Matriculation diploma		Advanced (5 units) math study	
School SES	Jewish	Arab	Jewish	Arab
Low	54	49	6	5
Mid	62	71	9	21
High	80	-	19	-
Total	64	51	11	6

Analysis based on the Ministry of Education's data

within each SES school level, with even Arab sector schools having an advantage over Jewish sector schools in the group of mid–high-SES Israeli schools (see also Blass, 2017).

Currently, Israel's minister of education identifies the strengthening of mathematic studies as a major goal. This is due to the belief that failure in a math matriculation exam is a major barrier for many students approaching the matriculation diploma. Thus, the Ministry of Education aims to increase the percentage of students who study toward five math units, e.g., by investing in math teachers' education and supporting schools toward achieving this goal. Table 21.1 presents data regarding the achievement of a five-units math diploma. Unlike achievements in the matriculation exams, the data show that overall, the sectorial difference in a five-units math diploma is not large (11 percent versus 6 percent). Moreover, in relatively high-SES schools in the Arab sector, the rate of students who apply for a five-units math diploma is higher than the rate among high-SES students in the Jewish sector.

Interestingly, while the majority of students in the Jewish and Arab sectors take matriculation exams, this is not the case in the Ultra-Orthodox sector, in which most students do not take these exams (68 percent), a very small percentage of them achieve the matriculation diploma (14 percent), and only 33 percent of this sector's students study for five units in math (Israel Central Bureau of Statistics, 2017). However, note that compared to the past, in which no Ultra-Orthodox Jewish students participated in matriculation exams, these rates represent a meaningful change toward better coordination with the state educational curriculum. Should this trend be constant and amplified in the future, this change would have tremendous implications for Israel's system of higher education and, following that, on Israel's labor market.

HIGHER EDUCATION

Israel has several institutions for higher education: eight universities, thirty-six academic colleges that provide professional education (e.g., law), and twenty-one academic colleges for teachers' education. These institutions enroll around 48 percent of high school graduates. Yet enrollment in these institutions is higher for students of higher SES than of low SES – i.e., 44 percent versus 17 percent in the Arab sector and 26 percent versus 48 percent in the Jewish sector (Blass, 2017). Significant differences in enrollment exist also once sectorial differences are taken into account – i.e., more Jewish students (48.4 percent) than students from other groups: Muslims (22.1 percent), Arab-Christians (42.9 percent), or Druze (28.5 percent) (Kranzler, 2018). Referring to the matriculation diploma as a prerequisite for being enrolled into higher education, 70.8 percent of Jewish students who achieve a matriculation diploma continue into higher education versus 52.4 percent of non-Jewish students (Israel Central Bureau of Statistics, 2017). Moreover, of those who achieved a five-units math diploma, the percentage of Jewish high school graduates who continue to higher education is even greater (i.e., Jewish girls, 93.8 percent; Jewish boys, 87.5 percent; Muslim girls, 88.7 percent; Muslim boys, 69.3 percent) (Kranzler, 2018). Nevertheless, it is important to note the steady increase in Arab representation in higher education, from 8.3 percent in 2000 to 15.2 percent in 2017 (Israel Central Bureau of Statistics, 2018).

In terms of preferred educational institutions and fields of study, Arab students tend to be enrolled in academic (nonuniversity) colleges of education, while the past couple of years have brought an increase in Israel's high school graduates' enrollment into universities and academic colleges (see also Ayalon & Yogev, 2017). Arab students are also more inclined to enroll in paramedical studies (15 percent versus 5 percent) (Israel Central Bureau of Statistics, 2018), while Jewish students tend to pursue engineering and architecture (21 percent versus 13 percent). Except for teaching, paramedical studies, engineering, and architecture, in other fields of study the differences between Jewish and Arab students are relatively small. Notably, Jewish men are more inclined to enroll in STEM fields, yet achieving a five-units math diploma decreases the Jewish–Arab gap, particularly among women (Kranzler, 2018). In addition, more former Jewish students than Arab students complete their five-units math diploma after school graduation than less-advantaged groups (Kimhi & Horovitz, 2015). These examples indicate that Jewish students find channels to increase their enrollment into fields that in the long run will enable them to attain better social rewards.

Among students of the Ultra-Orthodox sector the enrollment rate in higher education is the lowest; however, their number is constantly increasing, from 560 in 2000 to 9,400 in 2017. Most Ultra-Orthodox students enroll in nonuniversity (i.e., practice-oriented) colleges, with gender differences in their fields of study – i.e., women mainly enroll in paramedical studies, natural sciences, and mathematics while men tend to enroll in law and education and teacher training programs (Alon, 2018; Israel Central Bureau of Statistics, 2018).

Notably, sustaining students from lower-SES groups – i.e., generally speaking, Arab students and Ultra-Orthodox students – in higher education is an even greater challenge, as the dropout rates of these groups are high – i.e., 38 percent among Arab males and 48 percent among Ultra-Orthodox Jewish male students who do not complete the study requirements in order to merit a degree, compared to 24 percent among men in the (more secular) Jewish sector. A similar trend was found among women, but to a lesser extent (24 percent, 29 percent, and 18 percent, respectively) (Regev, 2016).

In summary, consistently across various parameters, students who study in high-SES schools have higher achievements (e.g., on standardized tests, matriculation entitlements, five math units, enroll into higher education) along the different levels of the educational system. Such dominance of SES in explaining educational inequality is evident across the different educational sectors in Israel, including the large gaps between the Jewish and Arab sectors and the application to STEM fields in higher education. Hence, speaking about Israeli children's well-being, it seems that social justice would be better achieved once interventions and educational policies are directed toward fostering children from lower-SES groups, rather than on the basis of other social identifications (e.g., ethnicity).

OVERCOMING THE SES BARRIER

The majority of Israel's school personnel are aware of the need to pursue social justice in education, and many Israeli schools activate various initiatives meant to increase disadvantaged students' ability to succeed in their studies (e.g., Erhard & Sinai, 2012). We discuss a few examples of these initiations in what follows.

PURSUING EQUALITY IN EDUCATION

Pursuing social justice via the improvement of educational abilities and opportunities takes many forms in Israel. Out of the hundreds of cases that have been and are still being implemented, the following represents two examples.

Tel Aviv University Project to Promote Adolescents from Disadvantaged Areas

The outreach program entitled "Tel Aviv University Project to Promote Adolescents from Disadvantaged Areas" (Smilansky & Israelashvili, 1990) was one of the interventions intended to foster low-SES high school students' achievements and their aspirations toward higher education. The project ran from 1983 to 1989 and was conducted in two large high schools located in a disadvantaged neighborhood of Tel-Aviv, the largest city and the financial center of Israel. The program was established through the collaboration of the Municipality of Tel-Aviv with the Israeli Ministry of Education (Ha'Aguda LeKidum HaChinuch). The project was based on the meritocratic approach, according to which each student has an equal educational opportunity based on his/her abilities and learning efforts, rather than on his/her descriptive characteristics (e.g., socioeconomic background, race, ethnicity, or gender). Thus, the aim of the program was to foster low-SES students who were in the top quarter of their school students' ability levels to apply for higher education and succeed there. Students' selection to the program was made when in the seventh grade, based on a combined criterion consisting of three components: students' achievements in a standardized IQ test (MILTA), teachers' evaluations of students' academic potential, and students' own motivation to take part in the program. This planned program ran for five years, incorporating in total about 800 students during this time period, with an additional 200 students serving as a comparison group. Each student was expected to participate in the program until the end of twelfth grade (i.e., a six-year program). During these years the program pursued the advancement of students' positive social and personal development alongside an effort to encourage the inclusion of higher education in their future planning (Smilansky & Israelashvili, 1990). In practice, the program included several activities conducted at school and at university: (1) Peer group support – Divided into groups of twenty students led by professional school counselors, the program participants discussed "the challenge of adolescence." Issues related to their relationships with parents or peers (of both genders) were addressed theoretically and practically, including roleplaying, homework, etc. This activity was held two hours per week. (2) Critical thinking and writing skills – Special learning materials were developed for that purpose. (3) Participation in advanced English and mathematics courses – Two academic hours per week in a group of twenty students. (4) Adults' support – Both parents and schoolteachers were invited occasionally to join the meetings in which issues related to adolescence, higher education, occupational choices and family–school relationships were discussed, followed by reports on students' activities and achievements in the outreach program. (5) Enrichment courses – Each student participated in two courses on various subject matters (e.g., law, medicine, psychology, etc.) of his/her choice. The teachers were university PhD students specializing in the given field of knowledge who were instructed on how to teach adolescents. (6) Preparation for university entrance exams – In cooperation with Tel-Aviv University's dean of students, the participants in the program were enrolled in a preparation course for university acceptance (similar to the US SAT). (7) Exposure to university life – Indirectly, another goal of students' participation in the enrichment courses was to expose them to the university's campus and to other regular students as it was assumed that many of them did not have a comprehension of what university may look like. In addition to its formal components, the program aimed to increase students' sense of responsibility for their studies and future plans (Smilansky & Israelashvili, 1990). Thus, the program provided an opportunity for introspection and social comparison with peers as a means of acquiring better insights regarding personal preferences and abilities.

A follow-up study (Addi-Raccah & Israelashvili, 2014) conducted twenty years later among former participants of the project, indicated that participation in this university outreach program was positively related to future enrollment in higher education and to the acquisition of academic degrees. The program's impact was particularly evident among former students whose preliminary ability (i.e., IQ score) was average. Thus, in agreement with Yeager and Walton's (2011) argumentation, the outreach program was a type of sociopsychological intervention that changed students' mindset, thereby helping them take greater advantage of available learning opportunities and benefit from them. Participants in the project came to embrace the view that continuing into higher education depends solely on the individual's determination and achievements. Interestingly, the study findings indicated that former participants who did not continue into higher education shared an equivalent opinion. These former participants attributed their failure to finally gain an academic degree more to their own personal actions rather than external obligations. Moreover, they did not doubt or criticize the outreach program for prevailing social inequalities in higher education, although they did express some disappointment at not having studied for academic degrees.

Governmental National Plan to Achieve Social Justice in Education

At the national level, for many years there were various projects that aimed to improve disadvantaged groups' achievements, both low-SES groups and disadvantaged ethnic minorities (e.g., Arabs), from early childhood on (e.g., long school day and low enrichment, 1997; low-price lunches, 2005). Following demonstrations (in 2014) and increasing public demand to reduce social gaps and promote equality, a comprehensive policy at the elementary and high school levels has been recommended (Israel Ministry of Education, 2014). This policy aims to reduce inequality through budgetary change (Blass & Shavit, 2017). Generally speaking, this initiative suggests a new model of resource allocation, in which low-SES schools will get more resources, which should be directed to encourage students through focusing on: teaching hours; defining minimum basic standards for each class, reflecting state obligations for each student, preserving a progressive funding approach, and inevitably providing additional resources for low-SES schools. Thus, school principals may be less dependent on bureaucratic mechanisms in addition to maintaining the uniqueness of special populations in schools (such as new immigrants, gifted, outstanding, and special education students) and gradually implementing the policy within the given school while providing supervision, reflective assessment, training, and empowerment to the comprehensive school staff, with special attention given to novice teachers.

In higher education, the government encourages programs for reaching out to low-SES, Arab, or Ultra-Orthodox groups through special programs based on affirmative action (e.g., reaching out to outstanding high school graduates from low-SES peripheral areas), or offering precollege programs that may assist further in the transition to higher education.

CONCLUSIONS

Israel is a very dynamic, diverse, and multicultural society with considerable social gaps along ethnic, religious, and socioeconomic lines. Focusing on the landscape of education, the current chapter has outlined the emergence of social injustice from childhood to adulthood, stemming from the educational experiences of individuals. First, the major impact of SES on the Israeli educational system was exemplified, showing that students of high-SES schools obtain higher educational achievements along the different levels of the educational system. Second, it was demonstrated that such SES impact exists across the board, for students from the Jewish sector as well as for those coming from the Arab sector. Thus, it was suggested that the prominent claim regarding Jewish students' better academic achievement over those in the Arab sector need to be reconsidered, as it appears to be dependent on SES rather than on other explanations (e.g., ethnic orientation, social discrimination, etc.). In line with these explanations it has been advocated and proved that the sectorial gaps are narrowing, or hardly found, once we control for school SES (RAMA, 2017b). Based on this notion, it has been argued that the evolving middle and high socioeconomic groups within Arab society, which reshape and increase the percentage of its students who study in high-SES schools (Agbaria, 2016), will probably lead to more social equality in terms of Israeli Arab students' enrollment in higher education and thus achieving a better life and more positive future orientation. Referring to the current pressure of the Israeli Ministry of Education on students to study in a five-unit math program, two aspects were elaborated. First, a five-unit math diploma does create a change in students' application to STEM fields. Second, considering recent evidence regarding students' reluctance to study math in spite of their high estimation of math's learning benefits (RAMA, 2017a) – as evident especially among females (Ayalon, 2002) – a question was raised regarding the potential human capital lost as a result of the obvious pressure put on schools and students to study math at its highest level. Paradoxically, it may turn out that by placing more pressure on pursuing a highest diploma in math, Israel's educational system perpetuates inequality rather than decreases it.

Alternatively, assuming that differences in students' – and hence schools' – levels of SES will always exist, it seems that social justice would especially be reached by focusing more on affirmative (or corrective) justice. It is suggested to move away from a standardized approach, reflecting procedural justice, which refers to educational gaps as a deficit of disadvantaged groups that needs to be corrected. This is due to the fact that in this standardized approach there is a great possibility of missing learners' abilities that are not taken into account in standard measures. Rather, it is suggested to adopt a diversified approach in which there is a great amount and types of scales for measuring learners' abilities and nurture each person's development according to his/her personal needs (Arcavi & Mandel-Levy, 2014). This approach is a precise case of acknowledgment that there can be pluralist definitions of evaluation that are of equal worth (Lamont, 2012).

The general approach suggested here can be called an edumetric approach (Carver, 1974). Unlike the psychometric approach, in the edumetric approach, the idea is to explore new ways to identify those students whose abilities are not yet evident in their current academic achievements, and who may benefit from receiving additional resources. Thus, for example, an edumetric approach will pay more attention to better (e.g., gradually) integrate all students into the school system, exploring carefully their performances under the best educational conditions, paying attention to their learning curves rather than immediate learning achievements, and being more flexible in meeting their desires and general needs. Thus, it is argued here that social justice will not occur by "coping with differences" but rather by "dignifying diversities" and finding ways to enable these diversities to turn into personal capital that fosters success.

Note

1. For gaining and being entitled to a matriculation diploma, students have to take tests in the following compulsory subjects: language, literature, civic education, history, Bible, English, and math. They also select additional subjects. In each school subject, it is possible to take tests at different levels repressed by units. One to three units are considered to be of low levels; four units and particularly five units are high levels.

REFERENCES

Addi-Raccah, A., Grinshtain, Y., & Bahak, H. (2015). *Trends in socioeconomic-based residential segregation/integration in Israel*. Jerusalem: Israel Academy of Science. http://education.academy.ac.il/SystemFiles/23118.pdf

Addi-Raccah, A., & Israelashvili, M. (2014). The long-term effects of a university outreach programme: Implications on higher education enrollment. *Higher Education Policy, 27*, 111–130.

Agbaria, A. K. (2016). The "right" education in Israel: Segregation, religious ethnonationalism, and depoliticized professionalism. *Critical Studies in Education*. doi:10.1080/17508487.2016.1185642

Alon, M. (2018). Ultra-Orthodox in Israel. Central Bureau of Statistics. www.cbs.gov.il/kenes/kns_2_45_16.pdf

Arcavi, A., & Mandel-Levy, N. (eds.). (2014). *Education for all and for each and every one in the Israeli education system*. Jerusalem: Israel Academy of Sciences and Humanities.

Ayalon, H. (2002).Mathematics and sciences course taking among Arab students in Israel: A case of unexpected gender equality. *Educational Evaluation and Policy Analysis, 24*, 63–80.

Ayalon, H., & Shavit, Y. (2004). Educational reforms and inequalities in Israel: The MMI hypothesis revisited. *Sociology of Education, 77*, 103–120.

Ayalon, H., & Yogev, A. (2017). The college revolution in Israel: Does structural change influence individual choice? ISF: Final Report Grant No. 918/13 (reprint).
Bar-Haim, E., Blank, C., & Shavit, Y. (2013). Educational opportunity, employment, and income: 1995–2008. In D. Ben-David (ed.), *State of the Nation Report 2013* (pp. 233–255). Jerusalem: Taub Center.
Blass, N. (2017). *The academic achievements of Arab Israeli pupils.* Jerusalem: Taub Center.
Blass, N., & Shavit, Y. (2017). Israel's education system in recent years: An overview. In A. Weiss (ed.), *The State of the Nation Report 2017* (pp. 3–17). Jerusalem: Taub Center.
Carver, R. P. (1974). Two dimensions of tests: Psychometric and edumetric. *American Psychologist, 29,* 512–518. http://dx.doi.org/10.1037/h0036782
Clark, A. E., Flèche, S., Layard, R., Powdthavee, N., & Ward, G. (2018). *The origins of happiness: The science of well-being over the life course.* Princeton, NJ: Princeton University Press.
Dar, Y., & Resh, N. (2003). Social disadvantage and students' perceived injustice in socially integrated schools in Israel. *Social Justice Research, 16,* 109–133. http://dx.doi.org/10.1023/A:1024248003808
Erhard, R. L., & Sinai, M. (2012). The school counselor in Israel: An agent of social justice? *International Journal for the Advancement of Counselling, 34,* 159–173. http://dx.doi.org/10.1007/s10447-012-9148-6
Factor, R., Castilo, J. C., & Rattner, A. (2014). Procedural justice, minorities, and religiosity. *Police Practice & Research: An International Journal, 15,* 130–142. http://dx.doi.org/10.1080/15614263.2013.874171
Feldman, G., Strier, R., & Schmid, H. (2016). The performative magic of advocacy organisations: The redistribution of symbolic capital. *British Journal of Social Work, 46,* 1759–1775. http://dx.doi.org/10.1093/bjsw/bcv088
Israel Central Bureau of Statistics (2017). *Statistical abstract of Israel 2017.* Jerusalem: Israel Central Bureau of Statistics.
Israel Central Bureau of Statistics (2018). *Higher education 2016/17.* Jerusalem: Israel Central Bureau of Statistics.
Israel Ministry of Education (2014). The national program to close gaps and promote equity within the educational system. http://meyda.education.gov.il/files/MinhalCalcala/Ikaretochnit_%20zimzumpearim.pdf
Israelashvili, M. (1997). Situational determinants of students' feelings of injustice. *Elementary School Guidance & Counseling, 31,* 283–292.
Kimhi, A., & Horovitz, A. (2015). *The importance of the level of high school math studies to the academic studies and future careers of Israeli students.* Jerusalem: Taub Center.
Kranzler, A. (2018). Trends in higher education in Israel. Central Bureau of Statistics. www.cbs.gov.il/kenes/kns_2_45_05.pdf
Kulik, L. (2017). Volunteering during an emergency: A life stage perspective. *Nonprofit and Voluntary Sector Quarterly, 46,* 419–441.
Lamont, M. (2012). Toward a comparative sociology of valuation and evaluation. *Annual Review of Sociology, 38,* 201–221.
Larsen, C. A. (2016). How three narratives of modernity justify economic inequality. *Acta Sociologica, 59,* 93–111. http://dx.doi.org/10.1177/0001699315622801
Malchi, A., & Ben-Porat, G. (2018). Home and away: Volunteering among Ultra-Orthodox men in Israel. *International Journal of Sociology and Social Policy, 38,* 411–425. https://doi.org/10.1108/IJSSP-06-2017-0086
Milgrom, M. (2015). Economic segregation in Israel, 1983–2008. Institute for Structural Reforms. http://reformsinstitute.org/cities/#/start

Myyry, L., & Helkama, K. (2002). Moral reasoning and the use of procedural justice rules in hypothetical and real-life dilemmas. *Social Justice Research*, 15, 373–391. https://doi.org/10.1023/A:1021271108440

National Authority for Measurement and Evaluation in Education (RAMA) (2017a) *International research to assess the knowledge and skills of eighth graders in mathematics and science*. Tel-Aviv: National Authority for Measurement and Evaluation in Education.

National Authority for Measurement and Evaluation in Education (RAMA) (2017b). *School efficiency and growth indices: Scholastic achievements*. Tel-Aviv: National Authority for Measurement and Evaluation in Education.

OECD (2018). *OECD Economic Surveys: Israel 2018*, OECD Publishing, Paris. http://dx.doi.org/10.1787/eco_surveys-isr-2018-en

Omer, A. (2013). *When peace is not enough: How the Israeli peace camp thinks about religion, nationalism, and justice*. Chicago, IL: University of Chicago Press.

Organisation for Economic Co-operation and Development (OECD) (2012). *Education at a glance: OECD indicators 2012*. Paris: OECD Publishing.

Regev, E. (2016). The challenges of integrating haredim into academic studies. In A. Weiss (ed.), *State of the Nation Report: Society, Economy and Policy* (pp. 219–268). Jerusalem: Taub Center.

Resh, N., & Sabbagh, C. (2014). Justice, belonging and trust among Israeli middle school students. *British Educational Research Journal*, 40, 1036–1056. http://dx.doi.org/10.1002/berj.3129

Sabbagh, C., Powell, L. A., & Vanhuysse, P. (2007). Betwixt and between the market and the state: Israeli students' welfare attitudes in comparative perspective. *International Journal of Social Welfare*, 16, 220–230. http://dx.doi.org/10.1111/j.1468-2397.2006.00473.x

Sabbagh, C., Resh, N., Mor, M., & Vanhuysse, P. (2006). Spheres of justice within schools: Reflections and evidence on the distribution of educational goods. *Social Psychology of Education*, 9, 97–118. http://dx.doi.org/10.1007/s11218-005-3319-9

Senor, D., & Singer, S. (2009). *Start-up nation: The story of Israel's economic miracle*. New York: Hachette.

Shavit, T., Lahav, E., & Shahrabani, S. (2014). What affects the decision to take an active part in social justice protests? The impacts of confidence in society, time preference and interest in politics. *Journal of Behavioral and Experimental Economics*, 52, 52–63. http://dx.doi.org/10.1016/j.socec.2014.06.004

Smilansky, M., & Israelashvili, M. (1990). Intellectual fostering of the more gifted among socially disadvantaged. *Gifted Education International*, 6, 108–117.

Swirski, S., Konor-Attias, E., & Zelinger, R. (2015). *The social situation 2015*. Tel-Aviv: Adva Center.

Tyler, T. R. (2006). Restorative justice and procedural justice: Dealing with rule breaking. *Journal of Social Issues*, 62, 307–326. http://dx.doi.org/10.1111/j.1540-4560.2006.00452.x

Walzer, M. (1983). *Spheres of justice: A defense of pluralism and equality*. New York: Basic Books.

Ward, V. (2018). What do we know about suicide bombing? Review and analysis. *Politics & Life Sciences*, 37, 88–112.

Yeager, D. S., & Walton, G. M. (2011). Social-psychological interventions in education: They're not magic. *Review of Educational Research*, 81, 267–301.

Zohar, N. J. (1998). A Jewish perspective on access to healthcare. *Cambridge Quarterly of Healthcare Ethics*, 7, 260–265.

22

Social Justice for Children and Young People in Mexico

María Elena Figueroa-Díaz and Liliana López Levi

INTRODUCTION

Children and young people in Mexico face problematic situations that threaten social justice. From poverty and child labor to vulnerability and criminality, such issues must be addressed by civil society, nongovernmental organizations, and public institutions. Circumstances are complex in a large and heterogeneous country, where the situation in the countryside varies from the one in the city, the north varies from the south, and the boys vary from the girls. In addition, immigrants, ethnic, and social groups respond to diverse factors and have multiple ways to visualize their needs.

The National Commission of Human Rights in Mexico established the following as basic rights of children and young people: the right to life, survival, and development; the right of priority; the right to identity; the right to live in a family; the right to substantive equality and to not be discriminated against; the right to a healthy integral development; the right to a life free of violence; the right to health protection; the right to inclusion of children and people with disabilities; the right to rest and leisure; the right to have ethical convictions, thought, conscience, religion, and culture; the right to participation; the right to association; the right to privacy; the right to legal security; the rights of children and migrant adolescents; and the right to access information technology and communication (General Law of the Rights of Girls, Children, and Adolescents [Ley General de los Derechos de Niños, Niñas y Adolescentes], 2017).

The beginning of an era when children and youth rights matter can be marked in 1990, when the country established a solid legal framework on the subject, through the endorsement of the Convention on the Rights of the Child (United Nations [UN] Office of the High Commissioner on Human Rights, 1989). Thirty years earlier, in 1959, Mexico had ratified the UN Declaration of the Rights of the Child; however, not until 1990 were these initial principles applied, along with the ratification of the Convention on the Rights of the Child (United Nations International Children's Emergency Fund [UNICEF], 2018). The latter was the first mandatory international treaty that established the rights of children and adolescents with legal support. This led to important changes in the Constitution of the United Mexican States regarding the protection of children; specifically, Article 4, which focuses on children's best interests.

Prior to 1990, some policies had been ratified, such as the Inter-American Convention on Adoption in 1987 and the Convention on the Minimum Age for Marriage in 1982 (Alto Comisionado de las Naciones Unidas para los Derechos Humanos [ACNUDH], 2019). A year earlier, Mexico had also ratified the International Covenant on Economic, Social, and Cultural Rights, which includes a section on the duty to protect children and adolescents, focused on the right to healthcare, the right to education, the right to nutrition, and the rights to housing and to dress (Consejo para la prevención y eliminación de la discriminación de la Ciudad de México [COPRED], 2018; Red por los Derechos de la Infancia en México [REDIM], 2018).

Throughout the past three decades, Mexico has adhered to UN guidelines and signed international treaties and agreements in favor of social justice for children and young people. After 1990, commitments were made in matters of international adoption and in prohibitions against the worst forms of child labor, the sale and trafficking of children, child prostitution, the use of children in pornography, and minors in armed conflicts. During this time, governments and society have expressed a growing interest to engage in the rights of children and youth, although a system of children's rights is still needed.

Prohibition, for instance, has not provided a solution these problems, as shown by activists such as journalist Lydia Cacho (2010), who have worked to denounce and fight problems such as pedophilia and sexual exploitation. The state has taken responsibility for guaranteeing the survival, protection, and development of children and young people, considering their needs and their opinions and putting aside an adult-centered vision. Great efforts have been made to work on a public policy aimed to guarantee social justice for children and young people. However, as explained before, much remains to be done.

MEXICO'S COUNTRY PARAMETERS

Mexico has more than 120 million people, of which 40 million are boys, girls, and adolescents (National Institute of Statistics, Geography and Informatics [INEGI], 2015). Twenty-one million more children and young people than adults live in poverty. According to the 2015 National Intercensal Survey, 39.2 million children and young people under age seventeen live in Mexico (32.8 percent of the total population). The states in Mexico with the largest number of children and young people are Chiapas (39 percent of the state's population), Guerrero (37 percent), and Aguascalientes, Durango, Puebla, and Oaxaca (35 percent). In 2015, the population representing the most common age group was children between twelve and seventeen years old (33.9 percent), followed by six- to eleven-year-olds (33 percent), and infants, toddlers, and children from zero to five years of age (32 percent). In 2010,

60 percent of households with children had children under the age of twelve; a third of the households with children under twelve were in a situation of food insecurity, 7.6 percent for which food insecurity was severe and implied hunger. In fact, 13.6 percent of children younger than five years of age suffer from chronic malnutrition (Arellano, 2005; UNICEF, 2010).

With regard to school-age children who do not attend school, 63 percent are three to five years old, 97.7 percent are six to eleven years old, and 16.2 percent are twelve to seventeen years old (INEGI, 2015). Of these young people who do not attend school, 56 percent completed elementary education (of six years), 41 percent did not complete elementary education, and 2.8 percent never studied (UNICEF, 2010). Regarding the use of information technologies, 60 percent of children and young people have access to a computer, and 69.8 percent have Internet access through a device (INEGI, 2015). The population who is not educated is more vulnerable because they tend to be poor and have not developed basic skills such as reading and writing that are necessary in life. In addition, they are likely to only have access to low-paying jobs, and may find it difficult to know their rights and exercise them.

In 2018, 2.48 million children and young people (five to seventeen years old) in Mexico worked in the informal economy, construction activities, agriculture, fishing, forestry, livestock, or domestic service in order to pay their expenses or to help their families. Child labor is one of the main factors that leads children to not study (24.9 percent of all cases) (INEGI, 2015). According to the Ministry of Labor and Social Security (Secretaría de Trabajo y Previsión) (STPS, 2015), the minimum legal working age in Mexico is fifteen years old. However, some boys and girls work from five years old. Although there are laws regarding child labor, it is a difficult phenomenon to solve. Many working children live in the countryside and help their families in agricultural activities, fishing, or livestock work, or do domestic work and care for their siblings. Others are in a street situation (e.g., they do not have a home, they have no family ties, and they live in the street) and they work selling products in an informal economy circuit. These children and adolescents are vulnerable to violence, abuse, prostitution, and drug trafficking. Despite the legislation, it is very difficult to enforce the law. The existence of criminal organizations and the lack of education, as well as corruption and in some cases unwillingness from the government, are obstacles to law enforcement.

Child labor is a reality in Mexico that interferes with children and young people's dignity and is detrimental to their physical and psychological development. Its eradication is decisive in overcoming the cycle of poverty (Gobierno de la República, 2014; INEGI, 2015; UNICEF, 2010). There have been many attempts to solve this problem. Over the years, for instance, dangerous, nocturnal child labor has been eliminated, the legal working age has been increased, and the hours allowed for a minor to work have been shortened. As mentioned, the government has passed legislation on this matter. The prohibition of infantile work before fifteen years of age is written in the Constitution of Mexico, the Law of Work, and the

General Law of the Rights of Girls, Children, and Adolescents. Besides the work they do outside of their homes, 1.68 million children and adolescents do housework under inadequate conditions (e.g., long hours, dangerous conditions).

Working illegally undermines children's and young people's health, moral integrity, and future opportunities. UNICEF (2010) statistics show that 12.5 percent of all children and adolescents are working in Mexico. The Constitution of the Republic accepts that adolescents of fifteen years or more can work no more than six hours a day, although the full age to join normal working hours is still eighteen years. Despite this, around 36.6 percent of children and youth work before the age of fifteen. Further, about 42.5 percent of the young working population does not receive any income, either because they work to help their parents and siblings, or because they are in some situation of exploitation and slavery. Of these children and young people who do not receive income for their work, 69.8 percent are boys and 30.2 percent are girls.

Around 9.6 percent of working children and adolescents only work, 9.7 percent work and study, 27 percent work in dangerous conditions (with dangerous machinery or tools, at night, or in the streets), and 53.3 percent work, study, and do housework (63.2 percent of all girls and 55.5 percent of all boys who are five to thirteen years old, but 93 percent of all girls and 69.3 percent of all boys who are fourteen to seventeen years old). Of all girls that do housework, 80 percent dedicate more than twenty-eight hours a week to domestic work, and 12.4 percent of girls and young women drop out of school due to pregnancy (UNICEF, 2010). Table 22.1 presents data on child labor in Mexico.

With regard to violence suffered by children and adolescents, the Social Cohesion Survey for the Prevention of Violence and Crime (2014) states that

TABLE 22.1 *Data on child labor in Mexico*

Child labor	Percent
Children and young people who work under age 15	36.6%
Children who work and do not receive any income	42.5%[1]
Children and young people who only work (and don't study)	9.6%
Children and young people who work and study	9.7%
Children and young people who work under dangerous conditions	27%
Children and young people who work, study, and do housework	53.3%[2]
Girls who do housework more than 28 hours per week	80%
Girls who drop out of school due to pregnancy	12.4%

Table created by chapter authors based on data from UNICEF, 2010.
[1] 69.8% boys and 30.2% girls
[2] 63.3% girls 5 to 13, 55.5% boys 5 to 13 and 93% girls 14 to 17, 69.3% boys 14 to 17

47.8 percent of the population aged twelve to seventeen years old were victims of some crime or mistreatment (e.g., by harassment due to attributes – bullying, hurtful nicknames, lies – nonviolent and violent robbery, damage to belongings, physical abuse, and threats). Regarding sexual violence, 5 percent have suffered offensive touching (of which 74 percent were girls) and 1.8 percent have suffered rape (of which 67 percent were girls). Of the youth population under seventeen years of age, 4.2 percent had a violent death, either by homicide or by suicide.

The situation of the indigenous population is even worse. Although an expansive definition of *indigenous* is beyond the parameters of this chapter, we can define the term as the original population linked to a territory, which is assumed as a national ethnic minority who share a story about their origin, a language, and a worldview. However, the most accepted definition among the Mexican people is that which defends self-ascription: indigenous is whoever he/she says he/she is. In Mexico, 4.6 million children and adolescents live in indigenous homes, of which 78.6 percent live in poverty. Twenty-one percent of indigenous people do not even have a birth record. This means that indigenous children and young people often are not counted among the nation's population because they do not have birth records, do not speak Spanish, and live in very small communities scattered far from cities. This population also suffers from discrimination, limited educational access, malnutrition, in some cases forced marriages at an early age, teenage pregnancy, child labor, lack of access to goods and services, and geographic isolation (Heredia, 2006; INEGI, 2015).

BARRIERS TO SOCIAL JUSTICE FOR YOUNG PEOPLE IN MEXICO

If we think of social justice as an instrument for the distribution of social goods, respect for human rights, and the generation of development opportunities, we must admit that for the most vulnerable groups (i.e., children and young people), Mexico faces many barriers to achieving justice. This is explained, in part, with the fact that the full inclusion into the legal framework of this segment of the population is very recent, as is explained in the next section.

The first and most important barriers are corruption and abuse of power, both significant obstacles to social development (Alianza por los Derechos de Niños, Niñas y Adolescentes [Alianza MX], 2014), followed by polarization, meaning the gap between those who have more and those who have less. Homes with children and adolescents where no one works, where there is a person with a disability, that have four or more members, whose head of household is sixty-five or older, or that live in poverty/extreme poverty are more likely to have vulnerable conditions (Alianza MX, 2014). In the case of the indigenous population, there has been an increase in children and adolescents in low-income vulnerable households, but at the same time, there has been also an increase in access to healthcare services, which has not grown significantly (Consejo Nacional de Evaluación de la Política de Desarrollo Social [CONEVAL]/UNICEF, 2014).

Other barriers are discrimination, insecurity due to organized crime, labor exploitation, and human trafficking (women and children), as well as ethnic, spatial,[1] socioeconomic, and gender inequality. For example, 28 percent of trafficking victims in Mexico are girls, boys, and adolescents under eighteen years of age; they are poor and mostly illiterate. They are often victims of mixed exploitation (e.g., sexual/labor) (Comisión Nacional de Derechos Humanos [CNDH], 2018). Migrant children who travel alone are often victims of organized crime (Crea, López, Taylor, & Underwood, 2017), and many become agricultural laborers under a system of exploitation (Vera-Noriega, Robles, & Lunes, 2009).

Currently, Mexico is in a deep human rights crisis. Government institutions, including security forces such as the police and the army, have fallen into disrepute and the population is fearful and distrustful of them. There are also cuts to public spending that directly affect programs, goods, and services aimed at this population and achieving social justice for them.

The National Commission of Human Rights (CNDH, 2017) reports that more than half (53 percent) of the young people under seventeen years old lack the minimum conditions to guarantee the exercise of at least one right (for example, the rights to integral development, healthcare, education, judicial security, rest and leisure, freedom of expression, intimacy, and a life without violence). Their home income is insufficient to cover their needs, and in the case of the indigenous population, this figure rises to almost 80 percent.

According to the National Council for the Evaluation of the Social Development Policy (CONEVAL) and the United Nations International Children's Emergency Fund (UNICEF), 30 percent of Mexican youth are in a vulnerable situation due to low income and insufficient access to healthcare, education, and other social services. These institutions also state that the levels of poverty among the population in Mexico have not changed since the global economic crisis of 2008 (CONEVAL/UNICEF, 2014). Alianza MX (a group of twenty-three civil society institutions in Mexico) contends that public institutions do not have the capacity to resolve or mitigate the situation of children and young people in extreme poverty, and that this is evident in their vulnerabilities, which include disappearances, confinements, malnutrition, and/or lack of education (Alianza MX, 2014).

Young people contend with another relevant problem. Justice for young criminals (under eighteen years of age) is still a matter of debate. There is a need to redefine policies on crimes they commit. This problem is more serious in the case of indigenous people, because there are no clear rules for this population who have special needs (for example, translation during trials), and there are no principles for social reintegration in the case of foreign migrants (Alianza MX, 2014). Alianza MX's report confirms the direct relationship between the inability to generate foundations for social justice and the prevailing level of poverty and inequality (Alianza MX, 2014). Where there is a lack of educational access, social deprivation, and a population living in small, isolated, and scattered localities, social justice is harder to achieve (Alianza MX, 2014).

Rebuilding Capacity

Mexico has signed several international treaties and agreements on children and youth matters. Among others, the following stand out: the International Convention for the Suppression of the Traffic in Women and Children, the United Nations Standard Minimum Rules for the Administration of Juvenile Justice ("The Beijing Rules"), the Declaration on Social and Legal Principles relating to the Protection and Welfare of Children, with Special Reference to Foster Placement and Adoption Nationally and Internationally, and the United Nations Convention on the Rights of the Child.

According to Ortega Soriano (2015), not until 1980 was a paragraph added to the Mexican constitution on the need for parents to preserve the rights of their children and the necessity for institutions to protect minors. In 2000, reforms to the penal code were made so as to protect children and adolescents from prostitution and pornography; in 2001, Mexico founded the National Institute for Women, which aims to protect girls, female adolescents, and adults. Table 22.2 presents a timeline of national and international instruments of social justice for young people as related to Mexico.

In recent years, UNICEF has supported the Mexican government in various tasks. For instance, it helped design a national plan to combat violence against youngsters and was present in the implementation of protection systems in 855 municipalities in thirty-two states. UNICEF also trained 350 officials to support – legally, psychologically, and/or medically – injured children, along with training an additional 2,000 officials to support migrant children.

In 2001, a network for the rights of children (Red por los Derechos de la Infancia en México [REDIM]) was constituted. Seventy-five civil organizations that had developed programs in favor of boys, girls, and youth united to work on infants' rights in sixteen states of the country. Among their achievements were several campaigns to raise awareness about the following: violence against children and adolescents; gender violence toward girls; being in favor of nondiscrimination; improving the nutrition of children; and protecting the rights of migrant children, among other issues. The REDIM network seeks to influence political policies in order to strengthen the rights of children through political agendas that are observed by governments. It has identified the need to develop an information system that gathers data on the situation of children and adolescents so as to detect situations of injustice, including abuse and rights violations, so that it can help improve public policies that affect children and youth.

TABLE 22.2 *Main instruments of the national and international legal framework in matters of justice for minors*

Year	Name
1962	Convention on Consent to Marriage, Minimum Age for Marriage and Registration of Marriages
1973	Convention 138 on the minimum age of the International Labour Organization
1974	Declaration on the Protection of Women and Children in Emergency and Armed Conflict
1980	Reform to the Political Constitution of the United Mexican States on the importance of protecting children
1981	International Covenant on Economic, Social and Cultural Rights establishes the duty to protect children and adolescents against economic and social exploitation
1985	United Nations Standard Minimum Rules for the Administration of Juvenile Justice (The Beijing Rules)
1987	Inter-American Convention on Conflict of Laws Concerning the Adoption of Minors
1990	Children's Rights Convention
1990	United Nations Rules for the Protection of Juveniles Deprived of their Liberty
1990	United Nations Guidelines for the Prevention of Juvenile Delinquency
1991	1980 Hague Convention on the Civil Aspects of International Child Abduction
1994	Inter-American Convention on the International Return of Children
2000	Protocol of the Convention on the Rights of the Child on the sale of children, child prostitution, and the use of children in pornography
2001	Convention 182 on the prohibition of the worst forms of child labor and immediate action for its elimination
2002	Protocol to the Convention on the Rights of the Child on the involvement of children in armed conflict
2003	Protocol to Prevent, Suppress and Punish Trafficking in Persons, Especially Women and Children
2008	The Rio de Janeiro Declaration and Call for Action to Prevent and Stop Sexual Exploitation of Children and Adolescents
2011	Reform of the Political Constitution of the United Mexican States, incorporation of Article 4 on the principle of the best interests of children
2014	General Law on the Rights of Girls, Boys and Adolescents, implies the creation of the National System of Integral Protection of the Rights of Girls, Boys, and Adolescents
2015	National System for the Integral Protection of Children and Adolescents

Authors' table and elaboration, based on data from COPRED, 2018; REDIM, 2018; UNICEF, 2008, 2016; Zariñán, 2016

In 2010, Mexico participated in the Towards a Childhood without Corporal Punishment world conference, which aims to completely prohibit corporal punishment as a corrective measure worldwide, and defends the human dignity and physical integrity of children. Between 2014 and 2015, Mexico adhered to the

Declaration of Action against online sexual exploitation, which is oriented to fight against criminal groups that engage with prostitution and pornography through the Internet, as well as the use of social networks as a means to access boys, girls, and adolescents for sexual exploitation. In 2016, Mexico became a guide country for the Global Alliance to end violence against children. This effort tries to eliminate all forms of violence against children and adolescents, a task that is part of the United Nation's Sustainable Development Goals.

PROGRAMMATIC EXAMPLES

Examples in this matter come from private, nongovernmental organizations and public policies. One of the most important actions that renews the way public policy is made has been the creation of the General Law for the Protection of the Rights of Children and Adolescents[2] in 2014. From this law, then derived in 2015, the National System for the Integral Protection of Children and Adolescents (SIPINNA, 2016) was developed so that "the State fulfills its responsibility to guarantee the protection, prevention and integral restitution of the rights of girls, boys and adolescents that have been violated" (General Law of the Rights of Children and Adolescents, 2017, p. 5).

This same year a national policy instrument was proposed titled the "25 to 25" strategy. This number refers to twenty-five objectives to be achieved by the year 2025 in order to guarantee the rights of boys, girls and youngsters. Objectives are organized into the following areas: survival (health, safety, food, nutrition, mortality, early childhood development, and adolescent pregnancy); development (nondiscrimination, poverty, education, supports for indigenous populations, housing, water, and safe environments); protection (identity, life free of violence, special protection for migrants and refugees, and against child labor, promotion of justice); and social participation (digital gap, culture, sports, media).

This program seeks to satisfy various international commitments, in accordance with the United Nations 2030 Agenda for Sustainable Development. For this purpose, several indicators have been developed along with goals for each objective. To monitor this, commissions that involve several government institutions have been formed. Currently, each of the thirty-two states of the Mexican Republic has its own laws for the protection of children and adolescents. Twenty-five states also have a justice law for teenagers.

In criminal matters, adjustments to the laws have been made to treat minors who break the law with dignity and respect (Correa García, n.d.). This includes imprisoning young people only for very serious crimes, involving them in community programs, and providing the support of mental healthcare institutions as well as government social assistance agencies. There have also been attempts to renew criminal justice systems for adolescents, where topics such as the protection of privacy, legal assistance, restorative justice, reparation, protection/support, and reliability of the child's declaration are considered (Ortega Soriano, 2015, Supreme Court of Justice, 2012). These efforts are under a model of restorative justice so that young people can reintegrate into society (Centro de Investigación para el Desarrollo [CIDAC], 2016).

Other examples are the production of books and digital resources, aimed at children according to their age, published by various public institutions such as the CNDH, or by international organizations such as UNICEF.

CONCLUSION

The aforementioned efforts imply a paradigm shift from the assistance perspective to one that assumes children and youth populations as a subject of rights and not as property or inferior beings who are recipients (or not) of public social policies (López Galicia, 2016). At a regional level, there's the need to approve the laws of the states in order to establish a legal framework for the rights of children and youth and generate mechanisms to guarantee true respect and protection of rights by the institutions at different governmental levels. Relatedly, it's important to establish bilingual study programs (e.g., the native indigenous language and Spanish) in indigenous communities so as not to discriminate against the population who speaks native languages; to educate the population in terms of respect and care for children within their homes; to avoid child labor, raise awareness of children's rights to rest, play, engage in recreation and receive formal education; and to continue working to generate total access to information through digital devices and the Internet. Groups like Alianza MX, which includes several civil society institutions and academics from four universities, can make effective viable recommendations regarding these considerations, from a nongovernmental and specialized view.

The CNDH, a governmental entity accredited by United Nations and responsible to protect human rights in Mexico, and Alianza MX underscore the need to guarantee the fair treatment of youth in conflict with the law. They establish the need to guarantee the rights of these young people, whether they are in prison or not; to create monitoring committees to ensure the agreements made under the Convention on the Rights of the Child are followed; and to respect and hear the opinions of children and young people, especially in matters that concern them.

According to Alianza MX, these are difficult issues that need to be addressed and require a stronger, concerted effort. One of them is the case of child laborers, who usually migrate from the south of the country to northern states in order to work in the countryside. Many begin to work as young as age five and perform jobs such as collection of fruits and vegetables in the fields, food preparation, loading boxes, cleaning and doing household labor, where their rights are violated in multiple ways.

Other delicate matters concern human trafficking. It is not clear what actions have been carried out to detect, prevent, and attend to cases where minors are involved. It is also necessary to effectively deal with the issue of the relationship between young people and organized crime. Similarly, the case of homeless children and adolescents is a complex and uncontrolled issue that must be addressed.

In this case, thousands of children and young people live and work in the streets for different reasons: migration, social disintegration, family violence, abandonment and poverty, among others. They are exposed to labor exploitation, violence, prostitution, drugs, criminal organizations, and police harassment. This is a severe structural problem that hasn't been solved, because the programs that address it only offer some services, such as medical services, food, clothing, and places to stay overnight. But there are no further solutions.

RESOURCES

In this final section, we present a short list of current institutions and digital resources aimed at social justice and human rights for Mexican children and young people (see Table 22.3).

The Mexican government has worked to improve social justice for children and adolescents, especially in terms of signing international agreements and assuming the responsibilities that come with those. However, much remains to be done in terms of healthcare, education, integrity, security, food, and welfare. Many problems that affect children are part of structural problems that Mexico has not been able to solve, such as poverty, marginalization, violence, insecurity, inequality, uneven distribution of wealth, and large abandoned territories. These problems have recently worsened, due to the lack of effective social policies.

In other words, although much has been done, there is still a long way to go. we need to close gaps in opportunities between rural and urban populations, as well

TABLE 22.3 *Resources for social justice and human rights for Mexican children and young people*

Alianza MX Alternative reports (www.uam.mx/cdi/pdf/s_doc/biblioteca/informe_ejec_alianzamx_esp.pdf)
General Law for the Protection of the Rights of Children and Adolescents
National Commission of Human Rights (www.cndh.org.mx)
National System for the Comprehensive Protection of Children and Adolescents
Network for the Rights of Children in Mexico (www.derechosinfancia.org.mx)
New criminal justice system for adolescents (http://200.33.14.34:1033/archivos/pdfs/lib_LeyGralCuidadoInfantil.pdf)
Strategy 25 to 25. National Objectives of the Rights of Children and Adolescents (www.gob.mx/segob/articulos/25al25-objetivos-de-mexico-para-garantizar-el-ejercicio-de-derechos-a-ninas-ninos-y-adolescentes)
UNICEF Mexico Reports (www.unicef.org/mexico/spanish/)

as between indigenous and nonindigenous populations; restructure public spending in order to strengthen the resources allocated to youth development programs; and stop criminalizing and therefore discriminating against young people, just for being in this age group. For example, some people assume that low-income youth tend to be delinquents, to consume drugs or alcohol, and drop their studies or work. The goal of the aforementioned efforts is to support young people, not to stigmatize them.

Notes

1. *Spatial inequality* refers to territorially uneven conditions that result from social injustice.
2. This system was created twenty-five years after its appearance in other countries. The indicators of rights of this population are inferior to those present in Colombia, Argentina, Uruguay, or Costa Rica (25 to 25, SIPINNA, 2016).

REFERENCES

Alianza por los Derechos de Niños, Niñas y Adolescentes (2014). *Informe Alternativo al cuarto y quinto Informe consolidado sobre el cumplimiento de los derechos del niño en México*. Mexico City: Alianza MX.

Alto Comisionado de las Naciones Unidas para los Derechos Humanos (ACNUDH) (2019). Convención sobre el consentimiento del matrimonio, la edad mínima para contraer matrimonio y el registro de los matrimonios. Retrieved from www.ohchr.org/SP/ProfessionalInterest/Pages/MinimumAgeForMarriage.aspx.

Arellano, A. (2005). La población infantil con discapacidad orgánica. In T. Mier & C. Rabell (eds.), *Jóvenes y niños: un enfoque sociodemográfico* (pp. 339–372). Mexico City: Cámara de Diputados LIX Legislatura/Facultad Latinoamericana de Ciencias Sociales, Universidad Nacional Autónoma de México.

Cacho, L. (2010). *Los demonios del Edén*. Mexico City: Editorial Debolsillo.

Centro de Investigación para el Desarrollo (CIDAC) (2016). *Justicia para Adolescentes, ¿se garantizan los derechos de los jóvenes?* Mexico City: Centro de Investigación para el Desarrollo/Embajada de Finlandia.

Comisión Nacional de Derechos Humanos (CNDH) (2016). *Reglas mínimas de las Naciones Unidas para la administración de justicia de menores*. Mexico City: Comisión Nacional de los Derechos Humanos.

Comisión Nacional de Derechos Humanos (CNDH) (2017). *Pobreza, pobreza extrema y violencia contra niños, niñas y adolescentes motivan foro de análisis sobre sus derechos y la agenda 2030 de desarrollo sustentable de la ONU*. Mexico City: Comunicado de Prensa.

Comisión Nacional de Derechos Humanos (CNDH) (2018). Informe Anual de Actividades. Retrieved from www.cndh.org.

Consejo Nacional de Evaluación de la Política de Desarrollo Social (CONEVAL)/Fondo Internacional de Emergencia de las Naciones Unidas para la Infancia (UNICEF) (2014). *Pobreza y derechos sociales de niños, niñas y adolescentes en México*. Mexico City: Consejo Nacional de Evaluación de la Política de Desarrollo Social and Fondo Internacional de Emergencia de las Naciones Unidas para la Infancia.

Consejo para la prevención y eliminación de la discriminación de la Ciudad de México (COPRED) (2018). Niñas, niños y adolescentes. Retrieved from https://copred.cdmx.gob.mx/storage/app/uploads/public/5ac/7ed/c11/5ac7edc11154136176494.pdf.
Correa García, S. (n.d.). *Diferentes instrumentos y modelos de justicia de menores*. Mexico City: Instituto de Investigaciones Jurídicas. Retrieved from https://archivos.juridicas.unam.mx/www/bjv/libros/6/2680/14.pdf.
Crea, T., López, A., Taylor, T., & Underwood, D. (2017). Unaccompanied migrant children in the United States: Predictions of placement stability in long term foster care. *Children and Youth Services Review*, 73, 93–99.
Franco, E., Griesbach, M., & Rojas, A. (2011). *La infancia y la justicia en México. El niño víctima y testigo del delito dentro del Sistema Penal Acusatorio*. Mexico City: National Institute of Criminal Sciences.
Gobierno de México (2012). Cruzada Nacional contra el Hambre. Retrieved from www.gob.mx/cms/uploads/attachment/file/120919/CruzadaNacionalContraElHambre.pdf.
Gobierno de la República/Secretaría del Trabajo y Previsión Social (2014). *El Trabajo Infantil en México: Avances y Desafíos*. Mexico City: Gobierno de la República/Secretaría del Trabajo y Previsión Social.
Heredia, E. (2006). Los pueblos indígenas de México y la CNDH. *Tiempo Laberinto*, 53, 53–61.
Herrera Bautista, E. (2011). Infancia y juventud en situación de calle. Retrieved from http://revistarayuela.ednica.org.mx/sites/default/files/Art.%20Elsa%20Herrera%20Bautista.pdf.
Ley General de los Derechos de Niños, Niñas y Adolescentes (2017). Mexico City: Gobierno de la República, Cámara de Senadores, Cámara de Diputados.
López Galicia, M. A. (2016). *Una mirada a los derechos humanos de las niñas y los niños: su resignificación*. Mexico City: Comisión Nacional de los Derechos Humanos.
National Institute of Statistics, Geography and Informatics (INEGI) (2014). Encuesta de Cohesión Social para la Prevención de la Violencia y la Delincuencia. Mexico: Instituto Nacional de Geografía, Estadística e Informática. Retrieved from: (ECOPRED). www.inegi.org.mx/programas/ecopred/2014/
National Institute of Statistics, Geography and Informatics (INEGI) (2015). *Encuesta Intercensal 2015*. Mexico City: Instituto Nacional de Estadística, Geografía e Informática. Retrieved from http://internet.contenidos.inegi.org.mx/contenidos/Productos/prod_serv/contenidos/espanol/bvinegi/productos/nueva_estruc/702825078836.pdf.
Ortega Soriano, R. (2015). *Los derechos de las niñas y los niños en el derecho internacional con especial atención al Sistema Interamericano de Protección de los Derechos Humanos*. Mexico City: Comisión Nacional de los Derechos Humanos.
Red por los Derechos de la Infancia en México (REDIM) (2018). Retrieved from www.derechosinfancia.org.mx/index.php.
Secretaría de Gobernación (SEGOB) (2016). *Sistema Nacional de Protección Integral de niños, niñas y adolescentes*. Mexico City: Secretaría de Gobernación. Retrieved from www.gob.mx/segob/documentos/sistema-nacional-de-proteccion-integral-de-ninas-ninos-y-adolescentes-sipinna.
Secretaría de Trabajo y Previsión Social (STPS) (2015). Resultados del Módulo de Trabajo Infantil 2015. Retrieved from www.stps.gob.mx/bp/gob_mx/Boletin%20STPS%20MTI%202015.pdf.
Sistema Nacional de Protección Integral de Niñas, Niños y Adolescentes (SIPINNA) (2016). *25 al 25. Objetivos Nacionales de Derechos de Niños, Niñas y Adolescentes*. Mexico City: Sistema Nacional de Protección Integral de Niñas, Niños y Adolescentes.

Suprema Corte de Justicia de la Nación (2012). *Protocolo de Actuación para quienes imparten justicia en casos que afecten a niños, niñas y adolescentes*. Mexico City: Suprema Corte de Justicia de la Nación.

United Nations International Children's Emergency Fund (UNICEF) (2008). The Rio de Janeiro Declaration and Call for Action to Prevent and Stop Sexual Exploitation of Children and Adolescents. Retrieved from www.unicef.org/protection/Rio_Declaration_and_Call_for_Action.pdf.

United Nations International Children's Emergency Fund (UNICEF) (2010). *Los derechos de la Infancia y la Adolescencia en México: una agenda para el presente*. Mexico City: United Nations International Children's Emergency Fund.

United Nations International Children's Emergency Fund (UNICEF) (2016). *Informe anual 2016*. Mexico City: United Nations International Children's Emergency Fund.

United Nations International Children's Emergency Fund (UNICEF) (2018). Convención de los derechos del Niño. Retrieved from www.unicef.org/mexico/spanish/mx_Convencion_Derechos_es_final.pdf.

United Nations [UN] Office of the High Commissioner on Human Rights (1989). Convention on the Rights of the Child. Treaty Series, 1577, 3.

Valázquez, M. E., & Iturralde, G. (2012). *Afrodescendientes en México. Una historia de silencio y discriminación*. Mexico City: Consejo Nacional para Prevenir la Discriminación and Instituto Nacional de Antropología e Historia.

Vera-Noriega, J. A., Robles, J. A., & Luna, M. E. (2009). Salud mental de niños y niñas jornaleros agrícolas migrantes. In A. Covarrubias & E. Méndez (eds.), *Estudios sobre Sonora* (pp. 333–347). Mexico City: El Colegio de Sonora.

Zariñán, L. (ed.) (2016). *Ley General de los Derechos de los Niños, las Niñas y los Adolescentes. Ley General de Prestaciones de Servicios para la Atención, Cuidado y Desarrollo Integral Infantil*. Mexico City: Comisión Nacional de los Derechos Humanos.

23

Social Justice for Children and Young People in Norway

Torill Larsen, Ingrid Holsen, and Helga Bjørnøy Urke

INTRODUCTION

Norway is a small country with approximately 5.3 million people, of which 21 percent (2018 estimations) are children under eighteen years of age (51 percent are boys and 49 percent are girls), with immigrant children accounting for 7.3 percent of the zero-to-seventeen years age group (Statistics Norway, 2018). Norway is a unitary state with well-developed welfare services and benefits, characterized by a social democratic welfare state model (Esping-Andersen, 1990). This comprises a strong public sector with a broad social security system and institutionalized social rights, along with universalism as the main approach. This is supposed to provide good conditions for social justice. Despite this, Norway is facing many of the same challenges as the rest of the world when it comes to protecting and facilitating a safe and just upbringing for children and young people. This chapter sheds light on: (1) some challenges in Norwegian society with regard to child welfare, youth delinquency, violence, mental health, child poverty, social inequalities, and education; (2) societal conditions for promoting social justice; (3) societal capacity for promoting positive mental health; and (4) examples of policies, actions, and programs in place.

CHALLENGES IN NORWAY AND IN NORWEGIAN SOCIETY

Concerning child welfare, an increasing number of families are in contact with the child welfare system, of which many have received support for several years. In 2010, 37,500 children and young people received measures (e.g., counseling, advisory services, aid measures, external support contacts, relief measures in the home like access to day care, institutional, or foster care placement) from the child welfare system, while, in 2015, the number rose to 53,440. Every fourth child (zero to eighteen years) receiving measures had an immigrant background. A comprehensive study of the coping capacity of adults who received such measures when they were children shows that they are significantly worse off than the rest of the population in areas such as education, unemployment, disability, income, and the use of social support schemes (Statistics Norway, 2016).

When we take into account population growth, in terms of young delinquents, after 2007, the number of penalties decreased across all age groups under the age of twenty-five years. This trend was repeated in 2015. To prevent further negative effects on young defenders, it has been an aim for the authorities that the prosecutor should change practice from imposing a court order to handing down a conditional sentence. Consequently, the court now largely applies community sanctions in serious criminal cases, and imposes far fewer prison sentences and rarely unconditional imprisonment. Very few persons under the age of eighteen are imprisoned. However, young people are clearly overrepresented among those punished for crimes, a situation that applies to both sexes. The proportion is greatest among men in the age range from nineteen to twenty-one years, where about 3 percent are registered as having been punished for one or more crimes in 2014 (Engvik, 2018). The punishment of the youngest age groups has changed considerably over time. Of all registered sentences given to fifteen- to seventeen-year-olds, nearly 40 percent were conditional. Forty-eight verdicts were reached relating to youth punishments in 2015. This new type of punishment requires the court to determine the duration of the sentence, while the content of the sentence, in terms of actions and conditions, is determined at a meeting under the guidance of the Conflict Council (Engvik, 2018). This procedure seems to offer important steps in rehabilitation and prevents further involvement in the criminal justice system.

Violence against women and children is still a major concern in society, with 4,550 individuals registered as victims of ill treatment within the context of close relationships in 2016, representing a 4.7 percent increase from the year before (Drager, Sten, & Fossanger, 2017). Following the new law on family abuse (from 2006), there has also been a redistribution in the registration of types of violent offenses, with an increase in reported cases of abuse in family relationships. Especially, the number of registered victims of abuse in family relationships increased in the years 2010–2013, by more than 30 percent. This occurred because more children and adolescents are registered as victims of family violence cases. In other words, from being an almost nonexistent group in the violence reports in the years before 2006, the new and improved documentation of offenses along with police practices – especially in recent years – have made children a visible and significant group among victims of violence in today's crime statistics. Among the victims of this type of violence in 2016, nearly 3,000 were aged zero to nineteen years, representing a threefold increase compared to 2010. The trend of an ever-increasing number of children and young people registered as victims continued throughout 2016. The statistics related to sexual abuse show that, by 2016, two-thirds of sexual abuse victims were under the age of eighteen at the time of the act (Drager et al., 2017). As both violence and sexual abuse remain a taboo topic to discuss or report to the police, it is reasonable to assume that a significant amount of underreporting occurs in this area. However, the law from 2006 seems to have had a positive effect on the numbers of reports.

The figures for child poverty and social inequality show that the proportion of children growing up in families with persistent low income increased from 8 percent in 2012 to 8.6 percent in 2013 (relative measures based on household incomes lower than 60 percent of the median income in Norway). Children from an immigrant background account for more than half of all children in economically disadvantaged families (Epland & Kirkeberg, 2015). However, compared to other European countries, children in the Nordic countries have a lower poverty risk. In most other European countries, the likelihood that children belong to a low-income group compared to adults is greater. In the Nordic countries, Iceland has the lowest proportion of children under the age of eighteen living in poverty at 10 percent, followed by Norway with 11 percent (Statistics Norway, 2011). One in every ten families with low income or with a single-parent household receives assistance through social support schemes. Fourteen percent of single parents and 8 percent of low-income families receive housing support. Among all couples with children, the share for both (housing and social) support schemes is 2 percent. Low-income families also receive cash benefits and unemployment benefit payments. In 2014, the proportion of low-income families receiving cash and unemployment benefits was twice as high (17 and 23 percent, respectively) as the corresponding share for all couples with children (9 and 11 percent). Low-income families and single parents have lower educational levels and less stable employment; they are also more likely to be the recipients of different social support schemes compared to other couples with children (Normann, 2016). A major challenge for these groups is that the labor market has become specialized, leaving fewer jobs available for people without education.

How to break this vicious circle is on the political agenda in Norway, with the discussion centering on redistribution of economic resources, a more inclusive labor market, early interventions for children, and family strengthening and support.

Likewise, mental health problems and disability pensions among young people are increasing. The proportion of mental health problems is highest among girls, but the latest national survey among young people shows that, in 2017, an increasing number of boys reported such problems (Bakken, 2017). Figures from the Norwegian Institute of Public Health (NIPH) also show an increasing use of antidepressants among young girls (NIPH, 2014). In recent years, we have seen a rise in the number of young people receiving disability pensions (Lunde, 2013). The number of young people with a disability has tripled over the past thirty years; for example, in 2011, 9,221 young people aged eighteen to twenty-nine years received disability pensions, which is a 17 percent increase from the previous year (Lunde, 2013). More young men than young women have a disability due to mental health problems. Since 2007, there has been a tendency toward larger numbers of new disability pension recipients each year (incidence), especially among younger women (Bragstad, Ellingsen, & Lindbøl, 2012). Six out of ten have a disability because of problems such as anxiety and depression or severe mental illness such as psychosis and schizophrenia (Lunde, 2013). In terms of the overall population with a disability, young people make up only a small percentage, but the numbers have increased due to earlier diagnosis. The level of mental health problems is a major concern for individuals as well as society as a whole. From a life course perspective, insufficient basic support for children and young people will influence their health, living conditions, and societal participation at later stages in their lives.

The right to education is an important prerequisite for social justice. As attending school is compulsory for all children in Norway, schools are therefore central institutions in the lives of children and young people and seen as important arenas for leveling out inequalities and stimulating positive development. Nevertheless, we see that schools are reproducing inequalities, and figures show a clear correlation between the educational level of the parents and the children's education, despite the fact that there is a clear goal for education to be accessible to all with a focus on social equalization (Dahl, Bergsli, & van der Wel, 2014). Of special concern is the dropout rate from upper secondary education. About 30 percent of students fail to complete upper secondary school within three years, and many of the young people who drop out have mental health problems or illnesses (Lillejord et al., 2015; Lunde, 2013). In response, school authorities nationwide have introduced new strict absentee reports, so that in the past two years the dropout rate has decreased from approximately 30 percent to about 20 percent, but the rate is still high. This group is at risk of being excluded from the workforce with negative consequences for the future.

In summary, all these challenges are interrelated, given that an upbringing characterized by significant social and economic problems can reduce children's ability to develop physically, mentally, and socially. It can also lead to understimulation and deficient language development, which in turn can result in weak school-based skills and poor self-esteem fostered by underperformance. It also appears that mental health and education are factors that are strongly related to all aspects of social justice. Taken together, this picture underscores the fact that social justice for all children is an everyday challenge in Norway.

SOCIETAL CONDITIONS FOR PROMOTING SOCIAL JUSTICE

Compared to other countries, Norway should have robust conditions for promoting social justice due to its fundamental welfare state ideas. The country has also been in the forefront in recognizing international conventions on humanitarianism, solidarity, equal rights and opportunities, and justice (Aadnesen & Hærem, 2007). In addition, laws and regulations are typically informed by principles of prioritizing the best interests of children, treating them as proper legitimate participants in society and embracing the notion of children as important social agents (Hollekim, Anderssen, & Daniel, 2016). The status of the child is also reflected in the relatively early recognition of various legal rights for children. Physical punishment of children by parents was made illegal in 1987, while an ombudsman for children (Department for Children and Equity) was established as early as 1981. The United Nations (UN) Convention on the Rights of the Child has, since 2003, been integrated into the Norwegian Human Rights Act and is given priority when conflicting with other policies or legislations (Hollekim et al., 2016). In addition, the Norwegian school system must secure equal rights for every child, independent of social class, gender, age, religion, or ethnicity. These core values are based on the United Nations Educational, Scientific and Cultural Organization's (UNESCO, 1994) Salamanca Statement and the UN Convention on the Rights of Persons with Disabilities. The latter was ratified in Norway in 2013 (Danielsen, 2017).

Furthermore, our welfare reforms have historically been pursued in the name of equality, with the core aim of all welfare policies being social security and income maintenance, without explicitly seeking to reshape the class structure within society by leveling out the gradient in social inequality. We now have access to data showing that raising the health status of less privileged socioeconomic groups to the level of more privileged groups needs to be a key objective in all international, national, and local health policies (Marmot, 2013). However, not until the last decades of the twentieth century did it become possible to detect a policy shift in favor of leveling out the gradient in inequality. These new policies have been implemented primarily through education reforms and efforts to reduce child poverty, but also through policies aimed at supporting female employment and gender equality (Esping-Andersen, 2015), as well as the new Public Health Act (2012). In Norwegian public health policy, a central objective is to reduce social inequalities without affecting the health status of anyone in a negative way. Yet, as presented previously, social inequalities can be observed in Norway, and, for some population groups, such as immigrants, social inequalities are in fact increasing (Dahl et al., 2014; Norwegian Directorate for Children, Youth and Family Affairs, 2017). We know that public expenditure linked to mitigating the effects of adverse development and facilitating positive development at an early age will be much more effective than attempting to deal with the consequences of social inequalities later on in a person's life.

Nevertheless, it remains a challenge to shift the focus and the money needed onto prevention and health-promoting efforts. The cost of mental health problems, in 2009, was estimated to be NOK 60–70 billion per year, which exceeded the costs associated with all other diseases (Ministry of Finance, 2009–2010), confirming that prevention is not only necessary in terms of health outcomes but also beneficial to the economy. Likewise, the number of young people on disability pensions is increasing. By April 2018, it was as high as 1.7 percent of the eighteen to twenty-nine years age group and 4 percent of the total population (Statistics Norway, 2018). Undermining the inability of large groups of children and young people to achieve their full potential in terms of mental, physical, and social well-being will lead to losses that societies cannot afford.

We know that the mental health and success of young people are determined by a balance between the settings in which they are raised (e.g., families, schools, and neighborhoods) and the strengths and vulnerabilities they bring to those settings (World Health Organization [WHO], 2014). Nevertheless, it seems fair to state that, although we have knowledge about how to promote mental health, applying this knowledge in practice is still lacking. This is linked to the political will to allocate the resources needed and for professions to change their perspective from disease and risk to more prevention with positive outcomes. Indeed, evidence supports the need for a shift in focus that moves beyond a negative view of young people toward an emphasis on the strengths, positive qualities, and outcomes that we wish them to develop. There is also a need for a critical mass of policy makers, researchers, public services, and practice to advance a shift in the paradigm from deficits to resources. In this regard, the challenge remains of encouraging policy makers, public services, researchers, school leaders, and teachers to embrace this perspective and create opportunities for children and young people to be advocates and influencers by becoming involved in articulating needs as policies are developed (WHO, 2014).

As schools (and kindergartens) are central institutions in the life of children and young people, these are important arenas, if not the most important arenas, for creating robust conditions for positive development, promoting a safe and secure learning environment, and facilitating engagement and participation. Norwegian authorities have an explicit goal of reducing the dropout rate from upper secondary education (Lillejord et al., 2015), as implementing measures to prevent school dropout rates is necessary for both economic and humanitarian reasons. Research shows a clear relationship between mental illness and absence and dropout rates among pupils in upper secondary education (Anvik & Gustavsen, 2012; Markussen & Seland, 2012). This is of concern to individuals and to society as a whole. Up to 50 percent of mental disorders have their onset during adolescence, and mental health problems can be identified in between 10 and 20 percent of young people, with even higher rates among disadvantaged population groups (NIPH, 2014; Reiss, 2013). Adolescence is therefore regarded as a crucial age for the prevention of mental health problems and the promotion of well-being. Young people who experience connectedness, feel a sense of community and social support, and engage in their schools and communities are less likely to use drugs and alcohol, less likely to drop out of high school, less likely to become involved in criminal behavior, and more likely to experience better mental health (Scales et al., 2016).

However, schools are part of the larger context of communities, and a sense of belonging and connectedness to both the community and school are fundamental to positive mental health and functioning (Putnam, 2016; I. Sarason, 2013). Feeling connected to one's community provides a sense of common good and allows people to recognize the important role they can play in the positive development of their surroundings and the society. A psychological sense of community is seen as the perception of similarity and interdependence with others, a reciprocity of expectations and willingness to giving to or doing for others what one expects from them, and the feeling that one is part of a larger dependable and stable structure (S. Sarason, 1974).

As the context for promoting mental health is important, both interdisciplinary and cross-sector cooperation is necessary. We need policies that facilitate better cooperation and more holistic approaches to improving the conditions in which children and young people are brought up, as well as acknowledging the interplay between individuals and their everyday context. According to WHO (2014), a paradigm shift is needed within mental health promotion that is more focused on structures and systems, such as understanding what kind of role the psychosocial environment plays in fostering positive mental health in our children and young people.

Thus, a major challenge within the promotion of positive mental health is to enable ways of nurturing a sense of community and connectedness to communities and schools, as well as building the capacity of children and young people to participate in self-regulation and civic engagement. For more than two decades, it has been a goal in Norway and across Europe to reorient societies toward applying health-promoting strategies with a resource and strength perspective and building capacity among individuals in order to improve the mental health of the whole of society. Even so, we are still far from reaching these goals and mental health problems are increasing, especially among young people.

SOCIETAL CAPACITY FOR PROMOTING POSITIVE MENTAL HEALTH

To meet the challenges of mental health problems, as well as to level out social inequality and promote social justice, there is a need for a broad approach with inter-sector and interdisciplinary collaboration (e.g., between all governmental departments, municipalities, mental healthcare services, child welfare organizations, communities, and schools). Similar to the situation in other countries, in Norway, numerous sectors "own" the mental health problems of children and young people, and this can be problematic in that no one entity sees itself as responsible for the outcomes. The good news is that there is movement in the right direction, with an emphasis on enhancing both interdisciplinary and inter-sector collaboration in new policies. Mental healthcare in school policies is one example of such a collaboration.

For more than a decade, national policy in Norway has centered on mental healthcare in schools through a partnership between the healthcare and education authorities and relevant nongovernmental organizations (NGOs). The overall focus of this policy has been to anchor mental health in schools as a public health concern, recognizing the interconnection between learning and education, while acknowledging the huge potential that schools have to promote mental health and well-being. To strengthen the efficacy of this work, several laws have been developed and implemented that support, prioritize, and regulate mental healthcare in schools. One such law is the Norwegian Education Act (§ 9), which ensures that all students have the right to a positive physical and psychosocial environment that promotes health, well-being, and learning (Ministry of Education, 2017). However, an evaluation of the programs included in the related Norwegian governmental initiative from 2004 to 2008 showed that the majority of them have no visible effects. They were seen as too short (e.g., lasting only one day), too narrow in focus (e.g., information on how to seek help or types of mental health problems), and not addressing the school as a whole (e.g., only for teachers or only for students) (Andersson, Kaspersen, & Bungum, 2010). The most recent report on the state of the art of mental healthcare promotion in schools confirmed some raised awareness of children's mental health, including both the ability to detect those who are struggling and the need to minimize mental health problems by creating a positive and safe learning environment within schools (Holen & Waagene, 2014). Yet the concept that mental healthcare promotion should be an integrated and systematic activity within schools is far from achieved in reality (Holen & Waagene, 2014).

One positive development is that the psychosocial environment and its influence on the mental health of children and adolescents has been highlighted in the most recent initiative in the new interdepartmental strategy on mental healthcare promotion from a life course perspective (Ministry of Health and Care Services, 2017–2022). Within this strategy, kindergartens are included, reflecting the importance of early prevention: "Children in Kindergarten should experience safe and good environments that help promote children and young people's coping and mental health. This also includes the psychosocial environment, including friendship, safe adults, and prevention of social exclusion, offense and bullying" (p.44). This strategy is strongly related to the revised national curriculum, to be implemented in 2020, where social emotional skills are to be incorporated, from a life course perspective, with a subject called "coping with life" to be taught at all levels.

EXAMPLES OF POLICIES, ACTIONS, AND PROGRAMS IN PLACE

In Norway, policies and measures are typically universal – i.e., addressing all children. However, according to Marmot (2013), there is a need for targeted efforts in combination with universal approaches to meet these challenges. In Norway, the use of more evidence-based knowledge, as well as indicated and selective programs to promote the mental health of children and young people, has become more frequent in recent years, alongside more cross-sectional and interdisciplinary collaboration. In the following, both universal and indicated measures and programs are briefly presented.

Among the most important universal policies or measures for the youngest children to support their upbringing and development are maternity leave measures, the right to a kindergarten place for every child, and a monthly paid child benefit. Mothers are entitled to twelve months (for most mothers, paid) of maternity leave, while fathers also have a legal right to paternity leave (currently, they can take 15 weeks of paternity leave). However, if a father does not use this leave, he will lose it. Every child is entitled to attend school/kindergarten from the age of one year; although it is not free, the cost of the scheme is based on income, with a maximum amount set at NOK 2,910 in 2018. The scheme applies to both private and municipal day care centers. A child benefit is received every month for all children from the age of one month until they are eighteen years old; the rate for one child is NOK 970 per month. In addition, education is available free to everyone from grade one through college and university, the latter two being voluntary; ensuring attendance from first grade through upper secondary school is a duty for parents and a right for every child.

Another important universal measure is that the healthcare system in Norway, which is free at the point of use, offers a well-developed universal healthcare program comprising fourteen meetings with a pediatric nurse during a child's first five years. In recent years, a competence program known as Early In has been implemented for pediatric and school nurses, preschool teachers, and teachers for the early detection of drug abuse, as well as violence and mistreatment. The aim of the program is to give participants the (a) courage to ask about alcohol, mental health, and violence, (b) courage to act on the basis of responses from the individual, and (c) knowledge of what can be done and whom to contact, as well as when it is appropriate to follow up concerning an individual, a family, or children (www.korusnord.no).

If problems are detected, indicated and selective measures such as early interventions for children at risk (TIBIR) are available. The aim of TIBIR is to prevent and remedy behavioral problems at an early stage (children aged three to twelve years), as well as to develop children's positive and prosocial behavior. Furthermore, it seeks to provide employees and managers who work with and have responsibility for children a common understanding of how behavioral problems arise and can be remedied. The TIBIR program has established a comprehensive action chain where interventions are in line with the needs of the target group (www.nubu.no). For older children (twelve years and older), the Parent Management Training – Oregon (Forgatch, 2002) approach is used. The Nurse Family Partnership (Olds, et al., 2014) is another early intervention program targeting at-risk, first-time parents that starts during pregnancy. Child welfare offers for vulnerable toddlers and all toddlers and their parents are also very important in this context, since the care given to children during this period is crucial to their further development. Furthermore, child welfare services must ensure that children and young people living under conditions that may harm their health and development receive the necessary assistance (Ministry for Children and Equality, 2015).

A review of relevant research published since 1990 reveals clear evidence that universal school-based interventions have a positive effect on the mental health of children and young people. A much-used universal program in the lower grades in primary schools is the social emotional learning program known as Zippy's Friends. It is lesson-based and aims to teach students how they can make friends and function effectively in a social context. Zippy's Friends is used in thirty countries. In Norway, 550 schools now use the program. The Norwegian partner is the Adults for Children NGO, and funding is provided by the Norwegian Directorate of Health (www.vfb.no).

Another universal initiative is the Olweus Program, which seeks to prevent bullying and antisocial behavior. The program, which is delivered in eighty-eight schools, has been evaluated through a series of impact studies and is classified as an evidence-based program in the highest category (http://olweusinternational.no/).

Psychological First Aid (PFA) is one of the latest programs aimed at strengthening the mental health of children and young people. The PFA program can be implemented either as a whole group/class program or on a selective and individual basis. It is available in three versions: a child version for those aged four to seven years, another child version for those aged seven to twelve years, and a youth version for those aged twelve to eighteen years. The program, which is delivered in kindergartens, child healthcare centers, and schools, is widespread among communities in Norway (www.vfb.no).

For older pupils, the Dream School is available, which is a universal program for secondary and upper secondary schools run by Adults for Children and part of the Norwegian Mental Health in School initiative. The program is schoolwide, but the most important element is the use of peer mentors, students who are one year older than their mentees who are educated by adults in how to become a good leader and implement activities in their classes and at school. Using students as mentors promotes the active application of students' own positive resources to improving the school and class environment. This also fosters a stronger sense of belonging, as they become involved across several levels at school, not just in their own class. The program is used in thirty-six schools.

The Mental Health Support Team (MHST) is a new initiative that is currently being tested together with the Dream School in six upper secondary schools through an randomized control trial. The aim of the team is to nurture a sense of belonging and good relationships with students struggling in upper secondary schools. The MHST is an indicated and selective measure (www.complete.w.uib.no).

While the list of policies, programs, and measures is by no means exhaustive, it offers a glimpse into some of the efforts undertaken to ensure that the right of children to an upbringing within a just and positive environment is respected.

RESOURCES

www.complete.w.uib.no
www.korusnord.no/Tidlig-identifikasjon/Tidlig-inn/
www.nubu.no/TIBIR/
http://olweusinternational.no/
www.regjeringen.no/en/id4/
www.ssb.no/
www.vfb.no

REFERENCES

Aadnesen, B. N., & Hærem, E. (2007). *Interkulturelt barnevernsarbeid* [Intercultural child welfare work]. Oslo: Universitetsforlaget.

Andersson, H. W., Kaspersen, S. L., & Bungum, B. (2010). *Evaluering av Psykisk helse i skolen* [Evaluation of mental health in schools]. Sintef: Trondheim. Accessed June 12, 2018, from www.sintef.no/globalassets/upload/teknologi_samfunn/rapport-a14919-psykisk-helse-i-skolen–sluttrapport.pdf.

Anvik, C., & Gustavsen, A. (2012). Ikke slipp meg – unge, psykiske helseproblemer [Don't let me go: Young, mental health problems, education and work]. *Utdanning og arbeid. Report*, 13, 8–22.

Bakken, A. (2017). *Ungdata. Nasjonale resultater 2017* [Data on young people: National results 2017]. NOVA Rapport 10/17. Oslo: NOVA.

Bragstad, T., Ellingsen, J., & Lindbøl, M. N. (2012). Hvorfor blir det flere uførepensjonister [Why are there more disability pensioners]? *Arbeid og velferd*, 2012(1), 26–39.

Dahl, E., Bergsli, H., & van der Wel, K. A. (2014). Sosial ulikhet i helse: En norsk kunnskapsoversikt [Social inequality in health: A literature review]. Accessed June 12, 2018, from https://fagarkivet.hioa.archive.knowledgearc.net/bitstream/handle/123456789/716/Internettvedlegg%201.%20Maal%20og%20anbefalinger.pdf?sequence=3&isAllowed=y.

Danielsen, A. G. (2017). *Eleven og skolens læringsmiljø* [The pupil and the school learning environment]. Oslo: Gyldendal.

Drager, R. H., Sten, R. J., & Fossanger, S. F. (2017). Færre tyveriofre, men flere utsatte barn i anmeldelsene [Fewer thieves, but more vulnerable children in the reviews]. Accessed June 12, 2018, from www.ssb.no/sosiale-forhold-og-kriminalitet/artikler-og-publikasjoner/faerre-tyveriofre-men-flere-utsatte-barn-i-anmeldelsene.

Ekren, R. (2014). Sosial reproduksjon av utdanning [Social reproduction of education]? *Samfunnspeilet*, 2014/5, 20–25. Accessed June 14, 2018, from www.ssb.no/utdanning/artikler-og-publikasjoner/_attachment/153399?_ts=144d059ffb8.

Engvik, M. (2018). Færre unge straffet også i 2015 [Fewer young punished also by 2015]. Accessed June 12, 2018, from www.ssb.no/sosiale-forhold-og-kriminalitet/artikler-og-publikasjoner/faerre-unge-straffet-ogsa-i-2015.

Epland, J., & Kirkeberg, M. I. (2015). Flere økonomisk utsatte barn [More economically vulnerable children]. Accessed June 7, 2018, from www.ssb.no/inntekt-og-forbruk/artikler-og-publikasjoner/flere-okonomisk-utsatte-barn.

Esping-Andersen, G. (1990). *The three worlds of welfare capitalism*. Cambridge: Polity Press.

Esping-Andersen, G. (2015). Welfare regimes and social stratification. *Journal of European Social Policy*, 25(1), 124–134.

Forgatch, M. S. (2002). *Implementing parent management training in Norway (Grant application RFA – DA – 02 – 004)* (No. NIDA NNPRI: Community Multisite Prevention Trials [CMPT]). Eugene.

Fossanger, S. F. (2018). Historisk få lovbrudd anmeldt i 2017 [Historically fewer offenses reported in 2017]. Accessed June 12, 2018, from www.ssb.no/sosiale-forhold-og-kriminalitet /artikler-og-publikasjoner/historisk-fa-lovbrudd-anmeldt-i-2017.

Holen, S., & Waagene, E. (2014). Psykisk helse i skolen: Utdanningsdirektoratets spørreundersøkelse blant lærere, skoleledere og skoleeiere [Mental health in schools: The Directorate of Education's survey among teachers, school administrators, and school owners]. *NIFU Report*, No. 48. Accessed May 29, 2018, from http://hdl.handle.net/11250/ 280087.

Hollekim, R., Anderssen, N., & Daniel, M. (2016). Contemporary discourses on children and parenting in Norway: Norwegian child welfare services meets immigrant families. *Children and Youth Services Review*, 60, 52–60.

Lillejord, S., Halvorsrud, K., Ruud, E., et al. (2015). *Frafall i videregående opplæring: En systematisk kunnskapsoversikt* [Dropouts in upper secondary education: A systematic review]. Oslo: Kunnskapssenter for utdanning.

Lunde, S. E. (2013). Unge uten jobb og skoleplass sliter med helsen [Young people without jobs and schooling struggle with their health]. *Samfunnsspeilet*, 3, 17–23.

Markussen, E., & Seland, I. (2012). Å redusere bortvalg-bare skolenes ansvar? En undersøkelse av bortvalg ved de videregående skolene i Akershus fylkeskommune skoleåret 2010–2011. [Is reducing dropout only the responsibility of schools? A survey of dropouts at secondary schools in Akershus County Council 2010–2011]. NIFU Report, 6/2012. Accessed June 14, 2018, from https://brage.bibsys.no/xmlui/bitstream/handle/11250/280856/NIFUrapport2012-6.pdf?sequence=1.

Marmot, M. G. (2013). *Review of social determinants and the health divide in the WHO European region: Final report*. Copenhagen: World Health Organization Regional Office for Europe.

Ministry for Children and Equality (2015). *Barn som lever i fattigdom. Regjeringens strategi (2015–2017)* [Children living in poverty: Government strategy (2015–2017)]. Oslo: Ministry for Children and Equality.

Ministry of Education (2017). The National Education Act. Section 9a: Students' working environment. Accessed May 14, 2018, from https://lovdata.no/dokument/NL/lov/1998-07-17-61/KAPITTEL_11#KAPITTEL_11.

Ministry of Finance (2009–2010). *Stortingsproposisjon nr. 1 (2009–2010), Nasjonalbudsjettet* [National budget]. Oslo: Finansdepartementet.

Ministry of Health and Care Services (2017–2022). *"Mestre hele livet" – Regjeringens strategi for god psykisk helse (2017–2022)* ["Mastering your entire life": The government's strategy for positive mental health (2017–2022)]. Oslo: Ministry of Health and Care Services.

Normann, T. M. (2016). Hver femte familie med lav inntekt har ikke råd til ferie [Every fifth family with a low income cannot afford a vacation]. Accessed June 7, 2018, from www.ssb .no/sosiale-forhold-og-kriminalitet/artikler-og-publikasjoner/hver-femte-familie-med-lav-inntekt-har-ikke-rad-til-ferie.

Norwegian Directorate for Children, Youth and Family Affairs (2017). *Oppvekstrapporten 2017. Økte forskjeller – gjør det noe* [Revenue report 2017. Increased differences: Does it matter?] Oslo: Norwegian Directorate for Children, Youth and Family Affairs.

Norwegian Institute of Public Health (NIPH) (2014). Psykiske plager og lidelser hos barn og unge [Mental disorders and disorders in children and adolescents]. Accessed January 27, 2016, from www.fhi.no/artikler/?id=84062.

Olds, D. L., Kitzman, H., Knudtson, M. D., et al. (2014). Effect of home visiting by nurses on maternal and child mortality: Results of a two-decade follow-up of a randomized clinical trial. *JAMA Pediatrics*, 168(9), 800–806.
Putnam, R. D. (2016). *Our kids: The American dream in crisis*. New York: Simon and Schuster.
Reiss, F. (2013). Socioeconomic inequalities and mental health problems in children and adolescents: A systematic review. *Social Science & Medicine*, 90, 24–31.
Sarason, I. G. (ed.). (2013). *Social support: Theory, research and applications* (vol. 24). Berlin: Springer Science & Business Media.
Sarason, S. B. (1974). *The psychological sense of community: Prospects for a community psychology*. San Francisco: Jossey-Bass.
Scales, P. C., Benson, P. L., Oesterle, S., et al. (2016). The dimensions of successful young adult development: A conceptual and measurement framework. *Applied Developmental Science*, 20(3), 150–174.
Statistics Norway (2011). Decline in household income (Nedgang i husholdningenes inntekter). Accessed June 14, 2018, from www.ssb.no/inntekt-og-forbruk/artikler-og-publikasjoner/nedgang-i-husholdningenes-inntekter.
Statistics Norway (2013). Gjennomstrømning i videregående opplæring, 2007–2012. *Elektroniskpublisering*. [Education statistics, 2007–2012. *Electronic Publishing*.] Accessed April 19, 2014, from www.ssb.no/vgogjen/.
Statistics Norway (2016). Children and the child welfare system. Accessed June 7, 2018, from www.ssb.no/a/barnogunge/2016/barnevern/.
Statistics Norway (2018). Children and young people in the population. Accessed June 12, 2018, from www.ssb.no/a/barnogunge/2018/bef/.
UNESCO (1994). *The Salamanca statement and framework for action on special needs education*. Paris, France: UNESCO.
Weare, K., & Nind, M. (2011). Mental health promotion and problem prevention in schools: What does the evidence say? *Health Promotion International*, 26(Suppl. 1), 29–69.
Whitehead, M., & Dahlgren, G. (2006). Levelling up (part 2): A discussion paper on European strategies for tackling social inequities in health. Geneva: World Health Organization.
World Health Organization (WHO) (2014). Health for the world's adolescents. A second chance in the second decade. Accessed July 13, 2015, from http://apps.who.int/adolescent/second-decade/.

24

Social Justice and Children in Pakistan

Sana Younus, Aisha Sanober Chachar, and Ayesha Irshad Mian

REGION/COUNTRY PARAMETERS

Case Vignette

Shamim is an eleven-year-old girl who attends a local nongovernmental organization (NGO)–based school in the predominantly low-income area of Karachi.[1] She dreams of becoming a deputy commissioner of her city when she grows up. She tops class tests and regularly helps classmates who are struggling with academics. Her elder brother, Rahman[2], studies in the same school. To the contrary, he often gets into trouble because of delinquent behavior and "bad company." His teachers have tried to convey the problem to the family but have failed to communicate with the parents due to their unavailability. Rahman has often been caught smoking cigarettes, which he used to buy from a *khokha* (small shop) near the school. He has been struggling in academics since the beginning. He is always restless and disinterested in studies. He is disliked by most of the teachers in school.

Shamim's family situation is very difficult. She has three younger siblings. Her father has substance-related problems, does not work, and is physically abusive. Her mother, on the other hand, is the sole bread earner of the family. Her grandmother lives with them and recently broke her hip and is bedridden. Shamim and her nine-year-old sister now look after her grandmother and do most of the housework.

Shamim loves studying, but because of the increasing pressure on her mother she feels she needs to earn money. As well as going to school, Shamim sews shopping bags for a local clothing brand. At noon, after she gets home from school, she sews until four or five in the afternoon with the help of her sister. She is paid approximately ten cents per bag.

Stories similar to Shamim and Rahman's are frequently reported by the media in Pakistan in an effort to highlight the situation of social justice in the country. But understanding this situation requires understanding the social fabric of Pakistan and of the various factors involved in shaping the existing social situation in the country.

Introduction

Pakistan is the sixth most populous country in the world with a population of approximately 200 million in 2018 (Junior, 2018). It gained the status of an independent state in 1947 after religious and ethnic conflicts in the Indo-Pak region. It has a rich history as an old civilization; remains from Stone Age hunter-gatherers are found on its Potohar Plateau. Similarly, Kot Diji in Sindh has evidence of an early Bronze Age culture (Hasan, 1997). Despite being rich in historical and cultural artifacts and having an abundance of natural resources, Pakistan has seen its economic and social development compromised time and again due to the political and military situation in the country. In addition to the wars of 1965 and 1971, Pakistan's involvement in the war against terrorism during the past two decades has taken a toll on the overall progress and development of the country. Due to geopolitical reasons, a large portion of the capital resources is directed toward defense in order to maintain regional stability (Ministry Justifies Defence Budget Hike, 2018). This situation makes the country struggle on various fronts like healthcare, education, and the fight against poverty, with significant effects on the well-being of its citizens.

Pakistan, being a federation, has four provinces: Sindh, Punjab, Balochistan, and Khyber Pakhtunkhwa. These provinces have considerable autonomy in terms of policy and legislation, and child protection falls within the provincial domain. The provinces differ significantly in demographic, political, socioeconomic, and cultural characteristics; therefore, progress in enacting child protection legislation varies from province to province (Table 24.1).

Children comprise approximately 48 percent of the total Pakistani population (National Institute of Population Studies & ICF International, 2013). The frugal

TABLE 24.1 *Provincial initiatives for the enactment of child legislation*

Sindh	Child Protection Authority Act 2011
	Sindh Child Marriage Restraint Act 2013
	Standard operating procedures (SOPs) for Child Protection Units at the district level
Punjab	Destitute and Neglected Children Act 2004 (revised in 2007)
	Child Marriage Restraint Act 2014
	Standard operating procedures (SOPs) for Child Protection Units at the district level
Khyber Pakhtunkhwa	Child Protection and Welfare Act 2010
	Child Protection and Welfare Rules 2013
	Standard operating procedures (SOPs) for Child Protection Units at the district level (in the process of adaptation)
Balochistan	Child Welfare and Protection (approved by cabinet, approval from provincial assembly awaited)

support from the government, layered on underlying poverty, leaves them deprived of their basic human rights like the right to survival, education, healthcare, and protection, which are promised in the constitution of Pakistan and in international treaties such as the United Nations Convention on the Rights of the Child (UNCRC) to which Pakistan is a party. This deprivation is exacerbated for children who reside in areas affected by armed conflict as a part of the war against terrorism and those who are displaced from their homes due to natural or man-made disasters.

Background: Children's Rights in Pakistan

The National Commission for Child Welfare and Development (NCCWD) was established by the government of Pakistan in 1979. Having functioned under different governing bodies, it is now housed under the Ministry of Human Rights. The NCCWD has the responsibility of monitoring and ensuring that children are receiving their constitutional, legal, and administrative rights. It also suggests amendments to the constitution and national laws when necessary and formulates national policies and legislation for child welfare, development, and protection. The NCCWD has recommended a number of modifications and revisions to existing laws and policies, some of which have been accepted as a part of the constitution and the Pakistan Penal Code (PPC) (NCCWD, n.d.). Pakistan has also taken some other policy initiatives that provide measures for the survival, development, and protection of children from neglect, abuse, and exploitation (Table 24.2). Despite these laws, implementation in practical terms still leaves much to be desired in improving the lives of children.

The next significant event in child welfare occurred when the government of Pakistan signed the UNCRC in September 20, 1990, and ratified it on November 12, 1990 (United Nations High Commissioner for Human Rights, 1990). By signing this document, the government of Pakistan committed to the principle that children everywhere have the right to survival, to develop to their fullest potential, to protection from harmful influences, abuse, and exploitation, and to participate fully in family, cultural, and social life. Pakistan's first periodic report highlighted deficiencies in the existing legislation and the inadequacy of its measures to ensure proper implementation of the UNCRC. The second submission, in 2002, again showed an

TABLE 24.2 *National policy initiatives for social justice*

National Plan of Action for Children 2006
National Policy and Plan of Action to Combat Child Labour 2000
National Education Policy 2009
National Policy and Plan of Action on Human Trafficking 2005
National Health Policy 2009
National Youth Policy 2009
National Policy and Plan of Action to Combat Bonded Labour in Pakistan
National Policy Guidelines on Vulnerable Groups in Disasters

inability to comply with most of the recommendations. Subsequently, in a combined third and fourth periodic report, the committee raised the concern that its recommendations were insufficiently addressed by the government of Pakistan (Convention on the Rights of the Child, 2009).

BARRIERS TO SOCIAL JUSTICE FOR YOUNG PEOPLE

Core areas where social justice is compromised for children in Pakistan include the following:

Health and Nutrition

Pakistan has a high neonatal mortality rate relative to neighboring countries (National Institute of Population Studies & ICF International, 2013). Pakistan stands third from the bottom among 193 countries in the context of newborn deaths. Pakistan ranks twenty-third in the world for under-five deaths. The nutritional status of children is also very poor: 35 percent of them are underweight, more than 50 percent suffer from stunted growth, and around 9 percent suffer from emaciation. The National Nutrition Survey (NNS) 2011 cites a rate of anemia of 62.5 percent, which could by itself be an alarming indicator of weak child health status in the country (Bhutta, Soofi, Zaidi, Habib, & Hussain, 2011).

The vaccination status of children is also not optimum. The Pakistan Demographic and Health Survey (PDHS) 2012–2013 revealed that the proportion of children fully vaccinated is lower for girls (52 percent) than for boys (56 percent). It is also considerably lower for children in rural areas (48 percent) than in urban areas (66 percent). One-fifth of children (21 percent) in the province of Balochistan reportedly have not received any vaccinations at all (National Institute of Population Studies & ICF International, 2013). Polio is still endemic in the country with 187 cases reported in October 2014 (March, 2014).

With limited to virtually no healthcare insurance and an inadequate public healthcare system, the predominant provider of healthcare in Pakistan is the private sector. This is understandably associated with costs that have to be borne out of pocket. Considering the fact that approximately a quarter of the country's population lives below the poverty line, access to quality healthcare is limited. The majority of the children in Pakistan do not get a fair opportunity to attain their full health potential (health equity) due to various determinants of poverty like geographical location, large household size, high dependency ratio, illiteracy, large informal sector employment, and lack of access to basic utilities. The social determinants of health inequality and morbidity are quite similar to the determinants of poverty. Hence a physically or mentally ill child may not be able to access healthcare because medical attention or treatment is not affordable, or because the health facilities are not easily accessible from their homes (particularly in rural areas). Parental lack of knowledge, limited awareness, and stigma associated with certain illnesses like epilepsy and psychiatric disorders could also be reasons for not seeking any advice or treatment. Privatization of the healthcare system is another factor detrimental to the health of poorer populations because it constrains their access to healthcare services. Gender of a child is also of particular importance in healthcare situations from a social perspective with the possibility of greater efforts toward acquisition of better healthcare for a male child as compared to a female child.

Education

The education system in Pakistan is overseen by both the federal and provincial governments. Children, mainly those from disadvantaged backgrounds, do not access schools due to various barriers including poverty, distance to schools with no transportation facilities, unavailability of schools, and lack of awareness of the value of education. It is also true that due to various reasons schools fail to retain children (Table 24.3), resulting in high dropout rates (Government of Pakistan, 2017). The constitution of Pakistan requires the state to provide free and compulsory quality education to children of the age group five to sixteen years. Despite this, only 71 percent of children attend primary school in Pakistan and that too varies considerably between urban and rural areas. This means that approximately 23 million children are deprived of education (Annual Status of Education Report Pakistan, 2015). Furthermore, the attendance rate for education is lower for girls than boys. Of those who are going to school, the difficulties of public education are numerous: lack of funding, dilapidated buildings, lack of chairs and tables, a lack of toilets, disinterested teachers, poor delivery of education, and transportation difficulties. Furthermore, teachers are underqualified in the public school system, and often children may graduate or leave school prematurely without achieving grade-appropriate milestones. This is the case for almost 50 percent of school-going children ages six to sixteen in Pakistan. Pakistan was ranked 113 out of 120 countries on the Education Development Index. The National Plan of Action (NPA) has identified a few reasons driving low enrollment rates in Pakistan (Tables 24.3 and 24.4) (Government of Pakistan, 2013).

TABLE 24.3 *Among children who never attended school*

Girls	Boys
"Parents did not allow" (40%)	"Child not willing" (37%)
"Too expensive" (16%)	"Too expensive" (21%)
"Child not willing" (10%)	"Has to help at work" (10%)
"Too far" (9%)	

TABLE 24.4 *Reasons for dropping out of school before completing primary education*

Girls	Boys
"Child not willing" (14%)	"Child not willing" (26%)
"Parents did not allow" (10%)	"Had to help at work" (7%)
"Too expensive" (7%)	

Radicalization

Since independence in 1947, Pakistan has been challenged by the intergenerational trauma inflicted by the mass murder of people migrating to the "new" country. The regional Soviet–Afghan war, which began in 1979, altered the very character of the existing Pakistani society. Postwar Pakistani society experienced weaponization, "Kalashnikov culture," and "Talibanization." Since the 9/11 incident, Pakistan has been intricately linked with the many facets of the "war on terrorism." Within the past decade, more than 47,000 people have been killed in terrorism-related violence in Pakistan (Portal, 2018).

A vast majority of Pakistani youth express their identification with religious-based value systems. This strong affiliation and sense of self can increase the tendency of this cohort to radicalization. For long, madrassas have been considered an important variable in the development of radicalization in the country. They have gained a reputation for having an influence on young impressionable Muslims (Nizami, Hassan, Yasir, Rana, & Minhas, 2018). These institutes offer free Islamic education, boarding, and lodging for poor students. Approximately 12,000 registered madrasas exist in Pakistan. These madrassas have their own syllabi and examinations. Wafaq ul Madaris Al-Arabia of Pakistan is the regulatory body for these institutes. However, many are unregulated and unregistered. This is an alarming situation as these institutes are speculated to operate as recruiting agencies for religious extremists. Despite increasing rates of youth being exploited, parents continue to send their children to these madrassas. Their reasons for enrolling their children in the madrassas vary from that the madrassas provide a good Islamic education or that they are low in cost or free, to that the madrassas provide food and clothing. Families living in harsh financial situations with limited formal educational resources use madrassas more often (Andrabi, Das, Khwaja, & Zajonc, 2005). But parents from high-income backgrounds also send their children to religious schools as a supplement to their mainstream education. In most of these cases, parents and families remain unaware that their children are recruited.

The radicalization of Pakistani youth emerges from a strict religious identity in individuals and the presence of strong and unchecked Islam-based religious parties (Haque, 2014). Deradicalization in Pakistan requires not only action against fundamentalist militant organizations but also strong political, social, and educational advocacy.

Legal Framework

Article 1 of the UNCRC says that "a child means every human being below the age of eighteen years unless under the law applicable to the child, majority is attained earlier" (UNICEF, 1989, p.2). Therefore an important question that comes up in legal matters involving children is "Who is a child under Pakistani law?"

The Juvenile Justice System Ordinance (JJSO) (2000) offers protection to juvenile prisons throughout the country. This ordinance emphasizes that juvenile courts should be established with exclusive jurisdiction for a child accused of committing an offense. According to JJSO Section 7, "If a question arises as to whether a person before it is a child for the purposes of this Ordinance, the Juvenile Court shall record a finding after such inquiry, which shall include a medical report for determination of the age of the child" (JJSO, 2000).

The Protection of Pakistan Act (2014) is regarded as an important step against violent extremism. Section 24 of the Act gives it an overriding effect over other laws including the JJSO (2000), which prohibits the preventive detention of children younger than fifteen years of age. Hence, as the law currently stands, children can be held in preventive detention regardless of Section 10 of the JJSO and they can be tried by antiterrorism courts noted as juvenile courts (Protection of Pakistan Act, 2014).

Currently, no exclusively juvenile courts have been established except one in Karachi. In the rest of the country, the respective high courts have conferred the powers of juvenile courts upon the courts of all the district, session, or civil judges. In Khyber Pakhtunkhwa, 146 courts have been conferred the powers of juvenile courts. Similarly, all other provinces have conferred the powers of juvenile courts upon the courts of all the district, session, or civil judges. However, only one children's court presently operates in Lahore, established under the Punjab Destitute and Neglected Children Act 2004 (Juvenile Justice Systems, n.d.).

The juvenile justice system of the country continues to face problems because of inadequate infrastructure and resources, overcrowded prisons, and lack of political will toward reforming the system. Although laws related to children exist, their implementation leaves much to be desired. Pakistan does not have separate courts for children despite a legislative mandate for this. This situation is compounded by the fact that members of law enforcement and the lower judiciary lack basic knowledge of the law. The loopholes in the current legal framework lead to significant violations of children's rights and places children in a susceptible position within the society. No practical steps have been taken to ensure provision of free legal aid to all children in contact with the law. Some of the outcomes of this flawed legal framework with respect to children are as follows.

Child Labor

As stated earlier in this chapter, given that a quarter of Pakistan's population lives below the poverty line, families are often forced to make their children work so as to make ends meet. The International Labour Organization (ILO) estimates that child labor in Pakistan has exceeded the 12 million mark (National Institute of Population Studies & ICF International, 2013). Many of these children are performing domestic tasks and working in factories and agricultural fields. Others work in the textile industry (specifically, making carpets), construction, or even the automotive industry. Children in carpet factories sometimes work up to twenty hours a day, seven days a week. Very often, sleeping, eating, and working are all done in the same place. This puts a considerable strain on children's health. It is not uncommon for them to suffer from respiratory and vision problems, or even deformities of the spinal column. In 2004, the ILO estimated that more than 264,000 children were working as child domestic workers in Pakistan in hazardous and deplorable conditions. In the past eight years, the media have reported approximately fifty cases of severe torture and abuse of child domestic workers. From the total, approximately thirty children have died as a direct result of violence inflicted on them by their employers (World Day against Child Labour, 2015).

Child Marriages

Despite the Child Marriage Restraint Act, which forbids the marriage of children, these marriages still take place in Pakistan. This law establishes the legal age of marriage as eighteen years for men and sixteen years for women, and failure to follow it could lead to sanctions. In practice, this law is not followed at all, and early marriages, both for girls and for boys, continues to be a common practice in the country (Child Marriage Restraint Act, 1929). It is estimated that child marriage represents around 32 percent of local marriages. A big number of these children, mainly girls, are married at an early age, even as young as seven years of age. The Pakistan Demographic and Health Survey (2006–2007) mentions in its section on teenage fertility that almost half of the girls of fifteen to eighteen years of age were pregnant or had a baby to take care of (National Institute of Population Studies & ICF International, 2008). The exact numbers of child or early marriages are not available due to lack of proper documentation and data collection. In rural areas, *vani* marriages are still observed, though infrequently, which involves giving a daughter in marriage in order to settle a dispute or a debt between two parties. The "aggressor" offers one of his family's daughters in compensation for a wrong caused.

Early or child marriages have various causes. The most frequent among these causes are brotherhood (*biradri*) expectations, extremely weak legislation, lack of implementation of the existing laws, children treated as commodities/slaves, the tribal and feudal structure of society, a lack of public awareness about the harmful effects of child marriages, extreme poverty, and internal trafficking. The birth registration system is also an important cause of child marriages as due to its inefficiency, registration of children, especially girls, is not prioritized, leading to manipulation of the age of the child at the time of marriage (Naveed & Butt, 2015).

Abuse

There is a troubling increase in the cases of sexual abuse, kidnapping, and violence toward children in Pakistan. From 2008 to 2010 there was a rise in reported cases of all varieties of abuse from 1,839 to 2,595 (Cruel Numbers, 2013). These data are even more alarming if one assumes that 80 percent of the cases are not reported. Following the floods that affected Pakistan in 2010, more cases surfaced where children were sold, rented, or even kidnapped in order to force them into begging, labor, and prostitution.

Poverty, physical and mental abuse, negligence by nuclear and extended family, and family conflicts are the major factors that lead children to take refuge in the streets. These street children are at a higher risk of deprivation in supports essential for development and of various forms of dangers. They are also at a greater risk of sexual exploitation. Around 90 percent of the 170,000 street children in Pakistan are subjected to the sex trade, and it is estimated that only 20 percent of sexual abuse cases are reported. Sixty percent of young victims accuse the police of being the perpetrators (Nazish, 2018).

Substance Abuse

According to a report of the Society for the Protection of the Rights of the Child, an estimated 1.2 million children are on the streets of Pakistan's major cities and urban centers. Most common substance abuse agents among street children in Pakistan under the age of fifteen years are solvents or inhalants. The use of opioids is also common, but these users are mostly older than fifteen years of age. The factors associated with use of these substances in children are complex. Some of the social etiological factors responsible for increased drug use in Pakistan are listed in what follows (Sherman, Plitt, ul Hassan, Cheng, & Zafar, 2005):

- Increased availability of drugs at low prices.
- Rapidly changing social norms that act as stressors for vulnerable individuals.
- Lack of jobs and economic frustration.
- Compromised educational system.
- Existence and operation of drug dens.
- Lack of drug education within the family and in educational institutions.
- Inadequate response of political leaders toward drug use in the community.

REBUILDING CAPACITY

Given that most of the issues highlighted earlier in this chapter are intertwined, addressing one without the other would be an ineffective use of time and resources. The difficulty of implementing laws related to education when infrastructure needs have not been addressed is a noteworthy example. Some important components that need immediate attention and that can be effective for the aforementioned barriers (healthcare, education, and the legal system) include the following:

Capital resources. One of the major struggles when working with children in Pakistan is the inadequate budget allocated by the government to develop required services for this cohort. Upsizing this budget is integral, but given the current geopolitical situation this may not be immediately possible. Funds and grants from national and international agencies can be helpful in initiating and maintaining various projects. The United Nations Educational, Scientific and Cultural Organization (UNESCO), the United Nations International Children's Emergency Fund (UNICEF), and the United States Agency for International Development (USAID) are a few of the organizations that have been working in the domain of healthcare and education for children in Pakistan. In the private sector Pakistan is considered one of the most charitable nations in the world. This is evident in the form of projects supported by philanthropic organizations spanning the country that provide education and legal services free of cost for those who cannot afford them. At present all such projects are working in silos, on various scales, each with its own methodology to achieve the common outcome of better education, healthcare, and legal systems for children. Quality and effectiveness may be internally audited by each project but are not monitored by any external regulatory body. It will be beneficial to have a centralized system that evaluates, audits, monitors, and oversees these programs in order to have better documentation of provided care and in the long run provide collective effort for the common cause. Once a pilot has proven effective, it is important to consider sustainability and how the project can be scaled up at a population level. Exploring mechanisms that promote voluntary collaboration between these private companies and NGOs is essential to build sustainable models.

Human resources. This is another area that requires simultaneous attention to improve the current situation. Consider an example where the administration of a tertiary care hospital has ample capital resources to build a child and adolescent mental healthcare department. In the absence of any postgraduate training in the country, the positions for child and adolescent psychiatrists for this program will now be dependent on foreign-trained professionals applying for these jobs. This cannot be a long-term solution for an existing need. Supporting a homegrown solution that serves as a pipeline for professionals who can work with children and families is strategic to the welfare of children. Such professionals will be culturally aware, professionally trained to overcome barriers, and better accepted by the indigenous population. Hence it is important to develop required training programs to fill the void of human resources in the healthcare, education, and legal systems. Many universities and institutions are now providing training programs consistent with international standards in these fields with the existing societal norms integral to the approach. One such example is the initiation of a fellowship in child and adolescent psychiatry at The Aga Khan University, which is now training these professionals and multiplying the existing number of child and adolescent psychiatrists in the country.

Infrastructure. These efforts related to capital and human resources will be in vain in the absence of the required infrastructure. Where the support from the government in this domain has a slow pace, various NGOs in the country have created many projects catering to the needs of those who cannot support themselves. Shaukat Khanum Memorial Cancer Hospital and Research Centre, the Indus Children Cancer Hospital, and schools run by The Citizens Foundation are some of the finest examples of infrastructure built for the progress of health and education of children in the country. Since the legal system requires significant support from government, its progress has lagged behind as compared to the progress made in the domains of healthcare and education. Greater advocacy is needed targeting government officials so as to enhance their efforts in creating juvenile courts, improvising and implementing the JJSO, and making the necessary amendments in the constitution of Pakistan related to minors.

Awareness and advocacy. It is essential to create awareness among the masses about matters pertinent to social justice. Limited insight about one's own rights and the disparity between what the rich and poor get are some of the barriers that hinder the provision of social justice. Mass campaigns highlighting the basic rights of children in the simplest language using communication strategies accessible to most will be one of the most effective ways to increase awareness related to social matters. Constant advocacy for these matters at governmental and nongovernmental levels is essential to continuously create and maintain momentum.

PROGRAMMATIC EXAMPLES

Analysis

In past few years various agencies and organizations from within civil society have worked on specific budgetary analysis focused on child health, education, or social protection. Some examples of such work are cited in what follows.

UNESCO in Pakistan has conducted a situation analysis of the education sector in Pakistan that also contains gaps analysis, and has proposed how much federal and provincial governments have to allocate to the education sector in order to meet the Millennium Development Goals (MDGs).

Similarly, in 2013, ActionAid in Pakistan published a paper on the public financing of primary education in Pakistan. Save the Children in Pakistan, in partnership with local NGOs and networks, has been conducting budget analysis from a children's rights perspective that includes national-, provincial-, and, in some cases, district-level analysis. The Pakistan Institute of Legislative Development and

Transparency (PILDAT) has also been playing an important role in budget reform and analysis in the educational sector for many years.

Implementation

Implementation remains an ongoing challenge. Despite the many challenges cited earlier in this chapter, multiple small grassroots-level organizations, NGOs, and sporadic government-level initiatives continue to work in the area of children's rights but make minor progress for the country for the reasons cited earlier.

Government-Led Initiatives

The National Institute of Child Health (NICH) is a 500-bed hospital that is currently managed by the health department of the government of Sindh, Pakistan. It is the first children's hospital in the country and presently one of the largest and the only children's hospital in Sindh. It provides tertiary care services for almost all types of pediatric diseases. It provides these services free of cost to individuals in need. Given its provincial location the financial and resource-related burden on the hospital is immense. The provincial funds along with donations from across the country make ends meet for this hospital. There are some limitations related to care provision at NICH like possible delays in receiving treatment, the quality of care provided, and cleanliness and comfort. Despite these limitations, it is an example where government funds and donations from philanthropists help this institute in providing healthcare to all children visiting the hospital. This highlights the possible effectiveness of creating public-private partnerships for government-based healthcare programs with existing infrastructure. These programs can benefit from the funds associated with NGOs and from the expertise of professionals in the private healthcare sector.

Nongovernmental Organizations

Save the Children works with children affected by or at risk of violence, abuse, exploitation, and neglect. Advocacy for policy change and support to the government for establishment of child protection systems at the community, district, provincial, and national levels are overarching components of this program. The organization has successfully implemented child protection, health, nutrition, education, emergency response, and economic opportunities programs in forty-five districts across Pakistan.

The Citizens Foundation (TCF) is a nonprofit organization that was established in 1995 with the mission to provide quality education to the less privileged and to create better opportunities for their future. At present the TCF has 1,482 school units with 220,000 enrolled students. These schools are located in urban slums and in rural areas. They provide customized books to their students and provide in-depth training to their teachers. They also provide functional literacy skills and vocational training within the school communities. In addition to their programs, they are developing a public-private partnership with the government and managing around 253 government schools in the country. Being a charitable organization, TCF counts on donations as the sole source of its income. The TCF's accounts are audited and available to the public. Over the past two decades the TCF has gained the trust of people, leading to regular donations to its program, in turn leading to its sustainability. By having ample human and capital resources, the TCF is making a huge contribution toward achieving the constitutional goal of education for every Pakistani child. The program is also helping in keeping a great number of children off the streets for a significant number of hours each day.

The Child Rights Movement (CRM) in Pakistan is a coalition of more than 200 civil society organizations working for the protection and promotion of children's rights across Pakistan.

RESOURCES

Some of the resources that can be helpful in addressing the matter of social justice in Pakistan are as follows.

http://crm.com.pk/about-us/
www.konpal.org/
http://sahil.org/
www.tcf.org.pk/
http://unesco.org.pk/
www.unicef.org/pakistan/partners_1790.html

Note

1. The cases under discussion have been dis-identified in order to maintain and protect confidential information.
2. The cases under discussion have been dis-identified in order to maintain and protect confidential information.

REFERENCES

Andrabi, T., Das, J., Khwaja, A. I., & Zajonc, T. (2005). *Religious school enrollment in Pakistan: A look at the data.* Washington, DC: World Bank.

Annual Status of Education Report Pakistan (2015). Retrieved from http://aserpakistan.org/document/aser/2015/reports/national/ASER_National_Report_2015.pdf.

Bhutta, Z., Soofi, S., Zaidi, S., Habib, A., & Hussain, M. (2011). Pakistan national nutrition survey, 2011. Retrieved from https://ecommons.aku.edu/cgi/viewcontent.cgi?article=1262&context=pakistan_fhs_mc_women_childhealth_paediatr.

Child Marriage Restraint Act (1929). Retrieved from www.refworld.org/pdfid/4c3f19a02.pdf.

Convention on the Rights of the Child (2009). Consideration of reports submitted by states parties under Article 44 of the Convention. Retrieved from www2.ohchr.org/english/bodies/crc/docs/co/CRC-C-PAK-CO4.pdf.

Cruel Numbers. (2013). Retrieved from http://sahil.org/cruel-numbers/.

Government of Pakistan (2013). National Plan of Action 2013–16. Retrieved from http://itacec.org/document/2015/8/nep/National_Plan_of_Action_Pakistan.pdf.

Government of Pakistan (2017). Pakistan Education Statistics 2015–16. Retrieved from http://library.aepam.edu.pk/Books/Pakistan%20Education%20Statistics%202015-16.pdf.

Haque, R. (2014). *Youth radicalization in Pakistan.* Washington, DC: United States Institute of Peace.

Hasan, S. K. (1997). Cultural heritage of Pakistan. *Journal of the Pakistan Historical Society, 45* (4), 327–335.

Junior, K. (2018). Countries with a population over 200 million. Retrieved from www.worldatlas.com/articles/countries-with-a-population-over-200-million.html.

Juvenile Justice System Ordinance (2000). Retrieved from www.ilo.org/dyn/natlex/docs/ELECTRONIC/81784/88955/F1964251258/PAK81784.pdf.

Juvenile Justice Systems (n.d.). Retrieved from www.hrw.org/reports/1999/pakistan2/Pakistan-06.htm.

March, S. (2014). Polio cases in Pakistan expected to hit record high after continued militant attacks on vaccination teams. ABC News. Retrieved from www.abc.net.au.

Ministry Justifies Defence Budget Hike (2018). Retrieved from www.dawn.com/.

National Commission for Child Welfare and Development (n.d.). Retrieved from www.mohr.gov.pk/index.php/home/pps_page/18.

National Institute of Population Studies & ICF International (2008). *Pakistan demographic and health survey 2006–07.* Islamabad: National Institute of Population Studies & ICF International.

National Institute of Population Studies & ICF International (2013). *Pakistan demographic and health survey 2012–2013.* Islamabad: National Institute of Population Studies & ICF International.

Naveed, S., & Butt, K. M. (2015). Causes and consequences of child marriages in South Asia: Pakistan's perspective. *South Asian Studies, 30*(2), 161–175.

Nazish, K. (2018). Pakistan's shame: The open secret of child sex abuse in the workplace. *The Guardian.* Retrieved from www.theguardian.com/global-development/2018/jun/15/pakistan-shame-open-secret-child-sex-abuse-workplace-kasur.

Nizami, A. T., Hassan, T. M., Yasir, S., Rana, M. H., & Minhas, F. A. (2018). Terrorism in Pakistan: The psychosocial context and why it matters. *BJPsych International, 15*(1), 20–22.

Portal, S. A. T. (2018). Fatalities in terrorist violence in Pakistan 2003–2013. Retrieved from www.satp.org/satporgtp/countries/pakistan/database/casualties.htm.

Sherman, S. S., Plitt, S., ul Hassan, S., Cheng, Y., & Zafar, S. T. (2005). Drug use, street survival, and risk behaviors among street children in Lahore, Pakistan. *Journal of Urban Health, 82*(4), iv113–iv124.

Protection of Pakistan Act (2014). Retrieved from www.na.gov.pk/uploads/documents/1404714927_922.pdf.

UNICEF (1989). Convention on the Rights of the Child.

United Nations High Commissioner for Human Rights (1990). Convention on the Rights of the Child. Retrieved from www.ohchr.org/en/professionalinterest/pages/crc.aspx.

World Day against Child Labour (2015). Retrieved from www.ilo.org/wcmsp5/groups/public/–asia/–ro-bangkok/–ilo-islamabad/documents/publication/wcms_388760.pdf.

25

The Impact of Decades of Political Violence on Palestinian Children in the Gaza Strip and the West Bank

Abdel Aziz Mousa Thabet

INTRODUCTION

In this chapter, we highlight the political and psychosocial context of Palestinian children and families living in the Palestine state. During the past three decades many political events have occurred, from the First Intifada to the Oslo Agreement, from the Al-Aqsa Intifada to factional fighting, and from the 2014 war on Gaza to the Great March of Return on March 30, 2018.

SOCIODEMOGRAPHIC CHARACTERISTICS

In 2017, according to the Palestinian Central Bureau of Statistics (PCBS) census, the population of Palestine was 4,705,601, of whom 2.4 million were males compared to 2.3 million females. The West Bank had 2.8 million inhabitants, 1.42 million being male and 1.38 million being female; the population of the Gaza Strip was 1.87 million, 39.9 percent of the total population of Palestine, of which about 950,000 were males compared to 924,000 females. The 2017 population pyramid showed that the Palestinian society is a young society. The population of the age under fifteen years was 38.6 percent of the total population in Palestine, 36.5 percent of those living in the West Bank, and 41.7 percent of residents in the Gaza Strip (PCBS, 2018).

In the past fifty-one years, Palestinians in the West Bank and the Gaza Strip have been victims of conflict and war, which increases the risk of mental health problems. This is a result of many factors such as high unemployment, poverty within families, large numbers of children, overcrowding in homes, direct exposure to traumatic events, and other sociocultural factors. Many studies have been carried out during this period to establish the connection between mental health factors such as family monthly income, gender, place of residence, types of violence, and other socio-economic factors. Mental health problem indicators such as rates of post-traumatic stress disorder (PTSD), depression, anxiety, and behavioral and emotional problems of children have also been reported. Investigations of the efficacy of treatment protocols in people with mental health problems have yielded promising results.

Many institutes and organizations in the area deliver training for professionals working in mental healthcare facilities, and others deliver primary-, secondary-, and tertiary-level services for target groups. All these studies converge to give us a clearer picture of Palestinian well-being in the area.

The aim of this chapter is to investigate the impact of political violence on Palestinian children, their resilience, and their coping styles in dealing with the consequences of war and political violence. The following objectives were core to this review:

1. To explore (a) the common adversities and causes of mental health problems in Palestinian society such as political, community, domestic, and personal violence; and (b) coping strategies and resilience in countering the negative effect of such adversities.
2. To investigate the effect of such adversities on the psychological well-being of Palestinian children.
3. To evaluate type and availability of intervention programs that help Palestinian children cope with such adversities.

In addition, the following topics were explored in the analysis:

1. What are the most common stressors rated by Palestinian children in the Gaza Strip and the West Bank related to political turmoil?
2. What are the types and severity of traumatic events due to different kinds of violence?
3. What are the most common mental health reactions rated in children such as PTSD, anxiety, depression, hyperactivity, conduct, and somatization?
4. Which intervention programs in the West Bank and the Gaza Strip may help Palestinian children be more resilient and have good psychological well-being?

Responses to these objectives are based on the combining and reanalysis of secondary data from previous work in the field of the psychosocial well-being of Palestinian children in the Gaza Strip and the West Bank.

The following tools were used to gather the data:

1. Autobiographies/biographies of the author and other coauthors in the area.
2. Web-based research including the Medline, Psycho info, OVID, Oxford University Press, and other available databases such as UN organizations' databases. This was done by using the following keywords: "Psychosocial well-being of Palestinians," "Interventions used in psychosocial problems in Gaza Strip and West Bank," "Trauma," "PTSD, Anxiety, Depression," "Mental health services in the Palestinians Territories," "Sociodemographic characteristics of Palestinians," and "Effect of war on Palestinians."

Previous reports of different community-based organizations (CBOs) and ministries dealing with psychological well-being were reviewed. The data taken from previous work were critiqued and positive and negative conclusions were drawn from previous work in the field of psychological well-being. For the reliability of the report, the researcher reviewed the previous papers published in judged journals, books, or reports by organizations working in the field of mental health. An understanding of the operational definitions of the research variables is important to understand the context of the information presented and the conclusions reached.

DEFINITION OF PSYCHOLOGICAL WELL-BEING

Psychological well-being is an attitude that includes people's cognitive and affective evaluations of their lives (Diener & Larson, 1993; Myers & Diener, 1995). The research in the field of stress shows a link between normative stressors and psychological well-being (Vanfosse, 1986).

DEFINITION OF VIOLENCE

The World Health Organization (WHO) promotes a broad definition of violence: the intentional use of physical force or power, threatened or actual, against oneself or another person, or against a group or community that either results in or has a high likelihood of resulting in injury, death, psychological harm, maldevelopment, or deprivation (WHO, 2002). This definition encompasses interpersonal violence as well as suicidal behavior and armed conflict. It also covers a wide range of acts, going beyond physical acts to include threats and intimidation. In addition to death and injury, this definition also includes the myriad and often less obvious consequences of violent behavior, such as psychological harm, deprivation, and maldevelopment, that compromises the well-being of individuals, families, and communities (WHO, 2002).

COMMUNITY VIOLENCE

Community violence is defined for this purpose as: violence between people who are not related, and who may or may not know each other (acquaintances and strangers). It generally, but not always, takes place outside the home, in public places. Political violence refers to acts of violence committed for political reasons such as riots, the repressive actions of security forces against people opposing the government, or battles between hostel dwellers and township residents (WHO, 2002).

EFFECT OF POLITICAL VIOLENCE

Palestinian families, like families in other societies, are subject to all forms of natural and man-made disasters and traumatic events. This background limits its discourse to stress, adversities due to environmental factors, traumatic events associated with political oppression, and military violence (injury and death resulting from exposure to warlike conditions, including the effects of factional fighting on Palestinians' well-being).

Review of the literature on the relationship between psychological disorders and exposure to political and military violence showed that anxiety, psychosomatic, and depression symptoms seem to be shared by most children subjected to political or military violence irrespective of their ethnic or cultural background.

Thabet, Tawahina, Sarraj, and Vostanis (2008) conducted a study of 200 families from north Gaza and east Gaza who had been exposed to continuous shelling in 2006. The sample included 197 children and 200 parents. Results showed that children experienced a mean number of eight traumatic events, 138 children out of 197 (70.1 percent) were likely to present with PTSD, 33.9 percent were rated as having anxiety symptoms of likely clinical significance, and 42.7 percent were rated as having significant mental health morbidity by their parents. Parents reported a mean number of eight and a half traumatic events; 60 percent of parents had symptoms of PTSD with a potential clinical significance, and 26.0 percent reported severe to very severe anxiety symptoms. The rates of PTSD and anxiety symptoms among parents and children were of sufficient severity to require assessment and intervention. Parents' and children's scores were significantly correlated for PTSD intrusion and arousal (but not for avoidance), as well as for anxiety symptoms. Overall, parental responses were found to contribute to children's PTSD and anxiety presentations.

Khamis (2008) studied the occurrence of PTSD and psychiatric disorders (i.e., anxiety and depression) in Palestinian adolescents following intifada-related injuries. The participants were 179 boys who were injured during the Al-Aqsa Intifada and as a result sustained a permanent physical disability. They ranged in age from twelve to eighteen years (M = 16.30). Questionnaires were administered in an interview format with adolescents at home. Approximately 76.5 percent of the injured victims qualify as having PTSD and the disorder had a heterogeneous course, with excess risk for chronic symptoms and comorbidity with other psychiatric disorders such as anxiety and depression. Among all the predictors in the PTSD, anxiety, and depression models, geographical location, fatalism, and negative coping were significant. The conclusions reached were that post-traumatic reactions and psychiatric disorders in adolescents involved in armed conflict can persist for several months.

Thabet, Tawahina, Sarraj, and Vostanis (2009a) tested 184 Palestinian children and adolescents in the Gaza Strip in November and December 2008. The children ranged from 8–18 years with mean age of 14.69 years. The results showed that the most common items endorsed (Siege of Gaza items) were: learning problems due to shortage of electricity and teachers unable to come to school (82.6 percent), "I feel I am in a big prison" (79.9 percent), "I quit purchasing daily needs because prices are very high" (79.3 percent), "I was not able to go to school due to shortage of fuel and absence of transportation" (75 percent), "I cannot find some of the necessary things for studying such as books and stationery" (68.5 percent). The children reported from one to nineteen siege items (mean = 9.07). The study showed that the mean score for the children's physical well-being was 11.03, the psychological well-being mean was 13.77, the moods and emotions mean was 12.53, the self-perception mean was 7.28, the autonomy mean was 9.56, the parent relations and home life mean was 14.75, the financial resources mean was 5.45, the peers and social support mean was 12.63, the school environment mean was 13.79, and the social acceptance (bullying) mean was 2.26. High scores were positively predicted by general mood and self-perception and negatively predicted by financial resources.

Thabet, Matar, Carpintero, Bankart, and Vostanis (2011) conducted a study to establish the association between labor-related variables and mental health problems among 780 children in the workforce (aged 9–18 years, mean 15.8) in the Gaza Strip. Ratings of mental health problems were predicted by different factors – i.e., total difficulties scores that children expressed as poor friendships, poor relationships, and lack of health insurance; anxiety scores expressed as selling goods in the streets, working to help family, low family income and lack of health insurance; and depression scores expressed by parents' dissatisfaction with their jobs and longer working hours.

Ingridsdatter et al. (2012a) studied a sample of 139 adolescents twelve to seventeen years old in the Gaza Strip. Results showed that 56.8 percent of adolescents reported elevated levels of intrusion, avoidance, and depression compared to low levels (6.3 percent) of these symptoms in communities not affected by war in the recent past. Significant risk factors for PTSD were exposure, female gender, older age, and an unemployed father. Risk factors for anxiety were exposure, female gender, and older age, whereas female gender ($\beta = < 0.238; p < 0.001$) was the only significant risk factor for depression.

Six months after the end of the war on Gaza that lasted for twenty-three days in 2009, Thabet et al. (2013) conducted a study of the entire Gaza Strip. The study sample included 410 children aged six to seventeen years. Using the *Diagnostic Manual of Mental Disorders-IV* (DSM-IV) criteria for PTSD, 39.3 percent of children reported partial PTSD and 9.8 percent of children reported the full criteria for PTSD. According to parents' report, the results showed 31.3 percent of children met the criteria for inattentive type (ADHD), 36.3 percent of children were impulsive (ADHD), and 29 percent met the criteria for combined type (ADHD). According to the children's report, the results showed 28.8 percent of children met the criteria for inattentive type, 37.3 percent of children were impulsive, and 28.3 percent met the criteria for combined type. Using the DSM-IV diagnostic criteria for conduct disorder and oppositional defiant disorder, the study showed that 38.1 percent of parents reported conduct disorder in their children and 46.3 percent reported oppositional defiant disorder while 39.3 percent of the children themselves reported conduct disorder and 44 percent of them reported oppositional defiant disorder, indicating little discrepancy from parents. The study showed that 5.1 percent of children had comorbidity of post-traumatic stress disorder and attention deficit disorder, 4.4 percent had comorbidity of PTSD and impulsivity-hyperactivity disorder, and 4.4 percent had comorbidity of PTSD and attention deficit with hyperactivity combined type. While 4.6 percent of children had comorbidity of conduct disorder and PTSD, 6.1 percent had comorbidity of oppositional defiant disorder and PTSD (Thabet et al., 2013).

Khamis (2013) investigated 600 children whose ages ranged from twelve to fifteen years (M = 12.83) and examined parents' sociodemographic status, daily stressors, family environment, and coping strategies, as well as academic achievement, cognitive functioning, and aggression in a sample of children at the intermediate grade levels from the Gaza Strip. Each of the predictor variables exhibited a different pattern of relations with the outcome domains. Although the study highlights the negative consequences of stress on children's development, certain daily stressors had a positive effect. Optimal family relationships predicted better developmental outcomes. The author opined that more emphasis on personal growth, control, and organization in the family predicted less optimal child development except for personal growth and achievement. Also, more reliance on positive coping and less reliance on negative coping is associated with better academic achievement.

Thabet, El-Buhaisi, and Vostanis (2014) examined a sample that consisted of 358 adolescents aged fifteen to eighteen years old, 44.1 percent boys and 55.9 percent girls. The study showed that the mean traumatic events reported by adolescent participants was 13.34 on the Gaza traumatic events checklist. The traumatic experiences reported by the adolescents in order were: 90.8 percent saw mutilated bodies on TV, 88.5 percent heard shelling of the area by heavy artillery, 86.6 percent saw the signs of shelling on the ground, and 86.0 percent heard the sonic sounds of the jetfighters. The results showed the mean total anxiety was 41.18, the obsessive compulsive subscale was 8.90, the generalized anxiety subscale was 4.46, social phobia was 6.99, separation anxiety was 6.16, physical injury fears were 5.48, and panic/agoraphobia was 5.4. The results showed that girls had more anxiety problems than boys, including all anxiety subscales. Regarding PTSD, the study showed that only 11.8 percent of adolescents reported no PTSD, 24.2 percent reported fewer than two clusters of symptoms, and 34.31 percent reported symptoms meeting criteria for partial PTSD, while 29.8 percent reported symptoms meeting criteria for full PTSD, according to DSM-IV-TR.

Results showed that girls reported more PTSD than boys. Palestinian adolescents mainly cope by developing social support, investing in close friends, and/or engaging in demanding activities. The study showed that adolescents who experienced traumatic experiences developed less social support and positively asked for more professional support as coping strategies. Adolescents with PTSD coped by ventilating feelings, developing social support, and avoiding problems, and adolescents with less PTSD were looking for more spiritual support for solving family problems. Adolescents with anxiety were ventilating feelings, developing social support, and engaging in demanding activities. Adolescents with less anxiety were seeking more spiritual support (Thabet et al., 2014).

In a 2015 study, Khamis investigated the long-term effects of the 2012 war on children's psychological health in the Gaza Strip. Participants were 205 males and females aged nine to sixteen years. Results indicated that approximately 30 percent of the Palestinian children who were exposed to higher levels of war traumas developed PTSD with excessive risk for comorbidity with other disorders such as emotional symptoms and neuroticism. The findings revealed that children with lower family income reported higher levels of emotional and behavioral disorders and neuroticism. While emotion-focused coping was positively associated with emotional and behavioral problems, neuroticism, and PTSD, problem-focused coping was negatively associated with neuroticism and PTSD (Khamis, 2015).

Thabet, Sneada, Khayyat, and Vostanis (2015) examined a study sample that consisted of 380 adolescents randomly selected from secondary schools in the Gaza Strip; of these 171 were boys and 209 were girls between fifteen and eighteen years. The most common reported traumatic events due to the war on Gaza were: seeing mutilated bodies and wounded people on TV (92.3 percent) and hearing shelling of the area by artillery (89.4 percent). The mean number of traumatic events experienced by Palestinian adolescents was 14. Boys reported significantly more traumatic events than girls. Adolescents from families with monthly incomes of less than $150 US experienced more traumatic events than the other groups. There was a significant relationship between traumatic experiences and psychosomatic symptoms (Thabet et al., 2015).

In another study, Thabet, Thabet, and Vostanis (2016a) selected 251 children from three summer camps in Gaza. This study showed that children commonly reported traumatic events such as hearing shelling of the area by artillery, hearing the sonic sounds of jetfighters, and seeing images of dead and injured people on TV. The number of traumatic events was associated with PTSD, avoidance, arousal symptoms, anxiety, and depression.

Thabet and Thabet (2017) studied the prevalence of PTSD, depression, and anxiety among orphaned children in the Gaza Strip; the study sample consisted of eighty-one orphaned children from the Al-Amal Institute for Orphans. The study indicated that 67.9 percent showed depression. Depression was more prevalent in children from north Gaza in comparison to than those coming from the other four areas of the Gaza Strip. Thirty point nine percent of children had anxiety and children thirteen to fifteen years old were most anxiety prone. Children coming from north Gaza had more anxiety than those coming from the other four areas of the Gaza Strip, which is a border area with more exposure to traumatic events. Results showed a positive correlation with statistical significance between depression and anxiety, intrusion, and avoidance. While total depression was negatively correlated with arousal symptoms of PTSD, anxiety was negatively correlated with PTSD and avoidance symptoms of PTSD.

In a study of 317 children and their parents living in Rafah, Thabet and Thabet (2017) aimed to explore the consequences of trauma, in particular the extent to which children suffering from a range of behavioral and emotional disorders become the primary drivers of violence at the individual, family, and community levels. Palestinian children reported a mean of 9.34 traumatic events. Boys reported more exposure to traumatic events than girls. Results showed 25.2 percent of children had PTSD. The study showed a prevalence of general mental health problems using the Strengths and Difficulties Questionnaire (SDQ) (Goodman, 1997; Goodman, Lamping, & Ploubidis, 2010; Goodman, Meltzer, & Bailey, 1998); self-reported, parents', and teachers' forms were high. The total score of anxiety was 41.15. Girls had more panic/agoraphobia and separation anxiety than boys. Children commonly coped with trauma by using and seeking professional support, seeking diversion, solving family problems, and developing social support. Boys had more coping skills than girls. There was a significant correlation between total trauma and PTSD, PTSD and total coping strategies, ventilating feelings and PTSD, social support and PTSD, and avoiding problems and PTSD.

Recently, Thabet (2019) studied all children attending an orphanage (the El-Amal Institute) in Gaza City (N = 83). The age group most symptomatic was twelve to fourteen, with 18.1 percent meeting full PTSD criteria. After the trauma, 78.3 percent said that they have a stronger religious faith, and 70.7 percent said they learned a great deal about how wonderful people in the world are.

Qeshta, Hawajri, and Thabet (2019) aimed to investigate the relationship between war trauma and PTSD, anxiety, and depression among secondary school students in the Gaza Strip. The study sample consisted of 408 randomly selected secondary school students (204 boys and 204 girls). The results showed that the most common reported traumatic experiences by adolescents were: seeing mutilated bodies on TV (93.1 percent), hearing shelling of the area by artillery (92.4 percent), hearing the loud voice of drones (90.4 percent), forced to leave their home with family members due to shelling (67.6 percent), and inhalation of bad smells due to bombardment (67.6 percent). Mean traumatic events were 10. There were statistically significant differences in higher rates in boys. Our results showed that 25.5 percent showed partial PTSD and 16.4 percent of children showed the full criteria for PTSD. PTSD was more in children with family monthly income less than $450. Using a cut-off point of the scale, 92 of the children reported anxiety (22.2 percent). There were statistically significant differences in anxiety in favor of girls. Anxiety was more common in children from poor families (monthly income less than $450). Using this as the cut-off point of the scale, 139 of the children reported depression (34.1 percent). Depression was more common in children from poor families (monthly income less than $451). The results showed a significant correlation between total traumatic events reported by children and total PTSD, reexperiencing, avoidance, and arousal. There was a statistical correlation between anxiety and depression and anxiety and PTSD, and a statistically significant correlation between PTSD and depression.

EFFICACY OF THERAPEUTIC MEASURES TO IMPROVE THE MENTAL HEALTH AND WELL-BEING OF PALESTINIAN CHILDREN

Scholars have conducted limited research on the effectiveness of specific psychological interventions for children living in war zones. However, a number of studies have described or evaluated different models of interventions for mental health problems among children who have suffered abuse or experienced natural disasters, political violence, or exposure to community violence.

Thabet, Khalid, and Vostanis (2005) looked at the impact of a short-term group crisis intervention for children ages nine to fifteen years from five refugee camps in the Gaza Strip during ongoing war conflict and did not find a significant impact of the intervention on children's post-traumatic or depressive symptoms. While Loughry et al. (2006) found a reduction in externalizing symptoms, there was improved parental support of the children but no change in hopefulness scores. The study showed that children themselves reported a decrease in all mental health problems after the intervention but parents did not.

Furthermore, in another intervention study, Thabet, Tawahina, Sarraj, and Vostanis (2009b) found that children themselves reported a decrease in all mental health problems after the intervention and, according to their parents' reports, children did not report any changes in mental health problems. In the study of the effectiveness of a student mediation program on children, no changes were noted in child mental health and hyperactivity symptoms after the intervention program (Thabet, Tawahina, Sarraj, & Vostanis, 2009c). In a study examining the effectiveness of psychodrama on adolescents, the results showed that total scores of child mental health problems and hyperactivity symptoms were less after the program (Thabet, Tawahina, Sarraj, & Vostanis, 2009d). Ingridsdatter et al. (2012b) reported on the effectiveness of writing from recovery as a trauma intervention. Results at post test showed a reduction in post-traumatic stress symptoms in both groups, an increase in depression in the intervention group, and no change in anxiety symptoms. At follow-up, a significant decline in depression scores was evident. However, pooling the results supported no evidence for improvements due to the intervention. More recently, in a study examining the effectiveness of writing from recovery as a trauma intervention, Thabet and Vostanis (2016) showed an increase in post-traumatic stress after the intervention, while anxiety was decreased in adolescents.

Qouta, Qouta, Diab, and Punamaki (2012) examined the effectiveness of teaching recovery techniques (TRT) in war-affected children. The intervention significantly reduced the proportion of clinical post-traumatic stress symptoms among boys, and a reduction of clinical post-traumatic stress symptoms in girls. In another study using TRT, Diab, Peltonen, Qouta, Palosaari, and Punamaki (2015) showed that the intervention did not statistically significantly increase the level of resilience, neither was the effect of the intervention moderated by maternal attachment responses or family atmosphere. Similarly, Barron, Abdallah, and Heltne (2016) examined the effectiveness of TRT on Palestinian adolescents; the study showed that adolescents reported significantly fewer post-traumatic stress symptoms post-intervention, but that depression and dissociation remained stable for treated adolescents, but worsened for those on the wait list.

CONCLUSION

This review focuses on the effect of violence on children, adults, and children in the context of war. The severity of violence changes from time to time, but the types of traumatic experiences are similar and include viewing mutilated bodies on TV, hearing and seeing shelling, exposure to sonic bombs, and witnessing home bombardment and demolition. These traumatic violent experiences affect the lives of Palestinian children and their well-being and increase the rate of psychological problems in the targeted group.

However, coping strategies, family, and social support were a protective factor for children with regard to overcoming the negative impact of trauma. Such findings were consistent with previous studies on the same topic that showed that Arabs commonly emphasize family life, value family cohesion and continuity, and practice mutual assistance within the family. They tend to put the well-being of the family as a whole above that of individual family members. Arab society stresses the importance of good relations between nuclear and extended families. Children's status is affected by the partial responsibility of the extended family (in cooperation with the parents) for their upbringing. In Arab families, fathers are commonly responsible for discipline and mothers support, educate, and raise the children. Children are supposed to obey their parents, submit to their demands, and fulfill their expectations (Haj-Yahia, 1995). Others postulate that childhood trauma associated with war violates children's sense of safety and trust in the world in which they live, reducing their sense of worth. It also increases their levels of emotional distress, shame, and grief, and their tendency to engage in destructive behaviors (Atkinson, Nelson, Brooks, Atkinson, & Ryan, 2014).

For primary intervention most of the organizations working in the West Bank and the Gaza Strip are delivering services through public meetings, workshops, home visits, and group interventions within the community and schools. This includes the United Nations Relief and Works Agency for Palestine Refugees (UNRWA), the Ministry of Education, counseling centers, and early childhood centers.

Studies of the impact of different types of interventions have increased within the past few years, including group crisis intervention, psychodrama, school mediation, noncurricular activities in schools and summer camps, and expressive writing therapy with promising results that reduce anxiety – these improve the general mental health of children and women victims of violence and abuse. Such intervention programs were a necessity given the trauma and violence that children, young people, and their families experienced. However, we recommend longer-term interventions to address the long-term impact of trauma on children and parents.

From a sociopolitical context, after long years of occupation and exposure to wars and stressors due to the siege status of the area, and sharing in the Great March of Return (March 2018), Palestinian children's understanding of their rights to return to a homeland are now deeply rooted in their memories. The Palestinian struggle for independence is central to a Palestinian child's experience. Participation in such struggles reinforces and challenges patriarchal family values (Abdo-Kaloti, 2001) because children assume active roles in the protection of cultural traditions and the assertion of political ideology.

RECOMMENDATIONS

It is recommended that international agencies and human rights organizations use persuasion that forces the region into implementing the fifty-four articles outlined in the UN Convention on the Rights of the Child (CRC) and to operationalize and implement a wide array of social policies related to managing complex emergency events such wars, conflicts, and violence to more mundane situations that affect children.

Our recommendations for policy makers in the Ministries of Health, Education, and Social Welfare and the UNRWA are the following:

1. Promote normalization of daily routines for children inside schools as soon as possible after traumatic events.
2. Conduct psychoeducation and parenting programs for parents in order to promote positive parenting skills and to increase their sense of well-being, self-confidence, and ability to care for their children in the face of such frequent trauma, and to support parents as well as extended family by developing programs that produce a sense of normalcy for children and families.
3. Schools can continue to increase extracurricular facilities, turning them into "recreation centers" where children can study, play, and socialize throughout the day.
4. Continue with training programs for schoolteachers and counselors to recognize the early symptoms of trauma and mental health problems. Train school counselors and teachers to deal with childhood disciplinary infractions in a nonviolent manner.

This review provides data on how ubiquitous war trauma has an impact on the lives of all children who live in the Palestine area. Their lives are scarred by witnessing horrific images through the media or by direct exposure to war and its aftermath. However, it is also a significant observation that many children are resilient and flourish despite these problems. Interventions are only partially successful. Creating normalcy out of abnormal conditions is a daunting task, but creating a framework may rescue generations of children from the social injustice of being born in a part of the world in which war has become a normal part of daily life.

Gaps in areas of research suggest that we explore:

1. Risk and protective factors that can give clear direction regarding mental health interventions with children perpetually exposed to warlike circumstances.
2. To understand the mental health needs of people with special needs and marginalized populations such as the elderly and very young children.
3. To investigate biological and organic factors at risk for mental health problems.
4. To conduct new controlled studies to evaluate the effectiveness of new protocols for psychosocial intervention such as cognitive behavior therapy, group intervention with bereaved people, expressive writing therapy, and other new techniques used in Western societies after adapting them to the Palestinian sociopolitical context.

REFERENCES

Abdo-Kaloti, R. (2001). Palestinian adolescents' exposure to violence in their families of origin: The rate of the problem and its psychological consequences. Unpublished master's thesis, Hebrew University of Jerusalem, Jerusalem, Israel.

Atkinson, J., Nelson, J., Brooks, R., Atkinson, C., & Ryan, K. (2014). Addressing individual and community transgenerational trauma. In P. Dudgeon, H. Milroy, & R. Walker (eds.), *Working together: Aboriginal and Torres Strait Islander mental health and wellbeing principles and practice* (pp. 289–307). www.telethon.

Barron, I., Abdallah, G., & Heltne, U. (2016). Randomized control trial of teaching recovery techniques in rural occupied Palestine: Effect on adolescent dissociation. *Journal of Aggression, Maltreatment & Trauma*, 25, 9. https://doi.org/10.1080/10926771.2016.1231149.

Diab, M., Peltonen, K., Qouta, S. R., Palosaari, E., & Punamaki, R. L. (2015). Effectiveness of psychosocial intervention enhancing resilience among war-affected children and the moderating role of family factors. *Child Abuse & Neglect*, 40, 24–35.

Diener, E., & Larsen, R. J. (1993). The experience of emotional well-being. In M. Lewis & J. M. Haviland (eds.), *Handbook of emotions* (pp. 405–415). New York: Guilford Press.

Goodman, R. (1997). The Strengths and Difficulties Questionnaire: A research note. *Journal of Child Psychology and Psychiatry*, 38, 581–586.

Goodman A., Lamping D. L., & Ploubidis G. B. (2010). When to use broader internalising and externalising subscales instead of the hypothesised five subscales on the Strengths and Difficulties Questionnaire (SDQ): Data from British parents, teachers and children. *Journal of Abnormal Child Psychology*, 38, 1179–1191.

Goodman R., Meltzer, H., & Bailey, V. (1998). The Strengths and Difficulties Questionnaire: A pilot study on the validity of the self-report version. *European Child and Adolescent Psychiatry*, 7, 125–130.

Ingridsdatter, I., Nielsen, L., Kolltveit, S., et al. (2012a). Risk factors for PTSD, anxiety, and depression among adolescents in Gaza. *Journal of Traumatic Stress*, 25, 164–170.

Ingridsdatter, I., Nielsen, L., Kolltveit, S., et al. (2012b). Short-term effects of a writing intervention among adolescents in Gaza. *Journal of Loss and Trauma*, 17(5), 403–422.

Haj-Yahia, M. (1995). Toward culturally sensitive intervention with Arab families in Israel. *Contemporary Family Therapy*, 17, 429–447.

Khamis, V. (2008). Post-traumatic stress and psychiatric disorders in Palestinian adolescents following intifada-related injuries. *Social Science & Medicine*, 67, 1199–1207.

Khamis, V. (2013). Stressors, family environment and coping styles as predictors of educational and psychosocial adjustment in Palestinian children. *Educational Studies*. doi:10.1080/03055698.2013.767185.

Khamis, V. (2015). Coping with war trauma and psychological distress among school-age Palestinian children. *American Journal of Orthopsychiatry*, 85(1), 72–79.

Loughry, M., Ager, A., Flouri, E., et al. (2006). The impact of structured activities among Palestinian children in a time of conflict. *Journal of Child Psychology and Psychiatry*, 47(12), 1211–1218.

Myers, D. G., & Diener, E. (1995). Who is happy? *Psychological Science*, 6(1), 10–19. doi.org/10.1111/j.1467-9280.1995.tb00298.x

Palestinian Central Bureau of Statistics (PCBS) (2018). *Population, housing and establishments census 2017, final results: Establishments report*. Ramallah: Palestinian Central Bureau of Statistics.

Qeshta, H., Hawajri A. M. A, & Thabet, A. M. (2019). The relationship between war trauma, PTSD, anxiety and depression among adolescents in the Gaza Strip. *Health Science Journal*, 13(1), 621.1–12.

Qouta, S. R., Qouta, S. R., Diab, M., & Punamaki, R. L. (2012). Intervention effectiveness among war affected children: A cluster randomized controlled trial on improving mental health. *Journal of Traumatic Stress*, 25(3), 288–298.

Thabet, A. A. (2019). Psychological well-being of Palestinian children and Adolescents in Gaza Strip and West Bank: Review Paper. *EC Psychology and Psychiatry*, 8(3), 197–205.

Thabet, A. A., el-Buhaisi, O., & Vostanis, P. (2014). Trauma, PTSD, anxiety, and coping strategies among Palestinians adolescents exposed to war on Gaza. *Arab Journal of Psychiatry*, 25(1), 71–82.

Thabet, A. A., Khalid, K., & Vostanis, P. (2005). Group crisis intervention for children during ongoing war conflict. *European Child and Adolescent Psychiatry*, 14, 262–269.

Thabet, A. A., Matar, S., Carpintero, A., Bankart, J., & Vostanis, P. (2011). Mental health problems among labour children in the Gaza Strip. *Child Care Health Developments*, 37(1), 89–95.

Thabet, A. A., Sneada, N. A., Khayyat, D. K., & Vostanis, P. (2015). Prevalence of psychosomatic symptoms among traumatized Palestinian adolescents in the Gaza Strip. *British Journal of Education, Society & Behavioural Science*, 8(2). 94–103. Article no. BJESBS.2015.103.

Thabet, A. A., Tawahina, A. A., El Sarraj, E., & Vostanis, P. (2008). Exposure to war trauma and PTSD among parents and children in the Gaza Strip. *European Child & Adolescent Psychiatry*, 17, 191–199.

Thabet, A. A., Tawahina, A. A., El Sarraj, E., & Vostanis, P. (2009a). Impact of siege on Palestinian children's quality of life in the Gaza Strip. *Arabpsynet E. Journal*, 24, 101–107.

Thabet, A. A., Tawahina, A. A., El Sarraj, E., & Vostanis, P. (2009b). Effectiveness of school-based debriefing sessions for Palestinian children affected by war and trauma. *Arabpsynet E.Journal*, 24, 46–49.

Thabet, A. A., Tawahina, A. A., El Sarraj, E., & Vostanis, P. (2009c). Effectiveness of student mediation program to decrease behavioural and emotional problems in Palestinian children affected by war and trauma in the Gaza Strip. *Arabpsynet E. Journal*, 24, 50–55.

Thabet, A. A., Tawahina, A. A., El Sarraj, E., & Vostanis, P. (2009d). Effectiveness of school-based psychodrama in improving mental health of Palestinian adolescents. *Arabpsynet E.Journal*, 24, 67–71.

Thabet, A. A., Tawahina, A. A., El Sarraj, E., et al. (2013). Comorbidity of post-traumatic stress disorder, attention deficit with hyperactivity, conduct, and oppositional defiant disorder in Palestinian children affected by war on Gaza. *Health*, 5(6), 994–1002. www.scirp.org/journal/health/

Thabet, A. A., & Thabet, S. S. (2017). Coping with trauma among children in south of Gaza Strip. *Psychology and Cognitive Sciences Open Journal*, 3(2), 36–47. Doi:10.17140/PCSOJ-3-122.

Thabet, A. A., Thabet, S., & Vostanis, P. (2016a). The relationship between war trauma, PTSD, depression, and anxiety among Palestinian children in the Gaza Strip. *Health Science Journal*, 1791–809X.

Thabet, A. A., Thabet, S., & Vostanis, P. (2016b). Effects of a writing intervention for Palestinian adolescent victims of political violence in Gaza Strip. *BAOJ Psychology*, 3(1) 012.

Vanfossen, B. (1986). Sex differences in depression: The role of spouse support. In S. Hobfoll (ed.), *Stress, social support and women* (pp. 69–84). Washington, DC: Hemisphere.

World Health Organization (WHO) (2002). Global consultation on violence and health. Violence: A public health priority. Geneva (document WHO/EHA/SPI.POA. 2).

26

Social Justice Issues for Children and Young People in Peru and Other Latin American Countries

Renato D. Alarcón

Without attempting to impose it as an irrefutable statement, it can be said that Peru may be considered a typical representative of past and current, positive and negative realities of Latin America as a continent. Its inclusion in a fairly high level among the so-called Low- and Middle-Income Countries (LMICs) by United Nations (UN)-qualified agencies may also justify the assertion (Fantom & Serajuddin, 2016; International Society for Clinical Biostatistics, 2017). Furthermore, as the historical setting of many pre-Columbian (i.e., prior to Columbus's arrival in what is now America) cultures, a good part of Peru's current territory was also the geographic bastion of the Inca civilization, which, together with Mayas and Aztecs in the Yucatán Peninsula and part of what is now Central America and the Republic of México, respectively, were established powers in the region for about three centuries before the arrival of the Spanish *conquistadores*. Viceroyalties and general captainships then certified the colonial presence of European powers (Spain and Portugal) in the New World for the next 300 years. In the 1800s, independence wars and movements allowed the creation of sovereign nations whose total number today is twenty-one. In contemporary times, approaches from international organizations and several academic disciplines focus on Latin America (Mexico and Central and South America) and thirteen sovereign island nations in the Caribbean region (Cuba, Dominican Republic, Jamaica, Haiti, Grenada, St. Lucia, Trinidad and Tobago, Aruba, Barbados, Antigua, Bahamas, Cayman, and St. Kitts) as a joint study area, mostly based on geographic, demographic, and socioeconomic perspectives.

SOCIAL CONTEXTS

Like their counterparts in other countries and world regions, Peruvian children and young people deal with a variety of circumstances and situations that configure both the socioenvironmental background of their everyday lives, and the psychosociocultural characteristics of the personal and collective styles used to confront it. Context is a healthy relativistic concept used by developmental psychologists, pioneering psychoanalysts, social scientists, and clinical psychiatrists to describe these factors. Knowledge of its features provides a valuable frame of reference that assists researchers, care providers, administrators, and the public to understand and manage more effectively, the resulting processes (Fabrega, 2001; Schacht, 1993).

For the purposes of this chapter, a number of contextual factors can be identified as relevant to social justice issues for children and youngsters in Peru and other Latin American countries. Taken individually, partly, or totally, these contexts can be acknowledged and managed in a positive or constructive fashion but may also become real threats against or barriers to a normal physical, psychological, behavioral, sociocultural, and ethical human development (World Psychiatric Association, 2015). They are:

1) Family life: Called the "micro-cultural" component of human life, the interactions from the beginning of life between children and adolescents with parents or parental figures set the stage for the modeling, orientation, and future-oriented guidance of long-term existential formulations, including resilience (Garrett et al., 2014; Postma et al., 2014).

2) Community and neighborhood: The first scenario of individual inquiries, explorations, findings, and more or less complex experiences with "the others" (Turiel, Hildrebrandt, & Wainryb, 1991), the first edge of "macro-cultural" influences that may variously impart lessons of tolerance, acceptance, understanding, or their respective opposite notions.

3) Education and learning opportunities: A more formal and extended context of family and community life in a setting that broadens children's or adolescents' perspectives by subjecting them to diverse models and norms. These factors offer possibilities for long-term friendships and self-esteem enhancement, while also exposing youth to the negative features of competition, confrontation, abuse, arbitrariness, or violence (Garbarino, 1998; Holland & Cortina, 2017). Identity-building and reaffirmation processes reach a crucial stage in this context (Riquelme, 1987).

4) Healthcare and protection services: Children, adolescents, and young adults start experiencing and exploring sensations like pain, fever, discomfort, or physical distress, as well as options of care. The latter, like all the other contexts, may reflect a variety of approaches, their advantages, and their limitations.

5) Societal involvement: A collective set of traits that reinforce pluses and minuses of personal identity through the impact of social and cultural features, rules dictated by sometimes omniscient agencies – i.e., religious beliefs and practices, political slogans, pronouncements of confrontational groups, or gender-determined situations (Cosman, 2001; Finkelhor, Wolak, & Berliner, 2001).

6) Safety and security issues: The preambles of future, more active involvements are included in notions such as citizenship, public well-being, quality of life, etc., generating the superior meaning of justice in general, and of social justice in particular (Finkelhor et al., 2001; Postma et al., 2014). Solidarity and resilience

become pillars of maturity, instruments of defense, and/or protection against new or still unknown adversaries (Garrett et al., 2014; Zaff, Kawashima-Ginsberg, & Lin, 2011).

To be sure, these contextual factors have a strong presence at a global level and, obviously, in Peru and Latin America. It can be said that all of them show, in no small measure, deficiencies and failures when applied to the Peruvian and Latin American populations, much more evident of course in relation to their young components. The contexts become threats and raise barriers against a fair social justice construct and structure, making children and adolescents their greatest, most vulnerable victims.

General Parameters

According to the most recent data (Instituto Nacional de Estadística e Informática [INEI], 2017), Peru's population adds up to 32,204,325 inhabitants with an annual growth rate of 1.1 percent (about 339,000), and a nativity rate of 18.87 percent. The total figure has registered an increase of almost 4 million in ten years, from 28,220,764 in 2007. Occupying a territory of 1,285,216 square kilometers, 30 percent of which are devoted to agriculture and livestock, Peru is one of the nineteen largest countries in the world, and the fifth most populated in Latin America. Up to the age of forty-four, 49.9 percent of the Peruvian population is female, but the figure moves up to 50.2 percent beginning at age forty-five and reaches 58.4 percent at age eighty and over.

More than half of the people (52.6 percent) live in cities or towns located in the coastal region near the Pacific Ocean (only 11.7 percent of the country's territory), whereas 38 percent reside in the Andean zone (Sierra) (30.5 percent of the territory), and just 9.4 percent live in the jungle region (Selva) that occupies the largest geographic area (62 percent of the territory). Lima, the country's capital, has almost 10 million inhabitants and, together with Callao (the main port), Trujillo and Chiclayo (northern subregion), and Arequipa (southern subregion) represent the main urban metropolitan areas, with 76 percent of the population. An important new demographic development is the massive influx of immigrants, particularly from Venezuela, country from which nearly 600,000 persons have entered Peru since 2016, according to the UN High Commission for Refugees Agency (2018).

From an ethnic perspective, the predominant group (51 percent of the population) is constituted by *mestizos*, a mix of White (European, mostly Spanish) and native Peruvians, followed by the Amerindios (32 percent), descendants of the properly native groups (Quechuas and Aymaras, primarily), Whites (17 percent), Blacks, and Asians (4 percent). This composition is reflected in the use of languages: 84 percent of the population speak Spanish, 14 percent speak Quechua (the original Inca language), and 2 percent speak Aymara, which used mostly by natives from the Altiplano region, the highest Andean lands in the country's south and southeast zones, at the border with Bolivia. Note, however, that up to seventy-two ethnolinguistic groups live across the country, most of them in tribal, jungle-based communities. In terms of religion, 82 percent of the population self-identify as Catholic, 12.5 percent self-identify as Evangelicals or Protestants (a growing subgroup), 3.3 percent profess other religions, and 2.9 percent are nonbelievers or atheists (INEI, 2017).

Closer to the purposes of this chapter, the age group distribution of the Peruvian population goes as follows: children between zero and ten years, 17 percent; adolescents eleven to eighteen years old, 16 percent; young people between nineteen and twenty-nine years old, 22 percent; adults thirty to sixty-four years old, 38 percent; elderly sixty-five years and over, 7 percent. Life expectancy for women (50.3 percent of the total population) is seventy-seven years, and for men (49.7 percent), seventy-two years. In 2014, there were 8 million households in Peru, 76 percent of them in urban areas. In 26.5 percent of the households, the household was led by a woman, an increase of 4.7 points since 2004. Interestingly, 38.2 percent of household heads were single (down from 41.3 percent in 2004), 28.1 percent were married (down from 30.8 percent ten years earlier), and in 20.4 percent of households, the household couple lived consensually together (up from 17.6 percent in 2004) (Encuesta Nacional de Hogares [ENAHO], 2017).

In the year 2010, about one-third (30 percent) of the population had superior (college- or university-based) education; 39 percent, secondary (high school); 21 percent, primary; 4 percent, initial; and 6 percent no education. These figures meant an overall literacy level of 94.2 percent, probably also reflected in the 73.6 percent of the economically active population, a GDP annual growth rate of 5 percent, and the 6 percent of the population dealing with unemployment – the latter being three times higher among the young subpopulation. Nevertheless, employment levels improved from 20 percent to 28.5 percent, and below-average wages decreased from 64.2 percent to 57.2 percent between 2004 and 2014 (Cruz & Huerta-Mercado, 2015; ENAHO, 2017).

In the midst of these at times surprising and conflicting findings, 30.8 percent of Peru's population is considered to belong to the "middle class," according to universal standards. Interestingly, growing numbers of Peruvians seem to be migrating to other countries, primarily for educational and occupational reasons, yet a number of them return – i.e., 242,621 returned between 2000 and 2012, almost one-third of them people between fifteen and twenty-nine years of age, most of them students. Chile is the country with the highest number of Peruvian migrants (34.5 percent), followed by the United States of America and Argentina. Students, housewives, and professionals are, in that order, the most frequent occupations in this group. From these figures, we can conclude that the older the age of migration, the lower the chances of return (Aramburu & Mendoza, 2015).

Specific Parameters

In spite of some of the encouraging findings presented earlier in this chapter, several areas in Peru's current reality raise justifiable concerns, particularly in connection with social justice issues for children and young people. A poverty index of 30 percent (55 percent in rural areas) and an indigence (extreme poverty) rate of 4.7 percent may be closely related to an infantile and child mortality rate of 18 percent and growing. Children and youth are a considerable proportion of the 11 percent of the population with so-called chronic conditions (including malnutrition, anemia, cognitive underdevelopment, autism, or hyperactivity), physical handicaps, and subsequent incapacities, the majority of them residing in urban areas (INEI, 2017). Similarly, those age groups are found in a majority of the 70,000 HIV patients in Peru, and sexually transmitted diseases (STDs) increased from 0.2 percent to 0.5 percent in people aged fifteen to twenty-four between 2004 and 2014 (Ministerio de Salud, 2011). Likewise, young subpopulations exhibit high rates of alcohol, tobacco, and drug abuse-related clinical conditions.

Adolescent fertility rates reached 48.5 per 1,000 among women aged fifteen to nineteen years in 2015, with a subsequent high number of unintended pregnancies in this subpopulation. In 2012, Peru was one of the worst-performing countries in the Programme for International Student Assessment (PISA), sponsored by the Organisation for Economic Co-operation and Development (OECD) (2012). In turn, more than 2.5 million children aged five to fourteen years represented one-third of the nation's workforce. The same year it was found that 58.6 percent of gang activity in poor metropolitan areas of the main cities (particularly Lima) had youths in leading roles, in addition to people fifteen to twenty-nine years of age showing the highest death rates associated with criminal acts (femicides being the most prominent in the prior two to three years), and those between eighteen and twenty-nine being the highest cohort among prison populations (Consejo Nacional de la Juventud [CONAJU], 2002).

THREATS AND BARRIERS TO SOCIAL JUSTICE

A variety of issues, born out of the realities described earlier in this chapter, constitute threats that disrupt the social equilibrium of child and young populations in Peru, and actually interfere with eventual, well-intentioned, solution-searching measures. These threats also represent dramatic violations of social justice against defenseless community groups:

1) Poverty: A factor of universal presence – i.e., in entire countries as well as among underprivileged subpopulations in the so-called developed countries – poverty threatens the physical and emotional health of billions of people, particularly children and youth (Garbarino, 1998). Its most damaging sequelae is de facto social exclusion and neglect from governments and other powers that be, which

include wealthy minorities protected by political connections and one-sided legislation and public administrative rules (Bregaglio, Constantino, & Chavez, 2014; Silva, Loureiro, & Cardoso, 2017). In spite of recent economic growth, Peru has had (and still has) poverty as a powerful reality throughout its history, particularly among its Andean, native, and rural population segments.

2) Corruption: Moving many times in a not-so-subtle way from the private to the public sector, corruption has become the number one threat to the stability and credibility of governments in many countries around the world, Latin American nations (Brazil, Argentina, Venezuela, Ecuador, Nicaragua, Honduras, El Salvador, and Guatemala, among the most impacted) being no exception. Corruption operates as a threat against the majority of the citizenship, deprived as much of decent incomes as of power, information, and, ultimately, dignity. And, by trafficking influence in order to prevent investigations, pursuit of justice, and legitimate punishment, corruption is also a barrier to corrective efforts (Ugaz, 2018). Recently, it has been found that five different government administrations of Peru during the past three decades have been involved in enormous schemes of corruption that have landed two former presidents currently in prison, seen two prohibited from leaving the country (one of them recently sought political asylum in a foreign embassy in Lima, which did not grant it), and resulted in one currently facing extradition procedures (Transparencia Internacional, 2017; Vega, 2018).

3) Violence: The level of violence across the world has unquestionably increased, and not only in connection with wars or armed conflicts within and between many countries, particularly in Africa, the Middle East, and Asia (Preski & Shelton, 2001; Rajani, 1998). Even though Peru had more than two decades (the 1970s to the early 1990s) of political violence, with the insurrection led by two extremist political groups (Sendero Luminoso [Shining Path] and the Túpac Amaru Revolutionary Movement), violence nowadays is mostly criminal in nature with homicides, assaults, robbery, and aggressions particularly in urban zones, extended to Andean and jungle areas where bands of organized crime (i.e., narcotic traffic) have established almost inaccessible headquarters (Vargas, 2014; Zapata, 2018). Reports have emerged of collaboration between these criminal organizations and military or police personnel. Other kinds of violence (domestic violence, sexual assault, racism, or gender-related abuse) have also multiplied with children, adolescents, and women as their main victims (Butcher, Galanek, Kretschmar, & Flannery, 2015; Finfgeld-Connett, 2017; Holland & Cortina, 2017; Michalec, Martimianakis, Tilbert, & Hafferty, 2017). Lack of expeditious legal rules, scarce public order forces, and limited public collaboration (originating in fear, doubts, distrust, or ignorance) are additional factors of public distress and actual danger in Peru.

4) Life in the streets and open areas: Closely related to the previous threat, what were once safe and preferred settings of healthy social interactions (streets, parks,

avenues, museums, entertainment places or settings, etc.) in countries like Peru are now just unavoidable places of brief ambulatory transactions or deserted and avoided (when not violent) areas in cities, towns, and villages. Another phenomenon in this connection is the presence of gangs or *pandillas*, primarily integrated by youngsters, children of broken homes, Andean migrants to the coastal cities, jobless or homeless adolescents, or early narcotic users or traffickers, among other people (INEI, 2018a). These gangs devote themselves to sometimes major criminal or violent acts. Their members personify a living social threat, and are, at the same time, a nation's testimony of yet another dramatic violation of social justice principles (Ryan, Williams, & Courtney, 2013).

5) Internal migrations: The civil war of the 1980s and 1990s displaced at least 3 million people (mostly children, adolescents, women, and mothers) from small Andean villages to coastal urban cities, primarily Lima. Both the demographic and the socioeconomic impacts of these forced migrations were quite significant (Vaughn, Salas-Wright, DeLisi, & Maynard, 2014). This phenomenon, however, only intensified a process that had been taking place for more than a century, characterized by the predominance of young people (56.3 percent among fifteen-to-nineteen-year-olds, and 36.5 percent of those between twenty-five and twenty-nine years of age) previously living in rural areas, migrating in search of better jobs but not always succeeding: thus, a good proportion of skilled internal migrants in Peru end up at lower labor levels and become exposed to social exclusion and compromising levels of demoralization (De Figueiredo, 2012).

6) Social interactions: The overall feature in this aspect of Peru's reality is the pervasive class divisiveness or separation with predictable inequities, mutual distrust, and other potentially damaging dynamics. Areas of the big cities "belonging" to upper-, middle-, and lower-social class members can be easily identifiable, and have their own sets of features, from public lighting to motor trafficking through safety rules and police presence. There has been some progress, to be sure, and, in fact, some collective occasions such as religious celebrations or international sport competitions may soften or dissimulate these gaps and their sequelae, but the potential threats and subsequent barriers against a fair and vigorous social justice are still operating.

7) Public health deficiencies: Numerous examples can apply here. From the increased prevalence of chronic and infectious diseases as a result of lack of preventive policies and management resources (National Institute of Mental Health, 2007) to the unrestricted sale of toxic pesticides causing predictable poisoning (Mulreany, Calikoglu, Ruiz, & Sapsin, 2006; Rosenthal, 2003), violations of fundamental human rights to life, health, and security are evident. Sewage systems in metropolitan areas and small towns are also potentially dangerous if building, maintenance, and supervision practices do not respond to well-delineated rules and schedules; for instance, recent events in an overpopulated Lima district resulted in streets flooded by tons of decomposed human excrements (Andina, 2019).

REBUILDING CAPACITIES

Poverty is undoubtedly one of the most frequently cited topics in all types and branches of political discourse. Being the most dramatic source of social inequities, its presence has pervaded the country's history, enhanced by the collusion of wealthy individuals, families, and corporations with unscrupulous government administrations, party leadership, and unethical public officers (Ugaz, 2018). Social class divisiveness became a deepening process and interclass resentments triggered bloody political conflicts. Social justice lost significant ground in Peru, even though the country's economic growth has been paradoxically consistent at a mild-to-moderate rhythm. The explanations for this phenomenon vary from the stamina of the Peruvian people, to the beneficial impact of economic crises elsewhere in the world, to pragmatic policies dictated by the public administration bodies at opportune (or opportunistic) times. Job offers in fields like mining, modern agricultural projects, civil construction, and technology-based employment, among others, have appealed to a growing social and human capital (working class), neutralizing the damage of political battles.

But not all is just casual social or public occurrences. Some groups and institutions foster principles like preprimary and universal primary education that allow children and adolescents to cultivate cognitive, behavioral, and social skills that, in turn, improve access, retention, and learning outcomes in future work and employment fields (CONAJU, 2002; Cuadros Tairo, 2018). This process, lasting no more than fifteen or twenty years, is not free of obstacles: need of better monitoring, inadequate pupil–teacher ratios, scarcity of classroom and laboratory equipment, teaching vocation shortages, and low morale (due to relatively low, although increasing salaries) occur within the context of a small education sector budget.

Governmental and private initiatives also point to improvement of career counseling, enlisting parents and families in improving role modeling and group-based attitudes, gender parity, and equality – strong women advancement movements have materialized in street manifestations and institutional pronouncements in the past two years (Gold, 2017; Quiroz-Pérez, 2017). Adaptability to local or regional realities and decentralization efforts reflected in regional governments with varying degrees of autonomy also have made educational changes a substantial priority.

Thus, all of these efforts represent an integrated, multidisciplinary approach to education (the so-called critical pedagogy) (Connolly & Harvey, 2018) as a key instrument for poverty reduction, in addition to improvement of employment strategies, social protection programs, and well-defined child-oriented healthcare, nutrition, and labor policies. Such an approach also applies to the overall labor field where income-based disparities interacting with wider, gender-based inequalities and disadvantages, uneven language development, literacy levels, and other factors may subject young people to unfair management practices.

Moreover, with education as a pillar of social justice, threats such as corruption and violence can also be decisively weakened in Peruvian society. Ethical components must also be implemented within educational policies and public health decisions (Mooney-Doyle, Keim-Malpass, & Lindley, 2018; Richter, Groft, & Prinsloo, 2007). The public is closely following the steps being taken inside the Peruvian judiciary, also a recent subject of denunciations and investigations for crimes such as the misuse of public funds, trafficking of influence, purposeful neglect of legal procedures and rules, and obstruction of justice, among other issues. The initial phases of parental education aimed at reduction of domestic or sexual violence include educational and community-based efforts (ENAHO, 2017), also oriented to the reduction of juvenile gangs and their crime-leaning activities. Leading legal and political entities are also working toward less punitive and more education- and rehabilitation-oriented norms to deal with this situation.

The rubric of internal migrations and their unbalancing impact in the life of Peruvian communities and society in general is probably the least affected by the series of corrective or compensatory capacity-rebuilding measures outlined here. On paper, and ruling out political instability as a factor, the main statement would be to stop them, but, as long as employment, education, social improvement, and a variety of opportunities look more promising in other areas of the country, internal migration will continue. The aforementioned regional governments are supposed to be a decisive instrument in the "retention process" of potential migrants by reinforcing the attractiveness of local education, labor, financial, and social life options. Communication means, traveling possibilities, arts' development, urban progress, and rural tourism improvements may all assist in this process, the ultimate objective of which would be to provide a peaceful, stable, just, and stimulating local life setting – social justice principles being also implemented in this context.

Programmatic Intervention Examples

In the policy and legislation areas, the first two decades of this century have witnessed a variety of initiatives evolving into the National Youth Strategy, 2012–2021 (CONAJU, 2002) that, with the participation of agencies of the Justice Ministry, youth groups, civil organizations, and indigenous communities, attempts to work on the formulation of norms and creation of space for consultations and deliberations. Although lacking in both administrative autonomy and decision-making power (a situation that creates frictions and overlaps at bureaucratic levels), the Strategy aims at playing a coordinating role in the interactions between central, regional, and municipal authorities across the country.

In 2013, the National Plan on Security and Health in the Workplace established measures of responsibility, universalization, integration, prevention, participation, and social dialogue to be assessed during five-year periods (Ministerio de Trabajo,

2013). Unfortunately, the disruption of the judicial system in the country during the past two years (due to the corruption of many in the system's leadership) has prevented a reasonable examination of the results of these occupational health programs. The same has occurred with youth volunteer programs and initiatives to prevent social or occupational exclusion of young internal migrants – i.e., those moving from rural to urban areas of the country and who are unable to find a job in spite of documented skillfulness (Secretaría Nacional de Juventudes [SENAJU], 2007).

In the healthcare area in general, and mental healthcare in particular, two programs (one in the capital city, led by Lima's municipal authority [the mayor and city council], and the other in several areas of the country, led by the Ministry of Health's Mental Health Division) have produced positive results. The former, started in 2004, gave place to the creation of so-called Solidarity Hospitals, neighborhood-based medical centers, recognized as public, decentralized agencies offering comprehensive care to both insured and noninsured members of the community in need of care that overcrowded public and Social Security hospitals could not provide. Currently, with thirty-three sites in Lima and eight in other provinces, reports about numbers of people who attended, conditions dealt with, and clinical results are highly encouraging (Municipalidad Provincial de Lima, 2018).

With regard to the latter, nearly 100 community mental health centers located in the three geographic regions of the country, with multidisciplinary personnel ready to offer a variety of outpatient diagnostic and management options (CONAJU, 2005; Ministerio de Salud, 2018), constitute a significant step forward in the unfinished task of ending many decades of care inequities and neglect of significant segments of the Peruvian population, particularly their younger members, and persons with mental health problems (Ministerio de Salud, 2015). The public receptivity to and the results of this approach operated by the Ministry of Health have been encouraging, in spite of bureaucratic/administrative norms (such as a pervasive lack of multidisciplinary approaches) and slogan-charged statements (i.e., "patient-centered" care) that carry isolating rather than integrating features.

OTHER LATIN AMERICAN COUNTRIES

General demographic and health indicators in the subcontinent reflect many aspects of the Peruvian data, even though the countries can be subgrouped according to economic, geographic, and ethnic parameters. Brazil and Mexico are the largest countries and, together with Chile, Colombia, Costa Rica, and Peru, have enjoyed a more or less consistent financial growth over the past two decades. Argentina and Paraguay's performance has decreased, and Bolivia, Panama, and Uruguay's has increased during the same period. Central American (particularly El Salvador, Nicaragua, Honduras, and Guatemala) and Caribbean (i.e., Haiti, Dominican Republic, Cuba, and Belize) countries exhibit high figures in detrimental social justice-related issues such as infant (under five years old) mortality, undernutrition, deficits in literacy and education, and general social and health conditions of indigenous communities (Economic Commission for Latin America and the Caribbean, 2014; Pan American Health Organization, 2018).

Decentralization efforts, particularly those aimed at improving adolescent perceptions of access to well-resourced schools, response to specific local needs, and increased public spending to finance "education for equity," have been successful in Brazil, thanks to the Fund for Maintenance and Development of Basic Education (Ministerio de Educacao de Brazil [FUNDEF], 1996; Thomas, 2017). Similar initiatives to raise quality and strengthen equity in public primary and secondary education have been implemented in Mexico, Argentina, and Colombia. Human rights groups have been present in countries like Mexico, Brazil, and Venezuela on issues like the decriminalization of abortion and related women's rights and responsibilities (Hautzinger, 1997; Rakowski, 1998; Siqueira, 1983). In Ecuador, socioeconomic inequalities in the use of healthcare services (lower economic status and indigenous ethnicity found as significant negative predictors) (Lopez-Cevallos & Chi, 2010) document a reality of continental dimensions. In Chile, the Ministry of Justice established in the early 1990s a series of regulating norms of a comprehensive support system for the care of minors in irregular situations – i.e., abandoned, neglected, or victimized by parents or other relatives (Ministerio de Justicia de Chile, 1991); the results have been encouraging.

Certainly, the most dramatic current situation in terms of cost-of-living increases, income-based disparities, public health figures, and quality of life for the whole population is taking place in Venezuela (Organization of American States, 2018). Several international organizations point out that income disparities interact with other inequalities and disadvantage markers related to gender, location (urban vs. rural), age (children and adolescents vs. adults), education, language, and work opportunities. Massive migrations to neighboring countries, lack of basic food and medication resources, abuse of political power by the governing party, growing international isolation of the country, and an extremely dangerous social divisiveness are some of the manifestations of this critical situation.

Heterogeneity remains, however, as a distinctive feature of social justice realities in many Latin American countries. A vivid example is given by the fact that children are forced to join the workforce to the detriment of their school attendance, up to 30 percent in countries like Nicaragua and Panama. There are discrepancies between levels of the gross enrollment ratio (GER) – i.e., total numbers of registered students – and the net enrollment ratio (NER) – i.e., the actual numbers of those who attend classes – in several Central American countries, a reality that disrupts the transition of students to upper education levels (UNESCO, 2009).

Nevertheless, tertiary education in the subcontinent has expanded from an average of 21 percent in 1993 to 36 percent in 2016, with the lowest (3 percent) registered in Belize, and the highest (up to 88 percent) in Argentina, Cuba,

Colombia, and Mexico. Access to university education for poor applicants is 6 percent for Black students and 20 percent for White students. In terms of gender, boys are, interestingly, underrepresented at the secondary and tertiary levels (with the exception of Brazil and Guatemala), with the opposite occurring with girls, particularly in Caribbean states and Guatemala in Central America. The socioeconomic context, reflected in occupational practices (i.e., a high number of young people in the workforce), plays an important role in keeping boys away from school.

DISCUSSION

Interventions aimed at correcting or alleviating the consequences of violations of social justice for young people in Peru, Latin America, and other world regions can be classified as general and specific. General interventions provide the basic principles for the conduction of recovery programs. They include, for instance, educational programs targeting adulthood preparation subject areas such as healthy relationships, adolescent development, parent–child communication, and healthy life skills (Burrus et al., 2018). Social inclusion entails investment in youth education programs, the challenges of adequate employment opportunities for internal and external migrants, and the conduction of reasonable urbanization initiatives (Alberti et al., 2018; Gold, 2017). Physician advocacy (Bagshaw & Barnett, 2017) or the active participation of professionals in health promotion and prevention campaigns in search of public support not only enhances the professional's standing, moral authority, and constructive potential but also can make possible a competent service for dispersed segments of the population (Leong, Pickren, & Vasquez, 2017). In turn, the ethical implications of these approaches have been recognized in what is known as "the bioethics of protection" and "shared moral public health literacy" (Schramm & Braz, 2008, see pages 73 and 79).

According to Segal, Guy, and Furber (2018), the developmental origins of mental illness underline the urgency of an adequate provision of comprehensive services "to avoid loss of life potential and reduce the pressures on the justice, child protection and welfare systems" (p. 163). Attention to cultural diversity and cultural adaptation of evidence-based interventions has been a long-standing priority in prevention science. In Latin America, there is also some evidence that the bioethical approach is grounded on social justice, equity, and human rights as guiding principles (Penchaszadeh, 2015). Furthermore, mental health research priorities in LMICs require a consensual agenda based on burden of disease criteria, social justice principles, and disposition of available funds (Sharan et al., 2009).

Trauma symptoms generated by exposure to violence require a culturally informed treatment that identifies protective factors (social relations and social support) in local contexts (Butcher et al., 2015). Critical conversations about issues such as poverty, racism, sexism, and other forms of discrimination, about how we might be perpetuating institutional inequities, and about the development of collaborative spaces across diverse sectors are crucial for creating equitable health conditions (Gifford-Smith, Dodge, Dishion, & McCord, 2005; Verbiest et al., 2016). Research in all these topics from psychosocial, equality, and distributive justice perspectives and conceptions of human behavior engaged in moral judgments are also mandatory in order to reinforce resistance and opposition to injustice (Petersen, Koller, Motti-Stefanidi, & Verma, 2016; Turiel, Chung, & Carr, 2016) and to favor relevant modalities of preparation of adolescents for a productive adulthood (Burrus et al., 2018; Osgood, Foster, & Courtney, 2010). In this context, even concepts eventually thought of as distant from this approach (i.e., civic engagement) can be extremely useful in the management of the needs of underserved populations (Zaff et al., 2011). A multidisciplinary, comprehensive approach is basic and mandatory (Bent-Goodley, 2017).

CONCLUSIONS

Studying the health (and mental health) status of a country or a subcontinent from the perspective of social justice is a complex enterprise, more so when the population on which the study is centered possesses the chronological, developmental, and interpersonal characteristics of childhood and adolescence. That is the main reason why Peru can be considered a typical representative of Latin American countries, and why Latin America can be seen as reflecting the realities of several other world regions that share in its various socioeconomic characteristics. Social justice provides unique tools to study contexts, threats, health viewpoints, and interventions that, being closely related to each other, show challenging and severe manifestations, as well as cogent reflections and hopeful possibilities. There are, in effect, testing realities that when confronted with determination and objectivity show results that, although still uncertain can be also cataloged as promising. Governments, international agencies, social assistance organizations, population committees, and private citizens join efforts through a variety of interventions targeting unfairness and injustice. Such has been the perspective of this report.

REFERENCES

Alberti, P. M., Sutton, K. M., Cooper, L. A., et al. (2018). Communities, social justice and academic health centers. *Academic Medicine*, 93(1), 20–24. doi:10.1097.ACM.0000000000001678

Andina, Agencia Peruana de Noticias (2019). Continúa emergencia por inundación en San Juan de Lurigancho. Lima, January 13, 2019. https://andina.pe

Aramburu, C. E., & Mendoza, W. (2015). El futuro de la población peruana: Problemas y oportunidades. *Debates en Sociedad*, 41, 5–24.

Bagshaw, P., & Barnett, P. (2017). Physician advocacy in Western medicine: A 21st century challenge. *New Zealand Medical Journal*, 130(1466), 83–89.

Bent-Goodley, T. B. (2017). Readying the profession for changing times. *Social Work* 62(2), 101–103. doi:10.1093/sw/swx014

Bregaglio, R., Constantino, R., & Chavez, C. (2014). *Políticas públicas con enfoque de derechos humanos en el Perú. El Plan Nacional de derechos Humanos y las experiencias de planes regionales*. Lima: Instituto de Democracia y Derechos Humanos de la Pontificia Universidad Católica del Perú.

Burrus, B. B., Krieger, K., Rutledge, R., et al. (2018). Building bridges to a brighter tomorrow: A systematic evidence review of interventions that prepare adolescents for adulthood. *American Journal of Public Health*, 108(S1), S25–S31.

Butcher, F., Galanek, J. D. Kretschmar, J. M., & Flannery, D. J. (2015). The impact of neighborhood disorganization on neighborhood exposure to violence, trauma symptoms, and social relationships among at-risk youth. *Social Science & Medicine*, 146, 300–306. doi:10.1016/j.socscimed.2015.10.013

Connolly, M., & Harvey, W. J. (2018). Critical pedagogy and APA: A resonant (and timely) interdisciplinary blend. *Adapted Physical Activity Quarterly*, 12, 1–15. doi:10.1123/apaq/2017-0106

Consejo Nacional de la Juventud (CONAJU) (2002). *Informe y formulación de estrategias 2006–2011 y 2012–2021*. Lima: Consejo Nacional de la Juventud.

Consejo Nacional de Salud (2005). *Comité Nacional de Salud Mental. Plan Nacional de Salud Mental*. Lima: Consejo Nacional de Salud.

Cosman, M. P. (2001). Psychiatric Darwinism = survival of the fittest + extinction of the unfit. *Issues in Law and Medicine*, 17(1), 3–34.

Cruz, J., & Huerta-Mercado, R. (2015). Occupational safety and health in Peru. *Annals of Global Health*, 81(4), 568–575. doi:10.1016/jagh.2015.08.027.

Cuadros Tairo, R. (2018). Perú, país de jóvenes: Una mirada desde la antropología de la salud y la demografía. *Diagnóstico*, 57(3), 148–152.

De Figueiredo, J. (2012). Deconstructing demoralization: Distress and subjective incompetence in the face of adversity. In J. B. Frank & R. D. Alarcón (eds.), *The psychotherapy of hope: The legacy of persuasion and healing* (pp. 107–124). Baltimore, MD: Johns Hopkins University Press.

Economic Commission for Latin America and the Caribbean (2014). *Guaranteeing indigenous people's rights in Latin America: Progress in the past decade and remaining challenges*. Washington, DC: Economic Commission for Latin America and the Caribbean.

Encuesta Nacional de Hogares (ENAHO) (2017). *INEI, Dirección Técnica de Demografía e Indicadores Sociales. Informe sobre condiciones de vida y pobreza 2015–2016*. Lima: Dirección Técnica de Demografía e Indicadores Sociales.

Fabrega, H. (2001). Culture and history in psychiatric diagnosis and practice. *Psychiatric Clinics of North America*, 24, 391–405.

Fantom, N., & Serajuddin, U. (2016, January 12). Classifying countries by income: A new working paper. *World Bank Data Blog*. No. WPS 7528. Washington, DC: World Bank Group. https://documents.worldbank.org/curated/en/408581467988942234/The-World-Banks-classification-of- countries-by-income

Finfgeld-Connett, D. (2017). Intimate partner violence and its resolution among Mexican Americans. *Issues in Mental Health Nursing*, 28(6), 464–472.

Finkelhor, D., Wolak, J., & Berliner, L. (2001). Police reporting and professional help-seeking for child crime victims: A review. *Child Maltreatment*, 6(1), 17–30.

Garbarino, J. (1998). The stress of being a poor child in America. *Child and Adolescent Psychiatric Clinics in North America*, 7(1), 105–119.

Garrett, M. T., Parrish, M., Williams, C., et al. (2014). Fostering resilience among Native American youth through therapeutic intervention. *Journal of Youth and Adolescence*, 43(3), 470–490. doi:10.1007/s10964-013-0020-8.

Gifford-Smith, M., Dodge, K. A., Dishion, T. J., & McCord, J. (2005). Peer influence in children and adolescents: Crossing the bridge from developmental to intervention science. *Journal of Abnormal Child Psychology*, 33(3), 255–265.

Gold, D. D. (2017). Make health and safety a part of global struggles against imperialism, racism, and other oppressions. *New Solution: A Journal of Environmental and Occupational Health Policy*, 27(1): 124–128. doi:10.1177/1048291117697111

Hautzinger, S. (1997). "Calling a state a state": Feminist politics and the policing of violence against women in Brazil. *Fem Issues*, 15(1–2), 3–30.

Holland, K. J., & Cortina, L. M. (2017). "It happens to girls all the time": Examining sexual assault survivors' reasons for not using campus supports. *American Journal of Community Psychology*, 59(1–2), 50–64. doi:10.1002/ajcp.12126

Instituto Nacional de Estadística e Informática (INEI) (2017). *Encuesta demográfica de salud familiar, ENDES*. Lima: Instituto Nacional de Estadística e Informática.

Instituto Nacional de Estadística e Informática (INEI) (2018a). *Informe técnico – Estadísticas de seguridad ciudadana*. Lima: Instituto Nacional de Estadística e Informática.

Instituto Nacional de Estadística e Informática (INEI) (2018b). *XII Censo de Población, VII de Vivienda y III de Comunidades Indígenas*. Lima: Instituto Nacional de Estadística e Informática.

International Society for Clinical Biostatistics (2017, July 1). *List of low, lower middle and upper-middle income economies according to the World Bank*. 38th annual conference. Vigo, Spain.

Leong, F. T. L., Pickren, W. E., & Vasquez, M. J. T. (2017). APA efforts in promoting human rights and social justice. *American Psychologist*, 72(8), 778–790. doi:10.1037/amp0000220

Lopez-Cevallos, D. F., & Chi, C. (2010). Health care utilization in Ecuador: A multilevel analysis of socio-economic determinants and inequality issues. *Health Policy Plan*, 25(3), 209–218. doi:10.1093.heapol/czp052

Michalec, B., Martimianakis, M. A., Tilburt, J. C., & Hafferty, F. W. (2017). Why it's unjust to expect location-specific, language-specific or population-specific service from students with underrepresented minority or low-income backgrounds. *AMA Journal of Ethics* 19(3), 238–244. doi:10.1001/journalofethics.2017.19.3.ecas1-1703

Ministerio da Educacao de Brazil (1996). *Fundo para Manutencao e Desenvolvimento do Ensino Fundamental a Valorizacao do Magisterio (FUNDEF)*. Rio de Janeiro: Ministerio da Educacao de Brazil.

Ministerio de Justicia de Chile (1991). Decree No. 1.373 of 29 October 1990 establishing support systems for the care of minors in irregular situation. Argent. Repub. Laws Statut. 98, 489–491.

Ministerio de Salud del Perú (2011). *Documento técnico: Análisis de situación de salud de las y los jóvenes. Una mirada al bono demográfico*. Lima: Ministerio de Salud del Perú.

Ministerio de Salud del Perú (2015, October 5). *Decreto Supremo de la Presidencia de la República*. Lima: Ministerio de Salud del Perú.

Ministerio de Salud del Perú (2018). *Plan Nacional de Fortalecimiento de Servicios de Salud Mental Comunitaria 2018–2021*. Lima: Ministerio de Salud del Perú.

Ministerio de Trabajo y Promoción del Empleo, Perú (2013, May 2). *Plan Nacional de Seguridad y Salud en el Trabajo, 2014–2017*. Lima: Ministerio de Trabajo y Promoción del Empleo, Perú.

Mooney-Doyle, K., Keim-Malpass, J., & Lindley, L. C. (2019). The ethics of concurrent care for children: A social justice perspective. *Nursing Ethics*, 26(5), 1518–1527. doi:10.1177/0969733018765308

Mulreany, J. P., Calikoglu, S., Ruiz, S., & Sapsin, J. W. (2006). Water privatization and public health in Latin America. *Pan-American Journal of Public Health*, 19(1), 23–32.

Municipalidad Provincial de Lima (2018). Hospitales de la Solidaridad realizan más de 120 millones de atenciones en salud por todo el país. http://solidaridadsalud.gob.pe

National Institute of Mental Health (2007). Ethical issues in the NIMH Collaborative HIV/STD Prevention Trial. *AIDS*, Suppl. 2, S69–S80.

Organisation for Economic Co-operation and Development (OECD) (2012). *Programme for International Students Assessment (PISA): Countries' performance report*. London: Organisation for Economic Co-operation and Development.

Organization of American States (2018, May 29). Panel of independent international experts finds "reasonable grounds" for crimes against humanity committed in Venezuela. Press release. Washington, DC.

Osgood, D. W., Foster, E. M., & Courtney, M. E. (2010). Vulnerable populations and the transition to adulthood. *Future Child*, 20(1), 209–229.

Pan American Health Organization (2018). *Health situation in the Americas: Core indicators*. Washington, DC: Pan American Health Organization.

Penchaszadeh, V. B. (2015). Ethical issues in genetics and public health in Latin America with a focus on Argentina. *Journal of Community Genetics*, 6(3): 223–230. doi:10.1007/s12687-015-0217-5

Petersen, A., Koller, S. H., Motti-Stefanidi, F., & Verma, S. (2016). Global equity and justice issues for young people during the first three decades of life. *Advances in Child Development and Behavior*, 51, 289–320. doi:10.1016/bs.acdb.2016.05.006

Postma, J., Peterson, J., Ybarra Vega, M. J., et al. (2014). Latina youth's perception of children's environmental health risks in an agricultural community. *Public Health Nursing*, 31(6), 508–516. doi:10.1111/phn.12112

Preski, S., & Shelton, D. (2001). The role of contextual, child and parent factors in predicting criminal outcomes in adolescence. *Issues in Mental Health Nursing*, 22(2), 197–205.

Quiroz-Pérez, L. (2017). Del centro a las márgenes: Los feminismos del Perú y México de los 70 a la actualidad. Amerika (en ligne), 16–2017, mis en ligne le 01 julliet 2017. http://journals.openedition.org/amerika/8056. doi:10.4000/Amerika/8056

Rajani, R. R. (1998). Child sexual abuse in Tanzania: Much noise, little justice. *Sexual Health Exchange*, 1, 13–24.

Rakowski, C. A. (1998). Unity in diversity and adversity: Venezuelan women's struggle for human rights. *INSTRAW News*, 28, 26–33.

Richter, M. S., Groft, J. L., & Prinsloo, L. (2007). Ethical issues surrounding studies with vulnerable populations: A case study of South African street children. *International Journal of Adolescent Medicine and Health*, 19(2), 117–126.

Riquelme, H. (1987). Latinoamericanos en Europa. Experiencia de desarraigo y proceso de identidad psico-cultural. *Acta Psiquiatrica y Psicológica de América Latina*, 33, 281–295.

Rosenthal, E. (2003). The tragedy of Tauccamarca: A human rights perspective on the pesticide poisoning deaths of 4 children in the Peruvian Andes. *International Journal of Occupational and Environmental Health*, 9(1), 53–58.

Ryan, J. P., Williams, A. B., & Courtney, M. E. (2013). Adolescent neglect, juvenile delinquency and the risk of recidivism. *Journal of Youth and Adolescence*, 42(3), 454–465. doi:10.1007/s10964-013-9906-8

Schacht, T. E. (1993). How do I diagnose thee: Let me count the dimensions. *Psychological Inquiry*, 4, 115–118.

Schramm, F. R., & Braz, M. (2008). Bioethics of protection: A proposal for the moral problem of developing countries? *Journal International de bioéthique*, 19(1–2), 73–86.

Secretaría Nacional de Juventudes (SENAJU) (2007). *2ª. Estrategia Nacional, 2012–2021*. Lima: Secretaría Nacional de Juventudes.

Segal, L., Guy, S., & Furber, G. (2018). What is the current level of mental health service delivery and expenditure on infants, children, adolescents, and young people in Australia? *Australian and New Zealand Journal of Psychiatry*, 52(2), 163–172. doi:10.1177/0004867417717796

Sharan, P., Gallo, C., Gureje, O., et al. (2009). Mental health research priorities in low- and middle-income countries of Africa, Asia, Latin America and the Caribbean. *British Journal of Psychiatry*, 195(4), 354–363. doi:10.1192/bjp.bp.108.050187

Silva, M., Loureiro, A., & Cardoso, G. (2017). Social determinants of mental health: A review of the evidence. *European Journal of Psychiatry*, 30(4), 259–292.

Siqueira, W. I. (1983). Latin American perspectives on the individual and the greater community. *Draper Fund Report*, 12, 16–18.

Thomas, K. J. (2017). Justice perceptions and demographics of privilege among Brazilian adolescents. *Psychological Reports*, 1. doi:10.1177/0033294117745886

Transparencia Internacional (2017). *Informe sobre la percepción de corrupción del sector público*. Berlin: Transparencia Internacional.

Turiel, E., Chung, E., & Carr, J. A. (2016). Struggles for equal rights and social justice as unrepresented and represented in psychological research. *Advances in Child Development and Behavior*, 50, 1–29. doi:10.1016/bs.acdb.2015.11.004

Turiel, E., Hildrebrandt, C., & Wainryb, C. (1991). Judging social issues: Difficulties, inconsistencies and consistencies. *Monographs of the Society for Research in Child Development*, 56(2), 104–116.

Ugaz, J. (2018, March 15). La corrupción en América Latina. *La Vanguardia*.

UNESCO Education for All (EFA) (2009). *Global monitoring report, regional overview: Latin America and the Caribbean*. Geneva: UNESCO.

United Nations High Commissioner for Refugees Agency (2018, October). *Refugees and migrants from Venezuela in Peru*. Geneva: United Nations High Commissioner for Refugees Agency.

Vargas, R. (2014, March 7). Los carteles de la droga. *El Comercio*.

Vaughn, M. G., Salas-Wright, C. D., DeLisi, M., & Maynard, B. R. (2014). The immigrant paradox: Immigrants are less antisocial than native-born Americans. *Social Psychiatry and Psychiatric Epidemiology*, 49(7): 1129–1137. doi:10.1007/s00127-013-0799-3

Vega, E. (2018). *La corrupción y el grave daño a la gobernabilidad*. Lima: Universidad Antonio Ruiz de Montoya, Instituto de Ética y Desarrollo.

Verbiest, S., Malin, C. K., Drummonds, M., & Kotelchuck, M. (2016). Catalyzing a Reproductive Health and Social Justice Movement. *Maternal and Child Health Journal*, 20(4), 741–748. doi:10.1007/s10995-015-1917-5

World Psychiatric Association (2015). *Position statement on social justice for persons with mental illness (mental disability)*. London: World Psychiatric Association.

Zaff, J. F., Kawashima-Ginsberg, K., & Lin, E. S. (2011). Advances in civic engagement research: Issues of civic measures and civic context. *Advances in Child Development and Behavior*, 41, 273–308.

Zapata, A. (2018). *La guerra senderista. Hablan los enemigos*. Lima: Editorial de Bolsillo.

27

Social Justice and Adolescent Health

A Case Study of Rwanda

Agnes Binagwaho, Kirstin Scott, and Kateri Donahoe

INTRODUCTION

Around the world, children and adolescents are uniquely vulnerable to structural violence and systemic injustice that put their health and human rights at risk. The youth of the world lack political agency relative to adults and are less able to independently mobilize in order to create an advocacy movement against barriers to social justice and human rights for themselves within government, civil society, community, and family. Particularly for adolescents between the ages of ten and nineteen, during a period of growth, they feel the tension of being more aware of their situation and formulating opinions, but do not have the necessary maturity, rights, or agency in society to act on their own behalf.

Most people assume that the nature of being "young" equates to being healthy. As such, adolescents who struggle with health challenges are especially vulnerable with respect to their human right to health. Because there is a global assumption that this population is healthy, fewer initiatives and resources are dedicated toward them. In recent years, through global initiatives such as the Millennium Development Goals (MDGs) (2018b) and now the Sustainable Development Goals (SDGs) (2018c), there has been a significant focus on reducing mortality of children under the age of five, who are at particular risk for infectious disease and perinatal complications. Further, those involved in healthcare have increased their efforts to bolster preventive health initiatives so as to combat noncommunicable diseases (NCDs) in both children and adults.

However, adolescent health seems to have fallen by the wayside as investments into global health tend to be directed toward these other age groups. According to the World Health Organization (WHO), 1.2 million adolescents died in 2015, mainly from treatable or preventable causes (WHO, 2018a). These deaths are a tragic reminder that we cannot take the health of adolescents for granted. One in six people in the world – or 1.2 billion lives – falls into this historically ignored group of individuals (WHO, 2018a). Thus, it is imperative to investigate ways in which we can take account for the state of their health and keep these young lives healthy.

Considerations should be made for the particular needs of adolescent populations with regard to health and social justice. In this chapter, we focus on the case study of Rwanda and provide an overview of this country's experience with working to improve adolescent health. Describing Rwanda's approach, challenges, and outcomes may help to outline a path forward in other settings for building capacity to ensure adolescents can live to their healthiest potential.

COUNTRY CONTEXT: RWANDAN DEMOGRAPHICS AND THE CONDITION OF ADOLESCENTS

Rwanda, a small country of around 12 million people located in East Africa, has witnessed remarkable gains in life expectancy and progress over the past two decades. The country suffered a tragic genocide in 1994 in which nearly 1 million Rwandans were killed and 2 million were displaced inside and outside the country. At the time, Rwanda was one of the least developed nations in the world; life expectancy at birth was just twenty-nine years, the lowest in the world, and the gross domestic product (GDP) was $126 USD per capita (United Nations Development Programme, 2018; World Bank, 2018). On average, a woman would expect to give birth 6.3 times over the course of her life, and the mortality rate of children under five years old was the second highest in the world, at 284 deaths per 1,000 live births (World Bank, 2018).

Fortunately, the harsh reality of the mid-1990s in Rwanda was not permitted to persist. Thoughtful planning, visionary leadership, and a national commitment to emerge stronger from this tragic past has resulted in incredible achievements in economic and human development throughout Rwanda. Today, while Rwanda is still a low-income country with an estimated GDP of approximately $800 per capita (according to the International Monetary Fund), the country has made great strides toward achieving the health-related MDGs and is committed to further gains through the SDGs (International Monetary Fund, 2018). Key health and development indicators show that the country is on an upward trajectory of wellness and prosperity for its citizens (Ndagijimana, 2015; World Bank, 2017, 2018). In just over twenty years, the life expectancy has more than doubled to sixty-seven years, and the under-five mortality rate has fallen at an unprecedented pace to 39 deaths per 1,000 live births. In the past, only 26 percent of women delivered in healthcare facilities, but now this has increased to more than 90 percent (World Bank, 2018). Beyond these population health gains, Rwanda has embraced a national health insurance model and more than 91 percent of Rwandans have health insurance.

Similar to the populations of other countries, adolescents constitute a sizable segment of the population in Rwanda, a total of 22 percent (World Bank, 2018). These young people are a source of great promise for the country's economic and social development. One method of monitoring adolescent health – and the well-being of all Rwandans – includes Rwanda's national health survey, the

Demographic and Health Surveys (DHS), which takes place every five years (DHS Program, 2018). With respect to education, the DHS has unveiled significant generational shifts. Between the 2010 and the 2015 DHS surveys, the percentage of Rwandan women and men, ages fifteen to forty-nine, who had completed primary school, while still low, increased from 13.9 percent to 21.6 percent and from 13.7 percent to 21.7 percent, respectively (DHS Program, 2012, 2016). In the 2015 DHS, among women age sixty-five and over, 75.1 percent had received no education; this figure dropped to 1.7 percent among girls ages ten to fourteen. Among young men in these age groups, the percentage with no education dropped from 40.5 percent to 2.9 percent.

Education in Rwanda is also trending toward greater gender equity. Whereas only 36.3 percent of women between the ages of twenty-five and twenty-nine had completed primary school or higher, compared with 42.8 percent of men in this age group, among women aged fifteen to nineteen, 57.1 percent had completed primary school or higher, compared to just 47.4 percent of men in this age group (DHS Program, 2016). Rwanda has also achieved gender parity in primary and secondary school enrollment. In fact, when considering just secondary school, the gender parity index (GPI) tips just slightly in favor of female students, to a GPI of 1.1, per World Bank data (World Bank, 2018).

Regarding literacy, in 2010, among youth age fifteen to twenty-four, there was complete gender parity in the literacy rate (World Bank, 2018). Despite these impressive gains, data on Rwandan adolescents' educational retention and completion rates are concerning and demonstrate a dire need to introduce policies that further reduce their vulnerability. For example, while 96 percent of primary-age schoolchildren are enrolled in primary education, only 67 percent of these children complete their primary education; among this group, only 72 percent actually continue on to the secondary level (World Bank, 2018). Only 28 percent of eligible Rwandan children are enrolled in secondary education (World Bank, 2018). Clearly, these results are unsatisfactory and should prompt a meaningful call to action.

All adolescents are in a vulnerable position regarding retention in education, which, in turn, has ripple effects in all aspects of the future of an adolescent's health and well-being. Higher educational attainment serves as a protective factor against nearly all the ills that one can think of in terms of risk factors that compromise reproductive and maternal health outcomes. For both young men and women, higher educational attainment is associated with fewer sexually transmitted infections (STIs) and a decreased prevalence of human immunodeficiency virus (HIV) (DHS Program, 2016). Adolescents who do not stay in school through the secondary level are at a higher risk of poor health outcomes and harmful interpersonal behaviors, negatively impacting their mental, social, and physical health.

Although adolescents are generally considered traditionally healthy and resilient, they are affected by unique health challenges that cause unnecessary mortality and morbidity. These include early pregnancy and childbirth, HIV/AIDS and STIs, mental health issues, accidents, injuries, and alcohol and substance use (WHO, 2018). In regard to decreasing some of these risky behaviors, Rwanda has made some impressive strides (DHS Program, 2016; Ministry of Health, 2012).

Let's assume that the outcomes of the HIV response among Rwandan adolescents serve as a reasonable proxy indicator of adolescents' access to relevant health information. Data from Rwanda's DHS show that comprehensive knowledge about AIDS and means of preventing new HIV infections has increased among adolescents (DHS Program, 2006, 2016). The power of making this information available to adolescents should be of interest in other settings as HIV is a known scourge to the well-being of adolescents globally. Worldwide, HIV is estimated to be the second leading cause of mortality among adolescents. Though the overall mortality rates of HIV are low, HIV-related deaths among adolescents are estimated to have increased since 2000 (WHO, 2014). In Africa, one in six adolescent deaths is due to HIV and 90 percent of the world's HIV-related adolescent deaths occur in Africa (WHO, 2014). However, in Rwanda, between the 2010 and 2015 DHS, the percentage of women ages fifteen to nineteen with comprehensive knowledge about AIDS increased from 49.3 percent to 61.6 percent. Similarly, among men in this age group, comprehensive knowledge of AIDS increased from 43.5 percent to 59.5 percent (DHS Program, 2012, 2016).

In 2015, a vast majority of both men and women ages fifteen to nineteen knew where to obtain condoms (84.6 percent for women and 93.6 percent for men) (DHS Program, 2016). There was also a marked increase in the proportion of the population who had been recently tested for HIV between 2005 and 2015. In 2005, only 12.7 percent of men and 26.9 percent of women ages fifteen to nineteen who had sexual intercourse in the previous twelve months reported both being tested for HIV in the year prior and knowing the results of this testing. In 2015, these figures increased to 29.4 percent and 61.3 percent, respectively (DHS Program, 2006, 2016).

In comparison, aggregate data collected between 2008 and 2012 from sub-Saharan Africa indicated that only 26 percent of adolescent girls and 36 percent of adolescent boys, ages fifteen to nineteen, had a comprehensive knowledge of HIV (see Table 27.1) (United Nations Children's Fund, 2013). Additionally, among high school students in the United States (generally fourteen to eighteen years old), an average of 22 percent of students (17 percent of male students and 27 percent of female students) who were sexually active had ever been tested for HIV, with no significant change in this figure between 2005 and 2013 (Van Handel, Kann, Olsen, & Dietz, 2016).

Though Rwanda has witnessed improving HIV awareness and education among adolescents, it has struggled in other areas of adolescent health and wellness. For example, while the age-specific fertility rate for women age fifteen to nineteen declined from 60 births per 1,000 women in 1992 to 40 births per 1,000 women in 2008, there has been an upswing in teenage childbearing in recent years. The 2015 fertility rate for women age fifteen to nineteen was 44 births per 1,000 women, with

TABLE 27.1 *Adolescent girls' (ages 15–19) comprehensive knowledge of HIV, between 2008 and 2012 (United Nations Children's Fund, 2013)*

	Percent of adolescent girls (ages 15–19) who have comprehensive knowledge of HIV
Rwanda	49%
Sub-Saharan Africa	26%
World	21%

continual increases since 2008 (DHS Program, 2016). This correlates with an increase in the percentage of women who have started to have children by the age of nineteen, which rose from 12.8 percent in 2005 to 20.8 percent in 2015 (DHS Program, 2016).

This trend is concerning for a number of reasons. First, pregnancy and childbirth in the teenage years are particularly risky for both mother and child. According to WHO, the leading cause of death for fifteen- to nineteen-year-old women globally is complications from pregnancy and childbirth (WHO, 2018). Second, a higher adolescent fertility rate may hinder greater educational attainment among young women, as early childbearing may negatively impact a woman's ability to consistently pursue an education (DHS Program, 2016). For example, an assessment focused on ten districts in Rwanda found that only 10 percent of girls who became pregnant between the ages of eleven and eighteen actually returned to school after their pregnancies (Collective of Leagues and Associations for the Defense of Human Rights in Rwanda [CLADHO], 2016).

Rwanda also faces challenges in optimal adolescent health with respect to substance use. A 2015 study found that, among Rwandan youth, the average age of onset of alcohol, tobacco, and other substance use was 11.4 years old and that dependence on alcohol, cigarettes, and cannabis among youth affected 7.5 percent, 4.9 percent, and 2.5 percent of youth, respectively (Kanyoni, Gishoma, & Ndahindwa, 2015). Young men are particularly vulnerable to substance use challenges as their rate of use is nearly double the rate of their female counterparts (Kanyoni et al., 2015). Additionally, youth that were not enrolled in school or who had never attended school had higher rates of substance use (Kanyoni et al., 2015). These findings suggest that while Rwanda has made progress in certain areas of adolescent health, other vulnerable behaviors continue to have an impact on the full realization of adolescents' human right to health.

From a policy-level standpoint in Rwanda, adolescent issues are governed by several ministries with partially overlapping policy jurisdictions. The most notable policy-making entity is the Ministry of Youth, which oversees the Youth Sector Strategic Plan (YSSP) and the National Youth Policy (NYP). These policies, most recently updated in 2013 and 2015, respectively, describe the primary vision of the Government of Rwanda to achieve a "HAPPI" generation of youth – Health, Aptitude/Attitude, Patriotism, Productivity, and Innovation. These policies aim to equip Rwandan youth with technical and relational skills so as to meet current and forecasted labor market needs, create interventions for increased youth employment and productivity, and improve the socioeconomic condition of Rwandan youth in general through greater involvement in private-sector activities.

An important clarification is that both the NYP and the YSSP define "youth" as persons between the ages of sixteen and thirty; this is a shift from earlier policies that had defined the "youth" as a broader segment of the population (ages fourteen to thirty-five) (Ministry of Finance and Economic Planning, 2013; NYP, 2015). Though the age range was narrowed for a number of reasons, including an attempt to have greater harmony with both international and local legal definitions of this subgroup, it still does not overlap perfectly with the WHO definition of adolescents, and obviously excludes a significant portion of people in adolescence (ten to nineteen years old). This is a case in point regarding the challenges related to "defining" adolescent health as varying policies capture different segments of this population, which we elaborate upon further later in this chapter.

As noted earlier in this chapter, when describing concerning trends in Rwanda's health and demographic data, the NYP identifies sexual and reproductive health, HIV/AIDS, and drug abuse as the greatest health challenges faced by Rwanda's youth (NYP, 2015). This is supported by the fact that 0.6 percent of persons ages fifteen to nineteen have HIV and 30 percent to 40 percent of adolescents ages ten to twenty report having used an illicit substance (DHS Program, 2016; Kanyoni et al., 2015). The YSSP, however, suggests that the major health problem faced by Rwanda's youth is a lack of youth-friendly health services that cater to the specific needs of young people. The plan also cites sexual and reproductive health and HIV/AIDS as key issues, and proposes youth-friendly service provision and increased access to health information as potential solutions (Ministry of Finance and Economic Planning, 2013).

Taken together, these documents seem to align their priorities for youth fairly well and indicate a significant amount of coordination between policy makers and implementers. These documents were also developed to align with Vision 2020, Rwanda's national strategic plan and development goals to achieve by the year 2020, the United Nations SDGs, and the Rwandan Economic Development and Poverty Reduction Strategy (EDPRS). Nearly every SDG related to youth health and well-being is part of the youth policy and strategy documents. The YSSP specified MDG Number 1 as focusing on the "eradication of poverty through youth employment promotion by supporting youth-led employment and entrepreneurial initiatives within rural and urban areas" and MDG Number 8 as providing for the "establishment of global partnership for development and decent/productive job creation for youth" (Ministry of Finance and Economic Planning, 2013, p. 4). Additionally, MDG Number 3 included targets for the ratio of girls to boys in primary and secondary education, as a measurement of gender equity (Ndagijimana, 2015).

Beyond the aforementioned specific national ministry policies, Rwanda is a signatory to several international treaties that relate to adolescents' right to health. These treaties include the Convention on the Rights of the Child (CRC) (ratified in 1991) (United Nations 2018b), the International Covenant on Economic, Social and Cultural Rights (United Nations 2018c), and the Convention on the Elimination of all Forms of Discrimination Against Women (ratified in 1981) (United Nations, 2018a). These aspirational and legally binding treaties include the key principles that all people have the right to gain the highest attainable standard of physical and mental health (Backman et al., 2008; Khan, 1999).

The right to health for adolescents encompasses many elements, including food, sanitation, clean water, and housing. Any failure of a government that can but does not provide adolescents these underlying determinants of health, as well as equal, open, and affordable access to quality healthcare services, compromises adolescents' human right to health (Backman et al., 2008). Specifically, Article 24 of the CRC explicitly mentions making provisions for family planning education and services as well as reducing infant and child mortality, both of which relate to the issue of sexual and reproductive health among adolescent girls (United Nations, 2018b).

The right to health enshrined in these treaties also includes access to medical care free from discrimination and stigma, which is important when considering the condition of adolescents who may face judgmental healthcare service provision for STI- and HIV-related services or family planning (Milliez, 2009; Shaw, n.d.). Rwanda, as a signatory of these agreements, has indicated a commitment to ensuring children's right to health through open, equitable, nondiscriminatory, and comprehensive healthcare delivery and health education, from which adolescents can and should also benefit. In spite of these advancements and commitments, challenges remain for adolescents in actualizing their full set of rights, including the human right to health.

BARRIERS TO ACTUALIZING ADOLESCENTS' RIGHT TO HEALTH

Despite Rwanda's national and international commitment to promoting health and human rights for all, including adolescents, numerous barriers remain in meeting these commitments and allowing adolescents to fully realize their human right to health. In this section, we describe five of these key barriers affecting Rwanda's experience: the variable definitions of "adolescence," fragmented policy planning and coverage, societal pressures and expectations, individual preferences, and gaps in data availability.

The Challenge of Defining Adolescent Health

Integral to these challenges is the inconsistency with which the international legal framework, agencies, funders, and even national policies define the term "adolescence." While the CRC defines childhood as the period prior to age eighteen, except where specified elsewhere earlier by national law, General Comment No. 20 on implementing the rights of the child in adolescence notes that defining adolescence is not a straightforward or clearly agreed-upon process. The Comment states that the transition from childhood to adulthood is influenced by a set of physical, contextual, and environmental factors. The Comment therefore does not seek to define adolescence but "instead focuses on the period of childhood from ten years until the eighteenth birthday to facilitate consistency in data collection" (United Nations, 2016, 2018b, p. 3).

However, not all international agencies adhere to this definition, creating significant discrepancies in the definition of adolescence. The UN agencies (e.g., United Nations Children's Fund [UNICEF], United Nations Population Fund [UNFPA], WHO) define adolescence as the period from age ten to nineteen. However, a separate UN institution – the Joint United Nations Programme on HIV/AIDS (UNAIDS) – subscribes to a different definition, which obviously is a probable cause of confusion for both policy makers and service providers. Specifically, UNAIDS reports "for the purposes of epidemiological monitoring, UNAIDS' estimates refer to children as those aged 0 to 14 years, adolescents as those aged 10 to 19 years, young people as those aged 15 to 24 years, and adults as those older than 15 years" (UNAIDS, 2016, p. 2).

Further, a recent study published in *The Lancet Child & Adolescent Health* argues for a broader definition of adolescence, shifting from ages ten to nineteen to ages ten to twenty-four, as more developmentally and socially accurate, according to new understandings of human growth periods and shifting cultural milestones that mark adulthood, such as marriage, completion of education, or parenthood (Sawyer, Azzopardi, Wickremarathne, & Patton, 2018). Within the current Rwandan legal framework, the Ministry of Health defines children services delivery as healthcare services provided to an individual under the age of fifteen, in contradiction with the CRC definition of children as a human being under the age of eighteen years. Additionally, Rwanda's Ministry of Health separates the adolescent population into three groups. The Adolescent Sexual and Reproductive Health and Rights Policy (ASRH&R Policy), issued by the Ministry of Health in 2012, adopted the WHO definition of adolescence as ages ten to nineteen; this is comprised of "young adolescents" ten to fourteen years old and "old adolescents" fifteen to nineteen years old. The Policy also stipulated that its strategic plan focuses on young people aged ten to twenty-four years old, including among adolescents the "young adults" aged twenty to twenty-four.

These broad definitions of adolescence and youth serve to increase the mandate of the Ministry of Health when planning for adolescent health programs, but also run the risk of overlooking the differences between the needs of young adolescents, as they are still developmentally in childhood, and the needs of young adults who are autonomous adults in the eyes of the law. Further complicating this policy planning, the NYP defined parameters for "youth" in 2015 as individuals aged sixteen to thirty years old in order to harmonize with the National Child Policy and other national and international documents (NYP, 2015). In Table 27.2, we outline the definitions of these terms and the national and international agencies that support them.

These varying definitions of "adolescence" and "youth" provided by normative agencies create discrepancies and confusion, which can lead to poorly informed policies and complicate national planning. When considering the issue of adolescent health, a clear definition should be agreed upon by international bodies so that

TABLE 27.2 *Varying definitions for terms related to child, adolescent, and youth health across national and international policies*

Term	Definition	Source
Children	Persons below the age of 18	United Nations Convention on the Rights of the Child (United Nations, 2018b) National Integrated Child Rights Policy, Ministry of Gender and Family Promotion, Republic of Rwanda (Ministry of Gender and Family Promotion) (MIGEPROF, 2011)
	Persons aged 0 to 14 years	UNAIDS (2016)
Adolescent	Persons between the ages of 10 and 19	UNICEF (2013) United Nations Children's Fund (UNICEF) World Health Organization (WHO) United Nations Population Fund (UNFPA) UNAIDS (2016)
Youth	Persons between the ages of 15 and 24	United Nations General Assembly resolution A/ RES/50/81 (UNAIDS, 2016)
	Persons from 16 to 30 years	National Youth Policy, Republic of Rwanda (NYP, 2015)
Young people	Persons between the ages of 10 and 24	United Nations Children's Fund (UNICEF) World Health Organization (WHO) United Nations Population Fund (UNFPA) (UNAIDS, 2016) Ministry of Health (2012)
	Persons aged 15 to 24 years	UNICEF (2013) UNAIDS (2016)
Young adolescents	Persons aged 10 to 14 years	Ministry of Health (2012)
Old adolescents	Persons aged 15 to 19 years	Ministry of Health (2012)
Young adults	Persons aged 20 to 24 years	Ministry of Health (2012)

this segment of the population does not fall victim to being unintentionally forgotten given that their population is poorly defined and thus it is difficult to find a true signal about their health amidst all the noise in the data. If this does not occur, adolescents will continue to be overlooked in the care of children, ignored in the realm of adulthood, and left to fend for themselves with regard to appropriate and comprehensive healthcare.

Furthermore, although international and national agencies tend to recognize adolescence as beginning around age ten, the health sector's most meaningful quantitative data collection begins at age fifteen. The Rwandan DHS reports, which are supported by the US Centers for Disease Control and Prevention (CDC), WHO, and the UN agencies, do not collect data specifically on adolescents, and data collection tends to begin at age fifteen (not at ten), including the information that is specifically relevant to adolescent health, such as HIV/AIDS knowledge and sexual and reproductive health behaviors.

In fact, reporting on "adult mortality" in the DHS begins at age fifteen. The Integrated Household Living Conditions Survey (EICV) conducts specific data collection on youth and follows the NYP's definition of this age group (ages sixteen to thirty, as of 2015), but does not collect data on adolescents aged ten to fifteen. Additionally, the Rwandan Ministry of Health Annual Statistics Booklet, which is a collection of the national Health Management Information System (HMIS) data initiative, includes information from monthly, quarterly, and annual HMIS reporting formats. However, monthly HIV reports, the electronic tuberculosis system, and the Performance-Based Financing (PBF) database for clinical care stemming from the HMIS do not make any explicit mention of adolescents.

These delineations, and the trend toward focusing on later adolescents and young people, is indicative of the codifying of societal and organizational neglect for this age group. This is particularly true in the case of young adolescents (ages ten to fourteen), who are not well represented in the considerations made for "young people" and within child health because they have aged out of the early years of childhood that are the focus of a great deal of health programming in Rwanda and worldwide. Further, even the care of adolescents between the ages of fifteen and nineteen who are hospitalized is difficult to track as they are typically included in adult wards and treated by the same doctors and with the same approach and considerations as adults.

In an effort to standardize care for this population, WHO has developed the Integrated Management of Adult and Adolescent Illness guidelines for "common presenting illnesses in adults and adolescents" (Vasan et al., 2013, p. 2). While such guidelines may be a helpful first step, they run the risk of lumping children, under the eyes of the law, in with adults in clinical settings when in reality they do not yet have the agency or maturity to serve as adequate advocates for their own health. Additionally, in HIV care settings, both patients and parents overwhelmingly report feeling the need to establish a separate adolescent ward (Binagwaho, 2009).

Fragmentation of Programs to Coordinate Policies to Improve Adolescent Health

As adolescents uniquely straddle this transition between childhood and adulthood, policy-making bodies must effectively coordinate efforts if they wish to meaningfully support them. Today, adolescent health in Rwanda is governed in a fragmented manner by many partially overlapping policies, and several ministries are directly or indirectly concerned with these issues. This necessitates an increased effort to bolster coordination and cooperation in order to remove the inconsistencies in definitions and actions for Rwandan governmental entities so that they can improve the efficiency and effectiveness of interventions.

Currently, several policies cover different aspects of adolescent health, the most important being the Adolescent Sexual Reproductive Health and Rights Policy and the NYP. While both cover adolescent health partially, they are lacking in a comprehensive analysis to improve the issues that are most burdensome for optimizing adolescent health. Other health policies exist but either do not cover the aspects of adolescent health at all or do so insufficiently. The same is true regarding Ministry of Health guidelines that define the standards of care for this group. With the exception of volume 6 of the guideline document, "Standard Procedures in Family Planning, Infertility, Youth Consultation, and Gender-Based Violence," adolescents are not covered explicitly by any procedures that acknowledge that this group's needs might differ from other subgroups.

On an organizational level, there is a lack of staff trained and dedicated to adolescent health and related policy mechanisms that coordinate interventions between ministries. Even though the Ministry of Youth has an individual person assigned to coordinate adolescent health issues, this is not true across all ministries. Although a large share of adolescent health activity is carried out by disparate task forces and sectors, Rwanda's Ministry of Health currently has no position to coordinate and provide guidance on adolescent health issues. The National Reproductive Health Policy calls for a mechanism under the Ministry of Health, but this is designed to cover only reproductive health and does not provide for a holistic approach to adolescent health.

On the other hand, the National Youth Steering Committee under the guidance of the Ministry of Youth is mandated to cover health only as a subtopic, and their coordination does not seem sufficient given the complexity and demanding nature of health-related interventions within the mandate of this ministry (Binagwaho, 2009). These overlapping, partial sets of responsibilities for adolescent health, with huge gaps in coordination and guidance for services delivery, can translate into an environment where no institution feels the full responsibility to ensure that comprehensive adolescent healthcare is accessible or even provided.

Cultural and Societal Barriers

In the realm of society and culture, adolescents face pressure from a multitude of social determinants and cultural norms that influence behavior. An example of this influence comes through in seeking reproductive healthcare. Examples in the realm of reproductive health suggest that young people, and young women in particular, feel social pressure regarding their sexuality and acceptable sexual behavior in Rwandan society. According to the 2015 DHS report, marriage remains the only legally and socially sanctioned setting for sexual intercourse in Rwanda (DHS Program, 2016). The average age of first reported sexual intercourse is 21.8 years for women and 22.5 years for men (DHS Program, 2016). However, when questioned in a setting where privacy has been ensured, adolescent girls reported younger age at first sexual intercourse, more comprehensive knowledge about condom sources, and a higher number of sexual partners (Binagwaho, 2009).

The surrounding social and cultural conditions and shifts may also influence riskier individual health behaviors among adolescents. For example, among currently married women and sexually active unmarried women, adolescent girls ages fifteen to nineteen have drastically lower contraceptive use rates as compared to women of all ages (35.3 percent against 53.2 percent and 11.6 percent against 35.6 percent, respectively) (DHS Program, 2016). Adolescent girls may be discouraged or disempowered from seeking reproductive healthcare and contraceptives due to stigma and social pressure regarding their sexual activity. There is a significant, seemingly counterintuitive gap between adolescent care-seeking for family planning (preventive care) compared to care for STIs and antenatal care (acute care), according to a 2007 Service Provision Assessment survey (USAID/Republic of Rwanda Ministry of Health, 2007).

A possible explanation for this gap is that adolescents are unwilling or unable to seek preventive services related to sexual activity due to societal pressures against adolescents' sexual activity. They may be willing to seek services only in cases of extreme need, such as pregnancy or an acute symptom of sexually transmitted diseases. Such trends suggest an increased need to improve access to comprehensive, adolescent-focused healthcare in order to better respond to the unique societal pressures and health challenges facing adolescents.

Individual Preferences

In addition to the governance, policy, and societal influences on adolescent health, individual factors obviously contribute to an adolescent's particular health outcomes. Adolescents' social capital and knowledge and attitudes regarding health and health determinants influence their risk behaviors and the degree to which they will seek preventive care (Basen-Engquist & Parcel, 1992; Binagwaho, 2009; Brooks, Magnusson, Spencer, & Morgan, 2012). For example, if a Rwandan adolescent girl engages in behavior that is perceived as culturally unacceptable but socially normal among her peers, such as premarital sex, she is caught at a crossroads of norms. This may lead to risky behaviors occurring outside of the public eye and without the benefit of comprehensive information, such as unprotected sex occurring due to girls' inability to negotiate condom use. As discussed before, this impacts the level of preventive versus curative services that Rwandan adolescents utilize. Further, a comprehensive literature review of adolescent health behaviors and outcomes in developing countries found that premarital sex, pregnancy and early childbearing, and not using condoms were related to nonsexual risk behaviors, namely alcohol and drug use (Mmari & Blum, 2009).

On the other hand, school enrollment and high educational aspirations were found to be protective factors against premarital sex (Mmari & Blum, 2009). Given this challenging combination of a high rate of early onset of alcohol and drug use and a low rate of secondary school enrollment and completion among Rwandan adolescents, this is a cause for concern in terms of the current status quo of policies that can influence these individual behaviors among adolescents.

Data Gaps

Unsurprisingly, given the challenges in defining who adolescents are in society not simply in Rwanda but also worldwide, this hamstrings policy makers' abilities to effectively monitor trends facing this population. For example, though mental health concerns and injuries and accidents are noted as key issues for this subgroup in particular, there is a relative dearth of data programs tracking these problems.

Specifically, in Rwanda, where transgenerational trauma exists and large-scale trauma is a major aspect of the recent past, there is a gap in understanding how the trauma of the 1994 genocide has impacted the psychosocial well-being of later generations (Basabose, 2017). As a result of these interconnected factors, Rwandan adolescents, like adolescents across the globe, are vulnerable to riskier individual-level decisions and behaviors because of inadequate health program design that does not account for the intersecting social, cultural, and governance level barriers to health. Yet people generally assume this is a healthy population. This assumption coupled with these data gaps are ingredients for a risky blind spot for policy makers: since no reliable data sets exist to showcase the health challenges facing adolescents (which are already a group poorly defined across global reports), then it is easier to reinforce the assumption that they are a healthy subgroup.

BUILDING CAPACITY FOR ADOLESCENTS' RIGHT TO HEALTH IN RWANDA

While we have explored a number of barriers facing adolescents and their ability to fully realize their human right to health, Rwanda is pursuing a number of initiatives to address these obvious barriers. For example, the fourth Health Sector Strategic Plan (HSSP4), which guides health planning from 2018 to 2024, prioritizes health for adolescents in several different ways. The HSSP4 includes revising training curricula and bolstering service provider education in order to capture adolescent sexual and reproductive health concerns, expanding coverage for sexual and reproductive healthcare by increasing youth-friendly health centers and areas, promoting the use of technology to reach adolescents, increasing investment in adolescent nutrition (as part of SDG Number 2) for greater coverage and uniformity of services, and expanding access to and promoting HIV prevention and treatment services.

The plan also cites human resources for health as a priority, stipulating that community health workers and palliative care workers should come from different age groups so as to better accommodate youth and the elderly (Ministry of Health, 2018). Other social sectors, including the Ministry of Education, have developed initiatives to curb HIV among adolescents, such as encouraging the development of anti-AIDS clubs and other peer-education programs in schools as well as HIV/AIDS training for teachers (Binagwaho, 2009). Youth Friendly Centers, administered by the National Youth Council (NYC), also exist to economically mobilize youth, provide vocational training, and promote innovation and business opportunities for youth (NYC, 2018).

Such services can help to address the larger socioeconomic issues that contribute to adolescent vulnerability if they provide young people with economically productive skills that increase their employability and value to the national labor market. Additionally, such trainings may serve to occupy adolescents that are out of school, decreasing the amount of time that they might otherwise spend engaging in risky behaviors. Other interventions that focus specifically on adolescent girls have been recently introduced that seek to improve retention in school, economic empowerment, sexual and reproductive health information and services, nutrition, bodily autonomy, freedom from violence, improved psychosocial well-being, and overall agency.

A review of these programs found that though impact evaluations are largely missing, they are associated with positive shifts in knowledge and attitudes, schooling, employment, and psychosocial outcomes (Stavropoulou, Gupta-Archer, & Marcus, 2017). Rwanda is also part of ALL IN to End Adolescent AIDS, a UNAIDS and UNICEF initiative designed to promote evidence-based policies that will combat this scourge among adolescents (Bains & Armstrong, 2017). The resulting data assessment demonstrated that low knowledge and utilization of sexual and reproductive healthcare services was contributing to an increasing rate of new HIV infections and pregnancy among adolescents.

These findings led to the creation of a national operational plan that established targets for bolstering the HIV response for adolescents in Rwanda (Bains & Armstrong, 2017). Finally, the Imbuto Foundation, an initiative of First Lady Jeannette Kagame, has developed a number of programs in recent years in order to address adolescent health issues in Rwanda. These programs aim primarily at improving adolescent sexual and reproductive health and reducing HIV infections among young people, with the goal of empowering young adolescent girls through youth mentorship and building life skills (Imbuto Foundation, 2018). These strides forward for adolescent health and access to health information resulted from key, intentional actions taken by the various ministries and other public institutions that oversee adolescent and youth issues in Rwanda, in coordination with international and national NGOs.

While much room remains for improvement, particularly in the area of coordination between ministries and increased access to adolescent-specific healthcare services, Rwanda has demonstrated an encouraging trajectory for improving adolescent health. To go even further, it is heartening that adolescents are demanding greater information about their right to health: a recent survey of girls age eleven to eighteen who had dropped out of school due to pregnancy found that 81 percent of respondents reported that they needed training on human rights principles (CLADHO, 2016).

In order to continue to build capacity, Rwanda needs multisectoral approaches that intersect health-sector interventions and programs conceived to support other aspects of adolescents' well-being, such as interventions developed by the youth and education sectors. Such solutions should support increasing adolescents' access to information and skills needed for healthy decision-making and a broad range of nonjudgmental, comprehensive healthcare services. These solutions should take place in and be facilitated by a social, legal, and regulatory environment that supports and protects adolescents and prioritizes the realization of their human right to health (Jamison et al., 2006). Fortunately, Rwanda's governing structure is ripe for this coordination for adolescent health as the various ministers of social programs meet regularly through the "Social Cluster" to identify opportunities for greater coordination of services across ministries. As such, the Social Cluster should review the national legal frameworks related to adolescent health and work on aligning definitions and synergy.

As demonstrated here, adolescents as a population are at a greater risk of being overlooked in their right to health because of individual, social, political, legal, cultural, and international contextual factors. However, there is much opportunity for change in this particular age group as many of these factors are not fixed and behaviors are not yet entrenched, thereby making educational and health initiatives more potentially accessible to these youth. Efforts to optimize the human right to health for adolescents and influencing their lifestyle and behaviors in positive ways are crucial components of ensuring a healthy workforce and adult population for Rwanda, and for the world – and are simply just the right thing to do (Binagwaho, 2009). To make progress, international governing bodies, including all of the UN agencies, must prioritize efforts to correct discrepancies in their definitions for adolescent health, which will inform not only Rwanda's policies to improve the lives of adolescents but also the policies of all countries. Taken together, this will help ensure that global health initiatives can be better developed to improve the lives of these young minds and sources of boundless energy, which the older generations will look toward for making the world a better place.

REFERENCES

Backman, G., Hunt, P., Khosla, R., et al. (2008). Health systems and the right to health: An assessment of 194 countries. *Lancet*, 372, 2047–2085. https://doi.org/10.1016/S0140

Bains, A., & Armstrong, A. (2017, December). Developing an adolescent operational plan: Rwanda. *ESA ALL IN Blog Series*. Retrieved from https://childrenandaids.org/sites/default/files/2017-12/All In ESA - Blog Rwanda 2017.pdf.

Basabose, J. de D. (2017). Coping with trans-generational trauma: A key feature of peace-building work in Rwanda. *Peace Insight*. Retrieved from www.peaceinsight.org/blog/2017/12/coping-trans-generational-trauma-key-feature-peace-building-work-rwanda/.

Basen-Engquist, K., & Parcel, G. S. (1992). Attitudes, norms, and self-efficacy: A model of adolescents' HIV-related sexual risk behavior. *Health Education Quarterly*, 19(2), 263–277. https://doi.org/10.1177/109019819201900209

Binagwaho, A. (2009). Report on adolescent health and HIV services in Rwanda, in the context of their human rights. *Health and Human Rights Journal*. www.hhrjournal.org/2009/10/adolescent-health-in-rwanda

Brooks, F. M., Magnusson, J., Spencer, N., & Morgan, A. (2012). Adolescent multiple risk behaviour: An asset approach to the role of family, school and community. *Journal of Public Health*, 34(S1), i48–i56. https://doi.org/10.1093/pubmed/fds001

Collective of Leagues and Associations for the Defense of Human Rights in Rwanda (CLADHO) (2016). Report on early/unwanted pregnancy for under 18 years in 10 districts of Rwanda: Advocating for girls' rights socio protection through fighting against early and unwanted pregnancies in Rwanda. A-SRH PROJECT/CLADHO – KNH. Kigali, Rwanda. Retrieved from www.cladho.org.rw/fileadmin/templates/document/REPORT_OF_THE_RAPID_ASSESSMENT_ON_TEENAGE_PREGNANCY.PDF.

Convention on the Rights of the Child (1990). New York: United Nations General Assembly. Retrieved from www.ohchr.org/Documents/ProfessionalInterest/crc.pdf.

DHS Program (2006). Rwanda demographic and health survey 2005. Retrieved from www.measuredhs.com/pubs/pdf/FR183/FR183.pdf.

DHS Program (2012). Rwanda demographic and health survey 2010. Retrieved from https://dhsprogram.com/pubs/pdf/FR259/FR259.pdf.

DHS Program (2016). Rwanda demographic and health survey 2014–15. Retrieved from https://dhsprogram.com/pubs/pdf/FR316/FR316.pdf.

DHS Program (2018). Rwanda: Standard DHS, 2014. Retrieved from https://dhsprogram.com/what-we-do/survey/survey-display-468.cfm.

Imbuto Foundation (2018). Health programmes. Retrieved from http://imbutofoundation.org/-health-projects-.html.

International Monetary Fund (2018). World economic outlook (October 2018): GDP per capita, current prices. Retrieved from www.imf.org/external/datamapper/NGDPDPC@WEO/OEMDC/ADVEC/WEOWORLD.

Jamison, D. T., Breman, J. G., Measham, A. R., et al. (2006). *Disease control priorities in developing countries* (2nd ed.). Washington, DC: World Bank and Oxford University Press. Retrieved from https://openknowledge.worldbank.org/handle/10986/7242.

Joint United Nations Programme on AIDS/HIV (UNAIDS) (2016). Ending the AIDS epidemic for adolescents, with adolescents: A practical guide to meaningfully engage adolescents in the AIDS response. Geneva. Retrieved from www.unaids.org/sites/default/files/media_asset/ending-AIDS-epidemic-adolescents_en.pdf.

Joint United Nations Programme on AIDS/HIV (USAID)/Republic of Rwanda Ministry of Health (2007). 2007 Rwanda Service Provision Assessment Survey.

Kanyoni, M., Gishoma, D., & Ndahindwa, V. (2015). Prevalence of psychoactive substance use among youth in Rwanda. *BMC Research Notes, 8*, 3–4. https://doi.org/10.1186/s13104-015-1148-2

Khan, S. (1999). Role of the Convention on the Elimination of All Forms of Discrimination Against Women (CEDAW) in realization of women's reproductive health, sexual health and reproductive rights. The Hague. Retrieved from www.un.org/popin/icpd/icpd5/hague/cedaw.pdf.

Milliez, J. (2009). FIGO Committee report: Adolescent and youth reproductive health care and confidentiality. *International Journal of Gynecology and Obstetrics, 106*, 271–272. Retrieved from https://ac-els-cdn-com.ezp-prod1.hul.harvard.edu/S0020729209001696/1-s2.0-S0020729209001696-main.pdf?_tid=ff1e1357-92a6-4322-aa6e-ee4d60c01ac7&acdnat=1528393566_766e460b2e4666afa52bc4ab1fa3746d.

Ministry of Finance and Economic Planning (2013). Youth sector strategic plan 2013–2018. Retrieved from http://extwprlegs1.fao.org/docs/pdf/rwa165155.pdf.

Ministry of Health (2012). Adolescent sexual reproductive health and rights policy: 2011–2015. Retrieved from www.moh.gov.rw/fileadmin/templates/policies/ASRH_and_Right_policy.pdf.

Ministry of Health (2018). Fourth health sector strategic plan July 2018–June 2024. Retrieved from www.moh.gov.rw/fileadmin/templates/Docs/FINALH_2-1.pdf.

Mmari, K., & Blum, R. W. (2009). Risk and protective factors that affect adolescent reproductive health in developing countries: A structured literature review. *Global Public Health, 4*(4), 350–366. https://doi.org/10.1080/17441690701664418

National Youth Council (NYC) (2018). Youth friendly centers. Retrieved from www.nyc.gov.rw/youth-services-project/youth-friendly-centers/.

National Youth Policy (NYP) (2015). National Youth Policy: Towards a HAPPI generation. Retrieved from www.nyc.gov.rw/fileadmin/templates/template_new/documents/National_Youth_Policy.pdf.

Ndagijimana, U. (2015). Update status & key messages: MDGs, EDPRS 2, Vision 2020. Retrieved from www.statistics.gov.rw/file/4433/download?token=a7VAE4 j_.

Republic of Rwanda, Ministry of Gender and Family Promotion (MIGEPROF) 2011. National Integrated Child Rights Policy. Retrieved from http://197.243.22.137/migeprof/fileadmin/_migrated/content_uploads/INTEGRATED_CHILD_RIGHTS_POLICY-2.pdf.

Sawyer, S. M., Azzopardi, P. S., Wickremarathne, D., & Patton, G. C. (2018). The age of adolescence. *The Lancet Child & Adolescent Health, 2*(3), 223–228. https://doi.org/10.1016/S2352-4642(18)30022-1

Shaw, D. (n.d.). Access to sexual and reproductive health for young people: Bridging the disconnect between rights and reality. *International Journal of Gynecology and Obstetrics, 106*, 132–136. https://doi.org/10.1016/j.ijgo.2009.03.025

Stavropoulou, M., Gupta-Archer, N., & Marcus, R. (2017). Adolescent girls' capabilities in Rwanda: The state of the evidence on programme effectiveness. Retrieved from www.gage.odi.org/sites/default/files/2018-02/Rwanda Interventions Report.pdf.

United Nations (2016). United Nations Convention on the Rights of the Child. General Comment No. 20 on the implementation of the rights of the child during adolescence. Retrieved from www.youthpolicy.org/library/wp-content/uploads/library/2016_General_Comment_20_Eng.pdf.

United Nations (2018a). Convention on the Elimination of All Forms of Discrimination against Women. In *United Nations Treaty Collection* (1,249th ed.). New York: United Nations.

United Nations (2018b). Convention on the Rights of the Child. In *United Nations Treaty Collection*. New York: United Nations. Retrieved from https://treaties.un.org/Pages/ViewDetails.aspx?src=IND&mtdsg_no=IV-11&chapter=4&lang=en.

United Nations (2018c). International Covenant on Economic, Social and Cultural Rights. In *United Nations Treaty Collection* (993rd ed.). New York: United Nations.

United Nations Children's Fund (UNICEF) (2013). Towards an AIDS-free generation: Children and AIDS: Sixth stocktaking report, 2013. Retrieved from www.unaids.org/sites/default/files/media_asset/20131129_stocktaking_report_children_aids_en_0.pdf.

United Nations Development Programme (2018). Human development index. Retrieved from http://hdr.undp.org/en/indicators/137506.

Van Handel, M., Kann, L., Olsen, M., & Dietz, P. (2016). HIV testing among US high school students and young Adults. *PEDIATRICS*, 137(2), 1–9. https://doi.org/10.1542/peds.2015-2700

Vasan, A., Anatole, M., Mezzacappa, C., et al. (2013). Baseline assessment of adult and adolescent primary care delivery in Rwanda: An opportunity for quality improvement. *BMC Health Services Research*, 13(518), 1–9. Retrieved from https://bmchealthservres.biomedcentral.com/track/pdf/10.1186/1472-6963-13-518.

World Bank (2017). The World Bank in Rwanda: Overview. Retrieved from www.worldbank.org/en/country/rwanda/overview.

World Bank (2018). World development indicators. Retrieved from http://databank.worldbank.org/data/reports.aspx?source=world-development-indicators.

World Health Organization (WHO) (2014). Mortality, morbidity and disability in adolescence: Mortality. Retrieved from http://apps.who.int/adolescent/second-decade/section3/page2/mortality.html.

World Health Organization (WHO) (2018a). Adolescents: Health risks and solutions. Retrieved from www.who.int/en/news-room/fact-sheets/detail/adolescents-health-risks-and-solutions.

World Health Organization (WHO) (2018b). Millennium Development Goals. Retrieved from www.who.int/topics/millennium_development_goals/en/.

World Health Organization (WHO) (2018c). Sustainable Development Goals (SDGs). Retrieved from www.who.int/sdg/en/.

28

Ending Mental Health Stigma and Discrimination

Young People Creating a Fairer Scotland

Amy Quinn, Ellie Moyes, Oliver McLuckie, Kirsten Roberts, and Doriana DeGradi, Supported by Laura Sharpe, Calum Irving, Wendy Halliday, and Clare McArthur

REGION/COUNTRY PARAMETERS

Scotland's population is estimated at 5.5 million: 4 million live in urban areas and 1.5 million in rural areas. Sixteen- to twenty-five-year-olds make up 500,000 of these and those under sixteen years total 1 million people (Gov.Scot, 2017). The health of the people of Scotland is improving: average life expectancy has increased to seventy-seven years for men and eighty-one for women (Mental Healthy, 2018). Health inequalities are a major public health challenge: in the most affluent areas of Scotland, men can experience twenty-four more years of good health and women twenty-two more years compared to the most deprived. The life expectancy of people who experience mental health problems is substantially shorter than the Scottish average. Further, those with mental illnesses are likely to die fifteen to twenty years prematurely because of physical ill health. Inequalities are evident in associations between mental health and age, gender, ethnicity, social class, disability, and looked-after and accommodated children (LAAC) (defined as those in the care of their local authority).

Given the direct link between the environment in which people live and work and their individual experiences of and access to services (NHS Health Scotland, 2015), addressing health inequalities (including mental health) and creating social justice is a priority for the Scottish government, the fourteen regional health boards, and the thirty-two local authorities.

Scotland is committed to improving children and young people's mental health and well-being as a social justice issue; as such it is a priority in the Mental Health Strategy. The Ministerial Task Force and Young People's Mental Health Commission have been formed, alongside the Audit Scotland report on Children and Young People's Mental Health, and a review of rejected referrals to child and adolescent mental health services (CAMHS) across Scotland. The review looked at the numbers of children and young people who were referred to but not seen by CAMHS, and explored the circumstances around why the referral was not progressed.

Empowering children and young people (CYP) to speak about issues that affect them, to have their voices heard, and to take action themselves has long been at the forefront of Scottish policy – this is crucial in addressing social injustice and inequalities, including mental health stigma and discrimination, that have an impact on CYP, creating barriers to help-seeking behaviour (NHS Health Scotland, 2019).

Unlike most physical health conditions, mental illness is often subject to stigma, a social process which associates a person with an unwanted label and affects emotional reactions and attitudes, which may lead to social disapproval (Goffman, 1963), prejudice, and discrimination (Corrigan, Edwards, Green, Diwan, & Penn, 2001). Negative stereotypes act as a barrier to seeking help for mental health conditions (Corrigan, Markowitz, Watson, Rowan, & Kubiak, 2003) because they reinforce public stigma by fuelling sensationalist stories that portray people with mental health conditions as unpredictable, aggressive, and dangerous (Corrigan, Watson, et al., 2005). Negative attitudes often result in social isolation and discriminatory behaviours towards CYP with mental health conditions. For instance, research has shown that 24 per cent of CYP would not confide in someone if they were experiencing a mental health problem (The Princes Trust MacQuarie, 2017). Social disapproval increases the chances of self-stigma, when a person starts to believe and internalise the public stigma associated with mental health issues. As identity is still being shaped during adolescence, one of the most debilitating effects of self-stigma on CYP is not seeking help, derived from a fear of negative outcomes and a lack of confidentiality being maintained, which is a potential breach of CYP rights.

Scotland spent £56.6 million on CYP mental healthcare services in 2016/17 (Audit Scotland, 2018). Estimates suggest that 20 per cent of CYP experience a mental health problem in any given year (McGinnity, Meltzer, Ford, & Goodman, 2005), with 10 per cent being clinically diagnosable (Audit Scotland, 2018). The Local Delivery Plan, established by the National Health Service (NHS) and the Scottish government, aims for 90 per cent of CYP to start treatment within eighteen weeks after being referred to CAMHS. However, data suggest that only 67.8 per cent are seen within this time frame and only four out of the fourteen health boards met this requirement by June 2018 (Gov.Scot, 2018b). Of these referrals, 21.6 per cent were rejected, a 24 per cent increase since 2013/14 (Audit Scotland, 2018), without providing CYP with any further guidance, leaving many unable to cope. The most common reason for declining a referral was that the person's mental health problem was not considered serious enough; this decision was usually made when there was a lack of suicidal ideation (Audit Scotland, 2018).

As services struggle to meet these demands effectively, there is greater emphasis on preventative action, so as to reduce the onset of mental illness and to provide intervention at the earliest experience of mental health difficulties. Prevention and early intervention are key features of the Scottish government's Mental Health Strategy 2017–2027. Organisations funded by the Scottish government, such as See Me, are developing education programmes and campaigns with this in mind.

Campaigns including Feels FM (https://feelsfm.co.uk/) and What's on Your Mind?, and training such as Scottish Mental Health First Aid (SMHFA) all aim to create conditions for preventative action, empowering CYP to seek help and supporting those around CYP in need to act in ways that best meet their needs.

BARRIERS TO SOCIAL JUSTICE FOR YOUNG PEOPLE

Social injustice occurs across the life course, but early and teenage years have particular significance in determining future outcomes. In the early years, adverse childhood experiences, such as bereavement or trauma, can have a direct and adverse impact on mental health and on life experience and long-term outcomes (Couper & Mackie, 2016). Half of all mental health problems develop by adolescence and three-quarters by the mid-twenties (NHS Health Scotland, 2013).

Recent studies suggest that adolescence is associated with poorer mental health and well-being. For example, CYP are more likely to self-harm so as to deal with distress and are more likely to develop schizophrenia at sixteen to twenty-five years than at any other age (Brown et al., 2016). This is compounded by a lack of awareness of rights, with only 27 per cent of CYP being aware that 'rights' are something they are entitled to (as defined by the United Nations Convention on the Rights of the Child [Ipsos MORI, 2017]) and reporting a reluctance to discuss mental health with adults around them due to concerns that confidentiality will not be maintained.

Gender can also be a barrier, with girls generally having poorer mental health and well-being than boys (Brown et al., 2016). There are marked differences in the mental health of CYP when considered alongside age and gender. A large-scale review of Scottish research found that older boys and girls generally have worse mental health than their younger counterparts (Cosma, Rhodes, Currie, Inchly, & HSBC Team, 2016a, 2016b), with fifteen-year-old girls more likely to report emotional problems than boys of the same age – 44 per cent and 21 per cent, respectively (Currie, Watson, & Rice, 2015). Further to this, young males are at a greater risk of suicide than any other group in society, and are almost four times more likely to take their own lives than females (Alexander, 2001). A supporting study found that suicide among young Scottish males increased for the third year in a row in 2017 (Samaritans, 2018). The literature suggests that higher rates of male suicide link to the stigma surrounding mental health issues and the social expectation of males – i.e., bravado, dominance, and strength (Rees, Jones, & Scott, 2005). This perceived need to cope can be damaging and can cause young men to internalise emotions, creating a barrier to potential help, with women twice as likely to visit their general practitioner (GP) as men (Scot.Gov, 2018).

Although one in ten CYP report experiencing a mental health condition, these statistics are not equally distributed across the population and thus socioeconomic status (SES) is another barrier faced by CYP. Research suggests that poor mental health is more prevalent and persistent in CYP of lower SES (Elliott, 2016).

Approximately one in four Scottish CYP are recognised as living in poverty (Child Poverty Action Group, 2018). This creates a harmful environment that can have a cumulative negative impact on health and development (Elliott, 2016), with CYP growing up in poverty two and a half times more likely to develop anxiety and depression due to a lack of basic needs such as food, shelter, and safety being met (Maslow, 1943, 1954). These individuals are also less able to access transport and healthcare services, meaning there is less opportunity to seek help or maintain treatment (Shavers, 2007). This results in inequalities in mental healthcare outcomes that pervade Scotland and arise from the unequal distribution of social and economic resources and opportunities (NHS Health Scotland, 2016).

Literature suggests a higher prevalence for mental health conditions in lesbian, gay, bisexual, and transgender (LGBT) youth than their heterosexual or cisgender counterparts due to discrimination. Specifically, higher rates of depression, eating disorders, suicidality, and self-harm occur among LGBT youth (Connolly, Zervos, Barone, Johnson, & Joseph, 2016). Moreover, 96 per cent of transgender and 84 per cent of LGBT CYP report experiencing mental health conditions and related behaviours, and 63 per cent and 50 per cent of transgender and LGBT young people experience suicidal ideation or behaviours (Lough Dennell, Anderson, & McDonnell, 2018). The same data suggest that 83 per cent of transgender and 73 per cent of LGBT young people reported having struggled with their mental health and that they had been bullied at school as a direct result of this.

High levels of homophobic bullying take place in Scottish education establishments, with 52 per cent of LGBT CYP (13–25) reporting being bullied. This can lead to negative consequences, including low academic attainment, a negative impact on CYP's mental health, low self-esteem, and greater absenteeism (Macpherson & Bond, 2009). Prolonged influences on CYP include isolation, reduced sleep and appetite, higher levels of risk-taking behaviour, and increased rates of completed and attempted suicide and self-harm (Dyson et al., 2003; Rivers & D'Augelli, 2001). Bullying during childhood and adolescence has been suggested to have an impact on an individual's mental health as an adult (Stonewall, 2007). For instance, 54 per cent of LGBT young people refrain from visiting their GP as they worry about how they will be perceived and treated (O'Neill, 2017). This suggests that healthcare services need to provide inclusive care so that LGBT CYP can seek effective, non-judgemental support.

Children and young people who are looked after and accommodated (LAAC) experience significant mental health issues and challenges, even when taking into account poverty and disadvantage. Looked-after children have poorer mental health than their non-looked-after peers (Priestley & Kennedy, 2015). These children can face multiple barriers when it comes to addressing mental health issues, including complex problems such as delayed identification of a mental health problem, long waiting times for appointments, their experience of service, service inflexibility, and the stigma surrounding mental health issues.

Children and young people who represent diverse racial/ethnic groups can also experience barriers when seeking advice and support for their mental health problems. These differences can be the result of a number of factors, including poverty. Mainstream services can fail to meet linguistic, cultural, and other needs and mental health problems may go unreported and untreated due to an understandable reluctance to seek support. It may also be the case that mental health problems are over-diagnosed in people whose first language is not English (Mind, 2009).

REBUILDING CAPACITY

The Scottish government continues to try to define, explain, and address the many barriers CYP face in relation to social justice and mental healthcare. These include developing frameworks and policy to improve outcomes for all and reduce the poverty-related attainment gap and to support public and third-sector organisations to create a common understanding, collective responsibility, and training underpinning the CYP sector.

The Fairer Scotland Action Plan sets out how to tackle poverty to reduce inequality and build a fairer and more inclusive Scotland. The aim is to work with partners in local government, the third sector, and communities to deliver this ambition and to recognise the importance of this activity in attaining good mental health for the whole of Scotland. This, alongside government programmes with a particular focus on closing the poverty-related attainment gap such as the Scottish Attainment Challenge, aims to achieve equity in education.

A CYP's well-being is influenced by their environment, experiences, and needs. Getting It Right for Every Child (GIRFEC) is the national approach to integrated support for children and young people, designed to improve outcomes for children and young people by offering the right help at the right time from the right people (Scottish Government, 2014). This policy empowers those working with children and families to operate across professional boundaries so as to provide support and identify and address needs at the earliest opportunity in order to prevent problems exacerbating (Gov.Scot, 2014). If successful it is hoped every child and young person has the same opportunity to succeed. It is underpinned by the National Improvement Framework – which measures and reports on progress of national and societal well-being, economic, social and environmental indicators, and targets aligned to a set of national outcomes – Curriculum for Excellence – the national curriculum to help young people and children obtain the attributes, skills, and knowledge necessary to equip them for life today – and GIRFEC.

The Scottish Government Mental Health Strategy for 2017 to 2027 (Gov.Scot, 2017) aims to combat the barriers CYP face when accessing help and support, including challenging mental health stigma and discrimination, as well as advocating for justice in relation to mental healthcare. The strategy details forty actions, with an increased focus on preventative measures, improving the capacity of and increasing the mental healthcare workforce, and involving people with lived experience in decision-making. The most critical for CYP include:

>Action 2 Roll out mental health training for those who support CYP in educational settings.
>
>Action 8 Work with partners to develop systems and multi-agency pathways that work cooperatively to support children's mental health and wellbeing.
>
>Action 17 Fund improved provision of services to treat child and adolescent mental health problems.
>
>Action 21 Improve quality of anticipatory care planning approaches for CYP leaving the mental health system entirely, and for CYP transitioning from CAMHS to Adult Mental Health Services.
>
>Action 32 Use a rights-based approach in the statutory guidance on the use of mental health legislation (Gov.Scot, 2017).

High levels of male suicide and a shifting focus towards prevention has been a top priority for governing bodies in recent years. The Scottish government's Action Plan on Suicide Prevention was informed by the views of people affected by suicide. One of the key findings of the Suicide Prevention Strategy Report was to address stigma, and the report acknowledged campaigns such as See Me and Finding Mike as good models through which to educate the public around stigma, a critical barrier to social justice, demonstrating the importance of such programmes.

With so many CYP in Scotland experiencing mental health problems (Gordon & Platt, 2017), it is vital that education staff be equipped to respond to mental health concerns. In 2017, 66 per cent of teachers in Scotland said they had not been trained sufficiently on mental health and only 1 per cent recalled receiving detailed training on mental health (Gordon & Platt, 2017). Such training will improve the confidence of education staff by increasing mental health literacy, encouraging open conversations, supporting recognition of mental health issues, and responding in a ways appropriate to the CYP. This is particularly important as stigma is one of the main barriers to help seeking that CYP face (Gordon & Platt, 2017).

The Scottish government has pledged significant investment in addressing mental health inequalities, including £250 million in funding, dedicated mental health counsellors in schools, extra training for teachers, and an additional 250 school nurses.

Through a strategic approach involving reviews of existing provision and commissioning of new services, the Scottish government is keen to ensure that the voices of CYP are included in the development of future provision and to deliver services that are evidence based, utilising improvement science and tests of change to support prevention and early intervention whilst ensuring causal factors and key barriers such as stigma and discrimination are embedded within approaches.

Ensuring that CYP voices are included in the decisions that affect their lives is pivotal to creating meaningful change. Scotland has specific provisions to ensure that young people understand their rights and are included in the decisions that affect their lives.

The Office of the Children and Young People's Commissioner for Scotland leads action on promoting and protecting CYP rights, consistent with the United Nations Convention of the Rights of the Child (UNCRC). They focus on supporting public services to uphold CYP's civic, cultural, economic, political, and social rights, and empowering CYP to claim their rights. This will be further supported through the principles of the UNCRC becoming enshrined into Scots law (Mental Health Strategy Progress Report, 2018). The government's vision with these actions is to continue and challenge the stigma and discrimination relating to mental health issues, as well as support parity of esteem with mental health considered in the same way as physical health.

The Scottish Government Youth Commission on Mental Health Services (YCMHS), led by young people, will review youth mental healthcare services in Scotland, ensuring that the voices and needs of CYP are central to the decisions being made that have an impact on their lives. The YCMHS will lead a study to reshape the available support, gather evidence on existing services, consult young people, and develop recommendations for ministers and service providers on how CAMHS can be improved. In addition to this, the Ministerial Task Force on Mental Health has been established. The Task Force will provide recommendations for improvements in provision for children and young people's mental healthcare in Scotland and, in partnership, develop a programme of sustainable reform (Mental Health Strategy Progress Report, 2018).

The Scottish government has also supported the 2018 Year of Young People (https://yoyp2018.scot/), a year-long opportunity for generations to come together and celebrate Scotland's young people. It is a platform for young people eight to twenty-six years, giving them a stronger voice on issues that affect their lives, showcasing their ideas and talents, and ultimately, aiming to challenge the status quo and create a more positive perception of CYP in society.

PROGRAMMATIC EXAMPLES

See Me is Scotland's national programme to end mental health stigma and discrimination. The See Me Education and Young People (EYP) programme has addressed key areas of focus in regard to mental health stigma and discrimination: education, campaigns, and social contact (Corrigan, Watson, et al., 2005). In a survey undertaken in April 2018, See Me consulted CYP across Scotland to find what the key issues for mental health stigma and discrimination were. With more than 1,400 responses from people aged twelve to twenty-six, See Me found that 67 per cent of young people would tell someone if they were struggling due to a physical condition or injury, yet only 31 per cent would tell someone that they had a diagnosed mental health condition and 26 per cent would share if they were struggling to cope. Current figures in relation to Scotland's CYP and their mental health demonstrate that CYP are experiencing barriers relating to stigma and discrimination towards mental health issues, which needs to be addressed. Further to this, 62 per cent of respondents said that they believe that people are treated unfairly for struggling with their mental health. This belief contributes to stigma and discrimination and can leave CYP feeling judged and invalidated, reinforcing barriers to help and support.

The See Me EYP programme aligns with the national framework and aims to help CYP understand the importance of good mental health, recognise how it affects them, and build confidence to talk openly about mental health. The programme works with volunteers who have lived experience of mental health conditions. It provides a peer-led model of training alongside resources for students and staff to address mental health stigma and discrimination. Through supporting and empowering CYP and staff members to advocate for their own mental health and that of their peers, See Me is embedding approaches to support a sustained cultural shift. Education and social contact models were comprehensively infused throughout schools given findings that taking a comprehensive approach is one of the best ways to implement projects that tackle stigma and discrimination to delivering mental health education in schools (Weist & Murray, 2008).

A social contact and education model was conducted in one local authority training 600 students and reaching 6,000 students experiencing some of the greatest barriers to social justice, including deprivation, rurality, and lack of services and long waits for CAMHS. The programme aimed to create lasting behavioural and attitudinal change for CYP and staff members within the school. Those trained reported that increasing knowledge and being able to help someone were key goals for the training. Initial analysis of the training suggests that staff and CYP feel more able and willing to tackle stigma at school and support peers (Mental Health Foundation, 2018). Longitudinal data continue to be gathered and are anticipated to demonstrate that the programme supports initial behavioural and attitudinal change within these schools; the sustainability of this continues to be evaluated. Stigma and discrimination towards mental health problems continues to be a social justice issue that has a negative impact on recovery and help-seeking behaviours and can exacerbate mental illness. With the current rates of CYP struggling with mental health in Scotland, it is essential that stigma and discrimination within education is tackled so as to improve mental health and well-being.

In 2018, See Me developed a national campaign, the world's first emoji-powered jukebox, otherwise known as 'Feels FM' (https://feelsfm.co.uk/). The online platform was created to help young people discuss mental health, stigma, and discrimination as part of the Scottish government's 'Year of Young People', an initiative created to give young people a voice on issues that affect their lives. See Me designed and coproduced the platform with young people, to host conversations with CYP about mental health and well-being and to identify key barriers and solutions. In the initial four-week phase of the campaign, from 17 September to 14 October, Feels FM was viewed 52,000 times by 29,000 different users. The findings will be reported to the Task Force on Mental Health in order to support recommendations to the Scottish government.

Through Feels FM, CYP were asked to choose an emoji to express how they were feeling and were asked a series of questions to which they gave open-ended responses in relation to mental health stigma and discrimination. It also encouraged CYP to give further feedback on what still needs to be done or what needs to change in Scotland to challenge mental health stigma and discrimination, providing an innovative way of giving CYP a voice in the decisions that have an impact on their lives. Whilst questions were answered, a music playlist was generated to mirror the emoji selected. Music was selected as it has been found to be a common coping strategy for those struggling with their mental health (McFerran, Garrido, & Saarikallio, 2016). It can also be an initial step to helping people understand and communicate feelings. The questions included:

> Q1: Does music affect how you are feeling, and if so, how?
> Q2: Music can help when you don't want to talk. What makes it difficult for YP to talk about their feelings?
> Q3: Sometimes it can be hard to describe in words how you're feeling. What helps YP talk about how they are feeling?

During the campaign, more than 4,800 young people answered the questions and took part in the conversation. Common themes included music as a popular coping strategy to deal with distress; however, music was also thought to be a trigger for certain feelings, for example listening to sad music triggering crying. The CYPs reported that judgement (such as being treated as dramatic or attention seeking), societal pressure, fear of unhelpful responses, not being taken seriously due to age, and feeling like a burden were contributors to making it difficult to talk about mental health, demonstrating that stigma and discrimination are still key barriers for CYP.

Children and young people also reported a lack of mental health literacy to express how they feel. They addressed key factors that can support feeling safe to talk about mental health, despite the barriers raised, including feeling respected, listened to, and understood. Confidentiality is a consistent issue for CYP. A lack of awareness in relation to rights compounds this as well as wider public stigma – all areas that need to be addressed before it will become any easier for CYP to talk about their mental health.

CONCLUSIONS

It is clear that CYP in Scotland face a multitude of barriers in relation to mental health stigma and discrimination, and that these barriers influence social justice. These barriers can include external factors beyond an individual's control, such as age, gender, prejudice and discrimination, or where they were born. However, despite a multitude of barriers, there are many advocates for CYP in Scotland, laying the foundations for whole-system improvement, including the government, health and social care, and third-sector organisations such as See Me, LGBT Youth, Children and Young People's Commissioner for Scotland, and the Scottish Youth Parliament – all of which aim to deliver social justice for CYP. Scotland is committed to achieving an ambitious social justice agenda through effective partnerships beyond traditional healthcare settings with a commitment to engaging and empowering individuals and communities as part of a rights-based approach and ensuring that the voices of those with lived experience of services can effectively inform the delivery. Much work still needs to be done so as to bridge the poverty-related attainment gap and address intersectional issues such as LGBT+ identity, LAAC, and diverse racial/ethnic groups, in order to understand the complex contribution of intersectionality that contributes to mental health concerns.

The Scottish government has provided substantial investment through which to address social justice issues and a commitment to continue the work of national programmes such as See Me, with a particular focus on young people. Programmes such as these have shown that CYP voices struggle to be heard, but that valuable work continues to take place to address this. However, there is still a long way to go to ensuring that all CYP are heard and as such, currently social justice for CYP may be achieved only for those already aware of services and their rights. We may be failing to reach the most vulnerable, stigmatised, and discriminated against due to lack of accessibility of services and campaigns. It is essential that effective partnerships facilitate lasting change and advocacy for CYP and continue to challenge stigma and discrimination. It is only through empowering individuals and providing access to human rights that social justice may be achieved, increasing the ability and accountability of individuals and institutions that are responsible for respecting, protecting, and fulfilling rights, and ensuring mental health stigma and discrimination end.

E-RESOURCES

https://feelsfm.co.uk/
www.seemescotland.org/media/8066/whats-on-your-mind-full-pack.pdf

REFERENCES

Alexander, J. (2001). Depressed men: An exploratory study of close relationships. *Journal of Psychiatric Mental Health Nursing*, 8, 67–75.
Audit Scotland (2018). Children and young people's mental health. Available at: www.audit-scotland.gov.uk/uploads/docs/report/2018/nr_180913_mental_health.pdf [Accessed 5 Nov. 2018].
Black, C., & Martin, C. (2015). Mental health and wellbeing among adolescents in Scotland: Profile and trends. Report produced by Ipsos MORI. Available at: https://dera.ioe.ac.uk/24715/1/00488358.pdf [Accessed 26 Oct. 2018].

Bmj.com (2018). Life expectancy gap widens between those with mental illness and general population. BMJ. Available at: www.bmj.com/press-releases/2013/05/21/life-expectancy-gap-widens-between-those-mental-illness-and-general-popula [Accessed 1 Nov. 2018].

Brown, L., Campbell-Jack, D., Gray, L., et al. (2016). *Scottish Health Survey 2015: Main report.* Edinburgh: A National Statistics Publication for Scotland.

Child Poverty Action Group (2018). Child poverty in Scotland. Available at: www.cpag.org.uk/scotland/child-poverty-facts-and-figures [Accessed 1 Oct. 2018].

Connolly, M. D., Zervos, M. J., Barone, C. J., Johnson, C. C., & Joseph, C. L. M. (2016). The mental health of transgender youth: Advances in understanding. *Journal of Adolescent Health*, 59, 489–495.

Corrigan, P. W., Edwards, A., Green, A., Diwan, S. E., & Penn, D. L. (2001). Prejudice, social distance, and familiarity with mental illness. *Schizophrenia Bulletin*, 27, 219–225.

Corrigan, P., Markowitz, F. E., Watson, A., Rowan, D., & Kubiak, M. A. (2003). An attribution model of public discrimination towards persons with mental illness. *Journal of Health and Social Behavior*, 44, 162–179.

Corrigan, P. W., Watson, A. C., Gracia, G., et al. (2005). Newspaper stories as measures of structural stigma. *Psychiatric Services*, 56, 551–556.

Cosma, A., Rhodes, G., Currie, C., Inchley, J., & HBSC Team (2016a). HSBC Briefing Paper 24. Mental and emotional well-being in Scottish adolescents. Child and Adolescent Health Research Unit (CAHRU), St Andrews.

Cosma, A., Rhodes, G., Currie, C., Inchley, J., & HBSC Team (2016b). HSBC Briefing Paper 25. Self-confidence and social wellbeing in Scottish adolescents. Child and Adolescent Health Research Unit (CAHRU), St Andrews.

Couper, S., & Mackie, P. (2016). *'Polishing the diamonds'. Addressing adverse childhood experiences in Scotland.* Edinburgh: Scottish Public Health Network.

Currie, C., Watson, L., & Rice, P. (2015). Adolescent health in the 21st century. *Journal of the Royal College of Physicians of Edinburgh*, 45(4), 258–260.

Dyson, S., Mitchell, A., Smith, A., et al. (2003). Don't ask, Don't tell. Hidden in the crowd: The need for documenting links between sexuality and suicidal behaviours among young people. *Monograph Series No. 45.* Melbourne: Australian Research Centre in Sex, Health and Society.

Elliott, I. (2016). *Poverty and mental health: A review to inform the Joseph Rowntree Foundation's anti-poverty strategy.* London: Mental Health Foundation.

Gale, F. (2007). Tackling the stigma of mental health in vulnerable children and young people. *Mental Health Interventions and Services for Vulnerable Children and Young People*, 58–80.

Goffman, E. (1963). *Stigma: Notes on the management of spoiled identity.* Harmondsworth, Middlesex: Penguin Books.

Gordon, J., & Platt, S. (2017). *Going to be all right? A report on the mental health of young people in Scotland.* Glasgow: Scottish Association for Mental Health.

Gov.Scot (2014). Children and Young People (Scotland) Act 2014. Available at: www.legislation.gov.uk/asp/2014/8/contents/enacted [Accessed 29 Oct. 2018].

Gov.Scot (2017). Age demographics. Available at: www2.gov.scot/Topics/People/Equality/Equalities/DataGrid/Age/AgePopMig [Accessed 22 Feb. 2019].

Gov.Scot (2018a). Education Scotland: National policy. Available at: https://education.gov.scot/ [Accessed 5 Nov. 2018].

Gov.Scot (2018b). Mental health strategy 2017–2027: First progress report. Available at: www.gov.scot/publications/mental-health-strategy-2017-2027-1st-progress-report/pages/4/ [Accessed 1 Nov. 2018].

Ipsos MORI (2017). Young People In Scotland Survey 2017. Available at: www.cypcs.org.uk/ufiles/Young-People-in-Scotland-Survey-2017-PDF-of-powerpoint-results.pdf [Accessed 5 Nov. 2018].

Lough Dennell, B. L., Anderson, G., & McDonnell, D. (2018). *Life in Scotland for LGBT young people*. Glasgow: LGBT Youth Scotland.

Macpherson, S., & Bond, S. (2009). Equality issues in Scotland: A review of research, 2000–08. Available at: www.equalityhumanrights.com/uploaded_files/Scotland/equality_issues_in_scotland_a_review_of_research.pdf [Accessed 12 Oct. 2018].

Maslow, A. H. (1943). A theory of human motivation. *Psychological Review*, 50, 370–396.

Maslow, A. H. (1954). *Motivation and personality*. New York: Harper & Row.

McFerran, K. S., Garrido, S., & Saarikallio, S. (2016). A critical interpretive synthesis of the literature linking music and adolescent mental health. *Youth & Society*, 48(4), 521–538.

McGinnity, Á., Meltzer, H., Ford, T., & Goodman, R. (2005). *Mental health of children and young people in Great Britain, 2004*, ed. H. Green. Basingstoke: Palgrave Macmillan.

Mental Health Foundation (2018). See Me evaluation of process and impact: Phase 2 Year 1. Available at: www.seemescotland.org/media/9188/mhf-see-me-report-public-summary-docmay-18.pdf [Accessed 26 Oct. 2018].

Mental Healthy (2018). Life expectancy for those with mental illness 15–20 years less that those without. Mental Healthy. Available at: www.mentalhealthy.co.uk/news/1281-life-expectancy-for-those-with-mental-illness-15-20-years-less-that-those-without.html [Accessed 26 Oct. 2018].

Mind (2009). Psychiatry, race and culture. Available at: www.mind.org.uk/media/192441/mind_think_report_4.pdf [Accessed 26 Oct. 2018].

NHS Health Scotland (2013). Scotland's mental health: Children and young people 2013. Available at: www.scotpho.org.uk/media/1169/scotpho131219-mhcyp2013-subnational.pdf [Accessed 13 Oct. 2018].

NHS Health Scotland (2015). *Good mental health for all*. Glasgow: Health Scotland.

NHS Health Scotland (2016). Good mental health for all. Available at: www.healthscotland.scot/media/1805/good-mental-health-for-all-feb-2016.pdf [Accessed 12 Oct. 2018].

NHS Health Scotland (2019). *Children and young people's mental health*. Glasgow: Health Scotland. Available at: www.healthscotland.scot/health-topics/mental-health-and-wellbeing/children

O'Neill, T. (2017). GPs at the deep end. Pioneer scheme day-release programme. Available at: www.gla.ac.uk/media/media_566450_en.pdf [Accessed 12 Oct. 2018].

Priestley, A., & Kennedy, L. A. (2015, July). *The health of looked after children and young people: A summary of the literature*. Glasgow: University of Strathclyde International Public Policy Institute, Centre for Health Policy. Available at: https://strathprints.strath.ac.uk/54056/ [Accessed 26 Oct. 2018].

The Princes Trust (2017). Stigma stopping young people talking about mental health. Available at: www.princes-trust.org.uk/about-the-trust/news-views/stigma-young-people-talking-about-mental-health [Accessed 26 Oct. 2018].

The Princes Trust MacQuarie (2017). *Youth Index 2017*. London: The Princes Trust London. Available at: www.princes-trust.org.uk/about-the-trust/research-policies-reports/youth-index-2017 [Accessed 26 Oct. 2018].

Rees, C., Jones. M., & Scott, T. (2005). Exploring men's health in a men-only group. *Nursing Standard*, 9, 38–40.

Rivers, I., & D'Augelli, A. R. (2001). *The victimization of lesbian, gay and bisexual youths: Lesbian, gay and bisexual identities and youth, psychological perspectives*. New York: New York University Press, pp. 199–223.

Samaritans (2018). Giving young people a space to talk about mental health. Available at: www.samaritans.org/news/giving-children-and-young-people-space-talk-about-mental-health [Accessed 20 Oct. 2018].

Samaritans (2018, December). *Suicide statistics report: Latest statistics for the UK and the Republic of Ireland*. Surrey, England: Samaritans.

Scottish Government (2014). *Getting it right for every child*. Edinburgh: Scottish Government. Available at: www.gov.scot/policies/girfec/ [Accessed 26 Oct. 2018].

Shavers, V. L. (2007). Measurement of socioeconomic status in health disparities research. *Journal of the National Medical Association*, 99, 1013–1023.

Stonewall (2007). *The Equalities Review: Sexual orientation research review*. London: Cabinet Office.

Weist, M. D., & Murray, M. (2008). Advancing school mental health promotion globally. *Advances in School Mental Health Promotion*, 1(sup1), 2–12.

29

Violence Exposure among Children and Young People

A South African Case Study

Theophilus Lazarus, Gershom Lazarus, Eugene Emory, Katelyn Reardon, and Eva Kuzyk

REGION/COUNTRY PARAMETERS

The mental health problems facing South Africans of all ages are well documented from various standpoints (Flisher et al., 2012). The persisting legacy of apartheid that legalized racial separation and discrimination continues to haunt South African society, as evidenced in the continuing verbal and violent racist attacks. The youth of South Africa, particularly those of previously socially disadvantaged backgrounds, face daunting challenges of poverty, lack of social support, and an emerging social class crisis that makes healthcare accessibility a serious issue (Das-Munshi et al., 2016).

The increasing burden of mental health problems arising from various socio-economic, medical, and congenital causes has received recognition in multiple ways. More than sixty years ago, the first director general of the World Health Organization (WHO), Dr. Brock Chisholm, argued that "without mental health, there can be no true physical health" (Chisholm, 1951, p. 3). Mental healthcare services can be viewed in terms of "a basic human right" when examining the definition of "mental health" provided by WHO: "a state of well-being in which every individual realizes his or her own abilities, can cope with the normal stresses of life, can work productively and fruitfully, and is able to make a contribution to his or her community" (WHO, 2001, p. 1).

Various reports have noted an alarming increase in the incidence of mental illness across the globe in developing and developed countries. The recognition of biological factors such as head trauma as causing or aggravating mental illness is also receiving more attention in nations around the world (Orlovska et al., 2014). Mental healthcare must consider interwoven factors that range from genetic to social influences when identifying etiology and developing appropriate treatments. One such factor that has emerged is the role of mild traumatic brain injuries in mental disorders (Haagsma et al., 2015; Zgaljardic et al., 2015).

South Africa is noted to have a high level of assaults and motor vehicle accidents that result in head injuries of varying levels of severity. While more severe head injuries are likely to receive the requisite medical attention, those of lesser severity (according to the medical parameters of loss of consciousness or negative initial CT brain scan findings) are managed, but to a lesser extent. A relevant concern in this context is the incidence of traumatic brain injury (TBI), which has an incidence of 150–170/100,000 in sub-Saharan Africa, compared to the global average of 106/100,000 (Hyder, Wunderlich, Puvanachandra, Gururaj, & Kobusingye, 2007). An increasing amount of attention has therefore been dedicated to this concern over the past several decades in order to guide clinicians in tackling this issue. Compounding this problem of a growing rate of TBI are the various barriers that reduce access to mental healthcare services in this population.

BARRIERS TO SOCIAL JUSTICE FOR YOUNG PEOPLE

Notwithstanding provision for protection against the lack of healthcare services as suggested in the South African constitution (see later in this chapter), children cannot access appropriate mental healthcare services if they come from previously disadvantaged backgrounds, which is a result of legally enforced discrimination (Szabo, Fine, Mayers, Naidoo, & Zabow, 2017). Research findings suggest that untreated adolescent mental problems persist into adulthood (Flisher et al., 2012) and pose an additional burden.

The most recent census of South Africa (2018) indicates that more than 30 percent of the child and adolescent population come from disadvantaged backgrounds. Given the emphasis of the current health initiatives in providing primary healthcare services in the form of medication for primary illnesses such as tuberculosis and HIV, there is a general lack of attention to the threat mild TBIs might pose to the mental and physical health of children and adolescents in this sector of South African society.

Due to this finding, a neurological insult such as a mild traumatic head injury or concussion in members of lower socioeconomic groups and in those who have a history of psychiatric illness is a significant risk factor in young children and adolescents, worsened in the South African context for the following reasons.

First, there is a lack of trained neurologists. Fewer than 500 neurologists serve a population of approximately 57 million people in South Africa. To a large extent, neurologists are based in private practice (independent or group) and not in hospitals where a large proportion of accident victims present. These victims of TBI do not receive a confirmatory diagnosis of concussion and so miss out on appropriate treatment (Rosman, 2006).

Second, it is widely recognized that while physical symptoms of concussion after a mild traumatic head injury are managed with medication and rest, the subtle cognitive and socio-behavioral disturbances that persist for years are not diagnosed (Corrigan, Selassie, & Orman, 2010).

One of the reasons for this difficulty is the lack of formal training and professional guilds for neuropsychological services in South Africa. This has led to reduced levels of compensation for conditions of disability and poor coverage of medical and neuropsychological rehabilitation for children and adolescents (Szabo et al., 2017). The society of the future will thus face a pool of survivors of mild TBIs with varying levels of cognitive, emotional, and social disability.

The following case study illustrates the intersection of mental health knowledge and the growing understanding of mild TBIs on mental healthcare and its dissemination to various social protection agencies and through appropriate legal procedures.

A fifteen-year-old male motor vehicle accident victim was taken to the emergency room a day after the incident.[1] As is customary triage in South Africa, particularly in rural communities, patients with injuries or illnesses are taken to a primary healthcare clinic for an initial assessment. The severity of the condition of the patient determines whether referral to a general or tertiary-level hospital is warranted. Since the child was conscious and aware of his surroundings, he was diagnosed with a post-concussion headache at the primary healthcare clinic and then sent home in the care of his mother, a single parent. The following day, the child complained of headaches that persisted and, according to his mother, displayed behavioral changes such as anger outbursts and tangential speech patterns, as well as offensive language that was considered uncharacteristic and atypical of the child. The consequent alterations in behavior resulted in altercations with community members, leading to the child's subsequent arrest by police authorities.

The child was then transferred to a psychiatric facility, without an appropriate history being taken by the police officers who arrested him. While awaiting psychiatric assessment, the child was sexually molested by patients awaiting psychiatric evaluation and investigations. When visiting her child, the mother observed blood on the child's clothing and complained to staff at the mental healthcare facility. A district surgeon's examination revealed that the child had previously received treatment for schizophrenia. The primary diagnoses in the district surgeon's report were mild head injury and sexual abuse, with a referral made for treatment to the psychiatric unit at a local government hospital.

Following the child's admission and conservative treatment for the head injury and sexual abuse, the following notes were entered into the medical charts: features of schizophrenia with psychotic thinking (paranoia) with violent and aggressive behaviors, noncompliance with medications, displaying poor insight and mild disorientation. The patient was started on psychotropic medication and discharged into the care of his mother while awaiting further legal investigations. A social worker was assigned to the mother for weekly visits in order to monitor the child's behavior.

Neuropsychological examination conducted one month following the accident confirmed that the child had a history of childhood schizophrenia that was treated with psychiatric medication dispensed by a local mental healthcare facility. The mother gave a history that, following the initiation of treatment for schizophrenia, the child attended a normal school with mainstream programs. Perusal of scholastic records revealed inconsistent academic performances but more specifically, significant behavioral difficulties with altercations with peers and disturbed behavior in classes. Notwithstanding these difficulties, the child was promoted at the end of the school year in successive fashion, despite failing semesters during the year.

Objective neuropsychological test results revealed a below average intellectual level of functioning. Appropriate levels of simple attention in visual and auditory modalities were noted, with the child being able to respond to instructions and to complete simple visual-linguistic tasks, such as naming objects portrayed in pictorial stimuli. His working memory and retention capacities in the verbal domain were poor while his visual retention and retrieval functions were mildly impaired for simple stimuli. Confusion while performing problem-solving tasks and the need for additional structure so as to complete tasks with complex visual stimuli was noted. A similar pattern was found for executive functions with complex tasks requiring structure and guidance. The child's social understanding was below average for his age and his reasoning in these contexts was concrete and rigid. Following the sexual assault diagnosed by the district surgeon, a legal case for damages against both the police authorities and the psychiatric institution was brought by the child's mother. As part of the neuropsychological work-up, assessment included a determination of whether the child could recognize social dangers in relation to his psychiatric incarceration and whether he had the requisite capacity to take self-protective actions.

Adverse factors such as low socioeconomic circumstances and a single-parent household are significant predictors of poor long-term outcomes in individuals with schizophrenia in rural communities (Ran et al., 2017). In this case study, a history of schizophrenia is a positive risk factor while the concussion forms the trigger for the cascade of psychological sequelae and vulnerability for sexual victimization while in detention. In terms of triage, the child was appropriately taken to the primary healthcare facility for initial assessment and management.

Several difficulties in the initial assessment become evident. First, the history taken at the primary healthcare facility did not contain information in regard to the psychiatric history of the patient. Second, the failure to alert the mother to possible behavioral sequelae of concussion poses a problem. While physical symptoms such as headaches are generally recognized in the context of a head injury and are treated with analgesics, the association of headaches with behavioral disorders after head trauma is less frequently documented. While the initial CT scan at the emergency room was negative, it is also clear that the patient was not evaluated by a neurologist.

Cognitive components of the concussion syndrome could be inferred from the association between difficulties on the Romberg Test (Khasnis & Gokula, 2003) and Tandem Gait (Margolesky & Singer, 2018) with task switching and increasing severity of post-concussion syndrome and delayed recovery.

The incidence of pediatric concussion in patients aged fourteen to nineteen years has been higher than expected (Cohen & Conidi, 2015). This case study highlights the urgent need to address these barriers to mental healthcare in South Africa, particularly in children and adolescents with TBI. The following sections of this chapter discuss healthcare barriers that must be addressed in order for the country to move forward and what the government has done to achieve those goals.

REBUILDING CAPACITY

Recognizing the importance of mental healthcare, Section 28 of the Constitution of the Republic of South Africa (1996, p. 12), in part, states: "Child has a right to be protected from maltreatment, neglect, abuse or degradation."

Mental healthcare services in South Africa attempt to integrate traditional and Western healthcare services (Campbell-Hall & Petersen, 2010). These two types of mental healthcare services are aimed at providing government-sanctioned medical, public health, and cultural-based healthcare. In rural areas of South Africa, the majority of practitioners practice in traditional rather than Western-based mental healthcare systems. Campbell-Hall and Petersen (2010), who studied the implementation of the mental healthcare services in Ghana, Uganda, South Africa, and Zambia, found that traditional practitioners attribute mental health problems to social and cultural factors, with two-thirds of participants choosing traditional and faith healing so as to address mental problems. Other findings, in contrast, suggest that participants view traditional practitioners as unable to actually cure serious mental health problems. It is for these reasons that attempts to sensitize mental healthcare practitioners to cultural as well as Western models of mental healthcare have been implemented.

PROGRAMMATIC EXAMPLES

Following the advent of the democratic South African government in 1994, policies aimed at impacting the mental healthcare of children and adolescents were formulated (Flisher et al., 2012). In 2003, the South African government issued policy guidelines for child and adolescent health, proposing the following five general intervention strategies (RSA Department of Health, 2003): (a) promotion of protective factors for children and adolescents, including a healthy, stable community, an encouraging, supportive home environment, and basic material resources, such as adequate food, water, electricity, transportation, education, and recreational facilities (RSA Department of Health, 2003); (b) provision of information on topics crucial to the healthy development, socialization, and empowerment of children and adolescents, including physical, psychological, and social development, physical and mental health, health risks and protective factors, and potential helpful resources (RSA Department of Health, 2003); (c) building developmental skills and personal capacities that are basic to one's independence (RSA Department of Health, 2003); (d) counseling; and (e) access to health services (RSA Department of Health, 2003). The guidelines proposed a model of care that incorporates healthcare services ranging from the primary to the super-specialist level in an attempt to increase accessibility of service (Flisher et al., 2012).

The Reconstruction and Development Programme (RDP) of South Africa forms the basis of a national program of action that outlines a set of goals for children as a means to establish their fundamental rights. In 1995, the government ratified the United Nations Convention on the Rights of the Child (CRC) and "pledged to enhance the survival, protection, and development of millions of children of South Africa" (RSA Department of Health, 2003, p. 10). The practical application of the ratification of the CRC was guided by the National Programme of Action for Children in South Africa (NPA) that was approved in 1996. The publication of the *White Paper for the Transformation of the Health System in South Africa* in 1997 paved the way for the development of community-based healthcare that was to be integrated with other healthcare services and implemented at national, provincial, district, and community levels (Flisher et al., 2012). The paper lists, among other functions, the development and promotion of specific programs that address "substance abuse, child abuse, and the management of the victims of violence" (RSA Department of Health, 2003, p. 10). More specifically, the stated goals were aimed at the treatment and prevention of mental health problems, with guidelines provided to strategically assist individuals and organizations working with children. The NPA identified all plans developed for children and ensured that they aligned with the existing framework of policy guidelines (RSA Department of Health, 2003).

The Child Care Act 74 of 1983 provides key legal structures to safeguard children, outlining the scope of the Commissioners of Child Welfare and Children's Courts operation. The Act guides the process following childhood cases of abuse, beginning with the investigative stage and proceeding to ultimately placing children in new homes or under the supervision of social workers. Section 42 of the Act mandates the reporting of suspected or alleged child mistreatment, particularly by individuals in positions of authority such as at schools, healthcare facilities, shelters for the homeless, and other facilities responsible for childcare. Section 50 of the Act provides the legal framework for prosecution in cases of mistreatment of children while Section 52A of the Act outlaws child labor (RSA Department of Health, 2003).

The Services for Children Section of the National Health Policy Guidelines for Improved Mental Health in South Africa prioritizes prevention and intervention in mental healthcare services for children, focusing on preventing developmental delays, beginning with fetal issues such as fetal alcohol syndrome and extending to life skills training (RSA Department of Health, 2003).

RESOURCES

According to Mayosi and colleagues (2012), the South African government agreed on seven main areas for health research with a result that the health research budget was increased to 2.0 percent of the national budget. The increased spending would aim to achieve Millennium Development Goals 4, 5, and 6 (Mayosi et al., 2012), which are focused on improving child survival (Bryce, Black, & Victora, 2013).

Despite the South African government's political commitment to improving mental healthcare, accessibility to mental healthcare services among those falling in the low socioeconomic status sector and/or rural areas remains a significant issue (Das-Munshi et al., 2016). A number of nongovernmental organizations have emerged to bridge the gap between public mental healthcare needs and available mental healthcare services. Two such organizations are the South African Depression and Anxiety Group and the South African Federation for Mental Health, which represent nonprofit organizations that aim to destigmatize mental illness, educate the public on a variety of mental health issues, and offer services to support those patients diagnosed with mental illness. One primary focus of these organizations is to connect individuals of all regions and socioeconomic backgrounds with appropriate healthcare, with the South African Depression and Anxiety Group organizing and operating support groups in the various provinces. In addition, they offer "helplines" (including specific helplines for youth and their families) that connect people to counselors (South African Depression and Anxiety Group, 2018). Similarly, the South African Federation for Mental Health offers many of the same services and provides referrals for those in need with more serious mental illness. They also run educational campaigns seeking to prevent teenage suicide (South African Federation for Mental Health, 2018). While these services are valuable and are widely accessible, very few resources are available for children and adolescents who have severe mental illness.

Another organization, Cape Mental Health, funded by the Department of Social Development, serves those patients suffering from debilitating mental illness, including those who have suffered intellectual disability. Counseling, rehabilitation, and care for people who experience difficulty coping with their mental health conditions is provided in an attempt to improve their daily functioning, ensure adequate care and protection, and develop self-reliant behavior. Cape Mental Health also provides training programs for service providers, parents, and caretakers and offers presentations and workshops to schools (Cape Mental Health, 2018).

The Sexual Abuse Empowerment Programme helps people with intellectual disabilities who have been sexually abused by providing counseling to the client and family, along with psychological assessment of the victim's intellectual functioning and ability to testify in court (Dickman & Roux, 2005).

All the aforementioned organizations refer those seeking acute mental healthcare and medical treatment to hospitals where treatment from a psychiatrist and team of professionals is available. However, access to mental healthcare facilities for youth in South Africa is markedly limited. Only three hospitals currently provide pediatric psychiatric in- and outpatient care: Red Cross War Memorial Children's Hospital, Tygerberg Hospital, and the Lentegeur Child and Family Unit. Due to this substantial inaccessibility of adequate care, particular challenges become evident when the patient is a child.

While 3,460 outpatient mental healthcare facilities are available in the country, only 1.4 percent are set up for children and adolescents. Of the eighty-day treatment facilities available in the country, approximately half are provided by the South African Federation for Mental Health. Of these, none are exclusively for children and adolescents. Of the forty-one community-based psychiatric inpatient units available in the country, representing a total of 2.8 beds per 100,000 population, 3.8 percent of these beds are reserved for children and adolescents only. South Africa has twenty-three mental healthcare hospitals, providing a total of 18 beds per 100,000 (population provincial range: 8–39), 1.4% of which are reserved for children and adolescents (WHO, 2007).

CONCLUSION

This case study has described attempts to highlight the hurdles facing previously disadvantaged communities who constitute a large percentage of the patient population dealing with head injuries in South Africa, due to their dependence on public transportation systems for commuting and thus falling victim to the increasing number of motor vehicle accidents prevalent in the country. In addition to motor vehicle accidents, the high level of interpersonal violence in socially and economically disadvantaged communities increases the number of head injuries, particularly those considered to be minor or mild in severity. The persisting social and economic disadvantages facing a large portion of South Africans and the structural barriers to accessing appropriate care due to lack of appropriately trained personnel therefore suggest that, although there is provision for legal recourse to financial compensation, the long and adversarial process denies this sector of South African society appropriate mental healthcare through appropriate diagnostic, treatment, and rehabilitation services. Article 12 of the International Covenant on Economic, Social and Cultural Rights (United Nations General Assembly, 1966), on which the South African constitution draws, provides for the "enjoyment of the highest attainable standard of physical and mental health conducive to living a life of dignity (p. 4)." Act 17 of the Mental Health Care Act of South Africa (Republic of South Africa, 2002) allows the best possible mental healthcare, treatment, and rehabilitation that available resources can afford and sets out the rights and duties of the mental healthcare user seeking respect and human dignity as well as privacy. Aligned to the Mental Health Care Act is the Correctional Services Act 111 (Republic of South

Africa, 1998) that places the duty on the Department of Correctional Services to provide all prisoners with adequate healthcare services. The objectives set out in the Health Care Act of the South African constitution aligns itself to the commitment document by WHO as articulated by Ghebreyesus (2017), who set out the 2030 Agenda for Sustainable Development as ensuring that no one is left behind in the provision of social healthcare. An initial step to redress the growing number of young children falling prey to criminal activities, both as perpetrators and victims, is reflected in the South African government's recent mobilization of the South African National Defence Force to assist communities in the Western Cape region in their fight against rising crime in daily life. These efforts, however, are proving ineffectual, prompting serious concerns that there will be an increase in the number of child victims such as the one described in this chapter. Urgent social and legal redress has now become paramount in South African society.

Note

1. The case has been de-identified to protect confidentiality.

REFERENCES

Bryce, J., Black, R. E., & Victora, C. G. (2013, October 16). Millennium Development Goals 4 and 5: Progress and challenges. *BMC Medicine*, 11(1), 1–4. doi.org/10.1186/1741-7015-11-225

Campbell-Hall, V., & Petersen, I. (2010). Collaboration between traditional practitioners and primary health care staff in South Africa: Developing a workable partnership for community mental health services. *Transcultural Psychiatry*, 47(4), 610–628.

Cape Mental Health (2018). Retrieved from www.westerncape.gov.za/facility/cape-mental-health.

Chisholm, B. (1951). *Outline for a study group on world health and the survival of the human race: Material drawn from articles and speeches.* Geneva: World Health Organization. Retrieved from https://apps.who.int/iris/bitstream/handle/10665/330666/MH.276.51-eng.pdf?sequence=1&isAllowed=y.

Cohen, D., & Conidi, F. (2015). Neurologic exam findings and clinical manifestations of post-concussion syndrome in a pediatric Population (P7.177). *Neurology*, 84(Suppl. 14).

Constitution of the Republic of South Africa (1996). *Government Gazette* (vol. 378, no. 17678, Act No. 108, Document No. 2083).

Corrigan, J. D., Selassie, A. W., & Orman, J. A. (2010). Epidemiology of traumatic brain injury: Erratum. *Journal of Head Trauma Rehabilitation*, 25(3), 224. doi:10.1097/htr.0b013e3181e5fdao

Das-Munshi, J., Lund, C., Mathews, C., et al. (2016). Mental health inequalities in adolescents growing up in post-apartheid South Africa: Cross-sectional survey, SHaW study. doi .org/10.1371/journal.pone.0154478

Dickman, B. J., & Roux, A. J. (2005). Complainants with learning disabilities in sexual abuse cases: A 10-year review of a psycho-legal project in Cape Town, South Africa. *British Journal of Learning Disabilities*, 33(3), 138–144. doi.org/10.1111/j.1468-3156.2005.00355.x

Flisher, A. J., Dawes, A., Kafaar, Z., et al. (2012). Child and adolescent mental health in South Africa. *Journal of Child & Adolescent Mental Health*, 24(2), 149–161. doi:10.2989/17280583.2012.735505

Ghebreyesus, T. A. (2017, December 10). Health is a fundamental human right. World Health Organization Media Centre Statement. Human Rights Day. Statement presented at the World Health Organization Media Centre.

Haagsma, J. A., Scholten, A. C., Andriessen, T. M. J. C., et al. (2015). Impact of depression and post-traumatic stress disorder on functional outcome and health-related quality of life of patients with mild traumatic brain injury. *Journal of Neurotrauma, 32*, 853–862. doi:10.1089/neu.2013.3283

Hyder, A. A., Wunderlich, C. A., Puvanachandra, P., Gururaj, G., & Kobusingye, O. C. (2007). The impact of traumatic brain injuries: A global perspective. *NeuroRehabilitation, 22*(5), 341–353.

Khasnis, A., & Gokula, R. M. (2003). Romberg's test. *Journal of Postgraduate Medicine, 49*(2), 169–172.

Margolesky, J., & Singer, C. (2018). How tandem gait stumbled into the neurological exam: A review. *Neurological Sciences, 39*(1), 23–29.

Mayosi, B. M., Lawn MRCP Paeds, J. E., van Niekerk, et al. (2012). Health in South Africa: Changes and challenges since 2009. *Lancet, 380*, 2029–2043. doi.org/10.1016/S0140-6736(12)61814-5

Orlovska, S., Pedersen, M. S., Benros, M. E., et al. (2014). Head injury as risk factor for psychiatric disorders: A nationwide register-based follow-up study of 113,906 persons with head injury. *American Journal of Psychiatry, 171*(4), 463–469. doi.org/10.1176/appi.ajp.2013.13020190

Ran, M. S., Yang, L. H., Liu, Y. J., et al. (2017). The family economic status and outcome of people with schizophrenia in Xinjin, Chengdu, China: 14-year follow-up study. *International Journal of Social Psychiatry, 63*(3), 203–211.

Republic of South Africa (1998). Correctional Services Act, No. 111 of 1998. *Government Gazette* (vol. 401, no. 19522, Act No. 111, Document No. 1543).

Republic of South Africa (2002). Mental Health Care Act, No. 17 of 2002. *Government Gazette* (vol. 449, no. 24024, Act No. 17, Document No. 1386).

Republic of South Africa (RSA) Department of Health (2003). *Policy guidelines: Child and adolescent mental health*. Pretoria: Government Printer.

Rosman, K. (2006). Neurology in South Africa. *World Neurology, 21*(2), 1–16. Retrieved from https://wfneurology.org/neurology-in-south-africa-2006.

South African Depression and Anxiety Group (2018). Retrieved from www.sadag.org/.

South African Federation for Mental Health (2018). Mental wellness is our concern. Retrieved from www.safmh.org.za/.

Szabo, C. P., Fine, J., Mayers, P., Naidoo, S., & Zabow, T. (2017). Mental health leadership and patient access to care: A public–private initiative in South Africa. *International Journal of Mental Health Systems, 11*.

United Nations (UN) General Assembly (1966). International Covenant on Economic, Social and Cultural Rights. Retrieved from www.ohchr.org/en/professionalinterest/pages/cescr.aspx.

WHO-AIMS Report on Mental Health System in South Africa, WHO and Department of Psychiatry and Mental Health, University of Cape Town, Cape Town, South Africa (2007). Retrieved from www.who.int/mental_health/evidence/south_africa_who_aims_report.pdf?ua=1.

World Health Organization (2001). *Mental health: New understanding, new hope. World Mental Health Report*. Geneva: World Health Organization.

Zgaljardic, D. J., Seale, G. S., Schaefer, L. A., et al. (2015). Psychiatric disease and post-acute traumatic brain injury. *Journal of Neurotrauma, 32*(23), 1911–1925.

30

Youth Participatory Action Research in Urban Public Education

Underrepresented Youth Addressing Social Justice in the United States

Jack Baker, Paul Flaspohler, Katelyn Wargel, and Tammy Schwartz

INTRODUCTION

In the United States, urban youth participate in public education systems that often fail to engage these children in their schooling. Youth participatory action research (YPAR), collaborations between youth, researchers, and community members designed to investigate social justice issues, can help to engage urban youth in education by creating conditions that promote learning. This chapter introduces YPAR as means to tailor education to the experiences of urban underrepresented youth. A case study is provided to illustrate how participants in YPAR become conscious of social justice issues, while increasing their sense of agency to confront these issues. The case study demonstrates how urban educators can adopt YPAR practices and principles to develop a more culturally responsive pedagogy. Challenges, progress, and lessons learned through the case study are discussed, as are recommendations for others attempting YPAR.

URBAN EDUCATION IN THE UNITED STATES

Significant disproportionality exists between urban and suburban education, making the public education provided to underrepresented youth living in low-income or urban communities a primary social justice concern in the United States. The economic recession of the late 2000s has caused urban neighborhoods in states such as Ohio, Pennsylvania, and New York to lose funding to higher-income areas. Several urban school districts in Indiana, for example, have seen per-student funding decrease by as much as 20 percent in the past eight years (Indiana Department of Local Government Finance, 2019). This financial impact has contributed to deteriorating facility conditions and fewer educational resources overall for urban underrepresented youth compared to their higher-income, White peers (Jordan & Kapoor, 2009; Wright, 2015). Additionally, urban underrepresented youth are often provided lower-quality instruction that includes limited instructional methods, irrelevant course content, and insufficient cultural awareness on the part of teachers (Atweh,

Kemmis, & Weeks, 1998; Daly, Buchanan, Dasch, Eichen, & Lenhart, 2010; Emdin, 2016; Holland & Mazzoli, 2001).

Disproportionality in education may lead to the disengagement of urban youth from their schools. For instance, urban underrepresented students graduate at a lower rate than their suburban peers (60.9 percent and 75.3 percent, respectively) (Swanson, 2009). In some cities, such as Cleveland, Ohio and Baltimore, Maryland, this disparity between urban and suburban graduate rates can exceed 35–40 percent (Swanson, 2009). Overall, the high school graduation rate for urban underrepresented students is declining, despite an increase in the national average in recent years (Emdin, 2016). Consequently, urban underrepresented students are subject to a growing achievement gap between themselves and their higher-income peers (Emdin, 2016; Morrel, 2004; Wright, 2015).

Urban underrepresented youth also display lower levels of school connectedness compared to students who are white or are from a higher socioeconomic group. For example, Black students in middle and high school scored significantly lower on a measure of school connectedness than did White students (14.7 versus 16.4, respectively, on a 25-point scale) (Bonny, Britto, Klostermann, Hornung, & Slap, 2000). In this same study, students from urban schools scored significantly lower on the same measure (14.7) than students from suburban schools (16.6). School connectedness is defined as "the belief by students that adults in the school care about their learning as well as about them as individuals" (Wingspread Declaration on School Connections, 2003, p. 233). Youth who report high levels of school connectedness show higher levels of positive interactions with teachers and administrators and report higher levels of belongingness to their school (Daly et al., 2010; Thompson, Iachan, Overpeck, Ross, & Gross, 2006). School connectedness has been shown to impact students' physical health, increase graduation rates, reduce engagement in violence and substance use, and lower risk for developing mental health issues (Blum, McNeely, & Rinehart, 2002; Resnick et al., 1997; Resnick, Harris, & Blum, 1993). While such benefits are often realized by students in higher-income areas or well-funded school districts, urban underrepresented youth may not incur these same benefits due to lower rates of school connectedness and engagement.

A POTENTIAL SOLUTION: PARTICIPATORY ACTION RESEARCH

One method to improve educational opportunities for urban underrepresented youth is through participatory action research (PAR), which is a collection of research methods used to investigate social justice issues within communities and to promote efforts to address these issues. Participatory action research promotes these goals through partnerships among researchers and members of the affected communities (Jordan & Kapoor, 2009). These partnerships afford attention to the voices and unique knowledge of individuals who directly experience the consequences of social injustice (Brown & Rodriguez, 2009). Within these partnerships, PAR participants learn how to gather information about a problem in their community, generate possible solutions, and perform actions to address the problem (Atweh et al., 1998).

Participatory action research has two distinguishing features. First, PAR targets social issues involving disadvantaged or oppressed groups. The PAR researchers embrace the perspectives of disadvantaged individuals and become civically engaged in order to effect change through public policy (Jordan & Kapoor, 2009). Second, PAR is action oriented. When working toward social justice, PAR researchers attempt to generate knowledge and awareness about social issues, while also instilling action to solve them. Because of these goals, PAR has been used globally to address a variety of social justice problems involving oppressed groups. These issues include the treatment of underrepresented citizens by law enforcement (Stoudt et al., 2019), adult literacy and education programs (Freire, 1985; Shizha, 2009), the promotion of women's advocacy groups (Chovanec & González, 2009; Mhina, 2009), and the reduction of adolescent homelessness (Conrad & Kendal, 2009). In each of these examples, affected community members collaborated with professional researchers to challenge issues facing their community. By doing so, they improved upon the negative health outcomes associated with social injustice.

YOUTH PARTICIPATORY ACTION RESEARCH

Based upon the use of PAR methodology in the alleviation of social injustices facing disadvantaged groups, it stands to reason that PAR can also be applied to the issue of urban underrepresented youth and their engagement in education. To do so, PAR researchers must partner with the youth themselves, forming the basis of youth participatory action research (YPAR).

Youth participatory action research partners youth with researchers and community members, and it often includes youth who have been marginalized, disadvantaged, or oppressed in some way. Several important principles inform YPAR approaches. These include an assets-based view of youth, asserting that youth are capable of accomplishing positive feats that benefit society, and the assumption that youth offer a unique perspective on issues facing their community (Brown & Rodriguez, 2009). The YPAR researchers work with youth and include their opinions and viewpoints in research that influences policy decisions.

Youth participatory action research provides opportunities for youth to learn to conduct research, operate within a team, engage in knowledge creation and self-reflection, and gain a fuller understanding of the social justice research topic. Ideally, youth then use their results to inform actions designed to solve real problems (Atweh et al., 1998). Throughout the YPAR process, youth form positive relationships with adults and peers who have experienced similar life circumstances (Lewis-Charp, Yu, & Soukamneuth, 2006). Youth also use self-reflection to explore the various social and political forces that affect their own identities (Flores-González, Rodríguez, & Rodríguez-Muniz, 2006).

Youth participatory action research is operationalized in a variety of ways. It can be conducted either as an extracurricular activity outside of school hours or within the school curriculum. For example, one YPAR program based in New Mexico was offered to Latinx youth as an extracurricular opportunity after school. Youth participants in this program became engaged in the creation and implementation of a new, culturally informed school curriculum that was relevant to the lives of Latinx youth (Cammarota & Romero, 2006). Other published research using YPAR in an extracurricular format documents youth inquiry into school- (bullying, nutrition, and physical facilities) and community-level (housing and homelessness, gun violence, food scarcity, and gentrification) issues (London, Zimmerman, & Erbstein, 2003; Ozer, Ritterman, & Wanis, 2010; Powers & Tiffany, 2006).

Youth participatory action research can alternatively be conducted as a cocurricular, educational method within the classroom. Jocson (2014) describes YPAR methodology as an integral part of one school's literature curriculum. During English and literature classes, youth learn to read, write, and analyze poetry as a means of not only gaining literacy skills but also developing awareness of social justice issues portrayed in the readings. In using these two YPAR methodologies (extra- and cocurricular), researchers, practitioners, and teachers can create conditions that better engage youth in education.

YPAR and Critical Race Theory. The inclusion of critical race theory (CRT) further enhances the success of YPAR programs. Critical race theory focuses on race and experiential knowledge in the context of research to challenge traditional or dominate social structures in society. Many YPAR projects with underrepresented youth incorporate CRT when addressing forms of oppression, such as poverty or gentrification, the process through which the desirability of urban neighborhoods increases housing costs, subsequently displacing low-income or working-class families (Hosang, 2006; Kwon, 2006). These projects integrate discussion of discrimination and racism, allowing youth to explore how these constructs affect them and their community. As such, the infusion of CRT into YPAR curricula can result in an increase in youths' critical consciousness. Critical consciousness is defined as the ability to locate, critique, and take action against social, political, and economic elements of oppression (Freire, 1985). Critical race theory–based YPAR scholars assert that increasing youths' critical consciousness is required for youth to understand how various societal forces contribute to social injustice in their community and identify solutions that can alleviate these conditions. In this way, CRT provides a framework for extending the social justice efforts of YPAR, allowing urban underrepresented youth to investigate and address the conditions that foster urban student disengagement.

OUTCOMES FOR YOUTH INVOLVED IN YPAR

Existing YPAR literature shows that youth achieve certain benefits from participating in YPAR projects, including critical consciousness. Critical consciousness is conceptualized and measured in a variety of ways (Diemer, Rapa, Park, & Perry,

2017). For example, Ginwright and Cammarota's Social Justice Youth Development Model (2002) divides critical consciousness into three subcomponents: self-awareness (an understanding of self and how social forces impact one's identities), social awareness (how social forces impact communities), and global awareness (how oppression manifests around the world). Under this model, subcomponents are primarily measured through qualitative means (observations and interviews of youth engaged in YPAR).

Youth agency is another documented outcome of YPAR. Youth agency is defined as a youth's ability to engage with social, political, and economic forces to produce knowledge and societal change or impact (Noguera, Ginwright, & Cammarota, 2006). Leadership ability, advocacy, and civic engagement are often included as pieces of youth agency (Anyon, Bender, Kennedy, & Dechants, 2018; London et al., 2003; Ozer et al., 2010). Youth agency goes beyond critical consciousness by extending the youths' increased knowledge of social injustice toward promoting action against such issues. Many YPAR scholars promote critical consciousness and youth agency as two central outcomes of YPAR (Anyon et al., 2018; Ginwright & Cammarota, 2002). Additional research identifies self-esteem, self-confidence, academic performance, and time management skills as further important YPAR outcomes (Flicker et al., 2008; Powers & Tiffany, 2006; Sallis, Millstein, & Carlson, 2011). Taken together, these outcomes suggest that YPAR may be a vehicle through which schools can engage urban underrepresented youth. Youth participatory action research provides culturally relevant learning opportunities and empowers students to take action against unjust conditions that lead to disengagement at school.

CASE STUDY: THE URBAN COHORT

The Urban Cohort (UC) is a university program that provides college students planning to work in urban settings with education and experiences in urban settings. Students apply to participate in the UC and those who are accepted collaborate with urban youth, educators, and other community members in curricular and extracurricular experiences. Most UC students are education majors, though other fields are represented (e.g., architecture, business, social work). Many urban teachers are unaware of the challenges facing urban youth and are not prepared to engage students whose culture differs from their own when they enter the profession (Emdin, 2016). A key principle of the UC program is that successful urban teacher preparation provides preservice teachers with experiences that foster partnership and engagement with urban communities (Borrero, 2009; Cochran-Smith et al., 2015; Noel, 2010). The Urban Cohort provides students with experiences to strengthen their ability to engage urban youth in the classroom and develops students' understanding of the sociopolitical and economic contexts of urban youth. The Urban Cohort also prepares future teachers to engage their students in critical thinking and socially meaningful work (Brown & Rodriguez, 2009).

In their first year of participation, UC students work with public school students during the academic year to complete research projects targeting issues like poverty, school discipline policies, and community food scarcity. Participating youth serve as mentors to the UC students in a reversal of the traditional concept that mentors are older than their mentees; in this context, youth are viewed as the experts on challenges that face their communities and thus serve as the mentors. The UC program theory is based on the idea that UC students should incorporate YPAR values into their own pedagogy to become more culturally aware educators. In other words, YPAR is used as a mechanism for improving urban education by including preservice teachers in the YPAR process, where they begin to cultivate a culturally responsive approach to teaching.

UC YPAR PROJECT: RESEARCHING THE INTERSECTION BETWEEN HOMELESSNESS AND VIOLENCE

The Urban Cohort sponsors several YPAR projects at multiple urban public schools each year. This case study is based on one YPAR project co-facilitated by a member of UC's formal evaluation team and a teacher from the host school. The youth and their UC student partners in this YPAR group chose to focus our project on the intersection of homelessness and violence. Youth self-selected to participate in YPAR projects, which were offered as after school extracurricular activities. Nine youth and four UC student mentees participated in our YPAR project throughout the school year. Youth and UC student attendance varied from week to week, with six youth and two UC mentees being present for most activities. All youth identified as African American and ranged in age from eleven to twelve years old. All youth attended the same school, located within a low-socioeconomic-status (SES) urban neighborhood. Two youth were enrolled in fifth grade, while the rest were enrolled in sixth grade.

The project took place over eight months and consisted of twelve after school sessions lasting two and a half hours and two additional weekend sessions, lasting about four to five hours. In total, the YPAR project team spent approximately forty instructional hours working together.

Youth participatory action research is designed to instruct youth to carry out the research process. When informed by CRT, this curriculum incorporates discussions of race and ethnicity. Youth and their UC college partners engaged in discussions addressing discrimination and racism. The youth defined and explained their own experiences of discrimination and racism, while also defining social justice and identifying potential research topics. During each session, youth and UC students participated in group activities to foster group unity and in self-reflective journaling to stimulate deep thinking about topics discussed.

Youth spent the last nine sessions learning specific research skills. Youth first learned how to design research questions and hypotheses. They also identified various types of research methods (surveys, interviews, etc.) available to use during their project. After choosing homelessness and violence as the target of their research, the youth reviewed literature to identify root causes and symptoms of these issues. With the help of their UC college mentees, youth designed and conducted an interview with the director of a local homeless shelter and a citizen currently experiencing homelessness. The youth reviewed an audio recording of the interview, taking note of responses relating to the original research question. They compiled these notes into an electronic presentation that several youth gave to other UC-sponsored YPAR groups and community members. The project concluded with youth creating an art-based awareness project for their school about their topic (see later in this chapter). They also participated in a focus group-style "reflection circle" through which youth expressed their feelings and opinions about the YPAR process.

CASE STUDY OUTCOMES FOR YOUTH

After each YPAR session, facilitators recorded implementation notes documenting the goals of the session, skills taught, activities carried out, and youths' responses to the activities. They also noted any challenges and difficulties that youth encountered with certain skills and lessons. In addition, facilitators reviewed the creation and outcome of the youths' final research products (formal presentation and art-based awareness project) and reflection circle. The team completed a qualitative analysis of these data sets and coded the data as they related to the predetermined themes of critical consciousness and youth agency (Braun & Clarke, 2006). All data were collected as part of a formal research study approved by the institutional review boards of both the authors' university and the youths' school district. Assent and consent from the youth and their parents respectively were received prior to pictures or notes being taken at each session and the reflection circle.

Outcome 1: Critical Consciousness. Data analysis followed the conceptualization of critical consciousness set forth by Ginwright and Cammarota (2002). Results indicated that each youth demonstrated self-awareness relative to discrimination and racism, as evidenced by their exploration of differences between their views of themselves and society's views of African American youth. For instance, one youth contrasted the way she views herself as "happy," "great," and having "style" to how she believes society views her as "small," "silent," and full of "drama." Youth could also provide explicit examples of social justice issues that have personally affected them, such as city efforts to demolish local parks and playgrounds to make room for new housing developments that are unaffordable to many families in the community.

Results indicated that each youth demonstrated social awareness of certain social, political, and economic forces that worsen social injustices facing their community, including gentrification and police brutality. Additionally, all youth experienced an increase in social awareness related to the intersection between homelessness and violence (their research topic). This was evident in part by youths' own acknowledgment of personal growth at the end of the project and through their final art project and awareness campaign. For this project, the youth constructed three model houses, each symbolizing one of the three branches of government: local, state, and federal. On each house, youth placed pictures of politicians, copies of newspaper articles, and symbolic items to demonstrate what they saw as a lack of progress in addressing homelessness and violence against citizens experiencing homelessness. Youth placed tape and bandages as symbols of various government policies that either helped to permanently end homelessness or provided only temporary relief, respectively. Next to these items, youth wrote the policy passed at each level of government, with stronger policies being linked to tape and weaker policies being connected to bandages. Youth also did this with various strategies that individuals use to help alleviate homelessness. For example, youth placed a bandage next to the written words "give spare change," while placing tape next to the words "provide someone with interview clothes for a job search."

Outcome 2: Youth Agency. Youth agency outcomes were defined as youths' ability to engage with social, political, and economic forces to produce knowledge and societal change through research. Results indicated variable uptake in research-related skills needed to produce knowledge through scientific research. All youth demonstrated an understanding of research skills related to formulating potential research topics, data collection methods, and hypotheses. However, most youth struggled to comprehend research skills related to designing interview questions and analyzing collected data (see Table 30.1).

As a group, the youth demonstrated agency through their ability to produce change by creating an awareness campaign for their school and delivering an electronic presentation detailing what they had learned during the YPAR project.

TABLE 30.1 *Research skills related to designing interview questions and analyzing collected data*

Topics/Skills Well Understood by All Youth	Topics/Skills Understood by at least Half the Youth	Topics/Skills Not Well-Understood by Most Youth
• Identifying Potential Research Topics	• Identifying the Research Question	• Designing Your Research Methodology
• Identifying Various Research Methods	• Identifying Root Causes and Symptoms of an Issue	• Using Data to Answer Your Research Question
• Generating Hypotheses	• Conducting Interviews	• Note Taking
• Displaying Results in a Final Product		• Public Speaking/Verbally Synthesizing Results

On an individual level, three youth stated that their ability to enact change increased by the end of the project, while one youth expressed skepticism in his ability to make an impact on his community. Three additional youth did not report an increase in their sense of agency, though this is potentially due to their high sense of agency at the beginning of the YPAR process.

DISCUSSION

This case study illustrates several points. First, YPAR can be used as a mechanism for engaging urban underrepresented youth with their education. Second, specific facilitation strategies can be used to increase the likelihood that youth participants will experience increases in critical consciousness and agency. Third, challenges arose during our YPAR project that are relevant for others conducting YPAR with urban underrepresented youth. We present these challenges along with suggestions for addressing them.

YPAR can reengage urban youth in education. Youth involved in our case study engaged in learning opportunities that are not afforded to many urban youth in the United States. The youth engaged in discussion, research, and action required to address challenges in their communities. Youth participatory action research can address social justice issues by giving youth time and space to research these topics and leverage their voices to affect change. In our case study, youth increased their ability to create knowledge using research skills applied to a topic they chose as relevant to their community. In this way, YPAR provides experiences that can make classroom material more culturally relevant.

Additionally, the value of urban public education depends in part upon the quality of instruction provided. Youth participatory action research provides a means through which educators can develop more culturally responsive pedagogy and increase the quality and relevance of instruction they provide. Preservice teachers in training participating in UC gained insight into the lives of urban youth and community members. This suggests that, when participating in YPAR, future teachers gain an understanding of barriers to learning and strategies to address them. Urban educators whose pedagogy incorporates the principles of YPAR may be more likely to connect with their students and provide culturally relevant instruction, leading to increased school connectedness among their students.

Useful YPAR facilitation strategies. Youth participatory action research requires high-quality facilitation strategies to increase the likelihood that youth will experience increases in critical consciousness, agency, and other cited outcomes. One such strategy is balancing flexibility and a structured curriculum. Youth participatory action research sessions can be unpredictable. We often arrived for a session with a detailed plan of action, but lessons did not always go according to plan. For example, sessions dedicated to skills labeled as "not well understood by most youth" in Table 30.1 required extra time to ensure student understanding. This was often unplanned and pushed back subsequent topics to later in the school year. As a result, several later topics (data analysis and public speaking) were rushed in order to allow youth the time to complete their final research products before the end of the program. While it is important to progress through the entirety of the research process, it is equally important not to sacrifice youths' understanding for the sake of moving forward in the curriculum. Youth in our study experienced difficulty in understanding complex research topics that stretched their current developmental capacity. We originally planned to dedicate a predetermined amount of time to each step of the research process so as to finish the project by the end of the school year. However, maintaining flexible facilitation allowed us to spend more time on steps that the youth found challenging. While this did result in less time being devoted to steps later in the research process, youths' mastery of earlier topics was enhanced.

Similarly, facilitators should be flexible in allowing time for youth to have fun, converse with one another and adult facilitators, and act in accordance with their age (Stillwell, 2016). Youth participatory action research facilitators working with younger youth should understand when lively, rowdy, or juvenile behavior is displayed, as this is to be expected and should be accounted for when making session agendas. In our case example, facilitators engaged youth in a variety of instructional methods and activities to keep youth energized and attentive. Facilitators utilized Socratic questioning to engage youth and stimulate critical thinking. This allowed facilitators to identify and address barriers that kept students from fully engaging in the work (e.g., learning disabilities or cognitive delays). Providing youth with opportunities for self-reflection helped them to solidify their thoughts and feelings regarding topics like discrimination and racism. The sessions also provided opportunities for team-building exercises that helped develop peer relationships and engage youth who had become inattentive during sessions.

Youth participatory action research facilitators should also analyze positionality in their work. Analyzing positionality entails recognizing what personal characteristics a student brings with him or her into the YPAR context. This may include being an outsider to the youths' community, in which case facilitators should acknowledge that youth will have greater insight into the issues facing their own community than facilitators. For facilitators who are of a different racial or ethnic background than the youth, analyzing positionality also entails recognizing historical and current power differentials between racial and ethnic groups (Stillwell, 2016). To address these aspects of positionality, or how one is positioned relative to study participants in regard to race, gender, and culture, facilitators can actively attempt to ground themselves in the community of their youth coleaders (St. Louis & Barton, 2002). For example, several UC college mentees did this by attending sporting events in which their youth mentors participated. Facilitators should also be willing to engage youth in conversations about inherent power differentials and how youth feel about coleading projects with adults from different racial backgrounds than their own.

Bridging agents were crucial to the success of this initiative. A bridging agent is someone who has experience from multiple perspectives. In our case, the bridging agent was the teacher co-facilitator, an African American community member who has been a part of the youths' school and community for many years. Her knowledge of the community and lived experiences with the youth participants bridged the gap between the evaluation team and the youth. When working with underserved and traditionally exploited communities, having a bridging agent can be critical.

POTENTIAL CHALLENGES WHEN CONDUCTING YPAR

Our case study involved several challenges that are relevant to any researcher, practitioner, or community member considering using YPAR to engage urban underrepresented youth. These challenges involve the outcomes evaluation and potential discrepancies between participants' developmental level and cognitive requirements of YPAR activities.

Evaluation of YPAR outcomes. Researchers from different perspectives (e.g., social justice, CRT, or traditional social science) often disagree about the targets and focus of YPAR. Depending upon their academic background, researchers may emphasize aspects of YPAR to varying degrees. For some, YPAR is conducted with an emphasis on research and action while addressing topics that affect all youth, such as bullying or climate change. Researchers may also choose to emphasis race and marginalization in YPAR work while addressing social justice issues with underrepresented youth. These differences in perspective can lead to conflict over several issues, including evaluation. For example, while several CRT scholars list critical consciousness as a primary outcome to emphasize in YPAR, 62 percent of published YPAR evaluations do not include critical consciousness as an outcome measure (Anyon et al., 2018). The use of quantitative scholarly inquiry into YPAR outcomes has also been met with criticism from CRT researchers, in part due to its positivist nature and inherent characteristic of illustrating social injustices through numbers rather than rich, qualitative depictions (Jordan & Kapoor, 2009; Kincheloe, 2009).

These differences in perspective manifested during our attempts to evaluate UC's YPAR efforts. The formal evaluation team was led by professional researchers (including authors JB and PF of this chapter), operating from a clinical psychology discipline. Meanwhile, partners in this evaluation included UC administrators (such as the director of the Urban Cohort, TS) and university faculty members serving as YPAR group facilitators. These stakeholders primarily operate through CRT, a framework different from the researchers' (JB and PF). As such, colleagues recommended that researchers take additional time exploring their positionality in this work as White men using traditional, Western research methodology (including quantitative measurement). Colleagues also suggested dedicating more time discussing how to blend varying perspectives of researchers and participants.

Several potential avenues for navigating these dilemmas are proposed. First, evaluators of YPAR programs should take time to self-reflect and examine how their positionality affects their investigation into outcomes (Giltrow, 2005). In projects involving social justice and traditionally exploited populations (such as urban youth), this examination of positionality becomes particularly important. Researchers may represent racial groups that have a history of mistreating vulnerable populations. Full acknowledgment of this representation is required when attempting to align oneself with underrepresented youth. Researchers should also reflect upon their professional frameworks and worldviews regarding what constitutes high-quality research. The propensity of many researchers from the United States to include quantitative methods of data collection, such as surveys, in research may be met with skepticism from researchers working with underrepresented youth and operating out of CRT. Such methodology may be reminiscent of times in which researchers took advantage of certain populations of people, including African American children (Kincheloe, 2009). By reflecting upon personal research philosophies, we can explore methodologies that bridge philosophical gaps and create ethical, high-quality evaluation strategies that help YPAR grow and provide valuable experiences for youth.

Second, we suggest that mixed-methods research may have utility as a YPAR evaluation strategy. Despite criticisms of quantitative methodology, several critical race theorists have stated that evaluation research should incorporate mixed methodology, while also being amenable to stakeholder opinions brought forth through open dialogue between researchers and community members (Kincheloe, 2009; McTaggart & Curró, 2009). As such, when planning an evaluation, one should pursue the opinions of the primary stakeholders involved in YPAR, the youth themselves. Interestingly, when asked to share their opinions about methods to include in future UC evaluations of YPAR, several youth involved in our case study recommended the use of surveys, suggesting that youth are amenable to quantitative measurement. Advancements in YPAR research have included the creation of culturally sensitive quantitative tools designed to measure constructs like critical consciousness and agency among urban underrepresented youth (Flores-González et al., 2006; Watts & Guessous, 2006). For example, the Critical Consciousness Inventory assesses two main subcomponents of the construct: sociopolitical development and social perspective-taking (Thomas et al., 2014). It is possible that these types of measurement may be more acceptable to CRT-informed YPAR stakeholders for evaluation.

Matching youths' developmental level to YPAR activities. As seen in Table 30.1, our case study revealed mixed results relative to youths' sense of agency and ability to create knowledge through formal research techniques. These results could stem from a mismatch between the youths' developmental level and activities used to explain various research methods. Research topics coded as "not well understood" were taught using lesson plans from external YPAR sources that were not designed for a specific age group. Similarly, during their initial introduction to YPAR, youth were presented with examples of YPAR in action that featured much older youth who were more developmentally able to accomplish significant change. Potentially, this negatively affected youths' sense of efficacy. These examples highlight the need for age-appropriate YPAR guidelines and lesson plans, specifically for youth under the age of thirteen. This conclusion is not entirely surprising, considering the relative lack of published YPAR research involving youth who are not yet adolescents.

Taking into consideration youths' developmental level, organizations can better define appropriate project goals. Because youth in elementary or middle school are in different developmental circumstances than their older, high school peers, it may be that YPAR projects with younger youth should work toward different goals than YPAR projects with older youth. If an organization struggles to fit an entire YPAR project into one year, it may behoove the organization to decide whether charging youth with the task of devising a full action plan by the end of the year is advisable. By adjusting such an expectation, YPAR leaders can allocate more time to research topics that younger youth have difficulty understanding. Leaders would also have more leeway to introduce a variety of activities and instructional styles that can more adeptly engage youth by balancing learning with enjoyment.

CONCLUSION

Urban underrepresented youth's low rates of school connectedness and high school graduation, compared to those of their suburban, White peers, suggest that such students are disengaged from their education. Through unjust, systematic processes, the education provided to urban underrepresented youth does not provide the same level of opportunity given to youth in more privileged circumstances. These students often are not able to study subjects that are relevant to their lived experiences and are often taught by teachers who are not prepared to educate underrepresented youth.

Youth participatory action research can be an effective and powerful experience that not only engages urban youth in a style of learning not traditionally housed within the current American education system but also has the potential to address political, social, and economic forces that contribute to oppression of urban underrepresented youth, limiting their educational opportunities. Our case study further demonstrates that YPAR can be utilized as training for future urban educators to help deepen their culturally competent pedagogy.

Despite these positive outcomes, YPAR is not a simple undertaking. Youth participatory action research can be challenging, for both youth and their adult coleaders. It is an experience that often pushes everyone involved to think in ways they have not previously. For example, the necessity of adult facilitators relinquishing power and control of projects to youth can be unsettling for both youth and adults alike (Stillwell, 2016). Interdisciplinary approaches to YPAR can be accompanied by additional challenges, including the ethical dilemmas our evaluation team faced when partnering with the Urban Cohort. Several of our colleagues within the realm of psychology have suggested that the disagreements between our evaluation team and UC were merely misunderstandings and not a question of ethics. This could be, in part, because our original evaluation proposal sufficiently met the standards set forth by the American Psychological Association's code of ethics. However, in this case study, we operated within an interdisciplinary environment, one in which more than one code of ethics exists to guide our work. As such, our UC colleagues countered the idea that our disagreements were "simple misunderstandings," suggesting that the use of the word "unethical" to describe our original evaluation proposal (one emphasizing quantitative measurement) was, in actuality, not strong enough.

As YPAR grows as a way of helping youth challenge the circumstances in which they live, it will begin to involve more adult allies from a variety of fields. Although this expansion will include growing pains, these challenges can provide us with the unique opportunity to engage in an analysis of our own positionality and critical consciousness in research. Ultimately, such an analysis helps us to more closely align ourselves with the youth with whom we stand in solidarity in their efforts to fight for social justice.

REFERENCES

Anyon, Y., Bender, K., Kennedy, H., & Dechants, J. (2018). A systematic review of youth participatory action research (YPAR) in the United States: Methodologies, youth outcomes, and future directions. *Health Education & Behavior, 45*(6), 865–878.

Atweh, B., Kemmis, S., & Weeks, P. (1998). *Action research in practice: Partnerships for social justice in education.* London: Routledge.

Blum, R. W., McNeely, C. A., & Reinhart, P. M. (2002). *Improving the odds: The untapped power of schools to improve the health of teens.* Minneapolis: University of Minnesota Center for Adolescent Health and Development.

Bonny, A. E., Britto, M. T., Klostermann, B. K., Hornung, R. W., & Slap, G. B. (2000). School disconnectedness: Identifying adolescents at risk. *Pediatrics, 106*(5), 1017–1021.

Borda, O. F., & Skiles, J. D. (1969). *Subversion and social change in Colombia.* New York: Columbia University Press.

Borrero, N. (2009). Preparing new teachers for urban teaching: Creating a community dedicated to social justice. *Multicultural Perspectives, 11,* 221–226.

Braun, V., & Clarke, V. (2006). Using thematic analysis in psychology. *Qualitative Research in Psychology, 3*(2), 77–101.

Brown, T. M., & Rodriguez, L. F. (2009). *Youth in participatory action research.* San Francisco, CA: Jossey-Bass/Wiley.

Cammarota, J., & Romero, A. (2006). A critically compassionate pedagogy for Latino youth. *Latino Studies, 4*(3), 305–312.

Chovanec, D. M., & Gonzalez, H. M. (2009). A participatory research approach to exploring social movement learning in the Chilean women's movement. In D. Kapoor & S. Jordan (eds.), *Education, participatory action research, and social change: International perspectives* (pp. 223–237). New York: Palgrave Macmillan.

Cochran-Smith, M., Villegas, A. M., Abrams, L., et al. (2015). Critiquing teacher preparation research: An overview of the field, part II. *Journal of Teacher Education, 66*, 109–121.

Conrad, D., & Kendal, W. (2009). Research and agency: The case of rural women and land tenure in Tanzania. In D. Kapoor & S. Jordan (eds.), *Education, participatory action research, and social change: international perspectives* (pp. 251–264). New York: Palgrave Macmillan.

Daly, B., Buchanan, C., Dasch, K., Eichen, D., & Lenhart, C. (2010). Promoting school connectedness among urban youth of color: Reducing risk factors while promoting protective factors.*Prevention Researcher, 17*(3), 18–20.

Diemer, M. A., Rapa, L. J., Park, C. J., & Perry, J. C. (2017). Development and validation of the critical consciousness scale. *Youth & Society, 49*(4), 461–483.

Emdin, C. (2016). *For white folks who teach in the hood ... and the rest of y'all too: Reality pedagogy and urban education (race, education, and democracy)*. Boston: Beacon Press.

Fetterman, D., Kaftarian, S., & Wandersman, A. (2014). *Empowerment evaluation: Knowledge and tools for self-assessment and accountability* (2nd ed.). Los Angeles: Sage Publications.

Flicker, S., Maley, O., Ridgley, A., et al. (2008). PAR: Using technology and participatory action research to engage youth in health promotion. *Action Research, 6*(3), 285–303.

Flores-González, N., Rodríguez, M., & Rodríguez-Muniz, M. (2006). From hip-hop to humanization: Batey Urbano as a space for Latino youth culture and community action. In S. Ginwright, P. Noguera, & J. Cammarota (eds.), *Beyond resistance! Youth activism and community change* (pp. 175–196). New York: Routledge.

Freiberg, H. J., Huzinec, C. A., & Templeton, S. M. (2009). Classroom management – a pathway to student achievement: A study of fourteen inner-city elementary schools. *Elementary School Journal, 110*(1), 63–80.

Freire, P. (1985). *Pedagogy of the oppressed*. Jakarta: LP3ES.

Giltrow, J. (2005). *Academic writing: An introduction*. Peterborough, ON: Broadview.

Ginwright, S., & Cammarota, J. (2002). New terrain in youth development: The promise of a social justice approach. *Social Justice, 29*(4), 82–95.

Holland, H., & Mazzoli, K. (2001). Where everybody knows your name. *Phi Delta Kappan, 83* (4), 294–303.

Hosang, D. (2006). Beyond policy: Ideology, race and the reimagining of youth. In S. Ginwright, P. Noguera, & J. Cammarota (eds.), *Beyond resistance! Youth activism and community change* (pp. 3–20). New York: Routledge.

Indiana Department of Local Government Finance (2019). Certified budget: Levy, CNAV, tax rate by fund. State of Indiana.

Jocson, K. (2014). Critical media ethnography: Researching youth media. In D. Paris & M. T. Winn (eds.), *Humanizing research: Decolonizing qualitative inquiry with youth and communities* (pp. 105–123). Thousand Oaks, CA: Sage.

Jordan, S., & Kapoor, D. (2009). *Education, participatory action research and social change: International perspectives*. New York: Palgrave Macmillan.

Kincheloe, J. L. (2009). Critical complexity and participatory action research: Decolonizing "democratic" knowledge production. In D. Kapoor & S. Jordan (eds.), *Education, participatory action research, and social change: International perspectives* (pp. 107–121). New York: Palgrave Macmillan.

Kwon, S. A. (2006). Youth of color organizing for juvenile justice. In S. Ginwright, P. Noguera, & J. Cammarota (eds.), *Beyond resistance! Youth activism and community change* (pp. 215–228). New York: Routledge.

Lange, E. (2009). Fostering a learning sanctuary for transformation in sustainability education. In J. Mezirow & E. Taylor (eds.), *Transformative learning in practice: Insights from* community, workplace, and higher education (pp. 193–204). San Francisco, CA: Jossey-Bass.

Lewis-Charp, H., Yu, H. C., & Soukamneuth, S. (2006). Civic activist approaches for engaging youth in social justice. In S. Ginwright, P. Noguera, & J. Cammarota (eds.), *Beyond resistance! Youth activism and community change* (pp. 21–36). New York: Routledge.

London, J. K., Zimmerman, K., & Erbstein, N. (2003). Youth-led research and evaluation: Tools for youth, organizational, and community development. *New Directions for Evaluation, 98*, 33–45.

McTaggart, R., & Curró, G. (2009). Action research for curriculum internationalization: Education versus commercialization. In D. Kapoor & S. Jordan (eds.), *Education, participatory action research, and social change: International perspectives* (pp. 89–105). New York: Palgrave Macmillan.

Mhina, C. H. (2009). Research and agency: The case of rural women and land tenure in Tanzania. In D. Kapoor & S. Jordan (eds.), *Education, participatory action research, and social change: International perspectives* (pp. 155–168). New York: Palgrave Macmillan.

Morrell, E. (2004). *Becoming critical researchers: Literacy and empowerment for urban youth.* New York: Peter Lang Publishing.

Noel, J. (2010). Weaving teacher education into the fabric of urban schools and communities. *Teacher Education Quarterly, 37*, 9–25.

Noguera, P., Ginwright, S. A., & Cammarota, J. (2006). *Beyond resistance! Youth activism and community change: New democratic possibilities for practice and policy for Americas youth.* New York: Routledge.

Nygreen, K., Ah Kwon, S., & Sánchez, P. (2006). Urban youth building community: Social change and participatory research in schools, homes, and community-based organizations. *Journal of Community Practice, 14*(1–2), 107–123.

Ozer, E. J., Ritterman, M. L., & Wanis, M. G. (2010). Participatory action research (PAR) in middle school: Opportunities, constraints, and key processes. *American Journal of Community Psychology, 46*(1–2), 152–166.

Powers, J. L., & Tiffany, J. S. (2006). Engaging youth in participatory research and evaluation. *Journal of Public Health Management and Practice, 12*, S79–S87.

Resnick, M. D., Bearman, P. S., Blum, R. W., et al. (1997). Protecting adolescents from harm. Findings from the national longitudinal study on adolescent health. *Journal of the American Medical Association, 278*(10), 823–832.

Resnick, M. D., Harris, L. J., & Blum, R. W. (1993). The impact of caring and connectedness on adolescent health and well-being. *Journal of Paediatrics and Child Health, 29*(S1), S3–S9.

Sallis, J. F., Millstein, R. A., & Carlson, J. A. (2011). Community design for physical activity. In H. Dannenberg, H. Frumkin, & R. Jackson (eds.), *Making healthy places: Designing and building for health, well-being, and sustainability* (pp. 33–49). Washington, DC: Island Press.

Shizha, E. (2009). Chara chimwe hachitswanyi inda: Indigenizing science education in Zimbabwe. In D. Kapoor & S. Jordan (eds.), *Education, participatory action research, and social change: International perspectives* (pp. 131–153). New York: Palgrave Macmillan.

St. Louis, K. & Barton, A. (2002). Tales from the science education crypt: A critical reflection of positionality, subjectivity, and reflexivity in research. *Forum Qualitative Sozialforschung / Forum: Qualitative Social Research, 3*(3), Art. 19.

Stillwell, C. (2016). Challenges to the implementation of youth PAR in a university-middle school partnership. *Inquiry in Education, 8*(1).

Stoudt, B. G., Torre, M. E., Bartley, P., et al. (2019). Researching at the community-university borderlands: Using public science to study policing in the South Bronx. *Education Policy Analysis Archives*, 27(56). doi:10.14507/epaa.27.2623

Swanson, C. (2009). *Closing the graduation gap: Educational and economic conditions in America's largest cities.* Bethesda, MD: Editorial Projects in Education.

Thomas, A. J., Barrie, R., Brunner, J., et al. (2014). Assessing critical consciousness in youth and young adults. *Journal of Research on Adolescence*, 24(3), 485–496.

Thompson, D. R., Iachan, R., Overpeck, M., Ross, J. G., & Gross, L. A. (2006). School connectedness in the health behavior in school-aged children study: The role of student, school, and school neighborhood characteristics. *Journal of School Health*, 76(7), 379–386.

Warren, M. R., & Mapp, K. L. (2011). *A match on dry grass: Community organizing as a catalyst for school reform.* New York: Oxford University Press.

Watts, R., Griffith, D. M., & Abdul-Adil, J. (1999). Sociopolitical development as an antidote for oppression-theory and action. *American Journal of Community Psychology*, 27(2), 255–271.

Watts, R. J., & Guessous, O. (2006). Sociopolitical development: The missing link in research and policy on adolescents. In S. Ginwright, P. Noguera, & J. Cammarota (eds.), *Beyond resistance! Youth activism and community change* (pp. 59–80). New York: Routledge.

Wingspread Declaration on School Connections (2004). *Journal of School Health*, 74(7), 233–234.

Wright, D. E. (2015). *Active learning: Social justice education and participatory action research.* New York: Routledge.

PART IV

Conclusion

31

Conclusion

Being a Change Agent for Social Justice for Children and Youth

Caroline S. Clauss-Ehlers, Mark D. Weist, Aradhana Bela Sood, and Cara Lomaro

In this edited volume – the first book on social justice for children and youth taking an international perspective – we have covered this critically important topic comprehensively. Following an introductory chapter, underscoring the neglect of this topic and its very high societal significance, including frameworks to move us forward, chapters have addressed fundamental themes: language, social determinants of health, using the health capability paradigm, children and poverty, educational access, children affected by war, lesbian, gay, bisexual, transgender, and queer (LGBTQ) youth, youth and families who are refugees or seeking asylum, young people with disabilities, improving school mental healthcare, family-school partnerships, the negative impact of exclusionary discipline practices, and body respect. Authors from around the world have highlighted unmet needs, disparities, clear examples of the consequences of failing to focus on social justice for our young people, and themes through which to make advancements in research, practice, and policy dimensions.

We have presented diverse case studies from countries around the world, shining the light on inequities and on the social justice needs of children and youth, and providing examples of ways to escalate progress. Country case studies reflect the experiences of low-income economies that include Ethiopia and Rwanda (World Bank, n.d.); lower-middle-income economies that include India, Pakistan, and Palestine (e.g., West Bank and Gaza; World Bank, n.d.); upper-middle-income economies that include Brazil, China, Colombia, Cuba, Mexico, Peru (other Latin American countries are also discussed that represent a range of country economies), and South Africa; and high-income economies that include Israel, Norway, Scotland (as part of the United Kingdom), and the United States (World Bank, n.d.; World Population Review, n.d.). Themes presented in this volume's chapters often repeat and resonate in the country case studies.

It has been a privilege for us as editors (CCE, ABS, MW) and an organizer (CL) to have interacted with leading scholars, practitioners, and policy makers from many countries in moving this book to completion over a three-year time period. We are grateful to Cambridge University Press for this opportunity.

As we bring this book to a close, all four of us are struck with this conclusion:

Significant problems exist with social injustice for children and youth all around the world, in less-developed and developed nations. This is a foundational human rights issue that should be prioritized in all communities, yet, in reality, progress has been very limited. While there is some emerging literature (as we have reviewed), important guiding policy documents, and a number of networks trying to deepen this work, there is a relative dearth of coordinated efforts taking this challenge head on so as to assure that policies and practices build a linked agenda that promotes wellness for children and youth, while assuring social justice for them.

Given this conclusion, we ask you, the reader, what actions you will take as a change agent to escalate progress in order to assure social justice for children and youth within your sphere of influence (SOI)? For example, consider these questions: What are the clear social justice inequities for the children and youth within your SOI? What policies and programs are in place to address them? Are these policies and programs contributing to progress or not? If they are in place, how can they be improved with a view toward enhancing and broadening impact? If they do not exist, what steps can you take to begin a change effort?

Our wish is that the impact of this book is not limited to enhancing the knowledge base, but actually contributes to meaningful policy and practice change. For children and youth in your SOI, be a change agent and organize a community of practice (see Wenger, McDermott, & Snyder, 2002). Convene a meeting with a small number of passionate, like-minded stakeholders. Identify the parameters of the problem; move from discussion to dialogue to collaboration to meaningful policy change and resource enhancement. The next section comprises a summary of lessons learned from working with our authors. Each theme is followed by potential actions that can be taken to promote children's social justice.

LESSONS LEARNED AND PROPOSED ACTION-ORIENTED STRATEGIES

Various themes stood out among the international collaboration that took place so as to make this book a reality. These themes fall under two categories: (1) themes related to engagement in social justice efforts for children and young people; and (2) themes related to supporting a global social justice infrastructure for children and young people. Table 31.1 provides a summary of key themes and related change-agent strategies for Category 1. Table 31.2 gives a synopsis of key themes and related change-agent strategies for Category 2.

CATEGORY 1 THEMES: THEMES THAT RELATE TO ENGAGEMENT IN SOCIAL JUSTICE EFFORTS FOR CHILDREN AND YOUNG PEOPLE

Theme 1.1. Some children's voices are not heard. As mentioned in our introduction, some of the authors we invited to write about their countries had to decline. They shared that they were afraid that if they authentically wrote about the status of social

TABLE 31.1 *Themes and action strategies related to engagement in social justice efforts for children and young people*

Theme	Related Action Strategies	Change-Agent Implications for Engagement
Theme 1.1. Some children's voices are not heard.	• Be aware of silent voices. • Engage in efforts to give voice when able to do so (e.g., reporting, writing).	• Extend collaborations and partnerships in anticipation of future participation.
Theme 2.1. Some children's voices are heard more than others.	• Conduct community-needs assessments so as to determine areas of unmet need. • Engage in grassroots interventions in order to address key issues. • Scale up interventions based upon needs assessments and grassroots efforts.	• Develop meaningful connections with communities that respect their historical experiences. • Consider the role of cultural adaptation when scaling up interventions.
Theme 3.1. Countries are committed to social justice for children and young people.	• Convene various constituencies. • Bring people together so as to promote social change.	• Take a multidisciplinary approach. • Meet people who represent a range of professions. • Engage in community-focused activities that bring stakeholders together.
Theme 4.1. Stigma continues to have an impact on social justice for young people.	• Promote media literacy campaigns. • Engage in public education campaigns. • Train journalists to appropriately report on mental health. • Provide parents and families with information.	• Be aware of your audience. • Identify local media outlets. • Develop innovative ways to provide communities with important health, educational, and mental health information.

TABLE 31.2 *Themes and action strategies related to supporting a global social justice infrastructure for children and young people*

Theme	Related Action Strategies	Change-Agent Implications for Developing a Social Justice Infrastructure
Theme 1.2. Share lessons learned across countries.	• Share information across countries via technology. • Create websites that countries participate in jointly. • Implement international conferences focused on social justice issues for young people.	• Importance of international communication. • Importance of having a formal forum focused on social justice issues for children and young people.
Theme 2.2. Share resources across countries.	• Create an online repository where international groups can share resources. • Provide networking opportunities via global conferences. • Engage in cultural adaptations of interventions from other nations. • Explore possibilities for scaling up such interventions.	• Need to share resources with multiple constituencies. • Importance of interdisciplinary collaborations. • Need for partnerships between researchers and policy makers.
Theme 3.2. Share public policy models.	• Governments can consider the relevance of other country policies as they relate to current issues in their countries. • Engage in cross-national consultation. • Consider implementation failure and aspects that promote policy success.	• Being open to learning from other models. • Awareness of barriers to policy implementation. • Engagement of youth in policy deliberation and development.
Theme 4.2. Develop a pipeline of professionals focused on social justice issues for children and young people.	• Provide mentoring. • Provide educational access. • Allocate funding for higher education and professional development. • Implement policy changes in order to make careers more attractive.	• Being intentional about professional pipelines that support youth social justice. • Importance of interdisciplinary mentoring throughout various developmental stages.

justice for children in their countries, they would lose their employment, lose funding for projects, see their families lose benefits, and even face deportation. Other authors wanted to contribute, but were unable to do so due to challenges such as having colleagues who engaged in social justice efforts removed from their positions – leaving no collective infrastructure for collegial communication.

Theme 1.1. Action-oriented strategies. No easy solution exists for countries without a free press and where communication is censored. Change-agent strategies need to consider the specific sociopolitical context of countries where communication is blocked. In discussions with authors who needed to decline, we valued their decisions as they were important for their own safety, as well as that of their families. As a result, this book describes only the experiences of children from countries where authors could speak for them.

Theme 2.1. Some children's voices are heard more than others. Having said that, as we read the country case studies, it also became clear that some children's voices are heard more than others. Inequities in social justice structures and related services for children reflect a vast range of supports. These differences are often related to country economies – with low-income economies and lower-middle-income economies often having fewer structures in place.

Despite this, however, many country initiatives gave expression to voices that are underrepresented. For instance, Chapter 8 highlights how the Transgender Persons Protection of Rights Act was passed in Pakistan in 2018. Chapter 18 shares how Cuba provided medical and psychological care to children and families affected by the Chernobyl disaster from 1990 to 2011. In yet another example, Chapter 28 talks about how Scotland's FeelsFM is the "world's first emoji-powered jukebox," used to decrease stigma and to encourage youth to talk about mental health. These initiatives provide us with hopeful examples of how change can occur.

On the other hand, high-income economies such as the economy of the United States provide some surprising inconsistencies. Despite mental health parity and greater access to mental healthcare services, for instance, many youth who have the resources to receive mental health treatment still do not do so (Clauss-Ehlers, Carpio, & Weist, unpublished manuscript). This speaks in part to the continued role of stigma (see Theme 4) and the importance of parental awareness (see Brazil country case study).

Theme 2.1. Action-oriented strategies. One action-oriented strategy utilized in order to address disparities in youth voices being heard is to conduct community-needs assessments so as to determine areas of unmet need. Such assessments can provide the groundwork from which to develop key policy initiatives. We see this in Chapter 28 where the country case study of Scotland provides an important example of this process. Through an understanding of the impact of mental health on young people, Scotland developed the Ministerial Task Force and the Young People's Mental

Health Commission. These initiatives are supported with ongoing needs assessments, as reflected in the Audit Scotland Children and Young People's Mental Health report and in a review of referrals to Child and Adolescent Mental Health Services (CAMHS) that were rejected.

While these efforts can be undertaken at a macro-policy level, for many of us, options for change lie in the smaller, community-based landscape. Rather than being overwhelmed at not being able to engage in large-scale initiatives, it's important to realize that such grassroots efforts often build the momentum needed to eventually scale up the provision of outreach and services. For instance, in Chapter 15, our country case study of Brazil, authors describe their research focused on providing early intervention and access to services for preschool children with language delays and behavioral problems. The researchers responded to this need – translating academic findings to the community – by subsequently developing a website with information for parents and teachers that presented strategies to promote language development and positive behavioral outcomes.

Theme 3.1. Countries are committed to social justice for children and young people. We also learned that countries are extraordinarily committed to supporting their youngest citizens. Many country efforts build upon one another, leading to a tiered process of working toward creating a social justice infrastructure. Chapter 22 talks about how Mexico has been building an infrastructure of support that started with Convention 138 of the International Labour Organization in 1973, and continued with supporting the National System for the Integral Protection of Children and Adolescents in 2015.

Theme 3.1. Action-oriented strategies. Country case studies tell us that forging commitments to social justice for young people takes the involvement of multiple stakeholders. In the case of Mexico, policies focused on children's rights increasingly grew alongside key stakeholder partnerships. Such partnerships spanned public, private, and governmental constituencies. For instance, Chapter 22 describes how Mexico's policy changed in conjunction with the development of the Red por los Derechos de la Infancia en México (REDIM) – a network of seventy-five civil groups that came together to support infant, child, and adolescent rights. The Mexican government also partnered with UNICEF to develop a national plan to fight violence against young people. UNICEF also trained 2,000 officials in ways to support migrant children (Clauss-Ehlers & Akinsulure-Smith, 2013).

This example demonstrates the important strategy of being a convener. By bringing groups together, individuals, communities, and governments engage in convening power. Our country case studies illustrate the power of bringing people together (Borgman, 2016; Karp, 2012). They show how convening often starts small and then grows as groups build momentum, ultimately inviting change and social impact.

Theme 4.1. Stigma continues to have an impact on social justice for young people. We define stigma as something that occurs beyond the individual level and that can be considered within a larger sociocultural context. From this perspective, stigma is "the cooccurrence of labeling, stereotyping, separation, status loss, and discrimination in a context in which power is exercised" (Hatzenbuehler, Phelan, & Link, 2013, p. 2). For instance, the South Africa case study presented in Chapter 29 presents strategies to destigmatize mental health issues so that people will access services. Similarly, Chapter 19 discusses how the prevailing stigma related to girls receiving an education in Ethiopia limits their educational access.

Stigma also plays a role among young people affected by war. In Chapter 7, for instance, Garbarino and colleagues describe the stigma and distrust that older children who have engaged in armed conflict may face from their communities. Such stigma has been found to lead to increased anxiety and depression (Betancourt, Agnew-Blais, Gillman, Williams, & Ellis, 2010). Further, Garbarino and colleagues discuss how educators may not know how to support children who have been sexually exploited during wartime. Children may be ashamed or even afraid to share what has happened to them.

Theme 4.1. Action-oriented strategies. Stigma in its many forms can be addressed through a range of interventions. Clauss-Ehlers and colleagues (unpublished manuscript) talk about media literacy campaigns as a way to provide communities with mental health information. The development of websites, such as illustrated in our country case study of Brazil, can provide parents with information that empowers them to help their children. Public education campaigns can provide the public with educational messages about the experience of being a child soldier, symptoms of post-traumatic stress disorder, and the trauma associated with witnessing and/or experiencing sexual violence.

Other strategies involve training reporters to provide fair and balanced reporting about mental health issues. This strategy is exemplified in the Rosalynn Carter Fellowships for Mental Health Journalism (see www.cartercenter.org/health/mental_health/fellowships/). Here fellows, both domestic and international, are trained on how to accurately report on mental health and related stigma. Each fellow has a media project focused on a specific mental health topic and reports on that topic during the fellowship year. Connecting people with accurate information via the media can further decrease stigma.

CATEGORY 2 THEMES: THEMES RELATED TO SUPPORTING A GLOBAL
SOCIAL JUSTICE INFRASTRUCTURE FOR CHILDREN AND YOUNG PEOPLE

Theme 1.2. Sharing lessons learned across countries in order to build a global infrastructure. A theme throughout the foundational chapters and country case studies explored in this volume is that, as nations, we need to share with one another what we know about how to support social justice for young people. For instance, while many Latin American countries face high poverty to the extent that, for some, children have had to give up their education in order to work, efforts have sought to increase equity in primary and secondary education. Such initiatives have been implemented in Brazil, Mexico, Colombia, and Argentina. In sharing what we know with one another, we can adapt policies, programs, and interventions for countries/cultures where the need for them resonates.

Theme 1.2. Action-oriented strategies. Information can be easily shared across borders given the role of technology. Community groups and countries can create joint websites so as to share information with one another. Community groups and countries can engage in conferences focused on sharing information about respective social justice efforts for young people.

Theme 2.2. Sharing resources across countries so as to build a global infrastructure. In addition to sharing ideas, we can share resources. Because different countries have various parameters and resources to offer, what one country can offer may complement what another country needs. By sharing resources, it is hoped, assets are maximized for the greatest gain. The Cuba country case study presented in Chapter 18 provides a critical example of sharing resources via its humanitarian program to treat children affected by the Chernobyl accident. Cuba was one of the first Caribbean islands to provide aid to Ukrainian people. This humanitarian program provided treatment for 20, 423 children affected by the Chernobyl accident (Labañino, 2016).

Theme 2.2. Action-oriented strategies. Having an online repository where community groups and countries can share information and resources is one way to make the availability of resources known. Developing global conferences focused on children's social justice provides networking opportunities where participants can learn about country resources. In addition, recent approaches talk about cultural adaptation of interventions (Bernal & Domenech Rodríguez, 2012). Effective interventions can be imported from other nations and culturally adapted as necessary. Subsequent to implementation, communities and governments can explore possibilities for scaling up interventions so that resources meet the needs of more young people within their sociocultural context.

Theme 3.2. Sharing public policy models in order to build a global infrastructure. Countries can also work together to build social justice capacity for young people by sharing public policy models with one another. Although such policies might need to be culturally adapted for varying country contexts, sharing how public policies have promoted change can provide useful cross-country models. For instance, as described in Chapter 8, many recent policies across countries have reversed discrimination experienced by LGBTQ individuals. While it might not be the case that countries were specifically talking with one another about public policies when they changed, Table 8.1 highlights how legislative cases of reversals of discrimination for LGBTQ people occurred in rapid succession in countries such as Nepal, Argentina, Bangladesh, Africa, South Africa, India, Mozambique, Malta, Chile, Colombia, and Pakistan.

Theme 3.2. Action-oriented strategies. Local, regional, and national governments can look to one another for policy examples connected to certain issues. Through this type of cross-national consultation, governments can explore and examine how other nations are responding to similar issues. Policy implementation can anticipate possible implementation failures and consider factors that promote success.

Theme 4.2. Develop a pipeline of professionals focused on social justice issues for children and young people. A critical theme that emerged across countries was the need to develop a pipeline of professionals focused on social justice issues for young people. This cadre of professionals includes mental health professionals, educators, nurses, physicians, crisis intervention workers, humanitarian aid workers, and legislators, among other areas of expertise. In Chapter 5, coauthors Nathalie O. Iotti and Tomas Jungert provide equity-focused principles that aim to address the complexities of structural poverty such as "increasing investment in equity-focused programs, so as to ensure that everyone is receiving the right kind of help" (see pp. 85–86 this volume).

Education. Increasing investment means having a workforce able to provide needed services. A UNESCO study found that by the year 2030, the world will be "off track in meeting its education commitments." More specifically, the world will need 69 million new teachers by 2030 in order to fulfill education goals. Thirty-three countries will not have enough teachers to educate all of their children by 2030 (see http://uis.unesco.org/en/topic/teachers).

Mental health. In another example, the World Health Organization's (WHO) (2018) *Mental Health Atlas 2017* published results demonstrating that, although many countries have developed structures through which to address mental health issues, "Globally, the median number of mental health workers is 9 per 100 000 population, but there is extreme variation (from below 1 in low-income countries to 72 in high-income countries)" (WHO, 2018, p. 2). In low-income economies, ratios of mental health workers can be as low as two providers for every 100,000 people.

Theme 4.2. Action-oriented strategies. Building a pipeline of professionals to provide services in education and mental health sectors (among others) is pivotal to social justice efforts for children and young people. Action-oriented strategies can start early in a young person's life. One such strategy can be to provide mentoring to young people about careers in education, mental healthcare, and related professions. This, in turn, relates to facilitating educational access to opportunities that support such mentoring and further student interest in these and related professions. Organizations and governments can allocate funding for higher education and professional development. Countries can also engage in policy changes that make careers such as those in education and mental healthcare more attractive for young people to pursue (e.g., higher national salaries, better benefits, prestige, value).

Make a difference for young people and help them to obtain the social justice they deserve, heeding the poignant words of Margaret Mead (1901–1978): "Never doubt that a small group of thoughtful, committed citizens can change the world. Indeed, it is the only thing that ever has."

We extend our thanks to you for reading this book, and we offer our best wishes to you in your efforts to improve social justice for children and youth.

REFERENCES

Bernal, G., & Domenech Rodríguez, M. M. (eds.). (2012). *Cultural adaptations: Tools for evidence-based practice with diverse populations*. Washington, DC: American Psychological Association.

Betancourt, T. S., Agnew-Blais, J., Gillman, S. E., Williams, D. R., & Ellis, B. H. (2010). Past horrors, present struggles: The role of stigma in the association between war experiences and psychosocial adjustment among former child soldiers in Sierra Leone. *Social Science Medicine*, 70, 17–26. doi:10.1016/j.socscimed.2009.09.038

Borgman, S. Z. (2016, March 9). The power of convening for social impact. Stanford Social Innovation Review. Retrieved from https://ssir.org/articles/entry/the_power_of_convening_for_social_impact.

Clauss-Ehlers, C. S., & Akinsulure-Smith, A. M. (2013). Working with forced migrant children and their families: Mental health, developmental, legal, and linguistic considerations in the context of school-based mental health services. In C. S. Clauss-Ehlers, Z. Serpell, & M. D. Weist (eds.), *Handbook of culturally responsive school mental health: Advancing research, training, practice, and policy* (pp. 135–146). New York: Springer.

Clauss-Ehlers, C. S., Carpio, M. G., & Weist, M. D. (unpublished manuscript). *Status of adolescent international mental health promotion*. Manuscript under review.

Hatzenbuehler, M. L., Phelan, J. C., & Link, B. G. (2013). Stigma as a fundamental cause of population health inequalities. *American Journal of Public Health*, 103(5), 813–821. doi:10.2105/AJPH.2012.301069

Karp, E. (2012, December 10). The power to convene. Forbes. Retrieved from www.forbes.com/sites/85broads/2012/12/10/the-power-to-convene/#e365e9e42326.

Labañino, A. (2016, April 25). Ukraine recalls Cuban humanitarian programme for Chernobyl children. Cubasi.com. Retrieved from http://cubasi.com/cuba/item/7580-ukraine-recalls-cuban-humanitarian-programme-for-chernobyl-children.

United Nations Educational, Scientific and Cultural Organization (UNESCO) (n.d.). New projections show the world is off track in meeting its education commitments by 2030. Retrieved from http://uis.unesco.org/en/news/new-projections-show-world-track-meeting-its-education-commitments-2030.

United Nations Secretary General (UNSG). (2008). *Guidance note of the secretary-general: UN approach to justice for children.* Retrieved from www.unicef.org/protection/RoL_Guidance_Note_UN_Approach_Justice_for_Children_FINAL.pdf.

Wenger, E., McDermott, R., & Snyder, W. M. (2002). *Cultivating communities of practice: A guide to managing knowledge.* Boston, MA: Harvard Business School.

World Bank (n.d.). *World Bank country and lending groups.* Retrieved from https://datahelpdesk.worldbank.org/knowledgebase/articles/906519-world-bank-country-and-lending-groups.

World Health Organization (WHO) (2018). *Mental health atlas 2017.* Retrieved from www.who.int/mental_health/evidence/atlas/mental_health_atlas_2017/en/.

World Population Review (n.d.). *High income countries 2019.* Retrieved from http://worldpopulationreview.com/countries/high-income-countries/.

CPSIA information can be obtained
at www.ICGtesting.com
Printed in the USA
LVHW010243200622
721630LV00001B/7